A Guide Book to

Edmund Beale Sargant

Bernhard Whishaw

Alpha Editions

This Edition Published in 2020

ISBN: 9789354216978

Design and Setting By
Alpha Editions
www.alphaedis.com
Email - info@alphaedis.com

PREFACE.

———◆———

In the large and increasing number of works, good, bad, and indifferent, which exist upon every subject, it is often difficult for the ordinary reader to choose the book he wants. Catalogues, which are comprehensive and not selective, are of little assistance. They seldom afford an indication of the nature and scope of the books named in them, nor do they discriminate between what has and what has not real merit; while bibliographies, besides being open to the same objections, are too voluminous to be of much service except to the student, and, moreover, are not always easily accessible.

The object of this little work is to place at the service of the reader the opinions of those who may be trusted to give sound advice as to the books which are of value in each department of knowledge. It is not always possible, even for specialists, to name the best works, but they can, at least, give an assurance that books which they recommend are thoroughly good. The list of names printed at the end of this preface will probably be a sufficient guarantee that reliance may be placed upon the information supplied.

Many works which are valuable in themselves, or historically interesting, will not be found in these pages. The idea in which the book has originated is precisely opposed to an enumeration of the whole literature upon any subject: its aim is to select as carefully as possible what is essential, and to omit all the remainder. This work is one of such difficulty, even in the hands of the most competent authorities, that the first issue is likely to be imperfect both by excess and defect: but the Editors hope, by inviting and noting criticisms and suggestions, to improve the book, should succeeding editions be called for.

Magazine articles, when not reprinted in book form, articles in encyclopædias and dictionaries, and special chapters of books or special papers published in volumes of collected essays, &c., have been, as a rule, omitted,

a 2

nor has any selection of school text-books been generally attempted. The prices quoted are, for English books, the published price ; for works published abroad, the nett cash price in London. Although the greatest trouble has been taken to ensure accuracy, the Editors cannot guarantee the correctness of all the prices given; and, moreover, from the fact that books are continually going out of print and new editions appearing, complete exactness in this respect is unattainable. The titles are not necessarily given in full, but frequently in an abbreviated form, sufficient for identification.

To the contributors named below the Editors desire to express their thanks, not only for the trouble taken in drawing up the lists of books, but for much valuable advice and criticism. Thanks are also due to many friends, whose names do not appear, for the kindly interest they have taken in the preparation of the Guide Book, and for many useful suggestions as to books, subjects and arrangement.

Contributors.

CAPT. W. DE W. ABNEY, R.E., C.B., D.C.L., F.R.S.

MR. R. ADAMSON, LL.D., Professor of Moral Philosophy, Owens Coll., Manchester.

„ WILLIAM ARCHER.

„ R. N. BAIN, British Museum.

„ T. HUDSON BEARE, B. Sc., Professor of Engineering, University Coll., London.

„ A. BEAZELEY, M. Inst. C.E. Librarian to the Royal Institute of British Architects.

MRS. HUGH BELL.

MR. A. BERRY, M.A., Fellow and Lecturer King's Coll., Cambridge.

„ W. C. A. BLEW.

„ JAMES BONAR, M.A.

„ H. COURTHOPE BOWEN, M.A., Cambridge. University Lecturer on the History and Theory of Education.

PROFESSOR BRIDGE, Mus. Doc., Organist of Westminster Abbey.

MR. H. L. BRÆKSTAD.

„ B. BROOMHALL.

„ JAMES BRYCE, M.P., D.C.L., Regius Professor of Civil Law, Oxford.

„ FRANK CAMPBELL, British Museum.

„ F. M. CAMPBELL.

REAR ADMIRAL COLOMB.

MR. P. COWELL, Librarian of the Liverpool Free Library.

RIGHT REV. M. CREIGHTON, M.A., Bishop of Peterborough.

MRS. CRAWFORD.

Mr. L. Cuthbert Cropper, Associate of the Institute of Chartered Accountants.

„ T. W. Rhys Davids, LL.D. Professor of Pali and Buddhist Literature, University Coll., London.

Right Rev. Randall T. Davidson, D.D., Bishop of Rochester.

Mr. R. K. Douglas, Professor of Chinese, King's Coll., London.

„ A. Dryden, Hon. Sec. Wimbledon Skating Club.

„ T. H. Eagles, M.A., Professor of Geometrical Drawing, Royal Indian Engineering Coll., Cooper's Hill.

„ John Earle, M.A., Professor of Anglo-Saxon, Oxford.

Mrs. Fawcett.

Mr. L. Fletcher, M.A., F.R.S., Keeper of Mineralogy, Natural History Museum.

„ H. O. Arnold Forster.

„ H. S. Foxwell, M.A., Professor of Political Economy, Univ. Coll., London.

Hon. C. W. Fremantle, C.B., Master of the Mint.

Miss Garrett.

Mr. Alfred Scott Gatty, F.S.A., York Herald, Herald's College.

„ Arch. Geikie, LL.D., F.R.S., Director-General of the Geological Survey.

„ Lawrence Gomme, F.S.A., Director of the Folk-Lore Society.

„ Walter T. Goolden, M.A., Member of the Institute of Electrical Engineers.

„ W. Gowland, Late Director of the Imperial Mint, Japan.

„ Joseph Griffiths, M.B., Assistant Professor of Surgery, Cambridge.

Sir George Grove, D.C.D., Director of the Royal College of Music.

Mr. J. W. Hales, M.A., Professor of English, King's Coll., London.

„ Frederick Harrison.

„ J. E. Harting, Librarian to the Linnæan Society.

Dr. N. Heinemann.

Miss L. Higgin.

Mr. J. E. Hodgson, R.A., Librarian to the Royal Academy.

„ J. R. Jackson, A.L.S., Curator of the Museums, Royal Botanic Gardens, Kew.

„ Henry Jones ("Cavendish").

„ J. Scott Keltie, Librarian to the Royal Geographical Society.

„ Dixon Kemp.

„ W. P. Ker, M.A., Professor of English Literature, University Coll., London.

Colonel C. Cooper King.

Mr. T. J. Kiernan, Assistant Librarian, Harvard University.

„ Joseph Knight, Secretary to the Vegetarian Society.

„ C. C. Lacaita.

„ E. Ray Lankester, M.A., LL.D., F.R.S., Professor of Zoology, University Coll., London.

„ C. G. Leland.

„ V. B. Lewes, Professor of Chemistry, Royal Naval Coll., Greenwich.

„ J. Norman Lockyer, F.R.S.

„ Robert W. Lowe.

Sir John Lubbock, Bart., M.P., D.C.L., F.R.S.

Hon. Alfred Lyttelton.

MRS. JOHN MACCUNN.

MR. W. MCTURK, Angelo's Royal School of Arms.

SIR PHILIP MAGNUS, City and Guilds of London Technical Institute.

MR. EIRÍKR MAGNUSSON, M.A., Sub-Librarian of the University Library, Cambridge.

„ D. S. MARGOLIOUTH, M.A., Laud's Professor of Arabic, Oxford.

„ J. E. MARR, M.A., Fellow and Lecturer, St. John's Coll., Cambridge. Secretary to the Geological Society.

„ A. MILNES MARSHALL, M.A., D.Sc., F.R.S., Professor of Zoology, Owens Coll., Manchester.

„ W. R. MORFILL, M.A., University Reader in Russian and the other Slavonic Languages, Oxford.

„ WILLIAM MORRIS.

„ F. MAX MÜLLER, M.A., Professor of Comparative Philology, Oxford.

„ G. NICHOLSON, A.L.S., Curator of the Gardens, Kew.

PROFESSOR D. OLIVER, F.R.S., Keeper of the Herbarium and Library, Royal Botanic Gardens, Kew.

MR. REGINALD F. D. PALGRAVE, C.B., Clerk of the House of Commons.

„ H. F. PELHAM, M.A., Camden Professor of Ancient History, Oxford.

REV. J. PERCIVAL, LL.D., Head Master of Rugby.

SIR FREDERICK POLLOCK, Bart., M.A., Corpus Professor of Jurisprudence, Oxford.

REV. T. G. P. POPE, English Chaplain, Lisbon.

MR. R. STUART POOLE, LL.D. Keeper of Coins, British Museum; Correspondent of the Institute of France.

REV. R. H. QUICK, M.A., Trinity Coll., Cambridge, Sometime University Lecturer on the History of Education.

MISS C. RADFORD.

MR. R. RAE, Secretary of the National Temperance League.

„ W. RAMSAY, Ph.D., F.R.S., Professor of Chemistry, University Coll., London.

„ T. A. REED.

„ JOHN RHYS, M.A., Professor of Celtic, Oxford.

„ D. A. RITCHIE, M.A., Fellow and Lecturer of Jesus Coll., Oxford.

„ R. D. ROBERTS, M.A., D.Sc., Fellow of Clare Coll., Cambridge; Sec. London Society for the Extension of University Teaching.

„ W. C. ROBERTS-AUSTEN, F.R.S., Professor of Metallurgy, Royal School of Mines.

SIR H. E. ROSCOE, M.P., D.C.L., LL.D., F.R.S.

MR. H. LING ROTH.

„ F. W. RUDLER, Curator of the Museum of Practical Geology, Jermyn Street.

„ E. M. SADLER, M.A., Sec. Oxford Society for the Extension of University Teaching.

„ GEORGE SAINTSBURY.

REV. W. SANDAY, M.A., Ireland Professor of Exegesis, Oxford.

MR. J. BURDON SANDERSON, M.A., Waynflete Professor of Physiology, Oxford.

MISS ETHEL SARGANT.

MR. J. R. SEELEY, M.A., Professor of Modern History, Cambridge.

„ W. SENIOR (" Red Spinner ").

„ A. SIDGWICK, M.A., Fellow and Tutor of Corpus Christi Coll., Oxford.

Mr. H. Sidgwick, D.Litt., Professor of Moral Philosophy, Cambridge.

Mrs. Henry Sidgwick.

Mr. F. Storr, M.A.

Right Rev. William Stubbs, D.D., Bishop of Oxford.

Mdlle. Souvestre.

Mr. A. W. Sunderland, M.A., Late Scholar of Trin. Coll., Cambridge. Fellow of [the Institute of Actuaries.

„ J. J. Sylvester, M.A., D.C.L., F.R.S. Savilian Professor of Geometry, Oxford.

„ J. Addington Symonds.

„ H. R. Tedder, Librarian to the Athenæum Club.

Sir Henry Thompson, F.R.C.S., M.B., Consulting Surgeon to University Coll. Hospital.

Mr. J. J. Thomson, M.A., F.R.S., Professor of Experimental Physics, Cambridge.

Sir William Thomson, LL.D., F.R.S., Professor of Natural Philosophy, Glasgow.

Mr. Andrew Tuer, F.S.A.

„ E. B. Tylor, M.A., D.C.L., F.R.S., Reader in Anthropology, Oxford.

Rev. E. Venables, Canon of Lincoln.

Mr. A. W. Verrall, M.A., D.Litt., Fellow and Lecturer of Trin. Coll., Cambridge.

„ A. H. Vesey, A.M.I.C.E.

„ Robt. Wallace, Professor of Agriculture, Edinburgh.

„ H. Marshall Ward, Professor of Botany, Royal Indian Engineering Coll., Cooper's Hill.

Rev. Wentworth Webster, M.A., Oxon., Corresponding Member of the Real Academia de la Historia, Madrid.

Mr. C. Welch, F.S.A., Librarian of the Guildhall Library.

„ E. H. Whinfield, M.A.

Mrs. Bernhard Whishaw.

Col. Sir Charles Wilson, K.C.B., K.C.M.G., R.E., D.C.L., F.R.S.

Mr. E. T. Wilson, B.A., M.B. (Oxon.), F.R.C.P.

„ W. T. Wilson, F.R.C.V.S., Professor of Veterinary Science, Royal Agricultural Coll., Cirencester.

Hon. Lewis Wingfield.

Mr. Justin Winsor, Librarian of Harvard University.

„ H. J. Wolstenholme.

Miss A. Romley Wright, Manchester School of Domestic Economy.

Contributors of Local Information.

Very Rev. Jas. Allen, M.A., Dean of St. David's.

Mr. Thos. Archer, C.M.G., Agent-General for Queensland.

„ Walter Baring, H.M. Chargé d'Affaires, Cettinje.

Hon. William A. C. Barrington, Secretary of Embassy, Madrid.

Hon. Frederick Bernal, H.M. Consul-General, Havre.

Sir George Bertram, Bailiff of Jersey.

„ G. F. Bonham, Bart., Secretary of Legation, Lisbon.

VERY REV. G. D. BOYLE, Dean of Salisbury.

    „   „   G. C. BRADLEY, D.D., Dean of Westminster.

MR. E. N. C. BRADDON, Agent-General for Tasmania.

    „ MONTAGU YEATS BROWN, H.M. Consul, Genoa.

    „ G. W. BUCHANAN, H.M. Chargé d'Affaires, Berne.

    „ S. DEERING, Assistant Agent-General for South Australia.

    „ D. DONOHOE, H.M. Consul, San Francisco.

    „ VICTOR DRUMMOND, H.M. Chargé d'Affaires, Munich.

VERY REV. GILBERT ELLIOT, D.D., Dean of Bristol.

MR. H. P. FENTON, Secretary of Legation, The Hague.

    „ A. DE FONBLANQUE, H.M. Consul, New Orleans.

    „ W. E. GOSCHEN, Secretary of Legation, Copenhagen.

    „ H. GRANT, H.M. Consul-General, Warsaw.

VERY REV. W. G. HENDERSON, D.D., Dean of Carlisle.

MR. W. R. HOARE, H.M. Consul, New York.

VERY REV. G. W. KITCHIN, D.D., Dean of Winchester.

    „   „ W. C. LAKE, D.D., Dean of Durham.

    „   „ H. G. LIDDELL, D.D., Dean of Christ Church.

REV. G. M. LIVETT, Precentor of Rochester.

SIR EDGAR MACCULLOCH, Bailiff of Guernsey.

MR. A. F. HASTINGS MEDHURST, H.M. Vice-Consul, Moscow.

VERY REV. CHAS. MERIVALE, D.D., Dean of Ely.

MR. A. W. MOORE, J.P., Member of the House of Keys.

VEN. F. J. MOUNT, Archdeacon of Chichester.

MR. J. NICHOLSON, Librarian of Lincoln's Inn.

SIR A. NICOLSON, K.C.I.E., H.M. Consul-General, Buda-Pesth.

MR. N. R. O'CONOR, C.B., C.M.G., H.M. Agent and Consul-General, Sofia.

    „ R. OTTLEY, H.M. Consul, Lyons.

MR. C. G. G. PERCEVAL, H.M. Consul, Marseilles.

RIGHT REV. J. J. STEWART PEROWNE, D.D., Bishop of Worcester.

LIEUT.-COL. SIR R. LAMBERT PLAYFAIR, K.C.M.G., H.M. Consul-General, Algiers

VERY REV. A. P. PUREY-CUST, D.D., Dean of York.

    „   „ E. H. PLUMPTRE, D.D., Dean of Wells.

SIR SAUL SAMUEL, K.C.M.G., Agent-General for New South Wales.

MR. T. B. SANDWITH, C.B., H.M. Consul-General, Odessa.

REV. W. SPARROW SIMPSON, D.D., Librarian of St. Paul's.

VERY REV. R. PAYNE SMITH, D.D., Dean of Canterbury.

    „   „ H. D. M. SPENCE, D.D., Dean of Gloucester.

MR. GEORGE STRACHEY, H.M. Chargé d'Affaires, Dresden.

    „ J. SPENCER B. TODD, C.M.G., Secretary to the Agency-General for the Cape Colony

HON. P. LE POER TRENCH, Secretary of Legation, Berlin.

SIR CHARLES TUPPER, G.C.M.G., High Commissioner for Canada.

MR. WILLIAM WARD, H.M. Consul, Bordeaux.

TABLE OF CONTENTS.

GUIDE BOOK TO BOOKS.

———◆———

A.

ABBEYS, *see* ARCHITECTURE III.

ABORIGINAL RACES, *see* ANTHROPOLOGY.

ABYSSINIA:

Blanford, W. T. Geology and zoology of Abyssinia. 8vo. *Macmillan.* 21*s.*
  Observations made during progress of British expedition, 1867-8.

Parkyns, Mansfield. Three years' residence in Abyssinia. p. 8vo. *Murray.* 7*s.* 6*d.*

Winstanley, H. Visit to Abyssinia. p. 8vo. 2 vols. *Hurst.* 21*s.*

Markham, C. R. History of the Abyssinian expedition, 1867-8. *Macmillan.*
  pub. 14*s.* O.P.

Rassam, H. British mission to Abyssinia. 8vo. 2 vols. *Murray.* illns. 28*s.*

ACCOUNTS, *see* BOOK-KEEPING.

ACOUSTICS, *see* PHYSICS VII.

ACTORS *and* ACTING, *see* STAGE.

ADMINISTRATION, LOCAL, *see* LOCAL GOVERNMENT.

ADRIATIC, *see* MEDITERRANEAN.

ADULTERATION, *see* CHEMISTRY IV.

ÆGEAN, *see* MEDITERRANEAN.

ÆSTHETICS, *see* ART IV.

AFGHANISTAN AND BALUCHISTAN:

Raverty, H. G. Afghanistan and part of Baluchistan. fo. 3 vols. *Trübner.* 10*s.*
  Sections i., ii., 2*s.*; iii., 5*s.*; iv., 3*s.* Notes extracted from writings of Afghan and Tagzik historians, geographers, etc.

Bellew, H. W. Afghanistan and the Afghans. 8vo. *Low.* 7*s.* 6*d.*

Malleson, G. B. Herat. d. 8vo. *Allen.* 8*s.*

Yate, A. C. Travels with the Afghan Boundary Commission. 8vo.
  Blackwood. illus. 21*s.*

Kaye, J. W. History of the war in Afghanistan. c. 8vo. 3 vols. *W. H. Allen.* 26*s.*

Thornton, T. Gazetteer of Afghanistan. d. 8vo. 2 vols. *W. H. Allen.* 25*s.*
Compiled for India Office.

Macgregor, C. M. Wanderings in Baloochistan. d. 8vo. *W. H. Allen.* 18*s.*
illus.

Floyer, E. A. Unexplored Baluchistan. r. 8vo. *Griffith.* illus. pub. 28*s.* O.P.
A journey through Western Baluchistan, Mekran, Bashakird, Persia, Kurdistan, and Turkey.

AFGHAN LANGUAGE :

Raverty, H. G. Dictionary of the Pushto, or Afghan language. 4to. (*London*). 70*s.*

,, Grammar of Afghan language. 4to. (*London*). 10*s.*

AFRICA :

See also ABYSSINIA, ALGIERS (with TUNIS and TRIPOLI), CAPE, EGYPT, MADAGASCAR. MOROCCO.

—I. GENERAL :

Reclus, E. Universal geography, vol. x., xi., xii., xiii. Ed. and tr. Keane. i. 8vo. 4 vols., 21*s.* each. *Virtue.* illus. and col. maps. 84*s.*
Vol. X. N.E. AFRICA. Nile basin, Great lakes, Abyssinia, Nubia, Egypt, and a general sketch of African geography. Vol. XI. N.W. AFRICA. Tripolitania, Fezzan, Tunisia, Algeria, Morocco, the Sahara. Vol. XII. W. AFRICA. African Islands, Senegal, Guinea, Niger basin, Congo basin. Vol. XIII. S. and E. AFRICA. Angola, Cape Colony, Natal, Dutch Republic, Mozambique, Zanzibar.

Stanford's Compendium of geography and travel: Africa. Ed. Johnston and Ravenstein. l. p. 8vo. *Stanford.* illus. and maps. 21*s.*

Murray, H., and others. Discovery and adventure in Africa from the earliest ages. 8vo. 2 vols. 1818. O.P.
With illustrations of the geology, mineralogy, and zoology.

D'Anvers, N. Heroes of North African discovery. c. 8vo. *Marcus Ward.* 3*s.* 6*d.*

,, Heroes of South African discovery. c. 8vo. *Marcus Ward.* 3*s.* 6*d.*

Les colonies portugaises. *Dulau.*

White, A. S. The development of Africa. *Philip.* 14*s.*

—II. NORTH :

Barth, H. Travels in North and Central Africa, 1849-55 (" Minerva library "). c. 8vo. *Ward, Lock.* 2*s.*

Nachtigal, G. Sahara und Sudan ; Ergebnisse sechsjähriger Reisen in Afrika. 8vo. 3 vols. (*Leipzig*). 15*s.*

Report on the Egyptian provinces of the Sudan, Red Sea, and Equator. 12mo. *Eyre.* 3*s.* 6*d.*
Compiled by the Intelligence Branch, Quartermaster-General's Department, War Office. Revised to July, 1884.

Beke, C. T. Sources of the Nile. 8vo. *Madden.* pub. 6*s.* O.P.
General survey and history of discovery.

—III. WEST :

Skertchley, J. A. Dahomey. 8vo. *Chapman.* pub. 21*s.* O.P.
Eight months' residence.

Forbes, F. E. Dahomey and the Dahomans. 8vo. 2 vols. *Longmans.* 1851.   O.P.
     Two Missions, 1849 and 1850.

Burton, R. F. Mission to Gelele, King of Dahomey. p. 8vo. 2 vols. *Tinsley.* pub. 25s.   O.P.

Faidherbe, Général. Le Sénégal. 8vo. *Hachette.* illus.   8s. 6d.

Büttikofer, J. Reisebilder aus Liberia. 8vo. 2 vols. (*Leyden*).   20s.

Wauvermans, H. Liberia: histoire de la fondation d'un état nègre libre. (*Brussels*).

Thomson, J. Mungo Park and the Niger ("Great Explorers," ser.). c. 8vo. *Philip.*   4s. 6d.

Burton, R. F. Abeokuta and the Cameroons mountains. 8vo. 2 vols. *Tinsley.*   25s.

Monteiro, J. J. Angola and the river Congo. 8vo. 2 vols. *Macmillan.*   21s.

Capello and Ivens. Benguella to Yacca; central and west Africa. 8vo. 2 vols. *Low.*   42s.

Baines, T. Journey and explorations in South West Africa. 8vo. *Longmans.* pub. 21s.   O.P.
     Walvisch Bay to Lake 'Ngami and the Victoria Falls.

Andersson, C. J. Lake 'Ngami. r. 8vo. *Hurst.*   O.P.
     Explorations and discoveries in S.W. Africa.

   ,,   Okovango river. 8vo. *Hurst.* pub. 10s. 6d.   O.P.

—IV. CENTRAL:

Schweinfurth, G. Heart of Africa. c. 8vo. 2 vols. *Low.*   15s.
     Three years' travel in unexplored regions; with introduction by Winwood Reade.

Dupont, E. Le Congo. 8vo. (*Brussels*).   12s. 6d.

Bentley, W. H. Life on the Congo. c. 8vo. *R. T. S.* illus.   1s. 6d.
     Introduction by Rev. Geo. Grenfell.

Stanley, H. M. The Congo, and its free state. 8vo. 2 vols. *Low.* illus.   42s.
     Cheaper edition, 21s.

   ,,   Through the dark continent. c. 8vo. *Low.* illus.   12s. 6d.

   ,,   In darkest Africa. 8vo. 2 vols. *Low.*   42s.

Ashe, R. P. Life by the shores of the Victoria Nyanza. c. 8vo. *Low.* illus.   6s.

—V. EAST:

James, F. L. Unknown horn of Africa (Somali land). m. 8vo. *Philip.* illus. and maps.   5s.

Drummond, H. Tropical Africa. c. 8vo. *Hodder.*   3s. 6d.

Burton, R. F. Zanzibar. 8vo. 2 vols. *Tinsley.* pub. 30s.   O.P.

Baines, M. J. Victoria Falls of the Zambesi River. *Day.* pub. 52s. 6d.   O.P.

Wagner, J. Deutsch Ost-Afrika. 8vo. *Dulau.*   2s. 6d.

AFRICAN ISLANDS, *see* ATLANTIC OCEAN, INDIAN OCEAN, MADAGASCAR.

AGRICULTURE:

See also DAIRY, FORESTRY, GARDENING, LIVE-STOCK.

—I. HISTORY AND THEORY:

Prothero, R. E. Pioneers of English farming. c. 8vo. *Longmans.*   5s.

Stephens, H. Book of the farm. 1. 8vo. 6 vols., 10s. 6d. each. *Blackwood.*
illus.   63s.
Most valuable book of reference.

Baldwin, J. Practical farming. *Macmillan.*   1s. 6d.
Specially written for Irish National Schools.

Wrightson, J. Principles of agricultural practice. c. 8vo. *Chapman.*   5s.

    ,,   Agricultural text-book. f. 8vo. *Collins.*   2s. 6d.

Clements, H. Fields of Great Britain. 12mo. *Lockwood.*   2s. 6d.
Valuable text-book.

Lloyd, F. J. Science of agriculture. 8vo. *Longmans.*   12s.

—II. CROPS :

See also BOTANY.

Wilson, J. Our farm crops. 2 vols. *Blackie.* pub. 11s.   O.P.
Standard work, but wants bringing up to date.

Johnson, S. W. How crops feed. c. 8vo. *Trübner.* pub. 10s.   O.P.

    ,,   How crops grow. c. 8vo. *Judd (U.S.).*   10s. 6d.

Crops of the farm. c. 8vo. *Vinton.*   2s. 6d.

Plant life of the farm. c. 8vo. *Vinton.*   2s. 6d.

Fream, W. Rothamsted experiment in growth of wheat and barley.
f. 8vo. *H. Cox.*   5s. 6d.

Buckman, J. Natural history of British meadow and pasture grasses. 8vo.
Hamilton, Adams.   O.P.

Stebler and Schroter. Agricultural grasses and forage plants. 4to. *Nutt.*
illus.   12s. 6d.
Adapted for England by A. McAlpine.

Gillitt, J. Gorse, furze, or whin. 16mo. (*Dublin*).   1s.
Cultivation and use as food for horses, cattle, and sheep; useful little manual.

Lawes and Gilbert. Rothamsted experiments in ensilage. *Harrison.*
Pamphlet of special value to dairymen.

Rew, R. H. Stack ensilage. c. 8vo. *Scott.*   1s.

Silos for British fodder crops. *H. Cox.*   6s.
Standard work.

Sutton, M. J. Culture of vegetables, etc. 8vo. *Hamilton, Adams.*   5s.

Smith, W. G. Diseases of field and garden crops. f. 8vo. *Macmillan.*
illus.   4s. 6d.

Ward, J. Flax; its cultivation and preparation. 8vo. *Orr.*   O.P.

Ormerod, Miss E. A. Manual of injurious insects. c. 8vo. *Simpkin.*   5s.
Best British work on the general subject.

Curtis, J. Farm insects, injurious to field-crops, etc. sup. r. 8vo. *Gurney.*
illus.   21s.

Ormerod, Miss E. A. Guide to methods of insect life (10 lectures).
c. 8vo. *Simpkin.*   2s.
See also *Insect Life*; monthly bulletin of U.S. Depart. of Agriculture, division of Entomology.

—III. SOILS :

See also GEOLOGY.

Fream, W. Soils and their properties. c. 8vo. *Bell.* illus.   2s. 6d.

Soil of the farm. c. 8vo. *Vinton.*   2s. 6d.

Crewe, A. W.   Manures.   c. 8vo.   *H. Cox.*   2*s.* 6*d.*

Chemistry of the farm.   c. 8vo.   *Vinton.*   2*s.* 6*d.*

Storer, F. H.   Agriculture; some of its relations to chemistry.   8vo.   2 vols.
Low.   25*s.*

Johnston and Cameron.   Agricultural chemistry and geology.   f. 8vo.
Blackwood. illus.   6*s.* 6*d.*

—IV. EQUIPMENT:

Scott, J.   Complete text-book of farm engineering.   12mo.   *Lockwood.*
illus.   12*s.*

Field and barn implements; Farm buildings; Draining and embanking; Irrigation and water supply; Farm roads, fences, and gates; Agricultural surveying.

Equipment of the farm.   c. 8vo.   *Vinton.*   2*s.* 6*d.*

Thomas, J. J.   Farm implements and machinery.   12mo.   *Orange Judd.*
(*U.S.*). illus.   7*s.* 6*d.*

Principles of construction and use.

Denton, J. B.   Agricultural drainage.   r. 8vo.   *Spon.*   3*s.*

French, H.   Farm drainage.   c. 8vo.   *Spon.*   7*s.* 6*d.*

Klippart, J. H.   Land drainage.   12mo.   (*Cincinnati*).   9*s.*

Ewart, J.   Land improver's pocket-book.   r. 32mo.   *Lockwood.*   4*s.*

Nesbit, A.   Practical land surveying.   Ed. W. Burness.   8vo.   *Longmans.*
illus.   12*s.*

—V. MANAGEMENT, ETC.:

Curtis, C. E.   Estate management.   d. 8vo.   *H. Cox.*   10*s.* 6*d.*

Labour of the farm.   c. 8vo.   *Vinton.*   2*s.* 6*d.*

Thomson, A. W.   Text-book of book-keeping (Land agents, etc.).   c. 8vo.
Bell.   5*s.*

Advanced double-entry system.

Dixon, H. H.   Law of the farm.   Ed. H. Perkins.   d. 8vo.   *Stevens.*   26*s.*

Bear, W. E.   British farmer and his competitors.   *Cassell.*   1*s.*

—VI. REFERENCE:

Cyclopædia of agriculture.   Ed. J. C. Morton.   r. 8vo.   2 vols.   *Blackie.*
illus. pub. 50*s.*   O.P.

The best book of the kind; though in some recent agricultural improvements behind the times. In the subject of Agricultural Botany it is yet unsurpassed.

McConnell, P.   Agricultural facts and figures for farmers.   r. 32mo.
Lockwood.   4*s.*

A most valuable pocket companion.

Morton, J. C.   Farmer's calendar.   d. 8vo.   *Warne.* illus.   15*s.*

Comprehensive.

ALBANIA, *see* TURKEY.

ALCHEMY, *see* CHEMISTRY I.

ALCOHOLISM:

Paget, J.   The alcohol question.   c. 8vo.   *Strahan.*   3*s.* 6*d.*

Magnan, V.   Alcoholism: forms and treatment.   Tr. W. S. Greenfield.
d. 8vo.   *Lewis.*   7*s.* 6*d.*

Kerr, Norman. Inebriety. c. 8vo. *Lewis.*   12s. 6d.

Gustafson, A. The foundation of death. *Paul.*   6s.

Barrett, E. R. Truth about intoxicating drinks. 8vo. *Nat. Temp. Pub. Depôt.*   2s. 6d.

Burns, Dawson. Temperance history. d. 8vo. 2 vols., 5s. each. *Nat. Temp. Pub. Depôt.*   10s.

Maguire, J. Life of Father Mathew. c. 8vo. *Longmans.* pub. 3s. 6d.   O.P.

ALGEBRA:

See also MATHEMATICS.

Smith, C. Elementary algebra. g. 8vo. *Macmillan.*   4s. 6d.

Hall and Knight. Elementary algebra for schools. g. 8vo. *Macmillan.*   4s. 6d.

Todhunter, I. Algebra for beginners. 18mo. *Macmillan.*   2s. 6d.

     ,,   Treatise on algebra. c. 8vo. *Macmillan.*   7s. 6d.

Hall and Knight. Higher algebra. c. 8vo. *Macmillan.*   7s. 6d.
Solutions of the examples. c. 8vo. 8s. 6d.

Chrystal, G. Algebra. (Advanced). p. 8vo. 2 vols. *Black.*   23s.

ALGIERS, TUNIS, AND TRIPOLI:

Murray's Handbook to Algeria and Tunis. Ed. R. L. Playfair. p. 8vo. *Murray.*   12s.
Twelve maps and plans; and short bibliography.

Harris, G. W. Practical guide to Algiers. 8vo. *Philip.*   3s.

Tchihatcheff, P. de. Espagne, Algérie, et Tunis. 8vo. (*Paris*).   10s.
Largely geographical.

Vignon, L. La France dans l'Afrique du Nord. 8vo. (*Paris*).   6s.
With preface by E. de Laveleye.

Seguin, L. G. Walks in Algiers and its surroundings. p. 8vo. *Daldy.* illus.   12s.
A very pleasant tourist's companion to Algiers.

Knox, A. The new playground; or wanderings in Algeria. c. 8vo. *Paul.*   6s.
A cleverly-written book of travels, by the well-known London police magistrate.

Playfair, R. L. Travels in the footsteps of Bruce in Algeria and Tunis. 4to. *Paul.*   63s.
Illustrated by fac-similes of Bruce's drawing.

     ,,   The scourge of Christendom. d. 8vo. *Smith, Elder.* illus.   14s.
The great interest of the work is the subject of Christian slavery.

Russell, M. History and present condition of the Barbary states. 12mo. (*Edinburgh*).   O.P.
In "Edinburgh Cabinet Library."

Poole, S. Lane. The Barbary Corsairs. c. 8vo. *Unwin.* illus.   5s.

Playfair, R. L. Bibliography of Algeria, from the Expedition of Charles V. in 1541, to 1887. 8vo. *Royal Geographical Society.*   4s.

Tissot, C. Exploration scientifique de la Tunisie. 4to. 2 vols., 15s. each. (*Paris*).   30s.
Largely archæological.

Graham and Ashbee. Travels in Tunisia. *Dulau.* illus.   25s.
With glossary, map, and bibliography, which is also published separately.

Broadley, A. M. Tunis, past and present. 8vo. 2 vols. *Blackwood.* illus. 25s.
    With a narrative of the French conquest.

Charmes, G. La Tunisie et la Tripolitaine. 12mo. (*Paris*). 3s.

Fournel, M. La Tripolitaine; les routes du Soudan. 8vo. (*Paris*). 2s. 6d.

Smith and Porcher. Recent discoveries at Cyrene. *Day.* pub. 126s. O.P.
    Expedition to the Cyrenaica in 1860-61. Superbly illustrated with 12 maps and plates, tinted
    lithographs, and wood-cuts.

Beechy, F., and H. Proceedings of the expedition to the N. Coast of Africa,
    from Tripoli, eastward, in 1821-22. 4to. *Murray.* illus. pub. 63s. O.P.
    Comprehending an account of the Greater Syrtis and the Cyrenaica. Nine maps.

Playfair, R. L. Bibliography of Tripoli and the Cyrenaica. *Royal Geo-
    graphical Society.* 3s.

ALLOTMENTS, *see* POLITICAL ECONOMY VII.

ALPS, *see* SWITZERLAND.

AMBULANCE:

Esmarck, F. First aid to the injured. Tr. by H.R.H. Princess Christian.
    f. 8vo. *Smith, Elder.* 2s.

Roberts, R. L. Lectures on ambulance work. c. 8vo. *H. K. Lewis.*
    illus. 2s. 6d.

Pye, W. Elementary bandaging. 18mo. *Houlston.* illus. 2s.

Heath, C. Manual of minor surgery and bandaging. f. 8vo. *Churchill.*
    illus. 6s.

Caird and Cathcart. Surgical handbook. *Griffin.* illus. 8s. 6d.
    Good, and well illustrated.

AMERICA, NORTH:

See also CANADA *and* UNITED STATES.

Reclus, E. Universal geography, vol. xv. i. 8vo. *Virtue.* 21s.
    Contains summary of American geography and exploration. Vol. xvii., to be issued shortly,
    will deal with the United States.

Stanford's Compendium; North America. Ed. Hayden and Selwyn.
    l. p. 8vo. *Stanford.* illus. and maps. 21s.

Catlin, G. North American Indians. r. 8vo. 2 vols. *Chatto.* col. plates. 63s.

Maclean, J. M. Twenty-five years' service in the Hudson's Bay Territory.
    8vo. 2 vols. *Bentley.* 1849. pub. 21s. O.P.
    Contains much information on Labrador.

Hind, H. Y. Explorations in the interior of Labrador. 8vo. 2 vols.
    Longmans. pub. 32s. O.P.
    The publications of the Royal Geographical Society, and the American Geographical Society,
    should be consulted on Labrador.

Hatton and Harvey. Newfoundland. d. 8vo. *Chapman.* 18s.

Hall, E. H. The Home Colony: a guide book to Newfoundland. 8vo.
    Stanford. 1s.

Pedley, C. History of Newfoundland. 8vo. *Longmans.* pub. 10s. O.P.

Campbell, D. History of Prince Edward Island. 12mo. (*Charlottetown*).
    CONSULT also the Bulletin of the American Geographical Society (N. York).

AMERICA, CENTRAL:

See also MEXICO.

Reclus, E. Universal geography, vol. xvi. i. 8vo. *Virtue.*   21*s.*

Stanford's Compendium: Central America, the W. Indies, and S. America.
Ed. H. W. Bates. l. p. 8vo. *Stanford.* illus. and maps.   21*s.*

Caceres, J. M. Geografia de Centro-America. 8vo. (*Paris*).   2*s.*

Brigham, W. T. Guatemala; the land of the Quetzal. d. 8vo. *Unwin.*   21*s.*

Bristowe and Wright. Handbook of British Honduras for 1889-90. c. 8vo.
Blackwood.   6*s.*
<small>Historical, statistical, and general information concerning the colony.</small>

Squier, E. G. Honduras. p. 8vo. *Trübner.* pub. 3*s.* 6*d.*   O.P.
<small>Descriptive, historical, and statistical.</small>

Soltera, M. A lady's ride across Spanish Honduras. 8vo. *Blackwood.*
illus.   12*s.* 6*d.*

Squier, E. G. Nicaragua. 8vo. 2 vols. *Harper.* illus. pub. 20*s.*   O.P.
<small>People, scenery, monuments, and the proposed inter-oceanic canal.</small>

Reyes, R. Apuntamientos estadisticos sobre la República del Salvador.
(*San Salvador*).
<small>Published for Paris Exhibition, 1889.</small>

Guzman, D. Topografia fisica de Salvador. (*San Salvador*).

AMERICA, SOUTH:

See also ARGENTINE, BRAZIL, CHILI, GUIANA, PERU.

—I. GENERAL:

D'Orbigny, A. Voyage dans l'Amérique méridionale. 7 vols. (*Paris*).
1833-47. illus   O.P.

Humboldt, A. von. Personal narrative of travels in America (1799-1804).
p. 8vo. 3 vols., 5*s.* each. *Bell (Bohn).*   15*s.*

Ball, J. Naturalist in South America. c. 8vo. *Paul.*   8*s.* 6*d.*

Vincent, F. Round and about S. America. 8vo. *Appleton.*   21*s.*

Watson, R. G. Spanish and Portuguese South America. p. 8vo. 2 vols.
Trübner.   21*s.*

—II. MINOR STATES:

COLUMBIA.

Pereira, R. S. États-Unis de Colombie. 8vo. *Marpon.*   8*s.* 6*d.*

COSTA RICA.

Calvo. Costa Rica. 12mo. (*Washington*).   10*s.* 6*d.*

ECUADOR.

Hassaurek, P. Four years among Spanish Americans. p. 8vo. *Low.*
pub. 7*s.* 6*d.*   O.P.

Simson, A. Travels in the wilds of Ecuador. c. 8vo. *Low.*   8*s.* 6*d.*

VENEZUELA.

Dance, C. D. Four years in Venezuela. p. 8vo. *H. S. King.*   7*s.* 6*d.*

Spence, J. M. Land of Bolivar. 8vo. 2 vols. *Low.* pub. 31*s.* 6*d.*   O.P.
<small>Adventure in Venezuela.</small>

Statistical Annuary of Venezuela. *Venezuelan Consulate (London)*.
To be had on application.

BOLIVIA.

Mathews, E. D. Up the Amazon and Madeira rivers, through Bolivia and
Peru. 8vo. *Low.*   18s.

Wiener, C. Perou et Bolivie. 8vo. *(Paris).* Maps and illus.   20s.

PATAGONIA.

Musters, G. C. At home with the Patagonians. p. 8vo. *Murray.* illus.   7s. 6d.

Dixie, F. Across Patagonia. 8vo. *Bentley.* illus.   15s.

Coppinger, R. W. Cruise of the " Alert." 8vo. *Sonnenschein.* illus.   6s.
Four years (1878-1882) in Patagonian, Melanesian, and Mascarene waters.

Beerbohm, J. Wanderings in Patagonia. c. 8vo. *Chatto.* illus.   3s. 6d.

ANATOMY, HUMAN :

—I. GENERAL :

Quain's Anatomy. Ed. Thomson, Schäfer, and Thane. 8vo. 2 vols., 18s.
each. *Longmans.* illus.   36s.

Knox, R. Manual of human anatomy. 12mo. *Renshaw.* 1852. illus.
pub. 12s. 6d.   O.P.

Gray, H. Anatomy, descriptive and surgical. r. 8vo. *Longmans.* illus.   36s.

Macalister, A. Text-book of anatomy. (Advanced). m. 8vo. *Griffin.*
illus.   36s.

Humphry, G. Human skeleton. m. 8vo. *Macmillan.* illus.   14s.
Advanced and philosophical.

Braune. Topographical anatomy. Tr. Bellamy. m. 8vo. *Churchill.*
illus.   40s.

Turner, W. Popular atlas of anatomy and physiology. fo. *Johnston.*   25s.
Very good.

Humphry, G. M. The human foot and human hand. f. 8vo. *Macmillan.*
illus.   4s. 6d.

Ellis, T. The human foot. d. 8vo. *Churchill.* illus.   7s. 6d.

Bell, C. The hand. p. 8vo. *Bell.*   5s.

Symington, J. Topographical anatomy of the child. fo. *Baillière.*   42s.

Flower, W. H. Diagrams of the nerves of the human body. r. 4to.
Churchill. illus.   12s.

Tomes, C. S. Dental anatomy. c. 8vo. *Churchill.* illus.   12s. 6d.

—II. HISTOLOGICAL :

Schäfer, E. A. Essentials of histology. c. 8vo. *Longmans.* illus.   6s.

Klein, E. Elements of histology. c. 8vo. *Cassell.* illus.   7s. 6d.
Medical elements of histology.

Klein and Smith. Atlas of histology. 4to. *Smith, Elder.*   84s.

Stricker, S. Manual of human and comparative histology. Tr.
H. Power. 8vo. 3 vols. *New Sydenham Soc.* To subscribers only.   31s. 6d.

Gibbs, H. Practical histology and pathology. c. 8vo. *H. K. Lewis.*   6s.
Medical.

Foster and Langley. Practical physiology and histology. c. 8vo. *Macmillan.*   7s. 6d.

—III. ARTISTIC:

Marshall, J. Anatomy for artists. c. 8vo. *Smith, Elder.* illus.	31*s.* 6*d.*
Duval, M. Artistic anatomy. Tr. Fenton. c. 8vo. *Cassell.* illus.	5*s.*
Bell, C. Anatomy and philosophy of expression. 8vo. *Bell.*	16*s.*

Also 12mo., 5*s.*

ANCIENT CIVILISATION, *see* ANTHROPOLOGY III.

ANEMONES, BRITISH, *see* ZOOLOGY VI.

ANGLING, *see* FISHING.

ANGLO-SAXON:

SUGGESTIONS TO BEGINNERS: First take Earle's *Short Grammar*, and after acquiring some knowledge of the grammatical forms of words, read the selections from the Gospels, with constant reference to the grammar, and parsing every word with the help of the glossary. Then take Sweet's *Reader* and read the pieces in prose. After this, take Plummer's *Chronicles* and read it well through with the help of his excellent glossary. After which, return to Sweet's *Reader*, and study the poetry, beginning with the Battle of Maldon. This done, the student will be able to guide himself.

—I. GRAMMARS AND READING BOOKS:

Marsh, F. A. Comparative grammar of the Anglo-Saxon language. 8vo. *Low.*   12*s.*

On a large scale.

Sievers, E. Old English grammar. Tr. A. S. Cook. 12mo. *Ginn.*   6*s.*

Chiefly phonetic.

Earle, J. Book for beginners in Anglo-Saxon. ex. f. 8vo. *Clar. Press.*   2*s.* 6*d.*

Short grammar, prose reading, and glossary.

  „   Philology of the English tongue. ex. f. 8vo. *Clar. Press.*   7*s.* 6*d.*

Sweet, H. History of English sounds. d. 8vo. *Clar. Press.*   14*s.*

Skeat, W. W. Principles of English etymology. c. 8vo. *Clar. Press.*

Ser. I. The native element, 9*s.* Ser. II. The foreign element, 10*s.* 6*d.*

Sweet, H. Anglo-Saxon reader in prose and verse. ex. f. 8vo. 2 vols. *Clar. Press.*   13*s.*

Vol. i., 8*s.* 6*d.*; vol. ii., 4*s.* 6*d.*

Zupitza. Old and middle English reader. Ed. Maclean. *Ginn.*   3*s.*

—II. DICTIONARIES AND REFERENCE:

Bosworth, J. Anglo-Saxon dictionary. Ed. and enlarged by T. N. Toller. sm. 4to. *Clar. Press.*

Parts i. to iii. down to Sár; 15*s.* each.

Leo, H. Angelsächsisches Glossar. r. 8vo. (*Halle*).   15*s.*

As yet, this is the only complete dictionary.

Mayhew and Skeat. Concise dictionary of Middle English. c. 8vo. *Clar. Press.*   7*s.* 6*d.*

Grein, C. W. Sprachschatz der angelsächsischen Dichter. 8vo. 2 vols. (*Cassel*).   O.P.

Wülcker, R. P., Grundriss zur Geschichte der angelsächsischen Literatur. 8vo. (*Leipzig*).   10*s.*

Good for bibliology; the criticism not always quite judicial.

Wright, T. Biographia Britannica literaria (Anglo-Saxon period). 8vo. *J. W. Parker.* 1842. pub. 12*s.*   O.P.

No later book covers the same ground for biographies.

—III. HISTORY AND CRITICISM:

Watson, R. S. Caedmon, the first English poet. c. 8vo. *Longmans.*
pub. 3s. 6d.   O.P.

Earle, J. Anglo-Saxon literature. f. 8vo. *S. P. C. K.*   2s. 6d.

Brink, B. ten, Early English literature. Tr. H. M. Kennedy p. 8vo.
Bell (Bohn).   3s. 6d.
<small>The Anglo-Saxon period forms the introductory part.</small>

Freeman, E. A. Old English history for children. ex. f. 8vo. *Macmillan.*   6s.

Bright, W. Chapters of early English church history. d. 8vo. *Clar.
Press.*   12s.

—IV. TEXTS:

Thorpe, B. Anglo-Saxon version of the gospels. *Rivingtons.* 1848.   O.P.

Caedmon. Angelsächsische biblische Dictungen. Ed. Bouterweck. 8vo.
2 vols. (*Elberfeld*). 1844–50.
<small>Since Thorpe's *Caedmon* was O.P. this has been the only separate edition.</small>

Schmidt, R. Die Gesetze der Angelsachsen. 8vo. (*Leipzig*).   20s.
<small>The only edition of Saxon laws in the market. Thorpe's edition (*Ancient laws and institutes*), from which it was made, may be seen in libraries.</small>

Wulfstan. Homilies: text. Ed. A. Napier. 8vo. (*Berlin*).   7s.

Be Domes Daege. (Early English Text Soc.). Ed. J. Lawson Lumby.
d. 8vo. *Trübner.*   2s.
<small>After Beda's *De die judicii.*</small>

Anglo-Saxon Life of St. Katherine: with Latin original. (Early English
Text Soc.). Ed. Einenkel. d. 8vo. *Trübner.*   12s.

Alfred's version of "Cura pastoralis." (Early English Text Soc.). Ed.
H. Sweet. d. 8vo. 2 vols., 10s. each. *Trübner.*   20s.

Alfred's version of Orosius. (Early English Text Soc.). Ed. H. Sweet.
d. 8vo. *Trübner.* Part i., 13s.

Oldest English texts. (Early English Text Soc.). Ed. H. Sweet. d. 8vo.
Trübner.   20s.

Old English vocabularies. Ed. Wright and Wulcker. 8vo. 2 vols.
Trübner.   28s.

Aelfric's Grammatik and Glossar: text. Ed. Zupitza. 8vo. (*Berlin*).   7s.

Lay of St. Andreas. Ed. W. M. Baskerville. 12mo. *Ginn.*   1s. 6d.

Aelfric's homilies. Ed. B. Thorpe. 2 vols. *Aelfric Soc.* 1844–6.   O.P.
<small>In libraries; there is no later edition.</small>

Beowulf and the Fight at Finnsburg. Ed. Harrison and Sharp. 12mo. *Ginn.*   6s.

Saxon Chronicles, A.D. 787–1001. Ed. C. Plummer. c. 8vo. *Clar. Press.*   3s.
<small>A revised text; with introduction, critical notes, and glossary.</small>

Saxon Chronicles; with English translation. Ed. and tr. B. Thorpe.
r. 8vo. 2 vols., 10s. each. *Eyre.*   20s.

Codex Exoniensis. Ed. and tr. B. Thorpe. 8vo. *Pickering.* 1842.
pub. 20s.   O.P.
<small>A collection of Anglo-Saxon poetry, from MS. of Dean and Chapter of Exeter. This text has since been embodied in the next book.</small>

Bibliothek der angelsächsischen Poesie. Ed. C. Grein. 8vo. 2 vols.
(*Cassel*).
<small>Vol. i., 12s.; vol. ii. (part 1), 8s.</small>

Cartularium Saxonicum. Ed. W. de Gray Birch. c. 8vo. 2 vols., 31s. 6d. each. *Whiting.*

<small>Vol. iii., in progress, 2s. 6d. per part. Nos. i. to xxvii., to A.D. 973.</small>

Earle, J. Handbook to the land charters. c. 8vo. *Clar. Press.*   16s.

Caedmon. Exodus and Daniel. Ed. Hunt. 12mo. *Ginn.*   3s. 6d.

Beowulf; fac-simile. (Early English Text Soc.). Ed. Zupitza. d. 8vo. *Trübner.*   25s.

Blickling homilies i.-iii. (Early English Text Soc.). Ed. R. Morris. d. 8vo. 3 vols. *Trübner.*   20s.

<small>Vol. i., 8s.; vol. ii., 4s.; vol. iii., 8s.</small>

Aelfric. Metrical lives of saints. (Early English Text Soc.). Ed. W. W. Skeat. d. 8vo. 3 vols. *Trübner.*

<small>Vol. i., 10s.; vol. ii., 12s.</small>

—V. TRANSLATIONS:

Weymouth, R. F. Literal translation of Cynewulf's "Elene." 8vo. *Stock.*   5s.

Low, W. H. Translation of Saxon Chronicles, from A.D. 787 to 1001. c. 8vo. *Clive.*   3s.

Garnett, J. M. Translation of the Beowulf. 12mo. *Ginn.*   5s. 6d.
<small>Translated line for line.</small>

,,   Translation of the "Elene," "Judith," "Athelstan," and "Byrhtnoth." c. 8vo. *Ginn.*   5s.

ANIMAL INTELLIGENCE, *see* MENTAL PHYSIOLOGY I.

,,   MAGNETISM, *see* PSYCHICAL RESEARCH.

,,   PHYSIOLOGY, *see* PHYSIOLOGY.

ANIMALS, DISEASES OF, *see* LIVE-STOCK *and* VETERINARY SCIENCE.

,,   DISTRIBUTION OF, *see* ZOOLOGY IV.

,,   DOMESTICATED, *see* LIVE-STOCK.

ANNUITIES, *see* ASSURANCE.

ANTARCTIC REGIONS, *see* ARCTIC.

ANTHROPOLOGY:

See also FOLKLORE.

<small>Tylor's *Anthropology* should be read first as an introduction: then Lubbock's *Origin of Civilisation*; afterwards Im Thurn's *Amongst the Indians of Guiana* may be studied for the daily life of a savage. The student will then appreciate Tylor's *Early History* and *Primitive Culture.* For an introduction to archæological anthropology Lubbock's *Prehistoric Times*, and for an introduction to philology Fr. Müller's *Grundriss* is recommended. The comparative study of man's physical characteristics is best given by Topinard, and the classification of mankind by De Quatrefages. Mr. Galton has made heredity and anthropometry his especial subjects. Lists of works relating to anthropology (and kindred subjects), compiled by Otis Mason, have appeared in the appendices to the Smithsonian Reports (*Washington*), 1879-86.</small>

—I. GENERAL:

Joly, N. Man before metals. ("Inter. Scient." ser.). c. 8vo. *Paul.*   5s.
<small>A good popular account of early man.</small>

Lubbock, J. Origin of civilisation and primitive condition of man. 8vo.
 Longmans. illus.   18*s.*
  See introductory remarks.

Tylor, E. B. Researches into the early history of mankind. 8vo. *Murray.*   12*s.*
  See introductory remarks.

  ,,   Anthropology. c. 8vo. *Macmillan.* illus.   7*s.* 6*d.*
  See introductory remarks.

  ,,   Primitive culture. 8vo. 2 vols. *Murray.*   24*s.*
  The standard work on primitive beliefs and customs.

—II. PREHISTORIC RACES AND THEIR MONUMENTS:

Lyell, C. Antiquity of man. 8vo. *Murray.* pub. 14*s.*   O.P.

Lubbock, J. Prehistoric times. 8vo. *Williams.*   18*s.*

Schrader, O. Prehistoric antiquities of Aryan peoples. Tr. F. B. Jevons.
 d. 8vo. *Griffin.*   21*s.*
  A manual of comparative philology and the earliest culture.

Dawkins, W. B. Cave hunting. 8vo. *Macmillan.* illus. pub. 21*s.*   O.P.
  Researches on the remains of prehistoric man in the bone caves of Europe.

  ,,   Early man in Britain. m. 8vo. *Macmillan.*   25*s.*

Evans, J. Ancient stone implements of Great Britain. r. 8vo. *Longmans.*
 illus. pub. 28*s.*   O.P.

  ,,   Ancient bronze implements of Great Britain and Ireland. 8vo.
 Longmans. illus. pub. 25*s.*   O.P.
  These works by Dawkins and Evans are suited to advanced students.

Greenwell, W. British barrows. m. 8vo. *Clar. Press.* illus.   25*s.*

Munro, R. Ancient Scottish lake-dwellings. d. 8vo. illus.   21*s.*

  ,,   Lake dwellings of Europe. 8vo. *Cassell.*   31*s.* 6*d.*

Keller, F. Lake-dwellings of Switzerland and of Europe. Tr. J. Lee. 8vo.
 2 vols. *Longmans.* illus. pub. 42*s.*   O.P.
  An important book for advanced students.

Nilsson, S. Primitive inhabitants of Scandinavia. Ed. J. Lubbock. 8vo.
 Longmans. pub. 18*s.*   O.P.
  Comparative ethnography in the N. of Europe during the Stone Age.

—III. ANCIENT RACES AND THEIR INSTITUTIONS:

Letourneau, C. La sociologie d'après l'ethnographie. 12mo. *Reinwald.*   4*s.* 6*d*

Spencer, H. Studies in sociology. ("Inter. Scient." ser.). c. 8vo. *Paul.*   5*s.*

Maine, H. Early history of institutions. 8vo. *Murray.*   9*s.*

Freeman, E. A. Comparative politics. 8vo. *Macmillan.*   14*s.*

Gomme, G. L. Literature of local institutions. f. 8vo. *Stock.*   4*s.* 6*d.*
  Applies only to English institutions, but it is the only bibliography.

Maine, H. Ancient law. 8vo. *Murray.*   9*s.*

  ,,   Early law and custom. 8vo. *Murray.*   9*s.*

Gomme, G. L. Primitive folkmoots. 8vo. *Low.*   12*s.*

Frazer, J. G. Totemism. c. 8vo. *Black.*   3*s.* 6*d.*

McLennan, J. F. Studies in ancient history. 8vo. *Macmillan.*   16*s.*

  ,,   The patriarchal theory. 8vo. *Macmillan.*   14*s.*

Pulszky, A. Theory of law and civil society. d. 8vo. *Unwin.*   18*s.*

Morgan, L. Ancient society. 8vo. *Macmillan.*   O.P.

Schrader, O.   Prehistoric antiquities of the Aryan peoples.   Tr.   8vo. *Griffin.*   21*s.*

Hearn, W. E.   Aryan household.   8vo.   *Longmans.*   16*s.*

Coulanges, F. de.   Aryan civilization.   Tr.   8vo.   *Parker.*   pub. 5*s.*   O.P.

Maine, H.   Village communities in the east and west.   8vo.   *Murray.*   9*s.*

Gomme, G. L.   The village community.   ("Contemp. science" ser.).   *Scott.*
illus.   3*s.* 6*d.*

Phear, J. B.   The Aryan village in India and Ceylon.   p. 8vo.   *Macmillan.*
pub. 7*s.* 6*d.*   O.P.

Laveleye, E. de.   Primitive property.   Tr.   8vo.   *Macmillan.*   pub. 12*s.*   O.P.

Seebohm, F.   English village community.   8vo.   *Longmans.*   16*s.*

Mayne, J. D.   Hindu law and usage.   r. 8vo.   *Stevens.*   32*s.*

Smith, W. Robertson.   Religion of the Semites; fundamental institutions.
d. 8vo.   *Black.*   15*s.*

    ,,   Kinship and marriage in early Arabia.   c. 8vo.   *Cambridge Press.*   7*s.* 6*d.*

O'Curry, E.   Manners and customs of the ancient Irish.   8vo.   3 vols.
Williams.   30*s.*

Fenton, J.   Early Hebrew life.   8vo.   *Trübner.*   pub. 5*s.*   O.P.

Wilkinson, J. G.   Manners and customs of the ancient Egyptians.
c. 8vo.   3 vols.   *Murray.*   illus.   84*s.*
A popular edition at 12*s.*

Mallet, P.   Northern antiquities.   Tr. Percy.   p. 8vo.   *Bell (Bohn).*   5*s.*
Ancient Scandinavian manners and customs.

—IV. MODERN ETHNOGRAPHY:

Wood, J. G.   Illustrated history of man.   r. 8vo.   2 vols.   *Routledge.*   28*s.*
A good popular account of savage and barbaric peoples.

Lane, E. W.   Manners and customs of the modern Egyptians.   Ed. E. S.
Poole.   c. 8vo.   2 vols.   *Murray.*   12*s.*

Dalton, E. T.   Descriptive ethnology of Bengal.   4to.   *Trübner.*   illus.   126*s.*

Elliott, H. M.   History, folklore, and distribution of the races of the
North-West Provinces of India.   d. 8vo.   *Trübner.*   illus.   36*s.*

Lewin, T. H.   Wild races of south-east India.   p. 8vo.   *Allen.*   pub. 10*s.* 6*d.*   O.P.

Man, E. H.   Aboriginal inhabitants of the Andaman Islands.   d. 8vo.
Trübner.   illus.   10*s.* 6*d.*

Nadaillac, Marquis de.   Prehistoric America.   Tr. N. D'Anvers.   8vo.
Murray.   illus.   16*s.*
For the general reader.

Bancroft, H. H.   Native races of the Pacific States.   r. 8vo.   5 vols.,
25*s.* each.   *Longmans.*   125*s.*
Vast collection of anthropological material as to the tribes and nations of the west side of
North America.

Schoolcraft, H. R.   Archives of aboriginal knowledge.   i. 4to.   6 vols.
Lippincott.   £15 15*s.*
All the original papers laid before the Congress respecting the history, antiquity, ethnology
of the Indian tribes of the United States.

Brinton, D. G.   Library of American aboriginal literature.   8vo.   7 vols.
Trübner.   82*s.*
Vols. i., ii., iv., v., vi., vii., 12*s.* each ; vol. iii., 10*s.*

Im Thurn, E. F.   Among the Indians of Guiana.   8vo.   *Paul.*   illus.   18*s.*
See introductory remarks.

Curr, E. M. Australian race. d. 8vo. 4 vols. *Trübner.* illus.   42*s.*
     Valuable treasury of native philology and custom. Conclusions not to be accepted implicitly.

Dawson, J. Australian aborigines. 4to. *Macmillan.*   14*s.*
     Description of natives of Western Victoria.

Smyth, R. B. Aborigines of Victoria. 4to. *Trübner.* illus.   63*s.*

Roth, H. Ling. Aborigines of Tasmania. 8vo. *Trübner.* illus. pub. 21*s.*   O.P.
     With preface by E. B. Tylor.

Turner, G. Samoa a hundred years ago. p. 8vo. *Macmillan.*   9*s.*
     Description of customs of the Navigator Islanders.

Notes and queries on anthropology for the use of travellers and residents in uncivilised lands. f. 8vo. *Stanford.*   5*s.*
     Prepared by a committee of the British Association. Of great value for travellers in savage and barbaric countries.

—V. PHYSICAL CHARACTERISTICS :

Topinard, P. Éléments d' anthropologie générale. 8vo. (*Paris*). illus.   20*s.*
     An exhaustive comparative study of the physical characters of man.

Haeckel, E. History of the evolution of man. Tr. p. 8vo. 2 vols. *Paul.* illus.   32*s.*
     To be read by students acquainted with technical zoology.

Quatrefages, A. De. Histoire générale des races humaines. l. 8vo. 2 vols. (*Paris*). illus.   22*s.*
     Latest contribution to the study of the classification of the races of man.

Beddoe, J. Races of Britain. r. 8vo. *Arrowsmith.* illus. and maps.   21*s.*
     Physical anthropology.

Darwin, C. Descent of man. c. 8vo. *Murray.* illus.   7*s.* 6*d.*
     This classical work should be read by all students who approach anthropology on the zoological side.

Roberts, C. Manual of anthropometry. d. 8vo. *Churchill.* illus.   8*s.* 6*d.*

Galton, F. Hereditary genius. 8vo. *Macmillan.* pub. 12*s.*   O.P.

Ribot, T. Heredity. r. 8vo. *H. S. King.*   9*s.*

Weissmann, A. Essays on heredity. (Advanced). 8vo. *Clar. Press.*   16*s.*

—VI. PHILOLOGICAL CLASSIFICATION :

Müller, F. Grundriss der Sprachwissenschaft. 8vo. 4 vols. (*Vienna*).   52*s.*
     An important general philological classification of peoples by languages. For advanced students.
     PERIODICALS : *L'Anthropologie* (Masson), fortnightly ; *Zeitschrift für Ethnologie* (Asher), monthly ; *Journal of the Anthropological Institute*, quarterly.

ANTILLES, *see* WEST INDIES II.

ANTIQUITIES, *see* ARCHÆOLOGY *and* ANTHROPOLOGY.

     „   POPULAR, *see* FOLKLORE.

ANTISEPTICS AND BACTERIOLOGY :

Trouessart, E. L. Microbes, ferments, and moulds. 8vo. *Paul.* illus.   5*s.*

Klein. Micro-organisms in disease. c. 8vo. *Macmillan.* illus.   6*s.*

Cheyne, W. Watson. Antiseptic surgery. d. 8vo. *Smith, Elder.* illus.   21*s.*

De Bary, A. Lectures on bacteria. Tr. Garnsey and Balfour. c. 8vo. *Clar. Press.*   6*s.*

APIARY, *see* BEES.

APPARITIONS, *see* PSYCHICAL RESEARCH.

ARABIA : GEOGRAPHY :

Reclus, E. Universal geography, vol. ix. Tr. i. 8vo. *Virtue.*   21*s.*

Palgrave, W. G. A year's journey through Central and Eastern Arabia (1862–63). c. 8vo. *Macmillan.*   6*s.*

Blunt, Lady Anne. Pilgrimage to Nejd, the cradle of the Arab race. 2 vols. *Murray.* illus.   21*s.*

Burton, R. F. Pilgrimage to El-Medina and Meccah. 3 vols. *Longmans.* illus. pub. 43*s.*   O.P.

Doughty, C. M. Travels in Arabia Deserta. 8vo. 2 vols. *Cambridge Press.* illus.   63*s.*

Hrugronje, C. S. Mekka. 8vo. 2 vols. (*Leyden*).   40*s.*
Vol. i., Die Stadt und ihre Herren ; vol. ii., Aus dem heutigen Leben. With atlas, 4to.

Glaser. Skizze der Geschichte und Geographie Arabiens. r. 8vo. *Dulau.*   21*s.*

ARABIA : LANGUAGE AND LITERATURE :

The student is recommended to master the selections in either Socin's or Lansing's manual, while making himself familiar with the grammatical paradigms and rules; to proceed thence through the reading-book of Forbes or Kosegarten; next to work through the grammar of Wright, and the reading-book of either Wright or De Sacy. He will then be in a position to study the original literature.

—I. GRAMMARS, DICTIONARIES, ETC. :

(A) CLASSICAL.

Socin, A. Arabic grammar. 8vo. *Williams.*   7*s.* 6*d.*
Contains Litteratura Arabica ; a bibliography of the literature.

Lansing, J. G. The Arabic manual. 8vo. *Nutt.*   10*s.* 6*d.*

Wright, W. Arabic grammar. Tr. from Caspari. 8vo. 2 vols. *Williams.* pub. 23*s.*   O.P.

Howell, M. S. Arabic grammar. 8vo. 3 vols. (*Allahabad*).   80*s.* 6*d.*
Vol. i. (1), 28*s.* ; (2), 21*s.* ; vols. ii., iii., 31*s.* 6*d.* Native system.

Wortapet and Porter. Arabic-English dictionary. 12mo. (*Cairo*).   22*s* 6*d.*

Abcarius, J. English-Arabic dictionary. 8vo. (*Beyrout*).   32*s.*

Steingass, F. English-Arabic dictionary. d. 8vo. *W. H. Allen.*   28*s.*

Lane, E. W. Arabic-English dictionary. Ed. Poole. 4to. 7 vols., 25*s.* each. *Williams.*   175*s.*
Unfinished.

Badger, G. P. English-Arabic dictionary. 4to. *Paul.*   189*s.*

Thornton, F. du Pré. Elementary Arabic reading lessons. c. 8vo. *W. H. Allen.* Part. i., 3*s.* 6*d.*
Grammatical analysis of parts of the Koran.

Forbes, D. Arabic reading lessons. r. 8vo. *W. H. Allen.*   15*s.*
With glossary.

Kosegarten, J. Chrestomathia Arabica. 8vo. (*Leipzig*). 1828.   12*s.*
Excellent collection. Glossary in Latin.

Sacy, S. de. Chrestomathie Arabe. r. 8vo. 3 vols. *Imprimerie du Roi.* 1827.   105*s.*
French translations.

Wright, W. Arabic reading book. 8vo. *Williams.*   7s. 6d.
Very advanced.

(B) MODERN.

Green, A. O. Practical Arabic grammar. c. 8vo. *Clar. Press.*   7s. 6d.
Dialect of Egypt.

Tien, A. Colloquial Arabic. f. 8vo. *W. H. Allen.*   7s. 6d.
Chiefly dialect of Syria.

Spitta-Bey. Grammatik des arabischen Vulgär-Dialectes von Ægypten. 8vo. (*Berlin*).   25s.

Newman, F. W. Arabic-English and English-Arabic dictionary. 8vo. *Trübner.*   6s.
Difficult system of transliteration.

Birdwood, A. Arabic reading book. 8vo. *W. H. Allen.*   5s.
Dialect of Egypt.

Machuel, L. Manuel de l'Arabisant. 8vo. (*Algiers*).   5s.
Dialect of Algiers.

Spitta-Bey. Contes arabes modernes. 8vo. (*Leyden*).   6s. 6d.
Dialect of Egypt. In European characters; of the greatest value.

—II. LITERATURE :

The Koran. (Arabic text). Ed. Flügel. 4to. (*Leipzig*).   20s.

,, ("Chandos Classics"). Tr. Sale. c. 8vo. *Warne.*   2s.

,, Tr. Palmer. d. 8vo. 2 vols. *Clar. Press.*   21s.

Selections from the Koran. Tr. E. W. Lane. 8vo. *Trübner.*   9s.

Elif Leila wa Leila. ("Arabian Nights"). Arabic text. 4 vols. (*Beyrout*).   24s.

Minhádj at-Tâlibin. Tr. into French by Van den Berg. r. 8vo. 3 vols. (*Batavia*).   50s.
Shâfeïte system.

Makainas of Hariri. Ed. Serkis. (*Beyrout*).

Assemblies of Hariri. Tr. Chenery. r. 8vo. *Williams.*   10s.
Elegant prose.

Kalila wa Dimna. (Bidpai's Fables). Arabic text. (*Beyrout*).

Diwan el-Mutanablî. Ed. Nasif el-Yazagi. 8vo. (*Beyrout*).   10s. 6d.

Lyall, C. J. Translations from ancient Arabian poetry. f. 4to. *Williams.*   10s. 6d.

Poetical works of Zoheir. Tr. Palmer. c. 4to. 2 vols., 10s. 6d. each. *Cambridge Press.*   21s.

Burckhardt, J. Arabic proverbs. 8vo. *Quaritch.*   10s.

—III. REFERENCE :

Haji Khalfa's Lexicon bibliographicum et encyclopædicum. Ed. and tr. into Latin by G. Flügel. 4to. 7 vols. (*Leipzig*). 1835–59.   126s.

Müller, A. Orientalische Bibliographie. 8vo. 4 vols. (*Berlin*).   28s.
Vol. i., 6s.; vol. ii., 6s.; vols. iii., iv., 8s. each. In progress.

Journal of Royal Asiatic Society. Ed. Rhys Davids. *Trübner.*
First series, complete in 20 vols., £10. New series, vol. i. (in two parts), 16s.; vol. ii., 16s.; vol. iii., 22s.; vol. iv., 16s.; vol. v., 18s. 6d.; vol. vi., 16s.; vol. vii., 16s.; vol. viii., 16s.; vol. ix., 18s. 6d.; vol. x., 22s.; vol. xi., 20s. 6d.; vol. xii., 23s.; vol. xiii., 31s.; vol. xiv., 31s. 6d.; vol. xv., 21s.; vol. xvi., 27s. 6d.; vol. xvii., 30s.; vol. xviii., 32s. 6d.; vol. xix., 40s.; vol. xx., 10s.

Arbuthnot, F. F. Arabic authors. 8vo. *Heinemann.*   10s.

ARABS, HISTORY OF, *see* MAHOMETANISM.

ARBORICULTURE, *see* FORESTRY.

ARCHÆOLOGY:

See also ANTHROPOLOGY II., *and* ARCHITECTURE III., ASSYRIA, EGYPT, GREECE, MEXICO, PALESTINE, PHŒNICIA, ROME.

Smith, W. Dictionary of Greek and Roman antiquities. 8vo. *Murray.*   28s.

Daremberg et Saglio. Dictionnaire des antiquités. 4to. (*Paris*).
Parts i. to xiii., 4s. 6d. each. In progress.

Rich, A. Dictionary of Greek and Roman antiquities. p. 8vo. *Longmans.*   7s. 6d.

Roscher, W. H. Lexicon der Mythologie. r. 8vo. (*Leipzig*).
Parts i. to xviii., 2s., each. In progress.

Baumeister, A. Denkmäler des classischen Alterthums. r. 8vo. 3 vols. (*Münich*).   87s.
Vol. i., 26s.; vol. ii., 23s.; vol. iii., 38s.

Babelon, E. Manual of Oriental antiquities. Tr. T. A. Evetts. 8vo. *Grevel.*   10s. 6d.

Perrot and Chipiez. L'art dans l'antiquité. 4to. *Hachette.* illus.
Vol. i., L'Egypte; vol. ii., Chaldée et Assyrie; vol. iii., Phénicie, Cypre; vol. iv., Judée, Sardaigne, Syrie, 21s. each. In progress. For English translation, *see* ART I. The chief treatises referred to by Perrot are the following: *Empire of the Hittites,* by W. Wright (Nisbet); *Reisen in Klein-Asien und Nordsyrien,* by Humann and Puchstein (Berlin); *Description de l'Asie-Mineure,* by C. Texier; *Exploration archéologique,* by Perrot, Guillaume, and Delbet; Ramsay's *Studies in Asia Minor and Phrygia* (in vols. iii. and v. of *Hellenic Journal,* Macmillan), and *Relations between Western Phrygia and Cappadocia* (Trübner); Sayce's *Karian language and inscriptions* (Trübner); and *Notes from journeys in the Troad and Lydia* (in vol. i. of *Hellenic Journal*).

Maspero, G. Histoire ancienne des peuples de l'orient. 12mo. *Hachette.*   5s.
GUIDES: Guide-books to British Museum, Louvre, and Berlin Museum.
JOURNALS: Publications of the German Archæological Institute; *Journal of Hellenic Studies* (Macmillan); *Bulletin de correspondence hellénique; Gazette archéologique; Comptes-rendus de l'Académie de St. Pétersbourg; Ephemeris archaiologike* (Greek); *Classical Journal.*

ARCHERY:

The most important treatises on Archery from an historical point of view are: (1) *Toxophilus,* by Roger Ascham; first edition, 1545; modern edition of Ascham's works in 4 vols., 12s. (Reeves, 196, Strand). (2) *The English Bowman,* by T. Roberts. 8vo. 1801.

Ford, H. Theory and practice of archery. 8vo. *Longmans.*   14s.

The Archer's Register. Ed. F. T. Follett. *H. Cox.*   3s. 6d.
Published annually; contains records of archery meetings through the year.

ARCHITECTURE:

For the professional student the best selection of reading is that contained in the *Kalendar* issued annually by the Royal Institute of British Architects. Those who desire to acquire a good general acquaintance with the subject, or to judge of their fitness for the profession, may well read the following books:—Tarver (*Guide*), Mitchell (*Manual*), Smith and Slater (*Classic and early Christian architecture*), Leeds (*Orders*); for Christian and Byzantine, Fergusson's *History*; for Saracenic, Smith and Slater's *Classic*; T. R. Smith (*Gothic*), Parker (*Introduction to Gothic*), Rickman (*Gothic in England*), Turner and Parker (*Domestic Architecture*), T. R. Smith (*Renaissance*), and Fergusson (*Modern styles*).

—I. HISTORY AND GENERAL:

Tarver, E. J. Guide to the study of the history of architecture. *Pettitt.*   O.P.
A handy and useful elementary book containing numerous bibliographical references.

Mitchell, T. Rudimentary manual of architecture. c. 8vo. *Longmans.* illus. pub. 10s. 6d.   O.P.

Fergusson, J. History of architecture. 8vo. 2 vols. *Murray.* illus.   63s.
New edition in preparation.

18

Freeman, E. A. History of architecture. d. 8vo. *Masters.* pub. 49*s.*   O.P.

Viollet-le-Duc, E. Lectures on architecture. Tr. Bucknall. 8vo. 2 vols., 31*s.* 6*d.* each. *Low.* illus.   63*s.*

—II. STYLES AND PERIODS:

These are treated of in the foregoing works, but specifically in the following.

Wilkinson, G. The architecture of ancient Egypt. 8vo. (*London*). 1850. illus.   O.P.

Leeds, W. H. The orders of architecture. p. 8vo. *Lockwood.*   1*s.* 6*d.*

Normand, C. New parallel of the orders of architecture. fo. Tr. Pugin. *Taylor.* illus.   O.P.

Mauch, J. M. von. Die architektonischen Ordnungen der Griechen und Römer. r. 8vo. (*Berlin*). illus.   14*s.* 6*d.*

Penrose, F. C. Principles of Athenian architecture. fo. *Macmillan.* illus.   147*s.*
Dilettanti Society's publication.

Stuart and Revett. Antiquities of Athens. fo. 5 vols. *Priestley and Weale.* 1841. illus.   O.P.

  ,, The same, abridged ed. p. 8vo. *Bell.* illus.   5*s.*
A handy summary of the larger work.

Taylor and Cresy. Architectural antiquities of Rome. fo. *Crosby, Lockwood.* illus.   63*s.*

Smith and Slater. Classic and early Christian architecture. 8vo. *Low.*   5*s.*

Texier and Pullan. Byzantine architecture. fo. *Day.* illus.   O.P.

Dartein, F. de. Étude sur l'architecture lombarde. 4to. plates fo. (*Paris*).   120*s.*)

Scott, Gilbert. Lectures on mediæval architecture. 8vo. 2 vols. *Murray.* illus.   42*s.*

Parker, J. H. Introduction to Gothic architecture. f. 8vo. (*Oxford*). illus.   5*s.*

Bloxam, M. H. Principles of Gothic ecclesiastical architecture. p. 8vo. 3 vols. *Bell.* illus.   22*s.* 6*d.*

Moore, C. H. Gothic architecture. m. 8vo. *Macmillan.*   18*s.*

Rickman, T. Attempt to discriminate the styles of architecture in England. d. 8vo. *Parker* (*Oxford*). illus.   16*s.*
Additions by J. H. Parker; contains pre-Norman work, omitted from 7th edition with a view to publication in separate form, an idea not yet carried out.

Turner and Parker. Domestic architecture in England. 3 vols. (*Oxford*). illus.   72*s.*
Vol. i., 21*s.*; vol. ii., 21*s.*; vol. iii., 30*s.*

Moller, G. Memorials of German Gothic architecture. Tr. Leeds. s. 8vo. *Weale.* 1824.   O.P.

Whewell and Lassaulx. Architectural notes on German churches. 8vo. (*Cambridge*). 1842.   O.P.

Ruskin, J. Stones of Venice. i. 8vo. 3 vols. *G. Allen.* illus.   89*s.*

Street, G. E. Gothic architecture in Spain. *Murray.* illus. pub. 30*s.*   O.P.

Smith, T. R. Gothic and renaissance architecture. c. 8vo. *Low.* illus.   5*s.*

Fergusson, J. Modern styles of architecture. 8vo. *Murray.* illus.   31*s.* 6*d.*
New edition in preparation.

Lübke, W. Ecclesiastical art in Germany. Tr. Wheateley. r. 8vo. (*Edinburgh*). illus.   21s.

Deals with transition from Byzantine to Gothic.

Berty, A. La renaissance monumentale en France. l. 4to. 2 vols. *Morel*. illus.   72s. 6d.

Grandjean de Montigny, and Famin. L'architecture toscane. fo. (*Paris*). illus.   60s.

III. CASTLES AND MONUMENTS:

Clark, G. T. Mediæval military architecture in England. 8vo. 2 vols. *Wyman*. illus.   31s. 6d.

M'Gibbon and Ross. Castellated and domestic architecture of Scotland. r. 8vo. 4 vols., 42s. each. *Douglas*.   168s.

Viollet-le-Duc, E. E. Military architecture of the middle ages. Tr. M. Macdermot. m. 8vo. *Parker*. illus.   10s. 6d.

Britton, J. Architectural antiquities of Great Britain. 4to. 5 vols. *Longmans*. 1807–26.   O.P.

Cutts, E. L. Sepulchral slabs and crosses of the middle ages. *Parker*. 1849.   O.P.

Rimmer, A. Ancient stone crosses of England. 8vo. *Virtue*. illus.   9s.

Non-sepulchral.

Haines, H. Manual of ornamental brasses. 8vo. 2 vols. *Parker*.   21s.

Creeny, W. F. Monumental brasses on the Continent. fo. *Goose* (*Norwich*).   50s.

A fine work; plates executed in facsimile from rubbings.

Fergusson, J. Rude stone monuments. r. 8vo. *Murray*. illus. pub. 24s.   O.P.

A perfect encyclopædia of so-called "Druidical remains."

Abbeys and churches of England and Wales. Ed. T. G. Bonney. *Cassell*. illus.   21s.

A popular account, illustrated with good wood-cuts. Ruined abbeys and churches, *i.e.*, such as are not now in use as places of worship, are expressly excluded.

IV. MISCELLANEOUS AND REFERENCE:

Garbett, E. L. Principles of design in architecture. 12mo. *Lockwood*.   2s. 6d.

Ruskin, J. Seven lamps of architecture. i. 8vo. *G. Allen*. illus.   21s.

Also p. 8vo., 7s. 6d.

Chambers, W. Decorative part of civil architecture. Ed. W. H. Leeds. 4to. *Lockwood*. illus.   21s.

Blackburne, E. L. Decorative painting applied to English architecture. fo. *Williams*. 1847. illus.   O.P.

Heideloff, C. von. Architectural ornaments of the middle ages in the Byzantine and Gothic style. Tr. 4to. (*Nuremberg*). illus.   30s.

Gwilt, J. Encyclopædia of architecture. 8vo. *Longmans*. illus.   52s. 6d.

Contains a bibliography, and a large number of brief biographical notices.

Parker, J. H. Glossary of terms used in architecture. d. 8vo. 3 vols. (*Oxford*). 1850. illus.   O.P.

,,   Concise glossary of terms used in architecture. f. 8vo. *Jas. Parker*. illus.   7s. 6d.

An abridgment of the larger work, without the plates.

Dictionary of architecture. *Architectural Publication Soc.* (9, *Conduit-street*, *W*.).

Seven volumes of text out of eight are already issued; and three vols. of illustrations. Price of the complete work to subscribers, £21.

Viollet-le-Duc, E. Dictionnaire raisonnée de l'architecture française du
    11ᵉ au 16ᵉ siècle. l. 8vo. 10 vols. (*Paris*). illus.   £12 12*s.*

Milizia, F. Lives of celebrated architects. Tr. Mrs. Cresy. 8vo. 2 vols.   O.P.
    Taylor. 1826.

> JOURNALS, ETC.: *Builder* (46, Catherine-street, W.C.); *Building News* (332, Strand,
> W.C.); *Proceedings and Transactions of the Royal Institute of British Architects*
> (9, Conduit-street, W.).

ARCTIC AND ANTARCTIC REGIONS:

Richardson, J. The polar regions; physical geography and ethnology.
    8vo. *Longmans.*   14*s.*

Arctic geography and ethnology. 8vo. *Murray.* maps.   7*s.* 6*d.*
    Selection of papers for the Arctic expedition of 1875.

Rink, H. Danish Greenland. Ed. Brown. p. 8vo. *King.*   10*s.* 6*d.*

Nansen, F. The first crossing of Greenland. 8 vols. 2 vols. *Longmans.*   36*s.*

Barrow, J. Voyages in the arctic regions. 8vo. *Murray.* 1818.   O.P.

    ,,   Voyages of discovery and research in the arctic regions from
        1818. 8vo. *Murray.* 1846.   8*s.*

    ,,   Discovery and adventure in polar seas and regions. Ed. Leslie and
        others. 12mo. *Harper.*   5*s.*

Nordenskjöld, A. E. von. Arctic voyages, 1858–79. Ed. A. Leslie. 8vo.
    Macmillan. illus.   16*s.*

    ,,   Voyage of the "Vega" round Asia and Europe. Tr. Leslie. 8vo.
        2 vols. *Macmillan.* illus.   45*s.*
        With review of all previous voyages along the north coast of the Old World.

Nares, G. S. Voyage to the polar sea in the "Alert" and "Discovery."
    8vo. 2 vols. *Low.*   42*s.*

Markham, A. H. The great frozen sea; voyage of the "Alert." c. 8vo.
    Paul.   6*s.*

Markham, C. R. The threshold of the unknown region. c. 8vo. *Low.*   10*s.* 6*d.*

Hall, C. F. Life with the Esquimaux. i. 8vo. *Bickers.* pub. 6s.   O.P
    Discovery of Frobisher's relics, etc.

    ,,   Second Arctic expedition of Charles F. Hall. Ed. J. Nourse.
        4to. *Trübner.*   28*s.*
        His voyage to Repulse Bay; sledge journeys to the Straits of Fury and Hecla, and to King
        William's Land; and residence among the Eskimo during the years 1864-9.

    ,,   Narrative of the expedition in the "Polaris." Ed. Davis. 4to.
        Trübner. illus.   28*s.*

Schley and Soley. The rescue of Greeley. 8vo. *Low.*   12*s.* 6*d.*
    With photos and maps.

Greeley, A. W. Three years of Arctic service; Lady Franklin Bay expedi-
    tion, 1881–4. r. 8vo. 2 vols. *Bentley.*   42*s.*
    With photographs taken by the party, and official maps and charts.

Weddell, J. Voyage towards the south Pole, 1822–24. 8vo. *Longmans.*
    1825.   O.P.

Ross, J. C. Voyages to Antarctic regions, 1839–43. 8vo. 2 vols. *Murray.*
    1847.   O.P.

McCormick, R. Voyages in the Antarctic Seas, 1839–43. r. 8vo. 2 vols.
    Low.   52*s.* 6*d.*

ARGENTINE REPUBLIC AND RIVER PLATE STATES:

Napp and others. Argentine Republic. (*Buenos Ayres*).

Mulhall, M. G., and E. T. Handbook of the River Plate. c. 8vo. *Trübner.*   8s.
    Comprising the Argentine Republic, Uruguay, and Paraguay.

Rumbold, H. Great silver river. c. 8vo. *Murray.* illus.   12s.

Uruguayan Republic, territory and conditions. c. 8vo. *Stanford.*   6s.
    By authority of Consulate-General of Uruguay.

ARITHMETIC:

Brook-Smith. Arithmetic in theory and practice. c. 8vo. *Macmillan.*   4s. 6d.
    Key, with each example completely worked out. c. 8vo. *Macmillan.* 10s. 6d.

Sonnenschein and Nesbitt. A.B.C. of arithmetic. 2 parts, 1s. each.
    Sonnenschein.   2s.
    For teachers of very young children.

    ,,   Science and art of arithmetic. c. 8vo. *Sonnenschein.*   5s. 6d.
    Chiefly for teachers.

De Morgan, A. Elements of arithmetic. 8vo. (*London*). 1848.   O.P.
    Though modern writers have drawn on De Morgan for their materials, this book is still of the greatest value to the student.

ARMENIA, TURKISH, *see* TURKEY.

ARMENIAN LANGUAGE:

Lauer, M. Grammatik der classischen Armenischen Sprache. (*Vienna*).   2s. 6d.

Calfa, A. Dictionnaire Arménien-Français. 12mo. (*Paris*).   21s.

ARMS AND ARMOUR:

    For general information, Lacombe, Luard, Scott; for special weapons, Egerton, De Cosson, Burton; for brief and useful reference, Demmin, Meyrick, Grose, Hewitt.

Lacombe, M. P. Arms and armour. Tr. Boutell. p. 8vo. *Reeves and Turner.* illus.   5s.
    Useful abstract for general reader; sketchy information.

Demmin, A. Arms and armour. Tr. Black. p. 8vo. *Bell.* illus.   7s. 6d.
    Valuable to the general collector. Inaccurate in some details, and with rather rough drawings.

Egerton, W. Handbook of Indian arms. 4to. *Trübner.*   2s. 6d.
    South Kensington Museum handbook; a very accurate and well-illustrated catalogue of the arms in the Indian Museum.

Luard, J. History of the dress of the British soldier. (*London*). 1852.   O.P.
    Beautifully illustrated history of the armour of the different races that have inhabited England (and to some extent India) since the Roman times.

Cosson, De. Ancient helmets, etc. *Archæological Institute.*   O.P.
    An exhaustive catalogue.

Meyrick, S. K. Ancient armour in Europe. i. 4to. 2 vols. *Bohn.* 1830. illus. pub. 94s. 6d.   O.P.
    Best account of arms and armour; specially of England to reign of Charles II.

Grose, F. Ancient arms and armour. (*London*). 1788. illus.   O.P.
    An old but useful book.

Scott, Sibbald. The British army; its origin and equipment. 2 vols. *Cassell.* illus.   42s.
    Good general account of weapons and armour used in the English army.

Burton, R. F. Book of the sword. 4to. *Chatto.* illus. 32s.
　　An exhaustive account of this special weapon.

Hewitt, J. Ancient armour and weapons in Europe. d. 8vo. 3 vols.
　　J. Parker. illus. 31s. 6d.
　　A valuable book of reference.

ARMY :

　　　Army regulations, drill books, handbooks, instructions, &c., are not noticed in the follow-
　ing list. A list of those published "by authority" will be found in the *Monthly Army
　List.* (*Eyre*; 1s. 6d. monthly).

—I. ARMS OF THE SERVICE :

Pratt, S. C. Field artillery; its equipment, organization, and tactics.
　　s. c. 8vo. *Paul.* 6s.

Kraft, Prince. Letters on artillery. Tr. Walford. c. 8vo. *Stanford.* 7s. 6d.

Mackinlay, E. Text-book of gunnery. *Eyre.* 4s.

Denison, G. A history of cavalry from the earliest times. 8vo. *Mac-
　　millan.* 18s.

Kraft, Prince. Letters on cavalry. Tr. Walford. *Stanford.* 6s.

Brack, F. de. Light cavalry outposts. Tr. Hale. *Mitchell.*

Kraft, Prince. Letters on infantry. Tr. Walford. *Stanford.* 6s.

Mayne, B. Infantry fire tactics. *Stanford.* illus. 6s.

Instructions in military engineering. 5 parts. *Eyre.* 12s. 6d.
　　Part i., 2s.; ii., 2s. 6d.; iii., 3s.; iv., 1s. 6d.; v., 3s. 6d.

Lewis, J. F. Permanent fortification for English engineers. *R. E. Institute,
　　Chatham.*

Clarke, G. S. Fortification, past and present. *Murray.* 15s.

Bucknill. Submarine mines and torpedoes. r. 8vo. *Office of "Engineering."* 12s. 6d.

Brackenbury, C. B. Field works. s. c. 8vo. 2 parts. *Paul.* 12s.

Walter. England's volunteer force. 12mo. *Clowes.* 5s.

Cooke, A. C. Aide-mémoire for the use of officers of Royal Engineers.
　　2 vols., 12s. 6d. each. *Eyre.* pub. 25s.
　　Technical. vol. i. o.p.

Wolseley, G. Soldier's pocket-book for field service. sq. 16mo. *Macmillan.* 5s.
　　General.

—II. ART OF WAR :

Hamley, E. B. The operations of war explained and illustrated. 4to.
　　Blackwood. 30s.

Shaw, W. Elements of modern tactics. s. c. 8vo. *Paul.* illus. 9s.

Clery, C. Minor tactics. c. 8vo. *Paul.* illus. 9s.

Verdy du Vernois. Studies in troop-leading (infantry). Tr. H. J. T.
　　Hildyard. 8vo. *King.* 7s. 6d.

　　,,　Studies in troop-leading (cavalry). Tr. W. H. Harrison. Ed. B. Bell.
　　8vo. *Eyre.* 5s.

Hamley, E. B. National defence. p. 8vo. *Blackwood.* 6s.

Frome, E. Outline of the method of conducting a trigonometrical survey,
　　etc. Revised C. Warren. 8vo. *Lockwood.* 1840. 12s.

Hutchinson, H. D. Military sketching made easy. 8vo. *Gale and Polden.* 4s.

23

Schellendorf, B. Von. Duties of the general staff. Tr. Hare. 8vo. 2 vols.
    Eyre.   15*s.*

Grierson, J. M. Staff duties in the field. *Harrison.*
    In press.

Furse, G. Military transport. 8vo. *Eyre.*   5*s.*

—III. MILITARY LAW AND HISTORY:

Buxton, J. W. Elements of military administration and law. s. c. 8vo.
    Paul.   7*s.* 6*d.*

Thring and others. Manual of military law. *Eyre.*   2*s.* 6*d.*
    Abbreviated 1888; 1*s.* 6*d.*

Pratt, S. C. Military law; its procedure and practice. s. c. 8vo. *Paul.*   4*s.* 6*d.*

Clode, C. M. The military forces of the crown. 8vo. 2 vols., 21*s.* each.
    Murray.   42*s.*
    Dealing with their relation to the Government.

Adams, C. Great campaigns. Ed. C. C. King. 8vo. *Blackwood.*   16*s.*
    A succinct account of the principal operations which have taken place in Europe from 1796 to
    1870.

Napier, W. F. P. History of the war in the Peninsula. c. 8vo. 3 vols.
    Routledge.   10*s.* 6*d.*
    Vol. i. (1807–10), 3*s.* 6*d.*; ii. (1810–12), 3*s.* 6*d.*; iii. (1812–14), 3*s.* 6*d.*

Chesney, C. C. Waterloo lectures; a study of the campaign. 8vo.
    Longmans.   10*s.* 6*d.*

Kaye, J. W. History of the war in Afghanistan. c. 8vo. 3 vols. *W. H.*
    Allen.   26*s.*

Hamley, E. B. The Crimean campaign.   5*s*

Kaye, J. W. History of the Sepoy war in India. d. 8vo. 3 vols. *W. H.*
    Allen.   58*s.*

Battles and leaders of the civil war (American). 8vo. 4 vols. *Unwin.*   105*s.*

The Franco-German war, 1870–71. Tr. from the German official account by
    F. C. H. Clarke. 8vo. 3 vols. *Eyre.*   131*s.* 6*d.*
    Also in 25 separate sections, from 2*s.* 6*d.* to 31*s.* 6*d.* each.

Greene, F. V. The Russian army and its campaigns in Turkey in 1877–8.
    r. 8vo. *Allen.*   32*s.*

Wilson, A. The ever victorious army. 8vo. *Blackwood.*   O.P.
    Suppression of the Taeping rebellion, by Colonel (afterwards General) Gordon.

—IV. BIOGRAPHY:

Series of military biographies. 4*s.* each vol. *Chapman.*
    Frederick the Great (Brackenbury), Washington (Cooper King), French revolutionary
    generals (Griffiths), Turenne (Hozier), Prince Eugene (Malleson), Parliamentary generals of
    civil war (Walford).

Coxe, W. Memoirs of the Duke of Marlborough. 8vo. 3 vols., 3*s.* 6*d.*
    each. *Bell (Bohn).*   10*s.* 6*d.*

Wrottesley, G. Life and correspondence of F.-M. Sir J. Burgoyne. 8vo.
    2 vols. *Bentley.*   30*s.*

Bourrienne, L. A. F. de. Memoirs of Napoleon Buonaparte. (Tr. from the
    French). Ed. R. W. Phipps. d. 8vo. 3 vols. *Bentley.*   42*s.*

Napier, W. Life and opinions of General Sir C. Napier. p. 8vo. 4 vols.
    Murray. 1847.   O.P.

Brialmont. Life of Arthur, first Duke of Wellington. Tr. C. R. Gleig.
    8vo. 4 vols. *Longmans.*   O.P.

Gurwood, J. Selections from the despatches of the Duke of Wellington.
r. 8vo. *Murray.* 1841.   O.P.

Shadwell. Life of Colin Campbell, Lord Clyde. 8vo. 2 vols. *Blackwood.*   36s.

Gordon, H. W. Events in the life of Charles George Gordon. d. 8vo.
Paul. illus.   7s. 6d.

—V. MISCELLANEOUS:

Maurice, J. F. Hostilities without declaration of war. 8vo. *Eyre.*   2s.

Blunt, S. E. Rifle and carbine firing for the United States army. *Low.*   8s. 6d.

Laidley, F. S. A course of instruction in rifle firing. 16mo. *Lippincott.*   7s. 6d.

Kitchener, H. E. Revolvers and their use. *Royal United Service Instit.*   O.P.

Farrow, E. S. Military encyclopædia. 4to. 3 vols. (*New York*).   170s.

> There is no bibliography of military books. The nearest approach to a bibliography are the
> catalogues of the War Office and Royal United Service Institution libraries.

ART—PICTORIAL AND PLASTIC:

—I. HISTORY AND GENERAL:

D'Anvers, N. Elementary history of art (architecture, painting, sculpture).
c. 8vo. *Low.* illus.   10s. 6d.
> Adopted as text-book at South Kensington.

Lübke, W. History of art. Tr. F. E. Bunnett. l. 8vo. 2 vols. *Smith,
Elder.* illus.   42s.
> Architecture, painting, sculpture.

Winckelman. History of ancient art. Tr. Lodge. 8vo. 2 vols. *Chapman.* 1851. illus.   O.P.

Perrot and Chipiez. History of art. Tr. W. Armstrong. i. 8vo. *Chapman.*
illus.
> In progress. Judæa, Sardinia, Syria, and Cappadocia, 2 vols., 42s.; Phœnicia, 2 vols., 42s.;
> Chaldæa and Assyria, 2 vols., 42s.; Egypt, 2 vols., 42s. A comprehensive and excellent work.
> Rather advanced for the general reader, perhaps, but eminently readable.

Labarte, J. Handbook of the arts of the middle ages. Tr. 8vo. *Murray.*
illus.   O.P.

Bibliothèque de l'enseignement des beaux-arts. 8vo. 34 vols., 3s. to 5s.
each. *Quantin.*

Newton, C. T. Essays on art and archæology. 8vo. *Macmillan.* illus.   12s. 6d.

Rayet, O. Monuments de l'art antique. fo. (*Paris*). illus.   120s.
> Art in chronological order, from earliest period to second century B.C.

Symonds, J. A. Renaissance in Italy. 8vo. *Smith, Elder.*   16s.

Scott, L. Renaissance of art in Italy. 4to. *Low.* illus.   31s. 6d.
> Avowedly written for the general reader.

Müntz, E. La renaissance en Italie et en France. r. 8vo. (*Paris*).   30s.

Pattison, Mrs. Mark. Renaissance of art in France. 8vo. 2 vols. *Paul.*
illus. (In progress).   32s.

Laborde, L. de. La renaissance des arts à la cour de France. (14th
century). 8vo. (*Paris*).   O.P.
> Biographical and critical; advanced.

Eastlake, C. L. Materials for a history of oil painting. Ed. (2nd vol.)
Lady Eastlake. *Longmans.*   O.P.
> Chiefly history of technique.

Woltmann and Woermann. History of painting. Ed. S. Colvin. 8vo.
Vol. i., 28s.; ii., 42s. *Paul.* illus.   70s.

Crowe and Cavalcaselle. A new history of painting in Italy from 2nd to 16th century. 8vo. 3 vols. *Murray.* illus.   O.P.

,,   History of painting in north Italy from 14th to 16th century. 8vo. 2 vols. *Murray.* illus.   42s.

Lanzi, L. History of painting in Italy. 8vo. 3 vols., 3s. 6d. each.   *Bell* (*Bohn*).   10s. 6d.

Walpole, H. Anecdotes of painting in England. 8vo. *Murray.*   6s.

Ottley, W. Y. Origin and early history of engraving on copper and wood. 4to. 2 vols. (*London*). 1816.   O.P.

Lübke, W. History of sculpture. Tr. Bunnett. i. 8vo. 2 vols. *Smith, Elder.* illus.   42s.

Perkins, C. C. Tuscan sculptors. 8vo. 2 vols. *Longmans.* pub. 63s.   O.P.

,,   Italian sculptors. 8vo. *Longmans.* pub. 42s.   O.P.

—II. SCHOOLS :

See also JAPAN.

Kugler, F. T. Handbook of painting. Ed. Layard. p. 8vo. 2 vols. *Murray.* illus.   30s.

Wornum, R. N. Epochs of painting. 8vo. *Chapman.* illus.   20s.

Siret, A. Dictionnaire historique des peintres de toutes les écoles. 8vo. (*Paris*). illus.   25s.

Smith, J. Catalogue raisonnée of Dutch, Flemish, and French painters. 8vo. 9 parts. *Smith.* 1829-42.
Invaluable to collectors, for identification of pictures.   O.P.

Kugler, F. T. Handbook of painting : German, Flemish, and Dutch schools. Ed. J. A. Crowe. c. 8vo. 2 vols. *Murray.*   24s.

Ruskin, J. Giotto and his works in Padua. 3 parts. *Arundel Society.* illus.   15s.

,,   Val d'Arno. 8vo. *G. Allen.* illus.   22s. 6d.
XIII. century art in Pisa and Florence.

—III. BIOGRAPHY :

Vasari, G. Le vite de' più eccellenti pittori, scultori, ed architetti. 15 vols. 12mo. (*Florence*).   48s.
Other editions. Also translated by Mrs. Foster ; p. 8vo. 6 vols. 3s. 6d. each. *Bell* (*Bohn*). 21s.

Charignarie and Aurray. Dictionnaire général des artistes de l'école française. r. 8vo. 2 vols. (*Paris*).   60s.

Redgrave, R. and S. A century of painters of the English school. 8vo. 2 vols. *Smith, Elder.*   32s.

Redgrave, S. Dictionary of artists of the English school. d. 8vo. *Bell.*   16s.

Cunningham, A. Lives of British painters, sculptors, and architects. p. 8vo. 3 vols., 3s. 6d. each. *Bell* (*Bohn*).   10s. 6d.

Strutt, J. Biographical dictionary of engravers. (*London*). 1785-6.   O.P.

Bryan, M. Dictionary of painters and engravers. Ed. Graves. 2 vols., 31s. 6d. each. *Bell.*   63s.

Ottley, H. Dictionary of painters and engravers. i. 8vo. *Bell.*
Supplement to Bryan.   12s.

Wilson, C. Michel Angelo. 8vo. *Murray.* illus.   15s.

Crowe and Cavalcaselle. Life and works of Raphael. 8vo. 2 vols. *Murray.*   33s.
Vol. i., 15s. ; vol. ii., 18s.

Müntz, E. Raphael, sa vie, son œuvre, et son temps. r. 8vo. (*Paris*). illus.   25s.

   ,,   Raphael; his life, works and times. Tr. i. 8vo. *Chapman*. illus.   25s.

Meyer, J. Correggio. Tr. Mrs. Heaton. i. 8vo. *Macmillan*.   31s. 6d.

Crowe and Cavalcaselle. Titian, his life and times. 8vo. *Murray*. illus.   21s.

Symonds, J. A. Benvenuto Cellini. 8vo. *Nimmo*. illus.   12s.

Maxwell, W. S. Annals of the artists of Spain. 8vo. 6 vols. *Nimmo*. illus.   126s.
     Vols. i. to iv. issued; v. and vi. shortly.

Curtis, C. B. Velasquez and Murillo. r. 8vo. *Low*.   31s. 6d.
     Few personal details, but valuable as a record of pictures.

Justi, C. Velasquez. Tr. A. H. Keane. r. 8vo. *Grevel*.   36s.

Thausing, M. Alb. Dürer. Ed. F. A. Eaton. 8vo. 2 vols. *Murray*. illus.   42s.

Wornum, R. N. Holbein. r. 8vo. *Chapman*.   31s. 6d.

Curtis, C. B. Rembrandt's etchings, with biography and notes. fo. illus. *Dodd, Mead & Co., N.Y.*   126s.

Vosmaer. Rembrandt, sa vie et ses œuvres. r. 8vo. (*The Hague*).   24s.

Sainsbury, W. Noël. Original and unpublished papers of Rubens. 8vo. *Bradbury*.   O.P.

Leslie, C. R. Constable. 4to. *Longmans*. 1845. pub. 21s.   O.P.

Fulcher, G. W. Gainsborough. c. 8vo. *Longmans*. pub. 6s.   O.P.

Rossi, G. Angelica Kauffman. 8vo. (*Florence*). 1810.   O.P.

Taylor, Tom. Sir Joshua Reynolds. 8vo. 2 vols. *Murray*. pub. 42s.   O.P.

Thornbury, W. Turner. 8vo. 2 vols. *Hurst*.   30s.

Smith, J. T. Nollekens. 8vo. 2 vols. *Colburn*. 1829.   O.P.

Plon, E. Thorwaldsen; sa vie et son œuvre. 8vo. (*Vienna*). illus.   15s.

—IV. THEORY, ÆSTHETICS AND CRITICISM:

Alison, A. Essays on the nature and principles of taste. 8vo. (*Edinburgh*). 1825.   O.P.

Lessing, G. E. Laoköon. Tr. T. Burbidge. 8vo. *Macmillan*.   12s.

Schlegel, F. Æsthetic and miscellaneous works. Tr. E. J. Millington. p. 8vo. *Bell (Bohn)*.   3s. 6d.

Taine, H. De l'idéal dans l'art. 12mo. (*Paris*).   2s. 6d.

Guizot, F. P. G. The fine arts; their nature and relations. Tr. G. Grove. 8vo. *Bosworth (London)*.   O.P.

Parry, T. G. The ministry of fine art. 8vo. *Murray*.   14s.

Fromentin, E. Les maîtres d'autrefois. 12mo. (*Paris*).   4s.
     A model of intelligent criticism.

Morelli, G. Italian masters in German galleries. Tr. Mrs. L. Richter. c. 8vo. *Bell*.   8s. 6d.
     Should be studied by collectors.

Ruskin, J. Modern Painters. i. 8vo. 5 vols. *G. Allen*. illus.   126s.

   ,,   Aratra Pentelici. 8vo. *G. Allen*.   22s. 6d.
     Elements of sculpture.

   ,,   Ariadne Florentina. 8vo. *G. Allen*.   22s. 6d.
     Florentine engraving—wood and metal.

   ,,   Elements of drawing. 8vo. *Smith, Elder*. 1857.   O.P.

—V. SYMBOLISM:

Jameson, Mrs.　Sacred and legendary art.　8vo.　4 vols.　*Longmans.*　illus.
　　Legends of the Saints and Martyrs, 2 vols, 20s.　Legends of the Madonna, 10s.　Legends of the Monastic Orders, 10s.

Didron, A. N.　Christian iconography.　Tr. Millington.　c. 8vo.　2 vols., 5s. each.　*Bell (Bohn).*　illus.　　　　　　　　　　　　　　　　　10s.

Jameson, Mrs., and Lady Eastlake.　History of the Saviour as exemplified in works of art.　8vo.　2 vols.　*Longmans.*　illus.　　　　　　20s.

—VI. TECHNIQUE:

Church, A. H.　Chemistry of paints and painting.　8vo.　*Seeley.*　　　5s.

Merrifield, Mrs.　Original treatises, from the 12th to the 18th century. 8vo.　2 vols.　*Murray.*　1849.　　　　　　　　　　　　　　　　　o.p.
　　On oil painting, miniature, mosaic, glass, gilding, dyeing, colours, and artificial gems.

Cennini, C.　Treatise on painting.　Tr. Mrs. Merrifield.　r. 8vo.　*Lumley.* 1844.　　　　　　　　　　　　　　　　　　　　　　　　　　　o.p.
　　Written in 1437.　Practical directions for painting, with the art of illuminating MSS.

Book of Art.　Ed. F. Knight Hunt.　4to.　*(London).*　1846.　illus.　　o.p.
　　Practical directions for preparing and painting in fresco.

Lippman, F.　Art of wood engraving in Italy in the 15th century.　Tr. *Quaritch.*　　　　　　　　　　　　　　　　　　　　　　　　　　25s.

—VII. PERSPECTIVE:

Hayter, C.　Introduction to perspective, practical geometry, drawing, and painting.　8vo.　*Bagster.*　illus.　　　　　　　　　　　　　　　　· ·
　　A good general manual, very suitable for ladies.

Burchett, R.　Linear perspective.　p. 8vo.　*Chapman.*　illus.　　　　7s.

Malton, T.　Compleat treatise on perspective.　fo.　*(London).*　1779-83. illus.
　　A valuable but very advanced treatise: thorough and comprehensive.

Ware, W. R.　Modern perspective.　12mo.　*Osgood (Boston).*　plates 4to.　25s.
　　The most recent advanced work.　High-class.

—VIII. DECORATION AND ORNAMENT:

Wornum, R. N.　Analysis of ornament.　r. 8vo.　*Chapman.*　illus.　　8s.
　　The first book to be read by a student beginning this subject.　There is nothing equal to it as an explanation of first principles.

Day, L. F.　Anatomy of pattern.　c. 8vo.　*Batsford.*　illus.　　　　3s. 6d.

　　,,　Planning of ornament.　c. 8vo.　*Batsford.*　illus.　　　　3s. 6d.

　　,,　Application of ornament.　c. 8vo.　*Batsford.*　illus.　　　3s. 6d.
　　These three are very useful little handbooks.

Dresser, C.　Art of decorative design.　c. 8vo.　*Cassell.*　illus.　　5s.

Ruskin, J.　The two paths.　8vo.　*G. Allen.*　　　　　　　　　　　13s.
　　Principles of decorative art.

Racinet, A.　Polychromatic ornament.　Tr.　fo.　*Sotheran.*　illus.　　126s.
　　A truly magnificent work, systematically arranged.　The text is instructive.　100 plates in gold, silver, and colours.

　　,,　L'ornement polychrôme (2me. séries).　*(Paris).*　　　　　130s.
　　A worthy continuation of the first series.

Semper, G.　Polychromy.　Tr.　8vo.　1851.　　　　　　　　　　　o.p.
　　In *Museum of Classical Antiquities.*　Classic work and classic revival.

Hittorf, J. C.　L'architecture polychrôme chez les Grecs.　4to.　*Didot.*　　o.p.

Field's Chromatography. Ed. Taylor. c. 8vo. *Winsor and Newton.* illus.   5*s.*

Magne, L. Œuvre des peintres verriers français. 2 vols. sm. fo. *Firmin-Didot.*   100*s.*
> The last two works are artistic and critical.

Lévy and Capronnier. Peinture sur verre, particulièrement en Belgique. (*Brussels*).
> Historical and critical.
> See also Labarte's *Handbook of the arts of the middle ages*, cited under Section I.

Church, A. H. Colour (elem.). *Cassell.*   3*s.* 6*d.*

Chevreul, M. E. La loi du contraste simultané des couleurs. text 8vo. plates 4to. (*Paris*). 1839.   O.P.

  ,,   The same. Tr. Martel. 8vo. *Bell* (*Bohn*). illus.   5*s.*

  ,,   The same. Tr. Spanton. c. 8vo. *Routledge.* illus.   3*s.* 6*d.*
> A standard work; neither of the translations is perfectly satisfactory, Martel's having no coloured plates, and Spanton's being abridged in the text.

Shaw, H. Decorative arts of the middle ages. 8vo. *Bell.*   21*s.*
> PERIODICALS, ETC.: *The Year's Art*; annual; (Virtue); illus. *Art Journal* (Virtue); monthly, 1*s.* 6*d. Magazine of Art* (Cassell); monthly, 1*s.*

ARTILLERY, *see* ARMY I.

ARTISTIC ANATOMY, *see* ANATOMY III.

ARTISTIC PROCESSES:

—I. ETCHING:

Hamerton, P. G. Etching and etchers. 8vo. *Macmillan.* illus.   O.P.
> Critical and historical.

  ,,   The etcher's handbook (elem.). c. 8vo. *Roberson.*   5*s.*
> Technique.

—II. PRINTS AND ENGRAVINGS:

Brown, W. N. Practical manual of wood engraving. c. 8vo. *Lockwood.*   2*s.*
> With brief historical introduction; good on technique.

Chatto and Jackson. Wood engraving, historical and practical. l. 4to. *Chatto.* illus.   28*s.*

Didot, A. F. Essai sur la gravure sur bois (advanced). 8vo. (*Paris*).   4*s.* 6*d.*
> Historical and critical; contains list of artists and bibliography.

Passavant, J. D. Le peintre graveur. 8vo. 6 vols. (*Leipzig*).   54*s.*
> Advanced criticism.

—III. ENGRAVED GEMS:

Billing, A. The science of gems. r. 8vo. *Bell and Daldy.*   21*s.*
> Scientific and critical; contains a little technique.

King, C. W. Antique gems and rings. r. 8vo. 2 vols. *Bell and Daldy.*   42*s.*
> Historical and critical; contains biographical notices, and a bibliography.

  ,,   Handbook of engraved gems. i. 8vo. *Bell.* illus.   16*s.*
> Historical and critical; contains a catalogue of ancient artists.
> See also Jacquemart's *History of furniture*, cited under BRONZES.

—IV. GOLD AND SILVERSMITHS' WORK:

Pollen, J. H. Gold and silversmiths' work (S. Kensington art handbook). l. 8vo. *Chapman.*   2*s.* 6*d.*
> Historical only.

Wheatley and Delamotte. Art work in gold and silver. 8vo. 2 vols., 2*s.* 6*d.* each. *Low.*   5*s.*
> Vol. i., Mediæval ; vol. ii., Modern. Historical and critical.

Gee, G. E. Goldsmiths' handbook. 12mo. *Lockwood.*   3*s.* 6*d.*

,,   Silversmiths' handbook. 12mo. *Lockwood.*   3*s.* 6*d.*
> Both the latter books are technical and practical.

Cripps, W. J. College and corporation plate (S. Kensington art handbook). l. c. 8vo. *Chapman.*   2*s.* 6*d.*
> Historical, descriptive, and critical handbook to copies and reproductions in the S. Kensington Museum.

,,   Old English plate. m. 8vo. *Murray.* illus.   21*s.*
> Historical and descriptive ; contains list of makers' marks, etc.

,,   Old French plate. 8vo. *Murray.*   8*s.* 6*d.*
> Handbook for collectors ; critical and historical ; contains list of marks (towns and makers), etc.

—V. JEWELLERY :

Wallis, G. Jewellery (in " British manufacturing industries " ser.). p. 8vo. *Stanford.*   3*s.* 6*d.*
> Technical.

Boutell, C. Gold working (in same series). p. 8vo. *Stanford.*   3*s.* 6*d.*
> Technical.

Metal work (technique). Ed. G. W. Yapp. *Virtue.*   O.P.
> Historical and descriptive ; very fine plates ; text rather slight, but edited by Yapp, who is a good authority.
> *See also* Gee's *Goldsmiths' handbook,* cited in the preceding section ; and Jacquemart's *History of furniture,* cited under BRONZES.

—VI. BRONZES :

Fortnum, C. D. E. Bronzes (S. Kensington art handbook). l. c. 8vo. *Chapman.*   2*s.* 6*d.*
> Historical and technical.

Jacquemart, A. History of furniture. Tr. Mrs. B. Palliser. i. 8vo. *Chapman.* illus. pub. 31*s.* 6*d.*   O.P.
> *See also* Yapp's *Metal Work,* cited in the preceding section ; and J. C. Robinson's *Treasury of ornamental art.* Day. illus. O.P. Description only ; text slight.

—VII. ENAMELLING :

Ferrand, J. P. L'art du feu, ou de peindre en émail. (*Paris*). 1732.   O.P.
> Technique in detail ; old-fashioned ; no illustrations ; the most practical work on the subject.

Goupil and Renauld. Manuel vulgarisateur des connaissances artistiques (elem.). 16mo. (*Paris*).   O.P.
> Technique ; wholly practical ; very brief (16 pp.) ; no illustrations.
> *See also* J. Labarte's *Handbook of the arts of the middle ages* (in ART. I.) ; and Jacquemart's *History of furniture,* cited under BRONZES.

—VIII. WOOD CARVING :

Miller, F. Wood carving (elem.). c. 8vo. *Wyman.*   5*s.*
> Technique good.

Wood carving for amateurs. *Upcott Gill.*   1*s.*
> Technique good.

Leland, C. G. Manual of wood carving. 4to. *Whittaker.*   5*s.*

—IX. ILLUMINATING :

Audsley, W., and G. Guide to the art of illuminating. 8vo. *Rowney.*   1*s.*
> Historical and technical.

Offor, E. Art of illuminating without a master. 8vo. *Bunyard.* 6*s.*
 Technical.

Tymms and Wyatt. Art of illuminating. r. 8vo. *Day.* pub. 21*s.* O.P.
 Historical, critical, and technical; text slight; splendid illustrations.

Shaw, H. Handbook of the art of illumination. i. 8vo. *Bell and Daldy.*
 illus. 21*s.*
 Historical and critical; a fine work for study.

Jones and Humphreys. Illuminated books of the middle ages. *Longmans.*
 1849. O.P.
 High-class illustrations; with explanatory text.

—X. TAPESTRY:

Champeaux, A. de. Tapestry (S. Kensington art handbook). c. 8vo.
 Chapman. 2*s.* 6*d.*
 Historical: some technique.

Müntz, E. Tapestry. Tr. Miss L. J. Davis. *Cassell.* 5*s.*
 Historical: Müntz is considered a good authority.

Godon, J. Painted tapestry and its applications. *Lechertier (London).* 6*s.*
 Technique and briefly historical; technique good. A revived art.

—XI. STAINED GLASS WINDOWS:

Miller, F. Glass painting. *Wyman.* 5*s.*
 Good practical technique.

Gessert and Fromberg. Glass staining, and art of painting on glass. Tr.
 12mo. *Lockwood.* 2*s.* 6*d.*
 Technique.

Winston, C. Difference of style in ancient glass paintings, especially in
 England. m. 8vo. 2 vols. *Parker.* illus. 31*s.* 6*d.*

ASCENSION ISLAND, *see* ATLANTIC.

ASIA:

See also AFGHANISTAN, BURMA AND SHAN STATES, CEYLON, CHINA,
COREA, INDIA, INDIAN ARCHIPELAGO, JAPAN, MALAY PENINSULA,
PALESTINE, PERSIA, RUSSIA IN ASIA, TURKEY.

—I. GENERAL:

Reclus, E. Universal geography. i. 8vo. *Virtue.* illus. and maps. 21*s.*
 Vol. vi., Asiatic Russia (Caucasia, Turkestan, and Siberia); vol. vii., East Asia (Chinese
 Empire, Corea, and Japan); vol. viii., India and Indo-China; vol. ix., South-Western Asia
 (Afghanistan, Beluchistan, Persia, Asiatic Turkey, Asia Minor, Cyprus, Syria, Palestine,
 and Arabia). The introductory chapter of vol. vi. gives a general account of the geography of
 Asia.

Stanford's Compendium. Asia; with ethnological appendix. Ed. Keane
 and Temple. l. p. 8vo. *Stanford.* 21*s.*
 JOURNALS of the Royal Asiatic Society. (*Trübner*). [For particulars *see* ARCHÆOLOGY.]

—II. CENTRAL:

 The student will consult the *Gazetteer of Central Asia*, published by the India Office;
 the *Annual Reports of the Survey of India*; and the *Journal and Proceedings of the Royal
 Geographical Society.*

Stumm, H. Russia in Central Asia. Tr. Ozanne and Sachs. 8vo. *Harri-*
 son. 15*s.*
 Historical sketch of Russia's progress in the East up to 1873.

Lansdell, H. Russian Central Asia. 8vo. 2 vols. *Low.* illus.   42*s.*
     A popular summary. Including Kuldja, Bokhara, Khiva, Merv.

Curzon, G. N. Russia in Central Asia in 1889. 8vo. *Longmans.*   21*s.*
     Anglo-Russian question ; deals especially with the Central Asian railway.

Burnaby, F. Ride to Khiva. c. 8vo. *Cassell.*   3*s.* 6*d.*

Vambéry, A. History of Bokhara. 8vo. *King.* pub. 18*s.*   O.P.

Huc, Abbé. Chinese Empire ; Tartary and Thibet. 8vo. 2 vols. *Long-*
     mans.   24*s.*

Prejevalsky, N. From Kulja, the Thian Shan, to Lob Nor. Tr. Morgan.
     8vo. *Low.*   15*s.*
     With notices of the Central Asian lakes by Sir D. Forsyth. For General Prejevalsky's later
     journeys, the proceedings of the Royal Geographical Society should be consulted.

Kuropatkin, A. N. Kashgaria. Tr. W. E. Gowan. r. 8vo. *Thacker.*   10*s.* 6*d.*
     Historical and geographical sketch of the country, etc.

Prejevalsky, N. Mongolia, the Tangut Country, Northern Thibet, etc.
     Tr. Morgan and Yule. 8vo. 2 vols. *Low.*   42*s.*

Gilmour, J. Among the Mongols. c. 8vo. *R. T. S.* illus.   1*s.* 6*d.*

Howorth, H. H. History of the Mongols. r. 8vo. 4 vols. *Longmans.*   98*s.*

Wood, J. Journey to the source of the Oxus, 1840. Ed. Yule. 8vo.
     Murray.   12*s.*
     With essay on the geography of the Oxus Valley, by Col. Yule.

Narratives of G. Boyle's mission to Thibet, 1774, and T. Manning's journey
     to Lhasa. Ed. Markham. 8vo. *Trübner.*   O.P.
     Contains a very complete sketch of the geography of Central Asia.

Desgodins, C. H. Le Thibet. 8vo. (*Paris*).   7*s.*

ASIA MINOR, *see* TURKEY.

ASSAYING, *see* METALLURGY.

ASSURANCE :

     Assurance being a business, there are no text-books in the ordinary sense of the term.
     Life Assurance is the only department which has, to any extent, been made the subject of
     theoretical treatment.

King, G. Theory of finance. d. 8vo. *Layton.*   4*s.*

Porter, J. B. Laws of insurance. 8vo. *Stevens and Haynes.*   21*s.*
     Fire, Life, Accident, and Guarantee.

Sutton, W. Institute of Actuaries' text-book, part i. m. 8vo. *Layton.*   10*s.* 6*d.*
     Interest and annuities certain.

King, G. Institute of Actuaries' text-book, part ii. m. 8vo. *Layton.*   31*s.* 6*d.*
     Life contingencies, annuities, and other money benefits dependent on life.

Institute of Actuaries' life-tables. d. 8vo. *Layton.*   21*s.*

Mortality experience of life assurance companies. d. 8vo. *Layton.*   30*s.*
     Collected by Institute of Actuaries.

Crawley, C. Law of life insurance. d. 8vo. *Clowes.*   12*s.* 6*d.*

Accounts of life assurance companies. fo. *Eyre.* (For 1889).   2*s.* 6*d.*
     Board of Trade annual blue-book.

Hardy, G. F. Friendly societies. m. 8vo. *Layton.*   2*s.*

McArthur, C. Policy of marine insurance. 8vo. *Layton.*   3*s.* 6*d.*
     Popularly explained.

Lowndes, R. Law of marine insurance. d. 8vo. *Stevens.*   12*s.* 6*d.*

Arnould, J. Law of marine insurance. r. 8vo. 2 vols. *Stevens.*   60*s.*

Lowndes, R. Law of general average. r. 8vo. *Stevens.*   30*s.*

Hare, F. A. C. Fire insurance manual. c. 8vo. *Layton.*   15*s.*

Campbell, D. Fire underwriters' companion. d. 8vo. *Layton.*   10*s.* 6*d.*

Bunyon, C. J. Law of fire insurance. d. 8vo. *Layton.*   18*s.*

Insurance cyclopædia. Ed. C. Walford. r. 8vo. 6 vols., 21*s.* each. *Layton.*   126*s.*
    Incomplete.

Walford, C. Insurance guide and handbook. d. 8vo. *Layton.*   10*s.* 6*d.*
    PERIODICALS, ETC., *Post Magazine Almanac* (Buckley). *Handy Assurance Directory* (Bourne). *Journal of the Institute of Actuaries* (Layton) ; Four parts yearly ; 2*s.* 6*d.* per part.

ASSYRIA :

—I. ARCHÆOLOGY :

Layard, A. H. Monuments of Nineveh. i. fo. *Murray.* 1849–53. illus.
    pub. 210*s.*   O.P.

Rawlinson, G. Five great monarchies. 8vo. 3 vols. *Murray.* illus.   42*s.*

Smith, G. Babylonia. Ed. A. H. Sayce. *S. P. C. K.*   2*s.*

  ,,   Assyria. *S. P. C. K.*   2*s.*

Ragozin, Z. A. Chaldea. ("Story of the nations" series). c. 8vo. *Unwin.* illus.   5*s.*

  ,,   Assyria. ("Story of the nations" series). c. 8vo. *Unwin.* illus.   5*s.*

Menant, J. Annales des rois d'Assyrie. l. 8vo. *(Paris).*   12*s.* 6*d.*

Layard, A. H. Nineveh and its remains. c. 8vo. *Murray.* illus.   7*s.* 6*d.*
    With account of a visit to the Chaldean Christians of Kurdistan, etc.

  ,,   Nineveh and Babylon. c. 8vo. *Murray.* illus.   7*s.* 6*d.*

Botta, P. E. Monument de Ninive. fo. 5 vols. *(Paris).* 1847–50. illus.   £72

Tiele, C. P. Babylonisch-Assyrische Geschichte. 8vo. 2 vols. *(Gotha).*   13*s.*
    Vol. i., 6*s.* ; vol. ii., 7*s.*

Perrot et Chipiez. Chaldea and Assyria (L'art dans l'antiquité, vol. ii.).
    Tr. Armstrong. *Chapman and Hall.*   42*s.*
    [For full particulars of the work *see* ARCHÆOLOGY, and ART I.]

Oppert, J. Expédition en Mesopotamie (1851–4). 4to. 2 vols. *(Paris).*
    illus.   100*s.*

Records of the Past. Ed. Birch. 12mo. 12 vols., 3*s.* 6*d.* each. *Bagster.*
    O.P., except vol. xii. For fuller particulars, *see* EGYPT II.

Records of the Past (Second series). Ed. Sayce. 4 vols., 4*s.* 6*d.* each.
    Bagster.   18*s.*

Smith, G. Chaldean Genesis. Ed. Sayce. 8vo. *Low.* illus.   18*s.*

Schrader, E. Cuneiform inscriptions and the Old Testament. Tr.
    8vo. 2 vols. *Williams.*   21*s.*

Menant, J. Bibliothèque de Ninive. 18mo. *(Paris).*   2*s.* 6*d.*
    PERIODICALS : *Transactions and proceedings of the Society of Biblical Archæology* (Trübner) ; *Zeitschrift für Assyriologie.* Ed. Bezold.

—II. LANGUAGE :

Sayce, A. H. Elementary Assyrian grammar and reading book. c. 4to.
    Bagster.   7*s.* 6*d.*

Delitzsch, F. Assyrian grammar. Tr. A. R. Kennedy. c. 8vo. *Williams.*   15*s.*

Lyon, D. G. Assyrian manual. 8vo. *Scribner.*   21*s.*
    Includes a vocabulary.

Delitzsch, F. Assyrisches Wörterbuch. 4to. 3 vols. (*Leipzig*). 91s. 6d.

Schrader, E. Keilinschriftliche Bibliothek. 8vo. 2 vols. (*Berlin*).
Vol. i., 9s. ; vol. ii., 12s. In progress.

Budge, E. A. History of Esarhaddon (reading book). p. 8vo. *Trübner*. 10s. 6d.

ASTRONOMY :

—I. TEXT-BOOKS AND TREATISES :

Lockyer, J. N. Elementary lessons on astronomy. f. 8vo. *Macmillan*. 5s. 6d.

Young, C. A. Elements of astronomy. c. 8vo. *Ginn*. 7s. 6d.

,, General astronomy. r. 8vo. *Ginn*. 12s. 6d.

Herschel, J. F. W. Outlines of astronomy (advanced). sq. c. 8vo. *Longmans*. illus. 12s.

Ball, R. S. Elements of astronomy (advanced). c. 8vo. *Longmans*. illus. 6s.

Godfray, H. Treatise on astronomy (mathematical, advanced). 8vo. *Macmillan*. 12s. 6d.

Watson, J. C. Theoretical astronomy (mathematical, advanced). i. 8vo. *Trübner*. 45s.

Chauvenet, W. Treatise on astronomy (mathematical, advanced). 8vo. 2 vols. *Lippincott*. illus. 31s. 6d.

Loomis, E. Practical astronomy (mathematical, advanced). r. 8vo. *Low*. illus. 8s. 6d.

—II. POPULAR WORKS :

Ball, R. S. Story of the heavens. 8vo. *Cassell*. illus. 12s. 6d.

Newcomb, S. Popular astronomy. 8vo. *Macmillan*. illus. 18s.

Ledger, E. Sun, moon, and planets. c. 8vo. *Stanford*. illus. 10s. 6d.

Guillemin, A. World of comets. Tr. J. Glaisher. c. 8vo. *Low*. illus. 12s. 6d.

—III. SPECIAL SUBJECTS :

Clerke, Agnes M. History of astronomy during the 19th century. 8vo. *Black*. 12s. 6d.

Wolf, R. Geschichte der Astronomie. 8vo. (*Munich*). 10s. 6d.

Grant, R. History of physical astronomy. 8vo. *Baldwin*. 1852. pub. 16s. O.P.

Webb, T. W. Celestial objects for common telescopes. c. 8vo. *Longmans*. illus. 9s.

Airy, G. B. Gravitation. c. 8vo. *Macmillan*. 7s. 6d.

Young, C. A. The sun. c. 8vo. *Paul*. illus. 5s.

Secchi, A. Le soleil. 8vo. 2 vols. *Gautier-Villars*. illus. 36s.

Lockyer, J. N. Contributions to solar physics. r. 8vo. *Macmillan*. illus. pub. 31s. 6d. O.P.

,, Chemistry of the sun. 8vo. *Macmillan*. illus. 14s.

Schellen, H. Spectrum analysis. Ed. W. de W. Abney. 8vo. *Longmans*. illus. 31s. 6d.

Nasmyth and Carpenter. The moon. 8vo. *Murray*. illus. 21s.

Godfray, H. Elementary treatise on the lunar theory. c. 8vo. *Macmillan*. 5s. 6d.

Neison, E. The moon (advanced). 8vo. *Longmans*. 31s. 6d.

Tisserand. Traité de mécanique céleste. 4to. *Gautier-Villars.*
Vol. i., 21*s.* Perturbations des planètes d'après la méthode des constantes arbitraires. (Mathematical).

Proctor, R. A. Saturn and its system. c. 8vo. *Simpkin.* illus.   10*s. 6d.*

Flight, W. A chapter in the history of meteorites. 8vo. *Dulau.* illus.   12*s. 6d.*

Proctor, R. A. Star atlas. sm. fo. *Stanford.* illus.   15*s.*
Also smaller ed., 5*s.*

—IV. BIOGRAPHY:

Morton, E. J. C. Astronomers (in "Heroes of science"). c. 8vo. *S. P. C. K.*   4*s.*

Brewster, D. Life of Sir Isaac Newton. c. 8vo. *Tegg.*   6*s.*

Holden, E. S. Sir William Herschel. c. 8vo. *Allen.*   6*s.*

Herschel, Mrs. J. Memoir of Caroline Herschel. c. 8vo. *Murray.*   7*s. 6d.*

ATHENS, HISTORY, *see* GREECE, HISTORY.

  ,,   ART, *see* GREECE (ARCHÆOLOGY AND ART), *and* ARCHITECTURE II.

ATHLETICS:

Shearman, M., and others. Athletics, football, and paper-chasing ("Badminton Library"). c. 8vo. *Longmans.*   10*s. 6d.*

Griffin, H. H. Athletics. ("All England" series). s. 8vo. *Bell.*   1*s.*

Westhall, C. The modern method of training. Ed. E. T. Sachs. f. 8vo. *Ward.*   1*s.*
With hints on exercise, diet, clothing, and advice to trainers.

ATLANTIC OCEAN:

See also GEOGRAPHY IV.

Agassiz, A. A contribution to American thalassography. 8vo. 2 vols. *Low.* illus.   42*s.*
Cruises of the U.S.S. "Blake," 1877-1880.

Ellis, A. B. West African islands. d. 8vo. *Chapman.*   14*s.*

Gill, Mrs. Six months in Ascension. c. 8vo. *Murray.*   9*s.*
Account of a scientific expedition.

Walker, W. F. Azores. 8vo. *Trübner.*   10*s. 6d.*

Lefroy, J. H. Discovery and early settlement of the Bermudas (1511–1687). r. 8vo. 2 vols. *Longmans.* pub. 90*s.*   O.P.
Vol. i. (1515-1652), 30*s.*; vol. ii. (1650-1687), 60*s.* A political, commercial, and geographical account; compiled from the Colonial Records and other original sources.

Whitington, G. F. The Falkland islands. 8vo. *Smith, Elder.* 1840.   O.P.

Brown, A. Samler. Madeira and the Canary islands. 12mo. *Low.*   2*s. 6d.*

Taylor, Ellen M. Madeira: its scenery, and how to see it. 8vo. *Stanford.*   7*s. 6d.*
Contains lists of flora, etc.

Johnson, J. Y. Madeira (handbook). 12mo. *Dulau.*   7*s. 6d.*

Melliss, J. C. St. Helena (description). sup. r. 8vo. *L. Reeve.* illus.   42*s.*

Stone, O. M. Teneriffe and the Canaries. 8vo. *M. Ward.*   15*s.*
Very complete account of the group.

Taylor, Ellen M. Madeira (with map). c. 8vo. *Stanford.*   7*s. 6d.*

Johnson, J. Y. Madeira, its climate and scenery. 12mo. *Dulau.* Maps
and illus.   10*s*.

Taylor, W. F. Account of Tristan d'Acunha.   O.P.

ATLAS MTS., *see* MOROCCO.

ATLASES :

A complete list of the best maps and atlases published will be found in the special catalogue of *Stanford.* An excellent selected list of the best maps of each country is contained in
the *Scottish Geographical Magazine* for June, 1890 (*Stanford*). For each country the best
maps are those of the official survey, where there is one ; they are sold in sheets at a very cheap
rate. The sheets of our own survey are dearer ; but *Stanford, Bartholomew,* and *Philip* pub-
lish reduced and comparatively cheap reproductions. As a rule, the maps in the atlases mentioned below may be obtained separately.

Cosmographic atlas. fo. *Johnston.*   21*s*.
This is the most comprehensive English atlas at the price.

Andrée, R. von. Hand-atlas. fo. *Trübner.*   24*s*.
The largest and best atlas published anywhere at the price. It is German, but there need be
no difficulty in using it.

Bartholomew, J. Library reference atlas. fo. *Macmillan.*   52*s.* 6*d*.
For quantity and quality this is the cheapest and best atlas published in England.

Johnston, K. The royal atlas. fo. *Johnston.*   126*s*.
This still maintains its place as, on the whole, the best English atlas.

   ., Handy royal atlas. fo. *Johnston.*   52*s*.
A cheaper form of the royal atlas.

Taschen Atlas. *Perthes (Gotha).*   2*s*.
Best and cheapest pocket atlas.

Clark and Green. Bible atlas. r. 4to. *S. P. C. K.*   14*s*.

Johnston, K. Bible atlas. 12mo. *Johnston.*   1*s*.

   ., School atlas of classical geography. i. 8vo. *Johnston.*   12*s.* 6*d*.

Smith, W. Atlas of classical geography. fo. *Murray.*   126*s*.
Largest and best of its kind.

Spruner, C. von. Historical atlas. ob. 4to. *Trübner.*   15*s*.
There is a large and a small school edition ; each by far the best of its class.

AUDITORS, *see* BOOK-KEEPING.

AUSTRALASIA :

—I. GENERAL :

Stanford's Compendium ; Australasia. Ed. A. R. Wallace. l. p. 8vo.
Stanford. illus.   21*s*.
With ethnological appendix by A. H. Keane.

Picturesque atlas of Australasia. 3 vols. *Woodcock (17, Farringdon-
street).*   £15 15*s*.

Bonwick, J. British colonies in Australasia. c. 8vo. *Low.*   1*s*.

Wilkins, W. Australasia ; descriptive and pictorial. c. 8vo. *Blackie.*
illus.   2*s.* 6*d*.

Westgarth, W. Half a century of Australasian progress. 8vo. *Low.*   12*s*.

Trollope, A. Australia and New Zealand. c. 8vo. 2 vols. *Chapman.*   7*s.* 6*d*.

Wallace, R. Rural economy and agriculture of Australia and New
Zealand. *Low.* Maps and illus. (In prep.).

Blair, D. Cyclopædia of Australasia. *Petherick.*   40s.
Dictionary of events, dates, persons, and places connected with the discovery, exploration, and progress of the British dominions in the South.

Australian Handbook. (Annual). 8vo. *Gordon and Gotch.*   18s.
Including New Zealand, Fiji, and New Guinea. A complete and trustworthy summary of the geography of the Australian Colonies, with good maps.
PERIODICAL: *Proceedings of the Royal Geographical Society of Australasia* (Sydney).

—II. AUSTRALIA; GENERAL:

Beete-Jukes, J. Physical structure of Australia. 8vo. *Boone.* pub. 6s.   O.P.

Wall-Beresford, H. De la Poer. Physical geography of Australia. *Petherick.*   3s. 6d.

Woods, J. E. Tenison. History of the discovery and explorations of Australia. 8vo. 2 vols. *Low.*   28s.

Favenc. History of Australian exploration, 1788 to 1888. r. 8vo. *Griffith.*   21s.
Brings the history down to the present date.

Rusden, G. W. History of Australia. d. 8vo. 3 vols. *Chapman.*   50s.

Curr, E. M. The Australian (aboriginal) race. 8vo. 4 vols. *Trübner.* illus.   42s.

Inglis, J. Our Australian cousins. 8vo. *Macmillan.*   14s.
Chapters on New South Wales and Queensland.

Hatton, H. Finch. Advance Australia. 8vo. *W. H. Allen.*   18s.
Eight years in Queensland, New South Wales, and Victoria.

Froude, J. A. Oceana. c. 8vo. *Longmans.* illus.   2s. 6d.

Heaton, J. H. Australian dictionary of dates and men of the time. r. 8vo. *Trübner.*   15s.

Silver. Handbook for Australia and New Zealand. c. 8vo. *Silver.*   5s.

Year-Book of Australia. Ed. E. Greville. d. 8vo. *Paul.*   10s. 6d.

—III. NEW SOUTH WALES:

Official history of New South Wales. Ed. G. B. Barton. d. 8vo. *Paul.* Vol. i., 15s.
Compiled chiefly from the official and parliamentary records of the colony.

Coghlan, T. A. (Government Statistician). Wealth and progress of New South Wales. 8vo. *Robertson* (17, *Warwick-square, London*).   8s. 6d.
With maps and tables.

Griffin, G. W. Commerce and resources of New South Wales. (*Sydney*).
SEE ALSO Publications of the Linnæan Society of New South Wales, and Royal Society of New South Wales.

—IV. VICTORIA:

Murray, R. A. F. Victoria: geology and physical geography. (*Melbourne*).

Hayter, H. H. Notes on the colony of Victoria. 8vo. *Petherick.*   3s.

Labilliere, F. P. Early history of Victoria (to 1856). 8vo. 2 vols. *Low.*   21s.

Illustrated Handbook of Victoria. *Petherick.*   5s.
Victorian year-book (published annually at Melbourne), contains sketch of geography, and history and information about the other colonies.

—V. QUEENSLAND:

Russell, H. S. The genesis of Queensland. r. 8vo. *Griffith.*   21s.

Lumholtz, C. Among cannibals. 8vo. *Murray.*   24s.

—VI. SOUTH AUSTRALIA:

South Australia. Ed. Harcus. 8vo. *Low.*   25s.
      Best and most complete work on South Australia.

Stow, J. P. South Australia: its history, productions, and natural resources. *Petherick.*   5s. 6d.

Sowden, W. J. Northern territory. (*Adelaide*).

Daly, Mrs. D. Digging, squatting, and pioneering life. 8vo. *Low.*   12s.

—VII. WEST AUSTRALIA:

Favenc. Western Australia. 8vo. (*Sydney*).   21s.

Nicolay, C. G. Handbook of Western Australia. (*Perth, W.A.*).   O.P.

—VIII. TASMANIA:

Walsh. Tasmanian guide book. (*Hobart*).   5s.

Just, T. C. Tasmaniana: a description of the island and its resources. 8vo. *Petherick.*   2s. 6d.

Johnston, R. M. Geology of Tasmania. *Simpkin.*   O.P.

Fenton, J. History of Tasmania (from 1642). 8vo. (*Hobart*).   16s.

West, J. History of Tasmania. 8vo. 2 vols. (*Tasmania*).   O.P.
      Tasmanian Official Record, sold at Tasmanian Government Agency, 5, Victoria-street, S.W.

—IX. NEW ZEALAND:

Hochstetter. New Zealand: its physical geography, geology, natural history, &c. Tr. Sauter. r. 8vo. (*Stuttgart*).   25s.

Green, W. S. High Alps of New Zealand. p. 8vo. *Macmillan.*   7s. 6d.

Rusden, G. W. History of New Zealand. 8vo. 3 vols. *Chapman.*   50s.

Gisborne, W. Colony of New Zealand. c. 8vo. *Petherick.*   7s. 6d.

Official Handbook of New Zealand. d. 8vo. 2 parts, 1s. each. *Stanford.*   2s.

—X. NEW GUINEA:

Macgillivray, J. Voyage of H.M.S. "Rattlesnake," 1846–50. 8vo. 2 vols. *Boone.* pub. 36s.   O.P.

Moresby, J. Discoveries and surveys in New Guinea. 8vo. *Murray.* pub. 15s.   O.P.

D'Albertis, L. M. New Guinea; what I did, and what I saw. 8vo. 2 vols. *Low.*   42s.

Chalmers and Gill. Work and adventure in New Guinea, 1875 to 1885. p. 8vo. *R. T. S.*   6s.

Chalmers, J. Pioneering in New Guinea. 8vo. *R. T. S.* illus.   16s.

Romilly, H. H. From my verandah in New Guinea. 8vo. *Nutt.*   7s. 6d.
      Sketches and traditions. Introduction by Andrew Lang.

Nachrichten aus Kaiser Wilhelms Land. (*Berlin*).
      Published at intervals, on German New Guinea. Price varies.
      SEE ALSO Annual Reports of the Administrator of British New Guinea, issued by the Colonial Office.

AUSTRIA-HUNGARY:

Murray's Handbook to South Germany, Austria, Hungary, Tyrol, etc. p. 8vo. 2 vols. *Murray.*   12s.

Baedeker's Southern Germany and Austria (including Hungary and Transylvania). 12mo. *Dulau.*   7s.

Physikalisch - statistischer Handatlas der oesterreich - ungarischen Monarchie. fo. (*Vienna*). Separate maps, 1s. 6d.   35s.

Führer durch Ungarn und seine Nebenländer. (*Buda-Pesth*).   3s. 4d.

Kay, D. Austria-Hungary. 8vo. *Low.*   3s. 6d.

Rudolf, Prince. Die oesterreich-ungarische Monarchie in Wort und Bild. 108 parts, 8d. each. (*Vienna*).   72s.

Jackson, T. G. Dalmatia, the Quarnero and Istria. d. 8vo. 3 vols. *Clar. Press.* illus.   42s.
 Elaborate and extensive work.

Gilbert and Churchill. The Dolomite mountains. 8vo. *Longmans.* illus. pub. 21s.   o.p.

White, W. Holidays in the Tyrol. p. 8vo. *Chapman.*   14s.

Gerard, E. Transylvania. 8vo. 2 vols. *Blackwood.* illus.   25s.

Patterson, A. J. The Magyars. their country and institutions. c. 8vo. 2 vols. *Smith, Elder.*   18s.

Magyarland. 2 vols. *Low.*   38s.
 Travels in the Carpathians, etc.

AUSTRIA-HUNGARY, HISTORY, *see* GERMANY *and* HUNGARY.

AUTOMATISM, *see* PSYCHICAL RESEARCH.

AVERROES AND AVERROISM, *see* CHURCH HISTORY III.

AZORES, *see* ATLANTIC.

B.

BABYLON, *see* ASSYRIA.

BACTERIOLOGY, *see* ANTISEPTICS.

BALEARIC ISLANDS, *see* MEDITERRANEAN.

BALKAN PENINSULA, *see* TURKEY *for general works ; and* BULGARIA, ROUMANIA, SERVIA.

BALUCHISTAN, *see* AFGHANISTAN.

BANKING, *see* POLITICAL ECONOMY IV.

BAPTISTS, *see* CHURCH HISTORY V. (D).

BARBARY, *see* ALGIERS.

BARROWS, BRITISH, *see* ANTHROPOLOGY II.

BASQUE LANGUAGE :

Van-Eys, J. W. J. Grammaire comparée des dialectes basques. (*Paris*).   12s. 6d.

 ,,   Dictionnaire Basque-Français. (*Paris*).   20s.

BASQUE LEGENDS, *see* FOLKLORE.

BATHS AND WELLS, *see* HEALTH RESORTS.

BAYONET AND SABRE, *see* FENCING.

BEES :

> **Cook,** A. J. Manual of the apiary. 8vo. *Trübner.*   6s.
>
> **Cheshire,** F. R. Bee-keeping; scientific and practical. l. p. 8vo. 2 vols. *Gill.* illus.   16s.
>> Vol. i , 7s. 6d.; vol. ii., 8s. 6d.

BEETLES, BRITISH, *see* ZOOLOGY VI.

BELGIUM, *see* NETHERLANDS.

BENGAL, ETHNOLOGY, *see* ANTHROPOLOGY IV.

    „   GEOGRAPHY, *see* INDIA, GEOGRAPHY.

    „   GAME, *see* SPORT.

BERMUDAS, *see* ATLANTIC OCEAN.

BÉZIQUE, *see* CARDS.

BIBLE :

See also THEOLOGY.

—I. GENERAL :

> **Smith,** W. Dictionary of the Bible. 8vo. 3 vols. *Murray.*   105s.
>> Now rather out of date; a new edition is in preparation.
>
> **Polyglottenbibel.** Ed. Stier and Theile. 8vo. 6 vols. *Nutt.*   42s.
>> Hebrew, Greek, Latin, and Luther's German in parallel columns: in the N. T., Greek, Latin, and German. Very useful for the student.
>
> **Reuss,** E. La Bible. r. 8vo. 19 vols. (*Paris*).   170s.
>> A complete critical commentary on the whole Bible and Apocrypha, with introduction and a new translation by a highly competent scholar, and in easy and readable French.
>
> **Cheyne,** Driver, and others. Variorum reference Bible. 8vo. *Eyre.*   8s.
>> Very brief notes, and various readings from the best authorities.
>
> **Helps** to the study of the Bible. 12mo. *Clar. Press.*   2s.
>
> **Aids** to the student of the Bible. (Various authors). *S. P. C. K.*   1s.
>> The *Helps* and *Aids* contain a concise summary of Biblical history, geography, etc.
>
> **Westcott,** B. F. History of the English Bible. p. 8vo. *Macmillan.*   10s. 6d.
>
> **Mombert,** J. I. Handbook of English Versions of the Bible. p. 8vo. *Bagster.*   6s.
>> By a very competent American scholar.
>
> **Robinson,** E. Biblical researches in Palestine. 8vo. 3 vols. *Murray.*   42s.
>> The first systematic exploration of Palestine: still a standard authority.
>
> **Thomson,** W. M. The Land and the Book. c. 8vo. *Nelson.*   7s. 6d.
>> Specially good for manners and customs.
>
> **Wilson,** C. Picturesque Palestine. 24mo. 5 vols. *Virtue.* illus.   31s. 6d.
>> For further works on the geography and antiquities of Palestine, *see* PALESTINE.
>
> **Tristram,** H. B. Natural history of the Bible. c. 8vo. *S. P. C. K.*   7s. 6d.
>> More elaborate scientific details are contained in the Palestine Exploration Fund Memoirs. *See* PALESTINE.

Ewald, H. Antiquities of Israel. Tr. H. S. Solly. 8vo. *Longmans.*   12s. 6d.

Edersheim, A. The Temple and its services. i. 16mo. *R. T. S.*   5s.

Arnold, M. Literature and dogma. c. 8vo. *Smith, Elder.*   2s. 6d.

  ,,   God and the Bible. c. 8vo. *Smith, Elder.*   2s. 6d.

  ,,   St. Paul and Protestantism. c. 8vo. *Smith, Elder.*   2s. 6d.
> The views put forward in these three books have not met with much acceptance, but they deserve to be read for the freshness of appreciation with which they are written, and for the effort to bring out the permanent value of Biblical ideas.

Lee, W. Inspiration of Holy Scripture. 8vo. (*Dublin*).   O.P.
> The standard presentation of the older view.

Ladd, G. T. Doctrine of sacred Scripture. 8vo. 2 vols. *Hamilton.*   28s.
> A very elaborate work, leaving no side of the question unexplained.

—II. OLD TESTAMENT :

> The present is a time of acute transition in regard to the Old Testament, and it is probable that the literature produced upon it in the next few years will be decidedly superior to most of that which has preceded. The student who wishes to understand the Old Testament in the light of present knowledge is advised first to read Dr. Robertson Smith's *Old Testament in the Jewish Church*, then to go at once to Dr. Driver's *Isaiah* (in *Men of the Bible* series); and then, if he desires a closer study, to read Dr. Cheyne's Commentary and Essays on the same prophet. He will find himself thus at the centre of the Old Testament, and from this point he will be able to turn in any direction he pleases.

(A) INTRODUCTORY ESSAYS, HISTORY, AND COMMENTARIES.

(1) *Conservative.*

Cave, A. Inspiration of the Old Testament. 8vo. *Cong. Union.*   10s. 6d.
> This book is placed first, not as likely to satisfy the enquirer, but as written with knowledge and candour, and containing an attempt to adopt modern results with as little change as possible in the traditional views.

Oehler. Theology of the Old Testament. Tr. 8vo. 2 vols. *T. and T. Clark.*   21s.
> The best manual for the Old Testament.

Mozley, J. B. Ruling ideas of the Old Testament. 8vo. *Longmans.*   10s. 6d.
> Suggestive; but needs supplementing by literary criticism.

Green, W. H. Moses and the prophets. 12mo. (*New York*).   7s. 6d.
> Dr. Green was chairman of the American Old Testament Revisers, and has the reputation of being the ablest advocate of the conservative position.

Curtiss, S. I. The Levitical priests. p. 8vo. *Hamilton.*   5s.

Green, W. H. The Hebrew feasts. p. 8vo. *Nisbet.*   5s.
> The two latter books discuss two of the burning questions of modern Pentateuchal criticism, with accuracy and knowledge.

Green and Harper. Discussion on the Pentateuch question (in *Hebraica*). Quarterly. *Low.* 13s. per annum.
> By far the most exhaustive treatment of the question in English : Dr. Green taking the older, and Prof. Harper the newer, view ; still proceeding.

Delitzsch, F. Messianic prophecy. Tr. 8vo. *Simpkin.*   5s.

Edersheim, A. Prophecy and history in relation to the Messiah. (Warburton lectures). 8vo. *Longmans.*   12s.

Perowne, J. J. The Book of Psalms. 8vo. 2 vols. *Bell.*   34s.
> Vol. i., 18s. ; vol. ii., 16s. Abridged edition, c. 8vo., 10s. 6d.

Alexander, W. The witness of the Psalms to Christ. 8vo. *Murray.*   14s.

Ginsburg, C. D. Ecclesiastes (Bampton lectures). 8vo. *Longmans.*   15s.

  ,,   Song of Songs. 8vo. *Longmans.*   10s.

Wright, C. H. Ecclesiastes. 8vo. *Hodder.*   12s.

  ,,   Zechariah (Bampton lectures). 8vo. *Hodder.*   14s.

Pusey, E. B. The minor prophets. 4to. *Parker.*   31*s.* 6*d.*
> Exhibits massive learning.

,,   Daniel. 8vo. *Parker.*   10*s.* 6*d.*

Men of the Bible ; Series by various authors. c. 8vo. 2*s.* 6*d.* each. *Nisbet.*
> Inexpensive, but well supplied with illustrative matter ; do not deal with critical questions. The following may be named in the present connection :—*Abraham*, Rev. W. J. Deane ; *Moses*, and *Kings* of Israel and Judah, Canon G. Rawlinson ; *Solomon*, Archd. F. W. Farrar ; *Elijah*, Dr. W. Milligan.

Maclear, G. F. Classbook of Old Testament History. 18mo. *Macmillan.*   4*s.* 6*d.*
> A brief manual, which is much used.

Speaker's Commentary. Ed. Canon Cook. r. 8vo. 6 vols. *Murray.*   135*s.*
> Vol. i., Gen. to Deut., 30*s.* ; vol. ii., iii., Josh. to Esther, 36*s.* ; vol. iv., Job to Song of Solomon, 24*s.* ; vol. v., Isaiah to Lament., 20*s.* ; vol. vi., Ezekiel to Malachi, 25*s.*

Cambridge Bible for Schools. Ed. J. J. S. Perowne. 12mo. Each vol., 1*s.* 6*d.* to 5*s.* *Cambridge Press.*
> Of these Commentaries the *Cambridge Bible* is perhaps to be preferred, especially for the historical books. Job, Micah, and Hosea are fully critical.

Keil and Delitzsch. Commentaries on the Old Testament. Tr. 8vo. 27 vols. *Clark.*   142*s.*
> Dr. Keil's editions cannot be regarded as satisfactory. Those by Delitzsch (*Genesis, Job, Song of Solomon, Isaiah*) are a mine of learning, and in their latest form make considerable advances towards the critical school.

Wordsworth, C. Commentary on the Old Testament. i. 8vo. 6 vols. *Rivington.*   120*s.*
> Not at all modern in its treatment, but shows special command of patristic literature.

(2) *Critical.*

Smith, W. Robertson. The Old Testament in the Jewish Church. p. 8vo. *Longmans.*   7*s.* 6*d.*
> The most comprehensive survey of the critical position ; suited to the general reader.

,,   Prophets of Israel. c. 8vo. *Longmans.*   7*s.* 6*d.*

,,   Religion of the Semites. 8vo. *Black.*   15*s.*
> An exploration of new ground, likely to develop in the future.

Cheyne, T. K. The hallowing of criticism. p. 8vo. *Hodder.*   5*s.*
> Dr. Cheyne is an accomplished scholar and writer, who follows the critical instinct wherever it seems to lead, but combines advanced views and strong religious sympathies.

,,   Isaiah. c. 8vo. *Macmillan.*   7*s.* 6*d.*
> A commentary, with important essays.

,,   Hosea. Micah. (In "Cambridge Bible"). c. 8vo. *Cambridge Press.*
> Hosea, 3*s.* ; Micah, 1*s.* 6*d.*

,,   Jeremiah. (In "Men of the Bible" series). c. 8vo. *Nisbet.*   2*s.* 6*d.*

Driver, S. R. Isaiah. (In "Men of the Bible" series). c. 8vo. *Nisbet.*   2*s.* 6*d.*
> A model book of its kind.

,,   Sunday school lessons from the Pentateuch. 12mo. *Scribner.*   4*s.*
> Slight, as the occasion necessitated, but, in the dearth of critical literature on the subject, will give some idea of the results arrived at.

Smith, G. A. Isaiah. (In the "Expositor's Bible"). p. 8vo. 2 vols. *Hodder.*   7*s.* 6*d.*
> A good example of the application of critical interpretation to homiletic purposes.

Briggs, C. A. Messianic prophecy. c. 8vo. *Scribner.*   12*s.* 6*d.*

Riehm, E. Messianic prophecy. Tr. J. Jefferson. c. 8vo. *Clark.*   5*s.*

Kalisch, M. M. Genesis (18*s.*) ; Exodus (15*s.*) ; Leviticus (i., 15*s.* ; ii., 15*s.*). 8vo. 4 vols. *Longmans.*   63*s.*
> A series of able commentaries, becoming more pronouncedly rationalistic as they proceed, and not quite corresponding with the present state of investigation, but still the best work on the Pentateuch in English.

Davidson, A. B. Job. (In "Cambridge Bible"). 12mo. *Cambridge Press.*   5*s.*
An admirable commentary.

Bradley, G. G. Job. c. 8vo. *Clar. Press.*   7*s.* 6*d.*

,, Ecclesiastes. c. 8vo. *Clar. Press.*   4*s.* 6*d.*
Attractive literary studies.

Schrader, E. The cuneiform inscriptions and the Old Testament. Tr.
O. C. Whitehouse. 8vo. 2 vols. *Williams.*   21*s.*
The standard authority on the relation of Assyrian discoveries to the Bible.

Sayce, A. H. Fresh light from the ancient monuments. c. 8vo. *R. T. S.*   3*s.*
A popular handbook of the same subject.

Stanley, A. P. Jewish Church. p. 8vo. 3 vols., 6*s.* each. *Murray.*   18*s.*

Renan, E. Histoire du peuple d'Israel. 3 vols. (*Paris*).
Vols. i., ii., 12*s.* 6*d.* For further works on Jewish history *see* JEWS.

Kuenen, A. H. Religion of Israel. Tr. A. H. May. 8vo. 3 vols.,
10*s.* 6*d.* each. *Williams.*   31*s.* 6*d.*
Another work from the extreme left, distinguished by clearness of exposition.

,, Historico-critical enquiry into the origin and composition of the Old
Testament. Tr. Wicksteed. 8vo. *Macmillan.*   14*s.*

Bleek, F. Introduction to the Old Testament. c. 8vo. 2 vols., 5*s.* each.
Bell (*Bohn*).   10*s.*

(B) TEXTS AND TRANSLATIONS.

Hebrew bibles differ very little from each other; the most exact are those now being issued by
S. Baer (*Leipzig*).

Hebrew text. Ed. Hooght. 4to. *Bagster.*   6*s.*

Fürst, J. Hebrew and Chaldean concordance. Tr. S. Davidson. r. 8vo.
Williams.   21*s.*

Greek (Septuagint). Vol. i. (Genesis to Kings); vol. ii., in preparation.
Ed. H. B. Swete. c. 8vo. *Cambridge Press.*   7*s.* 6*d.*
Elegantly printed, and marked by great care and accuracy.

Greek text. Ed. Tischendorf. 8vo. *Brockhaus.*   18*s.*
Best for use until the Cambridge edition is ready.

Trommius, A. Greek concordance (Septuagint). fo. 2 vols. (*Amsterdam*). 1718.   O.P.

Handy Concordance (Septuagint). r. 8vo. *Bagster.*   15*s.*
Accurate, but gives references only, not quotations, and does not include the Apocrypha.

Origen's Hexapla. Ed. Dr. Field. 4to. *Macmillan.*   30*s.*
A classical work on the other Greek versions besides the Septuagint.

Latin (Vulgate). Ed. Tischendorf. 8vo. 2 vols. *Brockhaus.*   15*s.*
Gives the various readings of one good MS. throughout, and of more in the early books.
There are many other editions.

Dutripon, F. P. Latin concordance to the Old and New Testaments.
i. 4to. (*Paris*).   32*s.*

(C) ENGLISH VERSIONS OF THE PSALMS.

Witt, J. de. Praise songs of Israel. 8vo. *Funk and Wagnalls.*   7*s.* 6*d.*
A striking modern version which well preserves the grand and solemn rhythm of the original.

Cheyne, T. K. Book of Psalms. p. 8vo. *Paul.*   6*s.*
The literary skill displayed in much of this version has hardly yet received due recognition.

—III. APOCRYPHA:

Speaker's commentary on the Apocrypha. Ed. Wace. m. 8vo. 2 vols.
Murray.   50*s.*
Much superior to the Speaker's Commentary on the Old Testament; a satisfactory book.

Bissell, E. C.   Apocrypha of the Old Testament.   i. 8vo.   *Clark.*   15s.
Based mainly on the German commentary of Fritzsche.

Deane, W. J.   The Book of Wisdom.   f. 4to.   *Clar. Press.*   12s. 6d.

Schodde, G. H.   The Book of Enoch.   12mo.   (*Andover, U.S.*).   9s.
A translation from the Ethiopic of this curious and interesting book, with introduction and notes.

—IV. NEW TESTAMENT:

There is not the same necessity in the case of the New Testament as in that of the Old, to distinguish between conservative and critical treatment. Most of those who deal with the New Testament now write in a more or less critical spirit, but the older verdicts do not seem to need so much revision. In England we have a number of good commentaries on single books, though first-rate commentaries are still needed on the Gospels of St. Matthew and St. Mark, the Acts, Ephesians, Thessalonians, the Pastoral Epistles, and some of the Catholic Epistles. We have also nothing which quite corresponds with the best German introductions to the New Testament.

(A) INTRODUCTIONS.

Westcott, B. F.   Canon of the New Testament.   c. 8vo.   *Macmillan.*   10s. 6d.
A scholarly sketch of the history of the canon.

Charteris, A. H.   Canonicity.   8vo.   *Blackwood.*   18s.
A collection of passages bearing on the history of the canon.

Salmon, G.   Introduction to the New Testament.   c. 8vo.   *Murray.*   9s.
An extremely vigorous treatment, especially of the books which have been more called in question, with a valuable sketch of the formation of the canon, and of the non-canonical books.

Weiss, B.   Introduction to the New Testament.   Tr. Miss Davidson.   c. 8vo. 2 vols., 7s. 6d. each.   *Hodder.*   15s.
The most scientific general introduction in English.

Dods, Marcus.   Introduction to the New Testament.   12mo.   *Hodder.*   2s. 6d.
Brief and popular, but well up to date in criticism.

Westcott, B. F.   Introduction to the study of the Gospels.   c. 8vo. *Macmillan.*   10s. 6d.
A close and scholarly study, now of some years' standing; rather difficult to grasp from its subtle thought and profuse details.

Sanday, W.   The gospels in the second century.   c. 8vo.   *Macmillan.* pub. 10s. 6d.   O.P.

Farrar, F. W.   Messages of the books.   8vo.   *Macmillan.*   14s.
Useful descriptive outlines of the books and their contents.

Watkins, H. W.   Modern criticism and the fourth Gospel.   8vo.   *Murray.*   15s.

Gloag, P. J.   Introduction to the Pauline epistles.   d. 8vo.   *Clark.*   12s.

  „   Introduction to the Catholic epistles.   d. 8vo.   *Clark.*   10s. 6d.
These two last named works are painstaking summaries of opinions.

(B) TEXTS WITH COMMENTARIES.

GENERAL NOTE.—The student who desires an exact knowledge will do well to use Meyer for St. Matthew and St. Mark; Meyer and Godet for St. Luke, Godet and Westcott for St. John, Meyer for Acts, the Speaker's Commentary for Romans and i. and ii. Corinthians; also Godet for Romans and i. Corinthians. If a fair scholar, Vaughan for Romans, Edwards for i. Corinthians, Lightfoot and Ellicott for the Epistles they have treated; Westcott for Revelation. The less advanced student may substitute the Cambridge Greek Testament for Gospels and Hebrews. The general reader had better study the Gospels in the lives of Christ (*Edersheim* and *Farrar*), and the Epistles in Farrar's *St. Paul* or *Early days of Christianity,* using the other books for reference.

Alford, H.   Greek Testament.   8vo.   4 vols.   *Rivington.*   102s.
Vol. i., Four Gospels, 28s.; vol. ii., Acts to ii. Corinthians, 24s.; vol. iii., Galatians to Philemon, 18s.; vol. iv., Hebrews to Revelation, 32s.
Still the best complete Greek Testament by a single hand; makes much use of German work.

Wordsworth, C.   Greek Testament.   i. 8vo.   2 vols.   *Rivington.*   60s.
Vol. i., Gospels and Acts, 23s.; Epistles, Apocalypse, and Index, 37s.
Not modern in its treatment, though the good Greek scholarship of the author should be recognised.

Meyer. Commentary on the New Testament (except Apocalypse). Ed. Dickson and Crombie. 8vo. *Clark.*   210s.

> Matt., 2 vols., 21s.; Mark and Luke, 2 vols., 21s.; John, 2 vols., 21s.; Acts, 2 vols., 21s.; Romans, 2 vols., 21s.; Corinthians, 2 vols., 21s.; Galatians, 10s. 6d.; Ephesians and Philemon, 10s. 6d.; Philippians and Colossians, 10s. 6d.; Thessalonians, 10s. 6d.; Pastoral Epistles, 10s. 6d.; Hebrews, 10s. 6d.; James and John, 10s. 6d.; Peter and Jude, 10s. 6d.
>
> Meyer is still a standard authority in German, but the English translation (which was carefully done) has not the additions which have kept the German editions up to date. Able, but inconveniently printed, and foreign in style.

Speaker's Commentary on the New Testament. Ed. F. C. Cook. m. 8vo. *Murray.*   91s.

> Vol. i., Matthew, Mark, and Luke, 18s.; vol. ii., John and Acts, 20s.; vol. iii., Romans to Philemon, 28s.; vol iv., Hebrews to Revelations, 28s.; also ed. in 2 vols., 7s. 6d. each.
>
> Unequal: the best are St. John, Romans, i. and ii. Corinthians, Philippians, James, Revelation.

Cambridge Bible for Schools. Ed. J. J. S. Perowne. ex. f. 8vo. *Cambridge Press.*

> The best are those by Archdeacon Farrar (St. Luke, 4s. 6d., and Hebrews, 3s. 6d.); Dr. Plummer (Gospel 4s. 6d., and Epistles 3s. 6d., of St. John); Mr. Moule (Romans, 3s. 6d., Ephesians, 2s. 6d., Philippians, 2s. 6d.); Dean Plumptre (James, 1s. 6d.; i. and ii. Peter, 2s. 6d.).

  ,,   Greek Testament. Ed. J. J. S. Perowne. *Cambridge Press.*

> Matthew, 4s. 6d.; Mark, 4s. 6d.; Luke, 6s.; John, 6s.; Acts, 6s.; i. Corinthians, 3s.; Hebrews, 3s. 6d.; Epistles of St. John, 4s.

Commentary for English readers. Ed. C. J. Ellicott. 3 vols. *Cassell.*

> Vol. i., Gospels: ii., Acts to Galatians: iii., Ephesians to Revelation, 21s. each. Not on the whole so good as the other works named; but Dean Plumptre's commentary on the first three Gospels and Acts is well suited to the general reader.

Popular Commentary on the New Testament. Ed. Schaff. i. 8vo. 4 vols., 12s. 6d. each. *Clark.*   50s.

> Vol. i., Synoptical Gospels; vol. ii., St. John and Acts; vol. iii., Romans to Philemon; vol. iv., Hebrews to Revelation. Plain and clear; justifies its title.

Bengel, J. A. Gnomon Novi Testamenti. 3 vols. *Clark.*   21s.

> This commentary (originally published in 1742) can never become antiquated. Its terseness, point, and depth will be appreciated best in the Latin.

Maldonatus, J. Commentarii in quatuor Evangelistas. Ed. J. M. Raich. r. 8vo. 2 vols. *Nutt.*   25s.

> Probably the best of the Roman Catholic commentaries, distinguished for clearness and exegetical tact.

McClellan, J. B. The four gospels. 8vo. *Macmillan.*   30s.

> Introduction, translation, harmony, and notes. Eccentric but accurate, and with much independently collected material; scholarly translation and notes, but not free from crotchets.

Morison, J. St. Matthew, 14s.; St. Mark, 12s. 8vo. *Hodder.*

> Good exegesis, but otherwise old-fashioned.

Godet, F. St. Luke. Tr. 8vo. 2 vols. *Clark.*   21s.

  ,,   St. John. Tr. 8vo. 3 vols. *Clark.*   31s. 6d.

  ,,   Romans. Tr. 8vo. 2 vols., 10s. 6d. each. *Clark.*   21s.

  ,,   i. Corinthians. Tr. 8vo. 2 vols. *Clark.*   21s.

> These works of Godet's are very thoughtful and thorough, but with peculiar views on textual criticism.

Westcott, B. F. St. John. 8vo. *Murray.*   10s. 6d.

  ,,   Hebrews. 8vo. *Macmillan.*   14s.

  ,,   Epistles of St. John. 8vo. *Macmillan.*   12s. 6d.

> Very close and scholarly exegesis, and excellent criticism, but rather difficult.

Lightfoot, J. B. Galatians. 8vo. *Macmillan.*   12s.

  ,,   Philippians. 8vo. *Macmillan.*   12s.

  ,,   Colossians and Philemon. 8vo. *Macmillan.*   12s.

> Admirably clear and lucid, with elaborate essays.

Ellicott, C. J.   Thessalonians.   8vo.   *Longmans.*   7s. 6d.

,,   Galatians.   8vo.   *Longmans.*   8s. 6d.

,,   Ephesians.   8vo.   *Longmans.*   8s. 6d.

,,   Philippians, Colossians, and Philemon.   8vo.   *Longmans.*   10s. 6d.

,,   Pastoral Epistles.   8vo.   *Longmans.*   10s. 6d.
Confined to close grammatical exegesis of the Greek; with slight introductions.

Vaughan, C. J.   Romans.   c. 8vo.   *Macmillan.*   7s. 6d.

,,   Philippians.   c. 8vo.   *Macmillan.*   5s.

,,   Hebrews.   c. 8vo.   *Macmillan.*   7s. 6d.
Finished scholarship rather than broad handling of the thought.

Beet, J. Agar.   Romans.   c. 8vo.   *Hodder.*   7s. 6d.

,,   i. and ii. Corinthians.   c. 8vo.   *Hodder.*   10s. 6d.

,,   Galatians.   c. 8vo.   *Hodder.*   5s.
Wesleyan; to be recommended rather for able treatment of particular passages than as a general commentary.

Jowett, B.   Romans, Galatians, i. and ii. Thessalonians.   8vo.   2 vols. *Murray.*   pub. 30s.   O.P.
Exegesis open to criticism, but with finely written and suggestive essays.

Stanley, A. P.   Corinthians i. and ii.   8vo.   *Murray.*   18s.
Also open to criticism in details, but brightly and picturesquely written; with a paraphrase which helps to bring home the meaning.

Edwards, T. C.   Corinthians i.   8vo.   *Hamilton.*   14s.
Welsh Presbyterian; full and able.

Dale, R. W.   Ephesians (doctrine and ethics).   c. 8vo.   *Hodder.*   7s. 6d.
An excellent presentation of the subjects with which it deals.

Davidson, A. B.   Hebrews.   12mo.   *Clark.*   2s. 6d.
Able grappling with the thoughts of the epistle; a book worth far more than its price.

Rendall, F.   Hebrews.   c. 8vo.   *Macmillan.*   7s. 6d.

(C) BIOGRAPHICAL AND EXPOSITORY WORKS.

Trench, R. C.   Notes on the parables.   p. 8vo.   *Paul.*   7s. 6d.

,,   Notes on the miracles.   p. 8vo.   *Paul.*   7s. 6d.

,,   Studies on the Gospels.   8vo.   *Macmillan.*   10s. 6d.
The works of a learned and accomplished theologian.

Bruce, A. B.   The parabolic teaching of Christ.   8vo.   *Hodder.*   12s.

,,   Miraculous element in the Gospels.   8vo.   *Hodder.*   12s.

,,   The Galilean Gospel.   8vo.   *Simpkin.*   3s. 6d.

,,   The training of the Twelve.   8vo.   *Clark.*   10s. 6d.
A series of thoughtful works, more modern than those of Archbishop Trench, but with a less distinguished stamp of scholarship.

Fairbairn, A. M.   Studies in the life of Christ.   8vo.   *Hodder.*   9s.

Edersheim, A.   Life and times of Jesus the Messiah.   8vo.   2 vols. *Longmans.*   24s.
Best of all the lives of Christ in its thorough knowledge of the historical background of Jewish life and thought.

Farrar, F. W.   Life of Christ.   8vo.   *Cassell.*   illus.   21s.

,,   Life of St. Paul.   12mo.   *Cambridge Press.*   3s. 6d.

,,   Early days of Christianity.   p. 8vo.   *Cassell.*   6s.
Picturesque and rather rhetorical description preponderates, but the work is that of a scholar. The later works rise in value.

Renan, E. Vie de Jésus. 8vo. (*Paris*).   6s. 6d.

,, S. Paul. 8vo. (*Paris*).   6s. 6d.

,, Les apôtres. 8vo. (*Paris*).   6s. 6d.

,, L'Antechrist. 8vo. (*Paris*).   6s. 6d.
  Brilliant as literature, and saved from some errors by critical good sense, though exposed to others by a tendency to sentimental romance.

Keim, T. Jesus of Nazara. Tr. 8vo. 6 vols., 10s. 6d. each. *Williams.*   63s.
  A work of much learning and ability ; perhaps the best specimen of rationalistic criticism.

Weiss, B. Life of Christ. 8vo. 3 vols. *Clark.*   31s. 6d.
  Critical, but more conservative than Keim.

Schürer, E. History of the New Testament times. 8vo. 3 vols. *Clark.*   31s. 6d.
  The standard work on the surroundings of the life of Christ (the life itself is excluded), studied rather more *ab extra* than in Dr. Edersheim's work ; learned, clear in statement, and judicious.

(D) LEXICONS AND GRAMMARS.

Greek-English lexicon of the New Testament ; enlarged translation of Grimm's Clavis Novi Testamenti. Tr. J. H. Thayer. d. 4to. *Clark.*   36s.
  The German original (in Latin) is cheapest, but the translation is much enlarged, and very carefully executed.

Cremer, H. Biblico-theological lexicon of Greek New Testament. Tr. Simon and Urwick. d. 4to. *Clark.*   38s.
  Full account of theological terms in New Testament.

Trench, R. C. Synonyms of the New Testament. 8vo. *Paul.*   12s.
  A standard work.

Hatch, E. Essays on Biblical Greek. 8vo. *Clar. Press.*   10s. 6d.
  Grinfield lectures, of which nearly half is taken up with a study of language : fresh and original.

Winer, G. B. Grammar of New Testament Greek. Tr. Moulton. 8vo. *Clark.*   15s.

Buttmann, A. Grammar of New Testament Greek. Tr. 8vo. (*New York*).   12s.

Simcox, W. H. Language of the New Testament. 12mo. *Hodder.*   2s. 6d.

McTurpie, D. Old Testament in the New. r. 8vo. *Williams.*   12s.

Toy, C. H. Quotations in the New Testament. 8vo. *Scribner.*   18s.
  The first of these two books has the more detailed comparison of texts ; the second deals more with the higher criticism.

Bruder, H. C. Concordantiae N. T. Graeci. 4to. (*Leipzig*).   30s.
  By far the most complete concordance.

(E) TEXTS AND VERSIONS.

  Editions of the text of the Greek Testament are extremely numerous, and many have some special feature not found so well in others. Stephen's text of 1550 (the basis of what is commonly called the Received Text) is conveniently printed by the *Clarendon Press.* The most scientific modern text is that of Drs. Westcott and Hort (larger editions with introductions and notes, 2 vols., 10s. 6d. each, also smaller edition, 5s. 6d., *Macmillan*) ; but this has met with considerable opposition. A useful compromise between the ordinary and the scientific texts is presented by the Greek text used by the revisers (*Clar. Press,* 10s. 6d.). A collation of the leading critical authorities is given by Scrivener (*Deighton*), or in a less convenient, but in some respects more trustworthy form by O. von Gebhart (*Tauchnitz*). Concise manuals of textual criticism are those by Warfield (*Hodder,* 2s. 6d.), and Hammond (*Clar. Press,* 3s. 6d.). Scrivener's introduction (*Deighton*), and Westcott and Hort's (*Macmillan*) are more elaborate.

Novum Testamentum Graece. Ed. Tischendorf. 8vo. (*Leipzig*).   45s.
  With prolegomena (still incomplete), by Dr. C. R. Gregory ; supersedes all other books as a collection and account of the critical materials. Smaller edition, 13s.

Novum Testamentum Latine. Ed. Tischendorf. 16mo. (*Leipzig*).   2s.
  A roughly corrected text of the Vulgate ; handy and inexpensive.

Novum Testamentum Latine. Ed. Wordsworth and White. 4to. *Clar. Press.*   12s. 6d.

> An elaborate critical edition, of which the first fascienlus only has appeared (12s. 6d.). The authorised Roman text published by command of Clement VIII. in 1592-8 may readily be had. (*Bagster*, 5s.).

Parallel New Testament. *Clar. Press* and *Camb. Press.*   from   1s. 6d.

> Authorised version of 1611, and revised version of 1881 in parallel columns ; the same may be had with the Greek text added. (12s. 6d.).

Burgon, J. W. The Revision revised. 8vo. *Murray.*   14s.

> The most elaborate and uncompromising criticism of the Revised Version, the merits of which are best pointed out in a series of articles by Dr. Westcott in the *Expositor* for 1887.

Lightfoot, J. B. A fresh revision of the English New Testament. p. 8vo. *Macmillan.* pub. 6s.   O.P.

> Perhaps the most important of a number of works advocating revision.

Schaff, P. Companion to the Greek Text and English Version. p. 8vo. *Harper.*   12s. 6d.

> A popular account of the Revised Version.

BIBLIOPHILIA ; AND HISTORIC AND ARTISTIC BINDINGS :

> All the books mentioned under this heading are of interest to the general reader, with perhaps the exception of the *Philobiblon* of Richard de Bury, and Dibdin's *Bibliomania.* The works of A. Lang and J. H. Burton are specially recommended.

Richard de Bury. Philobiblon. Ed. and Tr. Ernest C. Thomas. c. 8vo. *Paul.*   10s. 6d.

> Bishop of Durham, treasurer and chancellor of Edward III.

Burton, J. H. The book-hunter. c. 8vo. *Blackwood.*   7s. 6d.

Lang, A. The library. c. 8vo. *Macmillan.*   3s. 6d.

> With a chapter on modern English illustrated books by A. Dobson.

Ballads of books. Ed. Lang. f. 8vo. *Longmans.*   6s.

> A re-cast, with additions, of a volume under the same title, edited by W. B. Matthews, N.Y., 1857.

Ireland, A. The book lover's enchiridion. f. 8vo. *Simpkin.*   7s.

> Thoughts on the solace and companionship of books from writers of every age.

Dibdin, T. F. Bibliomania, or book-madness : a bibliographical romance. r. 8vo. *Chatto.* pub. 21s.   O.P.

> The source whence nearly all English writers, except Kerney, derive their information on bindings.

Blades, W. Enemies of books. 12mo. *Stock.*   4s. 6d.

Fitzgerald, P. The book fancier ; or the romance of book collecting. 12mo. *Low.*   5s.

Zaehnsdorf, J. W. The art of bookbinding. *Bell.* illus.   5s.

> Chiefly practical.

Cundall, J. Bookbindings, ancient and modern. i. 8vo. *Bell.*   31s. 6d.

Wheatley, H. B. Remarkable bindings in the British Museum. *Low.*

> Only 200 copies printed. 25 at 168s. ; 25 at 94s. 6d. ; 150 at 73s. 6d. and 63s.

Historical and artistic bindings. *Quaritch.* illus.   210s.

> A collection of facsimiles, illustrating the history of binding as a branch of decorative art. 103 plates, in colours, silver, and gold.
>
> The short introductory sketch, by M. Kerney, treats for the first time the history of bookbinding in a scientific manner. As the examples are very carefully classified, the book is undoubtedly the best on the subject in English. This is the only work which can be recommended to the student.

Vallée, L. Bibliographie des bibliographies (with supplement). 8vo. (*Paris*).   20s.

Petzholdt, J. Bibliotheca bibliographica. r. 8vo. (*Leipzig*).   12s.

Sabin, J. A bibliography of bibliography. 8vo. (*New York*).   6s.

Book prices current. d. 8vo. 3 vols. (annual), 27s. 6d. each. *Stock.*
Gives the current value of rare books. Vol. i., O.P.

PERIODICALS: The *Library* (Stock, 8d. monthly), the organ of the Library Association of the United Kingdom (20, Hanover-square, London, W.), devotes special attention to antiquarian bibliography. *See also* the *Library Journal* (Trübner), 1s. 6d. monthly.

BICYCLING, *see* CYCLING.

BILLIARDS:

Bennett, J. Billiards. Ed. Cavendish. e. 8vo. *De La Rue.* illus.	10s. 6d
Phelan, M. Billiards, the game of. 12mo. *Appleton.*	7s. 6d.

BILLS OF EXCHANGE, *see* POLITICAL ECONOMY IV.

     ,,   ,,   LAW OF, *see* ENGLAND, LAW VIII.

BIMETALLISM, *see* POLITICAL ECONOMY IV.

BIOLOGY, *see* ANTHROPOLOGY V., BOTANY, PHYSIOLOGY, ZOOLOGY.

BIRDS, *see* ZOOLOGY VI.

BLEACHING, *see* TEXTILE FABRICS.

BOATING, *see* ROWING *and* YACHTING.

BOHEMIA, HISTORY, *see* GERMANY, HISTORY.

BOHEMIA: LANGUAGE AND LITERATURE:

Vymazal, F. Böhmische Grammatik. 8vo. (*Brünn*).	3s.
Mourek, V. E. Dictionary, English and Bohemian. 8vo. (*Prague*).	O.P.
Wratislaw, A. H. The native literature of Bohemia in the 19th century. 12mo. *Bell.*	5s.
Jireček, C. J. Anthologie z Literatury Cesk (Anthology of Bohemian literature). 8vo. 3 vols. (*Prague*).	11s.

BOKHARA, *see* ASIA, CENTRAL.

BOLIVIA, *see* AMERICA, SOUTH.

BOOKBINDING, ARTISTIC, *see* BIBLIOPHILIA.

BOOK-KEEPING:

Hamilton and Ball. Book-keeping. ex. f. 8vo. *Clar. Press.*	2s.
Garcke and Falls. Factory accounts, principles, and practice. d. 8vo. *Lockwood.*	10s. 6d.
Gordon, W. J. Professional book-keeping. p. 8vo. *Wyman.*	2s.
Kain, G. J. Solicitors' book-keeping. 12mo. *Waterlow.*	6s.
Pixley, F. W. Auditors. d. 8vo. *Good.*	10s. 6d.

BOOTMAKING, *see* INDUSTRIES III.

BORNEO, *see* INDIAN ARCHIPELAGO V.

BOSNIA, *see* TURKEY.

BOTANY:

—I. TEXT-BOOKS:

Oliver, D. Elementary lessons in botany. f. 8vo. *Macmillan.*   4s. 6d.

Prantl, K. Elementary text-book of botany. Tr.Vines. d. 8vo. *Sonnenschein.*   9s.

Sachs, J. Text-book of botany. Ed. Bennett and Dyer. 3 vols. *Macmillan.*
   pub. 35s. 6d.   O.P.
     Vol. i., 10s. 6d.; vol. ii., 12s. 6d.; vol. iii., 12s. 6d.

Gray, A. Elements of botany. 8vo. *Trübner.*   12s.

Goebel, K. Classification and special morphology of plants. Tr. H.
   Garnsey. r. 8vo. *Clar. Press.* illus.   21s.

Sachs, J. Lectures on the physiology of plants. Tr. Marshall Ward.
   r. 8vo. *Clar. Press.* illus.   31s. 6d.

Gray, A. Text-book of botany. 8vo. *Macmillan.*   10s. 6d.
     Advanced. Vol. ii. Physiological botany by G. L. Goodale.

Bennett and Murray. Handbook of cryptogamic botany. c. 8vo. *Long-*
   mans. illus.   16s.
     With copious bibliographical references.

Bary, A. de. Comparative morphology and biology of fungi, etc. Tr.
   H. Garnsey. i. 8vo. *Clar. Press.* illus.   22s. 6d.

Bower, F. O. Course of practical botany. c. 8vo. *Macmillan.*   10s. 6d.
   For laboratory use.

—II. REFERENCE:

Lindley and Moore. Treasury of botany. c. 8vo. 2 vols. *Longmans.*
   illus.   12s.
     Much miscellaneous information brought together.

Bentham and Hooker. Genera plantarum. r. 8vo. 3 vols. *Williams.*   162s.
     Latin descriptions of all genera of flowering plants known to date of publication. Only for
     advanced students and specialists.

Le Maout and Decaisne. General system of botany. Tr. Mrs. Hooker.
   r. 8vo. *Longmans.* illus. pub. 31s. 6d.   O.P.

—III. BIOLOGICAL TREATISES:

Darwin, C. Fertilization of orchids. c. 8vo. *Murray.* illus.   7s. 6d.

  ,, Forms of flowers. c. 8vo. *Murray.* illus.   7s. 6d.

  ,, Movements of plants. p. 8vo. *Murray.*   6s.

  ,, Climbing plants. c. 8vo. *Murray.*   6s.

  ,, Insectivorous plants. c. 8vo. *Murray.*   9s.

  ,, Effects of cross and self-fertilization. c. 8vo. *Murray.*   9s.

Müller, H. Fertilisation of flowers. Tr. D'Arcy Thompson. m. 8vo.
   Macmillan.   21s.
     With bibliography.

Lubbock, J. British wild flowers in relation to insects. c. 8vo. *Macmillan.*
   illus.   4s. 6d.

Ward, H. Marshall. Diseases of plants. p. 8vo. *S. P. C. K.*   2*s.* 6*d.*

   ,,   Timber and some of its diseases. c. 8vo. *Macmillan.* illus.   6*s.*
     For further works on Timber, *see* FORESTRY.

—IV. GEOGRAPHICAL DISTRIBUTION:

Baker, J. G. Elementary lessons in botanical geography. *L. Reeve.*   3*s.*

Candolle, A. de. Origin of cultivated plants. ("Inter. Scient." ser.). Tr.
    c. 8vo. *Paul.*   5*s.*

Britten and Holland. Dictionary of English plant-names. (English Dialect
    Soc.). d. 8vo. *Trübner.* Part i., A–F, 8*s.* 6*d.*

Prior, R. C. Popular names of British plants. c. 8vo. *Williams.*   7*s.* 6*d.*

Hooker, J. D. Student's flora of the British Isles. g. 8vo. *Macmillan.*   10*s.* 6*d.*

Bentham, G. British flora. 8vo. 2 vols. *Bickers.* pub. 3*s.* 6*d.*   O.P.
     To enable one to find the name of any indigenous flowering plant. Very free from technicality.

Watson, H. C. Topographical botany of English plants. 8vo. *Quaritch.*   16*s.*
     Detailed treatment of geographical distribution of flowering plants in Great Britain.

More, A. G. Cybele Hibernica. 8vo. *Hodges.*   10*s.* 6*d.*
     Treats of the distribution of flowering plants in Ireland.

Moore, T. British ferns and their allies. sq. 12mo. *Routledge.* illus.   5*s.*
     Also c. 8vo., 3*s.* 6*d.*

Hobkirk, C. P. Synopsis of British mosses. c. 8vo. *L. Reeve.*   7*s.* 6*d.*

Braithwaite, R. British moss flora. i. 8vo. *L. Reeve.* illus.   50*s.*

Leighton, W. A. Lichen flora of Great Britain, Ireland, and Channel
    Islands. 8vo. *W. P. Collins (Shrewsbury).* pub. 31*s.* 6*d.*   O.P.

Cooke, M. C. Handbook of British fungi. 8vo. 2 parts, 4*s.* each. *Williams.*   8*s.*

Harvey, W. H. Phycologia Britannica. r. 8vo. 4 vols. *L. Reeve.* illus.   150*s.*

   ,,   Manual of British marine algae. 8vo. *Gurney and Jackson.* illus.   21*s.*
     With coloured illus., 31*s.* 6*d.*

Gatty, Mrs. Sea-weeds of Great Britain. sup. r. 8vo. 2 vols. *Bell.*   50*s.*
     The Phycologia Britannica in a popular form.

Nyman, C. F. Conspectus florae Europææ; with supplements. 8vo.
    5 vols. (*Sweden*).   30*s.*
     An enumeration of flowering plants, with their distribution in Europe.

Gray, A. Botany of the northern United States. Ed. Watson and Coulter.
    8vo. *Ivison (New York).* illus.   10*s.* 6*d.*

Chapman, A. W. Flora of the southern United States; with supplement.
    Ivison (New York).   20*s.*

Watson, C. Botany of California. 4to. (*Cambridge, U.S.*). illus.   42*s.*

Hooker, J. D. Botany of the Antarctic voyage of the "Erebus" and
    "Terror," 1839–43. 4to. 2 vols. *L. Reeve.* 1844–7. illus.   O.P.
     Pub. 150*s.*; coloured, 215*s.*

   ,,   Himalayan journals. 8vo. 2 vols. (*London*).   O.P.

—V. ECONOMIC BOTANY:

Bentley and Trimen. Medicinal plants. l. 8vo. 4 vols. *Churchill.* illus.   231*s.*

Official Guides to the Museums of economic botany.
     Sold at the museums. Though specially intended for visitors to the museums, they have much
     independent value in connection with economic uses.

Hemsley, W. B. Hardy trees and shrubs. r. 8vo. *Longmans.* illus.
    pub. 21*s.*   O.P.
     A handbook based on Decaisne and Naudin. For other works on trees, *see* FORESTRY.

—VI. HISTORY AND BIBLIOGRAPHY:

Sachs, J. History of botany. Tr. H. Garnsey. c. 8vo. *Clar. Press.*   10s.

Pritzel, G. A. Thesaurus literaturae botanicae. 4to. (*Leipzig*).   44s.
<small>Very careful and accurate enumeration of all independently published botanical works up to date.</small>

Jackson, B. D. Guide to the literature of botany. (Index society). s. 4to. *Dulau.*   31s. 6d.

Enumeration of Colonial and Indian Floras. (Kew Bulletin, No. 31, July, 1889). 8vo.
<small>Sold at the Museum. Nearly all the important floras are here given—that is, books to enable one to determine the plants of the respective countries.
PERIODICALS:—
Annals of Botany. Ed. Balfour and others. r. 8vo. *Clar. Press.* illus. .
   Vol. i., part i., 8s. 6d., part ii., 7s. 6d., part iii., and iv., 18s.; vol. ii., part v., 10s. 6d., part vi., 7s. 6d., part vii., 11s., part viii., 7s. 6d.; vol. iii., part ix., 11s. 6d., part x., 13s. 6d., part. xi., 18s., part xii. in press, part xiii., 12s. 6d., part xiv., 13s. 6d.
Original memoirs, with copious botanical bibliography.</small>

<small>   *The Journal of Botany*, British and Foreign, issued monthly (West, Newman), is specially useful to students of British botany. For original papers, etc., consult the *Journal* and *Transactions* of the Linnæan Society (botanical section).</small>

BOXING AND WRESTLING:

Donelly, N. Boxing. c. 8vo. *Weldon.*   2s. 6d.

Allanson-Winn, R. G. Boxing. ("All England" series). s. 8vo. *Bell.*   1s.

Armstrong, W. Wrestling. ("All England" series). s. 8vo. *Bell.*   1s.

BRAIN, *see* MENTAL PHYSIOLOGY.

BRASSES, *see* ARCHITECTURE III.

BRAZIL:

Smith, H. H. Brazil, the Amazon and the coast. m. 8vo. *Low.*   21s.

Fletcher and Kidder. Brazil and the Brazilians. 8vo. *Low.*   28s.
<small>Historical and descriptive sketches.</small>

Wells, J. W. Three thousand miles through Brazil. 8vo. 2 vols. *Low.* illus.   32s.

Dent, H. C. A year in Brazil. d. 8vo. *Paul.* illus.   18s.
<small>With notes on the abolition of slavery.</small>

Keller, F. The Amazon and Madeira rivers. 8vo. *Chapman.*   9s.

Mathews, E. D. Up the Amazon and Madeira rivers. 8vo. *Low.*   18s.
<small>Through Bolivia and Peru.</small>

Orton, J. Andes and Amazon. 8vo. (*New York*).   15s.

Brown and Lidstone. Fifteen thousand miles on the Amazon. d. 8vo. *Stanford.* illus.   21s.

Henderson, J. History of Brazil. *Longmans.* 1821.   O.P.

Levasseur, E. Brésil en 1889. 4to. (*Paris*). pub. 20s.   O.P.
<small>Maps, statistics, etc., prepared by the Franco-Brazilian Committee for the Paris Exhibition.</small>

Mulhall, M. G., and E. T. Handbook of Brazil. p. 8vo. *Trübner.*   O.P.
<small>Buenos Ayres, Rio Grande, etc.</small>

BREAD, *see* INDUSTRIES IV.

BRETON LANGUAGE, *see* CELTIC LITERATURE II.

BREWING, *see* INDUSTRIES VI.

BRICKS, *see* BUILDING.

BRIDGES, *see* BUILDING.

BRITISH ISLES, *see* ENGLAND. [For special works on Scotland, Ireland, Wales, Channel Islands, Isle of Man, *see* under those heads].

BRITISH MUSEUM, *see* LONDON VIII.

BRONZE IMPLEMENTS, ANCIENT, *see* ANTHROPOLOGY II.

BRONZES, *see* ARTISTIC PROCESSES VI.

BUDDHISM :

See also PALI.

> The first six books in this list deal with the original Buddhism.

Davids, T. W. Rhys. History of Indian Buddhism. (Hibbert Lectures, 1881). 8vo. *Williams.*	10s. 6d.
,, Buddhism. f. 8vo. *S. P. C. K.*	2s. 6d.
Oldenberg, H. Buddha. Tr. W. Hoey. 8vo. *Williams.* Manual, in greater detail : a standard work.	18s.
Davids, T. W. Rhys. Questions of King Milinda. (" Sacred books of the East." Vol. xxxv.). d. 8vo. *Clar. Press.* Series of discussions on vital points of Buddhism, written about A.D. 100.	10s. 6d.
Buddhist Suttas. (" Sacred books of the East." Vol. xi.). Tr. Rhys Davids. d. 8vo. *Clar. Press.*	10s. 6d.
Dhammapada, and Sutta Nipâta. (" Sacred books of the East "). Tr. Max. Müller and Fausböll. d. 8vo. *Clar. Press.* The two last are translations from the original sacred books of the Buddhists.	10s. 6d.
Rockhill, W. W. Life of Buddha, from Tibetan sources. 8vo. *Trübner.*	10s. 6d.
Edkins, J. Chinese Buddhism. 8vo. *Trübner.*	18s.
Beal, S. Catena of Buddhist scriptures, from the Chinese. 8vo. *Trübner.*	15s.
Nanjio, B. Catalogue of Chinese translations of the Buddhist Tripitaka. 4to. *Clar. Press.*	32s. 6d.

BUDDING *and* GRAFTING, *see* GARDENING.

BUILDING CONSTRUCTION :

Notes on building construction. 8vo. 3 vols. *Rivingtons.* illus. Vol i., Elementary, 10s. 6d. ; vol. ii., Advanced, 10s. 6d. ; vol. iii., Materials, 21s.	42s.
Tarn, E. Science of building. c. 8vo. *Lockwood.* Good elementary book for architectural students.	7s. 6d.
Fairbairn, W. Application of iron to buildings. 8vo. *Longmans.* pub. 16s.	O.P.
Matheson, E. Works in iron. (Bridges and roofs). r. 8vo. *Spon.* pub. 15s.	O.P.
Walmisley. Iron roofs. s. fo. *Spon.* illus.	63s.
Haupt, H. Bridge construction (American). 8vo. *Spon.*	16s.
Baker. Strength of arches. c. 8vo. *Spon.* pub. 9s.	O.P

Baker, I. O. Masonry construction. r. 8vo. *Trübner.*   21s.
    Very complete and valuable.

Davis, C. T. Manufacture of bricks. 8vo. *Low.*   25s.

Hull, E. Building and ornamental stones. 8vo. *Macmillan.*   12s.

Tredgold, T. Principles of carpentry. rev. by J. T. Hurst. c. 8vo. *Spon.*   12s. 6d.

Tredgold and Tarn. Elementary carpentry. 4to. *Lockwood.* illus.   25s.

Reid, H. Concrete. 8vo. *Spon.*   15s.

Gilmore, Q. A. Limes and mortars. r. 8vo. *Spon.* illus.   18s.

Reid, H. Portland cement. 8vo. *Spon.*   18s.

Leaning, J. Quantity surveying. 8vo. *Spon.*   9s.

Dobson and Tarn. Student's guide to measuring and valuing. 8vo. *Lockwood.*   9s.

BULGARIA:

—I. GEOGRAPHY:

Samuelson, J. Bulgaria, past and present. 8vo. *Trübner.*   10s. 6d.

Barkley, H. C. Between the Danube and the Black Sea. c. 8vo. *Murray.*   10s. 6d.
    Five years in Bulgaria.

Bleek, C. Commercial report for Bulgaria. 8vo. *Eyre.*   3½d.
    Foreign Office paper.

Sinclair and Brophy. Twelve years' study of the Eastern question in Bulgaria. 8vo. *Chapman.* pub. 9s.   O.P.

—II. HISTORY:

Jireček, C. J. Geschichte der Bulgaren. 8vo. (*Prague*).   8s.

Kanitz, F. Donau-Bulgarien. r. 8vo. 3 vols. (*Leipzig*).   58s.

Baker, V. Bulgarian war. 8vo. 2 vols. *Low.*   42s.

—III. LANGUAGE:

Vymazal, F. Die Kunst die bulgarische Sprache leicht und schnell zu lernen. 12mo. (*Vienna*).   2s.
    Contains some extracts from authors.

Bogoroff, U. A. Dictionnaire Bulgare-Français. 8vo. 2 vols. (*Vienna*).   36s.

Dozon, A. Chansons populaires bulgares. 12mo. *Maisonneuve.*   8s. 6d.

BURMA AND SHAN STATES:

Yule, H. Mission to the court of Ava, 1855. 8vo. *Smith, Elder.* illus.   3s. 6d.
    With notices of the country, government, and people.

Fytche, A. Burma, past and present. 8vo. 2 vols. *Paul.*   30s.

Forbes, C. J. British Burma and its people. c. 8vo. *Murray.* pub. 10s. 6d.   O.P.

Scott, J. G. Burma as it was, is, and will be. c. 8vo. *Redway.*   5s.

Colquhoun, A. R. Amongst the Shans. d. 8vo. *Tuer.*   O.P.

Hallett, H. S. A thousand miles on an elephant in the Shan States. 8vo. *Blackwood.* illus.   21s.

Colquhoun, A. R. Across Chrysê. 8vo. 2 vols. *Low.*   42s.
    Explorations in S. China and borderlands—Canton to Mandalay.

Gill, W. River of golden sand. c. 8vo. *Murray.*   7*s.* 6*d*
      Journey through China and E. Thibet to Burma.

BUTTERFLIES, BRITISH, *see* ZOOLOGY VI.

BUTTER-MAKING, *see* DAIRY.

BYZANTINE ARCHITECTURE, *see* ARCHITECTURE II.

C.

CALIPHS, *see* MAHOMETANISM.

CALVIN, *see* CHURCH HISTORY I .

CAMBRIDGE, *see* UNIVERSITIES.

CAMEROONS, *see* AFRICA III.

CANADA:

—I. GEOGRAPHY:

Reclus, E. Universal geography, Vol. xv. i. 8vo. *Virtue*   21*s*
      The best and fullest account of Canada in one volume.

Greswell, W. P. Geography of Canada and Newfoundland. 8vo. *Clar.*
    Press.   6*s.*

Selwyn and Dawson. Physical geography and geology of Canada. 8vo.
    (*Montreal*).
      Publication of the Canadian Survey.

Hurlbert, J. B. Physical atlas of Canada. (*Ottawa*).

Walker, H. B. Statistical atlas of the Dominion of Canada. fo. *Trübner.*   84*s.*

Silver's Handbook to Canada. c. 8vo. *Silver.*   5*s.*

Biggar, E. B. Canada; a memorial volume. 8vo. 10 parts. *Stanford.*   10*s.* 6*d.*
      Much useful information on each of the provinces.

Rae, W. Fraser. Columbia and Canada. p. 8vo. *Daldy.*   6*s.*

Cumberland, Stuart C. The Queen's highway. 8vo. *Low.* illus.   18*s.*

Grant, G. M. Picturesque Canada. 4to. 2 vols., 63*s.* each. *Cassell.* illus.   126*s*

Church, A. J. Making a start in Canada. 8vo. *Seeley.*   2*s.* 6*d.*

Fream, W. Canadian agriculture. 8vo.
      Official report, to be obtained from the High Commissioner, 17, Victoria-street, S.W.

Christy, R. M. Manitoba described. 8vo. *Wyman.*   1*s.*

Bryce, G. Manitoba. c. 8vo. *Low.*   7*s.* 6*d.*

Hardy, C. Forest life in Acadie (Nova Scotia). 8vo. *Chapman.* illu .
    pub. 18*s.*   O.P

Grant, G. M. Ocean to ocean. 8vo. *Low.*   O.P.

Wolley, C. P. A sportsman's Eden. 8vo. *Bentley.*   9*s.*

Rowan, J. J. Emigrant and sportsman in Canada. l. p. 8vo. *Stanford.*   10*s.* 6*d.*

Lovett's Gazetteer of British North America. Ed. P. A. Crossby. *Low.*   O.P.
    Descriptions of over 7,500 cities, towns, &c.

Englishman's Guide-book to U. S. and Canada. *Low.* illus.   7s. 6d.
    Appendix on shooting and fishing.
      PERIODICALS : *The official Handbook of Canada* for 1890 can be had post free on applica-
tion to the Canadian Government Offices, Victoria-street, S.W. The publications of the
Geological Survey of Canada and the transactions of the Royal Society of Canada are of
importance.

—II. HISTORY, GOVERNMENT, ETC. :

Parkman, F. Canada under French rule. p. 8vo. *Macmillan.*   7s. 6d.

MacMullen, J. History of Canada. 8vo. *Low.*   16s.

Kingsford, W. History of Canada. m. 8vo. Vol. I. *Trübner.*   15s.

Collins, J. E. Life and times of Sir J. A Macdonald. 8vo. (*Toronto*).

Bourinot, J. G. Federal government in Canada. 8vo. (*Baltimore*).   5s.

   ,,   Local government in Canada. 8vo. (*Baltimore*).
    John Hopkin's University Studies, 7th and 5th series.

Todd, A. Parliamentary government in the colonies. 8vo. *Little* (*Boston*).
   pub. 30s.   O.P.

Munro, J. E. C. Constitution of Canada. d. 8vo. *Cambridge Press.*   10s.

Russell, J. Schools of greater Britain. d. 8vo. *Collins.*   3s. 6d.
    PERIODICALS : Trade and Navigation Returns and Statistical Abstract and Record of
Canada (Queen's Printer, Ottawa). These, together with the statutes, blue-books of the
Dominion and provincial governments, and other works of reference, can be seen in the library
of the Office of the High Commissioner for Canada, 17, Victoria-street, S.W.

CANALS, *see* HYDRAULICS.

CANARY ISLANDS, *see* ATLANTIC.

CANDLE MANUFACTURE, *see* INDUSTRIES XVII.

CAOUTCHOUC, *see* ECONOMIC PRODUCTS II.

CAPE AND SOUTH AFRICA
    For detailed geography of special regions, consult recent vols. of the Proceedings of the Royal
Geographical Society, and blue-books from 1880, dealing with Bechuanaland, Transvaal, etc.

Reclus, E. Universal geography, vol. xiii. i. 8vo. *Virtue.*   21s.
    Latest and fullest.

Stanford's compendium ; South Africa. Ed. Keith Johnston. d. 8vo
   Stanford.   21s.

Juta. Map of South Africa. *Stanford.*   10s.
    Contains many printed notes.

Wilmot, A. Geography of South Africa. (*Cape Town*).   1s. 6d.
    For the use of higher classes in schools.

Trollope, A. South Africa. p. 8vo. 2 vols. *Chapman.*   30s.
    Cape Colony, Natal, Transvaal, Griqualand West, Orange Free State, Native Territories.

Greswell, W. Our South African empire. p. 8vo. *Chapman.*   21s.

Theal, G. McCall. History of South Africa. (1486–1872). d. 8vo. 5 vols.,
   15s. each. *Sonnenschein.*   75s.

Noble, J. South Africa, past and present. c. 8vo. *Longmans.*   7s. 6d.
    History of the European settlements. More succinct than Theal.

Brooks, H. Natal : history, description, and resources of the Colony.
   Ed. R. Mann. 8vo. *L. Reeve.* illus.   21s.

Peace, W.　Our colony of Natal.　c. 8vo.　*Stanford.*　　2*s.* 6*d.*

Norris-Newman, C. L.　With the Boers in the Transvaal and Orange Free State.　d. 8vo.　*Allen.*　　11*s.*

Theal, G. McCall.　History of the Boers in South Africa.　8vo.　*Sonnenschein.*　　15*s.*

Farrar, K.　Zululand and the Zulus.　f. 8vo.　*Kerby.*　　1*s.*

Silver's Handbook to South Africa.　c. 8vo.　*Silver.*　　5*s.*

　　PERIODICALS: The *Argus* annual and South African directory ; contains much information on all the South African countries.　The official *Handbook* of the history, productions, and resources of the Cape of Good Hope.
　　Cape of Good Hope *Statistical Register* ; sold at the Cape of Good Hope Government Agency, Victoria-street, S.W.

CAPITAL AND LABOUR, *see* POLITICAL ECONOMY III., VI. *and* IX.

CARDS :

Chatto, W. A.　Origin and history of playing cards.　8vo.　(*London*).　1848.　pub. 21*s.*　　O.P.
　　Rather behind time, but contains a bibliography.

Willshire, W. H.　Catalogue of playing cards.　8vo.　*British Museum.*　　21*s.*
　　Contains a concise general history of the subject.

Taylor and others.　History of playing cards.　f. 8vo.　*Chatto.*　　O.P.
　　Anecdotes of their use in conjuring, fortune-telling, and card-sharping.

Jeux de cartes tarots, et de cartes numérales du XIVme au XVIIIme siècle.　fo.　*Société des Bibliophiles Français (Paris).*　1844.
　　Contains bibliography.

Hoyle's games.　18mo.　*Whittaker.*　　5*s.*

"Trumps."　American Hoyle.　12mo.　(*N. York*).　illus.　　10*s.* 6*d.*

Bohn, H. G.　Handbook of games.　p. 8vo.　2 vols., 3*s.* 6*d.* each.　*Bell.*　illus.　　7*s.*

"Cavendish."　Round games at cards.　8vo.　*De La Rue.*　　1*s.* 6*d.*
　　Contains Loo, Vingt-et-Un, Poker, Napoleon, and minor games.

　　,,　Bézique.　8vo.　*De La Rue.*　illus.　　1*s.* 6*d.*

　　,,　Cribbage.　r. 16mo.　*De La Rue.*　illus.　　6*d.*

　　,,　Écarté.　8vo.　*De La Rue.*　illus.　　2*s.* 6*d.*

Leeds and Dwight.　Euchre.　18mo.　*Ticknor (Boston).*　　2*s.* 6*d.*

"Cavendish."　Euchre.　r. 16mo.　*De La Rue.*　　6*d.*

　　,,　Patience games.　d. ob. 4to.　*De La Rue.*　illus.　　16*s.*

　　,,　Piquet.　8vo.　*De La Rue.*　illus.　　5*s.*

Clay and Baldwin.　Short whist.　8vo.　*De La Rue.*　　3*s.* 6*d.*

"Cavendish."　Whist ; laws and principles.　8vo.　*De La Rue.*　illus.　　5*s.*
　　Contains a historical account, and hands played through.

Pole, W.　Philosophy of whist.　8vo.　*De La Rue.*　　3*s.* 6*d.*
　　Part i., Philosophy of whist playing ; part ii., Philosophy of whist probabilities.

"Cavendish."　Whist developments.　8vo.　*De La Rue.*　　5*s.*
　　American leads, and the unblocking game.

Rheinhardt, R. H.　Whist-scores and card-table-talk.　12mo.　(*Chicago*).　　12*s.* 6*d.*
　　With a bibliography of whist.
　　The *Field* (346, Strand), contains notes on whist and other games of cards.

CARPENTRY, *see* BUILDING *and* WORKSHOP.

CARRIAGE BUILDING, *see* INDUSTRIES VII.

CARTHAGE, *see* PHŒNICIA *and* ROME, HISTORY.

CASTLES, *see* ARCHITECTURE III.

CAT:

Mivart, St. G. The cat. 8vo. *Murray.* illus.   30*s.*
    Scientific work.

Chamfleury. The cat, past and present. Tr. Mrs. C. Hoey. c. 8vo. *Bell.*   6*s.*

CATHEDRALS AND CHURCHES, ENGLISH:

Murray's Handbooks to the English Cathedrals. *Murray.*

> Southern Cathedrals. illus. 2 vols. c. 8vo. 36*s.* (Winchester, Salisbury, Exeter, Wells, Rochester, Canterbury, Chichester, St. Alban's).
> Eastern Cathedrals. illus. c. 8vo. 21*s.* (Oxford, Peterborough, Ely, Norwich, Lincoln).
> Western Cathedrals. illus. c. 8vo. 16*s.* (Bristol, Gloucester, Hereford, Worcester, Lichfield).
> Northern Cathedrals. illus. 2 vols. c. 8vo. 21*s.* (York, Ripon, Durham, Carlisle, Chester, Manchester).
> Welsh Cathedrals. illus. c. 8vo. 15*s.* (Llandaff, St. David's, Bangor, St. Asaph's).

Britton, J. Cathedrals of England and Wales. 4to. 5 vols. *Longmans.*
    1836. pub. £12 12*s.*   O.P.

Abbeys and churches of England and Wales. Ed. T. G. Bonney. *Cassell.*
    illus.   21*s.*

Billings, R. W. History and description of Carlisle cathedral. 4to.
    Broome. 1840.   O.P.
    Architectural illustrations.

Willis, R. Architectural history of Canterbury cathedral. 8vo. *Parker.*
    1845.   10*s.* 6*d.*

    ,, Architectural history of conventual buildings of Christ Church,
    Canterbury. 8vo. (*London*).   O.P.

Stephens, W. R. Memorials of the see of Chichester. d. 8vo. *Bentley.* illus.   21*s.*

Greenwell, W. Durham cathedral. p. 8vo. *Andrews (Durham).*   2*s.*

Stewart, D. J. Architectural history of Ely cathedral. d. 8vo. *Van
    Voorst.* illus.   21*s.*

Haines and Waller. Guide to the cathedral church of Gloucester. d. 8vo.
    (*Gloucester*). illus.   1*s.* 6*d.*
    Admirable and exhaustive guide, but dry, and filled with many uninteresting details.

Paley, F. A. History and architecture of Peterborough cathedral.

Livett, G. M. Foundations of the Saxon cathedral church of Rochester.
    d. 8vo. *Kent Archæological Society.* illus.   2*s.*

Murray's Handbook to St. Alban's cathedral. c. 8vo. *Murray.*   6*s.*
    Published separately, but occurs in "Southern Cathedrals."

Jones and Price. History of St. David's. *Mason (Tenby).*   30*s.*

St. Paul's, *see* LONDON.

Freeman, E. A. History of the cathedral church of Wells. c. 8vo.
    Macmillan.   3*s.* 6*d.*

Westminster Abbey, *see* LONDON.

Milner, J. History and antiquities of Winchester. r. 8vo. (*Winchester*).
    1840.   O.P.

Loftie, W. J. Windsor. 8vo. *Seeley.*   6*s.*

Poole and Hugall. Historical guide to York cathedral. r. 8vo. (*York*).   O.P.

CATTLE, *see* LIVE-STOCK *and* VETERINARY SCIENCE.

CAUCASUS, *see* RUSSIA IN ASIA II.

CAVALRY, *see* ARMY I.

CELEBES, *see* INDIAN OCEAN.

CELTIC LITERATURE:

See also IRELAND, SCOTLAND, WALES, MAN, ISLE OF

—I. OLD CORNISH:

Williams, R. Cornish-English dictionary. 4to. *Trübner.*   42*s.*

Jago, W. P. English-Cornish dictionary. r. 8vo. *Simpkin.*   21*s.*

Norris, E. Ancient Cornish drama. 8vo. 2 vols. *Clar. Press.*   21*s.*
> With texts and translations and a sketch of Cornish Grammar (sold separately, 2*s.* 6*d.*).
> For further account of the Grammar, *see* Zeuss' *Grammatica Celtica* (IRELAND III).
> Nearly all Cornish literature is dramatic and in verse.

Life of St. Meriasek. Ed. and tr. Whitley Stokes. m. 8vo. *Trübner.*   15*s.*

—II. BRETON:

Le Gonidec. Dictionnaire Breton-Français, précédé de sa grammaire bretonne. 4to. 2 vols. (*Saint-Brieuc*).   50*s.*

Chants populaires de la Bretagne, recueillis et traduits par F. R. Luzel. 8vo. 2 vols. *Lorient.*   15*s.*

Ernault, E. Le mystère de Sainte Barbe. 4to. (*Paris*).   24*s.*
> Text, translation, and etymological dictionary. Only 120 copies printed.

CEMENT, *see* BUILDING.

CERAMICS, *see* POTTERY.

CEYLON:

Tennant, J. E. Ceylon: physical, historical, topographical, etc. 8vo. 2 vols. *Longmans.* pub. 50*s.*   O.P.

Haeckel, E. Visit to Ceylon. Tr. Clara Bell. p. 8vo. *Paul.*   7*s.* 6*d.*
> Specially important for the student.

Ferguson, A. M., & J. Ceylon: handbook and directory (Annual). p. 8vo. *Trübner.*   2*s.*

CHAIRMAN, *see* PUBLIC MEETINGS.

CHALDÆA, *see* ASSYRIA.

CHANCERY, INNS OF, *see* LONDON III.

CHANNEL ISLANDS:

Ansted and Latham. Channel Islands. 8vo. *Allen.* illus.   26*s.*

Le Quesne. Constitutional history of Jersey. *Longmans.* pub. 18*s.*   O.P

Dupont, G.　Histoire du Cotentin et de ses iles.　8vo.　4 vols., 6s. 6d. each.　(*Caen*).　　26s.

Havet, T.　Les Cours royales des iles normands.　8vo.　*Champion*.　　7s.

Tupper, F. B.　History of Guernsey, with notices of Jersey.　8vo.　*Simpkin*.　pub. 12s. 6d.　　O.P.

CHARITIES:

Loch, C. S.　Charities register and digest.　*Longmans*.　Annual.　　10s. 6d.

,,　　Charity organisation.　c. 8vo.　*Sonnenschein*.　　2s. 6d.

Low, S.　Handbook to the London charities.　Annual.　18mo.　*Low*.　　1s. 6d.
PERIODICAL: The *Charity Organisation Review*; quarterly.　(Longmans).

CHARTISM, *see* POLITICAL ECONOMY IX.

CHEESE-MAKING, *see* DAIRY.

CHEMISTRY:

For Technical Chemistry, see INDUSTRIES.

The general reader should begin with such a book as Muir's *Heroes of Science*, and read some short text-book, such as Remsen's *Inorganic Chemistry*. If he wish to study the subject further, it is essential to enter a laboratory, or do practical work under efficient supervision.

—I. HISTORY:

Thomson, T.　History of chemistry.　p. 8vo.　2 vols.　*Colburn*.　1830–31.　　O.P.

Rodwell, G. F.　Birth of chemistry.　p. 8vo.　*Macmillan*.　pub. 3s. 6d.　　O.P.
A popular account of alchemy.

Muir, M. M.　Heroes of science: Chemists.　c. 8vo.　*S. P. C. K.*　　4s.

Picton, H.　Story of chemistry　c. 8vo.　*Isbister*.　illus.　　3s. 6d.
The two last are short non-technical accounts of the development of chemical science.

Schorlemmer, C.　Rise and progress of organic chemistry.　8vo.　*Simpkin*.　pub. 2s. 6d.　　O.P.

Kopp, H.　Geschichte der Chemie.　8vo.　4 vols.　(*Brunswick*).　1843–7.
Vol. i., O.P.; vol. ii., 7s. 6d.; vol. iii., 6s.; vol. iv., 7s. 6d.　The standard work.

Meyer, E. V.　Geschichte der Chemie.　8vo.　(*Leipzig*).　　9s.
An excellent work; in course of translation.

—II. TEXT-BOOKS:

Roscoe and Schorlemmer.　Inorganic and organic chemistry.　8vo.　3 vols.　*Macmillan*.　illus.　　138s.
Vol. i., ii., Inorganic, 21s.; vol. iii. (five parts), Organic, 81s.　Large work, well arranged, and full in its treatment.

Miller, W. A.　Elements of chemistry.　Ed. H. McLeod.　8vo.　3 vols.　*Longmans*.　　71s. 6d.
Vol. i., Physics, 16s.; vol. ii., Inorganic, 24s.; vol. iii., Organic, 31s. 6d.

Fownes.　Manual of chemistry.　Ed. Tilden.　c. 8vo.　*Churchill*.　illus.　　18s. 6d.
Vol. i., Physical and inorganic, 8s. 6d.; vol. ii., Carbon compounds, 10s.

Bloxam, C. L.　Chemistry: inorganic and organic.　Ed. M. Thomson.　8vo.　*Churchill*.　　18s.
Well illustrated; adapted for experimental work.

Lewes, V. B.　Service chemistry.　d. 8vo.　*Whittingham*.　illus.　　15s.
Written specially for those who are interested in the practical applications of chemistry.

Remsen, J. Introduction to the study of inorganic chemistry. c. 8vo.
  Macmillan.   6s. 6d.
  One of the best elementary books.

Roscoe, H. E. Lessons in elementary chemistry. f. 8vo. *Macmillan.*
  illus.   4s. 6d.

Ramsay, W. Systematic inorganic chemistry. s. c. 8vo. *Churchill.*   4s. 6d.

Shepard, J. H. Elementary inorganic chemistry. p. 8vo. *Putnam.*   6s. 6d.
  The last two are arranged according to the periodic system.

Lewes, V. B. Inorganic chemistry. *Whittingham.*   3s. 6d.

Groves and Thorp. Chemical technology. r. 8vo. *Churchill.*   30s.

—III. PHYSICAL:

Meyer, L. Modern theories of chemistry. Tr. Bedson and Williams. 8vo.
  Longmans.   18s.
  A good translation of a standard work.

Muir, M. M. Principles of chemistry. d. 8vo. *Cambridge Press.*   15s.
  A fairly full treatise.

Ostwald, W. Allgemeine Chemie. 8vo. 2 vols. *Engelmann.*   20s.
  The standard work.

  ,,   Grundriss der allgemeinen Chemie. 8vo. *Engelmann.*   8s.
  In course of translation.

Remsen, J. Principles of theoretical chemistry. p. 8vo. (*Philadelphia*).   7s. 6d.

  ,,   Introduction to carbon compounds. c. 8vo. *Macmillan.*   6s. 6d.
  The best introductory work.

Bernthsen, A. Organic chemistry (elem.). Tr. McGowan. c. 8vo. *Blackie.*   9s.

Richter, V. von. Organic chemistry. Tr. Smith. 12mo. *Blakiston*
  (*Philadelphia*).   15s.

Reynolds, J. E. Experimental chemistry. f. 8vo. 4 vols. *Longmans*
  illus.   11s. 6d.
  A set of practical exercises in inorganic and organic chemistry. Part i., Introductory, 1s. 6d.;
  part ii., Non-metals, 2s. 6d.; part iii., Metals, 3s. 6d.; part iv., Carbon compounds, 4s.

—IV. ANALYTICAL:

Fresenius, C. R. Qualitative analysis. Tr. C. Groves. 8vo. *Churchill.*
  illus.   15s.
  The standard work.

Jones, F. Owen's College junior course of practical chemistry (qualitative).
  18mo. *Macmillan.*   2s. 6d.
  One of the best and cheapest of an enormous number of similar books.

Fresenius, C. R. Quantitative analysis. Tr. G. Vacher. d. 8vo. *Churchill.*
  illus.   15s.
  The standard work.

Thorpe, T. E. Quantitative chemical analysis. c. 8vo. *Longmans.* illus.   4s. 6d.

Dittmar, W. Quantitative chemical analysis. r. 8vo. *Williams.*   10s. 6d.

Hartley, W. N. Quantitative chemical analysis. gl. 8vo. *Macmillan.*   5s.
  ·The last three books give series of selected exercises.

Blyth, A. W. Foods: their composition and analysis. c. 8vo. *Griffin.*
  illus.   16s.

  ,,   Poisons: their effects and detection. c. 8vo. *Griffin.*   16s.
  The last two books are for the public analyst and medical practitioner.

König, J. Nahrungsmittel. 8vo. (*Berlin*).   25s.

Allen, A. H. Commercial organic analysis. d. 8vo. *Churchill.*
  Vol. iii. (1), 14s.; vol. i., ii., reprinting. Deals with adulterations.

Plattner, C. F. Analysis with the blowpipe. Tr. T. H. Cookesley. *Chatto.*
  pub. 21s.   O.P.

Sutton, F. Volumetric analysis. d. 8vo. *Churchill.* illus.   16s.
  The standard work.

Crookes, W. Select methods of chemical analysis. 8vo. *Longmans.* illus.   24s.

Winkler and Lunge. Technical gas analysis. c. 8vo. *Gurney.*   7s.

—V. REFERENCE AND BIOGRAPHY:

Watts, H. Dictionary of chemistry. Ed. Morley and Muir. 8vo. 4 vols.
  Longmans.
  Vol. i., ii., 42s. each; vol. iii., iv., in preparation. An almost re-written edition, with technical articles and physical memoirs cut out; much abridged; chiefly useful for reference.

  ,, Dictionary of chemistry. Ed. Thorpe. r. 8vo. 3 vols., 42s. each.
  Longmans.
  Technical dictionary. In course of publication. Vol. i., applied; vol. ii., pure.

Cundill. Dictionary of explosives. *Mackay (Chatham).*   6s.

Eissler, M. Handbook of modern explosives. 8vo. *Lockwood.*   10s. 6d.

Wilson, G. Life of the Hon. Henry Cavendish. d. 8vo. *Harrison.*   7s.

Davy, J. Life of Sir Humphrey Davy. 8vo. 2 vols. *Smith, Elder.* 1839.
  pub. 28s.   O.P.

Hervy, W. C. Life and scientific researches of John Dalton. d. 8vo.
  Harrison.   7s.

Jones, B. Life and letters of Faraday. 8vo. 2 vols. *Longmans.* pub. 28s.   O.P.

Gladstone, J. H. Michael Faraday. c. 8vo. *Macmillan.* pub. 4s. 6d.   O.P.

Tyndall, J. Faraday as a discoverer. f. 8vo. *Longmans.*   3s. 6d.

Hofmann, A. W. Life and work of Liebig. *Macmillan.*   5s.

  PERIODICALS AND TRANSACTIONS:
    —ENGLISH: *Transactions* and *Proceedings* of the Chemical Society of London, Ed. C. Groves; pub. since 1841; (Harrison). *Journal* of Society of Chemical Industry, Ed. Watson Smith; pub. since 1882; (Eyre); applied chemistry. *Chemical News,* Ed. W. Crookes; pub. since 1842; analytical and general chemistry. *American Chemical Journal,* Ed. J. Remsen; (Baltimore); bi-monthly; 15s. per annum; pure chemistry.
    —GERMAN: *Annalen der Chemie und Pharmacie* (Liebig's); conducted by a number of chemists; pub. since 1832; (Leipzig); issued in sets of four vols.; 24s. the set; pure chemistry. Many of the classical researches have been described in this journal. *Berichte der deutschen chemischen Gesellschaft,* Ed. F. Tiemann; (Berlin); 40s. per annum. *Journal für praktische Chemie,* Ed. E. V. Meyer; pub. since 1834; (Leipzig); 22s. per annum.
    —FRENCH: *Annales de chimie et physique;* pub. since 1789; 30s. per annum. The chief French journal. *Bulletin de la Société Chimique de Paris;* pub. since 1873; 25s. per annum.

CHESS:

Staunton, H. Chess-player's handbook. 8vo. *Bell.*   5s.

Cook, W. Synopsis of chess-openings. 8vo. *Simpkin.*   4s.

Chess-openings, ancient and modern. Ed. Freeborough and Ranken.
  l. p. 8vo. *Trübner.*   7s. 6d.

Green, R. F. Chess. 8vo. *Bell.* illus.   1s.
  Contains a bibliography.

Steinitz, W. Chess: modern instructor. 8vo. *Putnam.* Part i., 7s. 6d.
  PERIODICALS: *British Chess Magazine.* (Trübner). *Chess Monthly.* (Wade).

CHILDREN, MANAGEMENT OF, *see* DOMESTIC ECONOMY.

CHILDREN'S BOOKS :

This list is doubtless very incomplete, but it includes most of the time-honoured nursery classics. It is difficult to be consistent in matters of taste, but the attempt has been made to include only books of thoroughly wholesome tone. Many which possess great merit cannot be put into the hands of every child on account of one or two horrible stories or a few passages unfit for their age; these, if otherwise unobjectionable, have been marked with an asterisk as a danger signal, the probable age of the reader being taken as a guide. Thus, in the section " Fairy tales," regard has been had to the nerves of children from 8 to 10; but the standard under " Tales of adventure " has been the average boy of 12 or 14. " Grown-up " books, though suitable, have not, as a rule, been included in the list.

—I. FAIRY TALES :

(A) FOLKLORE.

Grimm, J., and W. German popular stories. Tr. E. Taylor. sq. 8vo. *Chatto.* illus. by Cruikshank.   6s. 6d.

***Wolff.** Fairy tales and stories (German legends). c. 8vo. *Routledge.*   2s. 6d.

***Dasent**, G. W. Popular tales from the Norse. *Douglas.*   10s. 6d.
Includes some rather terrible tales.

***Croker**, T. Crofton. Fairy legends and traditions of Ireland. p. 8vo. *Sonnenschein.*   2s. 6d.

Arabian nights' entertainments. i. 8vo. *Ward, Lock.*   10s. 6d.
Also *Routledge.* c. 8vo. 3s. 6d.

Frere, Mary. Old Deccan days. p. 8vo. *Murray.*   5s.
Indian fairy stories.

Steel and Temple. Wideawake stories. c. 8vo. *Trübner.*   9s.
Indian fairy stories charmingly arranged for children.

***Geldart**, E. M. Folklore of modern Greece. *Sonnenschein.* illus.   2s. 6d.

Griffis, W. E. Japanese fairy tales. 11 parts, 1s. each. *Dean.*   11s.
Parts sold separately.

Harris, J. C. Uncle Remus. c. 8vo. *Routledge.*   3s. 6d.
Negro stories in dialect.

Perrault and others. Fairy tales of all nations. Tr. J. R. Planché. p. 8vo. *Routledge.*   3s. 6d.

Tegg. Child's own book. c. 8vo. *Spencer Blackett.*   6s.
Fairy tales from all sources.

Lang, A. The blue fairy book. c. 8vo. *Longmans.*   6s.

,,   The red fairy book. c. 8vo. *Longmans.*   6s.

(B) ORIGINAL FAIRY TALES.

Andersen, Hans. Fairy tales. Tr. Mrs. Paull. d. 8vo. *Warne.* illus.   7s. 6d.
Also *Bell*, 3s. 6d.

Swift, J. Gulliver's travels. c. 8vo. *Blackie.*   6s.
Also *Routledge.* c. 8vo. 3s. 6d.

Baron Munchausen (" Daring deeds library "). c. 8vo. *Warne.*   2s. 6d

Kingsley, C. The water babies. c. 8vo. *Macmillan.* illus. Sambourne.   3s. 6d.

Ruskin, J. The king of the golden river. *G. Allen.* illus.   2s. 6d.

Thackeray, W. M. The rose and the ring. *Smith, Elder.*   .
In " Christmas books." c. 8vo. 7s. 6d. and 5s. ; or in one vol. with " Ballads," 3s. 6d. and 10s. 6d. Also pocket edition, 1s. 6d.

Holme Lee. Fairy tales.   O.P.

,,   Tuflongbo's adventures. f. 8vo.   O.P.
A selection from the " Fairy tales," forming a complete story.

Carroll, Lewis. Alice's adventures in wonderland. c. 8vo. *Macmillan.* illus.   2s. 6d. and 6s.

Carroll, Lewis. Through the looking-glass. c. 8vo. *Macmillan*. illus. 2*s*. 6*d*. and 6*s*.

Macdonald, G. At the back of the north wind. c. 8vo. *Blackie*.   5*s*.

Ewing, Mrs. Old-fashioned fairy tales. *S. P. C. K.*   3*s*. 6*d*.

Giles, Chauncey. The wonderful pocket.

    ,,   The magic shoes.
       Bright tales, well written but for a few Americanisms.

—II. TALES FROM THE CLASSICS:

Cox, G. W. Tales of ancient Greece. sm. c. 8vo. *Paul*.   6*s*.
     A number of myths briefly and well told.

Kingsley, C. Heroes. c. 8vo. *Macmillan*.   3*s*. 6*d*.
     A few tales from Greek mythology, told at length.

Hawthorne, N. Wonder-book for girls and boys. c. 8vo. *Routledge*.   1*s*. 6*d*.
     Greek myths re-told as modern fairy tales.

Witt, C. Tales of the Trojan war. Tr. Younghusband. c. 8vo. *Longmans*.   '2*s*.
     Tales from the *Iliad*.

    ,,   Wanderings of Ulysses. Tr. Younghusband. c. 8vo. *Longmans*.   3*s*. 6*d*.
     Tales from the *Odyssey*.

Church, A. J. Stories from the Greek tragedians. *Seeley*. illus.   5*s*.

    ,,   Stories from Herodotus. *Seeley*. illus.   5*s*.

Keary, A., and E. The heroes of Asgard. gl. 8vo. *Macmillan*.   2*s*. 6*d*.
     Tales from northern mythology.

Joyce, P. W. Old Celtic romances. p. 8vo. *Paul*. pub. 7*s*. 6*d*.   O.P.
     Irish legends of Finn Macoul.

*****Malory**, T. Morte d'Arthur. ("Globe" ed.). 8vo. *Macmillan*.   3*s*. 6*d*.
     The original text, very slightly expurgated.

King Arthur and his knights of the Round Table. *Griffith and Farran*.   O.P.
     A delightful setting of the principal adventures.

Cox and Jones. Popular romances of the middle ages. c. 8vo. *Paul*.   6*s*.
     Brief versions of Round Table and other legends.

Hope, A. R. Stories of old renown. c. 8vo. *Blackie*.   3*s*. 6*d*.
     Old stories told in a modern way.

*****Johnson**, R. Seven champions of Christendom. c. 8vo.   2*s*. 6*d*.

Kingston, W. H. G. Seven champions of Christendom. c. 8vo. *Griffith and Farran*.   O.P.
     Free and abridged version of Johnson for children.

Reynard the Fox. c. 8vo. *Sonnenschein*.   3*s*. 6*d*.

Storr and Turner. Canterbury chimes. f. 8vo. *Paul*. illus.   3*s*. 6*d*.
     Stories from Chaucer.

Lamb, C., and M. Tales from Shakespeare. c. 8vo. *Routledge*.   2*s*. and 3*s*. 6*d*.

—III. FABLES AND ALLEGORIES:

Æsop's fables. p. 8vo. *Murray*. illus. Tenniel.   2*s*. 6*d*.
     Also *Cassell*. 8vo. illus. E. Griset. 5*s*.

Gatty, Mrs. Parables from nature. 32mo. 5 series; i., 1*s*. 6*d*.; the rest 2*s*. each.   9*s*. 6*d*.
     Also sq. 16mo. 3*s*.

Fowler, W. W. Tales of the birds. c. 8vo. *Macmillan*. illus.   3*s*. 6*d*.
     Delightful stories of bird life.

Abbott, E. A. Parables for children. c. 8vo. *Macmillan*. pub. 3*s*. 6*d*.   O.P.

Wilberforce, S. Agathos. sm. 8vo. *Seeley*. illus.   1*s*. and 2*s*. 6*d*.

Bunyan, John. Pilgrim's progress. 8vo. *Cassell.* illus.   £s.
Also *Warne.* c. 8vo. 2s.

Carové. Story without an end. 4to. *Low.* illus.   7s. 6d.

Laboullaye, E. Abdallah, or the four-leaved shamrock ("Bayard series").
16mo. *Low.*   2s. 6d.

Craik, Mrs. The little lame prince. c. 8vo. *Macmillan.* illus.   3s. 6d.
A charming allegory.

—IV. TALES OF SCHOOL AND HOME:

(A) FOR LITTLE CHILDREN.

Barbauld, Mrs. Lessons for children. sm. 8vo. *Routledge.*   1s.

Prentiss, Mrs. Little Susy's six birthdays. p. 8vo. *Nelson.*   2s.

,,   Little Susy's six teachers. p. 8vo. *Nelson.*   1s.
Also *Routledge*, 1s.

,,   Little Susy's servants. p. 8vo. *Nelson.*   1s.
Also *Routledge*, 1s.

Edgeworth, Maria. Early lessons. c. 8vo. *Routledge.*   3s. 6d.

Bond, A. L. Tiny's natural history. f. 4to. *Routledge.* illus.   1s. 6d.

Trimmer, Mrs. Story of the robins. p. 8vo. *Routledge.*   1s.

Gwynfryn. Friends in furs and feathers. p. 8vo. *Bell.*   1s.

Howitt, Mary. Story of a happy home. p. 8vo. *Nelson.*   2s.
First published as "The children's year."

(B) FOR ELDER CHILDREN.

Edgeworth, Maria. Parent's assistant. c. 8vo. *Routledge.*   3s. 6d.

Day, T. Sandford and Merton. c. 8vo. *Warne.*   2s.

Martineau, Harriet. The Crofton boys. c. 8vo. *Routledge.* illus.   2s.

,,   Feats on the fiord. c. 8vo. *Routledge.* illus.   1s. and 2s.

*****Stowe**, Harriet B. Uncle Tom's cabin. c. 8vo. *Bell.*   3s. 6d.
Also *Warne*, 2s. Some scenes too painful for young or nervous children.

Craik, Mrs. Adventures of a brownie. *Macmillan.* illus.   4s. 6d.
Essentially domestic, in spite of the fairy machinery.

,,   A hero. *Routledge.* illus.   2s.

Gatty, Mrs. Aunt Judy's tales. f. 8vo. *Bell.* illus.   3s. 6d.

Ewing, Mrs. Mrs. Overtheway's remembrances. sm. p. 8vo. *Bell.* illus. 1s. and 3s.

,,   Six to sixteen. sm. p. 8vo. *Bell.* illus.   1s. and 3s.

,,   A great emergency, and other tales. sm. p. 8vo. *Bell.* illus.   1s. and 3s.

,,   Jackanapes. 8vo.   1s.

,,   Mary's meadow. 8vo. *S. P. C. K.*   1s.

Shaw, Flora. Castle Blair. c. 8vo. *Paul.*   3s. 6d.

Keary, Annie. A York and Lancaster rose. gl. 8vo. *Macmillan.*   2s. and 3s. 6d.
A modern tale of town life.

Alcott, Louisa M. Little women. *Ward, Lock.*   1s. 6d. and 2s. 6d.

,,   Good wives. *Ward, Lock.*   1s. 6d. and 2s. 6d.

,,   Little men. 16mo. *Low.*   2s. 6d.
New England life.

Coolidge, S. What Katy did. *Ward, Lock.*   2s.
American story for girls.

Hughes, T. Tom Brown's schooldays. c. 8vo. *Macmillan.* illus.   3s. 6d.
Also at 2s.

Hope, A. R. My schoolboy friends.   O.P.

Yonge, C. M. Countess Kate; and the Stokesley secret. c. 8vo. *Smith and Innes.*   5s.

,, Ben Sylvester's word. 18mo. *Smith and Innes.*   1s.

—V. TALES OF ADVENTURE:

Defoe, D. Robinson Crusoe. 8vo. *Cassell.*   5s.
Also *Warne*, 2s.

Swiss family Robinson. c. 8vo. *Warne.*   5s.
Also *Nelson*, 3s.; and others.

Marryatt, F. Masterman Ready. p. 8vo. *Bell (Bohn).*   3s. 6d.

,, Poor Jack. p. 8vo. *Bell.*   2s. 6d.

,, Settlers in Canada. p. 8vo. *Bell.*   3s. 6d.

* ,, Peter Simple. c. 8vo. *Routledge.*   2s. and 3s. 6d.
Broad humour; sometimes coarse.

Scott, Michael. Tom Cringle's log. c. 8vo. *Blackwood.*   3s.

Bowman, Annie. Esperanza. c. 8vo. *Routledge.*   2s. 6d.
Old-fashioned, but spirited.

Cooper, Fenimore. Leather stocking tales ("Deerslayer," "Last of the Mohicans," "Pathfinder," "Pioneers," "The Prairie"). c. 8vo. 2s. each. *Routledge.* Or in one vol.   5s.

Ballantyne, R. M. Coral island. p. 8vo. *Nelson.*   3s. 6d.

,, Ungava (Esquimau land). p. 8vo. *Nelson.*   3s. 6d.

,, Young fur traders. p. 8vo. *Nelson.*   3s. 6d.

Cottin, Mme. Elizabeth, or the exiles of Siberia. c. 8vo. *Nimmo.*   1s.

Stevenson, R. L. Treasure island. *Cassell.* illus.   5s.

,, Kidnapped. *Cassell.* illus.   5s.

Fenn, G. Manville. The golden magnet. c. 8vo. *Blackie.* illus.   6s.
Tale of gold diggings.

,, Dick o' the Fens. c. 8vo. *Blackie.* illus.   6s.
Tale of East Anglia in last century.

,, Devon boys. c. 8vo. *Blackie.* illus.   6s.

—VI. HISTORICAL TALES:

Kingsley, C. Hereward the Wake. c. 8vo. *Macmillan.*   3s. 6d.
A tale of the Conquest.

,, Westward ho! c. 8vo. *Macmillan.*   3s. 6d.
Elizabethan period.

Marryatt, F. Children of the New Forest. c. 8vo. *Routledge.*   5s.
A tale of the Great Rebellion. Also at 2s. 6d.

Porter, Jane. The Scottish chiefs. c. 8vo. *Routledge.* illus.   3s. 6d.
A tale of Wallace.

Yonge, C. M. The little duke. gl. 8vo. *Macmillan.* illus.   2s. 6d.
Normandy before the Conquest.

,, The lances of Lynwood. gl. 8vo. *Macmillan.* illus.   2s. 6d.
French wars of Edward III.

,, The pigeon pie. d. 8vo. *Smith and Innes.*   1s.
A cavalier story.

Peard, F. M. Mother Molly. sm. p. 8vo. *Bell.* illus.   3*s.*
    Plymouth in the time of Napoleon.

Henty, G. A. In freedom's cause. c. 8vo. *Blackie.* illus.   6*s.*

,,   Under Drake's flag. c. 8vo. *Blackie.* illus.   6*s.*

,,   The lion of the north. c. 8vo. *Blackie.* illus.   6*s.*
    A tale of the Thirty Years' War.

,,   Bonnie Prince Charlie. c. 8vo. *Blackie.* illus.   6*s.*
    Jacobite rising of '45.

—VII. BIOGRAPHY AND HISTORY:

Strickland, Agnes. Lives of the queens of England (abridged). p. 8vo.
    Bell.   6*s.* 6*d.*

Peake, Helena. Boy's book of heroes. c. 8vo. *Warne.* illus.   2*s.* 6*d.*
    Bayard, Bertrand du Guesclin, and others.

Yonge, C. M. Cameos from English history. ex. f. 8vo. 7 vols., 5*s.*
    each. *Macmillan.*   35*s.*

,,   Book of golden deeds. f. 8vo. *Macmillan.* ("Golden Treasury").   4*s.* 6*d.*

Hoare, G. T. True stories of brave deeds. c. 8vo. *Warne.* illus.   2*s.* 6*d.*

Frost, T. Half hours with early explorers. c. 8vo. *Cassell.*   2*s.* 6*d.*

Dickens, Chas. Life of, by his eldest daughter. c. 8vo. *Cassell.*   1*s.*
    Told for children.

—VIII. TRAVEL, SPORT, AND NATURAL HISTORY:

Cook's voyages. 8vo. *Bickers.*   7*s.* 6*d.*
    Also *Routledge,* 2*s.*

Mungo Park's travels. *Phillips.*   4*s.* 6*d.*
    Also *Cassell* (Selections), 1*s.*

Waterton, C. Wanderings in South America. Ed. J. G. Wood. c. 8vo.
    Macmillan. illus.   6*s.*
    Contains good biography of Waterton.

Whymper, E. Scrambles among the Alps. 8vo. *Murray.* pub. 21*s.*   O.P.

Dana, R. H. Two years before the mast. 12mo. *Blackwood.*   2*s.* 6*d.*

Greenwood, J. Wild sports of the world. c. 8vo. *Ward, Lock.* illus.   3*s.* 6*d.*

Darwin, C. Naturalist's voyage round the world. *Murray.*   3*s.* 6*d.*

Walton and Cotton. Complete angler. p. 8vo. *Bell (Bohn).* illus.   5*s.*

White, Gilbert. History of Selborne. Ed. J. G. Wood. c. 8vo. *Macmillan.*   6*s.*
    The three last books, though not specially designed for boys, are very interesting to those whose
    tastes lie in this direction.

Wallace, A. R. Malay archipelago. c. 8vo. *Macmillan.*   6*s.*

Wood, J. G. Illustrated natural history. c. 8vo. *Routledge.*   5*s.*

,,   Common objects of the country. c. 8vo. *Routledge.* illus.   3*s.* 6*d.*

,,   The brook and its banks. 4to. *R. T. S.*   6*s.*

,,   Common objects of the sea-shore. c. 8vo. *Routledge.* illus.   3*s.* 6*d.*

Cooke, M. C. Ponds and ditches. *S. P. C. K.*   2*s.* 6*d.*

Jefferies, R. Gamekeeper at home. c. 8vo. *Smith, Elder.*   5*s.*

,,   Amateur poacher. c. 8vo. *Smith, Elder.*   5*s.*

Sewell, Anna. Black Beauty. 12mo. *Jarrold.*   2*s.*
    The story of a horse sympathetically told.

Brightwen, Mrs. Wild nature won by kindness. c. 8vo. *Unwin.*   3*s.* 6*d.*

Ball, R. S. Starland. *Cassell.*   6*s.*

Lectures on astronomy for children.

—IX. POETRY:

(A) COLLECTIONS AND BALLADS.

Payne, J. Select poetry for children. 18mo. *Lockwood.*   2*s.* 6*d.*

Patmore, C. Children's garland. 18mo. *Macmillan.*   4*s.* 6*d.*

Trench, R. C. Household book of poetry. ex. f. 8vo. *Paul.*   7*s.* 6*d.*

The three last books contain selections of standard poetry for children.

Woods, M. A. Poetry books (First, 2*s.* 6*d.*; Second, 2*s.* 6*d.*; Third, 4*s.* 6*d.*). f. 8vo. *Macmillan.*   9*s.* 6*d.*

Small unhackneyed collections.

Taylor, A. and J. Original poems for infant minds. 18mo. *Nelson.*   1*s.*

Old-fashioned, but contains many charming pieces.

Stevenson, R. L. A child's garden of verses. sm. f. 8vo. *Longmans.*   5*s.*

****Percy's** Reliques of ancient poetry. p. 8vo. 2 vols., 3*s.* 6*d.* each. *Bell (Bohn).*   7*s.*

Unexpurgated.

The boy's "Percy." Ed. S. Lanier. c. 8vo. *Low.*   7*s.* 6*d.*

Carefully chosen specimens.

Aytoun, W. E. Lays of the Scottish cavaliers. f. 8vo. *Blackwood.*   3*s.* 6*d.*

Lockhart, J. G. Spanish ballads. c. 8vo. *Murray.* illus.   5*s.*

Scott, W. Lay of the last minstrel. 16mo. *Black.*   1*s.*

,,   Marmion. 16mo. *Black.*   1*s.*

,,   Lady of the lake. 16mo. *Black.*   1*s.*

Macaulay, T. B. Lays of ancient Rome. c. 8vo. *Longmans.* illus.   3*s.* 6*d.*

Longfellow, H. W. Hiawatha. *Routledge.*   1*s.*

(B) HUMOROUS.

Lear, E. Nonsense songs. f. 4to. *Warne.* illus.   2*s.* 6*d.*

,,   Book of nonsense. ob. 4to. *Warne.* illus.   6*s.*

,,   More nonsense. ob. 4to. *Warne.* illus.   6*s.*

****Barham,** R. H. D. Ingoldsby legends. c. 8vo. *Bentley.* illus.   2*s.* 6*d.*

Struwelpeter. 4to. *Griffith and Farran.* illus.   2*s.* 6*d.*

Good English translation.

(C) SONGS WITH MUSIC.

Hubbard, C. B. Merry songs and games.

Rossetti, Christina. Sing-song. 16mo. *Routledge.* pub. 2*s.* 6*d.*   o.p.

Gatty, A. S. Little songs for little voices. *Metzler.*   2*s.* 6*d.*

Reinecke, C. Fifty children's songs.

Baby's opera. sm. 4to. *Routledge.*   5*s.*

Baby's bouquet. sm. 4to. *Routledge.*   5*s.*

The time-honoured airs, well set and beautifully illustrated by Walter Crane.

—X. ILLUSTRATED BOOKS:

Caldecott, R. Picture books. *Routledge.* From 1*s.*   10*s.* 6*d.*

Greenaway, K. Under the window. *Routledge.*   6*s.*

,,   Mother Goose. *Routledge.*   1*s.* 6*d.* and 3*s.* 6*d.*

Greenaway, K. Pied piper of Hamelin. *Routledge.*   6*s*.

Crane, Walter. Baby's own Æsop. sm. 4to. *Routledge.*   5*s*.

—XI. MAGAZINES AND SERIALS :

Infants' magazine (monthly). *Partridge.* Annual vol.   2*s*.
  For very young children.

Child's pictorial (monthly). *S. P. C. K.* Annual vol.   2*s*. 6*d*.
  Excellent short stories.

Little Folks (monthly). *Cassell.* Half-yearly vol.   3*s*. 6*d*. and 5*s*.

Saint Nicholas (monthly). *Unwin.* Half-yearly vol.   8*s*.
  The American serial for children.

Aunt Judy's magazine. Ed. Mrs. and H. K. F. Gatty.   o.p.
  No longer published, but the bound volumes are full of delightful stories, including most of
  Mrs. Ewing's.

Good Words for the young.   o.p.
  The bound volumes contain good tales, some by George Macdonald.

CHILI :

Boyd, R. N. Sketches of Chili and the Chilians. c. 8vo. *Allen.*   10*s*. 6*d*.

Pissis, A. Geografía física de la República de Chile.

CHINA :

—I. GEOGRAPHY :

For Chinese Empire, see ASIA, CENTRAL ; *for routes to Burmah, see* BURMAH.

Reclus, E. Universal geography, vol. vii. i. 8vo. *Virtue.*   21*s*.

Richthofen, F. F. von. China, Ergebnisse eigener Reisen. 4to. 4 vols.
  (*Berlin*).
  Vols. i., ii., iv., 108*s*.; vol. iii., not issued ; atlas, 60*s*. By far the most complete and scientific
  work on China.

Williams, S. W. The middle kingdom. d. 8vo. 2 vols. *Allen.*   42*s*.
  The most satisfactory work for the general reader.

Douglas, R. K. China. p. 8vo. *S. P. C. K.*   5*s*.
  A popular account of the country and people.

Gray, J. H. China ; history, laws, manners, etc. Ed. W. G. Gregor. 8vo.
  2 vols. *Macmillan.* illus.   32*s*.

Playfair, G. M. H. Cities and towns of China.   Geographical dictionary.
  8vo. *Trübner.*   25*s*.

Thomson, J. Illustrations of China and its people. 200 photos with letterpress. i. 4to. 4 vols., 63*s*. each. *Low.*   252*s*.

Henry, B. C. Ling-Nam. c. 8vo. *Partridge.* illus.   5*s*.
  Southern China, including explorations in the hitherto untraversed Island of Hainan.

Little, A. J. Through the Yang-tse gorges. 8vo. *Low.*   10*s*. 6*d*.
  Trade and travel in Western China.

Hosie, A. Three years in Western China. d. 8vo. *Philip.*   14*s*.

Boulger, D. C. History of China. d. 8vo. 3 vols. *Allen.*   64*s*.
  Vol. i., ii., 18*s*. each ; vol. iii., 28*s*.
  NOTE : For outlying parts of China, and the Island of Formosa, *see* Journals and Proceedings
  of the Royal Geographical Society.

—II. LANGUAGE AND LITERATURE :

Williams, S. W. A syllabic dictionary of the Chinese language (Mandarin
  dialect). 4to. *Trübner.*   105*s*.

Williams, S. W. Tonic dictionary of the Chinese language (Canton dialect). 8vo. (*Canton*).   84*s.*
An excellent work.

Couvreur, S. Dictionnaire Français-Chinois (Langue mandarine). 8vo. *Maisonneuve*.   42*s.*
Very useful.

Julien, Stanislas. Syntaxe nouvelle de la langue chinoise. 8vo. 2 vols. (*Paris*).   30*s.*
An important work for students of Chinese literature.

Prémare, J. H. Notitia linguae Sinicae. Tr. J. G. Bridgman. 8vo. (*Canton*). 1847.   O.P.
A valuable work.

Edkins, J. Grammar of the Chinese colloquial language (Mandarin dialect). 8vo. *Trübner.*   30*s.*

Douglas, R. K. Chinese manual. 12mo. *W. H. Allen.*   10*s.* 6*d.*
Contains a condensed grammar, with idiomatic phrases and dialogues. A useful book for students of the Mandarin colloquial.

Wade and Hillier. Yü-Yen-Tzŭ êrh chi (colloquial Chinese). 4to. 3 vols. *W. H. Allen.*   63*s.*
Invaluable for Pekingese dialects.

Wên-chien Tzŭ êrh chi. Ed. Sir T. F. Wade. 4to. 3 vols. (*Trübner*).
A series of papers selected as specimens of documentary Chinese.

Hirth, F. Text-book of documentary Chinese. 4to. 2 vols. (*Shanghai*).   24*s.*
With valuable vocabulary.

   ,, Notes on the Chinese documentary style. 8vo. *Quaritch.*   3*s.* 6*d.*
Very useful.

Lacouperie, Terrien de. The languages of China before the Chinese. 8vo. *Nutt.*   10*s.* 6*d.*
Valuable philological work.

Edkins, J. Introduction to the study of Chinese characters. r. 8vo. *Trübner.*   18*s.*

Chalmers, J. Structure of Chinese characters. 8vo. *Trübner.*   12*s.* 6*d.*

Chinese classics. Ed. and tr. J. Legge. c. 8vo. 5 vols. *Trübner.*
Vol. i., Confucian analects, 42*s.*; vol. ii., Mencius, 42*s.*; vol. iii., Shoo-King, 2 parts, 42*s.* each; vol. iv., She-King, 2 parts, 42*s.* each; vol. v., The Dukes, 2 parts, 42*s.* each. With critical and exegetical notes, prolegomena, and copious indexes.

Zottoli, A. Cursus litteraturae Sinicae. r. 8vo. 5 vols., 50*s.* each. (*Shanghai*).   £12 10*s.*
Very valuable to beginners and advanced students.

Mayers, W. F. The Chinese reader's manual. 8vo. *Trübner.*   25*s.*
Biographical, historical, and general literary reference.

Wylie, A. Notes on Chinese literature. 4to. *Trübner.*   36*s.*
Bibliographical.

CHINA, *see* POTTERY.

CHURCHES, *see* CATHEDRALS.

CHURCH VESTMENTS, *see* COSTUME *and* NEEDLEWORK.

CHURCH HISTORY:

—I. GENERAL:

Fisher, G. P. History of the Christian Church. 8vo. *Hodder.*   12*s.*
A good text-book, especially for more modern times.

Allen, A. V. G.   Continuity of Christian thought. c. 8vo. (*Boston*).   5s.
An essay on the main features of theological developments.

Kurtz, J. H.   Church history. 3 vols., 7s. 6d. each. *Hodder.*   22s. 6d.
The best German history in small compass.

Mosheim, J. L.   Institutes of ecclesiastical history. 8vo. 3 vols.
Longmans. pub. 45s.   O.P.

Neander, A.   History of the Christian Church. Tr. p. 8vo. 10 vols.,
3s. 6d. each. *Bell (Bohn).*   35s.

—II. THE EARLY CHURCH TO 800 A.D.:

Schaff, P.   History of the Christian Church. ex. 8vo. 6 vols. *Clark.*   84s.
Vol. i., ii. (to A.D. 100), 21s.; vol. iii., iv. (100-325), 21s.; vol. v., vi. (325-600), 21s.; vol.
vii., viii. (590-1073), 21s. A useful handbook with copious bibliography.

Mahan.   Church history of the first seven centuries. 8vo. *Rivington.*
pub. 15s. (elem.).   O.P.

Farrar, F. W.   Early days of Christianity. 2 vols. *Cassell.*   24s.
Also 1 vol., 6s.

Döllinger, J.   First age of Christianity. c. 8vo. 2 vols. *Allen.*   18s.

Plummer, A.   Church of the early Fathers. f. 8vo. *Longmans.*
(elem.).   2s. 6d.

Simcox, W. H.   Beginnings of the Christian Church. c. 8vo. *Rivington.*   7s. 6d.

Bingham, J.   Antiquities of the Christian Church. d. 8vo. 10 vols.
Clar. Press.   63s.
A standard work for Christian institutions.

Mason, A. J.   Persecutions of Diocletian. d. 8vo. *Deighton Bell.*   10s. 6d.

Gwatkin, H.   The Arian controversy. (elem.). f. 8vo. *Longmans.*   2s. 6d.

    ,,   Studies of Arianism. 8vo. *Deighton Bell.*   10s. 6d.

Newman, J. H.   Arians of the 4th century. c. 8vo. *Longmans.*   6s.
To be compared with Gwatkin's work.

Hefele, C. J.   History of the Councils of the Church to 451. Tr. 8vo.
3 vols., 12s. each. *Clark.*   36s.
Vol. i., to 325; ii., 326-429; iii., 431-451. Forms part of a large work, *Conciliengeschichte,*
which carries the history of Councils to 1450.

Dale, A. W.   Synod of Elvira. c. 8vo. *Macmillan.*   10s. 6d.

Eusebius.   Ecclesiastical history; continued by Socrates, Sozomen,
Theodoret, and Evagrius. p. 8vo. 4 vols., 5s. each. *Bell (Bohn).*   20s.
These volumes contain translations of the earliest historical writings of the Church after the
Apostles, reaching to 544.

Broglie, Duc de.   L'église et l'empire romain au ive siècle. 12mo. 6 vols.
(*Paris*).   18s.
History of the 4th century.

The Fathers for English readers. f. 8vo. 12 vols., 2s. each ; 2 vols., 2s. 6d.
each. *S. P. C. K.*   29s.
A series containing the Apostolic Fathers, the Apologists, Augustine, Ambrose, Jerome,
Leo the Great, Gregory the Great, Basil, Synesius, and others.

Maclear and Merivale.   Conversion of the West. f. 8vo. 5 vols., 2s. each.
S. P. C. K. (elem.).   10s.
A series of vols. dealing with the Celts, Norsemen, Slavs, English and continental Teutons.

Bright, W.   Early English Church history. d. 8vo. *Clar. Press.*   12s.

Bede.   Ecclesiastical history of England. p. 8vo. *Bell (Bohn).*   5s.

Stokes, G. T.   Ireland and the Celtic Church. c. 8vo. *Hodder.*   9s.

Müllinger, J. Bass. Schools of Charles the Great. 8vo. *Longmans.*
pub. 7*s.* 6*d.*   o.p.
Contains a sketch of Christian education.

—III. MEDIÆVAL PERIOD, 800–1500:

Robertson, J. C. History of the Christian Church. c. 8vo. 8 vols., 6*s.*
each. *Murray.*   48*s.*
Reaches to 1517, and gives full details.

Milman, H. History of Latin Christianity. c. 8vo. 9 vols., 4*s.* each.
Murray.   36*s.*
Reaches to 1450; well written.

Greenwood, T. Cathedra Petri. 8vo. 6 vols. *Dickinson.*   o.p.
The political history of the Papacy to 1410.

Schmidt, C. Précis de l'histoire de l'église d'occident pendant le moyen
âge. 1. 8vo. (*Paris*).   10*s.*
A useful text-book.

Villemain, A. F., Life of Gregory VII. Tr. J. B. Brockley. 8vo. 2 vols.
Bentley.   o.p.

Church, R. W. St. Anselm. gl. 8vo. *Macmillan.*   5*s.*

Montalembert, Comte de. The monks of the west. Tr. 8vo. 7 vols.
Blackwood. pub. 77*s.* 6*d.*   o.p.
A history of monasticism, by a fervent believer: reaches to St. Bernard.

Maclear, G. F. History of Christian missions in the middle ages. *Macmillan.*   o.p.

Morison, J. C. Life of St. Bernard. c. 8vo. *Macmillan.*   6*s.*

Oliphant, Mrs. St. Francis of Assisi. c. 8vo. *Macmillan.*   6*s.*

Lacordaire, H. D. Life of St. Dominic. *Burns and Oates.*   6*s.* 6*d.*

Poole, R. L. Illustrations of the history of mediæval thought. 8vo.
Williams.   10*s.* 6*d.*
Essays chiefly on the 12th century.

Renan, E. Averroes et l'Averroisme. 8vo. *Léry.*   6*s.* 6*d.*
On the influence of the thought of the oriental philosophers.

Lea, H. C. History of sacerdotal celibacy. 8vo. *Houghton Mifflin.*   19*s.*

  ,, History of the mediæval Inquisition. 8vo. 3 vols. *Low.*   42*s.*
Full of information on mediæval sects, heresies, and their suppression.

Butler, Mrs. St. Catherine of Siena. p. 8vo. *Macmillan.*   6*s.*

Addison, C. G. History of the Knights Templars. c. 8vo. *Longmans.*
pub. 10*s.* 6*d.*   o.p.

Porter, W. History of the Knights of Malta. 8vo. *Longmans.*   o.p.

Platina, Bapt. Lives of the Popes. 1. c. 8vo. 2 vols., 1*s.* each. *Griffith.*   2*s.*
Written by the Papal librarian at end of XV. century.

Creighton, M. History of the Papacy during the Reformation. 8vo.
4 vols. *Longmans.*
From 1370 to 1517. In progress. Vol. i., ii., 32*s.*; vol. iii., iv., 24*s.*

Hunt, W. The English Church in the middle ages. f. 8vo. *Longmans.*
(elem.).   2*s.* 6*d.*
Extends to Wycliffe.

Poole, R. L. Wycliffe and the beginning of the Reformation. f. 8vo.
Longmans. (elem.).   2*s.* 6*d.*

Hook, W. F. Lives of the Archbishops of Canterbury. d. 8vo. 12 vols.
Bentley.   180*s.*
Vol. i., 15*s.*; vol. ii., 15*s.*; vol. iii., iv., 30*s.*; vol. v., 15*s.*; vol. vi., vii., 30*s.*; vol. viii., ix., x.,
xi., xii., 15*s.*, each.

Fosbrooke, T. D. British monachism. r. 8vo. *Bentley.*   o.p.

Lechler, G. V. John Wiclif and his English precursors. 8vo. *R. T. S.*
illus.   8s.

Loserth, J. Wiclif and Hus. Tr. M. J. Evans. p. 8vo. *Hodder.* pub.
7s. 6d.   o.p.

Stokes, G. T. Ireland and the Anglo-Norman church. c. 8vo. *Hodder.* 9s.
   From the English Conquest to the Reformation.

Muston, A. The Israel of the Alps. Tr. W. Hazlitt. 12mo. *Griffin.*
pub. 5s.   o.p.
   Treats of the Vaudois.

Kettlewell, S. Thomas à Kempis, and the Brothers of Common Life.
d. 8vo. 2 vols. *Paul.*   30s.

Ullmann, C. Reformers before the Reformation. 8vo. 2 vols. *Clark.* 21s.
   Deals chiefly with the theologians of N. Germany in the XV. century.

Schweinitz. History of the Moravians or United Brethren. 8vo.
   (*Pennsylvania*).   1s. 6d.

Villari, P. Life of Savonarola. Tr. Mme. Villari. d. 8vo. 2 vols. *Unwin.* 32s.

Hefele, C. J. Life of Cardinal Ximenez. Tr. Dalton. d. 8vo. *Dolman.* 10s. 6d.
   Contains much information about the Church in Spain.

Gams, P. B. Kirchengeschichte von Spanien. 8vo. 3 vols. (*Regensburg*). 39s.

Menendez y Pelayo. Historia de los heterodoxos Españoles. (*Madrid*).

Lea, H. C. Chapters from the religious history of Spain. (*Philadelphia*).

—IV. PERIOD OF THE REFORMATION, 1500–1600:

Häusser, L. Period of the Reformation. 8vo. *Gemmell.*   7s. 6d.
   A useful text-book, reaching to 1648.

Hardwick, C. History of the Christian Church during the Reformation.
c. 8vo. *Macmillan.*   10s. 6d.

Seebohm, F. The Oxford Reformers. 8vo. *Longmans.*   14s.
   An account of More, Colet, and Erasmus in England.

Drummond, R. B. Life of Erasmus. p. 8vo. 2 vols. *Smith, Elder.*
pub. 21s.   o.p.

Strauss, D. F. Ulrich von Hutten. 8vo. (*Bonn*).   7s.

Schaff, P. Modern Christianity. ex. d. 8vo. 2 vols. *Clark.*   21s.
   The German Reformation, 1517-30; with full bibliography. (Vol. v. of his *History of the
   Christian Church*).

Köstlin, J. Life of Luther. Tr. c. 8vo. *Longmans.* pub. 16s.   o.p.
   The standard life in Germany.

Beard, C. Martin Luther and the Reformation in Germany. d. 8vo. *Paul.* 16s.
   Only reaches to 1521. Valuable for the beginning of the Reformation movement.

   ,,   The Reformation of the 16th century. 8vo. *Williams.*   10s. 6d.
   Also at 4s. 6d. A good account of the relations of the Reformation movement to modern
   thought; from the standpoint of cultivated Unitarianism.

Aubigné, M. d'. History of the Reformation of the 16th century. 8vo.
R. T. S.   20s.
   Vol. i., ii., iii., 3s. each ; iv., 5s. ; v., 6s. A popular account with decided partisanship.

Stebbing. Life and times of Calvin. *Whittaker.*   o.p.

Willis, R. Servetus and Calvin. 8vo. *H. S. King.*   o.p.

Perry, G. C. The Reformation in England. (elem.). f. 8vo. *Longmans.* 2s. 6d.

Gasquet. Henry VIII. and the English monasteries. 2 vols. *Hodges.* 24s.
   Roman Catholic.

Dixon, R. W. History of the Church of England. d. 8vo. 3 vols., 16s. each. *Routledge*.   48s.
From 1529 to 1532.

Strype, J. Memorials of Cranmer. d. 8vo. 2 vols. *Clar. Press*.   11s.

McCrie, T. History of the Reformation in Italy. c. 8vo. *Blackwood*.   4s.

Benrath, K. Bernardino Ochino of Siena. 8vo. *Nisbet*.   9s.
The life of an Italian reformer.

Young, M. Life and times of Palcario. 8vo. 2 vols. *Bell*.   O.P.
An account of the Catholic reformers in Italy.

Rose, S. Ignatius Loyola and the early Jesuits. 8vo. *Longmans*. pub. 16s.   O.P.

Cartwright, W. C. The Jesuits. 8vo. *Murray*.   9s.
Deals with their organisation.

Coleridge, H. J. Life and letters of St. Francis Xavier. c. 8vo. *Burns*.   10s. 6d.

Dalton, H. John à Lasco. *Hodder*.   O.P.

Sander, N. Rise and growth of the Anglican schism. d. 8vo. *Burns*.   7s.
The view of a Roman Catholic contemporary.

Burnet, G. History of the reformation of the Church of England. Ed. N. Pocock. d. 8vo. 7 vols. *Clar. Press*.   30s.

Foxe, J. Acts and monuments. r. 8vo. 8 vols. *R. T. S.*   50s.
Often called the Book of Martyrs. An account by a fervent Protestant of the English Reformation.

Knox, J. History of the Reformation in Scotland. 8vo. *Blackie*.   O.P.

Strype, J. Annals of the Reformation under Elizabeth. 7 vols. *Clar. Press*.   O.P.

    ,,   Life of Archbishop Parker. 3 vols. *Clar. Press*.   O.P.

    ,,   Life of Archbishop Grindal. *Clar. Press*.   O.P.

    ,,   Life of Archbishop Whitgift. d. 8vo. 3 vols. *Clar. Press*.   16s. 6d.

Ward, A. W. The counter Reformation. (clem.). f. 8vo. *Longmans*.   2s. 6d.

Philippson. La contre-révolution religieuse. (*Brussels*).
Account of the Jesuits, Inquisition, and Council of Trent.

Simpson, R. Edmund Campion. 8vo. *Williams*.   O.P.
The coming of the Jesuits to England.

Jessopp, A. One generation of a Norfolk house. d. 8vo. *Burns*.   10s. 6d.
The life of an English Jesuit in the time of Elizabeth.

Letters of Cardinal Allen. Ed. T. F. Knox. 4to. *Nutt*.   30s.
With a valuable introduction on the Papal policy towards England.

Law, T. G. Jesuits and Seculars in the reign of Elizabeth. 8vo. *Nutt*.   15s.

Morris, J. Troubles of our Catholic forefathers. 3 vols., 14s. each. *Burns*.   42s.
Vol. i., o.p., contains full accounts of the position of the Roman Catholics.

Foley, H. Records of the English Province of the Society of Jesus. 6 vols. and vol. vii. 2 parts separate. *Burns*.   216s.
Vol. i., ii., iv., vi., vii. (1), vii. (2), 26s. each ; vol. iii., v., 30s. each.

—V. MODERN PERIOD, 1600–1880:

(A) ENGLAND.

Fuller, T. Church history of Britain (to 1648). Ed. J. S. Brewer. d. 8vo. 6 vols. *Clar. Press*.   39s.

Collier, J. Ecclesiastical history of Great Britain. 8vo. 9 vols. *Straker*. 1840–1.   O.P.

Dodd, C. Church history of England (to 1688). Ed. M. A. Tierney. d. 8vo. *Dolman.* 1849.   40s.
> The standard Roman Catholic history.

Wordsworth, C. Ecclesiastical biography. 8vo. 4 vols. *Rivington.* pub. 54s.   O.P.
> A collection of contemporary lives, beginning with Wolsey and ending with Tillotson.

Wakeman, H. O. The Church and the Puritans. (elem.). f. 8vo. *Longmans.*   2s. 6d.

Masson, D. Life of John Milton. 6 vols., 21s. each. *Macmillan.*   126s.
> The best source of information for the religious movements of the Commonwealth.

Heylyn, P. Cyprianus Anglus. fo. 1671.
> Life of Laud, by a contemporary.

Lathbury. History of Convocation. 8vo. *Leslie.* 1853.   O.P.

,,   History of the Nonjurors. 8vo. *Leslie.* 1845.   O.P.

Stoughton, J. History of religion in England from 1640. 3 vols., 7s. 6d. each. *Hodder.*   22s. 6d.
> With special reference to the Nonconformists.

Perry, A. History of the Church of England from 1603. 8vo. 3 vols. *Saunders.*   O.P.

Abbey and Overton. The English Church in the 18th century. c. 8vo. *Longmans.*   7s. 6d.

Plumptre, E. H. Life of Bishop Ken. d. 8vo. 2 vols. *Isbister.*   12s.

Curteis, G. H. Dissent in its relation to the Church of England. c. 8vo. *Macmillan.*   7s. 6d.

Tyerman, L. Life and times of John Wesley. 3 vols., 6s. each. *Hodder.*   18s.

Overton, J. H. The evangelical revival of the 18th century. (elem.). f. 8vo. *Longmans.*   2s. 6d.

Wilberforce, S. Life of William Wilberforce. c. 8vo. *Murray.*   6s.

Newman, J. H. Apologia pro vitâ suâ. c. 8vo. *Longmans.*   3s. 6d.

Ward, W. William George Ward and the Oxford movement. 8vo. *Macmillan.*   14s.

Church, R. W. The Oxford movement, 1833-45. 8vo. *Macmillan.*   12s. 6d.

Anderson, J. S. N. History of the Church of England in the colonies and dependencies. f. 8vo. 3 vols. *Rivington.* pub. 24s.   O.P.

Tucker, H. W. The English Church in other lands. (elem.). f. 8vo. *Longmans.*   2s. 6d.

(B) SCOTLAND.

Rankin, J. Handbook of the Church of Scotland. c. 8vo. *Blackwood.*   7s. 6d.

Spottiswoode, J. History of the Church of Scotland, to 1624. 8vo. 3 vols. *Oliver and Boyd.*   O.P.
> Written by an Episcopalian of the time.

Calderwood, D. History of the Church of Scotland to 1624. 8vo. 8 vols. *Wodrow Society (Edin.).*   O.P.
> Written by a Presbyterian of the time.

Wodrow, R. History of the sufferings of the Church of Scotland from 1660 to 1688. 8vo. 4 vols. (*Glasgow*). 1838.   O.P.

Cunningham, J. Church history of Scotland. p. 8vo. *Thin.*   16s.

Lawson, J. P. History of the Scottish Episcopalian Church. 8vo. (*Edin.*). 1843.   O.P.

(C) IRELAND.

Mant, R. History of the Church of Ireland (to 1800). 8vo. 2 vols. *J. W. Parker.* 1845.   34*s.*

Killen, W. D. Ecclesiastical history of Ireland. 8vo. 2 vols. *Macmillan.*   25*s.*

Brennan. Ecclesiastical history of Ireland (to 1829). 8vo. *Duffy* (*Dublin*).   O.P.
     Written by a Roman Catholic.

(D) NONCONFORMISTS.

Skeats, H. History of the Free Churches of England. 8vo. *Miall.*   O.P.
     A good general account.

Vaughan, R. English Nonconformity. 8vo. *Hodder.* pub. 7*s.* 6*d.*   O.P.
     A sketch.

Waddington, J. Congregational history. d. 8vo. 4 vols., vol. i., *J. Snow,* pub. 16*s.*; vol. ii., iii., iv., *Longmans.* pub. 15*s.* each.   O.P.
     Vol. ii. (1700-1800) ; vol. iii. (1800-1850) ; vol. iv. (1850-). Full details.

Neal, D. History of the Puritans (to 1688). 8vo. 2 vols. *Harper.*   20*s.*

Barclay, R. Inner life of the religious societies of the Commonwealth. 8vo. *Hodder.*   O.P.
     Especially useful for the growth of mysticism.

Autobiography of George Fox. Ed. H. Newman. f. 4to. *Partridge.*   6*s.*

Stoughton, J. William Penn. c. 8vo. *Hodder.*   7*s.* 6*d.*

Dexter, H. M. Congregationalism of the last 300 years. r. 8vo. *Harper.*   24*s.*
     Valuable for its survey of literature.

Crosby, T. History of the English Baptists. 8vo. 4 vols. (*London*). 1738.   O.P.
     A mass of material to 1717.

Bogue and Bennett. History of Dissenters (1688 to 1808). 8vo. 4 vols. (*London*). 1812.   O.P.

Bennett, J. History of Dissenters from 1808 to 1838. 8vo. (*London*). 1839.   O.P.

Brown, J. John Bunyan. d. 8vo. *Isbister.*   7*s.* 6*d.*

Stevens, A. History of Methodism. c. 8vo. 3 vols. *Wesleyan Conference Office.*   O.P.

Oliphant, Mrs. Life of Edward Irving. p. 8vo. *Hurst.*   5*s.*

Miller, E. History of Irvingism. l. p. 8vo. 2 vols. *Paul.*   15*s.*

Channing, sa vie et ses œuvres. Pref. by C. de Rémusat. 12mo. (*Paris*).   3*s.*

White, W. Life and writings of Swedenborg. 8vo. *Simpkin.*   7*s.* 6*d.*

(E) GERMAN PROTESTANTISM.

Dorner, J. A. History of Protestant theology. 8vo. 2 vols. *Clark.*   21*s.*

Neale, J. M. History of the Jansenist Church of Holland. 8vo. *Parker.*   10*s.* 6*d.*

Baur, W. Religious life in Germany during the wars of independence. p. 8vo. *Strahan.* pub. 7*s.* 6*d.*   O.P.
     Germany during the period of the French revolutionary movement.

Geffcken, H. Church and State. Tr. E. F. Taylor. 8vo. 2 vols. *Longmans.* pub. 42*s.*   O.P.
     Deals at length with Germany in the present century.

(F) CHURCH OF ROME.

Ranke, L. von. The Popes of Rome. Tr. 8vo. 3 vols. *Murray.* pub. 30*s.*   O.P.
     Also *Bohn.* 3 vol., 3*s.* 6*d.* each. The Papacy from 1520 to 1830.

Jervis, W. H. History of the Church of France. 8vo. 2 vols. *Murray.*   28*s.*

Jervis, W. H. The Gallican Church from 1516 to the Revolution. c. 8vo. 2 vols. *Murray.*   28s.

Lear, H. L. Bossuet and his contemporaries. c. 8vo. *Rivington.*   3s. 6d.

Schimmelpenninck, Mrs. Memoirs of Port Royal. c. 8vo. 3 vols. *Longmans.* pub. 21s.   O.P.

Beard, C. Port Royal. 8vo. 2 vols. *Williams.*   12s.

Coleridge, H. J. Life of St. Teresa. c. 8vo. 3 vols., 7s. 6d. each. *Burns.*   22s. 6d.

Weld, A. (S. J.) Suppression of the Jesuits in Portugal. c. 8vo. *Burns.*   7s. 6d.

Wiseman, Cardinal. Recollections of the last four Popes (1818-1837). *Hurst.*   5s.

"Leto." Rome during the Vatican Council. 8vo. *Murray.*   12s.
    By one who was opposed to the action of the Council.

"Janus." The Pope and the Council. *Rivington.*   O.P.
    An historical survey of the growth of the Papal power by a liberal Roman Catholic.

Manning, Cardinal. True story of the Vatican Council. *Burns.*   5s.

(G) EASTERN CHURCH.

Stanley, A. P. Lectures on the history of the Eastern Church. c. 8vo. *Murray.*   6s.
    A general sketch.

Neale, J. M. History of the Holy Eastern Church. d. 8vo. 5 vols. *Masters.* 1850.
    Vol. iii., iv., 24s. each; vol. i., ii., v., O.P.

Tozer, H. F. The Church and the Eastern Empire. (elem.). f. 8vo. *Longmans.*   2s. 6d.

Butler, A. T. Ancient Coptic Church of Egypt. d. 8vo. *Clar. Press.* illus.   30s.

Le Quien. Oriens Christianus. fo. 3 vols. 1740.
    The four Patriarchates.

—VI. BOOKS OF REFERENCE:

Hook, W. F. Church dictionary. m. 8vo. *Murray.*   21s
    Useful for general purposes.

Migné. Encyclopédie théologique. r. 8vo. 3 series. (*Paris*).
    1st series, 52 vols., £15 12s.; 2nd series, 53 vols., £16; 3rd series, 66 vols., £20. Separate vols. from 7s. to 10s. each.

Addis and Arnold. Catholic dictionary. d. 8vo. *Paul.*   21s.
    For Roman Catholic doctrine and ritual.

Dictionary of Christian antiquities. Ed. Smith. m. 8vo. 2 vols. *Murray.*   42s.
    Full information and references for the early Church.

    ,, of Christian biography. Ed. Smith and Wace. 4 vols. *Murray.*   136s. 6d.
    Vol. i., ii., iii., 31s. 6d.; vol. iv., 42s. Valuable for the first eight centuries.

Mansi. Concilia. fo. 37 vols. (*Lucca*). 1757-98.   O.P.
    A collection of all the documents bearing on the councils of the Church.

Haddan and Stubbs. Councils and ecclesiastical documents relating to Great Britain. r. 8vo. 3 vols. *Clar. Press.*   56s.
    Vol. i., 21s.; vol. ii. (part 1), 10s. 6d.; vol. ii. (part 2), 3s. 6d.; vol. iii., 21s. Period before the reign of Alfred.

Wilkins, D. Concilia Magnae Britanniae. fo. 4 vols. (*London*). 1737.   O.P.
    A collection of all councils and synods of the English Church.

Acta Sanctorum. Ed. Bolland and Henschenius. fo. 56 vols. (*Paris*).
   1734-1883.   £100
     A vast collection of the lives of all the saints of the Church, arranged according to the days
     of their festivals.

Magnum Bullarium Romanum. fo. 32 vols. (*Rome*). 1739-62.   £20
     A collection of Papal Bulls.

   ,,   (Continuation). fo. 19 vols. (*Rome*). 1835-57.   £13

Baronius. Annales ecclesiastici. i. 4to. 37 vols. (*Paris*).   £25
     Annals compiled from authorities on a large scale, begun by Baronius, continued by
     Raynaldus and Laderchius to 1571.

   ,,   The same; continued by Theiner. 3 vols. (*Rome*).   41s.

Gams, P. B. Series omnium episcoporum ecclesiae Catholicae. 4to.
   (*Ratisbon*).   34s. 6d.
     A list of all the Bishops of the Roman communion.

Stubbs, W. Registrum sacrum Anglicanum. s. 4to. *Clar. Press.*   8s. 6d.
     A catalogue of English Bishops.

Dugdale, W. Monasticon Anglicanum (with additions). fo. 8 vols.
   1817-30.   O.P.
     Documents relating to the English monasteries.

Gieseler, J. C. L. Compendium of ecclesiastical history. 8vo. 4 vols. *Clark.*   42s.
     A useful handbook for reference; with copious quotations from authorities, extending to
     the Reformation. The German edition, *Lehrbuch der Kirchengeschichte*, goes to 1840.

COLONIES: GENERAL:

Lucas, C. P. Historical geography of the British colonies. p. 8vo. *Clar.
   Press.* Vol. i., 5s.

Cotton and Payne. Colonies and dependencies. c. 8vo. *Macmillan.*   3s. 6d.

Hübner, Baron. Through the British Empire. p. 8vo. 2 vols. *Murray.*   24s.
     S. Africa, Australia, New Zealand, Straits Settlements, India, S. Sea Islands, California,
     Oregon, Canada, etc.

Martin, R. M. History of the British colonies. 8vo. 6 vols. *Tallis.*
1850. maps. pub. 84s. 　　　　　　　　　　　　　　　O.P.

Payne, E. J. History of European colonies. 12mo. *Macmillan.* maps. 　4s. 6d.

Bourne, F. Story of our colonies. p. 8vo. *Hogg.* 　　　　　　　6s.

Creasy, E. Imperial and colonial institutions of the British empire. 8vo.
Longmans. pub. 15s. 　　　　　　　　　　　　　　　O.P.

Seeley, J. R. Expansion of England. p. 8vo. *Macmillan.* 　　　4s. 6d.
An essay on the historical aspect of English colonisation.

Dilke, C. Problems of Greater Britain. c. 8vo. *Macmillan.* 　　12s. 6d.
A description of the present politics of the colonies.

Trendell, A. J. R. Colonial year-book. c. 8vo. *Low.* 　　　　6s.
JOURNAL: *Colonies and India;* weekly. (Silver).

COLUMBIA, BRITISH, *see* CANADA.

COLUMBIA, REPUBLIC, *see* AMERICA, SOUTH, II.

COMMERCE, *see* POLITICAL ECONOMY *and* ENGLAND, HISTORY V.

COMMERCIAL CORRESPONDENCE:

Commercial correspondence in fifteen languages. 8vo. 15 vols., 2s. 6d.
each. *Maier (Stuttgart).*
A series of letters, identical in all the fifteen languages, each language forming a separate
book: English, French, German, Dutch, Danish, Swedish, Italian, Spanish, Portuguese,
Polish, Russian, Hungarian, Czech, Servian, and Roumanian.

COMMON, RIGHT OF, *see* ENGLAND, LAW IV.

COMMONS, HOUSE OF, *see* PARLIAMENT.

COMPANY LAW, *see* ENGLAND, LAW VIII.

COMPASS, DEVIATION OF, *see* NAVY I.

COMTISM, *see* POSITIVISM.

CONCHOLOGY, *see* ZOOLOGY VI.

CONCRETE, *see* BUILDING.

CONGO, *see* AFRICA IV.

CONGREGATIONALISM, *see* CHURCH HISTORY V. (D).

CONJURING:

Hoffmann, L. Modern magic. 8vo. *Routledge.* 　　　　　　5s.

,, More magic. 8vo. *Routledge.* 　　　　　　　　　　7s. 6d.
Practical treatises on conjuring.

Sachs, E. Sleight of hand. 8vo. *Gill.* illus. 　　　　　　　7s. 6d.
Minute instructions for tricks of legerdemain.

Houdin, R. His memoirs as ambassador, author, and conjuror. c. 8vo.
2 vols. 　　　　　　　　　　　　　　　　　　　　　O.P.

CONTRACT, *see* ENGLAND, LAW VII.

CONVEYANCING, *see* ENGLAND, LAW IV.

CONVOCATION, HISTORY OF, *see* CHURCH HISTORY V. (D).

COOKERY AND FOOD:

—I. COOKERY:

> No good comprehensive treatise on the art of cookery, embracing first class cookery, exists in this country, nor any good work which also explains scientifically the processes necessary to render animal and vegetable products digestible and palatable.

Cassell's dictionary of cookery. 8vo. *Cassell.*   7*s.* 6*d.*
> An excellent epitome of English second class cookery. The principles of cookery are clearly, fully, and very correctly explained.

Cassell's shilling cookery. 8vo. *Cassell.*   1*s.*
> Principles and practice well given in small compass.

Mrs. Marshall's cookery book. c. 8vo. *Simpkin.*   5*s.*
> Higher-class cookery ; contains several modern recipes, particularly for cold entrées.

Reeve, Mrs. H. Cookery and housekeeping. c. 8vo. *Longmans.* illus.   5*s.*
> A useful guide written practically, with taste and judgment.

"Wyvern." Culinary jottings. 8vo. *Thacker.*   10*s.*
> Designed for Anglo-Indians ; full of valuable hints and recipes for cooks and housekeepers in any climate.

Kettner. Book of the table. Tr. Dallas. c. 8vo. *Dulau.*   10*s.* 6*d.*
> Practical ; but largely literary and historical.

William, W. M. Chemistry of cookery. c. 8vo. *Chatto.*   6*s.*
> Explains clearly certain scientific principles involved in the processes of cookery, with many practical hints.

Gouffé, J. Royal cookery book. Tr. r. 8vo. *Low.*   20*s.*
> Also household edition, 10*s.* 6*d.*

  ,,   Le livre de cuisine. r. 8vo. *Hachette.*   42*s.*
> Part i., La cuisine des ménages ; part ii., La grande cuisine.

Dubois and Bernard. La cuisine classique. 4to. 2 vols. *Dentu.* illus.   32*s.*
> The most complete treatise of the French school ; has partially superseded Gouffé's classical work.

Dubois, U. La cuisine d'aujourd'hui. 8vo. *Dentu.* illus.   12*s.* 6*d.*
> An admirable modern epitome.

Audot, L. E. La cuisinière de la campagne. 12mo. (*Paris*). illus.   3*s.*
> A good example of the common middle-class French cooking book.

Brillat-Savarin. Gastronomy as a fine art. Tr. Anderson. p. 8vo. *Chatto.*   2*s.*

Brotherton, Mrs. Vegetarian cookery. *F. Pitman.*   3*s.* 6*d.*

—II. FOODS:

Smith, E. Foods. ("Inter. Scient." ser.). c. 8vo. *Paul.* illus.   5*s.*

Thompson, H. Food and feeding. c. 8vo. *Warne.*   3*s.* 6*d.*

Yeo, J. B. Food in health and disease. 8vo. *Cassell.*   9*s.*

Roberts, W. Dietetics and dyspepsia. c. 8vo. *Smith, Elder.*   3*s.*

Church, A. J. Food : its sources, constituents, and uses. l. c. 8vo. *Chapman.*   3*s.*
> Manual published for Committee of Council on Education.

Bell, J. Foods. l. c. 8vo. 2 parts. *Chapman.*   5*s.* 6*d.*
> Part i., 2*s.* 6*d.* ; part ii., 3*s.*

Pavy, F. W. Food and dietetics. d. 8vo. *Churchill.*   15*s.*
> A standard work ; includes dietetics and natural history of foods.

Blyth, A. W. Foods : their composition and analysis. c. 8vo. *Griffin.* illus.   16*s.*

Kingsford, Anna. Perfect way of diet. sm. c. 8vo. *Paul.*   2*s.*

Newman, F. W. Essays on diet. sm. c. 8vo. *Paul.*   2*s.*
    The last two books advocate a vegetarian diet.

CO-OPERATION, *see* POLITICAL ECONOMY VI.

    „   IN UNITED STATES, *see* UNITED STATES HISTORY.

COPTIC:

Stern, L. Koptische Grammatik. (*Leipzig*).   18*s.*

Peyron, A. Lexicon Copticum. 4to. (*Turin*). 1835. pub. 35*s.*   O.P.

COPTIC CHURCH, ANCIENT, *see* CHURCH HISTORY V.

COPYHOLDS, *see* ENGLAND, LAW IV.

COPYRIGHT, *see* ENGLAND, LAW VI.

CORAL ISLANDS, *see* GEOLOGY II.

COREA:

Ross, J. History of Corea, with descriptions of manners and customs.
    8vo. *Houlston.*   12*s. 6d.*

Oppert, E. Voyages to the Corea. 8vo. *Low.* illus.   21*s.*

Lowell, P. Chosön, a sketch of Korea. l. 8vo. *Trübner.* illus.   24*s.*

Carles, W. R. Life in Corea. 8vo. *Macmillan.*   12*s. 6d.*

Griffis, W. E. Corea; the hermit nation. r. 8vo. *Allen.*   18*s.*

CORSAIRS OF BARBARY, *see* ALGIERS.

    „   OF FRANCE, *see* NAVY V.

CORSICA, *see* MEDITERRANEAN.

COSTA RICA, *see* AMERICA, SOUTH.

COSTUME, HISTORICAL:

See also NEEDLEWORK.

Planché, J. R. Cyclopædia of costume. r. 4to. 2 vols. *Chatto.* pub. 147*s.*   O.P.
    For general reference of a superficial kind. Vol. i., dictionary ; vol. ii., general chronological
    history of dress.

Luard, J. History of the dress of the British soldier. 8vo. *Clowes.*   O.P.

Hope, T. Costume of the ancients. 8vo. 2 vols. *Chatto.*   45*s.*
    Ancient Egypt, Greece, Rome, and Asiatic nations.

Rock, D. Church of our fathers; fashions and vestments. i. 4to. 3 vols.
    Dolman. 1849.   O.P.
    Ecclesiastical.

Pugin, W. Glossary of ecclesiastical ornament and costume. 8vo.
    Quaritch.   126*s.*
    Very complete.

Shaw, H. Dresses and decorations of the Middle Ages. 4to. 2 vols. *Pickering.* 1843.   145s.
<blockquote>Fragmentary, but useful, embracing engraved specimens of jewellery, as well as illustrations from missals.</blockquote>

Lacroix, P. Mœurs, usages, et costumes au moyen âge, et à l'époque de la Renaissance. 4to. *Didot.* illus.   24s.

Beck, W. Gloves: their annals and associations. c. 8vo. *Hamilton.* illus.   7s. 6d.

Greig, T. W. Ladies' old-fashioned shoes. fo. *Douglas.* illus.   31s. 6d

Uzanne, O. The fan. Tr. r. 8vo. *Nimmo and Bain.* illus.   31s. 6d.

Stewart, J. Plocacosmos, or the whole art of hairdressing. 1772.
<blockquote>In British Museum.</blockquote>

COTTAGE HOSPITALS, *see* HOSPITALS.

COTTON MANUFACTURE, *see* TEXTILE FABRICS.

COUNTERPOINT, *see* MUSIC II.

COUNTIES OF ENGLAND, *see* ENGLAND, HISTORY V.

COUNTY GOVERNMENT, *see* LOCAL GOVERNMENT.

CREMATION:

Eassie, W. Cremation of the dead. d. 8vo. *Smith, Elder.*   8s. 6d.

Thompson, H. Modern cremation. c. 8vo. *Paul*   2s. 6d.

CRETE, *see* MEDITERRANEAN.

CRIBBAGE, *see* CARDS.

CRICKET:

Lyttelton, E. Cricket. ("All England" ser.). sm. 8vo. *Bell.*   1s.

Steel and Lyttelton. Cricket. ("Badminton" ser.). c. 8vo. *Longmans.*   10s. 6d.

Lillywhite, J. Cricket scores and biographies. 8vo. 4 vols. *Longmans.* pub. 50s.   O.P.
<blockquote>Contains a good deal of interesting biographical matter, and many records of matches worth preserving.</blockquote>

CRIME (HISTORY OF) IN ENGLAND, *see* ENGLAND, LAW III.

CRIMEAN WAR, *see* ARMY III.

CRIMINAL LAW, *see* ENGLAND, LAW III.

CROATS, HISTORY OF, *see* HUNGARY, HISTORY.

CROPS, *see* AGRICULTURE II.

CROSSES, ANCIENT, *see* ARCHITECTURE III.

CRUSADES, *see* ENGLAND, HISTORY II. *and* EUROPE II.

CRYSTALLOGRAPHY:

Miller, W. H. A tract on crystallography. 8vo. *Parker.* pub. 9s.   O.P.

Gurney, H. P. Crystallography (elem:). f. 8vo. *S. P. C. K.*   1*s.*

Maskelyne, N. S. Treatise on crystallography. c. 8vo. *Clar. Press.*
    In press.

Groth, P. Physikalische Krystallographie. 8vo. (*Leipzig*).   16*s.*
    Elementary mathematics.

Mallard, E. Traité de cristallographie. 8vo. 2 vols. *Dunod.*   36*s.*
    High mathematics. Vol. i., Caractères crystallographiques, 20*s.*; vol. ii., Caractères optiques,
    16*s.*; vol. iii., in press.

Lang, V. von. Lehrbuch der Krystallographie. 8vo. (*Vienna*).   8*s.*
    PERIODICALS: *Mineralogical Magazine*; and *Journal of the Mineralogical Society of Great
    Britain.* 8vo. 8 vols. *Simpkin.* 13*s.* 6*d.* to 25*s.* per vol.

CUBA, *see* WEST INDIES II.

CURLING, *see* GAMES.

CURRENCY, *see* POLITICAL ECONOMY IV.

CUSTOMS, POPULAR, *see* ANTHROPOLOGY *and* FOLKLORE.

CYCLADES, THE, *see* MEDITERRANEAN.

CYCLING :

Bury and Hillier. Cycling. ("Badminton Library"). c. 8vo. *Longmans.*   10*s.* 6*d.*

Griffin, H. H. Cycling. ("All England" ser.). sm. 8vo. *Bell.*   1*s.*

Spencer, C. Cyclist's road-book. *Grube.*   1*s.*

CYPRUS, *see* MEDITERRANEAN.

CYRENAICA, *see* ALGIERS.

D.

DAHOMEY, *see* AFRICA III.

DAIRY :

Sheldon, J. P. Dairy-farming. 4to. *Cassell.* illus.   31*s.* 6*d.*

    ,,   The farm and the dairy. *Bell.* illus.   2*s.* 6*d.*

Long and Morton. The dairy. c. 8vo. *Vinton.*   2*s.* 6*d.*

Arnold, L. B. American dairying. 12mo. (*New York*).   6*s.*

Harris, J. B. The cheese and butter-maker's handbook. *Wright.*

Macgregor, A. Stewart. Milk supply of Copenhagen. *Scott, Ferguson*
    (*Edinburgh*). illus.   1*s.*

DALMATIA, *see* AUSTRIA.

DARWINISM, *see* ZOOLOGY I.

DECORATION, *see* ART VIII. *and* HOUSE DECORATION.

DEER STALKING, *see* SPORT.

DENMARK: GEOGRAPHY AND HISTORY:

Murray's Handbook for Denmark. p. 8vo. *Murray.* 6s.
 With Schleswig, Holstein, and Iceland.

Otté, E. C. Denmark and Iceland. c. 8vo. *Low.* 3s. 6d.

Andersen, L. Copenhagen and its environs. *Scott.* 3s. 6d.

Weitemeyer, H. Dänemark; Geschichte und Beschreibung. 12mo. *Höst.* 6s.

 ,, Le Danemark, histoire et géographie, langue, littérature et beaux arts, situation sociale et économique. *Höst.* 7s. 6d.
 English translation. *Heinemann.*

Pontoppidan, H. Landsbybilleder. 12mo. (*Copenhagen*). 4s. 6d.

Dahlmann, F. C. Geschichte von Dänemark. 8vo. 3 vols. (*Gotha*). 1840—43. 19s. 6d.

DENMARK: LANGUAGE AND LITERATURE:

 COURSE OF READING.—The student should begin with Holberg's comedies, which are very easy and simple; then take up Oehlenschläger's dramas, Andersen's fairy tales, then some of the modern novelists, and so on.

—I. GRAMMARS AND DICTIONARIES:

Otté, E. C. Simplified grammar of the Danish language. *Trübner.* 2s. 6d.

 ,, How to learn Danish (Ollendorffian system). *Trübner.* 7s. 6d.
 Key, 3s.

Rosing, S. Engelsk-Dansk Ordbog. 12mo. (*Copenhagen*). 7s. 6d.

Larsen, A. Dansk-Norsk-Engelsk Ordbog. 12mo. (*Copenhagen*). 9s.

Danish-English and English-Danish pocket dictionary. 16mo. *Tauchnitz.* 5s. 6d.

—II. HISTORY AND CRITICISM:

Petersen, N. M. Bidrag til den danske Literaturs Historie. 6 vols. (*Copenhagen*). pub. 63s. O.P.
 From the earliest period to 1800.

Hansen, P. Illustreret dansk Literatur historie. 8vo. 2 vols. (*Copenhagen*). 45s.
 Including Norway to 1814.

Brandes, G. Danske Digtere. 12mo. (*Copenhagen*). 7s.
 The greatest of Scandinavian critics.

 ,, Kritiker og Portrætter. 12mo. (*Copenhagen*). 7s. 6d.

—III. CLASSICS, ETC.:

Holberg, L. Comedier. 12mo. (*Copenhagen*). 5s.
 The Molière of the North. There are numerous cheap editions, and one *édition de luxe*, 4to. £5.

 ,, Peder Paars. 12mo. (*Copenhagen*). 2s. 6d.
 Satirical epic poem; the wittiest of Holberg's works.

Oehlenschläger. Heltedramaer (Hakon Jarl, 1s.; Axel og Valborg, 9d.; etc.). 12mo. (*Copenhagen*).
 Romantic poet.

 ,, Aladdin. 12mo. (*Copenhagen*). 3s. 6d.
 A fine dramatic poem.

Grundtvig, N. F. S. Optrin af Nordens Kjœmpeliv. 8vo. (*Copenhagen*).   12*s.*
  One of Denmark's most popular writers ; theologian, historian, and poet.

Kierkegaard, S. Enten-Eller. 8vo. 2 vols. (*Copenhagen*).   14*s.*

  ,,   Öieblikket. 12mo. (*Copenhagen*).   4*s.*
  The profoundest thinker and philosopher.

Andersen, Hans. Eventyr og Historier. 4 vols. (*Copenhagen*).
  The famous fairy-tale writer.

Winther, C. Hjortens Flugt. 12mo. (*Copenhagen*).   4*s.*
  Descriptive and lyrical poet.

—IV. MODERN NOVELS, DRAMAS, ETC. :

Ingemann, B. S. Historiske Romaner. 12mo. 4 vols. (*Copenhagen*).   14*s.*
  The Danish Walter Scott.

Müller, F. Paludan. Adam Homo. 8vo. (*Copenhagen*).   10*s.*
  A satirical poem.

Jacobsen, J. P. Fru Marie Grubbe. 12mo. (*Copenhagen*).   6*s.*
  For style, the best modern Danish novelist.

Hostrup, C. Komedier. 12mo. 3 vols. (*Copenhagen*).   9*s.*
  Popular dramatist.

Brandes, E. Et Besög. (*Copenhagen*).
  Best modern Danish dramatist.

Drachmann, H. Dœmpede Melodier. 12mo. (*Copenhagen*).   5*s.*
  Poet and novelist.

Ewald, H. F. Den skotske Kvinde paa Tjele. 12mo. 2 vols. (*Copenhagen*).   7*s. 6d.*
  Popular novelist.

—V. TRANSLATIONS :

Brandes, G. Eminent authors of the nineteenth century. 12mo.
  Crowell (*N. Y.*).   10*s.*

Oehlenschläger. Aladdin ; a dramatic poem. Tr. T. Martin. f. 8vo.
  Blackwood.   5*s.*

  ,,   Axel and Valborg ; a tragedy. Tr. H. W. Freeland. (*London*).

  ,,   Hakon Jarl ; a tragedy. Tr. J. Chapman. (*London*).   O.P.

  ,,   The gods of the North. Tr. W. E. Foye. (*London*). 1845.   O.P.

  ,,   Théâtre choisi. 8vo. (*Paris*).   5*s.*

Holberg, L. Journey to the world underground. (*London*). 1828.   O.P.

—VI. BIBLIOGRAPHY AND BIOGRAPHY :

Erslev, T. H. Almindeligt Forfatter Lexicon. 8vo. 3 vols. and supplement. (*Copenhagen*).   45*s.*

Dansk Bogfortegnelse (1841–80). 8vo. (*Copenhagen*).   90*s.*

DEVOTIONAL WORKS, *see* THEOLOGY IV.

DIET AND DIETETICS, *see* COOKERY.

DISPENSARIES, *see* HOSPITALS.

DISSENTERS, HISTORY OF, *see* CHURCH HISTORY V.

DOCKS, *see* HYDRAULICS.

DOG:

Jesse, G. R. Researches into the history of the British dog. 8vo. 2 vols. *Hardwick.*   32s.

Stables, G. Our friend the dog. 8vo. *Dean.* illus.   6s. 6d.

"Stonehenge." The dog, in health and disease. 8vo. *Longmans.* illus.   7s. 6d.

Steel, J. H. Diseases of the dog. 8vo. *Longmans.* illus.   10s. 6d.

"H. H." The scientific education of dogs for the gun. c. 8vo. *Low.*   6s.

Hutchinson, W. Dog breaking. 8vo. *Murray.* illus.   7s. 6d.

DOMESTIC ANIMALS, *see* HORSE, CAT, DOG, LIVE-STOCK.

DOMESTIC ECONOMY:

See also COOKERY, *and* HYGIENE.

Buckton, Mrs. Health in the house. c. 8vo. *Longmans.* illus.   2s.

Barnett, Mrs. The making of the home. (elem.). *Cassell.*   1s. 6d.

Lewes, G. H. Physiology of common life. c. 8vo. 2 vols. *Blackwood.*   O.P.

Johnston, J. H. Chemistry of common life. c. 8vo. *Blackwood.*   7s. 6d.

Barker, J. H. The hygienic management of infants and children. *Churchill.*   O.P.

Household medicine. Ed. J. Gardner. c. 8vo. *Smith, Elder.*   12s. 6d.

Family physician. r. 8vo. *Cassell.*   21s.

West, C. Mother's manual of children's diseases. c. 8vo. *Longmans.*   2s. 6d.

Wood, Catherine. Handbook for the nursing of sick children. *Cassell.*   2s. 6d.
    For other books on nursing, *see* NURSING.

Starr, L. Hygiene of the nursery. c. 8vo. *Lewis.* illus.   3s. 6d.

Money, A. Health of children. c. 8vo. *Lewis.*   6d.

Smith, Louisa E. Home washing. *Bemrose.*   1s.

Enquire within upon everything. c. 8vo. *Houlston.*   2s. 6d.

DRAINAGE, LAND, *see* AGRICULTURE IV.

     ,,   HOUSE AND TOWN, *see* HYGIENE.

DRAMA, *see* STAGE.

     ,,   CLASSIC, *see* GREECE, HISTORY III.

DRESS, HISTORIC, *see* COSTUME.

DRESSMAKING, *see* NEEDLEWORK.

DRINK, *see* ALCOHOLISM.

DRIVING, *see* HORSE V.

DUTCH LANGUAGE AND LITERATURE:

The books marked ◊ are recommended for young people. Beginning with the simple novels of Conscience, the student should go back to Vondel, after a careful perusal of whom he should be able to read anything.

Ahn, F. Concise Dutch grammar. c. 8vo. *Thimm.*   4s.

Jaeger, A. English-Dutch and Dutch-English pocket dictionary. 16mo. *Nutt.*   4s. 6d.

Vloten, L. Beknopte geschiedenis der nederlandsche letteren. 8vo. *Tiel.*   6s. 6d.

Schneider, L. Geschichte der niederlandischen Literatur. 8vo. (*Leipzig*).   12s.

Vondel, J. van. Meesterstucken uit zijne Werken. Ed. P. H. van Moerkerken. 8vo. (*Amsterdam*).   6s. 6d.

Hooft, P. C. Gedichten. Ed. Leendertz. 8vo. 2 vols. (*Amsterdam*).   16s.

§**Vondel**. Gedichte. Tr. into German by Grimmelt and Jansen. 12mo. (*Münster*).   2s.

     Vondel and Hooft are the great classical poets.

Cats, J. De volledige Werken. fo. 2 vols. (*Arnheim*).   28s.

     Popular poet.

Bilderdijk, W. Bloemlezing uit de Dichtwerken. 8vo. (*Arnheim*).   10s. 6d.

Conscience, H. Romantische Werken. 12mo. 41 vols., 3s. each. (*Leiden*).   123s.

     Popular novelist.

§ ,,   The happiness of being rich. f. 8vo. *Hodges.*   1s. 6d.

§ ,,   The lion of Flanders. *Burns and Oates.*   3s.

Cremer, J. J. Betuwsche novellen. 12mo. (*Leiden*).   2s.

§ ,,   An everyday heroine. (*London*).

Toussaint, Mme. Bosboom. Major Frans (novelle). 12mo. (*The Hague*).   4s.

     Historical novelist.

§ ,,   Major Frank ; a novel. Tr. Akeroyd. c. 8vo. *Unwin.*   6s.

Costa, J. de. Komplete Dichterwerken. 8vo. (*Arnheim*).   7s. 6d.

     Modern poet.

Aa, H. J. van der. Biographisch Woordenboek der Nederlanden. 8vo. 21 vols. (*Haarlem*).   £11 11s.

     Bibliography.

Ab Koude, J. van. Naamregister van de bekendste Neder'duitsche Boeken. (*Rotterdam*).   O.P.

Brinkman, C. C. Catalogue van Boeken in Nederland, 1850–1882. r. 8vo. (*Amsterdam*).   67s.

DYEING, *see* TEXTILE FABRICS.

DYNAMICS, *see* MATHEMATICS II. *and* PHYSICS.

DYNAMOS, *see* ELECTRICITY II.

E.

EARLY ENGLISH, *see* ANGLO-SAXON.

EARTHQUAKES, *see* GEOLOGY II.

EASTERN CHURCH, *see* CHURCH HISTORY V. (G).

EASTERN QUESTION, *see* TURKEY II.

ECARTÉ, *see* CARDS.

ECCLESIASTICAL HISTORY, *see* CHURCH HISTORY.

    ,,   LAW, *see* ENGLAND, LAW XI.

ECONOMICS, *see* POLITICAL ECONOMY.

ECONOMIC PRODUCTS, FOREIGN:

—I. CACAO:

Morris, D. Cacao; how to grow and how to cure it. (*Kingston, Jamaica*).

Mann, J. A. Cocoa: its cultivation, manufacture, and uses. (In *Journal of the Society of Arts*, Oct. 5, 1860).

—II. CAOUTCHOUC:

Collins, J. The caoutchouc of commerce. 4to. *W. H. Allen.* illus.   5*s.*

India-rubber. Reprinted from "Spon's Encyclopædia." r. 8vo. *Spon.*   4*s.*

—III. CINCHONA:

King, G. Cinchona cultivation in India. (For planters). *Govt. Print. Off.* (*Calcutta*).

—IV. COFFEE:

Coffee. Reprinted from "Spon's Encyclopædia." r. 8vo. *Spon.*   4*s.*

Sabonadiere, W. The coffee planter of Ceylon. p. 8vo. *Spon.* pub. 7*s.* 6*d.*   O.P.

Hull, E. C. P. Coffee planting in Southern India and Ceylon. p. 8vo. *Spon.* pub. 9*s.*   O.P.

—V. COTTON:

Royle, J. Forbes. Culture and commerce of cotton in India and elsewhere. 8vo. *Smith, Elder.* illus. pub. 18*s.*   O.P.

Cassels, W. R. Cotton; its culture in the Bombay Presidency. 8vo. *Smith, Elder.* pub. 16*s.*   O.P.
          Printed by order of the Indian Government.

Gibbs, J. Cotton cultivation. c. 8vo. *Spon.* pub. 7*s.* 6*d.*   O.P.

—VI. FIBROUS SUBSTANCES:

Fibrous substances. Reprinted from "Spon's Encyclopædia." r. 8vo. *Spon.*   4*s.*

—VII. MAIZE:

Simmonds, P. L. Tropical agriculture. 8vo. *Spon.*   21*s.*

—VIII. SILK:

Wardle, J. Silk. *J. Heywood.*

—IX. SUGAR:

Reed, W. History of sugar and sugar-yielding plants. c. 8vo. *Longmans.* pub. 5*s.*   O.P.

Gill, C. H. Manufacture and refining of sugar. 8vo. *Society of Arts.*   6*d.*

Lock and others. Sugar growing and refining. 8vo. *Spon.* illus.   30s.

Roth, H. Ling. Guide to the literature of sugar (bibliography.) *Paul.*   7s. 6d.

—X. TEA :

Money, E. Cultivation and manufacture of tea. d. 8vo. *Whittingham.*   10s. 6d.

Tea cyclopædia. 8vo. *Whittingham.*   28s.

Tea. (Reprinted from "Spon's Encyclopædia"). r. 8vo. *Spon.*   2s.

—XI. TOBACCO :

Tobacco. (Reprinted from "Spon's Encyclopædia"). r. 8vo. *Spon.*   4s.

Watson, Forbes. Report on the cultivation and preparation of tobacco in
India. *Trübner.*   5s.
    Appendix deals with tobacco cultivation in Hungary.

—XII. REFERENCE :

Spon's Encyclopædia of the industrial arts. Ed. C. G. Warnford Lock.
sup. r. 8vo. *Spon.* illus.   70s.
    Parts sold separately, 2s. each.

ECUADOR, *see* AMERICA, SOUTH.

EDINBURGH UNIVERSITY, *see* UNIVERSITIES.

EDUCATION :

See also UNIVERSITIES.

    For general reader.—Locke's *Thoughts* and *Conduct,* Montaigne's *Essays,* as in list,
Thring's *Theory and practice,* H. Spencer's *Education,* J. H. Newman's *Idea,* Painter's
History of Education, Pestalozzi's *Leonard and Gertrude,* Guimps' *Life of Pestalozzi,*
Quick's *Educational reformers.*

    For Teachers.—Fitch's lectures, Payne's lectures, Thring's *Theory and practice,* Spencer's
Education, Guimps' *Life of Pestalozzi, Leonard and Gertrude,* Trumbull's *Teaching and
teachers,* Montaigne's *Essays,* as in list, Locke's *Thoughts* and *Conduct,* Page's *Theory and
practice,* Parker's *Talks,* De Garmo's *Essentials,* Compayré's lectures, Sidgwick's lectures,
Cotterill's *School reforms,* Sully's *Psychology,* Marenholz-Bülow's *Child and child-nature,*
Quick's *Educational reformers,* Ascham's *Scholemaster.*

—I. HISTORY :

Compayré, G. History of pedagogy. Tr. W. H. Payne. 8vo. *Sonnenschein.*   6s.
    Covers the whole ground ; too condensed.

Painter, F. V. N. History of education. Ed. W. T. Harris. c. 8vo.
Appleton.   7s. 6d.
    A tolerable introduction to the subject.

Barnard, H. German educators. 8vo. 2 vols. (*Hartford, U.S.*).   O.P.

Quick, R. H. Educational reformers. 8vo. *Longmans.*   3s. 6d.

Guimps, R. de. Life of Pestalozzi. Tr. J. Russell. 8vo. *Sonnenschein.*   6s.

Stanley, A. P. Life of Dr. Arnold. c. 8vo. 2 vols. *Murray.*   12s.

Laurie, S. S. Life of Comenius. ex. f. 8vo. *Pitt Press.*   3s. 6d.

Leitch, J. Practical educationists. *Macmillan.* pub. 6s.   O.P.
    Good account of Wilderspin, Stow, etc.

Autobiography of Froebel. Tr. H. K. Moore. 8vo. *Sonnenschein.*   3s.

—II. THEORY :

Locke, J. Thoughts concerning education. ex. f. 8vo. *Pitt Press.*   3s. 6d.

Locke, J.   Conduct of the understanding.   Ed. T. Fowler.   ex. f. 8vo.
  Clar. Press.   2s. 6d.

Payne, J.   Lectures on science and art of education.   8vo.   *Longmans.*   9s.

Spencer, H.   Education.   8vo.   *Williams.*   6s.
  Also 12mo, 2s. 6d.   Makes much of science and nothing of literature.

Newman, J. H.   Idea of a university.   c. 8vo.   *Longmans.*   7s.

Milton, J.   Tractate on education.   ex. f. 8vo.   *Pitt Press.*   3s.
  A poet's scheme.

Montaigne.   Essays (Bk. i., Chaps. XXIV, XXV).   16mo.   *Routledge.*   2s. 6d.

Richter, J. P. F.   Levana.   Tr.   r. 8vo.   *Bell (Bohn).*   3s. 6d.

Payne, W. H.   Contributions to the science of education.   c. 8vo.   *Blackie.*   6s.

De Garmo, C.   Essentials of method (Psychological).   *Heath (Boston).*   3s.

Pestalozzi.   Leonard and Gertrude.   Tr. E. Channing.   *Heath (Boston).*   4s. 6d.

Preyer, W.   Mind of the child.   Tr. H. W. Brown.   c. 8vo.   2 vols., 7s. 6d.
  each.   *Appleton.*   15s.
  Scientific observation of children and other young animals.

Rosenkranz, J. R. F.   Philosophy of education.   Tr. A. C. Bracket.   c. 8vo.
  Appleton.   7s. 6d.

Latham, H.   Action of examinations.   p. 8vo.   *Bell.*   10s. 6d.
  Should be studied by all who wish to understand this subject.

Laurie, S. S.   Occasional addresses on educational subjects.   c. 8vo.   *Cambridge Press.*   5s.
  Theory and biography.

      ,,   The study of language.   ex. f. 8vo.   *Pitt Press.*   3s. 6d.

Rousseau, J. J.   Steeg's extracts from "Emile."   Tr. E. Worthington.
  c. 8vo.   *Isbister.*   3s. 6d.

Froebel, F.   Education of man.   Tr. W. N. Hailmann.   c. 8vo.   *Appleton.*   7s. 6d.

Sully, J.   Teacher's handbook of psychology.   c. 8vo.   *Longmans.*   6s. 6d.
  Indispensable for every teacher.

Marenholz-Bülow, B. von.   Reminiscences of Froebel.   12mo.   *(Boston).*   7s. 6d.

Shirreff, E.   Intellectual education.   c. 8vo.   *Smith, Elder.*   6s.

—III. THEORY AND PRACTICE:

Thring, E.   Theory and practice of teaching.   Ex. f. 8vo.   *Cambridge Press.*   4s. 6d.

Page, D. P.   Theory and practice of teaching.   12mo.   c. 8vo.   *Barnes (N.Y.).*   7s. 6d.
  Good book for young teachers.

Barnard, H.   English pedagogy.   8vo.   2 ser., 17s. 6d. each.   *Brown and
  Gross (Hartford).*   35s.

      ,,   German pedagogy.   8vo.   *Brown and Gross (Hartford, U.S.).*   17s. 6d.

Marenholz-Bülow, B. von.   The child and child-nature.   c. 8vo.   *Sonnenschein.*   illus.   3s.

Shirreff, E.   Kindergarten at home.   d. 8vo.   *W. H. Allen.*   illus.   6s.

Manuals of the science of teaching.   *Nat. Society.*
  Series i., Science of teaching, 5 parts, 6d. and 8d. each ; series ii., Art of teaching, 6 parts,
  6d. and 8d. each ; series iii., Advanced subjects, 9 parts, 8d. and 10d. each ; also in 2 vols.,
  5s. 6d. each—vol. i. being series i., ii. ; vol. ii. series iii.

Arnold, M.   School reports.   c. 8vo.   *Macmillan.*   3s. 6d.

Fearon, D. R.   School inspection.   c. 8vo.   *Macmillan.*   2s. 6d.

—IV. PRACTICE:

Fitch, J. G. Lectures on teaching. c. 8vo. *Cambridge Press.*   5*s.*

Parker, F. W. Talks on teaching. 16mo. *Kellogg (New York).*   3*s.* 6*d.*
     Excellent short book about elementary teaching.

Abbott, J. The teacher. 12mo. *Allman.* 1833.   O.P.

Compayré, G. Lectures on teaching. *Heath (Boston).*   7*s.*

Trumbull, H. Clay. Teaching and teachers. p. 8vo. *Hodder.*   5*s.*
     Good book for young teachers.

Sidgwick, A. Lecture on stimulus. ex. f. 8vo. *Pitt Press.*   1*s.*

   ,,   Lecture on form discipline. c. 8vo. *Rivingtons.*   1*s.* 6*d.*
     The last two books are excellent lectures based on schoolroom experiences.

Calderwood, H. On teaching. ex. f. 8vo. *Macmillan.*   2*s.* 6*d.*

Shaw and Donnell. School devices. 16mo. *Kellogg (New York).* illus.   6*s.*
     Practical suggestions for primary teachers.

Laurie, S. S. Language and linguistic method in the school. c. 8vo.
     Cambridge Press.   4*s.*

Geikie, A. Teaching of geography. gl. 8vo. *Macmillan.*   2*s.*

Landon, J. School management. c. 8vo. *Paul.*   6*s.*

Ascham, R. The scholemaster. Ed. J. E. B. Mayor. p. 8vo. *Bell (Bohn).*   1*s.*

—V. MISCELLANEOUS:

Craik, H. State and education. ("Eng. Citizen" ser.). c. 8vo. *Macmillan.*   3*s.* 6*d.*

Roberts, R. D. Eighteen years of University extension. c. 8vo. *Cambridge Press.*   1*s.*

Mackinder and Sadler. University extension : has it a future ? 8vo.
     Frowde.   1*s.*

Report of a conference on University extension teaching held in Oxford,
     April, 1887. *London Univ. Extension Soc., Charterhouse, E.C.*   6*d.*

Vincent, J. H. The Chatauqua movement (home reading). c. 8vo. *Home
Reading Union.*   5*s.*

—VI. REFERENCE, ETC.:

Report of the Royal Commission on elementary education (1861). 6 vols.
     Eyre.   18*s.* 3*d.*

   ,,   School enquiry Commission, 1868 (Endowed schools). 21 vols.
     Eyre.   68*s.* 9*d.*

   ,,   Royal Commission on technical instruction (1881). 5 vols. *Eyre.*   20*s.* 10*d.*

   ,,   Royal Commission on elementary education (1886). 10 vols.
     Eyre.   59*s.*
     All the volumes of these reports are sold separately.

Owen, H. Manual of the Education Acts. d. 8vo. *Knight.*
     Reprinting.

Sonnenschein, A. Foreign education codes. p. 8vo. *Sonnenschein.*   3*s.* 6*d.*

Cyclopædia of education. 8vo. *Sonnenschein.*   7*s.* 6*d.*

Hall and Mansfield. Bibliography of education. p. 8vo. *Heath (Boston).*   7*s.* 6*d.*

     PERIODICALS: *Journal of Education* ; monthly ; general. *Educational Times* ; monthly ;
organ of College of Preceptors. *Education* ; monthly. *New York School Journal* ; weekly
(Kellogg) ; 12*s.* 6*d.* per annum. *School Guardian* ; weekly ; organ of National Soc. *School
Board Chronicle* ; weekly. *Schoolmaster* ; weekly ; organ of elementary teachers.
University Extension Journal ; monthly (Charterhouse Press).
     See also the annual reports of the Committee of Council on Education (*Eyre*), and the list of
pamphlets on education issued by the National Technical Association, 14, Dean's-yard.

EDUCATION IN CANADA, *see* CANADA II.

　　　,,　　IN UNITED STATES, *see* UNITED STATES, HISTORY IX.

　　　,,　　IN GREECE, *see* GREECE, HISTORY III.

EGYPT:

—I. GEOGRAPHY AND DESCRIPTION:

Murray's Handbook for Egypt. p. 8vo. *Murray*　　　　　　15s.

Baedeker's Handbook of Egypt. 12mo. *Dulau.*　　　　　16s.
　　　Part i., Lower Egypt, etc.; part ii., Upper Egypt.

Reclus, E. Universal geography, vol. x. i. 8vo. *Virtue.* illus.　　21s.
　　　The whole of the Nile basin, the great lake region, Abyssinia, Kordofan, Darfur.

Edwards, Amelia B. A thousand miles up the Nile. r. 8vo. *Routledge.*　7s. 6d.
　　　Useful as a guide.

Lane, E. W. Modern Egyptians: their manners and customs. Ed.
　　　E. S. Poole. c. 8vo. 2 vols. *Murray.*　　　　　　12s.
　　　Written during 1825-28, and 1833-35.

Villiers-Stuart, H. Egypt after the war (1882). m. 8vo. *Murray.*　31s. 6d.

Wallace, D. M. Egypt and the Egyptian question. 8vo. *Macmillan.*　14s.

Bonomi and Sharpe. Egypt, Nubia, and Ethiopia. 4to. *Smith, Elder.*
　　　illus. pub. 63s.　　　　　　　　　　　　　　　O.P.

Zincke, F. B. Egypt of the Pharaohs and of the Khedive. d. 8vo. *Smith,*
　　　Elder. pub. 16s.　　　　　　　　　　　　　　O.P.

Moberly-Bell, C. F. From Pharaoh to Fellah. 4to. *Gardner.*　16s.

—II. ARCHÆOLOGY:

Maspero, G. Egyptian archæology. Tr. A. B. Edwards. p. 8vo. *Grevel.*
　　　illus.　　　　　　　　　　　　　　　　　10s. 6d.

Mariette, A. Monuments of Upper Egypt. p. 8vo. *Paul.*　　7s. 6d.

Wilkinson, J. G. Architecture of ancient Egypt. 8vo. (*London*). illus.
　　　pub. 63s.　　　　　　　　　　　　　　　　O.P.

Poole, R. Stuart. Cities of Egypt. c. 8vo. *Smith, Elder.*　　5s.

Perrot and Chipiez. History of art in ancient Egypt. Tr. Armstrong.
　　　i. 8vo. 2 vols. *Chapman.* illus.　　　　　　　　42s.

Renouf, P. Le Page. Religion of ancient Egypt (Hibbert lectures). 8vo.
　　　Williams.　　　　　　　　　　　　　　　10s. 6d.

　　　,,　　Book of the dead (Papyrus of Ani). fo. *British Museum.*　31s. 6d.

Erman, A. Aegypten und aegyptisches Leben. 8vo. 2 vols. (*Tübingen*).　18s.

Wilkinson, J. G. Manners and customs of the ancient Egyptians. Ed.
　　　Birch. c. 8vo. 2 vols. *Murray.*　　　　　　　　12s.

Brugsch, H. History of Egypt. Tr. P. Smith. 8vo. 2 vols. *Murray.*　32s.

Maspero, G. Histoire ancienne des peuples de l'orient. 12mo. (*Paris*).　5s.

Brugsch and Bouriant. Livre des rois. 8vo. Vol. i., 23s. (*Vienna*).

Records of the past. Ed. Birch. c. 8vo. 12 vols., 3s. 6d. each. *Bagster.*
　　　Vols. ii., iv., vi., viii., x., xii., are on Egypt; the others on Assyria. o.p., except vols. x., xi., xii.

　　　,,　　2nd series. Ed. A. H. Sayce. c. 8vo. 4 vols., 4s. 6d. each.
　　　Bagster.
　　　Vols. ii., iii., iv., mixed.

Lepsius, C. R. Denkmäler aus Aegypten und Aethiopen. e. fo. 12 vols.
  (*Berlin*). 1849–60. illus.   £33

Rosellini, I. Monumenti dell' Egitto e della Nubia. 8vo. 9 vols. (*Pisa*).
  1832–4. illus.   40s.

Champollion, J. F. Monuments de l'Egypte et de la Nubie. fo. 4 vols.
  (*Paris*). 1835–45. illus.   £20

—III. LANGUAGE, ANCIENT :

For Modern Egyptian, see ARABIA, LANGUAGE.

Renouf, P. Le Page. Elementary grammar. c. 4to. *Bagster.*   7s. 6d.

Rougé, E. de. Chrestomathie égyptienne (Grammar and reading book).
  4to. 4 vols. (*Paris*).   63s.

Pierret, P. Vocabulaire hiéroglyphique. 8vo. *Vieweg.*   50s.

Budge, E. A.   Sarcophagus of Anchnesraneferab (Reading book).   4to.
  Nutt.   15s.

> PERIODICALS, ETC.: Egypt Exploration fund, *Paul*; Society of Biblical Archæology,
> *Trübner*; Revue Egyptologique, 30s. per annum; Recueil de travaux, 30s. per annum
> (Egyptian and Assyrian archæology and philology); Mélanges d'archéologie, 10s. per vol.;
> Revue de l'histoire des religions, 25s. per annum.; Zeitschrift für aegyptische Sprache, 15s.
> per annum.

ELECTIONS, *see* LOCAL GOVERNMENT.

ELECTRICITY :

—I. THEORY :

Thompson, S. P. Elementary lessons in electricity and magnetism.
  f. 8vo. *Macmillan.* illus.   4s. 6d.
  > Clear, though not masterly.

Gerard, E. Leçons sur l'électricité. 8vo. *Gauthier-Villars.*
  > Vol. i., 10s. The best work; not requiring a knowledge of high mathematics.

Lodge, O. T. Modern views of electricity. c. 8vo. *Macmillan.*   6s. 6d.

Maxwell, J. Clerk. Electricity and magnetism. d. 8vo. 2 vols. *Clar.*
  Press. illus.   31s. 6d.
  > Requires high mathematical knowledge.

Thomson, W. Papers on electro-statics and magnetism. 8vo. *Macmillan.* 18s.

Wiedemann, G. Die Lehre von der Electricität. 8vo. 5 vols. *Vieweg.* 128s.
  > Vol. i., 20s.; vol. ii., 25s.; vol. iii., 24s.; vol. iv., 15s.; vol. v., 24s. The most complete work of
  > reference on the subject.

Everett, J. D. Units and constants. (elem.). gl. 8vo. *Macmillan.*   5s.

Gray, A. Theory and practice of absolute measurements in electricity
  and magnetism. c. 8vo. *Macmillan.* illus. Vol. i., 12s. 6d.

  ,,   Absolute measurements in electricity and magnetism. f. 8vo.
  Macmillan.   5s. 6d.

Mascart and Joubert. Electricity and magnetism (mathematical). Tr.
  G. Atkinson. d. 8vo. 2 vols., 21s. each. *De la Rue.* illus.   42s.

Reports of the committee on electrical standards. (*British Assoc.*).
  > Including report to Royal Society on units of electric resistance. Issued since 1881; 21s.
  > annually.

Catalogue of books and papers relating to electricity, magnetism, and
  electric telegraph. Ed. A. J. Frost. 8vo. *Spon.*   6s.

—II. ENGINEERING :

Thompson, S. P. Dynamo electric machinery. 8vo. *Spon.* pub. 16s. · O.P.

Kempe, H. R. Handbook of electric testing. c. 8vo. *Spon.* 16s.
Very technical.

Hospitalier, E. Formulaire pratique de l'électricien. (Annual). 12mo.
(*Paris*). 4s. 6d.

,, Modern applications of electricity. Tr. J. Maier. 8vo. 2 vols. *Paul.* 25s.

Swinburne, J. Practical electrical measurements. d. 8vo. *Alabaster.* O.P.

Slingo and Brooker. Electrical engineering. c. 8vo. *Longmans.* illus. 10s. 6d.
The only book on the subject.

Fleming, J. A. The alternate current transformer. d. 8vo. "*Electrician*"
Publishing Co. illus. Vol. i., 7s. 6d.

Preece and Sivewright. Telegraphy. c. 8vo. *Longmans.* illus. 5s.

Culley, R. S. Handbook of practical telegraphy. *Longmans.* illus. 16s.

Preece and Maiers. Telephone. c. 8vo. *Bell.* illus. 12s. 6d.

EMBROIDERY, *see* NEEDLEWORK.

EMBRYOLOGY, *see* ZOOLOGY V.

EMOTIONS, EXPRESSION OF, *see* ZOOLOGY.

EMPLOYERS' LIABILITY, *see* ENGLAND, LAW IX.

ENAMELLING, *see* ARTISTIC PROCESSES VII.

ENGINEERING :

See also BUILDING CONSTRUCTION, HYDRAULICS, HYGIENE, RAILWAYS,
STEAM-ENGINE, SURVEYING.

The best and most complete works on applied mechanics, the basis of scientific engineering,
are by French authors. The works of the late Professor Rankine are admirable. A certain
amount of mathematical knowledge is indispensable for any profitable reading of engineering
theory, but elementary text-books on mathematics are not included in this section.

—I. GENERAL :

Rankine, W. J. M. Applied mechanics. Ed. W. J. Millar. c. 8vo. *Griffin.*
illus. 12s. 6d.
Comprehensive, but highly condensed, and involves mathematical reasoning of advanced
character.

Cotterill, J. H. Applied mechanics. m. 8vo. *Macmillan.* 18s.

Alexander, T. Elementary applied mechanics, part i. c. 8vo. *Macmillan.*
pub. 4s. 6d. O.P.

Alexander and Thomson. Elementary applied mechanics, part ii. c. 8vo.
Macmillan. 10s. 6d.

Weisbach, J. Manual of mechanics of engineering and construction. Tr.
E. Coxe. 8vo. 2 vols. *Trübner.* 81s. 6d.
Vol. i., 31s. 6d.; vol. ii., 50s. Comprehensive, and treated as far as possible without the
calculus.

Clebsch, R. A. F. Théorie de l'élasticité des corps solides. Tr. from the
German. 8vo. *Dunod.* 32s.
Complete exposition of modern theory.

Navier and St. Venant. L'application de la mécanique à l'établissement des constructions et des machines. 8vo. *Dunod.* illus.
Vol i., 20s. Course given at L'école des Ponts et Chaussées. Contains an interesting historical summary.

Bresse, J. A. C. Cours de mécanique appliquée. 8vo. 3 vols. *Gauthier Villars.*
Vol. i., 13s.; vol. ii., 10s.; vol. iii., o.p.

Collignon, E. Cours de mécanique appliquée. 8vo. 2 vols., 11s. each. *Dunod.*   22s.
Course at L'école des Ponts et Chaussées. Clear and elegant demonstrations.

Poncelet, J. V. La mécanique industrielle. 8vo. *Gauthier Villars.*   10s.
Classical book on "principle of work."

Flamant, A. Résistance des matériaux. 8vo. *Baudry.* illus.   20s.

Graham, R. H. Graphic and analytic statics. 8vo. *Lockwood.*   16s.

Clarke, G. S. Graphic statics. 4to. *Spon.*   12s. 6d.

Merriman. Graphic statics (roofs and bridges). 8vo. *Wiley (New York).* 12s. 6d.

Smith, R. H. Graphics; part i., with atlas. 8vo. *Longmans.*   15s.
Calculation by diagram applied especially to mechanical engineering.

Stoney, B. Theory of stresses on girders. r. 8vo. *Longmans.* illus.   36s.

Barlow, P. Strength of materials. Ed. Humber. d. 8vo. *Lockwood.*   18s.

Unwin, W. C. Testing of materials of construction. 8vo. *Longmans.* illus.   21s.

Rankine, W. J. M. Useful rules and tables. c. 8vo. *Griffin.* illus.   10s. 6d.
With appendix for electrical engineers.

Clark, D. K. Manual of rules, tables, and data. 8vo. *Blackie.*   16s.

Eagles, T. H. Geometry of plane curves. c. 8vo. *Macmillan.*   12s.

  ,,   Descriptive geometry. c. 8vo. *Scott.*   3s. 6d.

Rankine, W. J. M. Civil engineering. Ed. W. J. Millar. c. 8vo. *Griffin.* illus.   16s.

Mahan, D. Civil engineering. 8vo. *Spon.*   21s.

Matheson, E. Aid book to engineering enterprise. 8vo. *Spon.*   21s.

—II. REFERENCE AND BIOGRAPHY:

Spon's Dictionary of engineering. r. 8vo. 4 vols. *Spon.*   145s.

Wershoven, F. J. Technological dictionary; English and German. 2 vols. *Whittaker.*   5s.

Ure, A. Dictionary of arts, manufactures, and mines. 8vo. 4 vols. *Longmans.* pub. 147s.   o.p.

Smiles, S. Lives of the engineers. c. 8vo. 5 vols., 7s. 6d. each. *Murray.* 37s. 6d.

Helps, A. Life and labours of T. Brassey. p. 8vo. *Bell and Daldy.*   10s. 6d.

Brunel, I. Life of I. K. Brunel. 8vo. *Longmans.* pub. 21s.   o.p.

Fairbairn, William, life of; partly an autobiography. Completed by W. Pole. 8vo. *Longmans.* pub. 18s.   o.p.

Smiles, S. Life of James Nasmyth. 8vo. *Murray.*   7s. 6d.

Pole, W. Life of Sir William Siemens. 8vo. *Murray.*   16s.

Smiles, S. Life of George Stephenson, with memoir of Robert Stephenson. c. 8vo. *Murray.* illus.   7s. 6d.

Jeaffreson, J. C. Life of Robert Stephenson. 8vo. 2 vols. *Longmans.*
pub. 32*s.*　　　　　　　　　　　　　　　　　　　　　　　　　O.P.

Smiles, S. Life of Telford. c. 8vo. *Murray.* illus.　　　　7*s.* 6*d.*
Extracted from the *Lives of the engineers.*

Muirhead, J. P. Life of James Watt. 8vo. *Murray.*　　　　O.P.
JOURNALS, ETC.: A mine of information exists in the volumes, now numbering a hundred, of the *Proceedings* of the Institution of Civil Engineers, in the journals of the Society of Mechanical Engineers and of the Iron and Steel Institute, and in *Van Nostrand's Magazine.* *Engineering,* published weekly, is perhaps the chief periodical.

ENGLAND: GEOGRAPHY:

—I. GENERAL:

Reclus, E. Universal geography, vol. iv. i. 8vo. *Virtue.*　　21*s.*

Ramsay, A. C. Physical geology and geography of Great Britain. p. 8vo.
Stanford. illus.　　　　　　　　　　　　　　　　　　7*s.* 6*d.*
Contains geological map.

Our own country. ex. c. 4to. 6 vols., 7*s.* 6*d.* each. *Cassell.* illus.　45*s.*

Jukes-Browne, A. J. The building of the British Isles. p. 8vo. *Bell.*
illus.　　　　　　　　　　　　　　　　　　　　　　　7*s.* 6*d.*
Study in geographical evolution.

Geikie, A. Elementary geography of the British Isles. 18mo. *Macmillan.*　1*s.*

Bartholomew, J. Gazetteer of the British Isles. r. 8vo. *Longmans.* pub. 36*s.*　O.P.

Richard, J. R., and A. S. Short geography of the British islands. f. 8vo.
Macmillan.　　　　　　　　　　　　　　　　　　　3*s.* 6*d.*
On the whole the best text-book.

—II. TOPOGRAPHY:

Baddeley's Thorough guide series. Ed. Baddeley and Ward. 12mo. *Dulau.*
English Lake District, 5*s.*: North Devon and North Cornwall, 3*s.* 6*d.*; South Devon and South Cornwall, 4*s.*; Peak District 2*s.* 6*d.*; Eastern Counties, 2*s.* 6*d.*
In course of publication. Specially valuable for their numerous excellent maps, and the clearness and minuteness of their directions.

Murray's Handbook for England and Wales. p. 8vo.　　　　　12*s.*

　,, 　English handbooks. p. 8vo. *Murray.*
Eastern Counties, 12*s.*: Kent, 7*s.* 6*d.*; Sussex, 6*s.*: Surrey and Hants, 10*s.*; Berks, Bucks, and Oxon, 9*s.*; Wilts, Dorset, and Somerset, 12*s.*; Devon, 7*s.* 6*d.*; Cornwall, 6*s.*; Gloucester, Hereford, and Worcester, 9*s.*; Northampton and Rutland, 7*s.* 6*d.*; Derby, Notts, Leicester, and Stafford, 9*s.*; Shropshire and Cheshire, 6*s.*; Lancashire, 7*s.* 6*d.*; Yorkshire, 12*s.*; Lincolnshire, Durham, and Northumberland, 9*s.*; Westmoreland and Cumberland, 7*s.* 6*d.*; Warwickshire (in preparation); Herts, Hunts, and Beds (in preparation).

Stanford's Tourist's guides. f. 8vo. *Stanford.*
Contain all that the majority of tourists want to know. Beds, Berks, Cambridge, Cornwall and Scilly Islands, Derbyshire, North Devon, South Devon, Dorset, Essex, Gloucestershire, Hants, Kent, Lake District, Norfolk, Somerset, Surrey, Sussex, Warwickshire, Wilts, Worcestershire, Yorks, North and East Riding, West Riding, 2*s.* each. Devonshire, 3*s.* 6*d.*

Anderson, J. Book of British topography. i. 8vo. *Satchell.* pub. 18*s.*　O.P.
A bibliography to be consulted whenever the names of books on special localities are needed.

ENGLAND: HISTORY:

—I. GENERAL HISTORIES:

Green, J. R. Short history of the English people. c. 8vo. *Macmillan.*
(elem.)　　　　　　　　　　　　　　　　　　　　　8*s.* 6*d.*

Bright, J. F. History of England. c. 8vo. 4 vols. *Rivington.* (elem.).　23*s.*
Vol. i. (449–1485), 4*s.* 6*d.*; vol. ii. (1485–1688), 5*s.*; vol. iii. (1689–1837), 7*s.* 6*d.*; vol. iv. (1837–80), 6*s.*
More facts than Green.

Green, J. R. History of the English people. 8vo. 4 vols., 16s. each. *Macmillan.*   64s.

Pauli, R. Geschichte von England (to 1509). 8vo. 5 vols. (*Gotha*).   49s.
     The fullest general history of the mediæval period.

Lingard, J. History of England (to 1689). 10 vols. *Nimmo.*   105s.
     By a fair-minded Roman Catholic.

Kennett. Complete history of England (to 1701). fo. 3 vols. (*London*). 1719.   O.P.
     A valuable collection containing Buck's *Richard III.*, Bacon's *Henry VII.*, Herbert's *Henry VIII.*, Godwin's *Mary*, Camden's *Elizabeth* and *James I.*; the third volume of Bishop Kennett is valuable for miscellaneous information.

Carte, T. History of England (to 1654). fo. 4 vols. 1747-55.   O.P.
     The best of the older histories.

Knight, C. Popular history of England. 8vo. 8 vols. *Bradbury and Evans.*   O.P.

—II. SPECIAL PERIODS IN CHRONOLOGICAL ORDER :

Elton, C. Origins of English history. 8vo. *Quaritch.*   21s.

Rhys, J. Celtic Britain. f. 8vo. *S. P. C. K.*   3s.

Scarth, H. M. Roman Britain. f. 8vo. *S. P. C. K.*   2s. 6d.

Wright, T. Celt, Roman, and Teuton. c. 8vo. *Trübner.* illus.   9s.

Freeman, E. A. Old English history. ex. f. 8vo. *Macmillan.* (elem.)   6s.

Green, J. R. Making of England. 8vo. *Macmillan.*   16s.

    ,,   Conquest of England. 8vo. *Macmillan.*   18s.

Freeman, E. A. History of the Norman conquest. d. 8vo. 6 vols. *Clar. Press.*   109s. 6d.
     Vol. i., ii., 36s.; iii., 21s.; iv., 21s.; v., 21s.; vi., 10s. 6d.

    ,,   Reign of William Rufus. 2 vols. *Clar. Press.*   36s.

Norgate, Miss K. England under the Angevin Kings. 8vo. 2 vols. *Macmillan.* illus.   32s.

Stubbs, W. The early Plantagenets. f. 8vo. *Longmans.* (elem.)   2s. 6d.

Archer, T. A. Crusade of Richard I. 16mo. *Nutt.*   2s.

Hutton, W. H. Misrule of Henry III. 16mo. *Nutt.*   1s.

    ,,   Simon de Montfort and his cause. 16mo. *Nutt.*   1s.
     The three last are selections from the Chronicles.

Prothero, G. W. The life of Simon de Montfort. c. 8vo. *Longmans.* pub. 6s.   O.P.

Seeley, R. B. Life and reign of Edward I. 8vo. *Seeley.*   6s.

Longman, W. Life and times of Edward III. 8vo. 2 vols. *Longmans.*   28s.

Wallon, H. Richard II. 8vo. 2 vols. *Hachette.*   12s. 6d.

Wylie, J. H. England under Henry IV. c. 8vo. *Longmans.*   10s. 6d.
     Vol. i. only, from 1399 to 1404.

Tyler, J. E. Life of Henry of Monmouth. 8vo. 2 vols. 1838.   O.P.

Gairdner, J. Houses of Lancaster and York. f. 8vo. *Longmans.* (elem.)   2s. 6d.

    ,,   Life and reign of Richard III. c. 8vo. *Longmans.*   10s. 6d.

    ,,   Henry VII. c. 8vo. *Macmillan.* (elem.)   2s. 6d.

Brewer, J. S. Reign of Henry VIII. 8vo. 2 vols. *Murray.*   30s.
     To 1530.

Creighton, M. Cardinal Wolsey. (elem.) *Macmillan.*   2s. 6d.

Friedmann, P. Anne Boleyn. 8vo. 2 vols. *Macmillan.*   28s.

Gasquet. Henry VIII. and the English Monasteries. 2 vols. *Hodges.*   24s.

Creighton, M. Age of Elizabeth. f. 8vo. *Longmans.* (elem.)   2s. 6d.

Froude, J. A. England from 1530 to 1588. c. 8vo. 12 vols., 3s. 6d. each.
   Longmans.   42s.

Brosch, M. Geschichte von England. 8vo. (*Gotha*).   13s.
      Continuation of Pauli, embracing the Tudor period.

Devereux, W. B. Lives of the Devereux, Earls of Essex. 8vo. 2 vols.
   Murray.   O.P.
      The Earls of Essex were important under Elizabeth, James I., and Charles I.

Spedding, J. Life of Francis Bacon. 8vo. 2 vols. *Trübner.*   21s.
      A mass of information about the end of Elizabeth and James I.

Gardiner, S. R. History of England, 1603-1640. c. 8vo. 10 vols., 6s. each.
   Longmans.   60s.

   ,, History of the great civil war. 8vo. *Longmans.*
      Vol. i., 21s.; vol. ii., 24s. Reaching to 1647.

Carlyle, T. Oliver Cromwell's letters and speeches. d. 8vo. 5 vols., 9s.
   each. *Chapman.*   45s.
      Also cheaper editions.

Harrison, F. Oliver Cromwell. c. 8vo. *Macmillan.* (elem.)   2s. 6d

Palgrave, R. F. D. Oliver Cromwell the Protector. c. 8vo. *Low.*   10s. 6d.
      Latest attack on Cromwell.

Gardiner, S. R. The first two Stuarts, and the Puritan Revolution (1603-
   1660). (elem.) f. 8vo. *Longmans.*   2s. 6d.

Clarendon. History of the Great Rebellion. Ed. Macray. c. 8vo.
   6 vols. *Clar. Press.*   45s.

Masson, D. Life of Milton. 6 vols. *Macmillan.*
      Vol. i., vi., 21s. each; vol. ii., o.p.; vol. iii., 18s.; vol. iv., v., 32s. Full of information
      about the intellectual movements of the Great Rebellion.

Ranke, L. von. History of England, principally in the 17th century.
   d. 8vo. 6 vols. *Clar. Press.*   63s.
      Especially valuable for foreign relations.

Burnet, G. History of his own times (1660-1713). 6 vols. *Clar. Press.*   O.P.
      A contemporary narrative of great value.

Coxe, W. Memoirs of the Duke of Marlborough. p. 8vo. 3 vols.,
   3s. 6d. each. *Bell.* illus.   10s. 6d.
      With a useful atlas of campaigns.

Diary of Samuel Pepys (1659-1669). Ed. Braybrooke. p. 8vo. 4 vols.,
   5s. each. *Bell (Bohn).*   20s.
      Fuller edition. Ed. Bright.

Diary of John Evelyn (1620-1706). Ed. W. Bray. p. 8vo. 4 vols.,
   5s. each. *Bell (Bohn).* illus.   20s.

Macaulay, T. B. History of England (from James II. to 1701). 8vo.
   5 vols. *Longmans.*   80s.
      Also cheaper editions.

Christie, W. D. Life of the first Earl of Shaftesbury. 2 vols. *Macmillan.*   O.P.

Harrop, R. Bolingbroke. 8vo. *Paul.*   O.P.

Wyon, F. W. Reign of Queen Anne. 8vo. 2 vols. *Chapman.* pub. 32s.   O.P.

Coxe, W. Memoirs of Sir R. Walpole. 8vo. (*London*). 1789.   O.P.

Lecky, W. E. H. England in the 18th century. 8vo. 8 vols., 18s.
   each. *Longmans.*   144s.

Stanhope, Lord. History of England, 1713-1783. p. 8vo. 9 vols., 5*s.* each. *Murray.*   45*s.*

Harvey, Lord. Memoirs of the reign of George II. *Bentley.* 1848.   O.P.

Walpole, H. Memoirs of the reign of George III. 8vo. 4 vols. *Bentley.* 1845.   O.P.

Thackeray, F. Life of Lord Chatham. 4to. 2 vols. 1827.   O.P.

Massey, W. England during the reign of George III. f. 8vo. 4 vols. *Longmans.* . pub. 24*s.*   O.P.

Thackeray, W. M. The four Georges. c. 8vo. *Smith, Elder.* illus.   10*s.* 6*d.*
     Also cheaper editions.

Russell, Earl. Life of Fox. p. 8vo. 3 vols., 12*s.* each. *Bentley.* pub. 36*s.*   O.P.

Stanhope, Lord. Life of William Pitt. 8vo. 3 vols. *Murray.*   36*s.*

Morley, J. Edmund Burke. g. 8vo. *Macmillan.*   5*s.*

Macknight, T. Life and times of Burke. 8vo. 3 vols. *Chapman.* pub. 50*s.*   O.P.

Martineau, Harriet. History of England 1800-1815. p. 8vo. *Bell.*   3*s.* 6*d.*

     ,, History of the thirty years' peace 1816-1846. p. 8vo. 4 vols., 3*s.* 6*d.* each. *Bell (Bohn).*   14*s.*

Walpole, S. History of England 1815-1858. c. 8vo. 6 vols., 6*s.* each. *Longmans.*   36*s.*

Stapleton, A. George Canning and his times. 8vo. *J. W. Parker.*   O.P.

Cory, W. Guide to modern English history 1815-1835. d. 8vo. 2 vols. *Paul.*   24*s.*
     Vol. i., 9*s.*; vol. ii., 15*s.* Epigrammatic and amusing.

McCarthy, J. History of our own times. d. 8vo. 4 vols., 12*s.* each. *Chatto.*   48*s.*
     Also at 6*s.* each.

Greville, C. C. F. Journals of the reigns of George IV., William IV., and Victoria. c. 8vo. 8 vols., 6*s.* each. *Longmans.*   48*s.*

Martin, T. Life of the Prince Consort. d. 8vo. 5 vols., 18*s.* each. *Smith, Elder.* illus.   90*s.*
     Also in 1 vol., 4*s.* 6*d.*

Ward, T. H. Reign of Queen Victoria. d. 8vo. 2 vols. *Smith, Elder.*   32*s.*
     Essays by various writers on the progress shown during the reign.

Dalling and Ashley. Life of Lord Palmerston. d. 8vo. 5 vols. *Bentley.*   75*s.*
     Vol. i., ii., 30*s.*; vol. iii., 15*s.*; vol. iv., v., 30*s.* Also in 2 vols., 12*s.* each.

Walpole, S. Life of Earl Russell. p. 8vo. 2 vols. *Longmans.*   12*s.*

—III. CONSTITUTIONAL HISTORY:

See also ENGLAND, LAW II.

Ransome, C. Rise of constitutional government. c. 8vo. *Rivingtons.* (elem.)   6*s.*

Taswell-Langmead, T. P. English constitutional history. 8vo. *Stevens and Haynes.*   21*s.*
     A general compilation.

Stubbs, W. Constitutional history of England to 1485. c. 8vo. 3 vols., 12*s.* each. *Clar. Press.*   36*s.*

Earle, J. Handbook to land charters and other Saxon documents. c. 8vo. *Clar. Press.*   16*s.*

Stubbs, W. Select charters. c. 8vo. *Clar. Press.*   8s. 6d.
Contains the chief documents of importance up to 1329.

Hallam, H. Constitutional history of England. 8vo. 3 vols. *Murray.*   30s.
Henry VII. to George II. Also cheaper editions.

Gardiner, S. R. Constitutional documents of the Commonwealth. c. 8vo.
Clar. Press.   9s.

May, T. E. Constitutional history of England. c. 8vo. 3 vols. *Longmans.*   18s.
From George III.

Gneist, R. History of the English constitution. Tr. P. A. Ashworth.
d. 8vo. 2 vols. *Clowes.*   32s.

  ,, History of the English Parliament. Tr. A. H. Keane. d. 8vo.
Clowes.   7s. 6d.

Todd, A. Parliamentary government in England. 8vo. 2 vols. *Longmans.*
pub. 54s.   O.P.
An account of the actual doings of Parliament since George III. Vol. i., 21s.; vol. ii., 30s.

Dicey, A. V. Law of the constitution. 8vo. *Macmillan.*   12s. 6d.

Bagehot, W. The English constitution. c. 8vo. *Paul.*   7s. 6d.
A survey of the constitution at present.

Anson, W. R. Law and custom of the constitution. d. 8vo. Part i., 10s. 6d.
Clar. Press.

—IV. ADMINISTRATION:

Dowell, S. History of taxes and taxation in England. 8vo. 4 vols.
Longmans.   42s.

Hall, H. History of the Customs revenue of England. d. 8vo. 2 vols.
Stock.   21s.

Campbell, Lord. Lives of the Lord Chancellors. c. 8vo. 10 vols., 6s.
each. *Murray.*   60s.

  ,, Lives of the Chief Justices. c. 8vo. 4 vols., 6s. each. *Murray.*   24s.

Foss, E. The Judges of England. 8vo. 9 vols. *Murray.*   O.P.

Eaton, Dorman B. Civil Service in Great Britain. 8vo. *Harper.*   12s. 6d.

—V. SOCIAL, ECONOMIC, AND INDUSTRIAL:

Hall, H. Court life under the Plantagenets. *Sonnenschein.* illus.   10s. 6d.

Browne, M. Chaucer's England. p. 8vo. 2 vols. *Blackett.*   O.P.

Jusserand, J. J. Wayfaring life in England in the 14th century. Tr.
L. T. Smith. 8vo. *Unwin.* illus.   12s.

Denton, W. England in the 15th century. d. 8vo. *Bell.*   12s.

Thornbury, W. Shakespeare's England. c. 8vo. 2 vols. *Longmans.*   O.P.

Hall, H. Society in the Elizabethan age. 8vo. *Sonnenschein.*   10s. 6d.

Bourne, H. R. Fox. English seamen under the Tudors. 8vo. 2 vols.
Bentley.   O.P.

Dyer, T. F. British popular customs. p. 8vo. *Bell (Bohn).*   5s.

Ashton, J. Social life in the reign of Queen Anne. c. 8vo. *Chatto*
illus.   7s. 6d.

Wright, T. England under the House of Hanover. 8vo. 2 vols. *Bentley.*
1848.   O.P.

Ashton, J. The dawn of the 19th century. c. 8vo. *Unwin.*   10s. 6d.

Cunningham. W. Growth of English industry and commerce during the early and middle ages. d. 8vo. *Cambridge Press.*   16s.

Ashley, W. J. English economic history and theory. *Longmans.*
Vol. i. (Middle Ages) issued. 5s.

Rogers, J. E. T. Six centuries of work and wages. d. 8vo. *Sonnenschein.*   15s.
A brief sketch of economic progress.

  ,,   History of agriculture and prices in England (1259-1793). d. 8vo. 6 vols. *Clar. Press.*   142s.
Vols. i. and ii., 42s.; iii. and iv., 50s.; v. and vi., 50s.

Seebohm, F. The English village community. 8vo. *Longmans.*   16s.

Gross, C. The gild merchant. 8vo. 2 vols. *Clar. Press.*   24s.

Macpherson, D. Annals of commerce. 4to. 4 vols. (*London*). 1805.   O.P.

Eden, F. M. State of the poor. 4to. 3 vols. (*London*). 1797.   O.P.

Popular county histories. A series now in progress. d. 8vo. 7s. 6d. each. *Stock.*
Norfolk (W. Rye); Derbyshire (J. Pendleton); Devon (R. N. Worth); Berkshire (C. Cooper King); Warwickshire (S. Timmins); Cumberland (R. S. Ferguson).

Historic towns. A series now in progress. c. 8vo. 3s. 6d. each. *Longmans.*
Exeter (E. A. Freeman); Bristol (W. Hunt); London (W. J. Loftie); Oxford (C. W. Boase); Colchester (E. L. Cutts); Cinque Ports (Montagu Burrows); Carlisle (M. Creighton).

--VI. REFERENCE, COLLECTIONS, ETC.:

Annals of England. d. 8vo. *Jas. Parker.*   12s.
An excellent text-book for students. (Also in five parts, 1s. 6d. each.)

Acland and Ransome. Handbook of the political history of England. c. 8vo. *Rivingtons.*   6s.
Chronological tables.

Gardiner and Mullinger. Introduction to the study of English history. l. c. 8vo. *Paul.*   9s.
General sketch with account of the authorities.

Dictionary of English history. r. 8vo. *Cassell.* (elem.)   10s. 6d.

Gairdner, J. Early chronicles of England. c. 8vo. *S. P. C. K.* (elem.)   4s.

Doyle, J. E. Official baronage of England. 8vo. 3 vols. *Longmans.* illus.   105s.
A valuable record of English noble families and the descent of titles.

Dictionary of national biography. Ed. Leslie Stephen. d. 8vo. 15s. each. *Smith, Elder.*
In course of publication; with full references to all sources of information.

Parry, C. H. Parliaments of England. 8vo. *Murray.* 1839.   O.P.
A handbook to Parliaments.

  ,,   Parliamentary history of England to 1803 r. 8vo. 36 vols. (*London*). 1806-20.   O.P.

Chronicles of Great Britain. r. 8vo. 10s. each. *Record Office.*
Published under the direction of the Master of the Rolls.

Calendar of State papers. i. 8vo. 15s. each. *Record Office.*
Published under the direction of the Master of the Rolls.
SEE ALSO Publications of the Camden Society; Reports of the historical MSS. Commission; *English Historical Review* (quarterly, 5s.).

ENGLAND: LAW:

See also LOCAL GOVERNMENT.

> Law books are very unlike other books, and the subject matter of legal literature is a constantly growing and changing one; hence a select list of books can be taken by the professed student of law merely as hints towards the art of using the resources of a law library. Laymen in search of information upon a special point will generally do well to consult a legal friend. In default of that counsel such a list as the present may possibly help them. Law books are always quoted among lawyers by the shortest form of the title which will identify the book. This professional usage has here been followed.
>
> As a rule books of earlier date than Blackstone's Commentaries are not included, nor books of practice, unless amounting in fact and in use to text-books of substantive law.

—1. GENERAL AND HISTORY:

Blackstone, W. Commentaries on the laws of England.
> An old edition, presenting the original text in full, is quite easily procurable for a few shillings. Best with Christian's notes.

Kent, J. Commentaries on American law. 8vo. 4 vols. (*Low*).   100*s.*
> With notes by O. W. Holmes, Junr. A classical work, not nearly so much used in England as it ought to be.

Stephen, H. J. New commentaries on the laws of England. 8vo. 4 vols. *Butterworth.*   84*s.*

Reeves, J. History of the English law. Ed. Finlason. 8vo. 3 vols. *Reeves.*   O.P.
> Old editions are quite as useful, and not scarce.

Brunner, H. The sources of the law of England (with bibliographical appendix by translator). Tr. W. Hastie. c. 8vo. *Clark.*   2*s.* 6*d.*

Holmes, O. W., Jun. The common law. 8vo. *Macmillan.*   12*s.*

Broom, H. Commentaries on the common law. Ed. Archibald and Green. 8vo. *Sweet and Maxwell.*   25*s*

Maitland, F. W. Justice and police ("English Citizen" ser.). c. 8vo. *Macmillan.*   3*s.* 6*d.*

—II. EARLY AND CONSTITUTIONAL:

See also ENGLAND, HISTORY III.

Dugdale, W. Origines juridiciales. fo. 3rd ed. 1680.
> The source of almost all the current information on English legal antiquities.

Essays in Anglo-Saxon law. m. 8vo. *Macmillan.*   18*s.*

Bigelow, M. M. Placita Anglo-Normannica. 8vo. *Low.*   18*s.*

  ,,   History of procedure in England. 8vo. *Macmillan.*   16*s.*
> The Norman period.

Pleas of the Crown for the County of Gloucester. Ed. F. W. Maitland. 8vo. *Macmillan.*   7*s.* 6*d.*

Select Pleas of the Crown (Selden Society). Ed. Maitland. *Quaritch.*   O.P.

Select Pleas in Manorial Courts (Selden Society). Ed. Maitland. *Quaritch.*   O.P.

Bracton's note book. Ed. Maitland. d. 8vo. 3 vols. *Cambridge Press.*   63*s.*

Forsyth, W. Cases and opinions on constitutional law. r. 8vo. *Stevens and Haynes.*   30*s.*

Broom, H. Leading cases on constitutional law. *Sweet and Maxwell.*   25*s.* 6*d.*

Traill, H. D. Central government ("English Citizen" ser.). c. 8vo. *Macmillan.*   3*s.* 6*d.*

Hearn, W. E. The government of England. 8vo. *Longmans.*   16*s.*

Broom, H. Constitutional law. Ed. G. O. Denman. 8vo. *Maxwell.*   31s. 6d.

May, T. E. Law, privileges, and proceedings of Parliament. 8vo.
Butterworth.   48s.

—III. CRIMINAL:

Stephen, J. F. Digest of the criminal law. 8vo. *Macmillan.*   16s.

,,   Digest of the law of criminal procedure. 8vo. *Macmillan.*   12s. 6d.

,,   History of the criminal law of England. 8vo. 3 vols. *Macmillan.*   48s.

,,   General view of the criminal law. 8vo. *Macmillan.*   14s.

Russell, W. O. Crimes and misdemeanours. Ed. S. Prentice. r. 8vo.
3 vols. *Stevens.*   115s. 6d.
An exhaustive book of reference.

Archbold. Pleading and evidence in criminal cases. Ed. Bruce. r. 12mo.
Sweet and Maxwell.   31s. 6d.

Roscoe. Digest of the law of evidence in criminal cases. Ed. Smith.
r. 12mo. *Stevens.*   31s. 6d.
"Archbold" and "Roscoe," notwithstanding their titles, deal largely with substantive law.

Wright, R. S. Law of criminal conspiracies and agreements. 8vo.
Butterworth.   O.P.

Pollock and Wright. Possession in the common law. d. 8vo. *Clar. Press.*   8s. 6d.
Contains full discussion of the law of theft.

Du Cane, E. F. The punishment and prevention of crime ("English
Citizen" ser.). c. 8vo. *Macmillan.*   3s. 6d.

Pike, L. O. History of crime in England. 8vo. 2 vols. *Smith, Elder.*   O.P.

—IV. REAL AND PERSONAL PROPERTY:

Coke. Commentary on Littleton. Ed. Hargrave and Butler. 8vo. (*London*).
1823.   O.P.
There is a critical edition of Littleton's French text, by Tomlin (1841).

Raleigh, T. Outline of the law of property. d. 8vo. *Clar. Press.*   7s. 6d.

Smith and Trustram. Compendium of the law of real and personal property.
d. 8vo. 2 vols. *Stevens.*   42s.

Digby, K. E. History of the law of real property. 8vo. *Clar. Press.*   10s. 6d.

Pollock, F. Land laws ("English Citizen" ser.). c. 8vo. *Macmillan.*   3s. 6d.

Challis, H. W. Law of real property.

Williams, J. Principles of the law of real property. Ed. T. C. Williams.
8vo. *Sweet and Maxwell.*   21s.

,,   Principles of the law of personal property. Ed. T. C. Williams.
d. 8vo. *Sweet and Maxwell.*   21s.

,,   Rights of common, etc. 8vo. *Sweet and Maxwell.*   14s.

Scrutton, T. E. Commons and common fields. d. 8vo. *Cambridge Press.*   10s. 6d.

Hood and Challis. Conveyancing and settled land acts. r. 8vo. *Reeves.*   15s.

Edwards, W. D. Compendium of the law of property in land. 8vo.   20s.

Leake, S. M. Digest of the law of property in land. d. 8vo. 2 vols.
Stevens and Haynes.   44s.

Elton, C. Copyholds and customary tenures. 8vo. *Wildy.*   20s.

Scriven, J. Copyhold and law of manors. Ed. A. Brown. 8vo. *Butterworth.*   30s.

Woodfall, W. Landlord and tenant. Ed. J. M. Lely. r. 8vo. *Sweet and Maxwell.*   38s.

Pollock and Wright. Possession in the common law. d. 8vo. *Clar. Press.*   8s. 6d.

Gale, C. J. Law of easements. Ed. Cave. r. 8vo. *Sweet and Maxwell.*   26s.

Goddard, J. L. Law of easements. d. 8vo. *Stevens.*   21s.

Shelford, L. Real property statutes. Ed. T. Carson. *Sweet and Maxwell.*
New edition in press.

Dart, J. H. Vendors and purchasers of real estate. Ed. Barber, etc. r. 8vo. 2 vols. *Stevens.*   75s.

Fry, E. Specific performance. r. 8vo. *Butterworth.*   36s.

Tudor, O. D. Leading cases on real property. r. 8vo. *Butterworth.*   52s. 6d.

V. TRUSTS, SETTLEMENTS, AND FAMILY RELATIONS:

Godefroi, H. Digest of the principles of the law of trust and trustees. d. 8vo. *Stevens.*   21s.

Lewin, J. Law of trusts. Ed. F. Lewin. r. 8vo. *Sweet and Maxwell.*   42s.

Ellis, A. L. Trustees' guide to investments. 12mo.   3s. 6d.

Smith, J. W. Manual of equity jurisprudence. Ed. Trustram. 12mo. *Stevens.*   12s. 6d.

Vaizey, J. S. Settlements of property. r. 8vo.   78s.

  ,, Investment of trust money. d. 8vo.   9s.
Mainly extracted from the author's larger work on settlements.

Williams, R. V. Executors and administrators. Ed. Williams. r. 8vo. 2 vols. *Stevens.*
In preparation.

Croswell, S. Executors and administrators. 8vo. (*Boston*).   31s. 6d.

Macqueen, P. J. Husband and wife. Ed. Russell. r. 8vo. *Sweet and Maxwell.*   25s.

Simpson, A. J. Infants. 8vo. *Stevens and Haynes.*   22s.
New ed. in preparation.

Schouler, J. Law of the domestic relations. 8vo (*Boston*).   31s. 6d.

Eversley, W. P. Law of the domestic relations. r. 8vo. *Stevens and Haynes.*   52s. 6d.

VI. COPYRIGHT, PATENTS, ETC.:

Copinger, W. A. Law of copyright. 8vo. *Stevens and Haynes.*   30s.

Shortt, J. Law of literature and art. d. 8vo. *Reeves and Turner.*   30s.

Scrutton, T. E. Law of copyright. 8vo. *Clowes.*   2s.
New and re-cast edition. More concise than the foregoing.

Aston, T. Patents, designs, and trade marks. r. 8vo. *Stevens.*   6s.

Daniel, E. M. Patents, designs, and trade marks. 8vo.   8s. 6d.

Mushet, R. S. Law of trade marks. c. 8vo. *Smith, Elder.*   5s.

VII. CONTRACT:

Anson, W. R. Principles of the English law of contract. d. 8vo. *Clar. Press.*   12s. 6d.

Addison, C. G. Contracts. Ed. H. Smith. r. 8vo. *Stevens.*   50s.

Chitty. Contracts. Ed. Lely and Geary. r. 8vo.   30s.
Chitty has been more lately re-edited than Addison.

Leake, S. M. Elementary digest of the law of contracts. d. 8vo. *Stevens.*   38s.
<small>An excellent book, but hardly elementary in the ordinary sense.</small>

Hare, J. Clark. Law of contracts. 8vo. *Low.*   26s.

Pollock, F. Principles of contract. d. 8vo. *Stevens.*   28s.

Langdell. C. C. Summary of the law of contracts. 12mo. (*Boston*).   12s. 6d.

Finch, G. B. Selection of cases on the English law of contracts. r. 8vo.
Cambridge Press.   28s.
<small>A selection of original authorities (not annotated) to be studied concurrently with a text-book.</small>

—VIII. COMMERCIAL :

Smith, J. Mercantile law. Ed. J. Macdonell. r. 8vo. 2 vols. *Stevens.*   42s.
<small>With new historical introduction.</small>

Story, J. Agency. 8vo. *Low.*   35s.
<small>A classical work in England as well as America.</small>

Benjamin, J. P. Sale of personal property. Ed. Pearson and Boyd. r. 8vo.
Sweet and Maxwell.   38s.

Blackburn, Lord. Contract of sale (of goods). Ed. J. C. Graham. r. 8vo.
Stevens.   21s.
<small>Benjamin and Blackburn cover the same ground to some extent, but a good lawyer ought to be familiar with both.</small>

Ker, W. C. Digest of the law of sale of goods. 8vo. *Reeves and Turner.*   6s.
<small>Concise and handy.</small>

Chalmers, J. Sale of goods. d. 8vo.   10s.
<small>Codified digest ; somewhat fuller than Ker.</small>

  ,,   Digest of the law of bills of exchange. d. 8vo. *Stevens.*   16s.

Maude and Pollock. Merchant shipping. r. 8vo. 2 vols. *Sweet and Maxwell.*   70s.

Maclachlan, D. Merchant shipping. r. 8vo. *Sweet and Maxwell.*   40s.

Arnould, J. Marine insurance. Ed. Maclachlan. r. 8vo. 2 vols. *Stevens.*   60s.

Tudor, O. D. Leading cases on mercantile and maritime law. r. 8vo.
2 vols. *Stevens.*   42s.

Lindley, Lord. Partnership. r. 8vo. *Sweet and Maxwell.*   35s.
<small>The fifth edition of "Lindley on Partnership," re-cast in 2 vols., each complete in itself.</small>

  ,,   Company law. r. 8vo.   50s. 6d.

Pollock, F. Digest of the law of partnership. d. 8vo. *Stevens.*   7s. 6d.
<small>Incorporating Partnership Act, 1890.</small>

Buckley, H. B. Companies Acts. r. 8vo. *Stevens and Haynes.*   32s.

Palmer and Macnaghten. Company precedents. r. 8vo. *Stevens.*   34s.

—IX. CIVIL WRONGS :

Bigelow, M. M. Elements of the law of torts. c. 8vo. *Cambridge Press.*   10s. 6d.

Addison, C. G. Wrongs and their remedies. Ed. Smith. r. 8vo. *Stevens.*   38s.

Pollock, F. Law of torts. 8vo. *Stevens.*   21s.

Cooley, T. M. Law of torts. 8vo. (*Chicago*).   35s.

Bigelow, M. M. Leading cases on the law of torts. 8vo. (*Boston*).   31s. 6d.

Roberts and Wallace. Duty and liability of employers. 8vo. *Reeves and
Turner.*   15s.

Beven, T. Negligence. r. 8vo. *Stevens and Haynes.*   42s.

Campbell, R. Negligence. 8vo. *Stevens and Haynes.*   12s.

Smith, H. Negligence. d. 8vo. *Stevens.*   12s. 6d.

Odgers, W. B. Libel and slander. r. 8vo. *Stevens.*   32s.

—X. LAW OF EVIDENCE:

Taylor, J. Pitt. Law of evidence. r. 8vo. *Sweet and Maxwell.*   75s.
Exhaustive.

Stephen, J. F. Digest of the law of evidence. c. 8vo. *Macmillan.*   6s.
Concise.

Best, W. Principles of evidence. Ed. J. M. Lely. r. 8vo. *Sweet and Maxwell.*   32s.

Bigelow, M. M. Law of estoppel. 8vo. *Low.*   31s. 6d.

Wharton, F. Evidence in civil cases. 8vo. 2 vols. (*Philadelphia*).   63s.

,,   Evidence in criminal cases. 8vo. (*Philadelphia*).   35s.

Greenleaf, S. Treatise on evidence. 8vo. 3 vols. *Low.*   84s.

—XI. SPECIAL JURISDICTIONS:

Story, J. Equity jurisprudence. Ed. Bigelow. 8vo. 2 vols. *Low.*   73s. 6d.

Spence, G. Equitable jurisdiction of the Court of Chancery.   O.P.
Easily accessible; still of great historical value.

Langdell. Equity pleading. 8vo. (*Cambridge, U.S.*).   15s.

Phillimore, R. Ecclesiastical law. Ed. Sir W. Phillimore. 8vo. 2 vols.
Sweet and Maxwell.   30s.

Williams and Bruce. Admiralty practice. 8vo. *Sweet and Maxwell.*   35s.

Thring and others. Manual of military law (official). *Eyre.*   2s. 6d.

—XII. REFERENCE:

Fisher's digest (with consolidated and annual supplements). Ed. Mews
and others. r. 8vo. 7 vols. *Sweet and Maxwell.*   £12 12s.
Fisher's *Digest* and the *Equity Index* are the working lawyer's guides to the great
bulk of modern law contained in reported cases. The *Digest to the Law Reports* contains
only cases reported in the *Law Reports* from 1865 onwards.

Chitty's "Equity Index." Ed. Hirst. r. 8vo. 9 vols. *Stevens.*   £12 12s.
Vol. i., ii., iii. v., vi., vii., viii., 31s. 6d. each; vol. iv., 12s.; vol. ix., "Names of cases," 21s.

Digest to the law reports (Annual). Ed. Emden and Thompson. r. 8vo.
Clowes.   About 6s.

Dale and Lehmann. Digest of cases over-ruled. r. 8vo. *Stevens.*   50s.

Williams' notes to Saunders' reports. Ed. E. V. Williams. r. 8vo. 2 vols.
Reeves and Turner.   50s.

Smith's leading cases. Ed. Collins and Arbuthnot. r. 8vo. *Sweet and
Maxwell.*   75s.
Both Williams', Saunders' and Smith's *Leading cases* are commentaries which have
outgrown their text and become repertories of miscellaneous learning; and both are as nearly
authoritative as it is possible for modern law books to be. The contents are made available by
full indexes.

Leading cases in equity. Ed. White and Tudor. r. 8vo. 2 vols. *Sweet
and Maxwell.*   84s.

Wallace. The reporters. Ed. Heard. 8vo. (*Boston*).   30s.
A bibliographical and antiquarian classic.

Sweet. Catalogue of modern law books. *Sweet.*   O.P.

Soule. Lawyer's reference manual of law books and citations. 8vo. *Soule*
(*Boston*).   21s.
Useful as general guides to legal bibliography, customary abbreviations in citing text-books
and reports, etc. Soule is naturally fuller as regards American law reports and literature, and
is altogether the more elaborate work. An annual continuation of Sweet's catalogue was pro-
jected, but not carried out.

Foss, E. Biographia juridica (a biographical dictionary of the judges of England). 8vo. *Murray.*   21s.

,,   Tabulae curiales. *Murray.*   O.P.
A most useful handbook of judicial chronology.

ENGLAND: LITERATURE:

See also ANGLO-SAXON.

—I. HISTORY AND CRITICISM:

Craik, G. L. History of English literature. r. 8vo. 2 vols. *Griffin.*   25s.

Taine, H. History of English literature. Tr. c. 8vo. 4 vols. *Chatto.*   30s.
Also in two vols., 15s.

Arnold, T. Manual of English literature. p. 8vo. *Longmans.*   7s. 6d.

Ward, A. W. History of English dramatic literature. 8vo. 2 vols. *Macmillan.*   32s.

Saintsbury, G. History of Elizabethan literature. c. 8vo. *Macmillan.*   7s. 6d.

Gosse, E. History of the literature of the eighteenth century. p. 8vo. *Macmillan.*   7s. 6d.

—II. 1100–1500. THE MIDDLE AGES:

Brink, B. ten, Early English literature. Tr. H. M. Kennedy. c. 8vo. *Bell (Bohn).*   3s. 6d.

Morley, H. English writers. p. 8vo. *Cassell.*   15s.
Vol. iii., Conquest to Chaucer; vol. iv., v., Fourteenth century. 5s. each.

Warton, T. History of English poetry. Ed. Hazlitt. r. 8vo. 4 vols. *Tegg.* pub. 42s.   O.P.

Altenglische Sprachproben. Ed. Mätzner. r. 8vo. *(Berlin).*   24s.

Morris and Skeat. Specimens of early English. ex. f. 8vo. 2 parts. *Clar. Press.*   16s. 6d.
Part i., 1150–1300, 9s.; part ii., 1298–1393, 7s. 6d.

Anglo-Saxon Chronicle. Ed. Thorpe. r. 8vo. 2 vols. *Rolls Series.*   20s.
Vol. i., Text, 10s.; vol. ii., Translation, 10s.

Two of the Saxon Chronicles; parallel. Ed. Earle. c. 8vo. *Clar. Press.*   3s.

Layamon's Brut. Ed. Madden. r. 8vo. 3 vols. *Soc. of Antiquaries.* 1847. pub. 63s.   O.P.

The Ormulum. Ed. White and Holt. ex. f. 8vo. 2 vols. *Clar. Press.*   21s.

Genesis and Exodus (Early English Text Society). Ed. Morris. d. 8vo. *Trübner.*   8s.

Old English homilies (E.E.T.S.). Ed. Morris. d. 8vo. 2 ser., 8s. each. *Trübner.*   16s.

An old English miscellany (E.E.T.S.). Ed. Morris. d. 8vo. *Trübner.*   10s.

Havelok the Dane (E.E.T.S.). Ed. Madden and Skeat. d. 8vo. *Trübner.*   10s.

Ancren Riwle. Ed. Morton. sm. 4to. *Camden Soc.*

Owl and nightingale. Ed. Stratmann. 8vo. *Kramer.*

Robert of Gloucester's chronicle. Ed. Wright. r. 8vo. *Rolls Series.*   10s.

Michel, D. Ayenbite of Inwyt (E.E.T.S.). Ed. Morris. d. 8vo. *Trübner.*   10s. 6d.

De Hampole, R. R. The prick of conscience. (Philol. Soc.). Ed. E. Morris. *Trübner.*   12s.

Cursor mundi (E.E.T.S.). Ed. Morris. *Trübner.*
> In course of publication. Part i., 10s. 6d.; part ii., 15s.; part iii., 15s.; part iv., 10s.; part v., 25s.

Mannyng (of Brunne), R. Handlyng synne. Ed. F. J. Furnivall. 4to. *Roxburghe Club.*

Minot, L. Poems. Ed. Hall. ex. f. 8vo. *Clar. Press.*   4s. 6d.

Wyclif, J. Select English works. Ed. Arnold. 8vo. 3 vols. *Clar. Press.*   21s.

   ,,   English works hitherto unprinted (E.E.T.S.). Ed. Matthew. d. 8vo. *Trübner.*   20s.

Lechler, G. V. John Wycliffe and his English precursors. Tr. Lorimer. 8vo. *R. T. S.*   8s.

Langland, W. Vision of William concerning Piers the ploughman. Ed. Skeat. 8vo. 2 vols. *Clar. Press.*   31s. 6d.
> Also *Trübner* (*E.E.T.S.*), 3 vols., 35s. 6d.

Chaucer, G. Poetical works. Ed. Morris. f. 8vo. 6 vols., 5s. each. *Bell.*   30s.
> Also in 6 vols., 1s. 6d. each; and in same type.

   ,,   Minor poems. Ed. Skeat. c. 8vo. *Clar. Press.*   10s. 6d.

   ,,   Legend of good women. Ed. Skeat. c. 8vo. *Clar. Press.*   6s.

   ,,   Prologue, Knightes Tale, Nonne Preestes Tale. Ed. Morris and Skeat. ex. f. 8vo. *Clar. Press.*   2s. 6d.

   ,,   Prioresses Tale, Sir Thopas, Monkes Tale, Clerkes Tale, Squieres Tale. Ed. Skeat. ex. f. 8vo. *Clar. Press.*   4s. 6d.

   ,,   Man of Lawes Tale, Pardoneres Tale, Second Nonnes Tale, Chanouns Yemannes Tale. Ed. Skeat. ex. f. 8vo. *Clar. Press.*   4s. 6d.

Brink, B. ten, Chaucer, Studien zur Geschichte seiner Entwickelung, etc. 8vo. (*Münster*).   4s.

Gower, J. Confessio amantis. Ed. Pauli. 8vo. 3 vols. *Daldy.* 1857. pub. 25s.   O.P.
> Also ed. Morley (*Routledge*), 8vo., 3s. 6d.

Mandeville, J. Voyage and travaile. Ed. Halliwell. 8vo. *Ellis.* 1839.   O.P.

Barbour, J. The Bruce (E.E.T.S.). Ed. Skeat. d. 8vo. 3 parts. *Trübner.*   37s.

James I. The king's quair. Ed. Skeat. 8vo. *Scottish Text Soc.*

Blind Harry. Wallace. Ed. Moir. *Scottish Text Soc.*

Hoccleve (or Occleve), T. Poems. Ed. Mason. (*London*). 1796.   O.P.

The governail of princes. Ed. Wright. *Roxburghe Club.*

Fortescue, J. The governance of England. Ed. Plummer. 8vo. *Clar. Press.*   12s. 6d.

Pecock, R. The repressor of over-much blaming of the clergy. Ed. Babington. r. 8vo. 2 vols., 10s. each. *Rolls Series.*   20s.

Chevy Chase (in "English and Scottish popular ballads"). Ed. Child. 4to. 8 parts. (*Boston*).   130s.

Malory, T. Morte d'Arthur. Ed. Sommer and Lang. r. 8vo. 3 vols.; 30s. (vol. iii. in prep.). *Nutt.*
> Also *Macmillan* (Globe series), 3s. 6d.

Skelton, J. Poems. Ed. Dyce. 8vo. 2 vols. *Bohn.* pub. 12s.   O.P.

Tyndale, W. Obedience of a Christian man. Ed. Lovett. 8vo. *R. T. S.*   2s. 6d.

More, T. History of Edward V. and Richard III. 8vo. *A. Murray.*   O.P.

Dunbar, W. Poems (Arber's reprints). Ed. Small and others. 12mo. *Arber.*   3s. 6d.

Surrey, Wyatt, etc. Tottel's Miscellany (Arber's reprints). 12mo. *Arber.*   2s. 6d.

Ascham, R. Toxophilus (Arber's reprints). 12mo. *Arber.*   3*s.*

,, The Scholemaster. 12mo. *Bell (Bohn).*   1*s.*

Sackville, T. Works. Ed. West. 12mo. *J. R. Smith.*   4*s.*

Udall, N. Roister Doister (Arber's reprints). 12mo. *Arber.*   1*s. 6d.*

Lyndsay, D. Works (E.E.T.S.). Ed. Small and others. 3 parts. *Trübner.*   9*s.*

The complaint of Scotland (E.E.T.S.). Ed. Murray. 2 parts. *Trübner.*   18*s.*

Elyot, T. The boke named the governor. Ed. Croft. 4to. 2 vols. *Paul.*   50*s.*

Douglas, Gavin. Works. Ed. Small. p. 8vo. 4 vols. *Sotheran.*   63*s.*

Pollard, A. W. Miracle plays. c. 8vo. *Clar. Press.*   7*s. 6d.*

—III. 1580–1630. AGE OF SHAKESPEARE AND BACON :

For Shakespeare, see SHAKESPEARE.

Spenser, E. Works. Ed. Grosart. r. 8vo. *Routledge.*   7*s. 6d.*

,, Works (Globe series). Ed. Morris. gl. 8vo. *Macmillan.*   3*s. 6d.*

,, Faerie Queen ; books i. and ii. Ed. Kitchen and Mayhew. ex. f. 8vo. 2*s. 6d.* each. *Clar. Press.*   5*s.*

Hooker, R. Ecclesiastical polity. Ed. Keble. m. 8vo. 3 vols. *Clar. Press.*   36*s.*

Bacon, F. Works. Ed. Spedding and others. 8vo. 7 vols. *Longmans.*   73*s. 6d.*

,, Essays ("Golden Treasury" ser.). Ed. Wright. 18mo. *Macmillan.*   4*s. 6d.*

,, Advancement of learning. Ed. Wright. ex. f. 8vo. *Clar. Press.*   4*s. 6d.*

,, Life of Henry VII. Ed. Lumby. ex. f. 8vo. *Pitt Press.*   3*s.*

Spedding, J. Letters and life of Francis Bacon. 8vo. 7 vols. *Longmans.*   84*s.*

Lily, J. Euphues (Arber's reprints). 8vo. *Arber.*   4*s.*

Sidney, P. An apologie for poetrie (Arber's reprints). 12mo. *A. Murray.*   6*d.*

Jonson, B. Works. Ed. Gifford and Cunningham. p. 8vo. 3 vols. *Chatto.*   18*s.*

Symonds, J. A. Ben Jonson ("English Worthies" ser.). f. 8vo. *Longmans.*   2*s. 6d.*

Beaumont and Fletcher. Works. Ed. Dyce. 8vo. 11 vols. *Moxon.* pub. 12*s.* each.   O.P.
Also r. 8vo. 2 vols. *Routledge.* 21*s.*

Marlowe, C. Works. Ed. Dyce. 8vo. *Routledge.*   7*s. 6d.*
Also c. 8vo. *Chatto.* 6*s.*

Chapman, G. Homer's Iliad and Odyssey. c. 8vo. *Chatto.*   6*s.*

Drayton, M. Complete works. Ed. Hooper. 12mo. 3 vols. *J. R. Smith.*   15*s.*

Daniel, S. Complete works in verse and prose. Ed. Grosart. 4to. 3 vols.
Printed for private circulation.

Raleigh, Wotton, etc. Poems. Ed. Hannah. f. 8vo. *Bell.*   2*s. 6d.*

Herbert, G. Poetical works. Ed. Grosart. f. 8vo. *Bell.*   2*s. 6d.*

Drummond, W. Poetical works. Ed. Turnbull. p. 8vo. *Reeves and Turner.*   4*s.*

Famous Elizabethan plays, expurgated and adapted for modern readers. Ed. Fitzgibbon. p. 8vo. *Allen.*   7*s. 6d.*
Plays of Dekker, Beaumont and Fletcher, Ben Jonson, Massinger, Ford.

—IV. 1630–60. AGE OF MILTON:

Milton, J. Poetical works. Ed. H. J. Todd. 8vo. 5 vols. *Rivington.*   42*s.*

   ,,   ,,   ,,   Ed. Masson. 8vo. 3 vols. *Macmillan.*   42*s.*
Also f. 8vo., 3 vols., 15*s.*, and "Globe" edition, 3*s.* 6*d.*

   ,,   Prose writings. Ed. Morley. l. c. 8vo. *Routledge.*   3*s.* 6*d.*

Cleveland, C. D. Complete concordance to the poetical works of Milton.
12mo. *Low.* pub. 6*s.*   O.P.

Masson, D. Life of John Milton. 8vo. 6 vols. *Macmillan.*
Vol. i. and vi., 21*s.*; vol. ii., O.P.; vol. iii., 18*s.*; vol. iv., v., 32*s.*

Marvel, A. Poetical works. p. 8vo. *A. Murray.*   2*s.* 6*d.*

Herrick, T. Poetical works. Ed. Hazlitt. 12mo. 2 vols. *J. R. Smith.*   8*s.*
Also selections ("Golden Treasury" ser.). *Macmillan.* 4*s.* 6*d.*

Clarendon. History of the Great Rebellion. Ed. Macray. c. 8vo. 6 vols.
Clar. Press.   45*s.*

Brown, Sir T. Works. Ed. Wilkin. p. 8vo. 3 vols., 3*s.* 6*d.* each. *Bell*
(*Bohn*).   10*s.* 6*d.*
Vol. i., Vulgar errors; vol. ii., Religio Medici or Garden of Cyprus; vol. iii., Urn burial,
tracts, and correspondence.

   ,,   Religio Medici, etc. ("Golden Treasury" ser.). Ed. Greenhill.
18mo. *Macmillan.*   4*s.* 6*d.*

Cowley, A. Essays. 18mo. *Low.*   2*s.* 6*d.*

The King and the Commons; Cavalier and Puritan song. Ed. Morley.
18mo. *Low.*   2*s.* 6*d.*

Hobbes, T. Leviathan. 8vo. *Routledge.*   1*s.*

Walton, I. Lives of Dr. Donne, Sir Henry Wotton, etc. Ed. Cooke. 12mo.
S. P. C. K.   4*s.*

Taylor, Jeremy. Liberty of prophesying. Ed. Cattermole. 12mo. *Virtue.*
1836.   2*s.* 6*d.*

Fuller, T. History of the worthies of England. Ed. Nuttall. p. 8vo.
3 vols. *Tegg.* pub. 18*s.*   O.P.

Vaughan, H. Silex scintillans. 8vo. *Bell.*   2*s.* 6*d.*

Orme, W. Life and times of Richard Baxter. 8vo.   O.P.

—V. 1660–1700. AGE OF DRYDEN:

Dryden, J. Works. Ed. Saintsbury. 8vo. 18mo. *Paterson.*   191*s.*
In course of publication.

   ,,   Poetical works. Ed. Hooper. f. 8vo. 5 vols., 5*s.* each. *Bell.*   25*s.*
Also cheap edition, 7*s.* 6*d.*, and in "Globe" series. *Macmillan.* 3*s.* 6*d.*

   ,,   Selected dramatic works. Ed. Seton. p. 8vo. *Hamilton, Adams.*   5*s.*

Butler, S. Hudibras. p. 8vo. *Bell (Bohn).*   5*s.*

Locke, J. Works. p. 8vo. 2 vols., 3*s.* 6*d.* each. *Bell (Bohn).*   7*s.*

Pepys, S. Diary. Ed. Braybrooke. c. 8vo. 4. vols. *Bell (Bohn).*   20*s.*
Also c. 8vo. *Warne.* 3*s.* 6*d.*

Evelyn, J. Diary. Ed. Bray and Wheatley. 8vo. 4 vols. *Bickers.*   48*s.*
Also c. 8vo. 4 vols. *Bell (Bohn).* 20*s.*

Bunyan, John. Pilgrims progress. etc. Ed. Venables. ex. f. 8vo. *Clar.*
Press.   5*s.*

Brown, J. John Bunyan, his life, times, and work. d. 8vo. *Isbister.*   7*s.* 6*d.*

Osborne, Dorothy. Letters. Ed. Parry. p. 8vo. *Griffith.*   6*s.*

Burnet, G. History of his own times. 8vo. 6 vols. *Clar. Press.*   O.P.

Congreve, W. Plays. Ed. Ewald. p. 8vo. *Vizetelly.*   2*s.* 6*d.*

VI. 1700–40. AGE OF ADDISON AND POPE:

Addison and Steele, etc. The Spectator. Ed. Morley. c. 8vo. 3 vols. *Routledge.*   10*s.* 6*d.*

Dobson, A. Life of Steele. f. 8vo. *Longmans.*   2*s.* 6*d.*

Macaulay, T. B. Essay on Addison. 8vo. *Longmans.*   1*s.*

Pope, A. Life and works. Ed. Croker, Elwin, and Courthope. 8vo. 10 vols., 10*s.* 6*d.* each. *Murray.*   105*s.*

     ,,   Works. c. 8vo. 4 vols., 5*s.* each. *Bell (Bohn).*   20*s.*
       Also "Globe" edition. *Macmillan.* 3*s.* 6*d.*

     ,,   Essay on man. Ed. Pattison. ex. f. 8vo. *Clar. Press.*   1*s.* 6*d.*

Defoe, D. Earlier life and works. Ed. H. Morley. p. 8vo. *Routledge.*   3*s.* 6*d.*

Minto, W. Daniel Defoe ("Eng. Men of Letters" ser.). c. 8vo. *Macmillan.*   1*s.* 6*d.*

Swift, J. Works. r. 8vo. 2 vols. *Bell.*   24*s.*

     ,,   Tale of a tub, and other works. Ed. H. Morley. l. c. 8vo. *Routledge.*   3*s.* 6*d.*

Craik, H. Life of Swift. 8vo. *Murray.*   18*s.*

Thackeray, W. M. The English humorists of the 18th century. l. 8vo. *Smith, Elder.* illus.   10*s.* 6*d.*
       Also at 3*s.* 6*d.*, and in cheaper editions.

—VII. 1740–90. AGE OF DR. JOHNSON:

Johnson, S. Lives of the poets. Ed. Mrs. Napier. c. 8vo. 3 vols., 3*s.* 6*d.* each. *Bell (Bohn).*   10*s.* 6*d.*

Boswell, J. Selected essays. Ed. Reid. 18mo. *Scott.*   1*s.*

     ,,   Life of Johnson. Ed. Croker. m. 8vo. *Murray.*   12*s.*

Goldsmith, O. Works. c. 8vo. 5 vols., 3*s.* 6*d.* each. *Bell (Bohn).*   17*s.* 6*d.*
       Also "Globe" edition. *Macmillan.* 3*s.* 6*d.*

Forster, J. Life of Oliver Goldsmith. d. 8vo. 2 vols. *Ward.*   10*s.*
       Also cheaper edition at 2*s.*

Burke, E. Select works. Ed. Payne. ex. f. 8vo. 3 vols. *Clar. Press.*   14*s.* 6*d.*

Richardson, S. Works. 8vo. 12 vols. (calf). *Sotheran.* pub. 126*s.*   O.P.
       Also (in rather small type), *Pamela, Sir Charles Grandison,* and *Clarissa Harlowe.* c. 8vo. 2*s.* each. *Routledge.* Second-hand copies of old editions can be frequently obtained at intermediate prices.

Fielding, H. Works. 8vo. 5 vols. *Routledge.*   25*s.*
       Also r. 8vo. *Bell.* 14*s.*

Smollett, T. Works. 8vo. 6 vols. *Routledge.*   30*s.*
       Also r. 8vo. *Bell.* 14*s.*

Sterne, L. Works. Ed. J. P. Brown. 4 vols. *Sotheran.* pub. 94*s.* 6*d.*   O.P.
       Also *Nimmo,* 5*s.*; and *Routledge,* 3*s.* 6*d.*

Traill, H. D. Sterne ("Eng. Men of Letters" ser.). c. 8vo. *Macmillan.*   1*s.* 6*d.*

Hume, D. Philosophical works. 8vo. 4 vols. *Longmans.*   56*s.*

     ,,   Essays. 8vo. *Warne.*   3*s.* 6*d.*

Huxley, T. H. Hume ("Eng. Men of Letters" ser.). c. 8vo. *Macmillan.*   1*s.* 6*d.*

Smith, Adam. Wealth of nations. Ed. Rogers. 8vo. 2 vols. *Clar. Press.*   21*s.*
       Also c. 8vo. *Routledge.* 3*s.* 6*d.*

Sheridan, R. B. Works. 8vo. 2 vols. *Bickers.*   21*s.*
       Also *Routledge,* 6*s.*; and *Bell (Bohn),* 3*s.* 6*d.*

Walpole, H. Letters. d. 8vo. 9 vols. *Bentley.*   94*s.* 6*d.*

Gray, T. Works. Ed. Gosse. gl. 8vo. 4 vols. *Macmillan.*   20*s.*
<small>Vol. i., Poems, journals, and essays; vols. ii. and iii., Letters (specially worth reading): ol. iv., Notes on Aristophanes and Plato.</small>

Chesterfield, Lord. Letters. Ed. Lord Carnarvon. r. 8vo. *Clar. Press.* illus.   . 21*s.*
<small>Also *Gibbings*, 7*s.* 6*d.*, and selection, *Low*, 2*s.* 6*d.*</small>

"Junius." Letters. c. 8vo. 2 vols., 3*s.* 6*d.* each. *Bell (Bohn).*   7*s.*
<small>Also c. 8vo. *Routledge.* 3*s.* 6*d.*</small>

Blake, W. Songs of innocence. Ed. Rossetti. f. 8vo. *Bell.*   2*s.* 6*d.*

Scott, W. Lives of eminent novelists and dramatists. c. 8vo. *Warne.*   2*s.*

Gibbon, E. Autobiography and correspondence. c. 8vo. *Warne.*   2*s.*

Oliphant, Mrs. Historical sketches. p. 8vo. *Blackwood.*   6*s.*

Seeley, L. B. Fanny Burney and her friends. 8vo. *Seeley.*   7*s.* 6*d.*

—VIII. 1790–1830. AGE OF BURNS, SCOTT, WORDSWORTH :

Burns, R. Works. c. 8vo. 3 vols., 5*s.* each. *Bell (Bohn).*   15*s.*
<small>Also Ed. Alex. Smith, in "Globe" series. *Macmillan.* 3*s.* 6*d.*</small>

Lockhart, J. G. Life of Burns. p. 8vo. *Bell (Bohn).*   3*s.* 6*d.*

Cowper, W. Poetical works ("Globe" ser.). Ed. Benham. gl. 8vo. *Macmillan.*   3*s.* 6*d.*

  ,,   Letters. Ed. Southey. p. 8vo. 4 vols., 3*s.* 6*d.* each. *Bell (Bohn).* illus.   14*s.*
<small>This edition, including poems, etc., is complete in 8 vols., 28*s.*</small>

Wordsworth, W. Poetical works (The Editio princeps). Ed. Knight. 8vo. 8 vols., 15*s.* each. *Paterson.*   120*s.*

  ,,   Poetical works. Ed. Rossetti. 8vo. *Ward.*   5*s.*
<small>Also Ed. John Morley. gl. 8vo. *Macmillan.* 7*s.* 6*d.*</small>

Wordsworth and Coleridge. Lyrical ballads. Ed. Dowden. 16mo. *Nutt.*   7*s.* 6*d.*

Wordsworthiana. Ed. Knight. c. 8vo. *Macmillan.*   7*s.* 6*d.*

Scott, W. Poetical works. f. 8vo. 12 vols. *Black.* illus. Turner.   38*s.*

  ,,   Poetical works. r. 8vo. *Black.* illus. Turner.   18*s.*
<small>Also "Globe" edition. Ed. Palgrave. *Macmillan.* 3*s.* 6*d.*</small>

  ,,   The Waverley novels. l. 8vo. 25 vols., 8*s.* 6*d.* each. *Black.* illus.   £10 12*s.* 6*d.*

  ,,   The Waverley novels. c. 8vo. 25 vols., 3*s.* 6*d.* each. *Black.* illus.   87*s.* 6*d.*
<small>Also several cheaper editions by *Black.*</small>

  ,,   Journals. 8vo. 2 vols. *Douglas.*   32*s.*

Lockhart, J. G. Life of Scott. f. 8vo. 10 vols. *Black.*   30*s*
<small>Abridged in one vol., 6*s.*</small>

Coleridge, S. T. Poetical works. f. 8vo. 4 vols. *Macmillan.*   31*s.* 6*d.*
<small>Also 2 vols. *Bell.* 5*s.*; and selections, with preface, by Swinburne. *Low.* 2*s.* 6*d.*</small>

  ,,   Biographia literaria. 12mo. *Bell.*   3*s.* 6*d.*

Byron, Lord. Works. 8vo. 6 vols. *Murray.*   45*s.*
<small>Also r. 8vo. (double columns, with rather small type). 7*s.* 6*d.*</small>

  ,,   Select poems ("Golden Treasury" ser.). Ed. Arnold. 18mo. *Macmillan.*   4*s.* 6*d.*

  ,,   Childe Harold. Ed. Tozer. ex. f. 8vo. *Clar. Press.*   3*s* 6*d.*

Shelley, P. B. Works. Ed. Forman. 8vo. 8 vols. *Reeves and Turner.*   100*s.*
<small>Also poetical works. 2 vols. 16*s.*</small>

  ,,   Poetical works. Ed. Dowden. gl. 8vo. *Macmillan.*   7*s.* 6*d.*
<small>Also selections ("Golden Treasury" ser.). *Macmillan.* 4*s.* 6*d.*</small>

Dowden, E. Life of Shelley. 8vo. 2 vols. *Paul.*   36*s.*

Keats, J. Works. Ed. Forman. 8vo. 4 vols. *Reeves and Turner.*   52*s.* 6*d.*
> Also Poetical works, in one vol. *Reeves and Turner*, 8*s.*; *Bell*, 2*s.* 6*d.* Selections ("Golden Treasury" ser.). *Macmillan*. 4*s.* 6*d.*

Hazlitt, W. Spirit of the age. p. 8vo. *Bell (Bohn).*   3*s.* 6*d.*

De Quincey, T. Select essays. Ed. Masson. c. 8vo. 2 vols. *Black.*   7*s.* 6*d.*

Lamb, C. Essays of Elia. Ed. Ainger. gl. 8vo. *Macmillan.*   5*s.*
> Also *Bell*, 3*s.* 6*d.*; and in "Pocket Library." *Routledge.* 1*s.*

Landor, W. S. Imaginary conversations (selected). ("Golden Treasury" ser.). 18mo. *Macmillan.*   4*s.* 6*d*

Bentham, J. Principles of morals and legislation. c. 8vo. *Clar. Press.* pub. 6*s.* 6*d.*   O.P.

Austen, Jane. Works. c. 8vo. 6 vols. *Bentley.*   36*s.*
> Also 5 vols., 2*s.* each (omitting *Lady Susan* and *The Watsons*). *Cassell.* 10*s.*

Smith, Goldwin. Jane Austen. c. 8vo. *Scott.*   1*s.*

—IX. VICTORIAN AGE:

For authors, see ESSAYS, NOVELS, *and* POETRY.

(A) BIOGRAPHY.

Gaskell, Mrs. Life of Charlotte Brontë. c. 8vo. *Smith, Elder.* illus.   5*s.*

Trevelyan, G. O. Life and letters of Lord Macaulay. 8vo. 2 vols. *Longmans.*   36*s.*
> Also edition at 2*s.* 6*d.*

Trollope, A. Thackeray ("Men of Letters" ser.). c. 8vo. *Macmillan.*   1*s.* 6*d.*

Forster, J. Life of Charles Dickens. d. 8vo. 2 vols. *Chapman.*   20*s.*
> Also c. 8vo. 2 vols., 7*s.*

Cross, J. W. Life of Geo. Eliot. c. 8vo. 3 vols. *Blackwood.*   15*s.*
> Also in 1 vol., 7*s.* 6*d.*

Froude, J. A. Life of Thomas Carlyle. 8vo. 4 vols. *Longmans.*   64*s.*
> Also 4 vols., 14*s.*

Celebrities of the century. Ed. Sanders. r. 8vo. *Cassell.*   10*s.* 6*d.*

(B) MISCELLANEOUS WRITERS.
> The works of living authors are excluded.

Brontë, Charlotte. Works. c. 8vo. 7 vols., 5*s.* each. *Smith, Elder.* illus.   35*s.*
> Also at 2*s.* 6*d.*, and cheaper editions.

Macaulay, T. B. Works. 8vo. 8 vols. *Longmans.*   105*s.*
> Also cheaper edition, 4 vols., 10*s.*

Thackeray, W. M. Works. l. 8vo. 26 vols., 10*s.* 6*d.* each. *Smith, Elder.*   £13 13*s.*
> Also 26 vols. at 3*s.* 6*d.* "Pocket" edition (rather small print), 27 vols. at 1*s.* 6*d.*, and many other editions.

Dickens, C. Works. p. 8vo. 30 vols. *Chapman.*   £12
> Also "Charles Dickens" edition. 21 vols. at from 3*s.* to 4*s.* each, the set 76*s.*; and "Pocket" edition (rather small print), 32 vols., 1*s.* 6*d.* each.

Eliot, George. Works. c. 8vo. 21 vols., 5*s.* each. *Blackwood.*   105*s.*
> Also cheaper editions, in 8 vols., from 2*s.* 6*d.* to 7*s.* 6*d.* each; the set, 34*s.* 6*d.*

Carlyle, T. Works. d. 8vo. 34 vols. *Chapman.*   £15 3*s.*
> Also cheaper editions, 37 vols., 1*s.* each.

Browning, R. Works. s. c. 8vo. 17 vols., 5*s.* each. *Smith, Elder.*   85*s.*
> Also Selections, 2 vols., 7*s.*; and "Pocket" edition, 1*s.*

Browning, E. B. Works. s. c. 8vo. 6 vols., 5*s.* each. *Smith, Elder.*   30*s.*
> Also Selections, 2 vols., 7*s.*; and "Pocket" edition, 1*s.*

Arnold, M. Works. c. 8vo. *Macmillan.*

Poetical works, 3 vols., 7*s.* 6*d.* each ; Essays on criticism, 9*s.* ; Essays on criticism, ser. ii., 7*s.* 6*d.* ; Higher schools and universities in Germany, 6*s.* ; Discourses in America, 4*s.* 6*d.* ; Reports on elementary schools, 3*s.* 6*d.*

Also Poetical works, 7*s.* 6*d.* ; and Selections ("Golden Treasury" ser.', 4*s.* 6*d.*

Rossetti, D. G. Works. Ed. W. M. Rossetti. p. 8vo. 2 vols. *Ellis.*   18*s.*

Also one vol. c. 8vo. 6*s.*

Newman, J. H. Works. c. 8vo. 21 vols., 3*s.* 6*d.* each. *Longmans.*   73*s.* 6*d.*

—X. SELECTIONS :

English verse. Ed. Linton and Stoddard. c. 8vo. 5 vols. *Paul.* pub. 5*s.*

each.   O.P.

Vol. i., Chaucer to Burns ; vol. ii., Translations ; vol. iii., Nineteenth century lyrics ; vol. iv., Dramatic scenes ; vol. v., Ballads and romances.

Percy's Reliques of ancient English poetry. Ed. Prichard. 8vo. 2 vols.

Bell (Bohn). 3*s.* 6*d.* each.   7*s.*

Minstrelsy of the Scottish border. Ed. Sir W. Scott. f. 8vo. 2 vols.

Black.   10*s.* 6*d.*

Ward, T. H. The English poets. c. 8vo. 4 vols., 7*s.* 6*d.* each. *Macmillan.*   30*s.*

Vol. i., Chaucer to Donne ; vol. ii., Ben Jonson to Dryden ; vol. iii., Addison to Blake ; vol. iv., Wordsworth to Rossetti.

Specimens of British poets. Ed. Campbell. r. 8vo. *Murray.* pub. 15*s.*   O.P.

Golden treasury of songs and lyrics. Ed. Palgrave. c. 8vo. *Macmillan.*   10*s.* 6*d.*

Also 18mo., 4*s.* 6*d.*

—XI. REFERENCE :

Murray, J. A. H. A new English dictionary on historical principles. i. 4to.

Clar. Press.   44*s.*

In course of publication : vol. i., A and B, 52*s.* 6*d.*

Whitney, W. D. The Century dictionary. *Unwin.*

To be completed in 6 vols., 42*s.* each ; 3 vols. already issued.

Skeat, W. W. Etymological dictionary of the English language. 8vo.

Clar. Press.

Also small ed., c. 8vo., 5*s.* 6*d.*

Chambers' Encyclopædia of English literature. r. 8vo. 2 vols. *Chambers.*   20*s.*

Halliwell (Phillips), J. O. Dictionary of old English plays. 8vo. *J. R.*

Smith.   O.P.

Adams, W. Davenport. Dictionary of English literature. ex. f. 4to.

Cassell.   7*s.* 6*d.*

Morris, R. Historical outlines of English accidence. ex. f. 8vo. *Mac-*

millan.   6*s.*

Oliphant, T. L. K. Old and middle English. gl. 8vo. *Macmillan.*   9*s.*

,, The new English. c. 8vo. 2 vols. *Macmillan.*   21*s.*

Marsh, G. P. Student's manual of the English language. Ed. Smith. p. 8vo.

Murray.   7*s.* 6*d.*

Sievers, E. Old English grammar. Tr. and Ed. Cook. c. 8vo. *Ginn*

(Boston).   6*s.* 6*d.*

Skeat, W. W. Principles of English etymology. c. 8vo. 2 vols. *Clar.*

Press.   19*s.* 6*d.*

Vol. i., The native element, 9*s.*; Vol. ii., The foreign element, 10*s.* 6*d.*

Hodgson, W. B. Errors in the use of English. c. 8vo. *Douglas (Edin.).*   3*s.* 6*d.*

ENGRAVING, *see* ARTISTIC PROCESSES II.

ENSILAGE, *see* AGRICULTURE II.

ENTOMOLOGY, *see* ZOOLOGY VI

ESCHATOLOGY, *see* THEOLOGY II.

ESKIMO, *see* ARCTIC REGIONS.

ESSAYS: ENGLISH:

Only names of essayists of the XIX. Century occur in this list.

Arnold, M. Essays on criticism (1st series, 9s.; 2nd series, 7s. 6d.). p. 8vo. *Macmillan.*	16s. 6d.
,, Irish essays. p. 8vo. *Smith, Elder.*	2s. 6d.
,, Mixed essays. p. 8vo. *Smith, Elder.*	9s.
,, Friendship's garland. p. 8vo. *Smith, Elder.*	O.P.
,, Discourses in America. p. 8vo. *Macmillan.*	4s. 6d.
,, Culture and anarchy. p. 8vo. *Smith, Elder.*	2s. 6d.
Bagehot, W. Literary studies. 8vo. 2 vols. *Longmans.*	28s.
Brown, J. Horae subsecivae. p. 8vo. 3 vols., 7s. 6d. *Douglas.*	22s. 6d.
Carlyle, T. Miscellaneous essays. p. 8vo. 7 vols., 1s. each. *Chapman.*	7s.
Church, R. W. Essays. p. 8vo. *Macmillan.*	5s.
Coleridge, S. T. Aids to reflection (religious). sm. 8vo. *Bell (Bohn).*	3s. 6d.
,, Lectures on Shakespeare, etc. 12mo. *Bell (Bohn).*	3s. 6d.
De Quincey, T. Essays. p. 8vo. 2 vols. *Black.*	7s. 6d.
Dowden, E. Studies in literature. 8vo. *Paul.*	6s.
Emerson, R. W. Essays. 8vo. *Macmillan.*	5s.
Gosse, E. Studies in northern literature. 8vo. *Paul.*	12s.
Hare, J. C., and A. W. Guesses at truth. 12mo. *Macmillan.*	4s. 6d.
Harrison, F. On the choice of books. p. 8vo. *Macmillan.*	6s.
Hazlitt, W. Winterslow. 8vo. *Bell (Bohn).*	3s. 6d.
,, The round table. c. 8vo. *Bell (Bohn).*	3s. 6d.
,, Table talk. c. 8vo. *Bell (Bohn).*	3s. 6d.
Helps, A. Friends in council. p. 8vo. *Smith, Elder.*	15s.
,, Companions of my solitude. p. 8vo. *Smith, Elder.*	7s. 6d.
,, Brevia. p. 8vo. *Bell.*	6s.
,, Essays written in the intervals of business. 12mo. *Smith, Elder.*	4s. 6d.
Hinton, J. The art of thinking, and other essays. p. 8vo. *Paul.*	8s. 6d.
Holmes, O. W. The autocrat of the breakfast table. c. 8vo. *Routledge.*	3s. 6d.
,, The professor at the breakfast table. c. 8vo. *Routledge.*	3s. 6d.
,, The poet at the breakfast table. c. 8vo. *Routledge.*	3s. 6d.
Pocket edition of the three series. 6 vols. *Douglas.* 6s.	
Hutton, R. H. Essays. c. 8vo. 2 vols., 6s. each. *Macmillan.*	12s.
Huxley, T. H. Lay sermons. p. 8vo. *Macmillan.*	7s. 6d.
Lamb, C. Essays of Elia. Ed. Ainger. gl. 8vo. *Macmillan.*	5s.
Pocket edition. *Routledge.* 1s.	
Landor, W. S. Imaginary conversations (selected). 18mo. *Macmillan.*	4s. 6d.

Macaulay, T. B. Essays. 8vo. 3 vols. *Longmans.*   36s.
       Also 4 vols., 21s., and cheaper editions.

Martineau, J. Essays. vol. i. *Longmans.*   7s. 6d.

Mill, J. S. Dissertations and discussions. 8vo. 4 vols. *Longmans.*   46s. 6d.

Pater, W. Appreciations. p. 8vo. *Macmillan.*   8s. 6d.

Saintsbury, G. Essays in English literature, 1780—1860. c. 8vo. *Percival.*   7s. 6d.

Seeley, J. R. Lectures and essays. p. 8vo.

Scott, W. Essays on chivalry, romance, etc. f. 8vo. *Black.*   2s. 6d.

Stephen, Leslie. Hours in a library. p. 8vo. 3 ser., 9s. each. *Smith, Elder.*   27s.

Stevenson, R. L. Virginibus puerisque, and other papers. c. 8vo. *Chatto.*   6s.

    ,,   Memoirs and portraits. c. 8vo. *Chatto.*   6s.

Swinburne, A. C. Essays and studies. p. 8vo. *Chatto.*   12s.

Thoreau, H. D. Walden. 8vo. *Harper (New York).*   7s. 6d.
       Also *Scott*, 1s.

Warner, C. D. My summer in a garden. 12mo. *Low.*   2s. 6d.
       Abounding in humour of a high order.

Wilson, J. Noctes ambrosianae. 8vo. *Clark.*   4s. 6d.

ESTATE MANAGEMENT, *see* AGRICULTURE V.

ETCHING, *see* ARTISTIC PROCESSES I.

ETHICS:

—I. GENERAL AND INTRODUCTORY:

Porter, N. Elements of moral science. 8vo. *Low.*   10s. 6d.

Calderwood, H. Handbook of moral philosophy. c. 8vo. *Macmillan.*   6s.

Bain, A. Moral science. c. 8vo. *Longmans.*   4s. 6d.
       Part ii. of *Mental and moral science* (10s. 6d.). Partly historical.

Wilson and Fowler. Principles of morals. (Part i.). 8vo. *Clar. Press.*   3s. 6d.
       Mainly historical or critical.

Sidgwick, H. Outlines of history of ethics. c. 8vo. *Macmillan.*   3s. 6d.
       Historical handbook.

—II. SYSTEMATIC TREATISES:

(A) TRANSCENDENTALIST OR INTUITIONAL.

Kant, Immanuel. Theory of ethics. Tr. (with the " Critique ") by Abbott. 8vo. *Longmans.*   12s. 6d.

Green, T. H. Prolegomena to ethics. Ed. Bradley. 8vo. *Clar. Press.*   12s. 6d.

Laurie, S. S. Ethica ; or ethics of reason. 8vo. *Williams.*   6s.

Martineau, J. Types of ethical theory. 8vo. 2 vols. *Clar. Press.*   15s.
       Largely historical and critical.

(B) UTILITARIAN.

Mill, J. S. Utilitarianism. 8vo. *Longmans.*   5s.

Sidgwick, H. Methods of ethics. 8vo. *Macmillan.*   14s.
       Largely critical.

Fowler, T. Principles of morals. 8vo. *Clar. Press.*   10s. 6d.
       Part ii. of Fowler and Wilson's *Principles.*

(C) EVOLUTIONAL.

Spencer, H. Data of ethics. 8vo. *Williams.*   8*s*.

Stephen, Leslie. Science of ethics. d. 8vo. *Smith, Elder.*   16*s*.

—III. MISCELLANEOUS:

Butler, Bishop. Sermons on human nature. 8vo. *R. T. S.*   1*s*.

Grote, G. Fragments on ethical subjects. 8vo. *Murray.*   7*s*. 6*d*.

Lecky, W. E. H. History of European morals. c. 8vo. 2 vols. *Longmans*   16*s*.

ETHIOPIA, *see* EGYPT.

ETHIOPIC LANGUAGE:

König, E. Neue Studien über Schrift der aethiopischen Sprache. 8vo. (*Leipzig*).   12*s*.

Dillman, A. Lexicon linguae Ethiopicae. 4to. 3 vols. (*Leipzig*).   80*s*.

ETHNOLOGY, *see* ANTHROPOLOGY.

ETRUSCAN ANTIQUITIES, *see* ITALY II.

EUCHRE, *see* CARDS.

EUCLID, *see* GEOMETRY.

EUROPE:

See also under the different countries.

—I. GEOGRAPHY:

Reclus, E. Universal geography. i. 8vo. 5 vols., 21*s*. each. *Virtue.*   105*s*.
Vol. i., Southern Europe, Greece, Turkey-in-Europe, Roumania, Servia, Italy, Spain, and Portugal; vol. ii., France and Switzerland; vol. iii., Central Europe, Austria-Hungary, Germany, Belgium, the Netherlands; vol. iv., British Isles; vol. v., Scandinavia and Russia.

Stanford's Compendium; Europe (with ethnological appendix by A. H. Keane). l. p. 8vo. *Stanford.* maps and illus.   21*s*.

Freeman, E. A. Historical geography of Europe. 8vo. 2 vols. *Longmans.*   31*s*. 6*d*.
Vol. ii. Atlas showing the changes in European States.

Droysen, G. Historischer Hand-Atlas. fo. (*Leipzig*).   30*s*.

Spruner, C. von. Historisch-geographischer Hand-Atlas. fo. (*Gotha*).   58*s*.
More detailed than Droysen.

—II. HISTORY:

Maine, H. Ancient law. 8vo. *Murray.*   9*s*.
Treats of the influence of Roman law on European institutions.

   ,,   Early law and custom. 8vo. *Murray.*   9*s*.

Freeman, E. A. General sketch of European history. 18mo. *Macmillan.* illus.   3*s*. 6*d*.

Bury, J. B. History of the later Roman Empire (400–800). 8vo. 2 vols. *Macmillan.*   32*s*.

Gibbon, E. Decline and fall of the Roman Empire. 8vo. 8 vols. *Murray.*   60*s*
Best edition; but there is a cheaper one by *Bell.*

Bryce, J. The Holy Roman Empire. c. 8vo. *Macmillan.*   7*s.* 6*d.*

A brilliant essay on the influence of the idea of the Empire.

Church, R. W. The beginning of the middle ages. (elem.). f. 8vo. *Longmans.*   2*s.* 6*d.*

A general sketch to 1000.

Mombert, J. I. The reign of Charlemagne. d. 8vo. *Paul.*   15*s.*

Latham, R. G. The nationalities of Europe. 8vo. 2 vols. *Allen.*   O.P.

Useful for the less important races.

Sybel, H. von. History and literature of the crusades. Tr. 8vo. *Chapman.*   10*s.* 6*d.*

A critical estimate of the authorities.

Kugler, B. Geschichte der Kreuzzüge. 8vo. (*Berlin*).   18*s.*

A good compendium of the whole period.

Wilken, F. Geschichte der Kreuzzüge. 8vo. 6 vols. (*Leipzig*). 1807–32.   O.P.

Fuller; most trustworthy.

Michaud, J. F. History of the crusades. Tr. Robson. c. 8vo. 3 vols. *Routledge.*   10*s.* 6*d.*

Not up to modern critical results, but the fullest account accessible in English.

Ranke, L. von. History of the Latin and Teutonic peoples 1494–1514. Tr. c. 8vo. *Bell* (*Bohn*).   3*s.* 6*d.*

Traces the formation of the modern conception of States.

Ruge, S. Geschichte des Zeitalters der Entdeckungen (In "Allgemeine Geschichte in Einzeldarstellungen"; ed. Oncken). (*Berlin*).   12*s*

A general account of the historical influence of maritime discoveries to 1600.

Hallam, H. View of the state of Europe during the middle ages. c. 8vo. 3 vols. *Murray.*   12*s*

The chapters relating to England have been superseded by more recent works.

Robertson, W. History of the reign of Charles V. c. 8vo. *Routledge.*   10*s*

Lodge, R. History of modern Europe (1453–1878). 8vo. *Murray.*   7*s.* 6*d.*

Dyer, T. H. History of modern Europe (1453–1871). d. 8vo. 5 vols. *Bell.*   52*s.* 6*d.*

Noorden, C. von. Europäische Geschichte im 18ten Jahrhundert. 8vo. (*Leipzig*).

Vol. i., 10*s.*; vol. ii., 12*s.*; vol. iii., 14*s.* In course of publication; has reached 1710.

Schlosser, F. C. History of the 18th century. Tr. 8vo. *Chapman.* 1843–52.   O.P.

Not up to date, but the best detailed account accessible in English.

Weir, A. Historical basis of modern Europe (1760–1815). 8vo. *Sonnenschein.*   4*s.* 6*d.*

A useful sketch of an important period.

Alison, A. History of Europe (1789–1815). c 8vo. 13 vols. *Blackwood.* illus.   51*s.*

Good in general military history.

  ,, The same continued (1815–22). c. 8vo. 8 vols. *Blackwood.* illus.   34*s.*

Fyffe, C. A. History of modern Europe. 8vo. 3 vols., 12*s.* each. *Cassell.*   36*s.*

Hertslet, E. The map of Europe by treaty. r. 8vo. 3 vols. *Butterworth.* pub. 94*s.* 6*d.*   O.P.

European history since 1814.

May, T. E. History of democracy in Europe. 8vo. 2 vols. *Longmans.*   32*s.*

Murdock, H. The reconstruction of Europe (1850–81). c. 8vo. *Watt.*   10*s.* 6*d.*

Mahan, A. T. Influence of sea power upon history (1666–1783). *Low.*   18*s.*

REFERENCE.

George, H. B. Genealogical tables. sm. 8vo. *Clar. Press.*   12*s.*

Blair, J. Genealogical tables. Ed. Rosse. p. 8vo. *Bell.*   10*s.*
    A cheap handbook.

Mas Latrie. Trésor de chronologie. fo. (*Paris*).   80*s.*
    The latest and most detailed information.

L'art de vérifier les dates. 8vo. 44 vols. (*Paris*). 1821–44.   o.p.
    Not superseded by Mas Latrie.

Potthast. Wegweiser durch die Geschichtswerke des Mittelalters.
    375–1500. 8vo. 3 vols. (*Berlin*).   18*s.*
    A list of all the authorities for the history of the middle ages.

Adams, C. K. Manual of historical literature. 8vo. *Low.*   12*s. 6d.*
    A compendious account of the best modern works.

EXAMINATIONS, *see* EDUCATION II.

EXCHANGE, *see* POLITICAL ECONOMY IV.

    ,,   BILLS OF, *see* ENGLAND, LAW VIII.

EXECUTORS, *see* ENGLAND, LAW V.

EXTRADITION, *see* LAW OF NATIONS I.

F.

FABLES, *see* FOLKLORE.

FACTORY LEGISLATION, *see* POLITICAL ECONOMY VI.

FAIRY TALES, *see* FOLKLORE *and* CHILDREN'S BOOKS.

FALCONRY:

Campbell, J. Treatise of modern falconry. 8vo. (*Edinburgh*). 1773.   o.p.

Bilany, J. C. Treatise upon falconry. 8vo. (*Berwick-on-Tweed*). 1841.   o.p.

Burton, R. F. Falconry in the valley of the Indus. p. 8vo. *Van Voorst*
    (now *Gurney*).   6*s.*

Salvin and Brodrick. Falconry in the British Isles. i. 8vo. *Gurney.* illus.   42*s.*

Freeman and Salvin. Falconry, its claims, history, and practice. 8vo.
    Longmans. illus. pub. 10*s. 6d.*   o.p.

Brodrick, W. Falconer's favourites. fo. *Gurney.* illus.   42*s.*

Freeman, G. E. Practical falconry. p. 8vo. *H. Cox.*   o.p.

Harting, J. E. Hints on the management of hawks. 8vo. *H. Cox.* illus.   3*s. 6d.*

    ,,   Bibliotheca accipitraria. *Quaritch.* illus.
    A catalogue of ancient and modern books relating to falconry. In preparation.

FALKLAND ISLANDS, *see* ATLANTIC.

FANS, *see* COSTUME.

FARMING, *see* AGRICULTURE, DAIRY, LIVE-STOCK.

FENCING AND SWORD EXERCISE:

Angelo, M. L'escrime. fo. (*London*). 1763. illus.   o.p
Original edition in folio: 47 engravings.

Prévost, Camille. Théorie pratique de l'escrime. l. 8vo. (*Paris*). illus.   10s.

Dunn, H. A. Colmore. Fencing. ("All England" ser.). sm. 8vo. *Bell.* illus.   1s.

Castle, E. Schools and masters of fence from the middle ages to 18th century. c. 4to. *Bell.* illus.   31s. 6d.

Chapman, G. Foil practice. 8vo.

Vigeant, A. La bibliographie de l'escrime ancienne et moderne. 8vo. (*Paris*). illus.   8s. 6d.

Waite, J. M. Sabre, single-stick; sabre and bayonet. c. 8vo. *Weldon.*   2s. 6d.

FERMENTATION, *see* PHYSIOLOGY III. *and* ANTISEPTICS.

FERNS, *see* BOTANY *and* GARDENING.

FIJI, *see* PACIFIC III.

FINANCE, *see* POLITICAL ECONOMY IV.

FINLAND: LANGUAGE:

Ujfalvy. Grammaire Finnoise. (*Paris*).   5s.

Ahlman. Svenskt Finskt Lexicon. (*Helsingfors*).   10s. 6d.

FIRE INSURANCE, *see* ASSURANCE.

FIREWORKS, *see* GAMES III.

FISHING AND FISHERIES:

See also ZOOLOGY.

For general essays and sketches on angling matters, the reader may be referred to the miscellaneous works of F. Francis, G. Rooper, "Red Spinner," Dr. Hamilton, Sir H. Davy, Dr. John Davy, Hofland, Stodhart, Stewart, Moffatt, Colquhoun, and others whose works are catalogued in *Bibliotheca piscatoria*.

Francis, F. A book on angling. c. 8vo. *Longmans.*   15s.
Complete treatise on the art of angling in every branch; thoroughly practical, and especially valuable in its list of salmon and trout flies.

Cholmondeley-Pennell, H. Fishing ("Badminton Library"). c. 8vo. 2 vols., 10s. 6d. each. *Longmans.*   21s.
Vol. i., Salmon and trout: vol. ii., Pike and coarse fish. Contribution by the best modern authorities, upon every method of angling.

Bickerdyke, J. The book of the all-round angler. c. 8vo. *Gill.* illus.   5s. 6d.
Deals with the coarse fish, pike, game-fish, and sea-fish. Profusely illustrated, and an excellent work for the beginner. Each division is published separately.

Cholmondeley-Pennell, H. Modern improvements in fishing-tackle. c. 8vo. *Low.*   2s.

  ,, The modern practical angler. c. 8vo. *Routledge.* pub. 5s.   o.p.

Keene, J. H. Fishing-tackle. c. 8vo. *Ward and Lock.* illus.   3s. 6d.
The last three are illustrated handbooks for amateur tackle-makers.

Halford, F. M. Floating flies, and how to dress them. 8vo. *Low.*   15s.

Halford, F. M.   Dry fly-fishing in theory and practice.   *Low.*   25*s.*
    Halford's books are beautifully illustrated works for the fly-fisher.

Pritt, T. E.   North country flies.   *Low.*   10*s.* 6*d.*

Theakston, M.   British angling flies.   Ed. Walbran.   c. 8vo.   *Low.*   5*s.*
    These last two are treatises on angling with hackle flies in north country streams.

Ronalds, A.   The fly-fisher's entomology.   8vo.   *Longmans.*   illus.   14*s.*
    Modern edition of an old standard work on the general flies known to trout fishers.

Day, F.   British and Irish salmonidæ.   i. 8vo.   *Cox.*   illus.   21*s.*
    The standard work on the history of the salmonidae.

Willis-Bund, J. W.   Salmon problems.   c. 8vo.   *Low.*   3*s.* 6*d.*

Traherne, Major.   The habits of the salmon.   c. 8vo.   *Chapman.*   illus.   3*s.* 6*d.*
    These two deal with many unsolved problems concerning the life history of the salmon.

Stone, L.   Domesticated trout.   c. 8vo.   *Low.*   illus.   12*s.* 6*d.*

Francis, F.   The practical management of fisheries.   p. 8vo.   *H. Cox.*   3*s.* 6*d.*
    illus.

Palmer, Black.   Scotch loch-fishing.   c. 8vo.   *Blackwood.*   4*s.*

Regan, Hi.   How and where to fish in Ireland.   c. 8vo.   *Low.*   3*s.* 6*d.*
    Indispensable to angler-tourists in Ireland.

Thomas, H. S.   The rod in India.   r. 8vo.   *Hamilton Adams.*   illus.   25*s.*
    Standard work on fish and fishing in India.

Senior, W.   Travel and trout in the Antipodes.   c. 8vo.   *Chatto.*   pub. 6*s.*   O.P.
    Trout streams of Tasmania and New Zealand.

Brown, J. J.   The angler's guide.   12mo.   *Appleton.*   illus.   10*s.* 6*d.*

Hallock, C.   Sportsman's gazetteer.   *Judd.*   15*s.*
    Handbooks to fish and fishing in N. America.

Angler's diary (annual).   p. 8vo.   *Cox.*   1*s.* 6*d.*
    A tourist fisherman's gazetteer of the rivers and lakes of the world; with carefully prepared
    divisions on Norway and Sweden, France and Switzerland.

Wilcocks, J. C.   The sea fisherman.   c. 8vo.   *Longmans.*   illus.   6*s.*
    Exhaustive and technical work.

Bickerdyke, J.   Angling in salt water.   (elem.).   c. 8vo.   *Gill.*   illus.   2*s.*

Manley, J. J.   Fish and fishing.   c. 8vo.   *Low.*   10*s.* 6*d.*
    Brightly written essays on British angling; with chapters on ichthyology, and angling
    literature.

Walton, I.   The compleat angler.   Ed. R. B. Marston.   r. 4to.   *Low.*   illus.   105*s.*
    "Lea and Dove" edition.

Oke's Fishery laws.   Ed. Willis-Bund.   p. 8vo.   *Butterworth.*   6*s.*
    The second edition contains a supplement relating to the Freshwater Fisheries Act, 1884.

Manley, J. J.   Literature of sea and river fishing.   *Clowes.*   O.P
    One of the handbooks of the Fisheries Exhibition of 1883.

Westwood and Satchell.   Bibliotheca piscatoria.   8vo.   *Satchell.*   15*s.*
    A carefully compiled catalogue; with descriptive commentary on all works upon angling, fish-
    culture, and fisheries, to date of publication.

      PERIODICALS, ETC.: *Sportsman's Guide* (monthly); Reports of the U.S. Commission
on fish and fisheries (*Washington*); Reports of the Fishery Commissioners (*Eyre*); Reports
of the Scotch Fishery Board (*Eyre*).

FIVES, *see* TENNIS.

FLAX, *see* AGRICULTURE II.

FLOUR, *see* INDUSTRIES IV.

FLOWERS, *see* BOTANY *and* GARDENING.

FODDER, *see* AGRICULTURE *and* LIVE-STOCK.

FOLKLORE:

—I. TREATISES:

See also ANTHROPOLOGY IV. *and* RELIGION.

> The beginner should take up the Folklore Society's *Handbook of folklore*, and then Campbell's *tales of the West Highlands*, with its clear and lucid introduction, and next Mrs. Hunt's translation of Grimm's *Household tales*, with Mr. Lang's introduction. Then turning to Sir George Cox's *Introduction to mythology and folklore* he will have gained an insight into the doctrines of the two chief schools of Folklore. From these he can proceed to the other volumes mentioned.
>
> The Folklore Society (director, Mr G. L. Gomme, 1, Beverley-villas, Barnes), has published twenty-five volumes (*Nutt*, 270, Strand), including a yearly volume of miscellanies (first called *The Folklore Record*, then the *Folklore Journal*, and now *Folklore*) and a handbook of Folklore.

Lang, A. Custom and myth. c. 8vo. *Longmans.*	7s. 6d.
,, Myth, ritual, and religion. c. 8vo. 2 vols. *Longmans.* pub. 21s.	O.P.
Clodd, E. Myths and dreams. c. 8vo. *Chatto.*	5s.
Frazer, J. G. The golden bough. d. 8vo. 2 vols. *Macmillan.*	28s.
Hartland, E. S. The science of fairy tales ("Contemp. Science" ser.). c. 8vo. *Scott.*	3s. 6d.
Gomme, G. L. Folklore relics of early village life. d. 8vo. *Stock.* In "Antiquary's Library." 3 vols. Not sold separately. These six books give the anthropological interpretation of folklore.	36s.
Cox, G. W. Introduction to mythology and folklore. c. 8vo. *Paul.* Philological interpretation of folklore.	7s. 6d.
Keary, C. F. Outlines of primitive belief. 8vo. *Longmans.* pub. 18s.	O.P.
Dorman, R. N. Origin of primitive superstitions. 8vo. *Lippincott.*	15s.
Callaway, Bishop. Religious system of the Amazulu. 8vo. *Trübner.* Parts i., ii., iii., 4s. each; part iv., 1s. 6d.	13s. 6d.
Clouston, W. A. Popular tales and fictions. c. 8vo. 2 vols. *Blackwood.* "Borrowing-theory" of folklore.	25s.
Gaster, M. Greeko-Slavonic literature. l. p. 8vo. *Trübner.* Literary origin of folklore.	7s. 6d.
Nutt, A. Studies in the legend of the Holy Grail (Folklore Soc.). 8vo. *Nutt.*	10s. 6d.
Rhys, J. Celtic heathendom (Hibbert lectures). 8vo. *Williams.*	10s. 6d.
,, Studies in the Arthurian legend. d. 8vo. *Clar. Press.*	12s. 6d.
Grimm, J. Teutonic mythology. Tr. J. S. Stallibrass. d. 8vo. *Bell.* Vol. i., ii., iii., 15s. each; vol. iv., 18s.	63s.
Brinton, D. G. (Ed.) Library of American aboriginal literature. 8vo. 7 vols. *Trübner.* Vol. iii., 10s.; the rest 12s. each.	82s.
,, Myths of the new world. r. 8vo. *Leypold* (*U.S.*).	12s. 6d.
Black, W. G. Folk medicine (Folklore Soc.) 8vo. *Nutt.*	13s. 6d.

—II. CUSTOMS AND SUPERSTITIONS:

Brand, J. Popular antiquities. Ed. Sir H. Ellis. c. 8vo. 3 vols., 5s. each. *Bell* (*Bohn*).	15s.
Henderson, W. The folklore of the northern counties (Folklore Soc.). 8vo. *Nutt.*	21s.

Gregor, W. Folklore of the north-east of Scotland (Folklore Soc.). 8vo. *Nutt.*   13s. 6d.

Napier, J. Folklore of the west of Scotland. c.8vo. *Gardner (Paisley).*   4s.

Dalyell, J. G. Darker superstitions of Scotland. *Griffin.*   o.p.

Burne, Miss C. S. Shropshire folklore. 8vo. 3 parts. *Trübner.*   22s. 6d.

Manners and customs, superstitions and traditions ("Gentleman's Magazine Library"). Ed. G. L. Gomme. 8vo. 4 vols., 7s. 6d. each. *Stock.*   30s.

Harland and Wilkinson. Lancashire folklore. c. 8vo. *J. Heywood.*   3s. 6d.

Hampson, R. T. Medii Ævi Calendarii (in English). d. 8vo. *Causton.*   o.p.

Roberts, P. Cambrian popular antiquities. *E. Williams.*   o.p.

Friend, H. Flowers and flower-lore. d. 8vo. *Sonnenschein.*   7s. 6d.

Bolton, H. C. Counting out rhymes of children. c. 4to. *Stock.*   9s.

Keightley, T. Fairy mythology. p. 8vo. *Bell (Bohn).*   5s.

Bleek, W. H. A brief account of Bushman folklore. fo. *Trübner.*   2s. 6d.

—III. COLLECTIONS OF TALES, ETC.:

Steel and Temple. Wide-awake stories. c. 8vo. *Trübner.*   9s.
Punjab and Kashmir.

Halliwell-Phillips, J. O. Nursery rhymes of England. f. 4to. *Warne.*   10s. 6d.

Popular rhymes of Scotland. Ed. R. Chambers. *Chambers.* 1841.   5s.

Campbell, J. F. Popular tales of the Western Highlands. d. 8vo. 4 vols. *Douglas.* pub. 32s.   o.p.
Now being reprinted. The first edition is very scarce and high-priced.

MacInnes and Nutt. Folklore and hero tales from Argyleshire. 8vo. *Nutt.*   15s.

Kennedy, P. Fireside stories of Ireland. 12mo. *McGlashan (Dublin).* pub. 1s.   o.p.

   ,, Legendary fictions of the Irish Celts. p. 8vo. *Macmillan.* pub. 7s. 6d.   o.p.

Croker, T. Crofton. Fairy legends and traditions of Ireland. p. 8vo. *Sonnenschein.*   2s. 6d.

Grimm, J. and W. Household tales. Tr. Mrs. Margaret Hunt. p. 8vo. 2 vols., 3s. 6d. each. *Bell (Bohn).*   7s.
Introduction by A. Lang. Anthropological basis.

Dasent, G. W. Tales of the Norse. c. 8vo. *Douglas.*   10s. 6d.

Ralston, W. R. S. Russian folk-tales. 8vo. *Smith, Elder.* pub. 16s.   o.p.

   ,, Songs of the Russian people. 8vo. *Ellis and Green.*   12s.

Wratislaw, A. H. Slavonic folk-tales. c. 8vo. *Stock.*   7s. 6d.

Kropf and Jones. Magyar folk-tales. 8vo. *Folklore Soc.*   15s.

Busk, R. H. Folk-songs of Italy. p. 8vo. *Sonnenschein.*   5s.

Crane, T. F. Italian popular tales. 8vo. *Macmillan.* pub. 14s.   o.p.

Stuart-Glennie, J. H. Greek folk-songs. d. 8vo. 2 vols. *Ward and Downey.*   7s. 6d.

Geldart, E. M. Folk-lore of modern Greece. *Sonnenschein.* illus.   2s. 6d.

Webster and Vinson. Basque legends. p. 8vo. *Griffith.* pub. 7s. 6d.   o.p.

Rink, H. Tales of the Eskimo. p. 8vo. *Blackwood.* illus. pub. 10s. 6d.   o.p.

Buddhist birth stories. Tr. Rhys Davids. *Trübner.* Vol. i.   18s.

Stokes, Maive. Indian fairy tales. Introduction by W. R. S. Ralston. 8vo.
Ellis and Elvey. pub. 7s. 6d.   O.P.

Frere, Mary. Old Deccan days. p. 8vo. *Murray.* illus.   5s.

Ralston, W. R. S. Tibetan tales. p. 8vo. *Trübner.*   14s.

Theal, G. McCall. Kaffir folklore. c. 8vo. *Sonnenschein.*   2s. 6d.

Callaway, Bishop. Zulu nursery tales. 8vo. *Trübner.* pub. 16s.   O.P.

Bleek, W. H. Reynard the fox in S. Africa. p. 8vo. *Trübner.*   3s. 6d.

Gill, W. Myths and songs of the S. Pacific. c. 8vo. *King.* pub. 9s.   O.P.

Chamberlain, B. H. Aino folk-tales. (Folklore Society). 8vo. *Nutt.*
To members only, 5s.

Bohn, H. G. Handbook of proverbs. p. 8vo. *Bell (Bohn).*   5s.

FOLKMOOTS, *see* ANTHROPOLOGY III.

FOOD, *see* COOKERY.

FOOTBALL:

Shearman, M., and others. Football ("Badminton Lib.") c.8vo. *Longmans.*   10s. 6d.

Vassall, H. Football; Rugby game ("All England" ser.). sm. 8vo. *Bell.*   1s.

Alcock, C. W. Football; Association game ("All England" ser.).
sm. 8vo. *Bell.*   1s.

FORESTRY:

Schlich. Manual of Forestry. *Bradbury, Evans.* pub. 7s. 6d.   O.P.

Hartig, R. Timbers, and how to know them. 12mo. *Simpkin.*   2s.

Fernandez and Smythies. Elements of sylviculture. Tr. Bagneris. *Rider.*   5s.

Des Cars, A. Pruning forest and ornamental trees. c. 8vo. *Trübner.*
pub. 4s.   O.P.

Macgregor, J. L. Organisation and valuation of forests. 8vo. *Wyman.*   16s.

FORTIFICATION, *see* ARMY I.

FOSSILS, *see* GEOLOGY IV.

FOWLING, WILD, *see* SHOOTING.

FRANCE: GEOGRAPHY:

—I. GENERAL:

Murray's Handbook for France. Part i. p. 8vo. *Murray.*   7s. 6d.
Normandy, Brittany, the Seine and Loire, Touraine, Bordeaux, the Garonne, Limousin, the Pyrenees, etc.

„ Handbook for France. Part ii. p. 8vo. *Murray.*   7s. 6d.
Central France, Auvergne, the Cevennes, Burgundy, the Rhone and Saone, Provence, Nimes, Arles, Marseilles, the French Alps, Alsace, Lorraine, Champagne, etc.

Baedeker's Guide-book to Northern France. 12mo. *Dulau.*   7s.

„ Guide-book; "Le Centre de la France" (in French). *Dulau.*   5s.

Guides Joanne. 7*s.* 6*d.* each, except "Nord," "Corse," and "Pyrénées." 16mo. *Hachette.*

> Savoie; Dauphiné et Hautes-Alpes; Franche-Comté et Jura; Provence; Corse (5*s.*), Auvergne et Centre; La Loire; De la Loire à la Gironde; Pyrénées (12*s.*); Gascogne et Languedoc; Cévennes; Bretagne; Normandie; Nord (9*s.*); Champagne et Ardennes; Vosges. Also each divided into smaller sections, 3*s.* to 4*s.* each.

Reclus, E. Universal geography, vol. ii. i. 8vo. *Virtue.*   21*s.*

Lebon and Pelet. France as it is. Tr. Mrs. W. Arnold. c. 8vo. *Cassell.*   7*s.* 6*d.*

—II. LOCAL:

PARIS.

Bemrose. Guide to Paris. Ed. Drewitt. *Neal (Rue de Rivoli).*   1*s.*

Baedeker's Guide to Paris and its environs. 12mo. *Dulau.*   6*s.*

Tours, C. de. Vingt jours à Paris. *Quantin.* illus.   3*s.* 6*d.*

Barron, L. Les environs de Paris. *Quantin.* illus.   30*s.*

Hugo, V. Paris. 18mo. *Hetzel.*   2*s.*

Menorval, G. de. Paris depuis ses origines, jusqu'à nos jours. 8vo. *Didot.*   6*s.*

Du Camp, M. Paris: ses origines, ses fonctions et sa vie dans la seconde moitié du 19e. siècle. 18mo. 6 vols. *Hachette.*   16*s.*

Hoffbauer. Paris à travers les âges. fo. 2 vols. *Didot.*   £15

> Or in 14 parts, 30*s.* each. With plans showing successive transformations of the city from the 13th century to the present day.

Vachon. L'ancien Hôtel de Ville de Paris. 4to. *Quantin.* illus.   60*s.*

Yriarte. Histoire de Paris.

> Only in the Bibliothèque Nationale and the library of the Hôtel de Ville.

Guilhermy, F. Itinéraire archéologique de Paris. (*Paris*).   O.P.

> Useful for reference.

BRITTANY.

Hutchinson, T. J. Summer holidays in Brittany. 8vo. *Low.* pub. 10*s.* 6*d.*   O.P.

HAVRE.

Braquehais. Guide au Havre. *Bourdignon.*   1*s.* 6*d.*

Borely. Histoire du Havre. *Lepelletrie.*   25*s.*

> Very complete.

ROUEN.

Rouen illustré. *Anger.*   25*s.*

BORDEAUX AND DISTRICT.

Guide (Joanne) à Bordeaux. 16mo. *Hachette.*   1*s.*

Gradis. Histoire de Bordeaux. (*Bordeaux*).   6*s.*

Drouyn, L. Variétés girondins; essai historique et archéologique. 3 vols. (*Bordeaux*).   54*s.*

Rebadien. La Guyenne d'autrefois. (*Bordeaux*).   5*s.*

CEVENNES.

Edwards, M. Betham. The roof of France (Lozère). d. 8vo. *Bentley.*   12*s.*

Stevenson, R. L. Travels with a donkey in the Cevennes. p. 8vo. *Chatto.*   2*s.* 6*d.*

LYONS.

Guide à Lyons. *Garnier.*   2*s.* 6*d.*

Niepce. L'archéologie lyonnaise. 3 vols. (*Lyons*).   27*s.* 6*d.*

PROVENCE.

Fabre. Histoire de Provence. 4 vols. (*Marseilles*).   25*s.*

FRANCE : HISTORY :

Coulanges, F. de. Histoire des institutions de l'ancienne France. 8vo. 3 vols., 6*s.* 6*d.* each. (*Paris*).   19*s.* 6*d.*

Guizot, W. History of civilization in France. Tr. W. Hazlitt. p. 8vo. 3 vols., 3*s.* 6*d.* each. *Bell* (*Bohn*).   10*s.* 6*d.*

Rambaud, A. Histoire de la civilisation française. 12mo. *Colin* (*Paris*).   11*s.*
     Vol. i., 3*s.* ; ii., 3*s.* 6*d.* ; iii., 4*s.* 6*d.*

Luchaire, A. Histoire des institutions monarchiques de la France. 987–1180. 8vo. 2 vols. (*Paris*).   15*s.*

Histoire de France racontée par les contemporains. Ed. Zeller. 16mo. 56 vols., 6*d.* each. *Hachette.*   28*s.*
     A valuable series of little volumes on separate epochs, consisting of extracts from the chronicles.

Kitchin, G. W. History of France (to 1793). c. 8vo. 3 vols., 10*s.* 6*d.* each. *Clar. Press.*   31*s.* 6*d*
     The best general history in English.

Sismondi, J. C. Histoire des Français (to 1789). 8vo. 31 vols. (*Paris*).   126*s.*
Michelet, J. Histoire de France. 12mo. 19 vols. (*Paris*).   66*s.* 6*d.*
Martin, H. Histoire de France (to 1789). 8vo. 17 vols. (*Paris*).   102*s.*
     Of the last three books Sismondi gives most details ; Martin is the most recent and judicious ; Michelet has great literary merits, but is sketchy, and falls off after the year 1600.

Wallon, H. Saint Louis et son temps. 8vo. 2 vols. (*Paris*).   15*s*

Joinville's Memoirs of Louis IX.
     An admirable contemporary memoir. Forms part of the volume entitled *Chronicles of the Crusades.* (Bohn's Lib., 5*s.*).

Langlois, V. Le règne de Philippe III. (1270–1285). 8vo. *Hachette.*   6*s.* 6*d.*

Boutaric. La France sous Philippe le Bel. 8vo. (*Paris*).   O.P.

Beaucourt, G. de. Histoire de Charles VII. 8vo. 4 vols., 8*s.* each. (*Paris*).   32*s*

Wallon, H. Jeanne d'Arc. 12mo. 2 vols. (*Paris*).   7*s.*

Michel, F. Histoire du commerce et de la navigation sous la domination anglaise. 8vo. 2 vols. (*Bordeaux*).   15*s.*

Luce, S. La France pendant la guerre de cent ans. 12mo. *Hachette.*   3*s.*
     Chiefly social.

Comines, P. de. Memoirs (for Louis XI. and Charles VIII.). Tr. A. R. Scoble. p. 8vo. 3 vols., 3*s.* 6*d.* each. *Bell* (*Bohn*).   10*s.* 6*d.*

Kirk, J. F. History of Charles the Bold. 8vo. 3 vols. *Murray.*   45*s.*

Hookham, Mrs. M. A. Life and times of Margaret of Anjou (1444–1482). d. 8vo. 2 vols. *Tinsley.* pub. 25*s.*   O.P.

Cherrier, C. de. Histoire de Charles VIII. 12mo. 2 vols. (*Paris*).   7*s*

Müntz, E. La renaissance en Italie et France à l'époque de Charles VIII. r. 8vo. (*Paris*).   30*s*

Ranke, L. von. Französische Geschichte (from 1550). 8vo. 6 vols. (*Stuttgart*).   60*s.*

Mignet, F. A. La rivalité de François I. et Charles V. 8vo. 2 vols. (*Paris*).   15*s.*

Baird, H. M. The rise of the Huguenots (1535–1574). 2 vols. *Hodder.*   O.P.

     ,,   The Huguenots and Henry of Navarre. 8vo. 2 vols. *Paul.*   24*s.*

Freer, M. W.   Henry III., King of France.   8vo.   3 vols.   *Hurst.*   O.P.

  ,,   History of the reign of Henry IV.   8vo.   4 vols.   *Hurst.*   O.P.

Sully, Duc de.   Memoirs of Henry IV.   Tr.   p. 8vo.   4 vols., 3*s.* 6*d.*
    each.   *Bell (Bohn).*   14*s.*
      The memoirs of the chief minister of the period.

Aumale, Duc d'.   Histoire des princes de Condé.   8vo.   4 vols., 7*s.* 6*d.* each.
    (*Paris*).   30*s.*

Voltaire.   Le siècle de Louis XIV.   12mo.   (*Paris*).   2*s.* 6*d.*

Perkins, J. B.   France under Richelieu and Mazarin.   l. 8vo.   2 vols.
    Putnam.   16*s.*

Jobez, A.   La France sous Louis XV.   8vo.   6 vols., 6*s.* each.   (*Paris*).   36*s.*

Broglie, Duc de.   The king's secret.   Tr.   8vo.   2 vols.   *Cassell.*   pub. 24*s.*   O.P.
      French ed., 2 vols., 12mo., 7*s.*   The diplomacy of Louis XV., 1752-1774.

  ,,   Frédéric II. et Marie Thérèse.   12mo.   2 vols.   (*Paris*).   7*s.*

Saint Simon.   Mémoires, 1692–1723.   12mo.   21 vols.   (*Paris*).   73*s.* 6*d.*

Morley, J.   Voltaire.   gl. 8vo.   *Macmillan.*   5*s.*

  ,,   Rousseau.   gl. 8vo.   2 vols.   *Macmillan.*   10*s.*

Aubertin, C.   L'esprit publique au XVIIIᵉ. siècle.   12mo.   (*Paris*).   4*s.*

De Tocqueville.   State of society in France before 1789.   8vo.   *Murray.*   12*s.*

Rocquain, F.   L'esprit révolutionnaire avant la révolution (1715–1789).   8vo.
    (*Paris*).   8*s.*

Gardiner, Mrs.   The French revolution.   (elem.).   f. 8vo.   *Longmans.*   2*s.* 6*d.*

Taine, H.   The ancient régime.   Tr.   8vo.   *Low.*   16*s.*
      Essays on the period without much detailed writing.

  ,,   The revolution.   Tr.   8vo.   2 vols., 16*s.* each.   *Low.*   32*s.*

Thiers, A.   History of the French revolution (1789–1794).   Tr.   d. 8vo.
    5 vols.   *Bentley.*   36*s.*

  ,,   Histoire du consulat et de l'empire.   8vo.   20 vols.   (*Leipzig*).   48*s.*
      Several other editions.

Sybel, H. von.   History of the French revolution, 1789-1795.   Tr.   4 vols.
    Murray.   pub. 48*s.*   O.P.
      German ed., 5 vols. (*Frankfort*), 36*s.*   Excellent for the political history of Europe generally,
      but very hard reading, and not broad enough in view.

Seeley, J. R.   Short history of Napoleon.   8vo.   *Seeley.*   5*s.*

Rémusat, Mme. de.   Memoirs, 1802-1808.   Tr.   8vo.   2 vols., 16*s.* each.   *Low.*   32*s.*
      An interesting account of Napoleon's character and court life.

Lanfrey.   History of Napoleon I.   Tr.   c. 8vo.   4 vols.   *Macmillan.*   30*s.*
      An unfavourable view.

Thureau-Dangin.   Histoire de la monarchie de Juillet.   8vo.   4 vols.
    (*Paris*).   28*s.*

Blennerhasset, Lady.   Life of Madame de Stael.   3 vols.   *Smith, Elder.*   O.P.
      Full of information about the thought and literature of the Napoleonic time.

Delord, Taxile.   Histoire du second empire.   8vo.   6 vols.   (*Paris*).   42*s.*

Jerrold, B.   Life of Napoleon III.   8vo.   3 vols.   *Longmans.*   pub. 54*s.*   O.P.

Block, M.   Le département.   12mo.   *Hetzel.*   1*s.* 6*d.*

  ,,   La commune.   12mo.   *Hetzel.*   1*s.* 6*d.*
      Recent and valuable works on French local administration.

Viollet, P.   Histoire des institutions politiques et administratives de la
    France.   (*Paris*).
      Development of feudal institutions.

—REFERENCE AND COLLECTIONS:

> The authorities for French history are scattered through several collections, none of which aims at completeness.

Monod. Bibliographie de l'histoire de France. 8vo. *Hachette.*   7s. 6d.

Masson, G. Early chroniclers of France. c. 8vo. *S. P. C. K.*   4s.
     A sketch of authorities to 1490.

Lalanne, L. Dictionnaire historique de la France. 8vo. (*Paris*).   17s.

Bouillet, N. Dictionnaire universel d'histoire et de geographie. r. 8vo. (*Paris*).   21s.

Recueil des historiens des Gaules et de la France (to 1328). Ed. Bouquet. 4to. 21 vols. 1738–1835.   O.P.

Collection complète de Mémoires (1120–1763). Ed. Petitot and Monmerqué. 8vo. 130 vols. 1825–30.   £27 10s.

     ,,   des chroniques nationales françaises (1520–1800.) Ed. Buchon. 8vo. 47 vols. 1825–34.   £22

Nouvelle collection de Mémoires (1200–1800.) Ed. Michaud and Poujoulat. r. 8vo. 34 vols. 1835–9.   £12 12s.

> PERIODICALS: *Revue historique* (30s. per annum); *Revue de questions historiques* (20s. per annum).

FRANCE: LANGUAGE AND LITERATURE:

Including (1) A larger and a smaller selection of works, with dictionaries, etc.; (2) Novels; (3) Books for young people; (4) A course of study for adult beginners; (5) Books for young children. The books marked (*) belong to the smaller collection. Those marked (§) are recommended as suitable for young people, in addition to the books named in the special list.

> GENERAL NOTE.—Read through one or other of the Primers recommended. Supplement it with one or more of the histories, and then follow, according to leisure and taste, with separate authors. Crépet's poets will suffice many readers for the whole poetical side of the literature, and will suggest to others where to fill in and extend. Purely critical works, such as Sainte-Beuve's, should be taken last of all, and after reading texts.

—I. DICTIONARIES, GRAMMARS, AND PRIMERS:

Vapereau, G. Dictionnaire universel des littérateurs. r. 8vo. *Hachette.*   24s.

     ,,   Dictionnaire des contemporains. r. 8vo. *Hachette.*   26s.

Littré and Beaujean. Dictionnaire de la langue française. r. 8vo. *Hachette.*   14s. 6d.
     All these are very valuable for reference.

*****Brachet.** Historical grammar. Tr. Kitchin. ex. f. 8vo. *Clar. Press.*   3s. 6d

*****Eve** and Baudiss. "Wellington" French grammar. 12mo. *Nutt.*   4s.

*****Masson,** G. French and English dictionary. c. 8vo. *Macmillan.*   6s.

*****Saintsbury,** G. Primer of French literature. ex. f. 8vo. *Clar. Press.*   2s.

*****Warren.** Primer of French literature. *Heath (Boston).*   4s. 6d.

*****Fasnacht,** G. E. French grammar. 8vo. *Macmillan.*   3s. 6d.

—II. HISTORY, CRITICISM, AND COLLECTIONS:

Géruzez. Histoire de la littérature française. 12mo. 2 vols. *Perrin.*   6s.

Demogeot, J. Histoire de la littérature française. 12mo. *Hachette.*   3s. 6d.

Saintsbury, G. Short history of French literature. c. 8vo. *Clar. Press.*   10s. 6d.

Paris, G. La littérature française du moyen age. 16mo. *Hachette.*   2s. 6d.

Hatzfeld and Darmesteter. Le seizième siècle en France. 12mo. *Delagrave.*   5s.
> Each of the two last is invaluable for its period. The second contains large extracts which will almost suffice for the Renaissance.

Bartsch, K. Chrestomathie de l'ancien Français. r. 8vo. *Vogel.*   10s.

Bartsch and Horning. La langue et la littérature françaises. 8vo. *Maisonneuve.*   12s. 6d.

Bartsch, K. Grundriss zur Geschichte der provençalischen Literatur. r. 8vo. (*Elberfeld*).   5s.

,, Chrestomathie provençale. 8vo. (*Elberfeld*).   9s. 6d.
> Bartsch's works supplement each other, and will together suffice for ordinary readers without further texts.

Sainte-Beuve, C. A. Premiers Lundis. 12mo. 3 vols. *Lévy.*   9s.

,, Causeries du Lundi. 12mo. 16 vols. *Garnier.*   48s.

,, Nouveaux Lundis. 12mo. 13 vols. *Lévy.*   39s.

* ,, Selected "Causeries." Ed. Saintsbury. ex. f. 8vo. *Clar. Press.*   2s.

Faguet, E. Les grands maitres du 17e siècle. Etudes littéraires et dramatiques. 12mo. *Lecène et Oudin.*   3s.

,, Notices littéraires sur les auteurs français, Corneille, Racine, Molière, La Fontaine, Boileau. 12mo. *Lecène et Oudin.*   2s. 6d.
> Deals with XVII., XVIII., and XIX. centuries.

Les poètes français. Ed. Crépet. 8vo. 4 vols., 6s. 6d. each. *Gide.* pub. 26s.   O.P.
> Almost indispensable.

Théâtre français du moyen age. Ed. Monmerqué et Michel. r. 8vo. *Didot.*   8s. 6d

Ancien théâtre français. Ed. Viollet-le-duc and Jacob. 12mo. *Bibliothèque Elzévirienne.*   16s.

Chefs d'œuvres comiques. 12mo. 8 vols., 2s. 6d. each. *Didot.*   20s.

Chefs d'œuvres tragiques. 12mo. 2 vols., 5s. each. *Didot.*   10s.

Chefs d'œuvres historiques. 12mo. 2 vols., 2s. 6d. each. *Didot.*   5s.
> Cheap and invaluable selections of complete plays and books.

***Specimens** of French literature. Ed. G. Saintsbury. c. 8vo. *Clar. Press.*   9s.

***La** lyre française. Ed. G. Masson. 18mo. *Macmillan.*   4s. 6d.

Crane, T. F. La société française au 17e siècle. 16mo. *Putnam.*   4s. 6d.

,, Le romantisme français. 16mo. *Putnam.*   4s. 6d.
> Excellent American handbooks to the respective periods.

Michaud and Poujoulat. Nouvelle collection de mémoires pour servir à l'histoire de France depuis le 13e siècle jusqu'à la fin du 18e siècle. r. 8vo. 34 vols. *Didot.* 1835-9.   £8
> Large body of texts, very useful to the student of means and leisure.

Tilley, A. A. Literature of the French Renaissance. c. 8vo. *Camb. Press.*   6s.

—III. TEXTS:
> It has seemed better to indicate, for the most part, editions of whole authors. The histories of literature recommended will guide the student as to the special works of each author which are best worth reading.

Chanson de Roland. Ed. L. Gautier. 12mo. (*Paris*).   4s. 6d.

***Extraits** de la chanson de Roland et de la vie de St. Louis. Ed. G. Paris. 16mo. *Hachette.*   2s. 6d.

Roman de la Rose. Ed. F. Michel. 12mo. 2 vols. *Didot.*   7s.

Froissart. Chronique. Ed. Buchon. r. 8vo. 3 vols. *Didot.*   18s. 6d.

Villehardouin. Œuvres. Ed. N. de Wailly. r. 8vo. *Didot.* 16*s.*

Joinville. Œuvres. Ed. N. de Wailly. r. 8vo. *Didot.* 16*s.*

Comines, P. de. Mémoires. Ed. Chantelauze. r. 8vo. *Didot.* 16*s.*

Villon. Œuvres. Ed. P. Jacob. 12mo. *Bibl. Elzev.* 16*s.*

"**Cent** Nouvelles Nouvelles." 12mo. *Garnier.* 2*s.* 6*d.*

Marot. Œuvres. Ed. Jannet. 12mo. 4 vols. *Lemerre.* 9*s.*

Rabelais. Œuvres. Ed. Jannet. 12mo. 7 vols. *Lemerre.* 15*s.*

* ,, Œuvres. Ed. Jannet. 12mo. 2 vols. *Didot.* 7*s.*

***Marguerite** de Valois. Heptameron. 12mo. *Garnier.* 2*s.* 6*d.*

Ronsard. Œuvres. Ed. Blanchemain. 12mo. 8 vols. *Bibl. Elzev.* 39*s.*
For most purposes the selection in Crépet will suffice.

Garnier. Les Tragedies. Ed. Förster. 12mo. *Henninger.* 12*s.*

Montaigne. Essais. Ed. Courbet et Roger. 8vo. 4 vols., 8*s.* 6*d.* each.
Lemerre. 34*s.*

* ,, Essais. Ed. Louandre. 12mo. 4 vols. *Charpentier.* 12*s.*

Brantôme. Œuvres. Ed. Buchon. 8vo. 2 vols. *Didot.* o.p.

***Satyre** Menippée. Ed. Labitte. 12mo. *Charpentier.* 3*s.*

Regnier. Œuvres. Ed. Poitevin. 12mo. *Garnier.* 2*s.* 6*d.*

Malherbe. Œuvres. Ed. Jannet. 12mo. *Lemerre.* o.p.

La Fontaine. Fables. r. 8vo. 2 vols. *Quantin.* illus. 120*s.*

,, Œuvres. Ed. Moland. 8vo. 7 vols., 7*s.* 6*d.* each. *Garnier.*
illus. 42*s.*

* ,, Fables. Ed. Sainte-Beuve. 12mo. (*Paris*). 3*s.*

***Boileau.** Œuvres. Ed. Amar. 12mo. *Didot.* 2*s.* 6*d.*

Voiture. Œuvres. Ed. Ubicini. 12mo. 2 vols. *Charpentier.* o.p.

Rotrou. Œuvres choisies. Ed. Ronchaud. 12mo. 2 vols. *Jouaust.* 12*s.* 6*d.*
Selected plays.

Corneille. Œuvres. Ed. Marty-Laveaux. 8vo. 12 vols. *Hachette.* 78*s.* 6*d.*

* ,, Théâtre. 12mo. 2 vols. *Didot.* 5*s.*

Racine. Œuvres. Ed. Mesnard. 8vo. 8 vols. *Hachette.* 58*s.*

* ,, Théâtre. 12mo. *Didot.* 2*s.* 6*d.*

Molière. Œuvres. Ed. Despois. 8vo. 10 vols., 6*s.* 6*d.* each. *Hachette.* 65*s.*

* ,, Théâtre. 12mo. 2 vols. *Didot.* 5*s.*

Regnard. Œuvres. 12mo. *Didot.* 2*s.* 6*d.*

Lafayette, Mme. de. La Princesse de Clèves. 12mo. *Lemerre.* o.p.

Perrault. Fables. Ed. Lefevre. 12mo. *Lemerre.* o.p.

,, Fables. Ed. Lang. ex. f. 8vo. *Clar. Press.* 2*s.*

Retz, Cardinal de. Œuvres. Ed. Feillet. 8vo. 10 vols., 7*s.* 6*d.* each. *Hachette.* 75*s.*

Sévigné, Mme. de. Œuvres. Ed. Monmerqué. 8vo. 14 vols. *Hachette.* 120*s.*

* ,, Lettres choisies. Ed. Suard. 12mo. *Didot.* 2*s.* 6*d.*

Saint Simon. Œuvres. Ed. Boislisle. 8vo. 30 vols., 7*s.* 6*d.* each. *Hachette.*
In course of publication.

Pascal. Pensées. Ed. Havet. 8vo. 2 vols. *Delagrave.* 7*s.*

* ,, Pensées. 12mo. *Didot.* 2*s.* 6*d.*

Pascal. Les provinciales. 12mo. *Didot.*   2s. 6d.

Larochefoucauld. Œuvres. Ed. Gilbert. 8vo. 3 vols. *Hachette.*   28s. 6d.

*   ,,   Maximes. 12mo. *Didot.*   2s. 6d.

La Bruyère. Œuvres. Ed. Servois. 8vo. 3 vols. *Hachette.*   27s. 6d.

Descartes. Œuvres. Ed. Simon. 12mo. *Charpentier.*   3s.

***Bossuet.** Œuvres. Ed. Girardin. r. 8vo. 4 vols. *Didot.*   32s.

Fénelon. Œuvres. Ed. Martin. r. 8vo. 3 vols. *Didot.*   24s.

Massillon. Œuvres. r. 8vo. 2 vols. *Didot.*   16s.

Bourdaloue. Œuvres. r. 8vo. 3 vols. *Didot.*   24s.

Chénier, A. Poésies complètes. Ed. G. de Chénier. 12mo. 3 vols., 5s. each. *Lemerre.*   15s.

***Le Sage.** Œuvres. Ed. Sainte-Beuve. r. 8vo. (*Paris*).   12s. 6d.

   ,,   Gil Blas. Ed. Poulet-Melassis. 16mo. *Lemerre.*   4s. 6d.

   ,,   Diable boiteux. Ed. Jannet. 12mo. 2 vols. *Lemerre.*   4s. 6d.

Voltaire. Œuvres complètes. r. 8vo. 13 vols. *Didot.* illus.   120s.

   ,,   Œuvres choisies. Ed. Bengesco. 16mo. 12 vols., 2s. 6d. each. *Jouaust.*   30s.

*   ,,   Romans. 12mo. *Didot.*   2s. 6d.

*   ,,   Siècle de Louis XIV. 12mo. *Didot.*   2s. 6d.

Diderot. Œuvres complètes. Ed. Assézat. 8vo. 20 vols. *Garnier.* illus.   140s.

*   ,,   Œuvres choisies. Ed. Genin. 12mo. 2 vols. *Didot.*   5s.

Rousseau, J. J. Œuvres. r. 8vo. 4 vols. *Didot.*   32s.

*   ,,   Confessions. 12mo. *Didot.*   2s. 6d.

*   ,,   Nouvelle Héloïse. 12mo. *Didot.*   2s. 6d.

Staël, Mme. de. Œuvres. r. 8vo. 3 vols. *Didot.*   24s.

*   ,,   Corinne. 12mo. *Didot.*   2s. 6d.

*   ,,   De l'Allemagne. 12mo. *Didot.*   2s. 6d.

Maistre, X. de. Œuvres. 12mo. *Charpentier.*   3s.

Vauvenargues. Œuvres. Ed. Gilbert. 8vo. 2 vols., 8s. 6d. each. *Furne.*   17s.

Chamfort. Œuvres choisies. Ed. Lescure. 12mo. 2 vols. *Jouaust.*   5s.

Rivarol. Œuvres choisies. Ed. Lescure. 12mo. 2 vols. *Jouaust.*   5s.

Joubert. Œuvres. Ed. P. Joynal. 12mo. 2 vols. *Charpentier.*   6s.

Montesquieu. Œuvres. Ed. Laboulaye. 8vo. 7 vols. *Garnier.*   52s. 6d.

Maistre, J. de. Du pape. 12mo. *Charpentier.*   3s.

   ,,   Soirées de St. Pétersbourg. 12mo. 2 vols. *Pelagaud.*   6s.

Chateaubriand. Œuvres. 8vo. 12 vols. *Didot.* illus.   60s

*   ,,   Les martyrs. 12mo. *Didot.*   2s. 6d.

*   ,,   Atala. 12mo. *Didot.*   2s. 6d.

Beyle, H. ("Stendhal"). Œuvres. 12mo. 7 vols., 3s. each. (*Paris*).   21s.

Buffon. Œuvres choisies. 12mo. 2 vols. *Didot.*   5s.

***Beaumarchais.** Le barbier de Séville. Ed. A. Dobson. ex. f. 8vo. *Clar. Press.*   2s. 6d.

***Prévost,** L'Abbé. Manon Lescaut. 12mo. *Charpentier.*   3s.

***Lespinasse**, Mlle. de. Lettres. Ed. Isambart. 12mo. 2 vols. *Lemerre.*   4s. 6d.

***Courier**, P. L. Œuvres. r. 8vo. *Didot.*   8s. 6d.

Béranger. Œuvres. 12mo. 5 vols., 3s. each. *Garnier.*   15s.

*   ,,   Chansons. 12mo. 2 vols., 3s. each. *Garnier.*   6s.

Lamartine. Œuvres. 12mo. 13 vols. *Lemerre.*   63s.

*   ,,   Méditations. 12mo. 2 vols., 5s. each. *Lemerre.*   10s.

Hugo, V. Œuvres complètes. 8vo. 54 vols., 6s. 6d. each. *Quantin.*
It is difficult to select two or three works of Victor Hugo for the smaller collection. Almost any one is characteristic, but hardly any one can be safely left out. [*See* Novels.]

Lamennais. Paroles d'un croyant. 12mo. *Garnier.*   2s. 6d.

Musset, A. de. Œuvres complètes. 12mo. 10 vols., 3s. each. *Charpentier.*   30s.

*   ,,   Poésies. 12mo. 2 vols., 3s. each. *Charpentier.*   6s.

Vigny, A. de. Œuvres. 12mo. 6 vols., 3s. each. *Charpentier.*   18s.

Baudelaire, C. Œuvres. 12mo. 7 vols., 3s. each. *Lévy.*   21s.

Nerval, G. de. Œuvres. 12mo. 6 vols., 3s. each. *Lévy.*   18s.

Dumas, père. Œuvres. 12mo. 303 vols., 1s. each. *Lévy.*   303s.

Mérimée, P. Œuvres. 12mo. 16 vols., 3s. each. *Lévy.*   48s.

Sand, George. Œuvres. 12mo. 59 vols., 1s. each, and 53 vols., 3s. each.

Gautier, T. Œuvres. 12mo. 28 vols., 3s. each. *Charpentier.*   84s.

Balzac. Œuvres. 8vo 24 vols.   154s.
For selected novels of Hugo, Dumas, Mérimée, Sand, Gautier, and Balzac, *see* Novels.

—IV. NOVELS:

Achard, A. Belle Rose. 12mo. *Lévy.*   3s.

Balzac. Les Chouans. 12mo. *Lévy.*   1s. 3d.

,,   La peau de chagrin. 12mo. *Lévy.*   1s. 3d.

,,   La cousine Bette. 12mo. *Lévy.*   1s. 3d.

,,   Le père Goriot. 12mo. *Lévy.*   1s. 3d.

,,   Le chef d'œuvre inconnu. 12mo. *Lévy.*   1s. 3d.

,,   Eugénie Grandet. 12mo. *Lévy.*   1s. 3d.

Bernard, C. de. L'écueil. 12mo. *Lévy.*   1s.

,,   Un homme sérieux. 12mo. *Lévy.*   1s.

,,   Gerfaut. 12mo. *Lévy.*   1s.

,,   Le paratonnerre. 12mo. *Lévy.*   1s.

Beyle, H. ("Stendhal"). Le rouge et le noir. 12mo. 2 vols., 1s. each. *Lévy.*   2s.

,,   La Chartreuse de Parme. 12mo. *Lévy.*   1s.

Boisgobey, F. du. Le crime de l'omnibus. 12mo. *Plon.*   3s.

,,   Margot la balafrée. 12mo. 2 vols. *Plon.*   5s.

Bourget, P. L'irréparable. 16mo. *Lemerre.*   5s.

Brète, J. de la. Mon oncle et mon curé. 12mo. *Plon.*   3s.

Capendu, E. Le roi des gabiers. 12mo. 3 vols. *Cadot.*   9s.

Cherbuliez, V. Le roman d'une honnête femme. 12mo. *Hachette.*   3s.

,,   Meta Holdenis. 12mo. *Hachette.*   3s.

,,   Samuel Brohl et Cie. 12mo. *Hachette.*   3s.

Cochin, H.   Le manuscrit de M. Larsonnier. 12mo. *Plon.*   2*s.* 6*d.*

Constant, B.   Adolphe. 12mo. *Jouaust.*   3*s.* 6*d.*

Daudet, A.   Tartarin de Tarascon. 12mo. *Marpon.* illus.   3*s.*

   ,,   Tartarin sur les Alpes. (*Paris*).   3*s.*

   ,,   Fromont jeune et Risler aîné. 12mo. *Charpentier.*   3*s.*

   ,,   Jack. 12mo. *Dentu.* illus.   3*s.*

§   ,,   Le petit chose. 12mo. *Lemerre.*   5*s.*

Droz, G.   Monsieur, Madame et Bébé. 12mo. *Havard.*   3*s.* 6*d.*

Dumas, père.   Les trois mousquetaires. 12mo. 2 vols. *Lévy.*   2*s.*

   ,,   Vingt ans après. 12mo. 3 vols. *Lévy.*   2*s.* 6*d.*

   ,,   Le vicomte de Bragelonne. 12mo. 6 vols. *Lévy.*   5*s.*

   ,,   La reine Margot. 12mo. 2 vols. *Lévy.*   2*s.*

   ,,   Les quarante-cinq. 12mo. 3 vols. *Lévy.*   2*s.* 6*d.*

   ,,   La dame de Monsoreau. 12mo. 3 vols. *Lévy.*   5*s.*

§   ,,   Le comte de Monte-Cristo. 12mo. 6 vols. *Lévy.*   5*s.*

Duruy, G.   L'unisson. 12mo. *Hachette.*   3*s.*

Feuillet, O.   Julia de Trécœur. 12mo. *Lévy.*   3*s.*

   ,,   La petite comtesse. 12mo. *Lévy.*   3*s.*

§   ,,   Le roman d'un jeune homme pauvre. 12mo. *Lévy.*   3*s.*

   ,,   M. de Camors. 12mo. *Lévy.*   3*s.*

Féval, P.   La fée des grèves. 12mo. *Plon.*   2*s.* 6*d.*

Feydeau.   Sylvie. 12mo. *Lévy.*   3*s.*

Flaubert, G.   Madame Bovary. 12mo. *Charpentier.*   3*s.*

   ,,   Salammbô. 12mo. *Charpentier.*   3*s.*

   ,,   Trois contes. 12mo. *Charpentier.*   3*s.*

   ,,   L'éducation sentimentale. 12mo. *Charpentier.*   3*s.*

France, A.   Le crime de Sylvestre Bonnard. 12mo. *Lévy.*   3*s.*

Gautier, T.   Le capitaine Fracasse. 12mo. 2 vols. *Charpentier.*   6*s.*

   ,,   Romans et contes. 12mo. *Charpentier.*   3*s.*

   ,,   Nouvelles. 12mo. *Charpentier.*   3*s.*

   ,,   Le roman de la Momie. 12mo. *Charpentier.*   3*s.*

Gréville, H.   Dosia. 12mo. *Plon.*   2*s.* 6*d.*

   ,,   Rose Rozier. 12mo. 2 vols. *Plon.*   6*s.*

"Gyp."   Le plus heureux de tous. 12mo. *Lévy.*   3*s.*

   ,,   Mademoiselle Eve. 12mo. *Lévy.*   3*s.*

Halévy, L.   La famille Cardinal. 12mo. *Lévy.*   3*s.*

Hugo, V.   Notre Dame de Paris. 12mo. 2 vols. (*Paris*).   3*s.* 6*d.*

   ,,   Les travailleurs de la mer. 12mo. 2 vols. (*Paris*).   3*s.* 6*d.*

   ,,   Quatre-vingt-treize. 12mo. 2 vols. (*Paris*).   3*s.* 6*d.*

Le Sage.   Gil Blas. 12mo. *Charpentier.*   3*s.*

   ,,   Le diable boiteux. 12mo. (*Paris*).   3*s.*

Loti, P.   Le mariage de Loti. 12mo. *Lévy.*   3*s.*

Loti, P. Mon frère Yves. 12mo. *Lévy*.	3s.
Mahalin, P. L'hôtellerie sanglante. 12mo. *Tresse*.	3s.
Maupassant, G. de. Pierre et Jean. 12mo. *Ollendorff*.	3s.
Mérimée, P. Colomba, etc. 12mo. *Lévy*.	3s.
,, Carmen, etc. 12mo. *Lévy*.	3s.
,, Chronique de Charles IX. 12mo. *Lévy*.	3s.
,, Dernières nouvelles. 12mo. *Lévy*.	3s.
Murger, H. La vie de Bohème. 12mo. *Lévy*.	1s.
,, Les buveurs d'eau. 12mo. *Lévy*.	1s.
Rabusson, H. Le mari de Madame Orgevault. 12mo. *Lévy*.	3s.
Reybaud, L. Jérôme Paturot. 12mo. *Lévy*.	1s.
Sand, George. Mauprat. 12mo. *Lévy*.	3s.
,, Lélia. 12mo. 2 vols. *Lévy*.	2s.
,, Lucrezia Floriani. 12mo. *Lévy*.	1s.
,, Consuelo. 12mo. 3 vols. *Lévy*.	2s. 6d.
,, La mare au diable. 12mo *Lévy*.	3s.
Sandeau, J. Le docteur Herbeau. 12mo. *Charpentier*.	3s.
§ ,, Mademoiselle de la Seiglière. 12mo. *Charpentier*.	3s.
,, Madeleine. 12mo. *Charpentier*.	3s.
,, Sacs et parchemins. 12mo. *Lévy*.	1s.
Souvestre, E. Le foyer breton. 12mo. 2 vols. *Lévy*.	2s.
Sue, E. Le Juif errant. 12mo. 4 vols. *Marpon et Flammarion*.	4s. 6d.
Theuriet, A. Michel Verneuil. 12mo. *Ollendorff*.	3s.
Voltaire. Romans. 12mo. *Didot*.	2s. 6d.

—V. COURSE OF STUDY FOR THE ADULT BEGINNER:

At least two of (A)—more if possible—should be worked carefully through with the notes, and the aid of dictionary and grammar. As many of (B) as can be should be read, for interest and exercise combined, with dictionary only. Use Masson's *Dictionary*, Fasnacht's *Grammar*, Saintsbury's *Short history of French literature*, and his *Specimens of French literature*, or Masson's *Lyre française*. [*See above*, Sec. I.]

(A)

Racine. Les plaideurs. Ed. Braunholtz. ex. f. 8vo. *Pitt Pr*.	2s.
Molière. L'école des femmes. Ed. Saintsbury. ex. f. 8vo. *Pitt Pr*.	2s. 6d.
Bonnechose. Lazare Hoche. Ed. Colbeck. ex. f. 8vo. *Pitt Pr*.	2s.
Voltaire. Mérope. Ed. Saintsbury. ex. f. 8vo. *Clar. Pr*.	2s.
Hugo, V. Les misérables. Ed. Boïelle. c. 8vo. 2 vols., 3s. 6d. each. *Williams*.	7s.

(B)

Dumas, père. Les trois mousquetaires. 2 vols. *Lévy*.	2s.
Thierry. Récits mérovingiens. 8vo. *Hachette*.	5s.
Mérimée. Lettres à une inconnue. 12mo. 2 vols. *Lévy*.	6s.
Michelet, J. La montagne. 12mo. *Lacroix*.	3s.
Musset. Comédies et proverbes. 12mo. 3 vols., 3s. each. *Charpentier*.	9s.
Quinet, E. Lettres à sa mère. *Alcan*.	3s.
Gautier. Voyage en Russie. 12mo. *Charpentier*.	3s.
,, Le capitaine Fracasse. 12mo. 2 vols. *Charpentier*.	6s.

—VI. BOOKS FOR THE YOUNG:

(In addition to those marked § in previous lists.)

Books marked † are suitable for children under twelve.

About, E. Le roi des montagnes. 12mo. *Hachette.*	2s.
Beauvoir, R. de. Voyage autour du monde. r. 8vo. (*Paris*).	20s.
Bernard, C. de. Le gentilhomme campagnard. 12mo. *Lévy.*	1s.
Cherbuliez, V. Le comte Kostia. 12mo. *Hachette.*	3s.
†Daudet, A. La belle Nivernaise. 12mo. *Flammarion.*	6d.
†Desnoyers, L. Aventures de Jean Paul Choppart. 12mo. *Hetzel.*	2s. 6d.
Dumas, père. La tulipe noire. 12mo. *Lévy.*	1s.
† ,, La bouillie de la comtesse Berthe. 12mo. *Lévy.*	1s.
Erckmann-Chatrian. Maître Daniel Rock. 12mo. (*Paris*).	2s. 6d.
,, La maison forestière. 12mo. (*Paris*).	2s. 6d.
,, Les deux frères. 12mo. (*Paris*).	2s. 6d.
Fabre, F. Mon oncle Célestin. 12mo. *Charpentier.*	3s.
,, L'abbé Tigrane. 12mo. *Charpentier.*	3s.
France, A. Le livre de mon ami. 12mo. *Lévy.*	3s.
Fromentin, E. Un été dans le Sahara. 12mo. 2 vols. (*Paris*).	7s.
,, Les maîtres d'autrefois. 12mo. (*Paris*).	3s. 6d.
†Girardin, J. Les braves gens. 16mo. *Hetzel.*	2s.
† ,, La toute petite. 8vo. *Hachette.*	3s. 6d.
Halévy, L. L'Abbé Constantin. 12mo. (*Paris*).	3s.
Hübner, Baron. Promenades autour du monde. 12mo. 2 vols. (*Paris*).	7s.
Hugo, V. Le dernier jour d'un condamné; Bug Jargal. 12mo. 2s. each. *Hetzel.*	4s.
Lamartine, A. de. Les confidences. 12mo. 2 vols., 3s. 6d. each. (*Paris*).	7s.
,, Jocelyn. 12mo. (*Paris*).	3s.
Loti, P. Pêcheurs d'Islande. 12mo. *Lévy.*	3s.
Malot, H. Sans famille. 12mo. 2 vols., 3s. each. *Charpentier.*	6s.
Michelet, J. L'oiseau. 12mo. *Hachette.*	3s.
†Perey, L. Zerbeline et Zerbelin. l. 8vo. *Lévy.* illus.	4s. 6d.
Pouvillon. Cesette. 12mo. *Lemerre.*	3s.
Rémusat, C. de. La Saint-Barthélemy. 12mo. *Lévy.*	3s.
Renan, E. Souvenirs d'enfance. 12mo. *Lévy.*	3s.
Sand, George. La famille de Germandre. 12mo. *Lévy.*	3s.
,, Les maîtres Sonneurs. 12mo. *Lévy.*	3s.
† ,, Histoire du véritable Gribouille. 12mo. (*Paris*).	1s. 6d.
Sandeau, J. Catherine. 12mo. *Lévy.*	1s.
,, J. La maison de Penarvan. 12mo. (*Paris*).	3s.
†Stahl, P. J. Maroussia. 12mo. *Hetzel.*	2s. 6d.
†Souvestre, E. Théâtre de la jeunesse. 12mo. (*Paris*).	1s.
Töpffer. Nouvelles Génevoises. 12mo. (*Paris*).	3s.
Verne, J. Michel Strogoff. 12mo. 2 vols., 3s. each. (*Paris*).	6s.

Vigny, A. de.   Servitude et grandeur militaires.   12mo.   (*Paris*).   3*s.*

,,   Stello.   12mo.   (*Paris*).   3*s.*

THÉÂTRE.

Augier, E.   La pierre de touche.   12mo.   (*Paris*).   2*s.*

,,   L'habit vert.   12mo.   (*Paris*).   2*s.*

,,   Le post-scriptum.   12mo.   (*Paris*).   2*s.*

Beaumarchais.   Le barbier de Séville.   32mo.   (*Paris*).   6*d.*

Erckmann-Chatrian.   Le Juif polonais.   12mo.   (*Paris*).   1*s.* 6*d.*

,,   La guerre.   12mo.   (*Paris*).   1*s.* 6*d.*

Feuillet, O.   Le village.   12mo.   *Lévy.*   1*s.* 6*d.*

Girardin, E. de.   La joie fait peur.   32mo.   (*Paris*).   6*d.*

Gondinet, E.   La cravate blanche.   12mo.   *Lévy.*   1*s.* 6*d.*

Hugo, V.   Hernani.   12mo.   *Lévy.*   1*s.*

,,   Ruy Blas.   12mo.   *Lévy.*   1*s.*

,,   Les Burgraves.   12mo.   *Lévy.*   1*s.*

Legouvé and Labiche.   La cigale chez les fourmis.   12mo.   *Lévy.*   1*s.*

Labiche, E.   La poudre aux yeux.   12mo.   *Lévy.*   2*s.*

,,   Les petits oiseaux.   12mo.   *Lévy.*   3*s.*

Legouvé, E.   Bataille de dames.   12mo.   *Lévy.*   1*s.*

Marivaux, P. C. de.   Les jeux de l'amour et du hasard.   12mo.   (*Paris*).   9*d.*

,,   Le legs.   12mo.   (*Paris*).   2*s.*

Pailleron.   L'étincelle.   12mo.   (*Paris*).   1*s.* 6*d.*

,,   Le monde où l'on s'ennuie.   12mo.   (*Paris*).   2*s.*

Sand, George.   Le mariage de Victorine.   32mo.   (*Paris*).   6*d.*

,,   Le marquis de Villemer.   12mo.   (*Paris*).   3*s.* 6*d.*

Scribe, E.   Le verre d'eau.   32mo.   (*Paris*).   8*d.*

Sedaine.   La gageure imprévue.   16mo.   1*s.*

—VII. NURSERY BOOKS:

Illustrated French primer.   sm. 8vo.   *Hachette.*   1*s.* 6*d.*

French nursery rhymes.   sm. 8vo.   *Hachette.*   1*s.*

Je saurai lire (with sequel).   4to.   *Garnier.*   illus.   5*s.*

Ségur, Mme. de.   Contes de fées.   12mo.   *Hachette.*   2*s.*

Perrault, Mme. d'Aulnoy, etc.   Contes de fées.   12mo.   *Hachette.*   2*s.*

Bell, Mrs. Hugh.   Petit théâtre des enfants.   f. 8vo.   *Longmans.*   1*s.* 6*d.*

Bawr, Mme. de.   Nouveaux contes.   12mo.   *Hachette.*   2*s.*

Berquin.   Choix de drames et de contes.   12mo.   *Hachette.*   2*s.*

Pape-Charpentier, Mme.   Histoire et leçons de choses.   12mo.   2 series.   *Hachette.*   2*s.*

Genlis, Mme. de.   Contes moraux.   12mo.   *Hachette.*   2*s.*

Carraud, Mme.   Historiettes véritables.   12mo.   *Hachette.*   2*s.*

Bert, Paul.   Première année de science.   12mo.   *Colin.*   1*s.*

Fleury, L. L'histoire racontée aux enfants. 18mo. 10 vols., 2s. each.
 Borrani. 20s.
  Ten little books on ancient and modern history.

Conversational first French reader. 16mo. *Hachette.* 10d.

La Fontaine. Fables. (*Paris*).
  Numerous editions, from 1s. 6d. upwards.

Ségur, Mme. de. Les malheurs de Sophie. 12mo. *Hachette.* 2s.

 ,, Petites filles modèles. 12mo. *Hachette.* 2s.

 ,, Les vacances. 12mo. *Hachette.* 2s.

 ,, Les deux Nigauds. 12mo. *Hachette.* 2s.

Carraud. Metamorphoses d'une goutte d'eau. 12mo. *Hachette.* 2s.

Esclangon. Petite anthologie des enfants. sm. 8vo. *Hachette.* 1s. 6d.

Les bébés des jardins de Paris. 4to. *Quantin.* illus. 2s.

La journée de bébé. 4to. *Quantin.* illus. 3s.

Les bébés d'Alsace-Lorraine. sm. 4to. *Quantin.* illus. 2s.

Malvin. First French reciter. *Hachette.* 1s. 3d.

La lyre enfantine. sm. 8vo. *Hachette.* 1s. 6d.

Images enfantines. fo. 5 vols., 3s. each. *Quantin.* 15s.
  Excellent series of picture books.

FRANCO-GERMAN WAR, *see* GERMANY, HISTORY.

FREE LIBRARIES, *see* LIBRARIES.

FREEMASONRY:

 Gould, R. F. History of Freemasonry. 4to. 6 vols., 12s. 6d. each. 78s.

 Mackey, A. G. Lexicon of Freemasonry. c. 8vo. *Griffin.* 6s.

FRIENDLY SOCIETIES, *see* ASSURANCE.

FRISIAN LANGUAGE:

 Cummins, A. H. Old Friesic grammar. c. 8vo. *Trübner.* 6s.

 Outzen, N. Glossarium der friesischen Sprache. (*Copenhagen*). 1837. 10s.

FRUIT GROWING, *see* GARDENING.

FURNITURE, *see* HOUSE DECORATION.

G.

GAELIC, *see* IRELAND *and* SCOTLAND.

GAME LAWS *and* GAME PRESERVING, *see* SHOOTING

GAMES AND PASTIMES :

See separate heads for games not mentioned below.

—I. OUTDOOR :

"Stonehenge." British rural sports. d. 8vo. *Warne.* illus.   21s.
> Cricket, football, fives, rackets, lawn tennis, badminton, golf, hockey, swimming, skating, bicycling, riding, driving, walking, running, leaping, throwing the hammer, putting the weight, training.

Boy's own book. 8vo. *Lockwood.* illus.   8s. 6d.
> Athletic and minor sports, indoor and drawing-room games, naturalist, scientific recreations, tricks, etc.

Book of sports and pastimes. 8vo. *Cassell.* illus.   3s. 6d.
> Outdoor games, toys, workshop, pets, etc.

Kerr, J. History of curling. d. 8vo. *Douglas.* illus.   10s. 6d.
> An elaborate and useful work somewhat marred by the efforts at humour.

Creswell, F. S. Hockey ("All England" ser.). sm. 8vo. *Bell.*   1s.

Sachs, E. Lacrosse for beginners. 8vo. (*New York*).   O.P.

Beers, W. G. Lacrosse. 12mo. *Low.* illus.   5s.
> Contains history of the game.

Younghusband, Capt. Polo in India. c. 8vo. *W. H. Allen.*   2s.

—II. INDOOR :

Bohn. Handbook of games. 2 vols., 3s. 6d. each. *Bell.* illus.   7s.
> Vol. i.: Billiards, chess, bagatelle, draughts, backgammon, dominoes, roulette, etc. Vol. ii.: Whist, piquet, ecarté, euchre, poker, cribbage, etc. Sold separately, 1s. each.

Cyclopædia of card and table games. Ed. "Hoffman." d. 8vo. *Routledge.*   10s. 6d.

"Hoffmann," Prof. Drawing-room amusements, and evening party entertainments. p. 8vo. *Routledge.* illus.   6s.
> Games of action, pen and pencil games, forfeits, miscellaneous amusements, amateur theatricals, tableaux vivants, waxworks, shadow pantomimes, drawing-room tricks, etc.

Lillie, A. Acting charades. 8vo. *Cox.*   3s. 6d.

Book of indoor amusements, card games, and fireside fun. 4to. *Cassell.* illus.   3s. 6d.
> Parlour games, toy games, toy making, puzzles, etc.

—III. MISCELLANEOUS :

Browne, W. H. Firework-making for amateurs. 8vo. *Upcott Gill.* illus.   2s. 6d.

Magic lantern, its construction and use. 12mo. *Perkins and Rayment.*   6d.

GARDENING :

Illustrated dictionary of gardening. Ed. G. Nicholson. l. p. 4to. 4 vols., 15s. each. *Gill.*   60s.
> General book of reference on everything relating to gardening.

Cassell's popular gardening. Ed. D. T. Fish. c. 8vo. 4 vols., 5s. each. *Cassell.*   20s.
> This includes articles on villa-gardening and window-gardening.

Bailey, L. H. Horticulturist's rule-book. *"Garden" Pub. Co.*

Kemp, E. How to lay out a small garden. 12mo. *Bradbury, Evans.*   3s. 6d.

  ,,   How to lay out a large garden. c. 8vo. *Bradbury, Evans.*   12s.

Robinson, W. English flower garden. 8vo. *Murray.* illus.   15s.
> Cultivation of out-door flowers.

Castle, Lewis. Town and suburban gardening. p. 8vo. *Sonnenschein.*   2s. 6d.

Burbidge, F. W. Cultivated plants, their propagation and improvement. c. 8vo. *Blackwood.* illus. | 12s. 6d.

Baltet, C. Art of grafting and budding. Tr. 12mo. *Macmillan.* | 5s.

André, E. L'art des jardins. r. 8vo. *Masson* (*Paris*). | 28s. 6d.
Best book on landscape gardening.

Milner, H. E. Art and practice of landscape gardening. 4to. *Simpkin.* | 31s. 6d.

Vilmorin-Andrieux, M. Vegetable garden. 8vo. *Murray.* illus. pub. 15s. | o.p.

Hogg, R. Fruit manual. *"Journal of Horticulture" Office.* | 16s.

Thomson, D. Fruit culture under glass. c. 8vo. *Blackwood.* illus. | 7s. 6d.

Rivers, T. Orchard house. c. 8vo. *Longmans.* illus. | 5s.

Barron, A. F. Vines and vine culture. *"Journal of Horticulture" Office.* | 5s.

Paul, W. Rose garden. 8vo. *Kent.* | 10s. 6d.

Smith, J. Ferns, British and foreign. c. 8vo. *Allen.* | 7s. 6d.

Watson and Bean. Orchids, their culture and management. d. 8vo. *Gill.* illus. | 15s. 6d.

Watson, W. Cactus culture for amateurs. l. p. 8vo. *Gill.* illus. | 5s.

Firminger, T. A. C. Indian gardening. c. 8vo. *Thacker.* | 21s.

PERIODICALS: *Gardener's Chronicle*; *The Garden*; the two best weekly papers. *Journal of the Royal Horticultural Society*, 117, Victoria-street, S.W.

GAS ANALYSIS, *see* CHEMISTRY IV.

„ ENGINES, *see* STEAM ENGINES.

„ MANUFACTURE, *see* INDUSTRIES X.

GASTRONOMY, *see* COOKERY.

GAZETTEERS, *see* GEOGRAPHY VII.

GEMS, *see* ARTISTIC PROCESSES III. *and* PRECIOUS STONES.

GENEALOGY, *see* HERALDRY II.

GENERAL AVERAGE, *see* ASSURANCE.

GEOGRAPHY:

See also under the different countries.

Under this head the aim has been to give the titles of the books that afford the best information up to date, on each section of the subject. No attempt is made to give a list of the best book of travel for each region; these will be found in the books mentioned under the head of "Reference." Anyone desiring a general knowledge of any particular region or country, would do well to start with the section dealing with the subject in Reclus' *Universal geography;* or in Stanford's *Compendium*, following up with the special books mentioned under the different heads, or in the references given in Reclus.

—I. HISTORY :

In the annual addresses of the presidents of the Royal Geographical Society, will be found a summary of each year's exploration and geographical work; these may be taken as supplementary to the works herein given.

Bunbury, E. H. History of ancient geography among the Greeks and Romans. 8vo. 2 vols. *Murray.* Maps. | 21s.

Saint Martin, V. de. Histoire de la géographie et des découvertes géographiques. 8vo. *Hachette.*   16s.
From the earliest time to the present day. On the whole, the best book on the subject. Includes historical atlas.

Cooley, W. D. History of maritime and inland discovery, 12mo. 3 vols. *Longmans.* 1831. pub. 10s. 6d.   O.P.

Murray, H. Historical account of discoveries in Africa, Asia, and North America, from the earliest times. 8vo. 7 vols. *Longmans.* 1818-29. pub. 96s.   O.P.

Lindsay, W. S. History of merchant shipping and ancient commerce. 8vo. 4 vols. *Low.*   50s.
Vol. i., ii., 22s. ; vol. iii., iv., 28s.

—II. VOYAGES AND TRAVELS:

Markham, C. R. Famous sailors of former times. p. 8vo. *Cassell.*   2s. 6d.

Yule, H. The book of Sir Marco Polo, the Venetian ; newly translated. m. 8vo. 2 vols. *Murray.*   63s.

Major, R. H. The life of Henry the navigator. i. 8vo. *Asher.* illus.   25s.

Vasco da Gama's three voyages. (*Hakluyt Soc.* vol. xlii.). Tr. from the Portuguese by H. E. J. Stanley. 8vo.

Columbus, Christopher. Select letters and other original documents relating to his four voyages to the New World. (*Hakluyt Soc.* vol. xliii.). Tr. R. H. Major. 8vo. illus.

Irving, Washington. Life and voyages of Christopher Columbus. p. 8vo. 2 vols., 3s. 6d. each. *Bell* (*Bohn*).   7s.

Harrisse, H. Christophe Colomb. r. 8vo. 2 vols. *Leroux.* illus.   80s.
From unpublished documents in the archives of Genoa, Madrid, etc.

   ,,   Cabot, Jean et Sebastian. l. 8vo. (*Paris*).   21s.
With maps, bibliography and chronology of north-western voyage.

Magellan's Voyage round the world ; from Pigafetta and other writers. (*Hakluyt Soc.* vol. liv.). 8vo.

Guillemard, F. H. Magellan ("World's Great Explorers" ser.). c. 8vo. *Philip.*   4s. 6d.

Markham, C. R. Life of John Davis, the navigator, 1550-1605 ("World's Great Explorers" ser.). c. 8vo. *Philip.* illus.   4s. 6d.

Markham, A. Voyages and works of John Davis. (*Hakluyt Soc.*). 8vo.

De Veer, Gerrit. Three voyages of William Barents to the Arctic regions, 1594—6. (*Hakluyt Soc.* vol. liv.). 8vo. illus.

Drake's Voyage round the world, 1577—80. (*Hakluyt Soc.* vol. xvi.). 8vo.

Drake's last voyage, and death. (*Hakluyt Soc.* vol. iv.). 8vo.

Barrow, J. Drake's life, voyages and exploits. p. 8vo. *Murray.*   2s.

Leo Africanus, John. Geographical historie of Africa. Tr. John Pory. 4to. Map. 1600.

Frobisher's three voyages in search of passage to Cathaia and India, 1576—8. Ed. R. Collinson. (*Hakluyt Soc.* vol. xxxviii.). 8vo.

Cayley, A. Sir Walter Raleigh. 2 vols. (*London*). 1806.   O.P.

Hawkins, Mary W. S. Plymouth Armada heroes ; the Hawkins family. *Brendon* (*Plymouth*).   12s. 6d.

Asher, G. M. Henry Hudson the navigator. (*Hakluyt Soc.*).

Valle, Pietro della. Travels in East India and Arabia Deserta ; also Sir Thomas Roe's voyage to the E. Indies. fo. Map. 1665.

Thévenot's Travels into the Levant. fo. 1687.

Tavernier's Travels in India. Tr. from the French of 1676, by V. Ball. 8vo. 2 vols. *Macmillan.*   42*s.*

Dampier, W. New voyage round the world. 8vo. 4 vols. 1729.

Walter, R. Anson's voyage round the world in the "Centurion," 1740—4. (*London*). Maps and plates. 1748.

Barrow, J. Life of Lord Anson. *Murray.* 1839. pub. 14*s.*   O.P.

Cook's Voyage towards the S. Pole, 1772—5. 4to. 2 vols. 1777.

     ,,   Voyage to the Pacific, 1776—80. 4to. 3 vols. Maps and plates. 1784.

Kippis, Andrew. Captain Cook. 4to. (*London*). 1788.   O.P.

Besant, W. Captain Cook. c. 8vo. *Macmillan.*   2*s.* 6*d.*
     Brief and popular.

Bruce, James. Travels to discover the source of the Nile, 1768—73. 4to. 5 vols. (*Edinburgh*). Maps and plates. 1790.

Vancouver, G. Voyage to the N. Pacific and round the world. 1790—5. 4to. 3 vols. Plates. 1798.

Park, Mungo. Travels in the interior of Africa. 1795—7. 8vo. 2 vols. Maps and plates. 1800.

Thomson, J. Mungo Park ("World's Great Explorers"). c. 8vo. *Philip.*   4*s.* 6*d.*

Lowenberg, J. Humboldt. Tr. Lassell. 8vo. 2 vols. *Longmans.* pub. 36*s.*   O.P.

Parry, W. E. Voyage for the discovery of a North-West passage, 1819—20. 4to. Charts and plates. 1821.

     ,,   Second voyage, 1821—3. 4to. Maps and plates. 1824.
     Appendix. 4to. 1825.

     ,,   Third voyage, 1824—5. 4to. Charts and plates. 1826.

     ,,   Attempt to reach the North Pole, 1827. 4to. Charts and plates. 1828.

Elder, W. Biography of Elisha Kent Kane. 8vo. (*Philadelphia*).   12*s.*

Franklin, J. Journey to the shores of the Polar Sea, 1819—22. 4to. Maps and plates. 1823.

     ,,   Second expedition, 1825—7. 4to. Maps and plates. 1828.

Markham, A. John Franklin and the North-West Passage. c. 8vo. *Philip.*   4*s.* 6*d.*

Voyages of the "Adventure" and "Beagle" to S. America and round the world, 1826—39. *Ward, Lock.*

Waterton, C. Wanderings in South America. c. 8vo. *Macmillan.* illus.   6*s.*

Corbin, Diana. M. F. Maury. 8vo. *Low.*   12*s.* 6*d.*

McIlraith, J. Life of Sir John Richardson. c. 8vo. *Longmans.* pub. 5*s.*   O.P.

Hitchman, F. Life and travels of R. F. Burton. 8vo. 2 vols. *Low.*   36*s.*

Life, letters, and journals of Sir Roderick J. Murchison. Ed. A. Geikie. 2 vols. *Murray.*   30*s.*

Blackie, W. G. Personal life of David Livingstone. c. 8vo. *Murray.* illns.   6*s.*

Montefiore, A. David Livingstone, his labours and his legacy. c. 8vo. *Partridge.* illus.   1*s.* 6*d.*

Johnston, H. H. Livingstone and Central Africa ("World's Great Explorers" ser.). c. 8vo. *Philip.*   4*s.* 6*d.*

Moffat, J. S. Lives of Robert and Mary Moffat. 8vo. *Unwin.*   3*s.* 6*d.*

Autobiography and reminiscences of Sir D. Forsyth. Ed. by his daughter. d. 8vo. *Bentley.*   12*s.* 6*d.*

COLLECTIONS.

Hakluyt, R. Voyages and discoveries.
> Black letter edition, 1599–1600. This is the original authority for the explorations of the 16th and previous centuries. Reprint 1809 in 5 vols. New edition, by subscr.; (*Goldsmid; Edinb.*); 1886.

Purchas, his pilgrims. 5 vols. 1625–26. illus.   O.P.
> To a considerable extent a supplement to Hakluyt.

Yule, H. Cathay, and the way thither: mediæval notices of China. (*Hakluyt Soc.*, vols. xxxvi. and xxxvii.). 8vo.

Pinkerton, John. Voyages and travels. 4to. 17 vols. *Longmans.* 1808–14. pub. £37 16*s.*   O.P.

Kerr, Robert. Collection of voyages and travels. 8vo. 17 vols. *Baldwin.* 1811–25. pub. £10 4*s.*   O.P.
> For ordinary purposes Pinkerton's and Kerr's collections will be found most useful.

Conder, Josiah. Modern traveller. 30 vols. 1831. maps and plates.   O.P.

Works issued by the Hakluyt Soc. (*Great Queen-st., W.C.*). Pub. since 1847.

—III. GENERAL GEOGRAPHY:

Strachey, R. Lectures on geography. c. 8vo. *Macmillan.*   4*s.* 6*d.*
> A useful summary of what subjects are included in geography to the modern student.

Huxley, T. H. Physiography. c. 8vo. *Macmillan.*   6*s.*
> This is the earliest work of the kind in England, and, on the whole, still the most satisfactory.

Hinman, R. Eclectic physical geography. c. 8vo. (*Cincinnati*).   5*s.*
> The clearest, most methodical, and most intelligible of physical geographies.

Our earth and its story. Ed. R. Brown. r. 8vo. *Cassell.*   9*s.*
> Based on a high-class German work, and more systematic and up to date than Reclus' "Earth" and "Ocean."

Reclus, E. The ocean, atmosphere, and life. Ed. A. H. Keane. i. 8vo. *Virtue.* illus.   21*s.*

  ,,   The earth and its inhabitants. Ed. Keane and Ravenstein. i. 8vo. *Virtue.* illus.   21*s.*
> General introduction to Reclus' "Universal geography."

  ,,   Universal geography. Ed. Ravenstein and Keane. i. 8vo. 17 vols., 21*s.* each. *Virtue.*   £17 17*s.*
> Vol. i., South Europe; vol. ii., France; vol. iii., Central Europe; vol. iv., N.W. Europe; vol. v., Scandinavia and Russia; vol. vi., Russian Asia; vol. vii., Eastern Asia; vol. viii., India and Indo-China; vol. ix., Western Asia; vol. x., North Africa (Nile Basin, etc.); vol. xi., North Africa (Algiers, Morocco, etc.); vol. xii., West Africa; vol. xiii., South and East Africa, in preparation; vol. xiv., Australasia, in preparation; vols. xv., xvi., xvii., America, in preparation.
>
> The best and most complete descriptive geography. For information required concerning any particular country this should be first referred to. The French original is better than the English translation.

Stanford's Compendium of geography and travel, with ethnological appendices. Ed. A. H. Keane. l. p. 8vo. 6 vols., 21*s.* each. *Stanford.*   126*s.*
> Europe, Asia, Africa, North America, Central and South America, Australasia.

Brown, R. The countries of the world. r. 8vo. 6 vols., 7*s.* 6*d.* each. *Cassell.* illus.   45*s.*
> More discursive and less systematic than Reclus.

Johnston, K.   Physical, historical, political, and descriptive geography.   Ed. E. G. Ravenstein. p. 8vo. *Stanford.*   12s.
    On the whole, the most satisfactory English text-book.

Chisholm, G. G.   Longman's school geography. p. 8vo. *Longmans.*   3s. 6d.
    The best text-book on the new lines.

Clyde, J.   School geography. 12mo. *Simpkin.*   4s.
    The best text-book on the old lines.

Mill, H. R.   Elementary class-book of general geography. c. 8vo. *Macmillan.* illus.   3s. 6d.
    A readable and interesting sketch.

    ,,   Elementary commercial geography. ex. f. 8vo. *Camb. Press.*   1s.

Chisholm, G. G.   Handbook of commercial geography. 8vo. *Longmans.*   16s.
    The best in existence. Smaller edition, 2s. 6d.

Keltie, J. Scott.   Applied geography. *Philip.*   3s. 6d.

Kiepert, H.   Manual of ancient geography. Tr. c. 8vo. *Macmillan.*   5s.

Lelewel, J.   Géographie du moyen âge. 8vo. 4 vols. (*Brussels*).   63s.

—IV. OCEANOGRAPHY :

Krümmel, O.   Der Ozean. 12mo. *Freitag.*   1s. 6d.
    Introduction to general oceanography.

Boguslawski, G. von.   Handbuch der Ozeanographie. 8vo. 2 vols. (*Leipzig*).   23s. 6d.

Depths of the sea. 8vo. *Macmillan.*   31s. 6d.
    General results of dredging cruises (1868-70) under the direction of Dr. W. B. Carpenter, Gwyn Jeffreys, and Sir Wyville Thomson.

Wharton, W. J. L.   Hydrographical surveying. 8vo. *Murray.*   15s.

Thoulet, J.   Océanographie. 8vo. *Dulau.* illus.   8s. 6d.

—V. SPECIAL TREATISES :

Peschel, O.   Neue Probleme der vergleichende Erdkunde. 8vo. (*Leipzig*).   5s.

    ,,   Abhandlungen zur Erdkunde. 3 vols. (*Leipzig*).   30s.

    ,,   Physische Erdkunde. 8vo. 2 vols. (*Leipzig*).   30s.
    Peschel's works must be studied by the student who desires to master the latest aspect of geography.

Ratzel, F.   Anthropologische Geographie. 8vo. *Engelhorn.*   10s.
    Sketch of application of geography to history.

Marsh, G. P.   The earth as modified by human action. 8vo. *Low.*   18s.

Hahn, F. G.   Inselstudien. 8vo. (*Leipzig*).   7s. 6d.

Wallace, A. R.   Island life. 8vo. *Macmillan.*   18s.
    Phenomena and causes of insular faunas and floras.

Ritter, K.   Comparative geography. Tr. F. Gage. f. 8vo. *Blackwood.*   3s. 6d.
    A translation of a few of Ritter's essays. The student should, if possible, study the whole of Ritter's works.

Wallace, A. R.   Geographical distribution of animals. 8vo. 2 vols. *Macmillan.*   42s.

Petherick.   Catalogue of the York Gate Library of S. W. Silver, Esq. 8vo. *Murray.*   42s.
    Silver's is probably the best private collection in the country : access is easily obtained by the studious.

    PERIODICALS, ETC.: The chief society is the Royal Geographical Society, whose *Journal* and *Proceedings* abound with papers and memoirs of great value. The Scottish Geographical Society also publish the *Scottish Geographical Magazine*, which contains many important papers. The *Journal* of the Manchester Geographical Society is strong in papers on commercial geography. The consular and other commercial reports published at frequent intervals by the Foreign Office, and those issued by the Colonial Office (*Eyre*), and costing usually a trifling sum, often contain new geographical information.

—VI. ETYMOLOGY:

Taylor, I. Words and places. gl. 8vo. *Macmillan.*   6s.
Etymological illustrations of history, ethnology, and geography.

Blackie, C. Geographical etymology. 8vo. *Murray.*   7s.

Yule and Burnell. Hobson-Jobson, a glossary of Anglo-Indian colloquial
    terms. 8vo. *Murray.*   36s.

Egli, J. J. Etymologisch-geographisches Lexikon. 8vo. (*Leipzig*).   12s.

—VII. REFERENCE :

There is no really first-rate English gazetteer up to date. Those given are, on the whole,
the best. The *Universal geography* might well be consulted (through its index) for gazetteer
information, and the geographical articles in the *Encyclopædia Britannica* and Chambers'
Encyclopædia. For the student, the copious bibliographies appended to St. Martin's
Nouvelle dictionnaire will be found most useful.

Martin and Rousselet. Nouveau dictionnaire de géographie universelle.
    4to. 5 vols. *Hachette.*
Vol. i. (A-C), 22s. 6d.; vol. ii. (D-J), 26s.; vol. iii. (K-M), 27s. 6d., in progress. The best
gazetteer in existence.

Bryce and Johnston. Library gazetteer of the world. r. 8vo. *Collins.*   15s.
A fairly satisfactory and succinct gazetteer.

Bartholomew, J. Century atlas and gazetteer of the world. 32mo.
    J. Walker.   2s. 6d.
A cheap and useful index to find where a place is.

Markham. Fifty years' work of the Royal Geographical Society. 8vo.
    Murray.   4s.
Contains a complete classified index to the Journal and Proceedings of the society. The vols.
from January, 1879, are supplied with lesser indices.

Statesman's year-book (annual). Ed. J. Scott Keltie. c. 8vo. *Macmillan.*   10s. 6d.

GEOLOGY :

Young students should read Geikie's *Primer.* All beginners must read a Physical
geography such as Page's *Introductory text-book,* or Huxley's *Physiography*; then read
Page and Lapworth's *Geology,* or the more expensive class-book by Geikie, followed by
Ramsay's *Physical geology and geography of Great Britain.* Geikie's *Field-work* will
teach how to observe. The science can only be learned in the museum and field. Lyell's
Principles should be read by those who desire a philosophical treatise, though it does not
include the latest discoveries. Geikie's *Scenery and geology of Scotland* will specially
interest those whose æsthetic perceptions are quickened by inquiry into causes.

—I. TEXT-BOOKS :

Geikie, A. Primer of geology. (elem.). 18mo. *Macmillan.* illus.   1s.

Page and Lapworth. Introductory text-book of geology. (elem.). f. 8vo.
    Blackwood. illus.   3s. 6d.

Geikie, A. Class-book of geology. c. 8vo. *Macmillan.* illus.   4s. 6d.

Lyell, C. Student's elements of geology. p. 8vo. *Murray.* illus.   9s.

   ,,   Principles of geology. 8vo. 2 vols., 16s. each. *Murray.* pub. 32s.   o.p.

Geikie, A. Text-book of geology. 8vo. *Macmillan.* illus.   28s.

Prestwich, J. Geology. 2 vols. *Clar. Press.* illus.   61s.
    Vol. i., 25s.; vol., ii., 36s.

Geikie, A. Outlines of field geology. c. 8vo. *Macmillan.* illus.   3s. 6d.

—II. PHYSICAL GEOLOGY (in addition to text-books above referred to) :

Gilbert, G. K. Geology of the Henry mountains. *Govt. Printing Office*
    (*Washington*). illus.

Green, A. H. Physical geology. 8vo. *Rivington.* illus.   21s.

Heim, A. Mechanismus der Gebirgsbildung. r. 8vo. 2 vols. (*Berlin*).   60*s.*
     With atlas of Alpine structure.

Judd, J. W. Volcanoes ("Inter. Scient." ser.). c. 8vo. *Paul.* illus.   5*s.*

Milne, J. Earthquakes ("Inter. Scient." ser.). c. 8vo. *Paul.* illus.   5*s.*

Darwin, C. Coral reefs. c. 8vo. *Smith, Elder.*   8*s.* 6*d.*

Dana, J. D. Corals and coral islands. c. 8vo. *Low.* illus. pub. 8*s.* 6*d.*   O.P.
     Structure and growth of corals and history of reefs, more generally useful than Darwin's
     classical essay.

—III. PETROGRAPHY:

Rutley, F. Rock-forming minerals. d. 8vo. *Murby.*   7*s.* 6*d.*

   ,,   Study of rocks. f. 8vo. *Longmans.* illus.   4*s.* 6*d.*

Teall. British petrography. r. 8vo. *Dulau.* illus.   63*s.*

Rosenbusch. Microscopic physiography of rock-making minerals. Tr. J. P
     Iddings. 8vo. *Macmillan.* illus.   24*s.*

—IV. PALÆONTOLOGY:

Nicholson and Lydekker. Manual of palæontology. 8vo. 2 vols. *Black-*
     wood. illus.   63*s*

Nicholson, H. A. Ancient life-history of the earth. (elem.). c. 8vo.
     Blackwood. illus.   10*s.* 6*d.*

—V. STRATIGRAPHY:

Harrison, W. J. Geology of the counties of England and Wales. 8vo.
     Kelly.   8*s*

Woodward, H. B. Geology of England and Wales. d. 8vo. *Philip.* illus.   18*s.*
     Contains geological map of England.

Phillips, J. Geology of Oxford and valley of the Thames. 8vo. *Clar. Press.*   21*s.*

—VI. COAL AND ORES:

Smyth, W. W. Coal and coal mining. 12mo. *Lockwood.*   4*s.*

Green and others. Coal: its history and uses. 8vo. *Macmillan.*   12*s.* 6*d.*

Hull, E. Coal-fields of Great Britain. d. 8vo. *Stanford.*   16*s.*

Phillips, J. Ore deposits. 8vo. *Macmillan.* illus.   25*s.*

—VII. GLACIAL PERIODS:

Geikie, J. Great ice age. 8vo. *Daldy.*   24*s.*

Croll, J. Climate and time. 8vo. *Daldy.*   24*s.*

Reid. Geology of the district around Cromer (Geol. Survey). *Stanford.*   6*s.*

Lubbock, J. Pre-historic times. 8vo. *Williams.*   18*s.*

Lyell, C. Antiquity of man. 8vo. *Murray.* pub. 14*s.*   O.P.

Evans, J. Ancient stone implements of Great Britain. r. 8vo. *Longmans.*
     pub. 28*s.*   O.P.

—VIII. SPECIAL REGIONS:

Geikie, A. Scenery and geology of Scotland. c. 8vo. *Macmillan.*   12*s.* 6*d.*

Kinahan, G. H. Geology of Ireland. p. 8vo. *Paul.*   15*s.*
     Deals with geology and minerals.

Hull, E. Geology of Ireland. p. 8vo. *Stanford.*   7*s.*
     Treats mainly of physical geography as dependent on the geology.

Ramsay, A. C.   Geology of North Wales (Geol. Survey).   *Stanford.*   21*s.*

Whitaker, W.   Geology of the London basin (Geol. Survey).   *Stanford.*   13*s.*

Geology of the Isle of Wight (Geol. Survey).   r. 8vo.   *Stanford.*   7*s.* 6*d.*

Dana, J. D.   Manual of geology.   8vo.   *Trübner.*   21*s.*
     Contains North American geology.

Lapparent, A. de   Géologie.   8vo.   *Sary.*   20*s.*
     Contains continental geology.

—IX. BIOGRAPHIES :

Life of Sir Charles Lyell.   Ed. Mrs. Lyell.   8vo.   2 vols.   *Murray.*   30*s.*

Geikie, A.   Sir R. Murchison and his contemporaries.   8vo.   2 vols.   *Murray.*   30*s.*

Clark and Hughes.   Life of Sedgwick.   d. 8vo.   2 vols.   *Cambridge Press.*   36*s.*

—X. MAPS AND BIBLIOGRAPHY :

Ramsay, A. C.   Geological maps of England and Wales (12 miles to inch).   *Stanford.*   21*s.*

Prestwich, J.   Geological map of Europe.   *Clar. Press.*   5*s.*

Geikie, A.   Geological map of Scotland (10 miles to inch).   *Stanford.*   21*s.*

Hull, E.   Geological map of Ireland (8 miles to inch).   *Stanford.*   30*s.*

Marcou.   Geological map of the world (8 sheets).   (*Zurich*).   16*s.*

Horizontal geological sections (Geol. Survey).   *Stanford.*
     Six inches to the mile.

District geological maps of the United Kingdom.
     (Geol. Survey, inch to mile, on sheets, 110 div.).   *Stanford.*   From 1*s.* 6*d.* to 8*s.* 6*d.* each sheet.

Catalogue of the library of the Geological Society (to 1880).   8vo.   *Geol. Soc.*   8*s.*
     PERIODICALS, ETC. :—*Geological Record* ; pub. since 1874, Vol. i., 15*s.* ; the rest 16*s.* each. (Taylor and Francis) ; *Geological Magazine* (Trübner), 1*s.* 6*d.* monthly ; *Quarterly Journal of the Geological Society* ; *Proceedings* of the Geologists' Association ; Palæontographical Society's monographs.

GEOMETRY :

For Analytical geometry, see MATHEMATICS.

Smith, Hamblin.   Elements of geometry (Euclid).   12mo.   *Rivington.*   3*s.*

Todhunter, I.   Euclid.   8vo.   *Macmillan.*   3*s.* 6*d.*

Casey, J.   Euclid (with exercises).   f. 8vo.   *Longmans.*   4*s.* 6*d.*
     First six books, and props. i. to xxi. of book xi. ; key to exercises, 6*s.*

  ,,   Sequel to Euclid.   c. 8vo.   *Longmans.*   3*s.* 6*d.*
     Contains theory of harmonic ratio.   Casey's books are very strongly to be recommended as the best books of their kind.

Elements of plane geometry.   (Association for improvement of geom. teaching).   c. 8vo.   2 parts, 2*s.* 6*d.* each.   *Sonnenschein.*   5*s.*
     Not to be used by those who wish to follow Euclid strictly.

Henrici, O.   Elementary geometry.   12mo.   *Longmans.*   1*s.* 6*d.*
     Departs altogether from Euclidean methods ; contains congruent figures.

Nixon, R. C. J.   Plane and solid geometry.   c. 8vo.   2 vols.   *Clar. Press.*   9*s.* 6*d.*
     Vol. i., Plane, Euclid, books i. to vi., 6*s.* ; also sold separately, book i., 1*s.* ; books i., ii., 1*s.* 6*d.* ; books i. to iv., 3*s.* ; books v., vi., 3*s.*   Vol. ii., Solid, books xi., xii., 3*s.* 6*d.*

Cremona.   Projective geometry (advanced).   Tr. Leudesdorf.   p. 8vo.   *Clar. Press.*   3*s.* 6*d.*

Drew, W. Geometrical treatise on conic sections. (elem.). c. 8vo. *Macmillan.*   5s.

Besant, W. H. Conic sections. f. 8vo. *Bell.*   4s. 6d.

Taylor, C. Geometrical conic sections. 8vo. *Bell.*   4s. 6d.

GEORGIA, *see* RUSSIA IN ASIA II.

GERMANY: GEOGRAPHY:

See also AUSTRIA-HUNGARY.

—I. GENERAL:

Murray's Handbook. The Rhine and North Germany. p. 8vo. *Murray.*   10s

  ,,   South Germany, Austria-Hungary, and Tyrol. p. 8vo. 2 parts. *Murray.*   12s

Baedeker. Northern Germany. 12mo. *Dulau.*   7s

  ,,   Southern Germany and Austria. 12mo. *Dulau.*   7s

Reclus, E. Universal geography, vol. iii. i. 8vo. *Virtue.*   21s

Neumann, G. Geographisches Lexicon des deutschen Reichs. 8vo. 2 vols. with atlas. *Bibliographisches Institut.*   15s

Baring-Gould, S. Germany past and present. p. 8vo. *Paul.*   7s. 6d.

Stieler, K. The Rhine, from its source to the sea. Tr. Bartley. 8vo. *Bickers.* illus.   52s. 6d.

Séguin, L. G. The Black Forest, its people and legends. *Strahan.*   12s.

—II. LOCAL:

BAVARIA AND MUNICH.

Lampers, F. Ober-Ammergau und sein Passionspiel. (*Munich*).   1s. 6d.

Acht Tage in München. (*Munich*).   2s

Führer durch München und seine Umgebung. (*Munich*).   2s.

München in guter alter Zeit. (*Munich*). illus.   16s.

München in der neuen Zeit. (*Munich*). illus.   10s.

König Ludwig I., und seine Kunstschöpfungen. (*Munich*). illus.   30s.

SAXONY AND DRESDEN.

Lehmann. Dresden und Sächs. Schweiz (Guide-book). 12mo. (*Leipzig*).   2s.

Schreyer, W. Landeskunde des Kgr: Sachsen. 8vo. (*Meissen*).   2s.

Lindau, M. Geschichte von Dresden. r. 8vo. (*Dresden*).   24s.

Mohr, K. Geschichte von Sachsen. 8vo. (*Leipzig*).   1s

Gebauer, H. Bilder aus dem sächsischen Berglande. 8vo. (*Leipzig*).   6s.

BERLIN.

Brasch and Rothenstein. Guide to Berlin. (*Berlin*).   2s.

Streckfuss, A. 500 Jahre Berliner Geschichte; vom Fischerdorf zur Weltstadt. 2 vols. (*Berlin*).   22s. 6d

Hennes, A. 150 Ausflüge in die Umgebung von Berlin (with map). (*Berlin*).   1s.

  ,,   32 Ausflüge in die weitere Umgebung von Berlin. (*Berlin*).   1s. 6d.

GERMANY : HISTORY :

Including Austria-Hungary. See also HUNGARY.

Dahlmann and Waitz. Quellenkunde der deutschen Geschichte. 8vo. (*Göttingen*).   5*s.*
Bibliography of the subject.

Wattenbach, W. Deutschlands Geschichtsquellen im Mittelalter. 8vo. 2 vols. (*Berlin*).   17*s.*
Critical account of the authorities to 1350.

Lorenz, O. Deutschlands Geschichtsquellen im Mittelalter. 8vo. 2 vols. (*Berlin*).   15*s.*
Continuation of the above, 1350-1160.

Allgemeine deutsche Biographie. 20 vols., 12*s.* each. (*Leipzig*).
Biographical dictionary, not quite completed.

Luden, H. Geschichte des teutschen Volkes. 8vo. 12 vols. (*Gotha*). 1825-37.   48*s.*

Greenwood, T. History of the Germans. 4to. *Longmans.* 1836.   O.P.
Only covers the early history, but does it in a way that no other accessible book does.

Waitz, G. Deutsche Verfassungsgeschichte. 8vo. 8 vols. (*Kiel*).
Vol. i., 12*s.*; vol. ii. (1), 16*s.*; vol. ii. (2), 10*s.*; vol. iii., 16*s.*; vol. iv., 16*s.*; vol. v., reprinting; vol. vi., 12*s.*; vol. vii.,.11*s.*; vol. viii., 13*s.* General constitutional history to 1200.

Maurer, G. L. von. Geschichte der Markverfassung in Deutschland. 8vo. (*Erlangen*).   O.P.

  ,, Geschichte der Dorfverfassung. 8vo. 2 vols. (*Erlangen*).   14*s.* 6*d.*

  ,, Geschichte der Städteverfassung. 8vo. 4 vols. (*Erlangen*).   46*s.*
Maurer's three books form together a history of German institutions, for a limited period and line of development.

Pütter, J. S. Germanic Empire. Tr. 8vo. 3 vols. 1790.   O.P.
Especially for constitutional points.

Kaufmann, G. Deutsche Geschichte. 8vo. 2 vols. (*Leipzig*).   15*s.*
Extremely good from about 370-800.

Giesebrecht, W. Geschichte der deutschen Kaiserzeit. 8vo. 5 vols. (*Brunswick*).   78*s.* 6*d.*
An excellent history of the great period, 919-1152.

Jahrbücher des deutschen Reiches. (*Leipzig*).
Vol. i. (1) (Henry I.), 2*s.*; vol. i. (2) (Otto I., 936-951), o.p.; vol. i. (3) (Otto I., 951-973), 3*s.*; vol. ii. (1) (Otto II.), 3*s.*; vol. ii. (2) (Otto III., 983-1002), 4*s.*; vol. iii. (1) (on the Chronicon Corbejense), 2*s.* An invaluable series of volumes by Waitz, Dümmler, Bernhardi, and others, treating in detail of German history to 1220.

Oliphant, T. L. K. Life of the Emperor Frederick II. (1194-1250). 2 vols. *Macmillan.*   O.P.

Coxe, W. History of the house of Austria (1218-1792). p. 8vo. 3 vols., 3*s.* 6*d.* each. *Bell* (*Bohn*).   10*s.* 6*d.*

Leger, L. Histoire de l'Autriche-Hongrie. 8vo. *Hachette.*   1*s.* 6*d.*

Palacky. Geschichte Böhmens. 8vo. 5 vols. (*Prague*).   53*s.* 6*d.*
Vol. i., 4*s.* 6*d.*; vol. ii. (1), 3*s.* 6*d.*; vol. ii. (2), 4*s.* 6*d.*; vol. iii. (1), 4*s.* 6*d.*; vol. iii. (2), 5*s.* 6*d.*; vol. iii. (3), 4*s.*; vol. iv. (1), 5*s.* 6*d.*; vol. iv. (2), 8*s.*; vol. v. (1), 6*s.*; vol. v. (2), 7*s.* 6*d.*

Wratislaw, A. H. John Hus. *S. P. C. K.*   3*s.* 6*d.*

Aschbach. Geschichte Kaiser Sigmunds (1350-1437). 8vo. 4 vols. (*Hamburg*). 1838.   33*s.*

Geiger. Die Renaissance und Humanismus in Italien und Deutschland. 8vo. (*Berlin*).   26*s.*

Ranke, L. von. Deutsche Geschichte im Zeitalter der Reformation. 8vo. 6 vols. (*Leipzig*).   30*s.*

Gardiner, S. R.   Thirty years' war.   (elem.).   f. 8vo.   *Longmans.*   2*s.* 6*d.*

Gindely, A.   History of the Thirty-Years' War.   Tr.   8vo.   2 vols.   *Putnam.*   20*s.*

Droysen, J. G.   Geschichte der prenssichen Politik.   8vo.   5 vols.   (*Leipzig*).   11*s.* 6*d.*
    Political history of the house of Brandenburg.

Ranke, L. von.   Memoirs of the house of Brandenburg.   3 vols.   *Murray.*   O.P.

Carlyle, T.   History of Frederick the Great.   d. 8vo.   10 vols., 9*s.* each.
    Chapman.   90*s.*
    Also cheaper editions.

Tuttle, H.   History of Prussia under Frederick the Great (1740–56).   8vo.
    2 vols.   *Longmans.*   18*s.*

Treitschke, H. von.   Deutsche Geschichte im 19ten Jahrhundert.   8vo.
    (*Leipzig*).   Vols. i.–iv.   39*s.*

Maurice, C. E.   The revolutionary movement of 1848–9, in Italy, Austria,
    Hungary, and Germany.   d. 8vo.   *Bell.*   16*s.*

Hooper, G.   Campaign of Sedan.   d. 8vo.   *Bell.*   14*s.*

Zimmern, Helen.   The Hansa Towns.   c. 8vo.   *Unwin.*   5*s.*

Seeley, J. R.   Life and times of Stein.   d. 8vo.   3 vols.   *Cambridge Press.*
    illus.   30*s.*
    A study of German history in the Napoleonic time.

Memoirs of Count Beust (1809–85).   Tr.   d. 8vo.   2 vols.   *Longmans.*   32*s.*

Freytag, G.   Bilder aus der deutschen Vergangenheit.   8vo.   4 vols.
    (*Leipzig*).
        Vol. i., Aus dem Mittelalter, 7*s.*; vol. ii. (1), Vom Mittelalter zur Neuzeit, 1200-1500,
    5*s.* 6*d.*; vol. ii. (2), Aus dem Jahrh. der Reformation, 1500-1600, 4*s.* 6*d.*; vol. iii., Aus dem
    Jahrh. des Grossen Krieges, 1600-1700, 6*s.*; vol. iv., Aus neuer Zeit, 1700-1848, 6*s.* Valuable
    studies, not simply popular essays. A portion has been trans. by Mrs. Malcolm (*Chapman*).

Pertz.   Monumenta Germanica historica.   fo.   43 vols.

        PERIODICALS: Sybel's *Historische Zeitschrift* (annual, 22*s.* 6*d.*). *Preussische Jahrbücher*
    (annual, 18*s.*).   *Archiv für oesterreichische Geschichte* (annual vol., 8*s.*).   *Neues Archiv für
    alte Geschichtskunde.*

GERMANY: LANGUAGE AND LITERATURE:

Including (1) a larger and a smaller selection of works, with dictionaries, etc. ;
    (2) Novels ; (3) Books for the young.   The books marked * belong to the
    smaller selection.   Those marked § are recommended for the young, in
    addition to those named in the special list in Section VII.

        The adult beginner of the language may first get up the necessary inflections from Eve's
    Short accidence, or from the larger *School German grammar*; or, if a book with exercises be
    desired, from Ane's smaller or larger German grammar; at the same time beginning to read
    something very simple,—Hauff's Märchen (*Die Karavane*, ed. Hager, *Macmillan*, 2*s.* 6*d.*), or,
    still simpler, Niebuhr's *Heroengeschichten*, ed. Buchheim, *Clar. Press*, 2*s.* Both these have
    notes, and a full vocabulary: Hager's is particularly good.   An easy play might follow;
    (Schiller's *Neffe als Onkel*; an edition with "crib" notes by Buchheim, *Williams*, 1*s.* 6*d.*, is
    a storehouse of idiomatic colloquial German, with very little that is obsolete); or novelette
    (e.g. Hauff's *Das Bild des Kaisers*; text in several cheap editions; annotated ed. in *Pitt Press
    Series*, 3*s.*); Whitney's dictionary being used.   A play or two of Benedix, a novelette or two
    of Heyse or Riehl, would be suited to this stage.   *Schiller's Prosa* (*Low*, 3*s.* 6*d.*) is the easiest
    introduction to classical prose; Goethe's is more difficult.   As an introduction to poetry,
    Sonnenschein's little volume of *Select poems of Goethe* (1*s.* 6*d.*), or Turner and Morshead's
    Selections from Schiller's lyrical poems (*Macmillan*, 2*s.* 6*d.*), may be recommended.   An
    easy introduction to dramatic poetry is Uhland's *Herzog Ernst von Schwaben*, *Pitt
    Press Series*, 3*s.* 6*d.*); Schiller's *Tell* (*Id.*) should not be read until later.   A student
    wishing to work his way to a thorough knowledge of the language by analytical study,
    will find an introduction to such study in the copious notes of the *Pitt Press* ed. of Riehl's
    Kulturgeschichtliche Novellen.   Buchheim's numerous editions of the classics and other
    works contain useful introductions and notes on the subject matter; but the notes on the text
    have too much of the mere crib, and leave the real student unsatisfied.   Of *Faust*, part i., two
    annotated editions may be mentioned, Morshead and Turner's (*Rivingtons*, 7*s.* 6*d.*), and
    Miss Lee's (*Macmillan*, 4*s.* 6*d.*).

—I. HISTORY OF THE LANGUAGE :

Rückert, H. Geschichte der neuhochdeutschen Schriftsprache. 8vo.
2 vols., 7s. each. *Weigel.*   14s.

Behaghel, O. Die deutsche Sprache. 12mo. *Freytag.*   1s. 4d.
> An excellent short sketch, recommended as an introduction to the subject. An English translation is announced.

Strong and Meyer. History of the German language. 8vo. *Sonnenschein.*   6s.
> Somewhat hasty and incomplete, but useful in the absence of anything similar in English.

—II. HISTORY OF THE LITERATURE :

Kurz, H. Geschichte der deutschen Literatur (to 1866). r. 8vo. 4 vols.
Teubner.   51s.
> With selected specimens.

Scherer, W. Geschichte der deutschen Literatur. 8vo. *Weidmann.*   10s.
> The best history of German literature in a moderate compass; a useful bibliography at the end.

  ,,   The same. Tr. Mrs. F. C. Conybeare. 8vo. 2 vols. *Clar. Press.*   21s.
> Good English style; original rather too freely handled.

Gostwick and Harrison. Outlines of German literature. 8vo. *Williams.*   10s.
> Good in parts, but includes much that lies outside literature, to the detriment of the latter.

Hettner, H. Literaturgeschichte des 18ten Jahrhunderts. 3 parts.
Vieweg.   46s. 6d.
> Part i., Die englische Literatur (1660-1770), 8s.; part ii., Die französische Literatur im 18 Jahrhundert, 8s.; part iii., Die deutsche Literatur (1648-1832), 4 vols, 30s. 6d.; the third and fourth vols. also issued separately under the title of *Goethe und Schiller*, 14s. 6d. A clear and interesting exposition of the literary and ethical movement of the 18th century, with its development in Germany, into the humanism and idealism of Goethe and Schiller. Contains some of the best German literary criticism.

Gottschall, R. Geschichte der deutschen Nationalliteratur des 19ten
Jahrhunderts. 8vo. 4 vols., 5s. each. (*Berlin*).   20s.

Brandes, G. Die Hauptströmungen der Literatur des 19ten Jahrhunderts. Tr. into German by Strodtmann. 8vo. 5 vols. (*Leipzig*).   29s.
> Vol. i., ii., iii., 4s. 6d. each; vol. iv., 7s. 6d.; vol. v., 8s. Vol. ii., *Die romantische Schule in Deutschland* is a brilliant study.

Koennecke, G. Bilderatlas zur Geschichte der deutschen Nationalliteratur. fo. (*Marburg*).   25s.
> Fac-similes of old literary documents, reproductions of illustrations, etc.

—III. OLD AND MIDDLE HIGH GERMAN :

(A) GRAMMARS AND DICTIONARIES.

Wackernagel, W. Altdeutsches Handwörterbuch. Ed. Rieger. r. 8vo.
(*Basle*).   8s.
> Concise; no illustrative passages.

Braune, W. Althochdeutsche Grammatik. r. 8vo. (*Halle*).   5s.

Paul, H. Mittelhochdeutsche Grammatik. 8vo. (*Halle*).   3s.

Lexer, M. Mittelhochdeutsches Taschenwörterbuch. 12mo. *Hirzel.*   5s.
> Concise and without illustrative passages, but comprehensive; very useful.

Lübben, A. Wörterbuch zu der Nibelunge Nôt (Liet). 8vo. (*Oldenburg*).   2s. 6d.

(B) TEXTS AND TRANSLATIONS.

Piper, P. Die älteste deutsche Literatur (to 1050; selected). 12mo.
Spemann.   2s. 6d.
> In *Deutsche Nationalliteratur*, a series well printed and got up. The works, by various editors, are of unequal value; some are very well edited by first-class authorities.

Der Nibelunge Noth (MS. A). Ed. K. Lachmann. 12mo. *Reimer.*   2s.
> Text only; there is a larger edition with various readings; also a vol. of notes (not elementary).

Das Nibelungenlied (MS. B). Ed. K. Bartsch. 12mo. *Brockhaus.*　　3*s.* 6*d.*
> In *Deutsche Classiker des Mittelalters* ; 3*s.* 6*d.* each. This series, well got up and handy, contains copious notes and explanations. They are intended in the first place rather for the general (German) reader, than for the student; but the latter, especially the foreign student of Middle High German, will also find them very useful in the earlier stages of his work.

Das Nibelungenlied. Tr. into New High German by L. Freytag. 8vo. (*Berlin*).　　4*s.*

The lay of the Nibelungers; otherwise, the Book of Chriemhild. Tr. W. Lettsom. 8vo. *Williams.*　　6*s.*

Kudrun (in "Deutsche Classiker des Mitt."). Ed. K. Bartsch. 12mo. *Brockhaus.*　　3*s.* 6*d.*

　　,,　Tr. into modern German by G. L. Klee. 8vo. *Hirzel.*　　2*s.*

Das deutsche Heldenbuch. (Selection with notes). Ed. E. Henrici. 12mo. *Spemann.*　　2*s.* 6*d.*

Hartmann von Aue. ("Deutsche Classiker"). Ed. F. Bech. 12mo. 3 vols. *Brockhaus.*　　10*s.* 6*d.*
> Vol. ii. contains *Lieder* and *Der arme Heinrich.*

Gottfried von Strassburg. Tristan und Isolde ("Deutsche Classiker"). Ed. R. Bechstein. 12mo. 2 vols., 3*s.* 6*d.* each. *Brockhaus.*　　7*s.*

　　,,　Tr. into modern German by W. Hertz. 8vo. (*Stuttgart*).　　8*s.*
> With additions after the old French of Thomas le Trouvère.

Wolfram von Eschenbach. Parzival und Titurel ("Deutsche Classiker"). Ed. K. Bartsch. 12mo. 3 vols. *Brockhaus.*　　10*s.* 6*d.*

　　,,　Tr. into modern German by San-Marte. 8vo. 2 vols. (*Halle*).　　10*s.*

Walther von der Vogelweide ("Deutsche Classiker"). Ed. F. Pfeiffer. 12mo. *Brockhaus.*　　3*s.* 6*d.*

　　,,　Tr. into modern German by K. Simrock. 16mo. *Hirzel.*　　5*s.*

—IV. EARLY NEW HIGH GERMAN:

Brant, Sebastian. Narrenschiff (in "Deutsche Dichter des 16 Jahrh."). Ed. Goedeke and Tittmann. 12mo. *Brockhaus.*　　3*s.* 6*d.*

　　,,　Narrenschiff. Tr. into modern German by K. Simrock. 4to. (*Berlin*).　　12*s.*

Luthers Schriften in Auswahl. Ed. J. Delius. *Perthes.*　　2*s.* 6*d.*

Köstlin, J. Luthers Leben. 8vo. (*Leipzig*).　　8*s.*

　　,,　Life of Luther. Tr. c. 8vo. *Longmans.* pub. 16*s.*　　O.P.

Sachs, Hans. Werke ("Deutsche Dichter des 16 Jahrh."). 12mo. 3 vols., 3*s.* 6*d.* each. *Brockhaus.*　　10*s.* 6*d.*
> Vol. i., Geistliche Lieder ; vol. ii., Spruchgedichte ; vol. iii., Dramatische Gedichte.

Fischart, J. Dichtungen ("Deutsche Dich des 16 Jahrh."). 12mo. *Brockhaus.*　　3*s.* 6*d.*

—V. NEW HIGH GERMAN :

(A) GRAMMARS AND DICTIONARIES.

*Whitney, W. D. Compendious German and English dictionary. c. 8vo. *Macmillan.*　　7*s.* 6*d.*
> The best small German-English dictionary ; the English-German part is too meagre.

*Cassell's New German-English and English-German dictionary. 8vo. *Cassell.*　　3*s.* 6*d.*
> On the whole, the most useful German-English and English-German dictionary of medium size. Some of the type, however, is rather faint and indistinct.

Heyne, M. Deutsches Wörterbuch. *Hirzel.* Vol. i.   10*s.*
> To be completed (in six half-vols. at 5*s.* each) within three years, on a similar plan to Grimm's great work, but more concise; giving briefly the etymology and history of each word, with illustrative examples, from its first occurrence to the present time. The most useful and compact work of its kind.

Sanders, D. Wörterbuch der deutschen Sprache. 4to. 3 vols. (*Leipzig*).   72*s.*
> Very useful for its clear definitions, and copious examples (which extend from Luther to the present time), but untrustworthy in its etymology, and often in the history of development of meaning and usage.

Kluge, F. Etymologisches Wörterbuch der deutschen Sprache. r. 8vo. (*Strassburg*).   12*s.* 6*d.*

Duden, K. Orthographisches Wörterbuch der deutschen Sprache. 8vo. (*Leipzig*).   2*s.*
> Follows the new official orthography.

Eberhard, J. A. Synonymisches Handwörterbuch. Ed. O. Lyon. 8vo. (*Leipzig*).   12*s.* 6*d.*

*****Aue.** German grammar (with exercises). 12mo. *Chambers.*   3*s.*
> Still one of the best for practical use.

　,,　Elementary German grammar. *Chambers.*   1*s.* 6*d.*

*****Eve,** H. W. School German grammar. 12mo. *Nutt.*   4*s.* 6*d.*
> On the whole, the best German grammar in English, for the ordinary student.

　,,　Short German accidence (abridged from the grammar). c. 8vo. *Nutt.*   2*s.*

Brandt, H. C. Grammar of the German language. 12mo. *Putnam.*   6*s.*
> Considerable space given to phonology, historical commentary on the accidence, and history of the language.

(B) TEXTS AND TRANSLATIONS.

*****Grimmelshausen,** H. J. C. Der abenteuerliche Simplicissimus. ("Deutsche Dichter des 17 Jahrh."). Ed. Goedeke and Tittmann. 12mo. 2 vols., 3*s.* 6*d.* each. *Brockhaus.*   7*s.*

　,,　The same; rendered into modern German. 12mo. 2 vols. *Spemann.*   2*s.*
> In *Hand- und Hausbibliothek*, a cheap series of handy volumes, fairly printed and bound, 1*s.* each.

Klopstock, F. G. Ausgewählte Werke. 12mo. 4 vols. *Cotta.*   4*s.*
> Vols. i., ii. Messias. In the *Cotta'sche Bibliothek der Weltlitteratur*; neat, handy vols., strongly bound and fairly printed, 1*s.* each; any vol. sold separately.

Wieland, C. M. Werke. 12mo. 40 vols. in 16. *Hempel.*   40*s.*
> In *Klassiker-Ausgaben*; Hempel's editions are complete and cheap, and some of them are very well edited; but the print is rather close, and the getting up but poor. Any work may be had separately.

　,,　Ausgewählte Werke. 12mo. 6 vols. *Cotta'sche Bibliothek.*   6*s.*
> Separate works, *Geschichte der Abderiten, Göttergespräche,* *Oberon*, etc., both in Hempel's and Cotta's editions.

Lessing, G. E. Sämmtliche Werke. Ed. Lachmann and Muncker. 8vo. 6 vols., 4*s.* 6*d.* each. (*Stuttgart*).
> In progress.

　,,　Sämmtliche Werke. Ed. Göring. 12mo. 20 vols., 1*s.* each. *Cotta'sche Bibl.*   20*s.*
> Separate works, * *Minna von Barnhelm,* * *Emilia Galotti,* * *Nathan der Weise,* *Laokoon,* * *Hamburgische Dramaturgie,* etc. (Hempel).

　,,　Dramatic works, complete. Tr. Ed. E. Bell. c. 8vo. 2 vols., 3*s.* 6*d.* each. *Bell (Bohn).*   7*s.*

　,,　Laokoon. Tr. T. C. Beesley; and dramatic notes tr. Helen Zimmern: in one vol. c. 8vo. *Bell (Bohn).*   3*s.* 6*d.*

　,,　Laokoon; separately. c. 8vo. *Bell (Bohn).*   1*s.* 6*d.*

　,,　Nathan the wise; and Minna von Barnhelm. Tr. in one vol. c. 8vo. *Bell (Bohn).*   1*s.* 6*d.*

*Zimmern, Helen. Life and works of Lessing. p. 8vo. *Longmans.*   10*s.* 6*d.*

Sime, J. Lessing ("English and Foreign Philosophical Lib."). 8vo. 2 vols. *Trübner.*   21*s.*

Herder, J. G. Sämmtliche Werke. Ed. B. Suphan. 8vo. *Weidmann.*
Over 30 vols. published, from 1*s.* to 9*s.* each ; well got up.

,,   Ausgewählte Werke. 12mo. 6 vols., 1*s.* each. *Cotta'sche Bibl.*   6*s.*
Separate works : ** Der Cid* ; *Fragmente zur Beförderung der Humanität* ; *Ideen zur Philosophie der Geschichte der Menschheit.*

Nevinson, H. Sketch of Herder and his times. d. 8vo. *Chapman.*   14*s.*

Bürger, G. A. Ausgewählte Werke. 12mo. 2 vols. *Cotta'sche Bibl.*   2*s.*

*   ,,   Gedichte. *Hendel.*   1*s.*
In *Hendel's Bibl. der Gesammtliteratur des In- und Auslandes* ; neat vols. in limp cloth, fairly printed and cheap. Most of the commoner classical works are to be had in this series.

Hölty, L. H. Gedichte. 18mo. *Hendel.*   1*s.* 6*d.*

Goethe. Werke. c. 8vo. *Böhlau (Weimar).*
In four sections : i., Werke im engeren Sinne, 50 vols., 2*s.* 6*d.* or 3*s.* each ; ii., Naturwissenschaftliche Schriften ; iii., Tagebücher ; iv., Briefe. The vols. in ii., iii., iv. cost 3*s.* or 4*s.* each. In course of publication ; well got up. Will be the definitive standard ed. of Goethe.

,,   Werke. 12mo. 23 vols. *Hempel's "Klassiker."*   60*s.*

,,   Lyrische Gedichte. Ed. Loeper and Strehlke. 12mo. 3 vols. *Dümmler.*   4*s.* 6*d.*
A reproduction, with more copious notes, of the first three vols. of *Hempel's* ed.
     Separate works (*Hempel* ; *Cotta* ; *Hendel*). **Hermann und Dorothea* ; **§ Dichtung und Wahrheit* (autobiography ; *Hempel's* ed. is valuable) ; *Dramen* (especially **Götz von Berlichingen* ; **Egmont* ; **Iphigenie in Tauris* ; **Torquato Tasso* ; **Faust,* part i.) ; **Wilhelm Meister's Lehrjahre* ; *Sprüche in Rosa* ; **Westöstlicher Divan.*

,,   Wilhelm Meister. Tr. T. Carlyle. c. 8vo. 3 vols., 1*s.* each. *Chapman.*   3*s.*

,,   Works. Tr. c. 8vo. 14 vols., 3*s.* 6*d.* each. *Bell (Bohn).*   49*s.*
i., ii., Autobiography ; v., Wil. Meister ; vii., Poems and Ballads, tr. Bowring ; viii., Dramas.

,,   Faust. Ed. G. von Loeper. 12mo. 2 vols., 3*s.* each. *Hempel.*   6*s.*
Valuable introductions and notes.

,,   Faust. Ed. K. J. Schröer. 8vo. 2 vols. *Henninger.*   9*s.*
More copious notes on the text than in any other German edition.

,,   Faust ; über die Entstehung und Composition des Gedichts. An essay by K. Fischer. c. 8vo. *Cotta.*   4*s.* 6*d.*
     TRANSLATIONS.—The merely English reader may be recommended to read first Hayward's literal prose version, and then Taylor's (which aims at being as literal as possible in metre) ; or Miss Swanwick's more flowing version.

,,   Faust ; part i. Tr. into prose by A. Hayward. f. 8vo. *Longmans.*   O.P.

,,   Faust ; parts i., ii. Translated in the original metres with notes, by Bayard Taylor. *Ward, Lock.*   3*s.* 6*d.*

,,   Faust ; parts i., ii. Tr. Miss A. Swanwick. c. 8vo. *Bell (Bohn).*   3*s.* 6*d.*

*   ,,   Briefwechsel mit Schiller. ("Hand- u. Hausbibl."). 12mo. 2 vols., 1*s.* each. *Spemann.*   2*s.*

,,   Correspondence with Schiller. Tr. Dora Schmitz. c. 8vo. *Bell (Bohn).*   3*s.* 6*d.*

,,   Briefwechsel mit Zelter. 8vo. 6 vols. *(Berlin).* 1832–4.   O.P.

,,   Correspondence with Zelter. (Zelter in extracts only). Tr. A. D. Coleridge. c. 8vo. *Bell (Bohn).*   3*s.* 6*d.*

*Eckermann, J. P. Gespräche mit Goethe. 12mo. 3 vols. *Brockhaus.*   6*s.*

,,   The same. Tr. J. Oxenford. c. 8vo. *Bell (Bohn).*   3*s.* 6*d.*

*Schäfer, J. W. Goethes Leben. 8vo. *(Leipzig).*   8*s.*
Perhaps the best biography in German for the general reader.

Lewes, G. H. Life of Goethe. 8vo. *Smith, Elder.*   ·16s.

    With all its faults, still the most readable life of Goethe.

  ,,   Story of Goethe's life. c. 8vo. *Smith, Elder.*   7s. 6d.

    Chapters on criticism omitted.

Scherer, W. Aufsätze über Goethe. 8vo. *Weidmann.*   6s.

*Grimm, H. Goethe. 8vo. (*Berlin*).   7s.

    Lectures, brilliant and interesting; but somewhat open to the charge of Goethomania.

  ,,   The same. Tr. S. H. Adams. c. 8vo. (*Boston*).   10s.

Schiller. Sämmtliche Werke. Ed. K. Goedeke and others. 8vo. 17 vols.

    Cotta.   60s.

    Generally accepted as the standard edition.

* ,,   Werke. 12mo. 15 vols., 1s. each. *Cotta'sche Bibl.*   15s.

    Separate works (*Cotta; Hempel; Hendel*). **Gedichte; Hauptdramen* (**Don Karlos;*

    **Wallenstein; Maria Stuart;* **Jungfrau von Orleans;* **Wilhelm Tell; Braut von Messina*);

    Geschichte des dreissigjährigen Krieges; Geschichte des Abfalls der vereinigten Nieder-

    lande; Kleinere Schriften.

  ,,   Works. Tr. E. A. Bowring, etc. c. 8vo. 7 vols., 3s. 6d. each.

    Bell (Bohn).   24s. 6d.

    Vol. v., Poems, tr. Bowring; vol. vii., *Wallenstein,* tr. Coleridge; and *William Tell,*

    tr. Sir T. Martin; vol. iii., other chief dramas; vol. vi., Essays, æsthetical and philosophical.

  ,,   Briefwechsel mit Körner. Ed. K. Goedeke. 8vo. (*Leipzig*).   8s.

  ,,   Briefwechsel mit W. von. Humboldt. 8vo. *Cotta.*   5s.

·Viehoff, H. Schillers Leben, Geistesentwickelung und Werke. 8vo.

    (*Stuttgart*).   7s. 6d.

    Based on the work of Hoffmeister (o.p.), which is still the best.

Goedeke, K. Goethe und Schiller. 8vo. (*Dresden*).   2s.

*Sime, J. Schiller ("Foreign classics for English readers"). c. 8vo.

    Blackwood.   2s. 6d.

    An excellent sketch.

Carlyle, T. Life of Schiller. c. 8vo. *Chapman.*   1s.

Richter, J. P. F. Werke. 12mo. 13 vols. *Hempel's "Klassiker."*   30s.

* ,,   Blumen-, Frucht-, und Dornenstücke. 12mo. *Hempel.*   2s.

  ,,   Flower, fruit, and thorn pieces. Tr. Ewing. c. 8vo. *Bell (Bohn).*   3s. 6d.

* ,,   Leben des Quintus Fixlein. 12mo. *Hempel.*   1s. 6d.

    Tr. by Carlyle, in "Translations from the German." *Chapman.*

  ,,   Levana. 12mo. *Hempel.*   1s. 6d.

  ,,   Levana, a treatise on education. Tr. c. 8vo. *Bell (Bohn).*   3s. 6d.

·Humboldt, A. von. Ansichten der Natur. *Cotta.*   3s.

§Humboldt, W. von. Briefe an eine Freundin. ("Hand- und Hausbibl.")

    12mo. 2 vols., 1s. each. *Spemann.*   2s.

Tieck, L. Ausgewählte Werke. 12mo. 8 vols., 1s. each. *Cotta'sche Bibl.*   8s.

    *Vols. i., iv., v.

Hölderlin, J. C. F. Ausgewählte Werke. Ed. C. Schwab. 18mo. *Cotta.*   2s. 6d.

Novalis (F. Hardenberg). Schriften. 12mo. 3 vols. (*Berlin*). 1837–46.   5s.

Hebel, J. P. Alemannische Gedichte. 24mo. *Hendel.*   8d.

    Very popular poems in dialect; published 1803.

*Kleist, H. von. Sämmtliche Werke. 12mo. 4 vols., 1s. each. *Cotta'sche*

    Bibl.   4s.

    Chief dramas:—*Käthchen von Heilbronn; Der zerbrochene Krug; Prinz Friedrich von*

    Homburg; Michel Kohlhaas (tale).

Brahm, O. H. von Kleist. (*Berlin*).   6s.

Schenkendorff, Max von. Gedichte. 24mo. *Hendel.*   1*s.* 6*d.*

Rückert, F. Gesammelte poetische Werke. 12mo. 12 vols., 3*s.* each. (*Frankfort*).   36*s.*

*   ,,   Gedichte (Selected by author). c. 8vo. (*Frankfort*).   5*s.*

   ,,   Liebesfrühling. 16mo. (*Frankfort*).   5*s.*

***Uhland**, L. Gedichte und Dramen. 16mo. *Cotta.*   5*s.*

Chamisso, A. von. Gedichte. 24mo. *Hendel.*   1*s.* 6*d.*

§   ,,   Peter Schlemihl. 24mo. *Hendel.*   8*d.*

***Eichendorff**, J. von. Gedichte. 24mo. *Hendel.*   1*s.* 6*d.*

Platen, A. von. Werke. 12mo. 4 vols., 1*s.* each. *Cotta'sche Bibl.*   4*s.*
     Poems in i. and ii.

Grillparzer, F. Sämmtliche Werke. 8 vols. *Cotta.*   20*s.*
     Chief dramas:—*Sappho, 2*s.* 6*d.*; **Das goldene Vliess*, 5*s.*; *Des Meeres und der Liebe Wellen* (*Hero und Leander*), 3*s.*, etc.

Laube, H. Grillparzers Leben. 8vo. *Cotta.*   4*s.*

Börne, L. Gesammelte Schriften. 12mo. 12 vols. (*Frankfort*).   30*s.*

Heine, H. Sämmtliche Werke. Ed. E. Elster. 12mo. 7 vols., 2*s.* 6*d.* each. *Bibliogr. Institut.*   17*s.* 6*d.*
     An excellent critical edition.

   ,,   Sämmtliche Werke. 12mo. 13 vols., 1*s.* each. (*Hamburg*).   13*s.*
     Neat handy volumes. Vol. i., *Buch der Lieder; vol. ii., *Neue Gedichte; vol. iii., *Romanzero; vol. iv., *Letzte Gedichte; vol. v., *Reisebilder, part i.; vol. vii., **Zur Geschichte der Religion und Philosophie in Deutschland*; *Die romantische Schule*; vol. xi., **Der Rabbi von Bacharach*; vol. xiii., Heines Biographie, by G. Karpeles.

   ,,   Ausgewählte. Ed. G. Karpeles. 12mo. (*Berlin*).   2*s.*

   ,,   Poems and ballads. Tr. Sir T. Martin. c. 8vo. *Blackwood.*   8*s.*

   ,,   Poems, selected ("Canterbury Poets"), various translators. Ed. Kate Kröker. 32mo. *Scott.*   1*s.*

   ,,   Wit, wisdom, and pathos, from Heine's prose. Tr. J. Snodgrass. p. 8vo. *Gardner (Paisley).*   6*s.*
     Mr. Snodgrass's translations rank among the best made from the German.

   ,,   Religion and philosophy in Germany ("English and Foreign Philos. Library"). Tr. J. Snodgrass. *Trübner.*   6*s.*

   ,,   Travel pictures. Tr. F. Storr. c. 8vo. *Bell (Bohn).*   3*s.* 6*d.*
     Tour in the Harz, Norderney, Book of Ideas, Romantic school. Distinctly above the average of prose translations.

Prölss, J. Heine, sein Lebensgang, etc. c. 8vo. (*Stuttgart*).   4*s.* 6*d.*

Sharp, W. Heine ("Great Writers"). *Scott.*   1*s.*
     A clever sketch, though very carelessly written.

Grün, Anastasius. Gesammelte Werke. 8vo. 5 vols.   18*s.*

Lenau, N. Sämmtliche Werke. 12mo. 4 vols., 1*s.* each. *Cotta'sche Bibl.*   4*s.*

Geibel, E. Gesammelte Werke. 12mo. 4 vols. *Cotta.*   24*s.*

*   ,,   Gedichte. 8vo. (*Stuttgart*).   4*s.* 6*d.*

Hebbel, F. Werke. 8vo. 6 vols. (*Hamburg*).   42*s.*

*   ,,   Die Nibelungen; ein Trauerspiel. c. 8vo. (*Hamburg*).   4*s.* 6*d.*
     Not a translation, but an independent dramatic work, dealing freely with the traditional material.

Kuh, E. Hebbels Biographie. 8vo. 2 vols. *Braumüller.*   15*s.*

Freiligrath, F. Gesammelte Dichtungen. 8vo. 6 vols. (*Stuttgart*).   10*s.*

*   ,,   Gedichte. 8vo. (*Stuttgart*).   4*s.* 6*d.*

Droste-Hülshoff, A. von. Gedichte. 12mo. *Schöningh.*   3s.
    The chief German poetess.

(C) MODERN LYRIC POETRY.

Keller, G. Gesammelte Gedichte. 8vo. *Hertz.*   7s.

*****Bodenstedt,** F. Die Lieder des Mirza Schaffy. 16mo. (*Berlin*).   3s.

*§**Scheffel,** V. von. Der Trompeter von Säkkingen. 12mo. (*Stuttgart*).   5s.

  ,, Gaudeamus! 12mo. (*Stuttgart*).   5s.

Hamerling, R. Ahasver in Rom. c. 8vo. (*Hamburg*).   4s.

  ,, Der König von Sion. c. 8vo. (*Hamburg*).   4s.

Jordan, W. Nibelunge. 12mo. 2 vols., 7s. each. (*Frankfort*).   14s.
    Vol. i., Sigfridsage; vol. ii., Hildebrands Heimkehr. Free epic treatment of the old saga.

*****Meyer,** C. E. Huttens letzte Tage. 12mo. (*Leipzig*).   3s.

Wolff, J. Der Rattenfänger von Hameln. 12mo. *Grote.*   4s.

  ,, Tannhäuser. 12mo. *Grote.*   7s. 6d.

(D) MODERN PLAYS.

Laube, H. Dramatische Werke. 12mo. 12 vols., 1s. each. (*Leipzig*).   12s.
    *Die Karlsschüler; *Graf Essex; *Prinz Friedrich, etc.

Gutzkow, K. Dramatische Werke. 8vo. 20 vols., 1s. 4d. each. *Costenoble.*   26s. 8d.
    *Zopf und Schwert; *Das Urbild des Tartüffe; *Uriel Acosta; etc.

Freytag, G. Dramatische Werke. c. 8vo. 2 vols. *Hirzel.*   7s.
    *Die Journalisten, 2s. 6d.; *Die Valentine, 2s. 6d.; *Graf Waldemar, 2s. 8vo. Hirzel.

Bauernfeld, E. von. Gesammelte Schriften. 12mo. 12 vols., 3s. each.
    Braumüller.   36s.
    Die Bekenntnisse; Bürgerlich und Romantisch; Ein Tagebuch; etc.

*****Ludwig,** O. Der Erbförster; Die Maccabäer, etc., in one vol. 8vo.
    Janke.   3s.

Benedix, R. Volkstheater (chief plays). c. 8vo. 20 vols., 1s. 4d. each.
    (*Leipzig*).   26s. 8d.
    Dr. Wespe; Der alte Magister; etc., 1s. 4d. each. c. 8vo. (Leipzig).

Wildenbruch, E. von. Die Quitzows; Harold; Christoph Marlow; 3s. each;
    or in 1 vol., 8vo., 2s. *Freund und Jeckel.*
    The most popular among the serious dramatists of the present time.

*****Deutsche** Lyrik der Gegenwart seit 1850 (anthology). Ed. F. Avenarius.
    8vo. (*Dresden*).   7s. 6d.

Die deutschen Volkslieder gesammelt. (*Basle*).

*****Auswahl** deutscher Gedichte. Ed. T. Echtermeyer. 8vo. (*Halle*).   5s.
    A good collection of German shorter poems for school and general use.

Hausschatz deutscher Prosa. Ed. Wolff. r. 8vo.   6s.

(E) ESSAYS, BIOGRAPHIES, ETC.

Grimm, H. Fünfzehn Essays. 8vo. (*Berlin*).   9s.

  ,, Neue Essays. 8vo. (*Berlin*).   8s. 6d.

Freytag, G. Die Technik des Dramas. 8vo. *Hirzel.*   5s.

  ,, Gesammelte Aufsätze. 8vo. 2 vols., 6s. each. *Hirzel.*   12s.

  ,, Erinnerungen aus meinem Leben. c. 8vo. *Hirzel.*   5s.

Schmidt, J. Porträts aus dem 19ten Jahrhundert. 8vo. *Hertz.*   8s.
    Byron, Carlyle, George Sand, etc.

Scherer, W. Vorträge und Aufsätze zur Geschichte des geistigen Lebens
    in Deutschland und Oesterreich. *Weidmann.*   8s.

Hillebrand, K. Lectures on German thought. p. 8vo. *Longmans.*   O.P.
> Delivered in 1879 before the Royal Institution; valuable to the student, and worth a little effort to the general reader.

Taylor, Bayard. Studies in German literature. 8vo. *Low.*   O.P.

Bulthaupt, H. Dramaturgie. 8vo. 3 vols., 5s. each. (*Oldenburg*).   15s.
> Vol. i., Lessing, Goethe, Schiller, Kleist; vol. ii., Shakespeare; vol. iii., Grillparzer, Hebbel, O. Ludwig, Gutzkow, Laube.

Allgemeine deutsche Biographie. 8vo. 2s. 6d. each part. (*Münich*).
> In progress; published down to *Rodbertus.*

Strauss, D. F. Ulrich von Hutten. 8vo. 3 vols. (*Leipzig*).   15s.

   ,, The same. Tr. Mrs. G. Sturge. p. 8vo. *Isbister.*   O.P.

Wilbrandt, A. Fritz Reuters Biographie.

Grimm, J. Auswahl aus den kleineren Schriften. 8vo. (*Berlin*).   4s.

*****Meissner,** A. Geschichte meines Lebens. 8vo. 2 vols. (*Vienna*).   10s.

Memoiren einer Idealistin. c. 8vo. 3 vols. (*Leipzig*).   9s.

Kügelgen, W. von. Jugenderinnerungen eines alten Mannes. c. 8vo. *Hertz.*   3s.
> A delightful book.

Hase, K. Ideale und Irrthümer; Jugenderinnerungen. 8vo. *Brockhaus.* pub. 6s.   O.P.

Sidgwick, Mrs. A. Caroline Schlegel and her friends. c. 8vo. *Unwin.*   7s. 6d.

Die deutschen Volksbücher für Jung und Alt wiedererzählt. Ed. G. Schwab. 8vo. *Bertelsmann.*   7s.
> *Herzog Ernst ; Die schöne Melusine,* etc.

Neue Folge (continuation of "Volksbücher"). Ed. G. Klee. 8vo. *Bertelsmann.*   4s.
> *Heinrich der Löwe ; Oberon,* etc.

*****Die** deutschen Heldensagen für Jung und Alt. Ed. G. Klee. *Bertelsmann.*   4s. 6d.

(F) REFERENCE.

Meyers Conversations-Lexicon. 8vo. 18 vols. *Meyer.*   £10 12s. 6d.

Kayser. Vollständiges Bücher-Lexicon. *Weigel.*
> Alphabetical list of all books published in Germany since 1750. A volume appears every few years.

Allgemeine Biographie für Deutschland. c. 8vo. (*Leipzig*).   Annual vol., 10s. 6d.
> Appears weekly, and in half-yearly volumes; alphabetically arranged.
> PERIODICALS : *Deutsche Rundschau.* Ed. Rodenberg. 8vo. (Berlin). monthly: per year, 28s. *Unsere Zeit.* Ed. Gottschall, 8vo. (Leipzig). monthly ; per year, 22s. *Westermann's illustrirte deutsche Monatshefte für das geistige Leben der Gegenwart.* Ed. Spielhagen and Glaser. 8vo. (Brunswick). monthly; per year, 20s. *Ueber Land und Meer.* fo. (Stuttgart). weekly; per year, 22s.

—VI. NOVELS:

> Many German novels, even the most popular, are never published in cheap editions. In the present list, economy is studied as far as possible.

Deutscher Novellenschatz. Ed. Heyse and Kurz. 12mo. 24 vols., 1s. each. (*Leipzig*).   21s.
> * Vols. iii., v., vi., vii., xiv., xvii., xviii. Neat, well-printed volumes, strongly bound; from two to four stories in each vol., selected from the best authors from Goethe down to the present time.

Neuer deutscher Novellenschatz. Ed. Heyse and Laistner. 12mo, 24 vols., 1s. each. (*Leipzig*).   21s.
> * Vols. i., v., viii., xi., xiii., xiv., xvii.

*__Auerbach__, B. Auf der Höhe. 8vo. 3 vols. *Cotta.*   10*s*

,,   The same (" On the heights," in "Tauchnitz collection "). Tr. F. E. Bunnett. 18mo. 3 vols., 2*s*. each. *Low.*   6*s*.

,,   Dorfgeschichten. c. 8vo. 10 vols. *Cotta.*   10*s*.
<blockquote>Among the most popular are :—‡*Barfüssele*, tr. (*Little Barefoot*). c. 8vo. *Routledge.* pub. 6*s*. O.P. **Die Frau Professorin.* 8vo. *Cotta.* 1*s*. 6*d*. §*Edelweiss* (in "Tauchnitz collection"). Tr. under the same title. 12mo. *Low.* pub. 5*s*. O.P. *Diethelm von Buchenberg* (vol. vii. of *Deutscher Novellenschatz*).</blockquote>

__Ebers__, G. Homo sum. c. 8vo. *Deutsche Verlags-Anstalt.*   6*s*.

,,   The same (in " Tauchnitz collection "). Tr. Clara Bell. 18mo. 2 vols., 2*s*. each. *Low.*   4*s*

__Ebner-Eschenbach__, Marie von. Dorf- und Schlossgeschichten. c. 8vo. (*Berlin*).   4*s*.
<blockquote>*Die Freiherren von Gemperlein* in vol. i.; and *Krambambuli* in vol. xxiii. of the *Neuer Deutscher Novellenschatz*.</blockquote>

*__Eichendorff__, J. von. Aus dem Leben eines Taugenichts. 32mo. *Hendel.*   8*d*.

__Elbe__, A. v. d. Lüneburger Geschichten. 12mo. *Spemanns Hand- und Hausbibl.*   1*s*.

*§__Fouqué__, F. de la Motte. Undine. 32mo. *Hendel.*   8*d*.

,,   The same (in " Tauchnitz collection "). Tr. 18mo. *Low.*   2*s*.

*__François__, Luise von. Die letzte Reckenburgerin. 12mo. *Janke.*   4*s*.

*§__Freytag__, G. Soll und Haben. c. 8vo. 2 vols. *Hirzel.*   5*s*.

,,   The same (" Debit and credit "). Tr. Mrs. Malcolm. c. 8vo. *Ward.*   2*s*. 6*d*.

,,   Die verlorene Handschrift. c. 8vo. 2 vols. (*Leipzig*).   6*s*.

,,   The same (" The lost manuscript"). Tr. c. 8vo. 3 vols. *Chapman.*   O.P

§   ,,   Die Ahnen. c. 8vo. 6 vols.
<blockquote>Vol. i., *Ingo und Ingraban*, 7*s*.; vol. ii., *Das Nest der Zaunkönige*, 6*s*.; vol. iii., *Die Brüder vom deutschen Hause*, 6*s*.; *vol. iv., *Marcus König*, 6*s*.; vol. v., *Die Geschwister*, *s*.; vol. vi., *Aus einer kleinen Stadt*, 6*s*. Vol. i. tr. by Mrs. Malcolm. p. 8vo. O.P.</blockquote>

__Gutzkow__, K. Durch Nacht zum Licht. (*Stuttgart*).   4*s*.

,,   The same (" Through night to light," in "Tauchnitz collection "). Tr. 18mo. *Low.*   2*s*.

__Hackländer__, F. W. Werke. 16mo. 60 vols. (*Stuttgart*).   72*s*.
<blockquote>The vols. are sold separately. **Handel und Wandel*; **Soldatenleben im Frieden*.</blockquote>

__Hauff__, W. Das Bild des Kaisers. 24mo. *Hendel.*   8*d*.

,,   Phantasien im Bremer Rathskeller. 24mo. *Hendel.*   8*d*.

*§__Hillern__, W. von. Die Geier-Wally. 12mo. (*Berlin*).   2*s*. 6*d*.
<blockquote>Much the best story of the authoress.</blockquote>

,,   The same (" The vulture maiden," in "Tauchnitz collection"). Tr. 18mo. *Low.*   2*s*.

__Heyse__, P. Gesammelte Werke. c. 8vo. 21 vols., 4*s*. each. *Hertz.*   84*s*.
<blockquote>*Vols. iv.-viii., and xv.-xix. are *Novellen*; a selection of these are translated in Low's *Tauchnitz collection*; vol. xi., xii., *Kinder der Welt*; vol. ix., x., xx., *Dramen.* No German author writes a style more correct, pure, and graceful than that of Heyse. His *Novellen* are more artistic, and, on the whole, more successful, than his longer *Romane*.</blockquote>

__Immermann__, K. Der Oberhof. 12mo. *Spemanns Hand- und Hausbibl.*   1*s*.

__Junghans__, Sophie. Helldunkel. c. 8vo. 2 vols. (*Leipzig*).   9*s*.
<blockquote>Historical: Germany, 17th century; vigorous style.</blockquote>

,,   Die Schwiegertochter. *Goldschmidt.*   1*s*. 6*d*.

__Keller__, G. Gesammelte Werke. c. 8vo. 10 vols. *Hertz*   30*s*.
<blockquote>Vols. not sold separately.</blockquote>

Keller, G. Die Leute von Seldwyla (Erzählungen). c. 8vo. 2 vols. *Hertz.*   6s.
> The best of these stories, *Romeo und Julie auf dem Dorfe*, is in vol. iii. of the *Deutscher Novellenschatz.*

Lewald, Fanny. Stella. c. 8vo. 3 vols. *Janke.*   12s.

,, The same (in "Tauchnitz collection"). Tr. Mrs. Marshall. 18mo. *Low.*   2s.

,, Helmar. 8vo. *Janke.*   6s.

*****Ludwig,** O. Zwischen Himmel und Erde. 24mo. *Janke.*   1s. 6d

Meissner, A. Die Sansara. c. 8vo. 4 vols. (*Leipzig*).   O.P

,, Novellen. c. 8vo. 3 vols. (*Leipzig*).   9s.
> One of the best, *Der Müller vom Höft*, is in vol. vi. of the *Deutscher Novellenschatz.*

Meyer, C. F. Jürg Jenatsch. c. 8vo. *Haessel.*   4s.

,, Der Heilige. c. 8vo. *Haessel.*   3s.

* ,, Novellen. 2 vols., 4s. each. *Haessel.*   8s.
> One of these, *Gustav Adolfs Page* is in vol. xiii. of the *Neuer deutscher Novellenschatz.*

Reuter, F. Sämmtliche Werke. 12mo. 15 vols., 4s. each. (*Hinstorff*).   60s.
> In low German. One of the most popular is *Ut mine Stromtid*; tr. under the title *An old story of my farming days.* ("Tauchnitz collection"). 18mo. 3 vols., 2s. each.

Riehl, W. H. *Geschichten aus alter Zeit; 2 vols., 9s.; Gesammelte Geschichten und Novellen, 2 vols., 6s.; Am Feierabend, 6s. c. 8vo. *Cotta.*
> Short stories from all periods of history, written throughout with the accurate and familiar knowledge of a historian, and, for the most part, with much liveliness and humour.

Roberts, A. von. *"Es" und Anderes, 3s.; "Unmusikalisch" und Anderes, 3s. c. 8vo. (*Leipzig*).
> Very short sketches and stories; written with a grace and lightness of touch not common in German authors.

Roquette, O. Grosse und kleine Leute in Alt-Weimar. c. 8vo. *Schottländer.*   5s.

*****Scheffel,** V. von. Ekkehard. 12mo. (*Stuttgart*).   5s.
> A story of the tenth century. The most popular German historical novel.

,, The same (in "Tauchnitz collection"). Tr. 18mo. 2 vols., 2s. each. *Low.*   4s.

*****Schweichel,** R. Der Bildschnitzer vom Achensee. 12mo. *Janke.*   2s.
> A decidedly good novel.

,, Der Wunderdoktor. 12mo. *Janke.*   1s.

* ,, Der Krämer von Illiez. 12mo. *Janke.*   1s. 6d.

Spielhagen, F. Ausgewählte Romane. 12mo. *Staackmann.*   28s.
> *Problematische Naturen*, 2 vols., 7s.; *Die von Hohenstein*, 3s. 6d.; *In Reih' und Glied*, 2 vols., 7s.; *Hammer und Ambos*, 3s. 6d.; *Sturmflut*, 2 vols., 7s.

* ,, Auf der Düne. 12mo. *Staackmann.*   1s. 3d.

,, Hans und Grete. 12mo. *Staackmann.*   1s. 3d.

Storm, T. Gesammelte Schriften. 12mo. 14 vols. *Westermann.*   31s. 6d
> P. Heyse calls Storm's stories "Die Novellen eines Lyrikers." There are several collections of the *Novellen* under various titles. Among the best are *Carsten Curator* and *Die Söhne des Senators. Eine Malerarbeit* is in vol. ix. of the *Deutscher Novellenschatz.*

—VII. BOOKS FOR THE YOUNG. (In addition to those marked § in the Literature list).

CHILDREN FROM 8 TO 12.

Andersen, Hans. Märchen. 8vo. (*Leipzig*).   4s. 6d

Grimm, J. and W. Kinder und Hausmärchen. 12mo. (*Berlin*).   6s.

Hauff, W. Märchen. 18mo. (*Leipzig*).   1*s.* 6*d.*

  ,,   W. Lichtenstein. 18mo. *Spemanns Hand- und Hausbibl.*   1*s.* 6*d.*

GIRLS FROM 12 TO 15.

Fouqué, F. de la Motte. Sintram und seine Gefärhten. 16mo. *Nutt.*   1*s.* 6*d.*

Helm, Klementine. Backfischen's Leiden und Freuden. 12mo.   *Wigand.*   3*s.*

Stein, A. Mädchens Tagebuch. 12mo. (*Berlin*).   3*s.*
     A charming book, though a little old-fashioned.

GIRLS OVER 15 AND YOUNG PEOPLE GENERALLY.

Andersen, Hans. Der Improvisator. 12mo. (*Leipzig*).   3*s.*

  ,,   Nur ein Geiger. 12mo. (*Leipzig*).   3*s.*

Baumbach, R. Sommermärchen. 4to.   17*s.*

Franzos, K. E. Ein Kampf ums Recht. 12mo. 2 vols. (*Leipzig*).   10*s.*

  ,,   Die Juden von Barnow. 8vo.   5*s.*

Heimburg, W. Gesammelte Romane und Novellen. 12mo. 10 vols., 4*s.* each.   40*s.*

Körner, T. Lustspiele. 12mo. (*Berlin*).   4*s.*
     Excellent for schoolroom acting.

Marlitt, E. Das Geheimniss der alten Mamsell. 12mo. 2 vols. *Dulau.*   7*s.*

Müller, F. Max. Deutsche Liebe. 8vo. *Brockhaus.*   3*s.*

Schubin, O. Ehre. 8vo. *Trübner.*   5*s*

  ,,   Unter uns. 8vo. *Trübner.*   7*s.* 6*d.*

Dahn, F. Ein Kampf um Rom. 12mo. 4 vols.   24*s.*

Ebers, G. Eine aegyptische Königstochter. 12mo. 3 vols *Deutsche Verlags-Anstalt.*   12*s.*

  ,,   Uarda. 12mo. 3 vols. *Deut. Ver. Anst.*   12*s.*

Blennerhasset, Lady. Mme. de Staël und ihre Zeitgenossen. 8vo. 3 vols.   31*s.*

Deutsche Lyrik ("Golden Treasury" ser.). Ed. C. A. Buchheim. 18mo. *Macmillan.*   4*s.* 6*d.*

Grimm, H. Michel Angelo. 8vo. 2 vols. (*Berlin*).   20*s.*

Hensel, S. Die Familie Mendelssohn. 8vo. 2 vols. (*Berlin*). illus.   12*s.*

Lewald, Fanny. Englische Reise. 8vo. 2 vols.   7*s.*

Polko, Elise. Dichtergruss. 16mo. (*Leipzig*).   6*s.*

Reumont, A. von. Charakterbilder aus der neueren Geschichte Italiens. 12mo. (*Leipzig*).   5*s.*

Riehl, W. H. Musikalische Charakterköpfe. 8vo. 3 vols.   15*s.*

Scherr, J. Schiller und seine Zeit. 16mo. (*Leipzig*).   4*s.* 6*d.*

GLASS-PAINTING, *see* ARTISTIC PROCESSES XI.

GLOVES (HISTORICAL), *see* COSTUME.

GOLD, *see* METALLURGY.

GOLDSMITHS' WORK, *see* ARTISTIC PROCESSES IV.

GOLF:

Golfiana miscellanea. Ed. J. L. Stewart. 8vo. *Hamilton Adams.*   4s. 6d.
     Collection of monographs.

Clerk. Royal and ancient game of golf.

Hutchinson, H. G. Hints on golf. f. 8vo. *Blackwood.*   1s. 6d.

Simpson, W. G. Art of golf. d. 8vo. *Douglas.* illus.   15s.
     PERIODICAL: *The Golfing Annual.* (H. Cox.) 2s. 6d. Contains history of golf clubs.

GOTHIC LANGUAGE:

Skeat, W. W. Gothic glossary. sm. 4to. *Asher.* pub. 9s.   O.P.
     With outline of grammar.

Braune, W. Gothic grammar with selections for reading, and a glossary.
     Tr. G. H. Balg. 8vo. *Low.*   3s. 6d.

Douse, T. le M. Introduction to the Gothic of Ulfilas. 8vo. *Taylor and*
     Francis.   10s. 6d.

Heyne, M. Ulfilas: Text, Wörterbuch, und Grammatik. 8vo. (*Paderborn*).   5s.

Skeat, W. W. Gospel of St. Mark in Gothic. ex. f. 8vo. *Clar. Press.*   4s.

Bosworth and Waring. Gothic and Anglo-Saxon gospels. 8vo. *J. R.*
     Smith. pub. 12s.   O.P.
     In parallel columns, with the versions of Wiclif and Tyndale.

GRAFTING AND BUDDING, *see* GARDENING.

GRASSES, *see* AGRICULTURE II.

GRAZING, *see* LIVE-STOCK I.

GREAT BRITAIN, *see* ENGLAND.

     For books relating especially to Scotland, Wales, Channel Islands, Man, Isle of; *see* under
     those heads.

GREECE (MODERN):

See also MEDITERRANEAN.

—I. GEOGRAPHY:

Murray's Handbook. p. 8vo. 2 vols. *Murray.*   24s.

Baedeker's Handbook (in German). 12mo. *Dulau.*   10s.

Neumann and Partsch. Physikalische Geographie von Griechenland, mit
     besondere Rücksicht auf das Alterthum. 8vo. (*Cologne*).   9s.

Geographia physike kai politike. 2 vols., 5s. each. (*Corinth*).   10s.
     A general geography for Greek schools, with geography of Greece given at length.

Mahaffy, J. P. Rambles and studies in Greece. c. 8vo. *Macmillan.*
     illus.   10s. 6d

Sandys, J. E. An Easter vacation in Greece. c. 8vo. *Macmillan.*   3s. 6d.
     Contains a bibliography of Greek travel and topography.

—II. LANGUAGE:

Vlachos, A. Modern Greek grammar. 12mo. *Thimm.*   4s.

Contopoulos, N. Modern Greek-English lexicon. 8vo. *Thimm.*   25s.

GREECE: ARCHÆOLOGY AND ART:

See also ARCHITECTURE II.

Smith, W. Greek and Roman antiquities. m. 8vo. *Murray*. illus.	28s.
Roberts, E. S. Introduction Greek epigraphy. 8vo. Part i. *Cambridge Press*.	18s.
Hicks, E. L. Manual of Greek historical inscriptions. d. 8vo. *Clar. Press*.	10s. 6d.
Head, B. V. Historia numorum. r. 8vo. *Clar. Press*.	42s.
Kroker, E. Katechismus der Archäologie. 12mo. (*Leipzig*).	3s.
Collingnon, M. Archéologie grecque. 8vo. (*Paris*).	4s. 6d.
,, Manual of mythology. Tr. Jane E. Harrison. 8vo. *Grevel*.	10s. 6d.
Schömann, G. F. Greek antiquities. Tr. Hardy and Mann. 8vo. *Rivington*.	18s.
Mahaffy, J. P. Antiquities (Primer). 18mo. *Macmillan*. illus.	1s.
Paris. Manual of ancient sculpture. Tr. Harrison. c. 8vo. *Grevel*.	10s. 6d.
Mitchell, Lucy. History of ancient sculpture. r. 8vo. *Paul*. illus.	42s.
Murray, A. S. Greek sculpture. r. 8vo. 2 vols. *Murray*.	31s. 6d.
Overbeck, J. Geschichte der Plastik. 8vo. 2 vols. *Dulau*. illus.	24s.
,, Schriftquellen. *Trübner*.	9s. 6d.
Müller and Wieseler. Denkmäler der Kunst. fo. (*Göttingen*). illus.	52s.
Brunn, H. Denkmäler der antiken Sculptur. fo. (*Berlin*).	
<small>To be completed in 80 parts at 20s. each; 21 parts issued.</small>	
Overbeck, J. Griechische Kunstmythologie. i. 8vo. (*Leipzig*).	
<small>In course of publication. 5 vols. issued, 11s. to 19s. each. Atlas and illustrations. i. fo. 28s. to 48s. each vol.</small>	
,, Pompeii. r. 8vo. (*Leipzig*).	20s.
Verrall and Harrison. Mythology and monuments of Athens. c. 8vo. *Macmillan*. illus.	16s.

GREECE: HISTORY:

—I. GENERAL:

Grote, G. History of Greece. p. 8vo. 10 vols. *Murray*. maps and plans.	50s.
Abbott, Evelyn. History of Greece. c. 8vo. *Longmans*.	10s. 6d.
,, Skeleton outlines of Greek history. 12mo. *Longmans*.	2s. 6d.
Curtius, E. History of Greece. Tr. A. Ward. d. 8vo. 5 vols., 18s. each. *Bentley*.	90s.
Smith, W. Student's manual of Greek history. p. 8vo. *Murray*.	7s. 6d.
,, Smaller history. 16mo. *Murray*.	3s. 6d.
Duncker. History of Greece. Tr. Alleyne and Abbott. 8vo. *Bentley*. Vol. i., 15s.	
Mahaffy, J. P. The Greek world under Roman sway. c. 8vo. *Macmillan*.	10s. 6d.
Finlay, G. History of Greece. B.C. 146 to A.D. 1864. Ed. H. F. Tozer. d. 8vo. 7 vols. *Clar. Press*.	70s.
Gregorovius, F. Geschichte der Stadt Athen. 8vo. 2 vols. (*Gotha*).	20s.

—II. SPECIAL PERIODS:

Cox, G. W. Greeks and Persians. f. 8vo. *Longmans*.	2s. 6d.

Sankey, C. Spartan and Theban supremacies. f. 8vo. *Longmans.*		2*s.* 6*d.*
Curteis, A. M. Macedonian empire. f. 8vo. *Longmans.*		2*s.* 6*d.*
Cox, G. W. Athenian empire. f. 8vo. *Longmans.*		2*s.* 6*d.*
Whitley. Political parties in the Peloponnesian war. 8vo. *Cambridge Press.*		2*s.* 6*d.*
Lloyd, W. Age of Pericles. 8vo. 2 vols. *Macmillan.*		21*s.*

—III. MISCELLANEOUS:

Mahaffy, J. P. Social life in Greece. c. 8vo. *Macmillan.*	9*s.*
Wilkins, A. Education in Greece. p. 8vo. *Isbister.*	5*s.*
Boeckh, A. Public economy of Athens. Tr. Lamb. (*Boston*).	O.P.
Becker, W. Charicles. p. 8vo. *Longmans.*	7*s.* 6*d*
Haigh, A. E. Attic theatre. d. 8vo. *Clar. Press.* illus.	12*s.* 6*d.*
Moulton, R. G. Ancient classic drama. c. 8vo. *Clar. Press.*	8*s.* 6*d.*

GREEK LANGUAGE AND LITERATURE:

—I. GRAMMARS, PHILOLOGY, AND DICTIONARIES:

Jelf, W. Greek grammar. 8vo. 2 vols. *J. Parker.*	30*s.*
Goodwin, W. W. Greek moods and tenses. 8vo. *Macmillan.* Best book on syntax of verbs.	14*s.*
,, Elementary Greek grammar (school). c. 8vo. *Macmillan.*	3*s.* 6*d.*
Thompson, F. E. Syntax of Attic Greek (school). c. 8vo. *Rivington.*	3*s.* 6*d.*
Curtius, G. Student's Greek grammar (school). Ed. Smith. p. 8vo. *Murray.*	6*s.*
Abbott, Evelyn. Elements of Greek accidence. *Longmans.*	4*s.* 6*d.*
King and Cookson. Greek and Latin philology. ex. f. 8vo. *Clar. Press.*	5*s.* 6*d.*
Henry, V. Comparative grammar of Greek and Latin. *Sonnenschein.*	7*s.* 6*d.*
Curtius, G. Principles of Greek etymology. Tr. Wilkins. 8vo. 2 vols. *Murray.*	28*s.*
,, The Greek verb. Tr. England and Wilkins. 8vo. *Murray.*	12*s.*
Liddell and Scott. Greek and English lexicon. 4to. *Clar. Press.* For all students. Abridged edition, 12mo., 7*s.* 6*d.*	36*s.*
Smith, W. Dictionary of Greek and Roman antiquities. m. 8vo. 2 vols. *Murray.* illus. Vol. i., 31*s.* 6*d.*; vol. ii. in press. Abridged edition, c. 8vo., 7*s.* 6*d.*	28*s.*
,, Dictionary of Greek and Roman biography. m. 8vo. 3 vols. *Murray.* illus.	84*s.*
,, Dictionary of Greek and Roman geography. m. 8vo. 2 vols. *Murray.* illus.	56*s.*
,, Classical dictionary. m. 8vo. *Murray.* illus. Abridged edition, c. 8vo., 7*s.* 6*d.*	18*s.*
Index in Tragicos Graecos. 2 vols. *Simpkin.* 1830.	O.P.

—II. HISTORY:

(A) GENERAL.

Muller and Donaldson. History of Greek literature. 8vo. 3 vols. *Longmans.* pub. 21*s.*	O.P.
Mure, W. History of Greek literature. 8vo. 5 vols. *Longmans.* pub. 69*s.*	O.P.

Mahaffy, J. P. History of Greek literature. c. 8vo. 2 vols., 9s. each. *Macmillan.*   18s.

Jevons, F. B. History of Greek literature. c. 8vo. *Griffin.*   8s. 6d.

Jebb, R. C. History of Greek literature (primer). 18mo. *Macmillan.*   1s.

(B) SPECIAL.

Symonds, J. A. Studies of Greek poets. 2 vols., 10s. 6d. each. *Smith, Elder.* vol. i. o.p.

Jebb, R. C. Attic orators. 8vo. *Macmillan.*   5s.

Abbott, E. Hellenica; essays on Greek literature. 8vo. *Rivington.*   16s.

Jebb, R. C. Homer. c. 8vo. *Maclehose.*   3s. 6d.

Butcher, S. H. Demosthenes. f. 8vo. *Macmillan.*   1s. 6d.

Ancient classics for English readers. Ed. L. Collins. c. 8vo. 28 vols., 2s. 6d. each. *Blackwood.*
> Homer, Herodotus, Xenophon, Euripides, Aristophanes, Plato, Lucian, Æschylus, Sophocles, Hesiod, Demosthenes, Aristotle, Thucydides, Pindar, Greek Anthology.

Bibliotheca scriptorum Graecorum. r. 8vo. *Didot.*
> From 12s. 6d. to 72s. per vol.

—III. GENERAL SCHOLARSHIP:

Hicks, E. L. Manual of Greek historical inscriptions. d. 8vo. *Clar. Press.*   10s. 6d.

Rutherford, W. G. New Phrynichus. 8vo. *Macmillan.*   18s.

Gow, J. Companion to school classics. c. 8vo. *Macmillan.*   6s.

—IV. COLLECTIONS:

Poetae scenici. Ed. W. Dindorf. i. 8vo. *J. Parker.*   21s.
> Contains the whole of Æschylus, Sophocles, Euripides, Aristophanes, and fragments.

Oratores Attici. Ed. J. Bekker. 8vo. 5 vols. (*Berlin*). 1823-4.   12s.
> Text only, of all the Greek orators extant.

Orators. Ed. Baiter and Sauppe. 16mo. 14 vols. (*Zürich*). 1838-43.   36s.

Anthologia Graeca. Ed. Dübner. r. 8vo. *Didot.*   36s.

Anthology, Select epigrams from. Ed. and Tr. J. W. Mackail. 8vo. *Longmans.*   16s.

Poetae lyrici Graeci. Ed. Bergk. 8vo. 3 vols. *Teubner.*
> Vol. i., o.p.; vol. ii., 10s.; vol. iii., 14s. Pindar, Elegiac, Iambic, and Lyric poets.

Comicorum Graecorum fragmenta. Ed. T. Kock. r. 8vo. 3 vols., 18s. each. (*Leipzig*).   54s.

Tragicorum Graecorum fragmenta. Ed. A. Nauck. 8vo. (*Leipzig*).   26s.

Philosophorum Graecorum fragmenta. Ed. F. Mullach. r. 8vo. 3 vols. *Didot.*   37s. 6d.

Bucolici poetae. Ed. H. Ahrens. 12mo. *Teubner.*   8d.
> Theocritus, Bion, Moschus.

—V. TEXTS AND TRANSLATIONS:

Homer. Iliad. Ed. D. B. Monro. ex. f. 8vo. 2 vols., 6s. each. *Clar. Press.*   12s.

,, Odyssey. Ed. W. W. Merry. 2 vols., 5s. each. *Clar. Press.*   10s.

,, Odyssey, books i.-xii. Ed. Merry and Riddell. d. 8vo. *Clar. Press.*   16s.

,, Iliad; with English notes. Ed. W. Leaf. 8vo. 2 vols., 14s. each. *Macmillan.*   28s.

German Editions :

Homer. Iliad. Ed. Fäsi. 12mo. 4 vols., 2*s.* each. *Weidmann.*   8*s.*

,,   Odyssey. Ed. Fäsi. 12mo. 4 vols., 2*s.* each. *Weidmann.*   8*s.*

,,   Iliad and Odyssey. Ed. Düntzer. 8vo. 12 vols. *Schöningh.*   17*s.*

,,   Iliad and Odyssey. Ed. Ameis and Hentze. 12 parts. *Teubner.*   16*s.*

,,   Iliad. Ed. La Roche. 6 parts, 1*s.* 6*d.* each. *Teubner.*   9*s.*

Translations :

,,   Iliad. Tr. into English prose by W. Leaf, E. Myers, and A. Lang. c. 8vo. *Macmillan.*   12*s.* 6*d.*

,,   Odyssey. Tr. into English prose by S. Butcher and A. Lang. c. 8vo. *Macmillan.*   6*s.*

Aids :

,,   Monro, D. B. Homeric grammar. 8vo. *Clar. Press.*   10*s.* 6*d.*

,,   Jebb, R. C. Homeric questions. c. 8vo. *Maclehose.*   3*s.* 6*d.*
    A general survey of the poems; their history, character, and questions connected with them.

,,   Dunbar, H. Concordance to Odyssey. 4to. *Clar. Press.*   21*s.*

,,   Prendergast, G. L. Concordance to Iliad. 4to. *Longmans.*   O.P.

Hesiod. Text; with English notes. Ed. F. A. Paley. d. 8vo. *Bell.*   5*s.*

Sappho. Text in Bergkh's Poetae lyrici Graeci, vol. iii. (*See* Sec. IV.).

Pindar. Text; with English notes. Ed. C. Fennell. c. 8vo. 2 vols. *Cambridge Press.*   9*s.*

,,   Tr. into prose, with notes, by E. Myers. c. 8vo. *Macmillan.*   5*s.*

,,   Olympian and Pythian odes. Tr. into verse by F. D. Morice. c. 8vo. *Paul.*   7*s.* 6*d.*

Æschylus. Text complete, scholia and synopsis of emendations. Ed. W. Wecklein. 8vo. 2 vols. (*Berlin*).   20*s.*
    The most valuable German edition for scholars.

,,   Text. Ed. F. A. Paley. d. 8vo. *Bell.*   8*s.*

,,   Agamemnon. Text with tr. by A. W. Verrall. 8vo. *Macmillan.*   12*s.*

,,   Seven against Thebes. Text with tr. by A. W. Verrall. 8vo. *Macmillan.*   2*s.* 6*d.*

,,   Agamemnon. Ed. F. A. Paley. f. 8vo. *Bell.*   1*s.* 6*d.*

,,   Prometheus. Ed. F. A. Paley. 18mo. *Macmillan.*   1*s.* 6*d.*

,,   Persae. Ed. F. A. Paley. f. 8vo. *Macmillan.*   3*s.* 6*d.*

,,   Septem contra Thebes. Ed. F. A. Paley. f. 8vo. *Macmillan.*   3*s.* 6*d.*

,,   Eumenides. Ed. F. A. Paley. 8vo. *Macmillan.*   5*s.*
    The above five plays, ed. by *Paley*, are school editions, with notes.

,,   Plays. Ed. and tr. by E. H. Plumptre. c. 8vo. *Isbister.*   4*s.* 6*d.*

,,   Agamemnon, Choephori, Eumenides. Tr. into verse by E. D. Morshead. c. 8vo. *Paul.*   7*s.* 6*d.*

,,   Plays. Tr. by F. A. Paley. 8vo. *Bell.*   7*s.* 6*d.*

Sophocles. Text, complete; with English notes. Ed. Campbell and Abbott. ex. f. 8vo. 2 vols. *Clar. Press.*   10*s.* 6*d.*

,,   Antigone; Œdipus Tyrannus; Œdipus Coloneus; Philoctetes; with English notes. Ed. and tr. R. C. Jebb. d. 8vo. 12*s.* 6*d.* each. *Cambridge Press.* Useful for all students.

,,   Ajax and Electra. Ed. R. C. Jebb. c. 8vo. 3*s.* 6*d.* each. *Rivington.*

,,   Plays (school edition). Ed. L. Campbell and E. Abbott. ex. f. 8vo. 7 vols. *Clar. Press.*   10*s.* 6*d.*
    Also sold separately, Œdipus Coloneus and Antigone, 1*s.* 9*d.* each; the others, 2*s.* each.

Sophocles. Tr. into verse by R. Whitelaw. c. 8vo. *Rivington.*   8s. 6d.
> Blank verse; with a few notes.

,,   Ed. and tr. into verse by E. H. Plumptre. c. 8vo. *Isbister.*   4s. 6d.
> Freer than Whitelaw's.

Euripides. Text, complete, with English notes. Ed. F. A. Paley. d. 8vo. 3 vols., 8s. each. *Bell.*   24s.

,,   Alcestis, Medea, Hippolytus, Hecuba, Bacchae, Orestes, Phœnissae, Troades. Ed. F. A. Paley. p. 8vo. 1s. 6d. each. *Bell.*

,,   Alcestis, 2s. 6d.; Helena, 3s.; Heracleidae, 3s.; Iphigenia in Tauris, 3s. Ed. C. S. Jerram. ex. f. 8vo. *Clar. Press.*

,,   Troades. Ed. Tyrrell. c. 8vo. *Hodges.*   1s.

,,   Medea (Critical ed.). Ed. A. W. Verrall. 8vo. *Macmillan.*   2s. 6d.

,,   Heracleidae (School ed.; with notes). Ed. E. A. Beck. ex. f. 8vo. *Pitt Press.*   3s. 6d.

,,   Bacchae (Critical ed.; with English notes). Ed. J. E. Sandys. c. 8vo. *Cambridge Press.*   12s. 6d.

,,   Hippolytus (School ed.) Ed. Hadley. ex. f. 8vo. *Pitt Press.*   2s.

,,   Hercules Furens (School ed.; with notes). Ed. Gray and Hutchinson. ex. f. 8vo. *Pitt Press.*   2s.

,,   Medea. Ed. M. G. Glazebrook. c. 8vo. *Rivington.*   2s. 6d.

,,   Alcestis. Tr. R. Browning; in "Balaustion's adventure." c. 8vo. *Smith, Elder.* Embedded in a poem which explains it.   5s.

,,   Hercules Furens. Tr. R. Browning; in "Aristophanes' apology." c. 8vo. *Smith, Elder.*   5s.

Herodotus. Text, with Latin notes. Ed. J. C. G. Bähr. 8vo. 4 vols. (*Leipzig*).   30s.
> There is no good English edition of the whole.

   Books i., ii.; with English notes. Ed. H. G. Woods. c. 8vo. 2 vols. Vol. i., 6s.; vol. ii., 5s. *Rivington.*

,,   Books ii., iii.; with English notes. Ed. Kenrick. 8vo. *Fellowes.* pub. 12s.   O.P.

,,   Tr. G. C. Macaulay. c. 8vo. 2 vols. *Macmillan.*   18s.

Thucydides. Text, with English notes. Ed. T. Arnold. 8vo. 3 vols. *J. Parker.*   36s.
> Half a century old, but good.

,,   Text, with German notes by J. Classen. p. 8vo. 8 parts, 2s. 6d. or 3s. each. *Weidmann.*

,,   Books vi., vii.; with English notes. Ed. P. Frost. f. 8vo. *Macmillan.*   3s. 6d.

,,   Tr. by B. Jowett. d. 8vo. 2 vols. *Clar. Press.*   32s.

Aristophanes. Text, with critical notes only. Ed. A. Meineke. 8vo. 2 vols. *Tauchnitz.*   7s. 6d.

,,   Clouds, 3s.; Frogs, 3s.; Acharnians, 3s.; Knights, 3s.; Birds, 3s. 6d. Ed. W. W. Merry. ex. f. 8vo. *Clar. Press.*

,,   Wasps, 3s. 6d. Ed. W. C. Green. *Rivington.*

,,   Peace, 2s. Ed. W. C. Green. *Hall (Cambridge).*

,,   Peace; Acharnians; Frogs (School ed., with notes). Ed. F. A. Paley. c. 8vo. 4s. 6d. each. *Bell.*

,,   Clouds, 2s.; Knights, 2s.; Frogs, 2s.; Birds, 2s. 6d.; with German notes. Ed. T. V. Kock. p. 8vo. *Weidmann.* Best German annotated edition.

,,   Acharnians, Knights, Birds, Frogs, Peace. Tr. J. H. Frere (Universal Library). c. 8vo. 1s. each. *Routledge.*

,,   Clouds, Wasps, Peace. Tr. B. B. Rogers. *Bell.*   O.P.

,,   Birds. Tr., with notes by B. H. Kennedy. c. 8vo. *Macmillan.*   6s.

,,   Dunbar. Concordance to Aristophanes. 4to. *Clar. Press.*   21s.

Xenophon. Text, complete. Ed. L. Dindorf and Hug. 5 vols. *Teubner.* 4s. 3d.

,,   Anabasis; with English notes. Ed. A. Pretor. ex. f. 8vo. Books i., iii., v., 2s. each; books ii., iv., vi., vii., 2s. 6d. each. *Pitt Press.*

,,   Agesilaus (School ed.; with English notes). Ed. R. W. Taylor. c. 8vo. *Rivington,* 2s. 6d.

,,   Cyropaedia (School ed.; with English notes). Ed. G. M. Gorham. f. 8vo. *Bell.* 3s. 6d.

,,   Cyropaedia; books vii., viii. Ed. W. W. Goodwin. f. 8vo. *Macmillan.* 2s. 6d.

,,   Economics; with English notes. Ed. H. Holden. f. 8vo. *Macmillan.* 5s.

,,   Hiero; with English notes. Ed. H. Holden. f. 8vo. *Macmillan.* 2s. 6d.

,,   Hellenics (School ed.; with English notes). Ed. H. Hailstone. f. 8vo. *Macmillan.* 2s. 6d.

,,   Selections from Hellenics (School ed.). J. H. Philpotts. ex. f. 8vo. *Clar. Press.* 3s. 6d.

,,   Memorabilia. Ed. J. Marshall. *Clar. Press.*

,,   Complete works. Tr. H. G. Dakyns. c. 8vo. *Macmillan.* vol. i., 10s. 6d.

Æschines. Text, complete. Ed. Francke. 12mo. *Teubner.*   1s.

,,   In Ctesiphontem; with De corona of Demosthenes. Ed. E. A. and W. H. Simcox. d. 8vo. *Clar. Press.* 12s.

,,   Text; German notes and translation. G. E. Benseler. 12mo. 3 vols. (*Leipzig*).   4s. 6d.

Demosthenes. Text; in "Oratores Attici." (*See Sec. IV.*)

,,   De corona; with English notes. Ed. A. Holmes. c. 8vo. *Rivington.* 5s.

,,   De falsa legatione, 6s. Olynthiacs, 2s. 6d. Philippics, 3s.; with English notes. Ed. G. H. Heslop. c. 8vo. *Rivington.*

,,   Androtion and Timokrates. Ed. W. Wayte. c. 8vo. *Cambridge Press.* 7s. 6d.

,,   Meidias; with English notes. Ed. E. A. Fennell. 12mo. (*Edinburgh*). 5s.

,,   Leptines; with English notes. Ed. B. W. Beatson. c. 8vo. *Bell.* 3s. 6d.

,,   Select Private Orations. Ed. Paley and Sandys. c. 8vo. 2 vols. Vol. i., 6s.; vol. ii., 4s. 6d. *Cambridge Press.* 10s. 6d.

,,   De corona. Tr. Simpson (*Oxford*). With English and Greek facing.

,,   Complete works. Tr. C. R. Kennedy. p. 8vo. 5 vols. *Bell (Bohn).* Vol. i., 3s. 6d.; vol. ii. to v., 5s. each.

Antiphon. Text; with German notes. Ed. Mätzner. 8vo. (*Berlin*). 1838. 4s.

Lysias. Selections; with English notes. Ed. E. S. Shuckburgh. f. 8vo. *Macmillan.*   5s.

,,   In "Selections from Orators." Ed. R. C. Jebb. f. 8vo. *Macmillan.* 6s.

Plato. Text, complete. Ed. Baiter, Orelli, and Winckelmann. 12mo. 4 vols. *Meyer (Zurich).*   O.P.

,,   Text. Ed. C. Hermann. 12mo. 6 vols. *Teubner.* 10s. 6d.

,,   Apology. (With valuable digest of idioms.) Ed. J. Riddell. d. 8vo. *Clar. Press.* 8s. 6d.

,,   Apology and Crito, 2s. 6d.; Phaedo, 5s. 6d. Ed. W. Wagner. c. 8vo. *Bell.*

,,   Protagoras. Ed. W. Wayte. c. 8vo. *Bell.* 4s. 6d.

,,   Philebus. Ed. E. Poste. d. 8vo. *Clar. Press.* 7s. 6d.

,,   Theaetetus, 10s. 6d.; Sophistes and Politicus, 18s. Ed. L. Campbell. d. 8vo. *Clar. Press.*

,,   Gorgias (o.p.); Phædrus, 5s. Ed. W. H. Thompson. d. 8vo. *Bell.*

,,   Euthyphro and Menexenus. Ed. C. E. Graves. 18mo. *Macmillan.* 1s. 6d.

,,   Republic; books i. to v. Ed. T. H. Warren. f. 8vo. *Macmillan.* 5s.

,,   Phaedo. Ed. R. Archer-Hind. 8vo. *Macmillan.* 8s. 6d.

,,   Euthydemus and Laches. Ed. G. H. Wells. c. 8vo. *Bell.* 4s.

Translations :

,,   Complete works; with introductions. Tr. B. Jowett. d. 8vo. 6 vols. *Clar. Press.*   70s.

,,   Philebus and Theaetetus. Tr., with notes by F. A. Paley. c. 8vo. 4s. each. *Bell.*

,,   Republic. Tr., with analysis and introduction, by B. Jowett. m. 8vo. *Clar. Press.* 12s. 6d.

,,   Euthyphro, Apology, Crito, and Phaedo. Tr. A. J. Church. 18mo. *Macmillan.* 4s. 6d.

,,   Gorgias. Tr. E. M. Cope. 8vo. *Bell.* 7s.

,,   Phaedo. Tr. E. M. Cope. d. 8vo. *Cambridge Press.* 5s.

,,   Phaedrus, Lysis, Protagoras. Tr. J. Wright. 12mo. *J. Parker.* pub. 3s. 6d. O.P.

Aristotle. Text, complete. Ed. J. Bekker. d. 8vo. 11 vols. *Clar. Press.*   50s.
　　Also sold separately (except vol ix.) at 5s. 6d. each.

,,　　Text, complete. Ed. Dübner and Heitz. r. 8vo. 5 vols. *Didot.*   64s.

,,　　Ethics; text. Ed. Bywater. p. 8vo. *Clar. Press.*   6s.

　　Politics; text. Ed R. Hicks after Susemihl. 8vo. *Macmillan.* In press.

,,　　De animâ; with English notes and tr. by E. Wallace. d. 8vo. *Pitt Press.*   18s.

,,　　Poetics; text. Ed. W. Christ. 12mo. *Teubner.*   8d.

,,　　Politics; text with German notes and tr. by F. Susemihl. 12mo. *Teubner.*   2s. 6d.

,,　　Organon; selections. Ed. J. Magrath. c. 8vo. *Rivington.*   3s. 6d.

,,　　Rhetoric; with English notes. E. M. Cope and J. Sandys. d. 8vo. 3 vols. *Cambridge Press.*   21s.

,,　　Politics; with intro. and notes. Tr. B. Jowett. m. 8vo. 2 vols. *Clar. Press.*   21s.

,,　　Nicomachean Ethics. Tr. F. H. Peters. c. 8vo. *Paul.*   6s.

,,　　Organon. Tr. E. Poste. 8vo. *Macmillan.*   8s. 6d.

　　Rhetoric. Tr. E. M. Cope. 8vo. *Macmillan.*   14s.

Aids :

,,　　Grote, G. Aristotle. 8vo. *Murray.*   12s.

,,　　Wilson, J. C. Aristotelian studies. d. 8vo. *Clar. Press.*   7s. 6d.

,,　　Wallace, E. Outlines of philosophy of Aristotle. ex. f. 8vo. *Pitt Press.*   4s. 6d.

,,　　Newman, W. L. Politics; with introduction and notes. m. 8vo. 2 vols. *Clar. Press.*   28s.

,,　　Mayor, J. E. B. Sketch of ancient philosophy. ex. f. 8vo. *Pitt Press.*   3s. 6d.

Theocritus, Bion, and Moschus. Text. Ed. H. Ahrens. 12mo. *Teubner.*   8d.

,,　　Text; with English notes (School ed.). Ed. Snow; revised by H. Kynaston. ex. f. 8vo. *Clar. Press.*   4s. 6d.

,,　　Text; with German notes. Ed. A. T. Fritzsche. 12mo. (*Leipzig*).   O.P.

,,　　Tr. into verse by C. S. Calverley. c. 8vo. *Bell.*   7s. 6d.

,,　　Tr. into prose by A. Lang. 18mo. *Macmillan.*   4s. 6d.

Aratus. Tr. E. Poste. c. 8vo. *Macmillan.*   3s. 6d.

Arrian. Anabasis. Ed. Abicht. 12mo. *Teubner.*   1s. 3d.

,,　　Scripta minora. Ed. Hercher. 12mo. *Teubner.*   2s.

Athenæus. Text. 12mo. 3 vols. vols. i. and ii., 5s. each; vol. iii., 7s. 6d.   17s. 6d.
Teubner.

Babrius. Text. Ed. W. G. Rutherford. 8vo. *Macmillan.*   12s. 6d.

Anacreon. Text; in "Poetae lyrici Graeci." (*See* Sec. IV.).

Bion. Text; in "Bucolici poetae." (*See* Sec. IV.).

Heraclitus. Fragments. Ed. T. Bywater. d. 8vo. *Clar. Press.*   6s.

Moschus. Text; in "Bucolici poetae." (*See* Sec. IV.).

Plutarch. Text. 12mo. 5 vols. *Teubner.*   8s. 6d.

,,　　Gracchi, 6s.; Nikias, 5s.; Sulla, 6s.; Timoleon, 6s. Ed. H. Holden. ex. f. 8vo. *Pitt Press.*

,,　　Lives. Tr. A. H. Clough. 8vo. 3 vols. *Low.*   42s.
　　Also in one vol., 18s.

Lucian. Text. Ed. C. Jacobitz. 12mo. 3 vols. *Teubner.*   6s. 6d.
　　Vol. i., Somnium and Charon; ii., Piscator; iii., De luctu.

,,　　Ed. W. Heitland. ex. f. 8vo. *Pitt Press.*   3s. 6d.

Pausanias. Text. Ed. J. Schubart. 12mo. 2 vols. *Teubner.*   4s.

Polybius. Text. Ed. Büttner and Dindorf. 12mo. 4 vols.   13s.
　　Vol. i., 3s. 6d.; vol. ii., 3s. 6d.; vol. iii., 3s.; vol. iv., 3s.

Theophrastus. Characters; text. Ed. Foss. *Teubner.*   O.P.

Theophrastus.   Text ; English notes and tr. by R. C. Jebb.   *Macmillan.*   O.P.

GREEK CHURCH, *see* CHURCH HISTORY V. (G).

  ,,   PHILOSOPHY, *see* PHILOSOPHY II.

GREENLAND, *see* ARCTIC REGIONS.

GROUSE DRIVING, *see* SHOOTING.

GUERNSEY, *see* CHANNEL ISLANDS.

GUIANA :

Whetham, J. W. B.   Roraima and British Guiana.   8vo.   *Hurst.*   15s.

Im Thurn, E. F.   Among the Indians of Guiana.   8vo.   *Paul.*   illus.   18s.
     Sketches, chiefly anthropological.

Dalton, H. G.   History of British Guiana.   r. 8vo.   2 vols.   *Longmans.*   52s. 6d.

Les colonies d'Amérique.   12mo.   *Quantin.*   3s. 6d.
     In vol. ii. of " Les colonies françaises."

Palgrave, W. G.   Dutch Guiana.   8vo.   *Macmillan.*   9s.

GUN, *see* SHOOTING.

GUNNERY, *see* ARMY I. *and* NAVY II.

GYMNASTICS :

Jenkin, A. F.   Gymnastics (" All England " ser.).   sm. 8vo.   *Bell.*   2s.

Ravenstein, E. G.   Gymnasium and its fittings.   8vo.   *Trübner.*   2s. 6d.

Puritz, L.   Code book of gymnastic exercises.   *Turner.*

Alexander, A.   Gymnastics.   8vo.   4 vols.   *Philip.*   illus.   12s. 6d.
     Vol. i., Musical drill for infants, 2s. 6d. ; vol. ii., Exercises for girls, 2s. 6d. ; vol. iii., Gymnastic exercises (elementary), 2s. 6d. ; vol. iv., Gymnastic exercises (advanced), 5s.

Lemaire, E. F.   Indian clubs.   4to.   *Iliffe.*   5s.

Mélio, G. L.   Swedish drill.   *Low.*   1s. 6d.

Noakes, S. G.   Free gymnastics.   32mo.   *Simpkin.*   1s.

GYPSIES AND GYPSY LANGUAGE :

Leland, C. G.   The gypsies.   c. 8vo.   *Trübner.*   10s. 6d.

  ,,   English gypsies and their language.   8vo.   *Trübner.*   7s. 6d.

  ,,   Gypsy sorcery and fortune telling.   4to.   *Unwin.*   16s.

  ,,   and Palmer. English gypsy songs ; with translations.   8vo.   *Trübner.*   7s. 6d.

Borrow, G.   The gypsies of Spain.   p. 8vo.   *Murray.*   2s. 6d.

  ,,   Word-book of the Romany.   8vo.   *Murray.*   pub. 10s. 6d.   O.P.

H.

HARBOURS, *see* HYDRAULICS.

HAWAII, *see* PACIFIC II.

HAWKING, *see* FALCONRY.

HAYTI, *see* WEST INDIES II.

HEALTH, *see* HYGIENE.

HEALTH RESORTS:

Yeo, J. B. Climate and health resorts. p. 8vo. *Chapman.*   10s. 6d.

Braun and Hermann. Curative effect of baths and waters. d. 8vo. *Smith,*   18s.
Elder.
    A handbook to the Spas of Europe.

Wilson, W. S. The ocean as a health resort. c. 8vo. *Churchill.* illus.   7s. 6d.

McPherson, J. Baths and wells of Europe. p. 8vo. *Stanford.*   6s. 6d.

Bennet, H. Winter and spring on the shores of the Mediterranean. p. 8vo.
Churchill. illus.   12s. 6d.

Sparks, E. I. The Riviera. c. 8vo. *Churchill.* pub. 8s. 6d.   O.P.
    Health resorts on the North Mediterranean coast.

Wise, A. T. Alpine winter. d. 8vo. *Churchill.* illus.   2s. 6d.
    Medical aspects; with notes on Davos Platz, Wiesen, etc.

Walker, A. D. Egypt as a health resort. f. 8vo. *Churchill.*   3s. 6d.

Illustrated handbook of American winter and summer resorts. c. 8vo.
2 vols., 4s. each. *Appleton.* illus.   8s.

Grabham, M. C. Madeira: climate and resources.   5s.
    Special reference to the welfare of invalids.

Moore, W. J. Health in the tropics. 8vo. *Churchill.*   9s.

   ,,   Health resorts for tropical invalids in India, at home, and abroad.
p. 8vo. *Churchill.*   5s.

Tilt, E. T. Health in India for British women. c. 8vo. *Churchill.*   5s.

HEAT, *see* PHYSICS V.

HEBREW:

    The student who is ignorant of the German language is recommended to make himself
master of the elements of the grammar, and then work through Genesis with the
assistance of Mr. Spurrell's notes. For the remaining books of the Bible he will find the
translations in Messrs. Clark's " Foreign Theological Library" of great value.

—I. GRAMMARS AND DICTIONARIES:

Gabriel, H. Rudiments of Hebrew grammar. (elem.). 8vo. (*Freiburg*).   2s.
    Contains some account of the syntax, which is wanting in the next book.

Strack, H. L. Hebrew grammar, with exercises. (elem.). c. 8vo. *Williams.*   4s. 6d.
    Contains a bibliography of Biblical literature.

Ball, C. J. Merchant Taylors' Hebrew grammar. (elem.). d. 8vo. *Bagster.*   6s.

Gesenius, W. Student's Hebrew grammar. Tr. B. Davies. 8vo. *Asher.*   7s. 6d.

Land, J. P. Principles of Hebrew grammar. Tr. Lane-Poole. c. 8vo.
Trübner.   7s. 6d.
    Deals specially with the accidence.

Ewald, H. Syntax of the Hebrew language. Tr. J. Kennedy. d. 8vo.
Clark.   8s. 6d.

Harper, W. R. Elements of Hebrew syntax. 8vo. *Nutt.*   7s. 6d.

Driver, S. R.   Treatise on the use of the tenses in Hebrew.   ex. f. 8vo.
  Clar. Press.   7*s.* 6*d.*

Wickes, W.   Hebrew accentuation of Psalms, Proverbs, and Job.   d. 8vo.
  Clar. Press.   5*s.*

  „   Hebrew prose accentuation.   d. 8vo.   *Clar. Press.*   10*s.* 6*d.*

Siegfried and Strack.   Lehrbuch der neuhebräischen Sprache.   12mo.
  (*Carlsruhe*).   3*s.* 6*d.*

Davies, B.   The student's Hebrew lexicon.   8vo.   *Asher.*   12*s.*

Gesenius, W.   Handwörterbuch über das alte Testament.   Ed. Mühlau and
  others.   8vo.   (*Leipzig*).   15*s.*

Buxtorf, J.   Lexicon Talmudicum et Rabbinicum.   4to.   (*Leipzig*).   70*s.*

Jastrow, M.   Lexicon to the Talmud (unfinished).   d. 4to.   3 parts, 5*s.*
  each.   *Trübner.*

Lederer, P.   Lehrbuch zum Selbstunterricht im babylonischen Talmud.
  8vo.   3 vols.   (*Frankfurt*).   6*s.*

—II. HISTORY OF LITERATURE, CRITICISM, ETC.:

Zunz.   Die gottesdienstlichen Vorträge der Juden.   8vo.   (*Berlin*).   1832.   O.P.

Delitzsch, F.   Zur Geschichte der jüdischen Poesie.   8vo.   (*Leipzig*).
  1836.   4*s.*

Ginsburg, C. D.   The Kabbala ; its origin, etc.   8vo.   *Longmans.*   pub. 7*s.* 6*d.*   O.P.

Bleek, F.   Introduction to the Old Testament.   p. 8vo.   2 vols., 5*s.* each.
  Bell (Bohn).   10*s.*
  Later German editions, revised by Wellhausen.

Kuenen, A.   Historico-critical inquiry into the origin and composition of
  the Old Testament.   Tr. Wicksteed.   8vo.   *Macmillan.*   14*s.*
  Latest school.

—III. READING BOOKS AND TRANSLATIONS:

Spurrell, G. J.   Notes on the Hebrew text of Genesis.   c. 8vo.   *Clar. Press.*   10*s.* 6*d.*

Fürst, J.   Aramäische Chrestomathie.   8vo.   (*Leipzig*).   1836.   4*s.*

Taylor, C.   Sayings of the Jewish fathers.   d. 8vo.   *Cambridge Press.*   10*s.*

Hershon, P. I.   Treasures of the Talmud.   d. 8vo.   *Nisbet.*   12*s.* 6*d.*

Talmud Jerushalmi.   Tr. K. M. Schwabe.   f. 4to.   *Williams.*
  Part i., 9*s.*

Ibn Ezra.   Commentary on Isaiah (Soc. of Hebrew literature).   Ed. and
  tr. M. Friedländer.   d. 8vo.   3 vols.   *Trübner.*   22*s.*
  Vol. i., 10*s.* 6*d.* ; vol. ii., 4*s.* 6*d.* ; vol. iii., 7*s.*

Maimonides.   "Guide of the perplexed."   Ed. and tr. M. Friedländer.
  d. 8vo.   3 vols.   *Trübner.*   31*s.* 6*d.*

—IV. REFERENCE:

Davidson, B.   Concordance to Hebrew and Chaldee scriptures.   r. 8vo.
  Bagster.   42*s.*

Kitto, J.   Biblical encyclopædia.   8vo.   *Black.*   10*s.* 6*d.*

Smith, W.   Bible dictionary.   8vo.   3 vols.   *Murray.*   105*s.*
  Vol. i., 42*s.* ; vols. ii., iii., 63*s.*

Schenkel.   Bibel-Lexicon.   8vo.   5 vols.   *Brockhaus.*   50*s.*

Riehm, E.　Handwörterbuch des biblischen Alterthums.　8vo.　(*Leipzig*).　　37*s*.
　　Antiquities only.

Hamburger, J.　Real-Encyclopädie für Bibel und Talmud.　8vo.　2 vols.
　　(*Neustrelitz*).　　　　　　　　　　　　　　　　　　　　　　　　40*s*.
　　Includes the later literature.

Strack, H. L.　Abriss der neuhebräischen Literatur.
　　In Siegfried's grammar.

Orientalische Bibliographie.　Ed. A. Müller.　8vo.　4 vols.　(*Berlin*).
　　Vol. i., ii., 6*s*.; vol. iii., iv., 8*s*. each.　In progress.

Lippe, C. D.　Bibliographisches Lexicon der gesammten jüdischen Literatur
　　der Gegenwart.　8vo.　(*Vienna*).　　　　　　　　　　　　　　12*s*.
　　In progress.
　　　PERIODICALS: *Zeitschrift für alttestamentliche Wissenschaft* (10*s*. per annum).
　　Jewish Quarterly review (London); *Hebraica* (Scribner); *Transactions* of the Society of
　　Biblical Archæology (Longmans).

HELMETS, ANCIENT, *see* ARMS.

HERALDRY AND GENEALOGY :

—I. HERALDRY :

　　　As no official list of those who have a right to coat armour has ever been issued by the
　　College of Arms, all printed lists must necessarily be incorrect and incomplete.　The laws of
　　arms are vested in the five Kings of Arms (three for England, one for Scotland, and one for
　　Ireland), and no official work has been issued by them on the subject.

Burke, B.　General armoury.　sup. r. 8vo.　*Harrison*.　　　　52*s*. 6*d*.

Boutell, C.　Heraldry.　p. 8vo.　*Reeves and Turner*.　illus.　　3*s*. 6*d*.

Papworth.　Ordinary of arms.　*Richards*.　　　　　　　　　　　O.P.

Planché, J. R.　Pursuivant of arms.　c. 8vo.　*Chatto*.　illus.　　7*s*. 6*d*.

Moule, T.　Bibliotheca heraldica.　(*London*).　　　　　　　　　O.P.

Glossary of terms used in British heraldry.　d. 8vo.　*Jas. Parker*.　illus.
　　In press.

— II. GENEALOGY :

　　　The chief trustworthy sources from which family pedigrees are constructed are original
　　evidences, such as parish registers; wills at Somerset House and other probate offices;
　　records deposited in the Record Office and College of Arms; original family papers in proper
　　legal custody; all the Harleian and similar societies' publications; all topographical and
　　county histories, etc., etc.

Sims, R.　Manual for the genealogist.　8vo.　*A. R. Smith*.　pub. 15*s*.　O.P.

Marshall, G. W.　Genealogist's guide.　d. 8vo.　*Bell*.　　　　31*s*. 6*d*.

Anderson, J. P.　Book of British topography.　4to.　*W. Satchell*.　pub. 18*s*.　O.P.

Burke, B.　Peerage and baronetage (annual).　r. 8vo.　*Harrison*.　　38*s*.

　　,,　　Dormant and extinct peerages.　r. 8vo.　*Harrison*.　　42*s*.

　　,,　　Landed gentry.　r. 8vo.　2 vols.　*Harrison*.　　　　63*s*.

　　,,　　Extinct baronetcies.　r. 8vo.　　　　　　　　　　　　O.P.

Doyle, J. E.　Official baronage of England.　4to.　3 vols.　*Longmans*.　illus.　105*s*.

HERAT, *see* AFGHANISTAN.

HEREDITY, *see* ANTHROPOLOGY V.

HERZEGOVINA, *see* TURKEY I.

Highways (England), *see* Local Government.

Hindi, *see* India, Languages I.

Hindu law and usage, Ancient, *see* Anthropology III.

Hindustani, *see* India.

Histology, *see* Anatomy II.

HISTORICAL NOVELS:

These novels are not selected so much for their literary excellence as for their use in giving children an interest in history.

—I. GREAT BRITAIN AND IRELAND:

Crake, A. D.   Camp on the Severn.   *Mowbray.*   3*s.* 6*d.*
III. Century. Introduction of Christianity.

Church, A. J.   Count of the Saxon shore. 8vo.   *Seeley.*   5*s.*
Early V. Century. Departure of the Romans.

Henty, G. A.   Dragon and the Raven. c. 8vo.   *Blackie.* illus.   5*s.*
Late IX. Century. Times of Alfred.

Crake, A. D.   First Chronicle of Aescendun. c. 8vo.   *Rivingtons.*   3*s.* 6*d.*
Middle X. Century. Times of Edwy.

    ,,   Second Chronicle of Aescendun. c. 8vo.   *Rivingtons.*   3*s.* 6*d.*
Early XI. Century. Times of Edmund Ironside.

Lytton, Lord.   Harold. c. 8vo.   *Routledge.*   2*s.*
Middle XI. Century.

Kingsley, C.   Hereward. c. 8vo.   *Macmillan.*   3*s.* 6*d.*
Middle XI. Century. Norman conquest.

Crake, A. D.   Third Chronicle of Aescendun. c. 8vo.   *Rivingtons.*   3*s.* 6*d.*
Late XI. Century. Norman conquest.

    ,,   Brian Fitz-Count. c. 8vo.   *Rivingtons.*   3*s.* 6*d.*
Middle XII. Century. Days of Stephen.

Edgar, J. G.   Runnymede and Lincoln Fair. d. 8vo.   *Ward.*   5*s.*
Early XIII. Century. Times of John.

    ,,   How I won my spurs. d. 8vo.   *Ward.*   5*s.*
Middle XIII. Century. Barons' War.

Crake, A. D.   House of Walderne. c. 8vo.   *Rivingtons.*   3*s.* 6*d.*
Middle XIII. Century. Barons' War.

Henty, G. A.   In freedom's cause. c. 8vo.   *Blackie.*   6*s.*
Late XIII. Century. Wallace and Bruce.

Porter, Jane.   Scottish chiefs. c. 8vo.   *Ward.*   5*s.*
Late XIII. Century. Wallace.

Aguilar, G.   Days of Bruce. c. 8vo.   *Routledge.*   5*s.*
Late XIII. Century.

Holt, E. S.   In convent walls. c. 8vo.   *Shaw.*   5*s.*
Early XIV. Century. The Despensers.

Henty, G. A.   St. George for England. c. 8vo.   *Blackie.* illus.   5*s.*
Middle XIV. Century. Crecy and Poictiers.

Edgar, J. G.   Crecy and Poictiers. d. 8vo.   *Ward.*   5*s.*
Middle XIV. Century.

Ainsworth, H.   Merrie England. c. 8vo.   *Routledge.*   2*s.*
Late XIV. Century. Peasant revolt.

Minto, W.   Mediation of Ralph Hardelot. c. 8vo. 3 vols.   *Macmillan.*   31*s.* 6*d.*
Late XIV. Century. Peasant revolt.

Gilliatt, E. John Standish.
Late XIV. Century. Peasant revolt.

James, G. P. R. Forest days. c. 8vo. *Routledge.* pub. 2s.   O.P.
Late XIV. Century. Robin Hood, etc.

Giberne, A. Coulyng Castle. *Shaw.*   O.P.
Early XV. Century. Lollards.

Guernsey, L. E. Sword of De Bardwell. *Shaw.*   O.P.
Early XV. Century. Agincourt.

Yonge, C. M. Caged lion. c. 8vo. *Macmillan.*   3s. 6d.
Early XV. Century. Captivity of James I.

Stevenson, R. L. Black Arrow. c. 8vo. *Cassell.*   5s.
Middle XV. Century. Wars of the Roses.

Church, A. J. Chantry priest of Barnet. 8vo. *Seeley.*   5s.
Late XV. Century. Wars of the Roses.

Lytton, Lord. Last of the Barons. c. 8vo. *Routledge.*   2s.
Late XV. Century. Wars of the Roses.

Cowper, F. Captain of the Wight. 8vo. *Seeley.*   5s.
Late XV. Century. Times of Henry VII.

Ainsworth, H. Tower of London. c. 8vo. *Routledge.*   2s.
Middle XVI. Century. Lady Jane Grey.

Whyte-Melville, G. J. Queen's Maries. c. 8vo. *Longmans.*   1s.
Middle XVI. Century. Mary, Queen of Scots.

Yonge, C. M. Unknown to history. c. 8vo. *Macmillan.*   3s. 6d.
Middle XVI. Century. Mary, Queen of Scots.

Corbett, Julian. For God or gold. c. 8vo. *Macmillan.*   6s.
Late XVI. Century. Days of Drake.

Kingsley, C. Westward Ho! c. 8vo. *Macmillan.*   3s. 6d.
Late XVI. Century. Armada.

Lovett, R. Drake and the Dons. c. 8vo. *R. T. S.* illus.   3s. 6d.
Late XVI. Century. Armada.

Ainsworth, H. Guy Fawkes. c. 8vo. *Routledge.*   2s.
Early XVII. Century.

James, G. P. R. Arabella Stuart. *Routledge.* pub. 2s.   O.P.
Early XVII. Century.

Scott, W. Fortunes of Nigel. *Black.* illus.   3s. 6d.
Early XVII. Century. James I.

   ,,   Legend of Montrose. *Black.* illus.   3s. 6d.
Middle XVII. Century. The Covenanters.

Church, A. J. With the King at Oxford. 8vo. *Seeley.*   5s.
Middle XVII. Century. Civil War.

Whyte-Melville, G. J. Holmby House. c. 8vo. *Longmans.*   1s.
Middle XVII. Century. Civil War.

Shorthouse, J. H. John Inglesant. c. 8vo. *Macmillan.*   6s.
Middle XVII. Century. Civil War.

Charles, Mrs. On both sides the sea. c. 8vo. *Nelson.*   5s.
Late XVII. Century. Commonwealth.

Field, Mrs. Ethne. l. c. 8vo. *Wells, Gardner.*   6s.
Late XVII. Century. Cromwell's settlement of Ireland.

Tytler, S. Duchess Frances. c. 8vo. 2 vols. *Low.*   21s.
Late XVII. Century. Times of Charles II.

Rowsell, M. C. Traitor or Patriot. c. 8vo. *Blackie.* illus.   3s. 6d.
Late XVII. Century. Rye House plot.

Manning, Miss. Cherry and Violet. c. 8vo. *Roper and Drowley.* illus.   2s. 6d.
Late XVII. Century. The Plague and Fire.

Scott, W.   Peveril of the Peak.   *Black.*   illus.   3s. 6d.
    Late XVII. Century. Isle of Man.

Doyle, A. C.   Micah Clarke.   c. 8vo.   *Longmans.*   3s. 6d.
    Late XVII. Century. Monmouth's rebellion.

James, G. P. R.   The fate.   O.P.
    Late XVII. Century. Revolution of 1688.

Banim, J.   Boyne-Water.   *Duffy.*   O.P.
    Late XVII. Century. Battle of the Boyne.

Henty, G. A.   Orange and green.   c. 8vo.   *Blackie.*   illus.   5s.
    Late XVII. Century. Battle of the Boyne.

Thackeray, W. M.   Esmond.   c. 8vo.   *Smith, Elder.*   5s.
    Early XVIII. Century. Times of Queen Anne.

Henty, G. A.   Cornet of horse.   sm. p. 8vo.   *Low.*   2s. 6d.
    Early XVIII. Century. Marlborough's Wars.

Ainsworth, H.   Preston fight.   c. 8vo.   *Routledge.*   2s.
    Early XVIII. Century. " The 1715."

Scott, W.   Waverley.   *Black.*   illus.   3s. 6d.
    Middle XVIII. Century. " The 1745."

Henty, G. A.   Bonnie Prince Charlie.   c. 8vo.   *Blackie.*   illus.   6s.
    Middle XVIII. Century. Fontenoy and Culloden.

    ,,   With Wolfe in Canada.   c. 8vo.   *Blackie.*   illus.   6s.
    Late XVIII. Century.

Grant, J.   Romance of war.   c. 8vo.   *Routledge.*   2s.
    Early XIX. Century. Peninsular War.

Banim, J.   The croppy.   3 vols.   *Colburn.*   1828.   O.P.
    Late XVIII. Century. Irish insurrection, 1798.

Henty, G. A.   One of the 28th.   c. 8vo.   *Blackie.*   illus.   5s.
    Early XIX. Century. Waterloo.

Wingfield, Lewis.   Lords of Strogue.   *Bentley.*   O.P.
    Early XIX. Century   Emmett, 1803.

Kingsley, H.   Ravenshoe.   *Macmillan.*   2s. 6d.
    Middle XIX. Century. Crimean War.

Whyte-Melville, G. J.   Interpreter.   c. 8vo.   *Longmans.*   1s.
    Middle XIX. Century. Crimean War

—II. INDIA:

Henty, G. A.   With Clive in India.   c. 8vo.   *Blackie.*   illus.   6s.
    Middle XVIII. Century.

Groves, J. P.   Duke's Own.   c. 8vo.   *Griffith.*   illus.   5s.
    Late XVIII. Century. Fall of Tippoo Sahib.

"A.L.O.E."   War and peace.   p. 8vo.   *Nelson.*   illus.   3s.
    Middle XIX. Century. Retreat from Cabul, 1842.

Chesney, C. C.   The dilemma.   *Blackwood.*   O.P.
    Middle XIX. Century. The Mutiny.

Taylor, Meadows.   Seeta.   c. 8vo.   *Kegan, Paul.*   6s.
    Middle XIX. Century. The Mutiny.

Henty, G. A.   In times of peril.   c. 8vo.   *Griffith.*   5s.
    Middle XIX. Century. The Mutiny.

Groves, J. P.   A soldier born.   c. 8vo.   *Griffith.*   illus.   5s.
    Middle XIX. Century. The Mutiny.

Henty, G. A.   For name and fame.   c. 8vo.   *Blackie.*   5s.
    Late XIX. Century. Afghan War.

—III. UNITED STATES:

Webb, Mrs. J. B.   Pilgrims of New England.   O.P.
      Middle XVII. Century.   Plymouth Colony.

Jones, J. R.   Quaker soldier.   8vo.   12mo.   (*Philadelphia*).   7s. 6d.
      Late XVII. Century.   Philadelphia.

Kingston, W. H. G.   A true hero.   c. 8vo.   *Sunday School Union.*   2s. 6d.
      Late XVII. Century.   Early settlers.   Pennsylvania.

James, G. P. R.   Ticanderoga.   *Routledge.*   pub. 2s.   O.P.
      Middle XVIII. Century.   French War.

Kingston, W. H. G.   Hurricane Harry.   c. 8vo   *Griffith.*   illus.   3s. 6d.
      Late XVIII. Century.   War of Independence.

Henty, G. A.   True to the old flag.   c. 8vo.   *Blackie.*   6s.
      Late XVIII. Century.   War of Independence.

Gleig, G. R.   The subaltern.   f. 8vo.   *Blackwood.*   1s. 6d.
      Early XIX. Century.   War of 1812.

James, G. P. R.   The old dominion.   f. 8vo.   *Routledge.*   2s.
      Middle XIX. Century.   Southampton massacre, 1831.

Lanier, S.   Tiger lilies.   c. 8vo.   *Low.*   12s. 6d.
      Late XIX. Century.   Civil War.

Verne, Jules.   North against south.   l. i. 16mo.   *Low.*   illus.   7s. 6d.
      Late XIX. Century.   Civil War.

Henty, G. A.   With Lee in Virginia.   c. 8vo.   *Blackie.*   6s.
      Late XIX. Century.   Civil War.

—IV. FRANCE:

Yonge, C. M.   The little duke.   gl. 8vo.   *Macmillan.*   2s. 6d.
      Middle X. Century.   Richard the Fearless, of Normandy.

James, G. P. R.   Philip Augustus.   f. 8vo.   *Routledge.*   2s.
      Early XIII. Century.

    ,,   The Jacquerie.   c. 8vo.   *Routledge.*   2s.
      Late XIV. Century.

Charles, Mrs.   Joan the Maid.   c. 8vo.   *Nelson.*   4s.
      Middle XV. Century.   Joan of Arc.

James, G. P. R.   Agnes Sorrel.   O.P.
      Middle XV. Century.   Charles VII.

Scott, W.   Quentin Durward.   *Black.*   illus.   3s. 6d.
      Late XV. Century.   Louis XI.

Yonge, C. M.   The chaplet of pearls.   c. 8vo.   *Macmillan.*   3s. 6d.
      Late XVI. Century.   St. Bartholomew.

James, G. P. R.   Henry of Guise.   c. 8vo.   *Routledge.*   2s.
      Late XVI. Century.   St. Bartholomew.

Holt, E. S.   Sister Rose.   c. 8vo.   *Shaw.*   5s.
      Late XVI. Century.   St. Bartholomew.

Vigny, A. de.   Cinq Mars.   *Dulau.*   3s. 6d.
      Late XVI. Century.   Days of Louis XIII.

Weyman, S.   For the cause.
      Late XVI. Century.   Henry of Navarre.

James, G. P. R.   Richelieu.   c. 8vo.   *Routledge.*   2s.
      Early XVII. Century.

Grant, J.   Arthur Blane.   c. 8vo.   *Routledge.*   2s.
      Early XVII. Century.   Scottish guard.

Tytler, S.   Huguenot family.   p. 8vo.   *Chatto.*   2s.
      Middle XVII. Century.

Coape, H. C. The Chateau de Louard. c. 8vo. *R. T. S.*   5s.
Late XVII. Century. Edict of Nantes.

Peard, F. M. Jeannette. *Nat. Society.*   O.P.
Late XVII. Century. Huguenots.

Dumas, père. The iron mask.
Late XVII. Century. Days of Louis XIV.

Stuart, Esmé. Isabeau's hero. c. 8vo. *S. P. C. K.*   3s. 6d.
Early XVIII. Century. Camisard Revolt, 1702.

James, G. P. R. Ancient régime. c. 8vo. *Routledge.* pub. 2s.   O.P.
Early XVIII. Century. Louis XV.

Dumas, père. Queen's necklace. c. 8vo. *Routledge.*   1s.
Late XVIII. Century. Court of Louis XVI.

Baring, Gould, S. In exitu Israel. c. 8vo. 2 vols. *Macmillan.*   21s.
Late XVIII. Century. Court of Louis XVI.

Erckmann-Chatrian. Story of a peasant. c. 8vo. *Ward.*   2s.
Late XVIII. Century. Revolution.

,,   Madame Thérèse. c. 8vo. *Ward.*   2s. 6d.
Late XVIII. Century. Revolution, 1792.

,,   Year one of the republic. c. 8vo. *Ward.*   2s. 6d.
Late XVIII. Century. Revolution, 1793.

Trollope, A. La Vendée. c. 8vo. *Ward.*   2s. 6d.
Late XVIII. Century. Revolution, 1793.

Tytler, S. Citoyenne Jacqueline. p. 8vo. *Chatto.*   2s.
Late XVIII. Century. Revolution, 1793.

Roberts, Miss. Atelier de Lys. c. 8vo. *Longmans.*   2s. 6d.
Late XVIII. Century. Revolution, 1793.

,,   On the edge of the storm. c. 8vo. *Warne.*   3s. 6d.
Late XVIII. Century. Revolution, 1793.

,,   A child of the Revolution. *Warne.*   O.P.
Late XVIII. Century. Revolution, 1793.

Henty, G. A. In the Reign of Terror. c. 8vo. *Blackie.*   5s.
Late XVIII. Century. Revolution, 1793.

Erckmann-Chatrian. Citizen Buonaparte. c. 8vo. *Ward.*   2s. 6d.
Late XVIII. Century. Revolution, 1794.

,,   The blockade. c. 8vo. *Ward.*   2s. 6d.
Late XVIII. Century. Revolution, 1799.

Giberne, A. Detained in France. *Shaw.*   O.P.
Early XIX. Century. The Empire.

Yonge, C. M. Kenneth. *Smith and Innes.*   O.P.
Early XIX. Century. Russian Campaign.

Erckmann-Chatrian. The conscript. c. 8vo. *Ward.*   2s. 6d.
Early XIX. Century. 1813.

,,   Great invasion. c. 8vo. *Ward.*   2s. 6d.
Early XIX. Century. 1813.

,,   Waterloo. c. 8vo. *Ward.*   2s. 6d.
Early XIX. Century. 1815.

,,   A man of the people.
Middle XIX. Century. Revolution, 1848.

Henty, G. A. The young Francs-Tireurs. c. 8vo. *Griffith.*   3s. 6d.
Late XIX. Century. Franco-German war.

Cobb, J. F. In time of war. *Wells, Gardner.*   O.P.
Late XIX. Century. Franco-German war.

Grant, J. Six years ago. c. 8vo. *Routledge.*   2s.
Late XIX. Century. Franco-German War.

Cobb, J. F. Workman and soldier. *Wells, Gardner.*   o.p.
   Late XIX. Century. The Commune.

—V. GERMANY AND AUSTRIA:

Scheffel, J. F. Ekkehard. 18mo. 2 vols. *Low.*   4*s.*
   X. Century.

Yonge, C. M. Dove in the eagle's nest. c. 8vo. *Macmillan.*   3*s.* 6*d.*
   Late XV. Century. Domestic life.

Roberts, Miss. In the olden time. c. 8vo. *Longmans.*   2*s.* 6*d.*
   Early XVI. Century. Peasants' War, 1525.

Charles, Mrs. Chronicles of the Schönberg-Cotta Family. c. 8vo. *Nelson.*
   1890. illus.   5*s.*
   Early XVI. Century. Reformation.

Grant, J. Philip Rollo. c. 8vo. *Routledge.*   .   2*s.*
   Early XVII. Century. Thirty Years' War.

James, G. P. R. Heidelberg. c. 8vo. *Routledge.* pub. 2*s.*   o.p.
   Early XVII. Century. Thirty Years' War.

Manning, Miss. In the year '9. *Roper and Drowley.*   o.p.
   Early XIX. Century. Revolt in Tyrol.

   ,,   Interrupted wedding. *Roper and Drowley.*   o.p.
   Middle XIX. Century. Civil War: Hungary, 1848.

—VI. GREECE:

Lytton, Lord. Pausanius the Spartan. c. 8vo. *Routledge.*   2*s.*
   V. Century, B.C.

Becker, W. Charicles. p. 8vo. *Longmans.*   7*s.* 6*d.*
   II. Century, B.C.

Leslie, Emma. Glaucia. i. 16mo. *R. T. S.*   3*s.* 6*d.*
   I. Century, A.D. Christianity at Athens.

—VII. ITALY:

Henty, G. A. Young Carthaginian. c. 8vo. *Blackie.*   6*s.*
   III. Century, B.C. Days of Hannibal.

Becker, W. Gallus. p. 8vo. *Longmans.*   7*s.* 6*d.*
   I. Century, B.C. Domestic life.

Church, A. J. Two thousand years ago. c. 8vo. *Blackie.* illus.   6*s.*
   I. Century, B.C. Last days of the Republic.

Westbury, H. Acte. c. 8vo.   6*s.*
   I. Century, A.D. The Rome of Nero.

Graham, J. W. Neaera. c. 8vo. *Macmillan.*   6*s.*
   I. Century, A.D. Times of Tiberius.

Whyte-Melville, G. J. The gladiators. c. 8vo. *Longmans.*   1*s.*
   I. Century, A.D. Rome and Jerusalem.

Lytton, Lord. Last days of Pompeii. c. 8vo. *Routledge.*   2*s.*
   I. Century, A.D.

Crake, A. D. Aemilius. *Mowbray.*   3*s.* 6*d.*
   Early III. Century. Decian and Valerian persecutions.

Newman, J. H. Callista. *Burns and Oates.*   5*s.* 6*d.*
   Middle III. Century. Persecutions.

Webb, Mrs. J. B. Martyrs of Carthage. c. 8vo. *Ward.*   3*s.* 6*d.*
   Middle III. Century. Persecutions.

Crake, A. D. Evanus. *Mowbray.*   3*s.* 6*d.*
   Early IV. Century. Days of Constantine.

Wiseman, Cardinal. Fabiola. f. 8vo. *Burns and Oates.*   3*s*. 6*d*.
    Early V. Century. The Catacombs.

James, G. P. R. Attila. f. 8vo. *Routledge.*   2*s*.
    Late V. Century. The Gauls.

Collins, Wilkie. Antonina. c. 8vo. *Chatto.* illus.   3*s*. 6*d*.
    Middle VI. Century. Fall of Rome, 1*5d*.

Lytton, Lord. Rienzi. c. 8vo. *Routledge.*   2*s*.
    Middle XIV. Century.

Hood, G. P. J. The Roman students. i. 8vo. *Unwin.*   3*s*. 6*d*.
    Early XV. Century. Renaissance.

Eliot, George. Romola. f. 8vo. *Smith, Elder.*   2*s*. 6*d*.
    Late XV. Century. Savonarola, etc.

Trollope, T. A. Catherine de Medici.   O.P.
    Early XVI. Century.

Frith, H. Under Bayard's banner. *Routledge.*   O.P.
    Middle XVI. Century. French Wars.

Grant, J. The aide-de-camp. c. 8vo. *Routledge.*   2*s*.
    Early XIX. Century. Campaign of Maida, 1806.

Mademoiselle Mori. c. 8vo. *Longmans.*   2*s*. 6*d*.
    Middle XIX. Century. Roman Revolution, 1848.

—VIII. NETHERLANDS :

Wallis, A. In troubled times. c. 8vo. *Sonnenschein.*   2*s*.
    Middle XVI. Century. Duchess Margaret.

Ebers, G. The burgomaster's wife. c. 8vo. *Macmillan.*   4*s*. 6*d*.
    Late XVI. Century. Siege of Leyden, 1574.

Walshe and Sargent. Within sea walls. i. 16mo. *R. T. S.*   2*s*. 6*d*.
    Late XVI. Century. Rise of the Republic.

Henty, G. A. By pike and dyke. c. 8vo. *Blackie.*   6*s*.
    Late XVI. Century. Rise of the Republic.

   ,,   By England's aid. c. 8vo. *Blackie.*   5*s*.
    Early XVI. Century. Freeing of the Netherlands.

Bray, Mrs. White hoods. *Chapman.*   3*s*. 6*d*.
    Late XVI. Century. Civil wars.

—IX. RUSSIA :

Helps, A. Ivan de Biron. c. 8vo. *Chatto.*   3*s*. 6*d*.
    Middle XVIII. Century. Court life.

Cobb, J. F. Story of the great Czar. *S. P. C. K.*   1*s*.
    Early XVIII. Century. Peter the Great.

—X. SPAIN AND PORTUGAL :

Aguilar, G. Vale of cedars. c. 8vo. *Routledge.*   5*s*.
    Late XV. Century. Expulsion of Jews from Spain, 1492.

Lytton, Lord. Leila. c. 8vo. *Routledge.*   2*s*.
    Late XV. Century. Conquest of Granada.

Burke, U. The Great Captain. c. 8vo. *S. P. C. K.*   2*s*.
    Late XV. Century. Gonsalvo de Cordova.

Cooper, Fenimore. Mercedes of Castile. c. 8vo. *Routledge.*   3*s*. 6*d*.
    Late XV. Century. Columbus, etc.

Hood, G. P. J. The Spanish brothers. c. 8vo. *Nelson.*   4*s*.
    Middle XVI. Century. Inquisition.

Milman, E. A. The wayside cross. p. 8vo. *Murray.*   2*s*.
    Middle XIX. Century. Carlist War, 1833.

—XI. EGYPT AND THE EAST:

Whyte-Melville, G. J. Sarchedon. c. 8vo. *Ward, Lock.*   2s.
   2000 B.C. Assyria.

Ebers, G. Uarda. 18mo. 2 vols. *Low.*   4s.
   1480 B.C. Egypt.

Church and Seeley. The Hammer. 8vo. *Seeley.* illus.   5s.
   II. Century, B.C. Maccabean times.

Church, A. J. Last days of Jerusalem. 8vo. *Seeley.*   3s. 6d.
   I. Century, A.D. Fall of Jerusalem.

Henty, G. A. For the Temple. c. 8vo. *Blackie.*   6s.
   I. Century, A.D. Fall of Jerusalem.

Kingsley, C. Hypatia. c. 8vo. *Macmillan.*   3s. 6d.
   Early V. Century. Egypt.

Manning, Miss. Harun al Raschid. *Shaw.*   O.P.
   Late VIII. Century. Bagdad.

Scott, W. Count Robert of Paris. *Black.* illus.   3s. 6d.
   Late XI. Century. First Crusade.

   ,, The Talisman. *Black.* illus.   3s. 6d.
   Late XII. Century. Third Crusade.

Holt, E. S. Lady Sybil's choice. c. 8vo. *Shaw.*   5s.
   Late XII. Century. Third Crusade.

Edgar, J. G. Crusades and Crusaders. c. 8vo. *Ward.*   5s.
   Middle XIII. Century. Seventh Crusade.

Everard, W. Sir Walter's ward. c. 8vo. *Blackie.* illus.   3s. 6d.
   Middle XIII. Century. Seventh Crusade.

Yonge, C. M. The prince and the page. gl. 8vo. *Macmillan.*   4s. 6d.
   Late XIII. Century. Eighth Crusade.

James, G. P. R. Bertrand de la croix.   O.P.
   Early XVI. Century. Siege of Rhodes, 1522.

—XII. MISCELLANEOUS:

Helps, A. Casimir Maremma. *Chatto.*   O.P.
   XV. Century. Poland.

Wallace, L. The fair God. c. 8vo. *Warne.*   2s.
   Early XVI. Century. Conquest of Mexico.

Ingraham, J. H. Montezuma.   O.P.
   Early XVI. Century. Conquest of Mexico.

Ballantyne, R. M. The Cannibal Islands. 16mo. *Nisbet.* illus.   1s.
   Late XVIII. Century. Captain Cook.

Porter, Jane. Thaddeus of Warsaw. c. 8vo. *Routledge.*   2s.
   Late XVIII. Century. Poland, 1791.

Kingston, W. H. G. The young Llanero. c. 8vo. *Nelson.*   4s.
   Early XIX. Century. War in Venezuela.

Martineau, Harriet. The hour and the man. f. 8vo. *Routledge.*   2s.
   Early XIX. Century. Hayti. Toussaint L'Ouverture.

Thomson, J. Ulu. c. 8vo. *Low.*   6s.
   Late XIX. Century. Africa.

Henty, G. A. By sheer pluck. c. 8vo. *Blackie.* illus.   5s.
   Late XIX. Century. Africa. Ashanti War.

—XIII. BIBLIOGRAPHY:

Bowen, H. Courthope. A descriptive catalogue of historical novels and
   tales. d. 8vo. *Stanford.*   1s. 6d.
   Contains about 1,600 entries.

HISTORY :

See also the different countries.

—I. SCIENCE OF HISTORY :

Hegel, G. W. F. Philosophy of history. Tr. Sibree. p. 8vo. *Bell.*   5*s.*

Schlegel, F. Philosophy of history. Tr. p. 8vo. *Bell.*   3*s.* 6*d.*

Montesquieu. Esprit des lois. 12mo. (*Paris*).   2*s.* 6*d.*

Buckle, H. T. History of civilization. c. 8vo. 3 vols. *Longmans.*   24*s.*

Smith, Goldwin. Lectures on the study of history. 8vo. *James Parker*   (*Oxford*).   2*s.* 6*d.*

—II. GENERAL HISTORY :

Laurent, F. Études sur l'histoire de l'humanité. 8vo. 18 vols. (*Brussels*).   162*s.*

Ranke, L. von. Weltgeschichte. 8vo. 6 vols. (*Leipzig*).   113*s.*
> Part i., Ancient and Greek, 2 vols., 18*s.*; part ii., Roman Republic, 2 vols., 20*s.*; part iii., Roman empire, 2 vols., 21*s.*; part iv., Eastern empire, 20*s.*; part v., Arabian supremacy and Charles the Great, 17*s.*; part vi., Dissolution of the Carlovingian empire, extending to Charles the First, 17*s.*

Weber, G. Allgemeine Geschichte. 8vo. 20 vols. (*Leipzig*).   147*s.*

Prévost-Paradol. Essai sur l'histoire universelle. 12mo. 2 vols. (*Paris*).   6*s.*

Freeman, E. A. General sketch of European history. (elem.). 18mo. *Macmillan.*   3*s.* 6*d.*

Universal history, ancient and modern. 8vo. 60 vols. 1779–84.

HOLLAND, *see* NETHERLANDS.

  ,,   LANGUAGE, *see* DUTCH.

HOLY LAND, *see* PALESTINE.

HOME READING, *see* EDUCATION V.

HONDURAS, *see* AMERICA, CENTRAL.

HORSE :

See also LIVE-STOCK.

—I. GENERAL :

Youatt, W. Treatise on the horse. 8vo. *Longmans.*   7*s.* 6*d.*

Robertson, J. P. Equine medicine. 8vo. *Baillière.*   21*s.*

Day, W. The horse : how to rear and breed him. 8vo. *Bentley.*   16*s.*
> Excellent in all matters relating to the breeding and rearing of thorough-bred horses.

Fitzwygram, J. Horses and stables. 8vo. *Longmans.* illus.   5*s.*
> Excellent book.

Fleming, G. Practical horse keeper. p. 8vo. *Cassell.*   7*s.* 6*d.*

Armatage, G. Horse owner and stableman's companion. c. 8vo. *Warne.*   5*s.*

Saunders, A. Our horses. 8vo. *Low.*   6*s.*
> Embraces several subjects.

Sidney, S. Book of the horse. 4to. *Cassell.*   35*s.*
> Embraces all divisions and subjects.

—II. RIDING :

Neville, G. Riding. 8vo. *Longmans.*   6s.

Anderson, E. L. Modern horsemanship. 8vo. *Douglas.*   21s.
     Suitable for advanced horsemen only.

     ,,   How to ride and school a horse. p. 8vo. *Douglas.*   2s. 6d.
     Advanced and technical.

Martinengo, Count. Function of the hands in riding. 8vo. *Turnbull and Spears.*
     Advanced and technical.

Dwyer, F. Seats and saddles. p. 8vo. *Whittingham.*   7s. 6d.
     Excellent book.

Hayes, M. H. Riding on the flat and across country. p. 8vo. *Thacker.*   10s. 6d.
     Chiefly with reference to steeple-chasing.

—III. HUNTING :

Beaufort, Duke of, and M. Morris. Hunting ("Badminton Library"). c. 8vo. *Longmans.*   10s. 6d.

Beckford, P. Thoughts on hunting. 8vo. *Toovey.*   14s.
     Reprint of old book.

—IV. RACING :

Beaufort, Duke of, and others. Racing ("Badminton Library"). c. 8vo. *Longmans.* illus.   10s. 6d.
     Chiefly historical.

Day, W. Racehorse in training. 8vo. *Chapman.*   9s.
     Historical and anecdotal.

—V. DRIVING :

Beaufort, Duke of. Driving ("Badminton Library"). c. 8vo. *Longmans.* illus.   10s. 6d.
     Chiefly historical.

HORTICULTURE, *see* GARDENING.

HOSIERY, *see* TEXTILE FABRICS.

HOSPITALS :

See also NURSING.

Oppert, F. Hospitals, infirmaries, and dispensaries. r. 8vo. *Churchill.* illus.   12s.
     Construction, internal arrangement, and management.

Nightingale, Florence. Notes on hospitals. 4to. *Longmans.*   18s.

Burdett, H. C. Cottage hospitals. p. 8vo. *Churchill.*   14s.
     General, fever, and convalescent.

Thorne, T. Hospitals for infectious disease. 8vo. *Eyre.* illus.   14s. 6d.
     10th Annual Report of Local Government Board, 1880 and 1881.

HOUSE DECORATION :

The industrial arts.—Historical sketches. l. c. 8vo. *Chapman.*   3s.
     South Kensington handbook.

Garrett, R. and A. House decoration ("Art at Home" series). 12mo. *Macmillan.* illus. pub. 2s. 6d.   O.P.

Richardson, C. J. Studies from old English mansions. 4to. 3 vols., 42*s.*
each. *Maclean.* 1841. pub. 126*s.* O.P.

Pollen, J. H. Ancient and modern furniture and woodwork. c. 8vo.
Chapman. 2*s.* 6*d.*
South Kensington handbook.

Shaw, H. Specimens of ancient furniture. 4to. *Bohn.* 1836. pub. 42*s.* O.P.

Gruner, L. Fresco decoration. fo. *Willis.* pub. 168*s.* O.P.

HUNGARY, GEOGRAPHY, *see* AUSTRIA.

HUNGARY : HISTORY :

See also GERMANY, HISTORY.

Vambéry, A. Hungary ("Story of the Nations"). c. 8vo. *Unwin.* illus. 5*s.*

Patterson, A. The Magyars: their country and its institutions. c. 8vo.
2 vols. *Smith, Elder.* pub. 18*s.* O.P.

Sayous, E. Histoire des Hongrois et de leur littérature politique de 1790 à
1815. 12mo. *Alean.* 3*s.*

Howath, M. Fünf-und-zwanzig Jahre aus der Geschichte Ungarn. 8vo.
2 vols. *Brockhaus.* 15*s.*

Hunfalvy, P. Die Ungarn oder Magyaren. 8vo. (*Vienna*). 4*s.* 6*d.*

Vilovsky, T. Die Serben im südlichen Ungarn. 8vo. (*Vienna*). 5*s.*

Schwicker, J. Die Zigeuner in Ungarn und Siebenburgen. 8vo. (*Vienna*). 1*s.*

Staré, J. Die Kroaten. 8vo. (*Vienna*). ?*s.*

Slavici, J. Die Rumänen in Ungarn und Siebenburgen. 8vo. (*Vienna*). 4*s.* 6*d.*

Life of Francis Deak. 8vo. *Macmillan.* 12*s.* 6*d.*

Kossuth, L. Memoirs of my exile. 8vo. *Cassell.* 10*s.* 6*d.*

HUNGARY : LANGUAGE AND LITERATURE :

—I. GRAMMARS AND DICTIONARIES :

Czuczor and Fogorasi. A magyar nyélv szótara. 6 vols. (*Pesth*).
The great dictionary of the Hungarian Academy.

Bizonfy, F. English-Hungarian and Hungarian-English dictionary. 8vo.
(*Pesth*). 13*s.* 6*d.*
A very good and cheap dictionary.

Singer, I. Hungarian grammar. 8vo. *Trübner.* 4*s.* 6*d.*

—II. HISTORY OF LITERATURE AND CRITICISM :

Toldy, F. A magyar nemzeti irodalom története. 12mo. (*Buda Pesth*). 5*s.*
Abbreviated history of literature.

Salamon, F. Összegyüjtött kisebb müvei (collected lesser works). 12mo.
(*Buda Pesth*). 3*s.* 6*d.*
Literary critic.

Erdélyi, J. Asthetikai elötanulmányok. 12mo. (*Buda Pesth*). 8*s.*
Aesthetic dissertations and lectures.

Beöthy, Zs. A magyar nemzeti irodalom történeti ismertetése. 12mo.
(*Buda Pesth*). 10*s.*
Historical accounts of the national literature.

Ferenczy, J. A magyar hirlapirodalom története. 8vo. (*Buda Pesth*). 10*s.*
History of the Hungarian press.

—III. TEXTS:

Arany, J. Toldi. 8vo. (*Pesth*).   7*s*. 6*d*.
> The great national modern epic. Innumerable editions.

Petöfi, S. Összes költeményei (collected poems) 8vo. (*Pesth*).   5*s*. 6*d*.
> The Hungarian Burns. Innumerable editions.

Kisfaludy, K. Válogatott munkai (selected works). 12mo. 2 vols. (*Pesth*).   3*s*. 6*d*
> The great dramatist.

Szigligeti, E. A mama (3-act comedy). 16mo. (*Pesth*).   1*s*. 6*d*.

Jokai, M. Ujabb munkai (latest works). 16mo. 53 parts, 1*s*. 6*d*. each.
(*Pesth*).   79*s*. 6*d*.
> The great novelist : of European reputation.

Mikszath. Munkai (works). (*Pesth*).
> Novelist ; suitable for girls.

—IV. TRANSLATIONS INTO ENGLISH OR FRENCH:

Jokai, M. The new landlord. Tr. Patterson. p. 8vo. 2 vols. *Macmillan.*
pub. 21*s*.   O.P.
> Nearly all Jokai's works are translated into German.

   ,,   Timar's two worlds. Tr. Mrs. Kennard. c. 8vo. 3 vols. *Blackwood.*   25*s*. 6*d*.

   ,,   Le tapis vert. (*Paris*).
> Adaptation by Ulbach of " Szabadság a hó alatt."

   ,,   Le fils de l'homme au cœur de pierre. 12mo. (*Paris*).   3*s*.

   ,,   Hungarian sketches in peace and war. p. 8vo. *Hamilton.*   3*s*. 6*d*.
> Vol. i. of " Constable's Miscellany."

Petöfi, S. Translations from, by Sir J. Bowring. 12mo. *Trübner.*   5*s*.

Arany, J. Legend of the wondrous hunt. Tr. E. D. Butler. c. 8vo.
Trübner.   2*s*. 6*d*.
> A good book for beginners, as the translation is literal, and the Hungarian text faces it.

—V. REFERENCE:

Kertbeny, K. M. A magyar nemzeti és nemzétközi irodalom Könyvészete.
(*Buda Pesth*).
> PERIODICALS: *Ungarische Revue* (literary) ; *Budapesti Szemle* (political, critical, etc.).

HUNTING, *see* HORSE III.

HYDRAULICS:

De Voisins. Hydraulics. Tr. Bennett. *Van Nostrand.*

Downing, S. Practical hydraulics. 8vo. *Longmans.* illus.   5*s*. 6*d*.

Bresse, J. A. C. Waterwheels or hydraulic motors. Tr. Mahan. 8vo. *Spon.*   10*s*. 6*d*.

Cullen, W. Turbines. 4to. *Spon.*   12*s*. 6*d*.

Bodmer, G. R. Hydraulic motors. c. 8vo. *Whittaker.* illus.   14*s*.

Harcourt, L. F. Rivers and canals. d. 8vo. 2 vols. *Clar. Press.* illus.   21*s*.

   ,,   Harbours and docks. d. 8vo. 2 vols. *Clar. Press.* illus.   25*s*.

Jeans, F. S. Waterways and water transport in different countries. 8vo.
Spon. illus.   14*s*.

Allen, J. R. Design and construction of dock walls. r. 8vo. *Spon.*   6*s*.

HYDROSTATICS, *see* MATHEMATICS II.

184

HYGIENE:

Wilson, G   Hygiene and sanitary science.   c. 8vo.   *Churchill.*   illus.   10*s*. 6*d*.

Corfield, W.   Health.   c. 8vo.   *Paul.*   6*s*.
     Deals with personal health.

Book of health.   Ed. M. Morris.   r. 8vo.   *Cassell.*   21*s*.
     Very comprehensive.

Parkes, E. A.   Practical hygiene.   Ed. F. de Chaumont.   m. 8vo.
     Churchill.   illus.   18*s*.

Wilson, G.   Healthy life and healthy dwellings.   f. 8vo.   *Churchill.*   5*s*.

Murphy, S.   Our homes, and how to make them healthy.   r. 8vo.   *Cassell.*   15*s*.

Teale, T. P.   Dangers to health.   d. 8vo.   *Churchill.*   illus.   10*s*.
     A pictorial guide to domestic sanitary defects.

Vacher, F.   Defects in plumbing and drainage work.   *Heywood.*   illus.   1*s*.

Latham, B.   Sanitary engineering.   8vo.   *Spon.*   pub. 30*s*.   O.P.
     A guide to the construction of sewerage and house drainage.

Farquharson, R.   School hygiene and diseases.   c. 8vo.   *Smith, Elder.*   7*s*. 6*d*.

Hime, T. W.   Public health.   *Baillière.*   5*s*.
     Handy reference to Public Health Acts.

Guy, W. A.   Public health.   p. 8vo.   *Renshaw.*   5*s*.
     A popular introduction to sanitary science.

Parkes, L. C.   Hygiene and public health.   c. 8vo.   *H. K. Lewis.*   illus.   9*s*.

Simon, J.   English sanitary institutions.   d. 8vo.   *Cassell.*   18*s*.

Richardson, B. W.   National health (abridged from Chadwick's "Health
     of nations").   c 8vo.   *Longmans.*   4*s*. 6*d*.

Boulnois, H. P.   Municipal and sanitary engineer's handbook.   d. 8vo.   *Spon.*   12*s*. 6*d*.

Hughes, S.   Waterworks for the supply of towns.   12mo.   *Lockwood.*   3*s*.

Chaumont, F. de.   Lectures on state medicine.   d. 8vo.   *Smith, Elder.*   10*s*. 6*d*.

Newsholme, A.   Elements of vital statistics.   p. 8vo.   *Sonnenschein.*   7*s*. 6*d*.

Farr, W.   Vital statistics.   Ed. Humphry.   8vo.   *Stanford.*   30*s*.
     Mass of information from Census.
     OFFICIAL PUBLICATION : Registrar-General's Returns (Annual).   *Eyre.*

HYMNOLOGY, *see* THEOLOGY VI.

HYPNOTISM, *see* PSYCHICAL RESEARCH.

I

ICELAND:

—I. GEOGRAPHY:

Lock, W. G.   Guide to Iceland.   8vo.   (*Hertford*).
     Published by the author.

Burton, R. F.   Ultima Thule; a summer in Iceland.   8vo.   2 vols.   *Nimmo.*   32*s*.

Lock, C. G. W.   Home of the Eddas.   Ed. C. C. Neve Foster.   8vo.
     Low.   pub. 16*s*.   O.P.
     With a chapter on the Sprengisandr.

Coles, J. Summer travelling in Iceland. 8vo. *Murray.*   18*s.*

Dufferin, Lord. Letters from high latitudes. f. 8vo. *Murray.*   7*s.* 6*d.*

—II. LANGUAGE AND LITERATURE:

(A) GRAMMARS AND DICTIONARIES.

Wimmer, L. T. A. Fornnordisk formlära. 8vo. (*Lund*).   3*s.* 6*d.*

Noreen, A. Altisländische Grammatik. 8vo. (*Halle*).   4*s.*

Cleasby and Vigfusson. Icelandic-English dictionary. 4to. *Clar. Press.*   67*s.*

Egilsson, S. Lexicon poeticum antiquae linguae septentrionalis. 4to. (*Hafniae*). pub. 84*s.*   O.P.

Fritzner, J. Ordbog. 8vo. (*Christiania*).
New edition in progress; 18 parts issued, 2*s.* 6*d.* each.

(B) LITERATURE.

Edda Sæmundar fróða. Ed. Sophus Bugge. 8vo. (*Christiania*).   16*s.*

,,   Snorra Sturlusonar. 8vo. 3 vols. (*Hafniae*).
Vol. i., o.p.; vol. ii., 9*s.*; vol. iii., 7*s.* 6*d.*

Islandske Annaler indtil 1578. Ed. G. Storm. 8vo. (*Christiania*).   10*s.* 6*d.*

Egils saga Skallagrímssonar. Ed. F. Jónsson. 8vo. (*Copenhagen*).   11*s.*

Eyrbyggja saga. Ed. G. Vigfusson. 8vo. (*Leipzig*).   6*s.*

Gísla saga Súrssonar. Ed. K. Gíslason. 8vo. (*Copenhagen*). 1849.   4*s.* 6*d.*

Grettis saga. 8vo. 2 vols. (*Copenhagen*).
Vol. i., o p.; vol. ii., 4*s.* 6*d.*

Gunnlaugs saga Ormstungu. Ed. E. Mogk. 12mo. (*Halle*).   1*s.* 6*d.*
This, out of many editions, is easiest to obtain.

Snorri Sturluson. Heimskringla. Ed. C. R. Unger. 8vo. (*Christiania*). pub. 10*s.*   O.P.

Ari the learned. Landnámabók, with Islendingabók. Ed. J. Sigurðsson. 8vo. (*Copenhagen*). 1843.

Laxdœla saga. Ed. K. Kålund. 8vo. (*Copenhagen*).
In progress, 2 parts issued, 13*s.*

Orkneyinga saga. Ed. G. Vigfusson. 8vo. (*London*).

Sturlunga saga. Ed. G. Vigfusson. 8vo. 2 vols. *Clar. Press.*   4 *s.*

Njáls saga. Ed. K. Gíslason. 8vo. 2 vols. (*Copenhagen*).   28*s.*

Jónsson, Karl. Sverris saga. Ed. C. R. Unger. 8vo. (*Christiania*).

Hákonar saga Gamla. Ed. G. Vigfusson. 8vo. (*London*).

Homilubók. Ed. T. Wisén. 4to. (*Lund*).   12*s.*

Stjórn. Gubernatis mundi. Ed. C. R. Unger. 8vo. (*Christiania*).   15*s.*

Grágás (ancient laws of Iceland). Ed. V. Finsen. 8vo. 5 vols. (*Copenhagen*).   17*s.* 6*d.*

Espolin, J. Islands árbœkr. 4to. 12 vols. (*Copenhagen*). 1821-55.
Vols. i.-ix., o.p.; vol. x., 2*s.* 6*d.*; vol. xi., 3*s.* 6*d.*; vol. xii., 3*s.* 6*d.*

Jónsson, F. Historia ecclesiastica Islandiae (to 1740). 4to. 4 vols. (*Havniae*). 1722-8.   O.P

Safn til sögu Islands. 8vo. 2 vols. (*Copenhagen*).   9*s.*
In progress.

Diplomatarium Islandicum. 8vo. (*Copenhagen*).
One volume issued 1876; in progress.

Islenzkar þjóðsögur og æfintýri. Ed. J. Arnason. 8vo. 2 vols. (*Leipzig*).

Vigfusson and Powell. Corpus poeticum boreale. d. 8vo. 2 vols. *Clar. Press.*   42s.

Biskupa, Sögur. 8vo. 2 vols. *Copenhagen.*
> BIBLIOGRAPHY.—A "Guide-book to Books" Bibliography of Icelandic literature, by Eiríkr Magnússon, in preparation. (*Frowde*).

ICHTHYOLOGY, *see* FISHING *and* ZOOLOGY.

ICONOGRAPHY, CHRISTIAN, *see* ART V.

IDIOCY, *see* MENTAL PHYSIOLOGY.

ILLUMINATING, *see* ARTISTIC PROCESSES IX.

INDIA : GEOGRAPHY AND GENERAL :

Murray's Handbooks to India. p. 8vo. 4 vols. *Murray.*   s.
> Bengal, North-West Provinces and Burmah, 20s.; Punjab, Kashmir, etc., 15s.; Bombay, 15s.; Madras, 15s.

Hints to travellers in India. f. 8vo. *W. H. Allen.*   1s.

Reclus, E. Universal geography; vol. viii. i. 8vo. *Virtue.*   1s.

Smith, G. Political and physical geography of British India. p. 8vo. *Murray.* illus.   7s. 6d.
> The best text-book.

Strachey, J. India. d. 8vo. *Paul.*   15s.
> Contains full details as to administration.

Blanford, H. F. Guide to the climates and weather of India, Ceylon, and Burma; and the storms of the Indian seas. 8vo. *Macmillan.*   12s. 6d.

Ball, V. Jungle life in India. 8vo. *De la Rue.* pub. 25s.   O.P.
> The journeys and journals of an Indian geologist.

Ross, D. Land of the Five Rivers, and Sindh. 8vo. *Chapman.*   12s.

Drew, J. The Jummoo and Kashmir territories. 8vo. *Stanford.* Maps and illus.   42s.

Cooper, T. T. The Mishmee Hills. p. 8vo. *H. S. King.*   7s. 6d.
> Account of an attempted journey to Thibet from Assam.

Logan, W. Malabar. 2 vols. *Gov. Press (Madras).*

Marshall, W. E. A phrenologist amongst the Todas of South India. 8vo. *Longmans.* illus. pub. 21s.   O.P.

Wallace, R. India in 1887 (agriculture). 8vo. *Simpkin.* illus.   21s.
> Deals mainly with native agriculture and native breeds of cattle, and other farm live-stock.

Nicholson, E. Indian snakes. 8vo. (*Madras*).   14s.

Günther, A. C. Reptiles of British India. fo. (*Ray Society*).   63s.

Fayrer, J. Thanatophidia of India. fo. (*London*).   147s.

Moore, W. J. Manual of family medicine for India. p. 8vo. *Churchill.* illus.   12s.

Hunter, W. W. Imperial gazetteer of India. 8vo. 14 vols. *Trübner.*   63s.
> There are separate official gazetteers for most of the provinces. The fullest information is given on all the tributary states and dependencies of India. Under the article "India" will be found a complete account of the country in all its aspects. The article forms one volume, and can be had separately.
>
> Reports of the survey of India are published annually, and abound in information for the student.

INDIA: HISTORY:

Hunter, W. W. Brief history of the Indian people. c. 8vo. *Trübner.*   3s. 6d.

Elphinstone, M. History of India to 1761. 8vo. *Murray.*   18s.
An account of the native states.

Owen, S. J. India on the eve of the British conquest. p. 8vo. *Allen.*   8s.
A lively account of the circumstances which led to English intervention.

Malleson, G. B. The French in India (1674–1761). r. 8vo. *Longmans.*
pub. 16s.   O.P.

Mill, Jas. History of British India to 1805. c. 8vo. 9 vols. *Allen.*   50s.
Vols. vii., viii., ix., contain a continuation by H. H. Wilson (1805–1835).

Strachey, J. India. d. 8vo. *Paul.*   15s.

Trotter, L. J. History of the British Empire in India (1844–62). d. 8vo.
2 vols. *Allen.*   30s.

Kaye, J. W. History of the Sepoy war. d. 8vo. 3 vols. *Allen.*   58s.
Vol. i., 18s.; vol. ii., 20s.; vol. iii., 20s.

Malleson, G. B. History of the Indian Mutiny. 8vo. 3 vols. *Allen.*   60s.

Lyall, A. C. Asiatic studies. 8vo. *Murray.*   12s.
Illustrative of Hindoo thought.

Trotter, L. J. Warren Hastings. c. 8vo. *W. H. Allen.*   9s.

,, Life of Lord Dalhousie ("Statesmen" ser.). c. 8vo. *W. H.*
Allen.   2s. 6d.

Smith, R. Bosworth. Life of Lord Lawrence. c. 8vo. 2 vols. *Smith, Elder.*   21s.

INDIA: LANGUAGES:

See also SANSKRIT *and* PALI.

—I. HINDI AND HINDUSTANI:

Kellogg, S. H. Grammar of the Hindi language. 8vo. (*Allahabad*).   21s.

Platts, J. T. Grammar of the Hindustani or Urdû language. 8vo. *Allen.*   12s.

,, Urdû, Hindi, and English dictionary. sup. r. 8vo. *Allen.*   63s.

—II. TAMIL:

Pope, G. U. First lessons in Tamil. 12mo. *Clar. Press.*   7s. 6d.

,, Tamil handbook (3 parts). 8vo. *W. H. Allen.*   12s. 6d.
Part iii. contains Tamil-English and English-Tamil dictionary.

,, Sacred "Kurral of Tiruvaḷḷuva Nûyanâr." 8vo. *W. H. Allen.*   24s.
Deals with the higher grammar; contains lexicon.

—III. TELUGU:

The beginner should take Arden's *Grammar*, then Campbell's. Brown's Telugu *Reader* is essential, his Telugu *Dictionary* and *Mixed Dialects Dictionary* are useful, but absolutely unscientific.

Arden, A. H. Progressive grammar of the Telugu language. r. 8vo.
Trübner.   18s.

Campbell, A. D. Grammar. 4to. *Dulau.* 1820.   21s.
Very good.

Brown, C. P. Grammar of the Telugu language. 8vo. *W. H. Allen.*   21s.
Contains a mass of quite priceless information.

,, Telugu-English, English-Telugu dictionary. r. 8vo. 3 vols. in 2.
W. H. Allen.   100s.

Vemana (with translation). Ed. C. P. Brown. 8vo. (*Madras*). 1829.   O.P.
Most useful.

Brown, C. P. Dictionary of mixed dialects and foreign words used in
Telugu. 8vo. (*Madras*).   12s.

  ,,   Teloogoo reader. 8vo. 2 vols. *Allen*.   11s.

INDIA : LAW :

Anglo-Indian codes. Ed. Whitley Stokes. d. 8vo. 2 vols. and supp. *Clar.
Press.*   67s. 6d.
Vol. i., 30s.; vol. ii., 35s.; Supplement, 2s. 6d.

Indian penal code. Ed. J. D. Mayne. d. 8vo. (*Madras*).   30s.

  ,,   Ed. Morgan and Macpherson. (*Calcutta*).   O.P.

Collett, C. Comments on the Indian penal code.

Macaulay, T. B. Notes on the Indian penal code. c. 8vo. *Longmans.*
In vol. vii. of collected works, 8 vols., 48s.

Mayne, J. D. Hindu law and usage. 8vo. *Stevens.*   32s.

Macnaghten, W. Hindoo and Mohammedan law. Ed. Wilson. 8vo.
Williams.   6s.

Hindu law books. Ed. Whitley Stokes. 4to. (*Madras*).   O.P.
Translated from Sanskrit.

Rumsey, A. Moohummudan law of inheritance. 8vo. *Allen*.   12s.

Indian evidence act. Ed. J. F. Stephen. 8vo. *Macmillan.* pub. 12s. 6d.   O.P.
With introduction on principles of judicial evidence.

INDIA, RACES OF, *see* ANTHROPOLOGY IV.

INDIAN OCEAN AND ARCHIPELAGO :

—I. GENERAL:

Keane, A. H. Eastern geography (with map). c. 8vo. *Stanford.*   5s.
Malay Peninsula, Indo-China, Eastern Archipelago, Philippines, New Guinea.

St. John, H. The Indian Archipelago. p. 8vo. 2 vols. *Longmans.* pub.
21s.   O.P.

Rosenberg, C. B. H. von. Der malayische Archipel ; with preface by Prof.
Veth. r. 8vo. *Weigel.*   18s.

Crawfurd, J. History of the Indian Archipelago. 8vo. 3 vols. *Allen.*
1820. pub. 52s. 6d.   O.P.

  ,,   Indian islands and adjacent countries. 8vo. *Bradbury.*   16s.
Descriptive dictionary.

Guillemard, F. H. Cruise of the "Marchesa." 8vo. *Murray.* illus.   21s.
Important for the Loochoo and Sooloo islands.

Wallace, A. R. The Malay Archipelago. p. 8vo. *Macmillan.*   6s.

Forbes, H. O. Naturalist's wanderings in the Eastern Archipelago. 8vo.
Low.   21s.

Findlay, A. G. Directory for the navigation of the Indian Archipelago.
r. 8vo. *R. H. Laurie.*   28s.

—II. MAURITIUS:

Pike, N. Sub-tropical rambles. 8vo. *Low.*   18s.

—III. MALDIVES:

Bell, H. C. P.　Maldive Islands.　fo.　*Trübner.*　　　　　　10*s.* 6*d.*

—IV. SUMATRA:

Marsden, W.　History of Sumatra.　4to.　(*London*).　1783.　　　o.p.

—V. BORNEO:

Jacob, Gertrude L.　Sir J. Brooke (Raja of Sarawak).　8vo.　2 vols.　*Mac-
　millan.*　　　　　　　　　　　　　　　　　　　　　25*s.*

St. John, S.　Life in the forests of the far east.　8vo.　2 vols.　*Smith,
　Elder.*　illus.　pub. 32*s.*　　　　　　　　　　　　　o.p.
　Chiefly Borneo.

Burbidge, F. W.　Gardens of the sun.　c. 8vo.　*Murray.*　illus.　14*s.*
　A naturalist's journal of travels in Borneo and the Sulu Archipelago.

Hatton, J.　The new Ceylon.　c. 8vo.　*Chapman.*　　　　　6*s.*
　North Borneo or Sabah.　From official and other exclusive sources of information.

Handbook of British North Borneo.　c. 8vo.　*Clowes.*　　2*s.* 6*d.*

—VI. JAVA:

Veth, P. J.　Java : geographisch-ethnologisch-historisch.　8vo.　3 vols.
　(*Haarlem*).　　　　　　　　　　　　　　　　　　55*s.*

Raffles, T. S.　History of Java.　8vo.　2 vols.　*Murray.*　illus.　pub. 28*s.*　　o.p.

—VII. CELEBES:

Hickson, S. J.　Naturalist in north Celebes.　8vo.　*Murray.*　illus.　16*s.*
　Narrative of travels in Minahassa, the Sangir, and Talant Islands ; with notes on the fauna,
　flora, and ethnology.

—VIII. PHILIPPINES:

Bowring, J.　A visit to the Philippine islands.　8vo.　*Smith, Elder.*　pub.
　18*s.*　　　　　　　　　　　　　　　　　　　　　　o.p.

Jagor, F.　Travels in the Philippines.　Tr.　8vo.　*Chapman.*　illus.　16*s.*

Montano, J.　Voyage aux Philippines et en Malaisie.　12mo.　*Hachette.*　3*s.* 6*d.*

Guerra, J. A.　Viages por Filipinas.　8vo.　(*Madrid*).　　　• 9*s.*

—IX. LA RÉUNION:

Colonies de l'océan indien.　Ed. L. Henrique.　12mo.　*Quantin.*　3*s.* 6*d.*
　Vol. i. of " Les colonies françaises."

INDIANS, AMERICAN, *see* ANTHROPOLOGY IV.

INDIAN CLUBS, *see* GYMNASTICS.

INDIA-RUBBER, *see* ECONOMIC PRODUCTS II.

INDIES, WEST, *see* WEST INDIES.

INDOOR GAMES. *see* GAMES II.

INDUSTRIES:

　　For industries not mentioned here, see under their respective heads.

—I. GENERAL:

Bevan, P. British manufacturing industries. 12mo. 12 vols., 3s. 6d. each. *Stanford.*   42s.
South Kensington handbooks.

Encyclopædia of industrial arts and manufactures. Ed. C. G. W. Lock. r. 8vo. 2 vols. *Spon.*   70s.

Yeats, J. Technical, industrial, and trade education. 8vo. 4 vols., 6s. each. *Philip.*   24s.
Vol. i., Natural history of the raw materials of commerce ; vol. ii., Technical history of commerce ; vol. iii., Growth and vicissitudes of commerce in all ages; vol. iv., Recent and existing commerce, with statistical supplement, maps showing trade-areas, and tabulated lists of places important in business or trade. The completest text-book of what is known as commercial geography, but in some respects behind date.

—II. ALKALI:

Lomas, J. Manual of the alkali trade. r. 8vo. *Lockwood.*   52s. 6d.

Lunge, G. Manufacture of sulphuric acid and alkali. 8vo. 3 vols. *Gurney.*   96s.
Vol. i., 36s.; vol. ii., 36s.; vol. iii., 24s.

—III. BOOTS AND SHOES:

Hill and Yeoman. Boot and shoe manufacture. d. 8vo. (9, *St. Bride's avenue, E.C.*).   4s.

Hannibal, A. Last fitting and pattern cutting. d. 8vo. (9, *St. Bride's avenue, E.C.*).   3s.

—IV. BREAD AND WHEAT:

Jago, W. Wheat, flour, and bread-making, etc. *Maclaren (Glasgow).*   12s. 6d.

  ,,   Chemistry of wheat flour and bread : bread-making, etc. *Simpkin.*   12s. 6d.

—V. BREWING:

Hooper, E. G. Brewing, scientific and technical. p. 8vo. *Sheppard.*   7s. 6d.

—VI. CLOCKS AND WATCHES:

Glasgow, D. Watch and clock-making. 12mo. *Cassell.*   4s. 6d.

Saunier, C. Modern horology. Tr. Tripplin and Rigg. p. 8vo. *Lockwood.*   9s.

—VII. COACH-BUILDING:

Thrupp, G. A. History of coach-building. 8vo. *Kerby and Endean.* illus.   6s.

Philipson, J. Coach body making. *Kemp.* illus.   4s.

Foggett, J. S. Wheel-making. *Kemp.* illus.   2s. 6d.

—VIII. COAL TAR:

Lunge, G. Distillation of coal-tar and ammoniacal liquors. 8vo. *Gurney.*   31s. 6d.

Mills, E. J. Destructive distillation. d. 8vo. *Gurney.* illus.   4s.

Knecht, E. Chemistry of coal tar colours. sm. p. 8vo. *Bell.*   6s. 6d.

—IX. ELECTRO-CHEMICAL:

Gore, G. Electro-chemistry. d. 8vo. *"Electrician" Pub. Co.*   2s.

Watt, A. Electro-metallurgy practically treated. c. 8vo. *Lockwood.*   3s. 6d.

Gore, G. Art of electro-metallurgy. c. 8vo. *Longmans.* illus.   6s.

Urquhart, J. W. Electro-plating. c. 8vo. *Lockwood.* 5*s.*

,, Electro-typing. c. 8vo. *Lockwood.* 5*s.*

Watt, A. Electro-deposition. c. 8vo. *Lockwood.* 12*s.* 6*d.*

—X. GAS:

Richards, W. Gas manufacture. d. 8vo. *Spon.* illus. 28*s.*

Newbigging, T. Handbook for gas engineers. f. 4to. *King.* illus. 15*s.*

—XI. GLASS:

Powell and Chance. Principles of glass-making. sm. p. 8vo. *Bell.* 3*s.* 6*d.*

—XII. LEATHER:

Watt, A. Art of leather manufacture. p. 8vo. *Lockwood.* 9*s.*

Proctor, H. Handbook of tanning. c. 8vo. *Spon.* 7*s.* *d.*

—XIII. OILS AND VARNISHES:

Cameron, J. Oils and varnishes. p. 8vo. *Churchill.* 7*s.* 6*d.*

—XIV. PAPER:

Cross and Bevan. Paper-making. c. 8vo. *Spon.* 12*s.* 6*d.*

Hofmann, C. Manufacture of paper. 8vo. *Low.* 73*s.* 6*d.*

—XV. PLUMBING:

Hellyer, S. S. The plumber. r. 8vo. *Batsford.* illus. 10*s.* 6*d.*

Davies, P. J. Standard practical plumbing. r. 8vo. *Spon.* 7*s.* 6*d.*

Maguire, W. R. Domestic sanitary drainage and plumbing. 8vo. *Paul.* 12*s.*

—XVI. SAW MILLS:

Bale, M. P. Saw mills. c. 8vo. *Lockwood.* 10*s.* 6*d.*

—XVII. SOAP:

Cameron, J. Soaps and candles. c. 8vo. *Churchill.* illus. 7*s.*

Carpenter, W. Soaps, candles, and lubricants. c. 8vo. *Spon.* 10*s.* 6*d.*

Watt, A. Art of soap-making. p. 8vo. *Lockwood.* 7*s.* 6*d.*

INTERNATIONAL LAW, *see* LAW OF NATIONS.

INVENTIONS, LAW RELATING TO, *see* ENGLAND, LAW VI.

IONIAN ISLANDS, *see* MEDITERRANEAN.

IRELAND:

See ENGLAND, *for books relating to England also.*

—I. GEOGRAPHY:

Baddeley and Ward. "Thorough Guide" series. 12mo. 2 parts. *Dulau.*   9s.
  Part i., North, 4s.; part ii., East, West, and South, 5s.

Hall, Mr. and Mrs. S. C. Ireland; its scenery, character, etc. r. 8vo. 3 vols. *How.* illus.   O.P.
  Vol. i., ii., pub. 25s. each; vol. iii., 30s.

—II. HISTORY:

O'Curry, E. Manners and customs of the ancient Irish. 8vo. 3 vols. *Williams.*   30s.

Lawless, Emily. Ireland. c. 8vo. *Unwin.* illus.   5s.

Richey, A. G. Short history of the Irish people to 1608. Ed. R. R. Kane. 8vo. *Hodges.*   14s.
  The best account of the period.

Bagwell, R. Ireland under the Tudors. 8vo. 3 vols. *Longmans.*   50s.
  Vol. i., ii., 32s.; vol. iii., 18s.

Froude, J. A. The English in Ireland. c. 8vo. 3 vols. *Longmans.*   18s.
  To be compared with the chapters on Ireland in Lecky's "History of the 18th Century."

Ball, J. T. Historical review of the legislative system in Ireland (1172-1800). 8vo. *Longmans.*   6s.

Hassencamp, R. History of Ireland (1530–1800). Tr. E. A. Robinson. 8vo *Sonnenschein.*   9s.
  Gives a German view of Irish history.

Lecky, W. E. H. Leaders of public opinion in Ireland. p. 8vo. *Longmans.* pub. 7s. 6d.   O.P.

Two centuries of Irish history. 1689–1870. Ed. J. Bryce. 8vo. *Paul.*   16s.

—III. LITERATURE: OLD AND MEDIÆVAL:

  In this list the grammars and texts are arranged in the order of a course of mediæval Irish study. For old Irish the same grammars have to serve, and for texts *Goidelica* (ed. Stokes), and *Codice Irlandese* (ed. Ascoli); *see* below.

Windisch, E. Short Irish grammar. (elem.). Tr. Dr. Norman Moore. c. 8vo. *Pitt Press.*   7s. 6d.

Stokes, Whitley. Celtic declension. (elem.). (*Göttingen*).

Zeuss, J. C. Grammatica Celtica. Ed. Ebel. r. 8vo. (*Berlin*).   30s.

Windisch, E. Irische Texte; mit Wörterbuch. 8vo. (*Leipzig*).   24s.

Zimmer, H. Keltische Studien. 8vo. 2 vols. (*Berlin*).   9s.

Irische Texte; mit Uebersetzungen und Wörterbuch (2nd series, parts i. and ii.). Ed. W. Stokes and E. Windisch. 8vo. (*Leipzig*).   11s.

Tripartite life of St. Patrick. Ed. W. Stokes. r. 8vo. *Rolls Series.*   10s.
  All Stokes' Irish texts are accompanied with translations into English, notes, explanations, and indices.

Lives of saints from the Book of Lismore. Ed. Stokes. c. 4to. *Clar. Press.*   31*s.* 6*d.*
"Anecdota Oxoniensia;" series "Mediæval and modern;" part v.

Three Irish Glossaries (including Cormac's). Ed. Stokes. 8vo. *Williams.*   10*s.* 6*d.*
Also a translation of Cormac by O'Donovan. Ed. Stokes. *(Calcutta).* Has more interest than an ordinary glossary, as it contains very curious archæological and mythical articles.

Passions and Homilies from Leabhar Breac. Ed. R. Atkinson. 8vo.
Royal Irish Academy.   30*s.*
Todd's lecture series; vol. ii. Text, translation, and glossary.

Joyce, P. W. Old Celtic romances. p. 8vo. *Paul.* pub. 7*s.* 6*d.*   O.P.

Leabhar na h-Uidhre. (Book of the Dun). fo. *Hodges.*   63*s.*
Lithographed facsimile of the oldest Irish MS. of any considerable size.

Goidelica. Ed. W. Stokes. m. 8vo. *Trübner.*   18*s.*

Codice Irlandese dell' Ambrosiana. Ed. Ascoli. 8vo. *(Rome).*
Vol. v., vi., of the Archivio Glottologico Italiano; issued in parts, about 10*s.* each.

ELAND, CHURCH OF, HISTORY, *see* CHURCH HISTORY V. (C).

IRON AND STEEL :

—I. METALLURGY :

Percy, J. Iron and steel. 8vo. *Murray.*   30*s.*

Greenwood, W. H. Steel and iron. 12mo. *Cassell.*   5*s.*

Howe, H. Metallurgy of steel. sm. fo. *Low.*   52*s.* 6*d.*
An elaborate treatise of much value.

—II. MANUFACTURE :

Practical iron founding. *Whittaker.*   4*s.*

Bell, J. H. Manufacture of iron and steel. *Routledge.*   21*s.*
Of special interest to blast furnace managers, and to others engaged in the production of pig iron.

Millis, C. T. Metal plate work. c. 8vo. *Spon.*   9*s.*
PERIODICAL: *Journal of the Iron and Steel Institute* (London).

IRRIGATION, *see* AGRICULTURE IV.

IRVINGITES, *see* CHURCH HISTORY V. (D).

ISLAM, *see* MAHOMETANISM.

ITALY : GEOGRAPHY AND DESCRIPTION :

—I. GENERAL :

Murray's Handbook for Italy. p. 8vo. 3 vols. *Murray.*   32*s.*
North Italy, 10*s.*; Central Italy (2 parts), 10*s.*; South Italy and Sicily, 12*s.*

Baedeker's Handbook for Italy. 12mo. 3 vols. *Dulau.*   18*s.*
North Italy, 6*s.*; Central Italy, 6*s.* South Italy, 6*s.*

Lobley, J. Logan. Vesuvius. 8vo. *Stanford.*   5*s.*

Rodwell, G. F. Etna. p. 8vo. *Paul.*   9*s.*

Lund, T. W. M. Como, and Italian lake-land. p. 8vo. *Allen.* illus.   10*s.* 6*d.*

Beauclerk, W. N. Rural Italy. 8vo. *Bentley.*   9*s.*
Account of the present agricultural condition of the kingdom.

Symonds, J. A. Sketches and studies in Italy. p. 8vo. *Smith, Elder.*   10*s.* 6*d.*

—II. ARCHÆOLOGICAL AND LOCAL:

Martha, J. Manuel d'archéologie étrusque et romaine. 8vo. (*Paris*)   3s. 9d.

Dennis, G. Etruria. 8vo. 2 vols. *Murray.*   21s

Ruskin, J. Mornings in Florence. 12mo. 6 parts, 10d. each. *G. Allen.*   5s.
Studies of Santa Croce, the Spanish Chapel, and Giotto's Campanile.

Oliphant, Mrs. Makers of Florence. c. 8vo. *Macmillan.*   10s. 6d.

Lemesurier, E. A. Genoa; her history, as told in her monuments. (*Genoa*).   6d.

Dyer, T. H. Pompeii; its history, buildings, and antiquities. p. 8vo. *Bell (Bohn).* illus.   7s. 6d.
An excellent description up to date of publication (1868).

Burn, R. Rome and the Campagna. 4to. *Deighton, Bell.* illus.   21s.

Middleton. Ancient Rome in 1889. p. 8vo. *Black.*   21s.

Ruskin, J. St. Mark's rest. 12mo. 6 parts, 1s. each. *G. Allen.*   6s.
History of Venice from her monuments.

Oliphant, Mrs. Makers of Venice. c. 8vo. *Macmillan.*   10s. 6d.

Ruskin, J. Guide to the principal pictures in the Academy of Fine Arts, Venice. 8vo. *G. Allen.*   1s.

ITALY: HISTORY:

Quinet, E. Les révolutions d'Italie. 8vo. 2 vols. (*Paris*).   12s.
An interesting general sketch of the tendencies of Italian history.

Leo, H. Geschichte der italienischen Staaten. 8vo. 5 vols. (*Hamburg*). 1829–32.   38s.
The best general history in reasonable compass.

Balzani, U. Early chronicles of Italy. c. 8vo. *S. P. C. K.*   4s.
An account of the authorities to 1300.

Milman, H. History of Latin Christianity to 1450. c. 8vo. 9 vols., 4s. each. *Murray.*   36s.

Guicciardini, F. Storia d' Italia. 12mo. 4 vols. (*Milan*).   6s.

Hodgkin, T. Italy and her invaders (376–553). d. 8vo. 4 vols. *Clar. Press.* illus.   68s.
Vols. i., ii., 32s.; vols. iii., iv., 36s.

Sismondi, J. C. The Italian republics. c. 8vo. *Longmans.*   3s. 6d.
A brief text-book.

  ,,   Les républiques italiennes du moyen âge (to 1748). 8vo. 10 vols. (*Paris*). 1840. pub. 90s.   O.P

Delarc, O. Les Normands en Italie. 8vo. (*Paris*).   10s.

Amari, M. Storia dei Mussulmani di Sicilia. 8vo. (*Milan*).   32s.

  ,,   La guerra del Vespro Siciliano. 12mo. 2 vols. (*Milan*).   8s.

Cipolla. Storia delle Signorie Italiane (1313–1530). 8vo. (*Milan*).   40s.
A mine of accurate information for a complicated period.

Ricotti, E. Storia delle Compagnie de Ventura. 12mo. 4 vols. (*Turin*).   10s.
An account of the military adventurers and their fortunes.

Temple-Leader and Marcotti. Sir John Hawkwood. 4to. *Unwin.* illus.   21s.
Life of an English adventurer in Italy, XIV. Century.

Creighton, M. History of the Papacy during the Reformation (1370–1518). 8vo. 4 vols. *Longmans.*
Vols. i., ii. (1378–1464), 32s.; vols. iii., iv. (1464–1518), 24s.

Ranke, L. von. The Popes of Rome. Tr. 8vo. 3 vols. *Murray.* pub. 30*s.*   O.P.
Also *Bell* (*Bohn*). 3 vols., 3*s.* 6*d.* each. The Papacy from 1520 to 1830.

Machiavelli, N. History of Florence to 1492. Tr. c. 8vo. *Bell* (*Bohn*).   5*s.*

Capponi, G. Storia della Republica di Firenze. sm. 8vo. 3 vols. (*Florence*).   12*s.*

Roscoe, W. Life of Lorenzo de Medici. c. 8vo. *Bell* (*Bohn*).   3*s.* 6*d.*

   ,, Life of Pope Leo X. c. 8vo. 2 vols. *Bell* (*Bohn*).   3*s.* 6*d.*

Burckhardt, J. Civilization of the period of the Renaissance in Italy. Tr. 8vo. 2 vols. *Paul.*   24*s.*
An admirable study of the social and artistic life of the period.

Symonds, J. A. Renaissance in Italy. d. 8vo. 7 vols. *Smith, Elder.*   112*s.*
Vol. i., Age of the despots, 16*s.*; vol. ii., Revival of learning, 16*s.*; vol. iii., Fine arts, 16*s.*; vols. iv., v., Italian literature, 32*s.*; vols. vi., vii., Catholic reaction, 32*s.* A survey of politics and literature in connection with one another.

Villari, P. Life of Machiavelli. Tr. L. Villari. p. 8vo. 2 vols. *Paul.*   24*s.*

Napier, H. E. Florentine history to 1815. p. 8vo. 6 vols. *Moxon.*   O.P.

Hazlitt, W. Carew. History of the Venetian Republic to 1469. d. 8vo. 4 vols. *Smith, Elder.* pub. 56*s.*   O.P.

Yriarte, C. La vie d'un patricien de Venise. r. 8vo. (*Paris*). illus.   30*s.*
Exemplifies the working of Venetian institutions in a typical life.

   ,, Venice: its history, art, and life. Tr. F. J. Sitwell. fo. *Bell.* illus.   63*s.*

Brown, H. F. Venetian studies. p. 8vo. *Paul.*   7*s.* 6*d.*
Excellent sketches of the most important epochs.

Yriarte, C. Rimini. fo. (*Paris*). illus.   30*s.*
Contains a history of the Malatesta lords.

Denistoun, J. Memoirs of the dukes of Urbino (1440-1630.) 8vo. 3 vols. *Longmans.* 1850. pub. 21*s.*   O.P.

Bent, J. T. Genoa: how the republic rose and fell. 8vo. *Paul.* illus.   18*s.*

Gregorovius, F. Geschichte der Stadt Rom. 8vo. 8 vols. (*Stuttgart*).   90*s.*

Brosch, M. Geschichte des Kirchenstaates. 8vo. (*Gotha*).   8*s.* 6*d.*

Hübner, Baron. Life and times of Pope Sixtus V. Tr. 8vo. 2 vols. *Longmans.* pub. 24*s.*   O.P.

Reumont, A. von. Geschichte Toscanas. 8vo. 2 vols. (*Gotha*).   27*s.*

Colletta, P. History of the kingdom of Naples (1734-1825). Tr. 8vo. 2 vols. (*Edinburgh*).   24*s.*

Freeman, E. A. History of Sicily from the earliest times. d. 8vo. 2 vols. *Clar Press.*   42*s.*
Vol. i., The native nations; vol. ii., Beginning of Greek settlement to beginning of Athenian intervention.

Cantù, C. Storia di cento anni (1750-1850). 12mo. 3 vols. (*Florence*).   12*s.*

Mazade, C. de. Life of Count Cavour. Tr. 8vo. *Chapman.*   16*s.*

Godkin, G. S. Life of Victor Emmanuel. c. 8vo. 2 vols. *Macmillan.*   16*s.*

Autobiography of G. Garibaldi. Tr. A. Werner. 8vo. 3 vols. *Smith and Innes.*   31*s.* 6*d.*

Mazzini. Life and writings. Ed. Mme. Venturi. p. 8vo. 6 vols., 9*s.* each. *Smith, Elder.*   54*s.*

Trollope, T. A. Life of Pius IX. 8vo. 2 vols. *Bentley.*   26*s.*

Probyn, J. W. Italy from 1815-78. 8vo. *Cassell.*   7*s.* 6*d.*

Rerum Italicarum Scriptores. Ed. Muratori. fo. 31 vols. (*Milan*).   £45
A collection of the Chronicles to 1500.

Monumenta historiae patriae. fo. 17 vols.

Storia documentata di Venezia. Ed. Romanin. 10 vols.

    PERIODICALS: Archivio Storico Italiano; Rivista Storica Italiana; Archivio Venito; Archivio Lombardo; Archivio Romano; Archivio Napolitano; each 20s. per annum.

ITALY : LANGUAGE AND LITERATURE :

    In addition to library editions of authors, cheaper editions of whole works or of selections will be found. These, with the cheaper grammars and dictionaries, etc., will provide a book-shelf of Italian literature for the student who is beginning to read the language.

—I. GRAMMARS AND DICTIONARIES :

Sauer, C. M. Italian conversation grammar. c. 8vo. *Hirschfeld.*   5s. 6d.
    Very good.

Demattio. F. Grammatica storica della lingua italiana. 8vo. (*Innsbruck*).   5s. 6d.
    An advanced school book. Part i., Fonologia, 1s. 6d.; part ii., Morphologia, 2s.; part iii., Sintassi, 2s.

Baragiola, A. Italienische Grammatik, mit Berücksichtigung des lateinischen und der romanischen Schwestersprachen. 8vo. (*Strassburg*).   5s.
    Advanced school book.

Diez, F. Grammatik der romanischen Sprachen. 8vo. *Nutt.*   21s.

Casini, T. Notizia sulle forme metriche italiane. 16mo. (*Florence*).   1s. 6d.
    Advanced school book.

Zambaldi, F. Vocabolario etimologico italiano. 8vo. (*Città di Castello*).   7s. 6d.

Fanfani, P. Vocabolario della lingua italiana. 8vo. (*Florence*).   15s.
    The most useful.

Millhouse, J. New pronouncing and explanatory English-Italian, and Italian-English dictionary. 8vo. 2 vols. (*Milan*).   12s.
    The student will find no Italian-English dictionary equal to the better French-English, German-English, or even Spanish-English dictionaries.

Graglia, C. Italian-English dictionary. 16mo. *Nutt.*   4s. 6d.

Loretz, P. Corrispondenza commerciale inglese con vocabolario mercantile. 12mo. *Nutt.*   1s. 5d.

—II. HISTORY OF LITERATURE :

Tiraboschi. Storia della letteratura italiana (in "Classici Italiani"). 8vo. 16 vols. (*Milan*). 1816.   63s.
    Work of reference. Most other writers depend on Tiraboschi for their facts.

Ancona, A. d'. Studii sulla letterartura italiana dei prima secoli. 16mo. (*Ancona*).   5s.

Sanctis, F. de. Storia della letteratura italiana. 16mo. 2 vols. (*Naples*).   8s.

Torraca, F. Manuale della letteratura italiana ad uso delle scuole secondarie. 16mo. 3 vols. (*Florence*).   12s.

Mestica, G. Manuale della letteratura italiana nel secolo XIX. 8vo. 2 vols. (*Florence*).   5s. 6d.

Symonds, J. A. Italian literature. d. 8vo. 2 vols. *Smith, Elder.*   32s.

  ,,   The Catholic reaction. d. 8vo. 2 vols. *Smith, Elder.*   32s.
    These books form parts iv. and v. of the author's "Renaissance in Italy." See ITALY, HISTORY.

—III. COLLECTIONS :

Classici Italiani. l. 8vo. 439 vols. (*Milan*). 1802–50   £40
    For full list of contents see ." List of the books of reference in the Reading-room of the British Museum."

Parnaso Italiano. 8vo. 56 vols. (*Venice*). 1781–1802.   £12

Raccolta de' novellieri italiani. 16mo. 27 vols. (*Milan*). 1816.   90*s.*
>Cheap edition. l. 8vo. 2 vols. 1833. 30*s.* The list of authors will be found in Symonds' chapter on novelists.
>The three works last named are for reference.

Nannucci, V. Manuale della letteratura del primo secolo della lingua italiana. 12mo. 2 vols. (*Florence*).   8*s.*

I quattro poeti classici italiani (Dante, Petrarca, Ariosto, Tasso). 32mo. 5 vols.   16*s.*

Teatro tragico italiano.   28*s.*

Scelta poesie liriche del primo secolo della lingua fino al 1700.   32*s.*
>The two works last named are useful collections, and form part of the "Biblioteca del viaggiatore." *Lemonnier* (*Florence*).

Poeti italiani contemporanei. r. 8vo. (*Paris*).   15*s.*

Canti e racconti del popolo italiano. Ed. Comparetti and d'Ancona. 8vo. (*Turin*).
>In progress. Vol. i., Canti Monferrini, 2*s.*; vol. ii., iii., Canti delle provincie meridionali, 9*s.*; vol. iv., Canti Marchigiani, 4*s.*; vol. v., Canti di Rovigno, 5*s.*; vol. vi., Novelline popolari italiane, 4*s.*; vol. vii., Fiabe mantovane, 5*s.*; vol. viii., Canti popolari della montagna lucchese.

—IV. POETS:

Dante. La divina commedia. Ed. Scartazinni. 8vo. 3 vols. (*Leipzig*).   27*s.*
>Vol. i., Inferno, 5*s.*; vol. ii., Purgatorio, 10*s.*; vol. iii., Paradiso, 12*s.*

,, La divina commedia. Ed. P. Fraticelli. 12mo. (*Florence*).   4*s.* 6*d.*
>Best handy edition.

,, Opere minori. Ed. P. Fraticelli. 12mo. 3 vols., 4*s.* each. (*Florence*).   12*s.*
>Vol. i., Canzoniere, Rime sacre, Poesie latine; vol. ii., Vita nuova, Vulgari eloquio de monarchia, e La questione de aqua et terra; vol. iii., Convito e epistole.

,, Inferno : text, notes, and prose translation by J. A. Carlyle. 8vo. (*London*). 1849.   O.P.

,, Purgatory : text, notes, and prose translation by A. J. Butler. c. 8vo. *Macmillan*.   12*s.* 6*d.*

,, Paradise : text, notes, and prose translation by A. J. Butler. c. 8vo. *Macmillan*.   12*s.* 6*d.*

,, Readings on the Purgatorio ; text, prose translation, commentary, and notes, by W. W. Vernon. c. 8vo. 2 vols. *Macmillan*.   24*s.*

,, The Vision ; or Hell, Purgatory, and Paradise. Tr. Cary. p. 8vo. *Bell* (*Bohn*).   3*s.* 6*d.*

,, The divine comedy. Tr. Longfellow. *Routledge*.   3*s.* 6*d.*
>There are several other editions by Routledge.

Blanc, C. L. Vocabolario Dantesco. 12mo. (*Florence*).   4*s.*

Symonds, J. A. Introduction to the study of Dante. p. 8vo. *Smith, Elder*. pub. 7*s.* 6*d.*   O.P.

Petrarca. Le rime. Ed. Leopardi. 12mo. (*Florence*).   2*s.* 6*d.*

,, Le rime. Ed. Leopardi and Ambrosoli. 12mo. (*Florence*).   1*s.* 6*d.*

,, Sonnets, etc. Tr. Cayley. c. 8vo. *Longmans*. pub. 10*s.* 6*d.*   O.P.

Foscolo, U. Essay on Petrarch. *Murray*. 1823.   O.P.

Poliziano. Le stanze, l'Orfeo, e le Rime. Ed. G. Carducci. 12mo. (*Florence*).   4*s.*

,, Opere volgari. Ed. J. del Lungo. 12mo. (*Florence*).   4*s.*

Ariosto. Orlando furioso ; and O. innamorato di Bojardo. 12mo. 4 vols. *Pickering*. 1834. pub. 21*s.*   O.P.
>The best edition ; contains an essay on the romantic narrative poetry of the Italians, etc., by Antonio Panizzi.

Ariosto. Orlando Furioso. 12mo. 2 vols. (*Florence*).   8*s.*

,,   Orlando Furioso (ad uso della gioventù). Ed. Bolza. 12mo. (*Florence*).   2*s.* 6*d.*
Suitable for girls.

,,   Orlando Furioso. Tr. W. Rose. p. 8vo. 2 vols., 5*s.* each. *Bell* (*Bohn*).   10*s.*

Berni. Opere, colle poesie burlesche. 12mo. (*Milan*).   2*s.* 6*d.*

Michael Angelo Buonarroti. Le rime. Ed. C. Guasti. 4to. (*Florence*).   20*s.*
The best edition.

,,   Rime e lettere. 32mo. (*Florence*).   2*s.* 6*d.*
With life by Condivi.

Tasso. Opere. Ed. G. Rosini. 8vo. 33 vols. (*Pisa*). 1821–33.   110*s.*
Library edition.

,,   Gerusalemme liberata ; with intro. by U. Foscolo. 12mo. (*Florence*).   4*s.*

Tasso. Gerusalemme liberata (School ed.). Ed. C. Carbone. 12mo. (*Florence*).   1*s.* 6*d.*

,,   Lettere. Ed. C. Guasti. 12mo. 5 vols. (*Florence*).   20*s.*

,,   Jerusalem delivered. Tr. Sir K. James. 12mo. 2 vols. *Long-mans.* pub. 14*s.*   O.P.

Cecchi, P. L. Tasso è la vita italiano nel secº. xvi. 12mo. (*F ence*).   3*s.*

Filicaia. Poesie e lettere. 32mo. (*Florence*).   2*s.* 6*d.*

Parini. Versi e prose. 12mo. (*Florence*).   4*s.*
With life by C. Guasti.

,,   Poesie. 32mo. (*Florence*).   2*s.* 6*d.*

Alfieri. Opere complete. Ed. G. Rosini. 8vo. 4 vols. (*Pisa*). 1828.   21*s.*
Library edition.

,,   Tragedie. 12mo. 2 vols. (*Florence*).   8*s.*

,,   Vita, giornale, lettere. Ed. E. Teza. 12mo. (*Florence*).   4*s.*

,,   Vita. 12mo. (*Milan*).   1*s.* 6*d.*

,,   Tragedies. Tr. E. A. Bowring. p. 8vo. 2 vols., 3*s.* 6*d.* each. *Bell* (*Bohn*).   7*s.*

Monti. Poesie. Ed. G. Carducci. 32mo. (*Florence*).   10*s.*
Vol. i., ii., Canti e poemi, 5*s.*; vol. iii., Poesie liriche, 2*s.* 6*d.*; vol. iv., Tragedie, drammi, e cantate, 2*s.* 6*d.*

Foscolo, U. Poesie. 12mo. (*Florence*).   4*s.*

Manzoni. Opere complete. 12mo. (*Milan*).   8*s.* 6*d.*
Vol. i., I promessi sposi ; with life by Carcano, 2*s.* 6*d.*; vol. ii., Storia della colonna infame, 3*s.* 6*d.*; vol. iii., Tragedie e poesie, 2*s.* 6*d.*

,,   Poesie. Ed. Mestica. 32mo. (*Florence*).   2*s.* 6*d.*

Leopardi. Opere (except "Epistolario"). 12mo. 2 vols. (*Florence*).   8*s.*

,,   Epistolario. 12mo. 2 vols. (*Florence*).   8*s.*
These together form a complete edition.

,,   La poesie. Ed. Mestica. 32mo. (*Florence*).   2*s.* 6*d.*

Giusti. Versi editi ed inediti. 12mo. (*Florence*).   4*s.*

,,   Epistolario. Ed. G. Frassi. 12mo. 2 vols. (*Florence*).   8*s.*

,,   Lettere scelte. Ed. G. Rigutini. 12mo. (*Florence*).   4*s.*

Carducci. Poesie. 16mo. 8 vols. (*Bologna*).   21*s.* 8*d.*
Juvenilia, 4*s.*; *Odi barbare*, 3*s.*; *Nuovi odi barbare*, 3*s.*; *Satana e polemiche Sataniche*, 1*s.* 6*d.*; *Levia gravia*, 3*s.*; *A. G. Garibaldi*, 8*d.*; *Giambi ed epodi*, 3*s.*; *Nuove poesie*, 3*s.* 6*d.*

Carducci. Opere. 12mo. 4 vols., 4*s*. each. (*Bologna*).
In progress.

—V. PROSE:

See Section IV. for Dante (*Opere minori*); Tasso (*Lettere*); Alfieri (*Vita*); Leopardi (*Prose* in Opere, and *Epistolario*); Giusti (*Epistolario*); Manzoni (*I promessi sposi* and *Storia della colonna infame*).

Francesco d' Assisi. I fioretti di San Francesco. 18mo. (*Turin*).	1*s*. 6*d*.
Boccaccio. Opere volgari. 8vo. 17 vols. (*Florence*). 1827–31.	52*s*. 6*d*.
Library edition.	
,, Decamerone. Ed. U. Foscolo. 8vo. 3 vols. *Pickering*. 1825.	O.P.
With the editor's *Discorso storico sul testo del Decamerone.* The best edition.	
,, Il Decamerone. Ed. P. Fanfani. 12mo. 2 vols. (*Florence*).	8*s*.
,, Novelle (School ed.) Ed. Dazzi. 12mo. (*Florence*).	1*s*. 4*d*.
,, Decameron. Tr.	
Cellini, Benvenuto. Vita. 8vo. 2 vols. (*Florence*). 1832.	O.P.
Best edition ; with old orthography.	
,, The same. Ed. Branchi. 12mo. (*Florence*).	4*s*.
Machiavelli, N. Opere. Ed. Passerini and Milanesi. 12mo. 6 vols. (*Florence*).	21*s*.
The best edition.	
,, Le istorie fiorentine. 12mo. (*Florence*).	4*s*.
With life by Niccolini.	
,, Il principe, e discorso sopra la prima deca di Tito Livio. 12mo. (*Florence*).	4*s*.
,, The prince. Tr. sm. c. 8vo. *Paul*.	6*s*.
Guicciardini, F. Storia d' Italia. Ed. Rosini. 8vo. 10 vols. (*Pisa*). 1820.	50*s*.
Also in one vol. 8vo. In "Bib. del Viaggiatore" series, 30s.	
Caro, A. Lettere. 8vo. 3 vols. (*Padua*). 1763.	O.P.
,, Lettere scelte. Ed. Marcucci. 16mo. (*Florence*).	1*s*. 6*d*.
Sarpi, F. Istoria del Concilio Tridentino. 12mo. 4 vols. (*Florence*).	16*s*.
Vasari, G. Opere. Ed. G. Milanesi. 8vo. 9 vols. (*Florence*).	72*s*.
Library edition.	
Galilei. Opere complete. Ed. Alberi. 8vo. 16 vols. (*Florence*). 1842-56.	105*s*.
Library edition.	
,, Prose scelte (School ed.) Ed. Conti. 16mo. (*Florence*).	1*s*. 6*d*.
Gozzi, G. Scritti. Ed. Tommaseo. 12mo. 3 vols. (*Florence*).	10*s*. 6*d*.
,, L'osservatore ; with life by Gherardini. 16mo. (*Florence*).	2*s*.
,, Favole novelle e lettere. Ed. Mestica. 16mo. (*Florence*).	1*s*. 6*d*.
,, Ragionamenti, dialoghi, sermoni. Ed. Mestica. 16mo. (*Florence*).	2*s*.
Beccaria. Memoirs. Tr. J. A. Symonds. 2 vols.	
Goldoni. Commedie scelte. 12mo. *Didot*.	3*s*.
Villari, P. Giralamo Savonarola e suoi tempi. 12mo. 2 vols. (*Florence*).	8*s*.
,, Life and times of Savonarola. Tr. Mme. Villari. d. 8vo. 2 vols. *Unwin*.	32*s*.
Azeglio, M. d'. I miei ricordi. 12mo. (*Florence*).	4*s*.
Settembrini, L. Ricordanze della mia vita. 8vo. 2 vols. (*Naples*).	9*s*.

—VI. NOVELS:

Modern Italian novels do not occupy a position in Italian literature as high as that occupied by English and French novels in their respective literatures. The list of novels is therefore short.

Manzoni. I promessi sposi. 12mo. (*Milan*).   2*s.* 6*d.*

Grossi. Marco Visconti. 12mo. (*Florence*).   3*s.* 6*d.*

Azeglio, M. d'. Niccolò de' Lapi. 12mo. (*Leipzig*).   3*s.* 6*d.*

,, Ettore Fieramosca. 16mo. (*Florence*).   1*s.* 6*d.*

Amicis, E. de. Bozzetti; La vita militare. 12mo. (*Florence*).   4*s.*

Venosta, G. Visconti. Novelle.   O.P.

Colombi. Un matrimonio in provincia. 12mo. (*Florence*).   3*s.*

Farina, S. Il mio figlio. 12mo. (*Milan*).   5*s.*
For girls.

,, Amore cendato. 12mo. (*Milan*).   4*s.*
For girls.

Thouar, P. Racconti popolari. 12mo. (*Florence*).   4*s.*
For girls.

,, Novelle. 2 vols. (*Paris*). 1847.   O.P.

Italian novelists. Tr. W. Roscoe. c. 8vo. *Warne.*   2*s.*

J.

JAMAICA, *see* WEST INDIES II.

JAPAN:

For a bibliography of Japan *see* vol. xiv. of Transactions of the Asiatic Society of Japan (Yokohama).

—I. GEOGRAPHY AND HISTORY:

Murray's Handbook. Ed. Satow and Kawes. *Murray.*   O.P.

Whitney, W. N. Concise dictionary of Japan. 8vo. 2 vols. *Trübner.*   *s.*
Chief roads, towns, population, etc.

Hassenstein, B. Atlas von Japan. *Perthes.*   12*s.*
Excellent maps.

Rein, J. J. Japan: travels and researches. *Hodder.*   25*s.*
A very complete account of the country in its various aspects.

Eden, C. H. Japan: historical and descriptive. c. 8vo. *Marcus Ward.*   3*s.* 6*d.*
A cheap popular summary.

Bird, Isabella L. Unbeaten tracks in Japan. c. 8vo. *Murray.*   7*s.* 6*d.*

Dixon, W. G. Land of the morning. p. 8vo. *Gemmell (Edin.).* illus and map.   O.P.

Griffis, W. E. The Mikado's empire. 8vo. *Low.*   21*s.*
A history of Japan; with personal experiences, observations, etc.

Adams, F. O. History of Japan. 8vo. 2 vols., 21*s.* each. *Paul.*   42*s.*

Reed, E. J. Japan. 8vo. 2 vols. *Murray.*   28*s.*

    A popular account of the history, traditions, and religions.

Franchet and Savatier. Enumeratio plantarum in Japonia sponte cres-

    centium. r. 8vo. 2 vols. (*Paris*).   40*s.*

—II. ART:

Audsley and Bowes. Ornamental arts of Japan. fo. 2 vols. *Low.*   £23 2*s.*

Anderson, W. Descriptive catalogue of Japanese pictures in the British

    Museum. 4to. *Longmans.*   21*s.*

    Valuable for its history of painting and legends.

Rein, J. J. The industries of Japan. *Hodder.*   30*s.*

Anderson, W. Pictorial arts of Japan. 4 parts. *Low.*   168*s.*

Franks, A. W. Japanese pottery. c. 8vo. *Chapman.* illus.   2*s.* 6*d.*

Bowes. Japanese pottery. i. 8vo. *Howell* (*Liverpool*). illus.   52*s.* 6*d.*

Gonse, L. L'art japonais. fo. 2 vols. *Quantin.*   160*s.*

—III. LANGUAGE AND LITERATURE:

Aston, W. G. Grammar of the Japanese spoken language. c. 8vo. *Trübner.*   12*s.*

Hepburn, J. C. Japanese-English and English-Japanese dictionary. d. 8vo.

    Trübner.   30*s.*

    Abridged edition, 14*s.*

Chamberlain, B. H. Handbook of colloquial Japanese. 8vo. *Trübner.*   12*s.* 6*d.*

The Ko-ji-ki, or Records of ancient matters. Tr. B. H. Chamberlain.

    8vo. *Trübner.*   20*s.*

    In vol. x. of Transactions of the Asiatic Soc. of Japan. Mythology and early mythical

    history of Japan.

Chamberlain, B. H. Classical poetry of the Japanese. p. 8vo. *Trübner.*   7*s.* 6*d.*

Mitford, A. B. Tales of old Japan. c. 8vo. *Macmillan.*   3*s.* 6*d.*

JAVA, *see* INDIAN OCEAN VI.

JERSEY, *see* CHANNEL ISLANDS.

JERUSALEM, *see* PALESTINE.

JESUITS, *see* CHURCH HISTORY IV.

    „   IN NORTH AMERICA, *see* UNITED STATES, HISTORY III.

JEWELLERY, *see* ARTISTIC PROCESSES V.

JEWS:

    For Language and Literature, see HEBREW.

—HISTORY:

Ewald, H. History of Israel. 8vo. 8 vols. *Longmans.*   118*s.*

    Down to Apostolic age. Vols. i., ii., 21*s.*; vols. iii., iv., 21*s.*; vol. v., 18*s.*; vol. vi., 16*s.*; vol.

    vii., 21*s.*; vol. viii., 18*s.*

Edersheim, A. History of Judah and Israel. (In "Bible History" ser.).

    c. 8vo. *R T. S.*   13*s.*

    Vols. iii., iv., v., vi., 2*s.* 6*d.* each; vol. vii., 3*s.*

Schürer, E. History of the Jewish people at the time of Christ. 8vo.

    3 vols., 10*s.* 6*d.* each. *Clark.*   31*s.* 6*d.*

Edersheim, A.　Life and times of Jesus the Messiah.　8vo.　2 vols.
　　Longmans.　　　　　　　　　　　　　　　　　　　　　　24*s.*
　　　　Also 1 vol. c. 8vo. 7*s.* 6*d.*

Milman, H.　History of the Jews.　p. 8vo.　3 vols.　*Murray.*　　12*s.*
　　　　After the fall of Jerusalem.

Grätz, H.　Geschichte der Juden von den ältesten Zeiten.　8vo.　11 vols.
　　(*Leipzig*).　1863.　　　　　　　　　　　　　　　　　71*s.* 6*d.*
　　　　Vol. i., 5*s.*; vol. ii. (1), 6*s.*; vol. ii. (2), 6*s.*; vol. iii., 11*s.*; vol. iv., 6*s.*; vol. v., 6*s.*; vol. vi., 5*s.*;
　　　　vol. vii., 5*s.*; vol. viii., 8*s.* 6*d.* ; vol. ix., o.p. ; vol. x., 6*s.*; vol. xi., 7*s.*

　　,,　　The same.　Tr. B. Lowy.　d. 8vo.　5 vols.　*Nutt.*
　　　　In progress ; vols. i. and ii., 10*s.* 6*d.* each.

Kuenen, A.　Religion of Israel.　8vo.　3 vols.　*Williams.*　　31*s.* 6*d.*

Ewald, H.　Antiquities of Israel.　Tr. H. S. Solly.　8vo.　*Longmans.*　12*s.* 6*d.*

Jost, J. M.　Geschichte des Judenthums.　8vo.　3 vols.　(*Leipzig*).　19*s.* 6*d.*

JUDÆA, *see* PALESTINE.

JURISPRUDENCE, *see* LAW I.

K.

KABBALA, *see* HEBREW.

KASHGARIA, *see* ASIA II.

KHIVA, *see* ASIA II.

KINDERGARTEN, *see* EDUCATION.

KNOTS, *see* YACHTING.

KORAN, *see* ARABIA, LANGUAGE II.

L.

LABOUR AND CAPITAL, *see* POLITICAL ECONOMY VI. AND IX.

LACE, *see* NEEDLEWORK.

LA CROSSE, *see* GAMES I.

LAKE-DWELLINGS, *see* ANTHROPOLOGY II.

LAND TENURE, *see* POLITICAL ECONOMY VII.

LANGUAGE, *see* PHILOLOGY.

LA PLATA, *see* ARGENTINE REPUBLIC.

LATIN :

—I. GRAMMARS AND COMPOSITION :

Madvig, J. Latin grammar. Tr. G. Woods. d. 8vo. *J. Parker.*   12s.

Roby, H. J. Latin grammar. c. 8vo. 2 vols. *Macmillan.*   19s. 6d.

  Vol. i., 9s.; vol. ii., 10s. 6d.

Kennedy, B. H. Revised primer. f. 8vo. *Longmans.*   2s. 6d.

Postgate, J. P. New primer. *Cassell.*   2s. 6d.

Sonnenschein, E. A. Elementary grammar. *Sonnenschein.*   2s. 6d.

  The last three grammars are especially for school use.

Postgate, J. P. Sermo Latinus. gl. 8vo. *Macmillan.*   2s. 6d.

Bradley. Aids to Latin prose. 12mo. *Longmans.*   5s.

Potts, A. W. Hints towards Latin prose composition. gl. 8vo. *Macmillan.*   3s.

Preston, G. Exercises in Latin prose composition. gl. 8vo. *Macmillan.*   2s. 6d.

—II. DICTIONARIES :

Lewis and Short. Latin dictionary. 4to. *Clar. Press.*   25s.

Lewis, C. Latin dictionary for schools. s. 4to. *Clar. Press.*   18s.

Gow, J. Companion to school classics. c. 8vo. *Macmillan.*   6s.

Smith, W. Dictionary of Greek and Roman antiquities. m. 8vo. *Murray.* illus.   28s.

  Smaller edition, c. 8vo., 7s. 6d.

  ,, Dictionary of Greek and Roman biography. m. 8vo. 3 vols. *Murray.* illus.   84s.

  ,, Dictionary of Greek and Roman geography. m. 8vo. 2 vols. *Murray.* illus.   56s.

  ,, Classical dictionary. 8vo. *Murray.* illus.   18s.

  Smaller edition, c. 8vo., 7s. 6d.

Kiepert, H. New atlas antiquus. fo. *Williams.*   7s. 6d.

Butler, G. Public school atlas of ancient geography (24 maps). r. 8vo. *Longmans.*   7s. 6d.

—III. LITERATURE : HISTORY AND CRITICISM :

Cruttwell, C. T. History of Roman literature. c. 8vo. *Griffin.*   8s. 6d.

Nettleship, H. Essays on Latin literature. c. 8vo. *Clar. Press.*   7s. 6d.

Sellar, W. Y. Roman poets of the republic. c. 8vo. *Clar. Press.*   10s.

  ,, Roman poets of the Augustan age : Virgil. c. 8vo. *Clar. Press.*   9s.

Verrall, A. W. Studies in the odes of Horace. 8vo. *Macmillan.*   8s. 6d.

—IV. COLLECTIONS :

Poetarum Latinorum corpus. Ed. Weber. i. 8vo. 1833. pub. 45s.   O.P.

  There is no satisfactory edition in print of the Latin poets in one volume. An edition by J. Postgate is in preparation.

Fragmenta poetarum Latinorum (Comicorum fragmenta, etc.). Ed. A. Bährens. 12mo. (*Leipzig*).   4s. 6d.

Remnants of early Latin, selected and explained for the use of students. Ed. F. D. Allen. 16mo. *Ginn and Heath.*   4s. 6d.

Selections from less known Latin poets, with English notes. Ed. North Pinder. d. 8vo. *Clar. Press.*   15s.

—V. TEXTS AND TRANSLATIONS:

Plautus. Ritschl's Text. Ed. Löwe, Götz, and Schöll. 8vo. 12 vols., from 2s. 6d. to 7s. each. (*Leipzig*).

,,   Text, complete, with Latin notes. Ed. Ussing. 8vo. 5 vols. (*Copenhagen*).   76s.
     Vol. i., 11s.; vol. ii., 14s.; vol. iii. (1), 6s.; (2), 11s. 6d.; vol. iv. (1), 10s.; (2) 10s.; vol. v., 13s. 6d.

,,   Miles gloriosus; with English notes. Ed. R. Y. Tyrrell. f. 8vo. *Macmillan*.   3s. 6d.

,,   Amphitryo; with English notes. Ed. A. Palmer. f. 8vo. *Macmillan*.   3s. 6d.

Terence. Text, complete; with English notes. Ed. W. Wagner. p. 12mo. *Deighton Bell*.   2s.

     Phormio. Ed. Bond and Walpole. f. 8vo. *Macmillan*.   2s. 6d.

Lucilius. Fragments. Ed. L. Müller. 8vo. (*Leipzig*).   9s.

Lucretius. Text, with English notes and translation by H. A. Munro. p. 12mo. *Deighton Bell*.   2s.

,,   Books i.-iii.; with notes. Ed. J. H. Warburton-Lee. f. 8vo. *Macmillan*.   3s. 6d.

,,   Books i., iii., and v.; with notes. Ed. Kelsey. *Allyn and Bacon* (*U.S.*).   9s.

,,   Book v.; with notes. Ed. Duff. ex. f. 8vo. *Pitt Press*.   2s.

,,   Mallock, W. H. Lucretius ("Ancient Classics for English Readers"). f. 8vo. *Blackwood*.   2s. 6d.

Catullus. Text. Ed. L. Schwabe. 8vo. *Weidmann*.   1s. 6d.

,,   Text. Ed. J. P. Postgate. 8vo. *Bell*.   3s.

,,   Commentary on; by R. Ellis. 8vo. *Clar. Press*.   16s.

,,   Selections; with notes. Ed. F. P. Simpson. f. 8vo. *Macmillan*.   3s. 6d.

,,   Tr. Sir Theo. Martin. p. 8vo. *Blackwood*.   7s. 6d.

Cicero. Text. Ed. C. F. Müller. 12mo. 11 vols. *Teubner*.   22s. 6d.
     This is not yet complete, and may be supplemented from the text edited by Baiter and Kayser.

,,   Text. Ed. J. Baiter and C. Kayser. 8vo. 11 vols. *Tauchnitz*.   46s. 6d.

,,   Pro Balbo; with English notes. Ed. J. S. Reid. ex. f. 8vo. *Pitt Press*.   1s. 6d.

,,   Pro Archia; with English notes. Ed. J. S. Reid. ex. f. 8vo. *Pitt Press*.   2s.

,,   Pro Sulla; with English notes. Ed. J. S. Reid. ex. f. 8vo. *Pitt Press*.   3s. 6d.

,,   Pro Murena; with English notes. Ed. W. Heitland. *Pitt Press*.   3s.

,,   Pro Rabirio. Ed. W. Heitland. d. 8vo. *Cambridge Press*.   7s. 6d.

,,   Pro Cluentio. Ed. W. T. Fausset. *Longmans*.   6s.

,,   Pro Roscio Amerino. Ed. E. H. Donkin. f. 8vo. *Macmillan*.   2s. 6d.

,,   In Catilinam'; with English notes. Ed. A. S. Wilkins. f. 8vo. *Macmillan*.   2s. 6d.

,,   Pro lege Manilia. Ed. A. S. Wilkins. f. 8vo. *Macmillan*.   2s. 6d.

,,   Philippics; with English notes. Ed. J. R. King. d. 8vo. *Clar. Press*.   10s. 6d.

,,   Philippics II.; with English notes. Ed. J. E. B. Mayor. f. 8vo. *Macmillan*.   3s. 6d.

,,   Pro Plancio; with English notes. Ed. H. Holden. ex. f. 8vo. *Pitt Press*.   4s. 6d.

,,   Pro Sestio; with English notes. Ed. H. Holden. f. 8vo. *Macmillan*.   3s. 6d.

,,   Divinatio in Q. Cœcilium, et In Verrem I.; with English notes. Ed. Heitland and Cowie. ex. f. 8vo. *Pitt Press*.   3s.

,,   De natura deorum; with English notes. Ed. J. E. B. Mayor. 3 vols. *Cambridge Press*. Vol. i., 10s. 6d.; vol. ii., 12s. 6d.; vol. iii., 10s.   33s.

,,   De officiis; with English notes. Ed. H. Holden. ex. f. 8vo. *Cambridge Press*.   9s.

,,   De amicitia; with English notes. Ed. J. S. Reid. ex. f. 8vo. *Pitt Press*.   3s. 6d.

,,   De senectute; with English notes. Ed. J. S. Reid. ex. f. 8vo. *Pitt Press*.   3s. 6d.

,,   De finibus; with Latin commentary. Ed. J. Madvig. 8vo. (*Copenhagen*).   22s.

,,   De finibus. Ed. and tr. J. S. Reid. *Cambridge Press*. Vol. iii.   8s.

,,   Academica; with English notes. Ed. J. S. Reid. 8vo. *Macmillan*.   15s.

,,   Academica. Tr. J. S. Reid. 8vo. *Macmillan*.   5s. 6d.

Cicero. De oratore; with English notes. Ed. A. S. Wilkins. 2 vols. *Clar. Press.*   12*s.* 6*d.*
Vol. i., 7*s.* 6*d.*; vol. ii., 5*s.*

,,   De oratore; with English notes. Ed. J. E. Sandys. ex. f. 8vo. *Cambridge Press.*   16*s.*

,,   Brutus. Ed. Kellogg. 12mo. *Ginn and Heath.*   6*s.* 6*d.*

,,   Tusculanae disputationes; with Latin notes. Ed. R. Kühner. 8vo. (*Jena*)   8*s.*

,,   Somnium Scipionis; with English notes. Ed. W. Pearman. ex. f. 8vo. *Cambridge Press.*   2*s.*

,,   De legibus; with English notes. Ed. W. D. Pearman. *Hall (Cambridge).* c. 8vo.   4*s.* 6*d.*

,,   Letters; with English commentary. Ed. R. Y. Tyrrell. 8vo. 2 vols., 12*s.* each. *Hodges.*   24*s.*

,,   Selection of letters; with English notes. Ed. A. Watson. d. 8vo. *Clar. Press.*   18*s.*

,,   Letters. Selected and tr. G. E. Jeans. c. 8vo. *Macmillan.*   16*s.* 6*d.*

Aids.

,,   Forsyth, W. Life of Cicero. c. 8vo. 2 vols. *Murray.*   O.P.

,,   Munk, E. Student's Cicero. Ed. W. Y. Fausset. *Sonnenschein.*   2*s.* 6*d.*
Adapted from the German. A general account.

Cæsar. De bello Gallico, with English notes. Ed. A. G. Peskett. ex. f. 8vo. *Pitt Press.*   10*s.*
Book i., 1*s.* 6*d.*; book ii., 2*s.*; book iii., 2*s.*; books i., ii., iii. (in one vol.), 3*s.*; books iv., v., 2*s.*; book vi., 1*s.* 6*d.*; book vii., 2*s.*; book viii., 1*s.* 6*d.*

,,   De bello civili; with English notes. Ed. C. E. Moberly. ex. f. 8vo. *Clar. Press.*   3*s.* 6*d.*

Sallust. Text. Ed. G. Long. 16mo. *Bell.*   1*s.* 6*d.*

,,   Catiline; with English notes. Ed. A. M. Cook. f. 8vo. *Macmillan.*   2*s.*

,,   Jugurtha. Ed. W. P. Brooke. *Longmans.*   *s.* 6*d.*

,,   Catiline and Jugurtha. Tr. A. W. Pollard. c. 8vo. *Macmillan.*   6*s.*

Livy. Text. Ed. Madvig and Ussing. 8vo. 4 vols., in 8 parts. (*Copenhagen*).   23*s.*
Vol. i. (1), 3*s.* 6*d.*; (2), 2*s.*; vol. ii. (1), 3*s.* 6*d.*; (2), 3*s.*; vol. iii. (1), 2*s.*; (2), 3*s.*; vol. iv. (1) 3*s.*; (2), 2*s.*

,,   Text; with German notes. Ed. Weissenborn and Müller. 20 parts, sold separately. *Weidmann.*   40*s.*

,,   Book i.; with English commentary. Ed. J. R. Seeley. d. 8vo. *Clar. Press.*   6*s.*

,,   Books ii., iii.; with English notes. Ed. H. Stephenson. f. 8vo. *Macmillan.*   3*s.* 6*d.*

,,   Book iv.; with English notes. Ed. H. Stephenson. ex. f. 8vo. *Pitt Press.*   2*s.* 6*d.*

,,   Books v., vi., vii. Ed. Cluer and Matheson. ex. f. 8vo. *Clar. Press.*   5*s.*

,,   Books xxi., xxii.; with English commentary. Ed. W. W. Capes. f. 8vo. *Macmillan.*   4*s.* 6*d.*

,,   Books xxiii., xxiv.; with English notes. Ed. G. C. Macaulay. f. 8vo. *Macmillan.*   3*s.* 6*d.*

,,   Books xxi., xxv. Tr. Church and Brodribb. c. 8vo. *Macmillan.*   7*s.* 6*d.*

Horace. Text; with Latin notes. Ed. Orelli and Hirschfelder. 8vo. (*Berlin*).   42*s.*

,,   Text; with English notes. Ed. E. C. Wickham. d. 8vo. *Clar. Press.*   24*s.*
Vol. i., Odes, Epodes and Carmen seculare, 12*s.*; vol. ii., Satires, Epistles, and De arte poetica, 12*s.*

,,   Satires; with English notes. Ed. A. Palmer. f. 8vo. *Macmillan.*   5*s.*

,,   Epistles; with English notes. Ed. A. S. Wilkins. f. 8vo. *Macmillan.*   5*s.*

,,   Satires. Tr. in verse, J. Conington. f. 8vo. *Bell.*   6*s.* 6*d.*

,,   Odes. Tr. in verse, J. Conington. f. 8vo. *Bell.*   5*s.* 6*d.*

,,   Odes. Tr. in verse, Sir Theo. Martin. c. 8vo. 2 vols. *Blackwood.*   21*s.*

,,   Odes, Englished and imitated by various hands. Selected by C. Cooper. c. 8vo. *Bell.*   6*s.*

Virgil. Text; with English commentary. Ed. J. Conington. d. 8vo. 3 vols., 10*s.* 6*d.* each. *Bell.*   31*s.* 6*d.*

Virgil. Bucolics. Ed. A. Sidgwick. ex. f. 8vo. *Pitt Press.*   1s. 6d.

,,   Georgics. Ed. A. Sidgwick. 2 vols. ex. f. 8vo. *Pitt Press.* Books i., ii., 2s.; books iii., iv., 2s.   4s.

,,   Æneid; with English notes. Ed. A. Sidgwick. ex. f. 8vo. 12 books, 1s. 6d. each. *Pitt Press.*   18s.

,,   Eclogues and Georgics. Tr. into prose by J. W. Mackail. *Longmans.*   5s.

,,   Æneid. Tr. into prose, J. W. Mackail. c. 8vo. *Macmillan.*   7s. 6d.

,,   Æneid. Tr. into prose, Lee and Lonsdale. gl. 8vo. *Macmillan.*   3s. 6d.

,,   Æneid. Tr. into verse, Sir C. Bowen. 8vo. *Murray.*   12s.

Propertius. Text. Ed. A. Palmer. f. 8vo. *Bell.*   3s. 6d.

,,   Text; with English notes. Ed. F. A. Paley. d. 8vo. *Bell.*   5s.

,,   Selections; with English notes. Ed. J. P. Postgate. f. 8vo. *Macmillan.*   5s.

Tibullus. Text. Ed. E. Hiller. 8vo. *Tauchnitz.*   1s.

Tibullus and Propertius. Selections; with English notes. Ed. G. G. Ramsay. ex. f. 8vo. *Clar. Press.*   6s.

Ovid. Text. Ed. Ewald and Merkel. 12mo. 3 vols. *Teubner.*   3s.

,,   Heroides; with English notes. Ed. E. S. Shuckburgh. f. 8vo. *Macmillan.*   3s. 6d.

,,   Tristia; books i., iii. Ed. S. G. Owen. d. 8vo. *Clar. Press.*   16s.

,,   Fasti. Ed. F. A. Paley. f. 8vo. *Bell.*   3s. 6d.

,,   Fasti; book vi. Ed. A. Sidgwick. *Cambridge Press.*   1s. 6d.

Petronius. Text. Ed. F. Bücheler. 8vo. *Weidmann.*   3s.

Seneca (the elder). Rhetoris. Ed. A. Kiessling. 12mo. *Teubner.*   4s. 6d.

Seneca (the younger). Text. Ed. F. Haase. 12mo. 3 vols. (*Leipzig*).   8s.

,,   On benefits. Tr. A. Stewart. *Bell.*   3s. 6d.

Lucan. Pharsalia; with English notes. Ed. C. E. Haskins. d. 8vo. *Bell.*   14s.

,,   Pharsalia, book i. Ed. Heitland and Haskins. f. 8vo. *Cambridge Press.*   1s. 6d.

Juvenal. Satires; with English commentary. Ed. J. E. B. Mayor. c. 8vo. 2 vols., 10s. 6d. each. *Macmillan.*   21s.

,,   Satires; with English notes (School edition). Ed. C. Pearson and A. Strong. c. 8vo. *Clar. Press.*   6s.

,,   Satires. Tr. into prose by Strong and Leeper. c. 8vo. *Macmillan.*   3s. 6d.

Martial. Epigrams. Ed. W. Gilbert. 12mo. *Teubner.*   2s. 6d.

,,   Selections; with English notes. Ed. F. A. Paley and W. H. Stone. d. 8vo. *Bell.*   4s. 6d.

,,   Selections; with English notes. Ed. H. Stephenson. f. 8vo. *Macmillan.*   5s.

Persius. Satires. Notes and tr. by J. Conington. Ed. H. Nettleship. d. 8vo. *Clar. Press.*   7s. 6d.

Tacitus. Text. Ed. C. Halm. 12mo. 2 vols. *Teubner.*   2s. 6d.

,,   Annals; books i.-vi.; with English commentary. Ed. H. Furneaux. d. 8vo. *Clar. Press.*   18s.

,,   Annals; with German notes. Ed. C. Nipperdey. p. 8vo. 2 vols. *Weidmann.* Vol. i., 3s.; vol. ii., 2s. 6d.   5s. 6d.

,,   Annals; with French notes. Ed. E. Jacob. l. 8vo. 2 vols. (*Paris*).   12s. 6d.

,,   Histories; with English notes. Ed. A. D. Godley. 2 vols. *Macmillan.* Vol. i. (books i., ii.), 3s. 6d.; vol. ii. (books iii., iv.), 3s. 6d.   7s.

,,   Germania and Agricola; with English notes. Ed. Church and Brodribb. f. 8vo. *Macmillan.*   3s. 6d.

,,   Histories; with English notes. Ed. K. Heraeus. 8vo. 2 vols., 2s. each. *Teubner.*   4s.

,,   Works. Tr. by Church and Brodribb. c. 8vo. 3 vols. *Macmillan.*   18s.

   History, 6s.; Annals, 7s. 6d.; Germania and Agricola, 4s. 6d.

Pliny (the elder). Text. Ed. D. Detlefsen. p. 8vo. 6 vols. *Weidmann.*   16*s.*
Vol. i., 2*s.*; vol. ii., 2*s.* 6*d.*; vol. iii., 2*s.* 6*d.*; vol. iv., 2*s.* 6*d.*; vol. v., 2*s.* 6*d.*; vol. vi., 4*s.*

Pliny (the younger). Text. Ed. H. Keil. 12mo. *Teubner.*   1*s.* 3*d.*

,,   Letters, books i., ii. with English notes. Ed. J. Cowan. f. 8vo. *Macmillan.*   3*s.*

,,   Letters, book iii.; with English notes. Ed. J. E. B. Mayor. f. 8vo. *Macmillan.*   3*s.* 6*d.*

,,   Church and Brodribb. Pliny's Letters ("Ancient Classics for English Readers").
f. 8vo. *Blackwood.*   2*s.* 6*d.*

Suetonius. Text. Ed. L. Roth. 12mo. *Teubner.*   1*s.* 6*d.*

Quintilian. Text. Ed. F. Bonnell. 12mo. 2 vols. *Teubner.*   2*s.* 6*d.*

,,   Institutiones; with French notes. Ed. Hild. 8vo. (*Paris*).   3*s.*

Valerius Maximus. Works. Ed. Kempf. 12mo. *Teubner.*   4*s.* 6*d.*

,,   School selection. Ed. W. R. Inge. *Longmans.*   3*s.* 6*d.*

Quintus Curtius. History of Alexander the Great. Ed. Foss. 12mo.
Teubner.   1*s.* 3*d.*

,,   Alexander in India; with English notes. Ed. Heitland and
Raven. ex. f. 8vo. *Pitt Press.*   3*s.* 6*d.*

Aulus Gellius. Noctes Atticae. Ed. Hertz. 12mo. 2 vols. *Teubner.*   4*s.* 6*d.*
Vol. i., 2*s.*; vol. ii., 2*s.* 6*d.*

Statius. Text. Ed. Bährens and Kohlmann. 12mo. 2 vols. *Teubner.*   3*s.* 9*d.*
Vol. i., 2*s.*; vol. ii., 1*s.* 9*d.*

Valerius Flaccus. Text. Ed. Bährens. 12mo. *Teubner.*   1*s.* 6*d.*

Pervigilium Veneris. Ed. Bücheler. 12mo. *Teubner.*   1*s.*

Apuleius. Text. Ed. G. Hildebrand. 8vo. 2 vols. (*Leipzig*).   30*s.*

Manilius. Text. Ed. F. Jacob. 8vo. (*Berlin*).   2*s.* 6*d.*

Silius Italicus. Text (French edition). Ed. Lemaire. 8vo. 2 vols.   O.P.

Ausonius. Text. Ed. Schenkl. 4to. (*Berlin*).   10*s.*
In "Monumenta Historiae Germanicae."

Claudian. Text. Ed. Jeep. 8vo. 2 vols. (*Leipzig*).   21*s.*

Prudentius. Text. Ed. Dressel. 8vo. (*Leipzig*).   7*s.* 6*d.*

Sidonius Apollinaris. Text (French edition). Ed. Barret. 8vo. (*Paris*).   13*s.* 6*d.*

Calpurnii et Nemesiani Bucolica. Ed. Schenkl. 8vo. (*Leipzig*).   6*s.*

LAW:

For works on ROMAN LAW, *and on the law of* ENGLAND, SCOTLAND, UNITED
STATES, INDIA, *see under those heads.*

—I. GENERAL JURISPRUDENCE AND EARLY HISTORY OF LAW:

Hobbes, T. Leviathan ("Morley's Universal Library"). c. 8vo. *Routledge.*   1*s.*

Bentham, J. Theory of legislation. 8vo. *Trübner.*   7*s.* 6*d.*

,,   Principles of morals and legislation. c. 8vo. *Clar. Press.*   6*s.* 6*d.*

,,   Fragment on government. 8vo. *Clar. Press.*   7*s.* 6*d.*

Austin, J. Jurisprudence. 8vo. 2 vols. *Murray.*   32*s.*
Student's edition. c. 8vo. 12*s.*

Holland, T. E. Elements of jurisprudence. (elem.). d. 8vo. *Clar. Press.*   10*s.* 6*d.*

Markby, W. Elements of law. d. 8vo. *Clar. Press.*   12*s.* 6*d.*

Clark, E. C. Practical jurisprudence. c. 8vo. *Cambridge Press.*   9*s.*

Pollock, F. Essays in jurisprudence and ethics. 8vo. *Macmillan.*   10*s.* 6*d.*

Pollock, F. Oxford lectures, etc. 8vo. *Macmillan.*　　9*s.*

Maine, H. Ancient law. 8vo. *Murray.*　　9*s.*

,,　　Early history of institutions. 8vo. *Murray.*　　9*s.*

,,　　Village communities. 8vo. *Murray.*　　9*s.*

,,　　Early law and custom. 8vo. *Murray.*　　9*s.*

—II. REFERENCE :

　　The leading law publishers issue annual catalogues, which give information of new works.

Douthwaite, W. R. Catalogue of the library of Gray's Inn. 8vo. *Librarian, Gray's Inn.*

Griswold, S. B. Catalogue of the New York State Library. (*Albany, N.Y.*).　　21*s*
　　Subject index of Law Library.

Elphinstone and others. Glossary of law terms and interpretation of deeds. 8vo. *Maxwell.*　　25*s*
　　The nearest approach to a scientific law glossary.
　　　PERIODICALS : *Law Magazine and Review ; Law Quarterly Review.* A list of current British, American, and foreign law reviews, with their contents, is published at the end of every number of the *Law Quarterly Review. American Law Review* (St. Louis, U.S.), *Harvard Law Review* (Cambridge, U.S.).

LAW OF NATIONS :

—I. INTERNATIONAL LAW :

Hall, W. E. International law. d. 8vo. *Clar. Press.*　　22*s. 6d.*
　　References to the leading continental authors will be found in Mr. Hall's book. Some knowledge of modern languages, or at least of French, is necessary for the profitable study of this subject.

Wheaton, H. Elements of international law. Ed. Boyd. r. 8vo. *Stevens.*　　30*s.*

Woolsey, T. D. Introduction to international law. 8vo. (*New York*).　　18*s.*

Phillimore, R. International law. 8vo. 4 vols. *Butterworth.*　　34*s.*

Maine, H. International law. 8vo. *Murray.*　　7*s. 6d.*
　　Published from the author's MS. lectures after his death.

Wheaton, H. History of international law. 8vo. *Stevens.*　　30*s.*

Clarke, Sir E. Law of extradition. 8vo. *Stevens and Haynes.*　　20*s.*

Calvo, C. Le droit international. 8vo. 4 vols. (*Paris*).　　60*s.*

Heffter, A. W. Das europäische Völkerrecht der Gegenwart. 8vo. (*Berlin*).　　12*s.*

—II. CONFLICT OF LAWS :

Westlake. J. Private international law. 8vo. *Maxwell.*　　15*s.*

Foote, J. A. Private international jurisprudence. 8vo. *Stevens and Haynes.*　　25*s.*

Dicey, A. V. The law of domicile. *Stevens.*

Nelson, H. Select cases, etc. r. 8vo. *Stevens.*　　21*s.*

Savigny, F. Private international law. Tr. Guthrie. 8vo. (*Edinburgh*).　　21*s.*
　　Vol. viii. of the *System des heutigen römischer Rechts.*

LAWN-TENNIS :

Heathcote and others. Tennis, lawn-tennis, rackets, and fives. ("Badminton Library"). c. 8vo. *Longmans.* illus.　　10*s. 6d.*

" **Cavendish.**" Game of lawn-tennis. 8vo. *De la Rue.*　　1*s. 6d.*

Brownlee, W. Methven.   Lawn-tennis; its rise and progress.   c. 8vo.
   Arrowsmith.   1*s.* 6*d.*
     Championship meetings; eminent players, with portraits; a treatise on the game.

Wilberforce, H. W. W. Lawn-tennis, with a chapter for ladies. ("All
   England" ser.). sm. 8vo. *Bell.*   1*s.*
     PERIODICALS: *Field,* weekly; *Pastime,* weekly; *Lawn-Tennis Annual* (principally reports
     of last year's matches: contains list of lawn-tennis clubs).

LEATHER, *see* INDUSTRIES XII.

LEEWARD ISLANDS, *see* WEST INDIES 1.

LEGENDS, *see* FOLKLORE.

LEGERDEMAIN, *see* CONJURING.

LEGISLATION, THEORY OF, *see* LAW I.

LIBEL, *see* ENGLAND, LAW IX.

LIBERIA, *see* AFRICA II

LIBRARIES:

Slater, J. Herbert. Library manual. *Upcott Gill.*   2*s.* 6*d.*
Wheatley, H. B. How to form a library. f. 8vo. *Stock.*   4*s.* 6*d.*
Blackburn, C. F. Hints on catalogue titles. r. 8vo. *Low.*   14*s.*
Greenwood, T. Free public libraries. c. 8vo. *Simpkin.*   5*s.*

LICHENS, *see* BOTANY.

LIFE ASSURANCE, *see* ASSURANCE.

LIGHT, *see* PHYSICS VI.

LINCOLN'S INN, *see* LONDON III.

LITHOGRAPHY, *see* PRINTING I.

LITU-LETTISH LANGUAGES, *see* SLAVONIC.

LITURGIES, *see* THEOLOGY V.

LIVE-STOCK:

See also HORSE, DOG, *and* VETERINARY SCIENCE.

—I. GENERAL:

Wallace, R. Farm live-stock of Great Britain. p. 8vo. *Simpkin.*   7*s.* 6*d.*
Youatt, W. The complete grazier. 8vo. *Lockwood.*   30*s.*
Carrington and others. Live-stock of the farm. c. 8vo. *Vinton.*   2*s.* 6*d.*
Brown, Prof. Animal life of the farm. c. 8vo. *Vinton.*   2*s.* 6*d.*
Seller and Stephens. Physiology at the farm. p. 8vo. *Blackwood.* illus.
   pub. 16*s.*   O.P.
     Aid to rearing and feeding the live-stock. A standard work, though not new.

Gamgee, J. Our domestic animals in health and disease. Ed. MacLachlan
and Stuart. 8vo. *Simpkin.*   22*s.*

Cobbold, T. S. Internal parasites of domesticated animals. p. 8vo. *H. Cox.*
pub. 5*s.*   O.P.
A book of reference.

Armsby, H. P. Manual of cattle-feeding. c. 8vo. *J. Willey.* illus.   12*s.* 6*d.*
Chemistry of feeding-stuffs, etc.; appendix of useful tables.

—II. SPECIAL:

Coleman, J. The cattle, sheep and pigs of Great Britain. 8vo. *H. Cox.* illus.   12*s.* 6*d.*
Good, though somewhat old in style.

Macdonald and Sinclair. History of Hereford cattle. *Vinton.* illus.   10*s.* 6*d.*

  ,,   History of polled cattle. c. 8vo. *Vinton.* illus.   12*s.* 6*d.*

Aberdeen Angus polled cattle. *Aldine Co. (Detroit).*
History of the breed in England and America, with an introduction by Judge Goodwin.

History of improved shorthorn or Durham cattle. (*N. Engd. Farm Office*).
From notes by the late T. Bates, with memoir by T. Bell.

Allen, L. F. History of the shorthorn cattle. 8vo. (*Buffalo, N.Y.*).   24*s.*

Clater's cattle doctor. Ed. Armatage. d. 8vo. *Warne.* illus.   21*s.*

Steel, J. H. Treatise on the diseases of the ox. 8vo. *Longmans.* illus.   15*s.*

  ,,   Diseases of sheep. 8vo. *Stock.*   12*s.*

Lawes, J. B. Tables for estimating dead-weight and value of cattle from
live-weight. 16mo. *Royal Agric. Soc. of England.*   1*s.*
Most valuable.

Sidney, S. The pig. *Routledge.* illus.   1*s.*

Tegetmeier, W. B. Poultry book. r. 8vo. *Routledge.*   21*s.*

Wright, L. Illustrated book of poultry. 4to. *Cassell.*   31*s.* 6*d.*

  ,,   Practical poultry keeper. c. 8vo. *Cassell.*   3*s.* 6*d.*

Wilson, Mrs. M. A. The A-B-C poultry book. 12mo. *Cassell.*   1*s.*

Fulton, R. The pigeon book. 4to. *Cassell.*   31*s.* 6*d.*

LIVERY COMPANIES, *see* LONDON II.

LOCAL GOVERNMENT:

In matters coming under this head, the statements of even the most recent text-books and
editions are specially liable to be superseded or affected by current legislation. In some
cases it is also necessary to make inquiry as to local orders or regulations.

Bazalgette and Humphreys. Local and municipal government. sup. r. 8vo.
Stevens.   63*s.*
Comprising the statutes relating to public health, municipal corporations, highways, etc.

Smith, J. Toulmin. Local self-government and centralization. p. 8vo.
Chapman. 1851. pub. 5*s.*   O.P.
Deals with general principles. The examples in many cases are no longer applicable owing to
changes in the law.

Glen, W. C. and A. Public health, local government, etc. 8vo. *Butter-*
worth.   36*s.*

Chalmers, M. D. Local government ("English Citizen" ser.). c. 8vo.
Macmillan.   3*s.* 6*d.*

Rathbone, W. Local administration ("Imperial Parliament" ser.). c. 8vo.
Sonnenschein.   1*s.*

Goschen, G. J.　Reports and speeches on local taxation.　8vo.　*Macmillan.*　　5s.
　　An important review of the financial principles involved.

Sargant, C. H.　Urban rating.　8vo.　*Longmans.*　　6s.

Bazalgette and Humphreys.　County councils.　r. 8vo.　*Stevens.*　　7s. 6d.

Pulling, A.　Handbook for county authorities.　d. 8vo.　*Clowes.*　　7s. 6d.

Smith, J. Toulmin.　The parish.　8vo.　*Sweet.*　　18s.

Glen, W. C. and A.　Highways.　12mo.　*Butterworth.*　　3s. 6d.

Rogers, F. N.　Elections.　d. 8vo.　2 parts, 21s. each.　*Stevens.*　　42s.

Arnold-Forster, H. O.　Laws of everyday life.　*Cassell.*　　1s. 6d.

　　,,　　Citizen reader.　8vo.　*Cassell.*　　1s. 6d.
　　The last two are elementary books for children.

Glen and Cunningham.　Law of county government.　d. 8vo.　*Knight.*　　42s.
　　Local Government Act, 1888.

Local government directory (annual).　d. 8vo.　*Knight.*　　8s. 6d.

LOCOMOTIVES, *see* STEAM ENGINE.

LOGIC:

—I. DEDUCTIVE:

(A) GENERAL.

Keynes, J. N.　Formal logic. (elem.).　8vo.　*Macmillan.*　　10s. 6d.

Bain, A.　Logical deduction. (elem.).　p. 8vo.　*Longmans.*　　10s. 6d.

Jevons, W. S.　Studies in deductive logic.　p. 8vo.　*Macmillan.*　　6s.

Bowen, F. E.　Treatise on logic.　12mo.　(*Boston*).　　7s.

Lotze, H.　Logic. (advanced).　Ed. B. Bosanquet.　p. 8vo.　*Clar. Press.*　　12s.

Bradley, F. H.　Principles of logic. (very advanced).　8vo.　*Paul.*　　16s.

Bosanquet, B.　Logic. (very advanced).　8vo.　2 vols.　*Clar. Press.*　　21s.

Whateley, R.　Elements of logic.　8vo.　*Longmans.*　　4s. 6d.
　　Mainly of historical interest; not an advanced treatise.

Hamilton, W.　Lectures on logic.　8vo.　4 vols.　(*Edinburgh*).　　24s.

Newman, J. H.　Grammar of assent.　p. 8vo.　*Longmans.*　　3s. 6d.

(B) MATHEMATICAL.

Boole, G.　Laws of thought.　8vo.　*Macmillan.*　　14s.

De Morgan, A.　Formal logic.　*Taylor and Walton.*　1847.　　o.p.

Venn, J.　Symbolical logic.　p. 8vo.　*Macmillan.*　　10s. 6d.

　　,,　　Logic of chance.　12mo.　*Macmillan.*　　10s. 6d.

　　,,　　Empirical logic.　8vo.　*Macmillan.*　　18s.
　　Mathematical and inductive.

—II. INDUCTIVE:

Bain, A.　Logical induction. (elem.).　p. 8vo.　*Longmans.*　　6s. 6d.

Mill, J. S.　System of logic.　c. 8vo.　*Longmans.*　　5s.

Taine, H.　A study of John S. Mill.　Tr. Haze.　c. 8vo.　*Simpkin.*　pub. 1s.　　o.p.

Jevons, W. S.　Principles of science.　p. 8vo.　*Macmillan.*　　12s. 6d.

Herschel, J. F. W. Introduction to the study of natural philosophy. 12mo. *Longmans.* 1840. pub. 3s. 6d.   O.P.

Whewell, W. History of scientific ideas. p. 8vo. *Parker.*   14s.

Bacon, A. F. Novum organum (vols. i., ii. of "Complete works"). Tr. and ed. Ellis and Spedding. 8vo. 10s. 6d. each. *Longmans.*

LONDON :

—I. GENERAL AND SUBURBS :

Baedeker's London. 12mo. *Dulau.*   6s.

Murray's Handbook of the environs of London. p. 8vo. 2 parts. *Murray.*   21s.

Metropolitan Yearbook. *Cassell.*   1s.
     A guide to imperial, municipal, local, commercial, educational, and social London.

Loftie, W. J. History of London. p. 8vo. 2 vols. *Stanford.*   32s.

     ,,   London (in "Historic Towns"). 8vo. *Longmans.*   3s. 6d.

Wheatley, H. B. London, past and present. 8vo. 3 vols. *Murray.*   63s.

Thornbury and Walford. Old and new London. 4to. 6 vols., 9s. each. *Cassell.*   54s.
     Descriptive.

Walford, E. Greater London : a narrative of its history, people, and its places. r. 8vo. 2 vols., 9s. each. *Cassell.* illus.   18s.

Timbs, J. Curiosities of London. c. 8vo. *Virtue.*   21s.

Buxton, E. N. Epping Forest. 12mo. *Stanford.*   2s.

Taunt. Illustrated guide to the Thames. *Philip.*   8s. 6d.
     Most useful in boating expeditions. Larger edition, with photographs, 15s.

—II. CITY :

     For the bibliography of the City, *see* Catalogue of the Guildhall library.

Norton, G. Commentaries on the history, constitution, and chartered franchises of the City of London. 8vo. *Longmans.* pub. 14s.   O.P.
     Constitution and government.

Birch, W. de Gray. Historical charters and constitutional documents of the City of London. r. 8vo. *Whiting.*   31s. 6d.

Pulling, A. Laws, customs, and regulations of the City and Port of London. 8vo. *Stevens and Norton.* 1842. pub. 18s.   O.P.

Memorials of London. Ed. H. T. Riley. i. 8vo. *Longmans.*   21s.
     London life in the 13th, 14th, and 15th centuries, being extracts from the early archives of the City.

Herbert, W. History of the twelve great livery companies. 2 vols. *Bohn.* pub. 16s.   O.P.
     Historical and antiquarian ; the only published book of value on the subject.

Welch, C. Bibliography of the Livery Companies. *Bale* (87, Great Tichfield-street).   1s.

Stow, J. Survey of London (1598). Ed. H. Morley. 8vo. *Routledge.*   2s. 6d.

City of London livery companies' Commission report. fo. 5 vols. *Eyre.*   33s. 8d.
     Historical enquiry, followed by statistics furnished by the companies, varying much in completeness.

Mackmurdo, A. H. Wren's City churches. 8vo. *G. Allen.*   5s.

City of London Directory. *Collingridge.*   10s. 6d.
     Annual ; concise particulars of each company, with arms, and lists of governing body and members.

—III. INNS OF COURT AND CHANCERY:

Herbert, W. Antiquities of the Inns of Court and Chancery. (*London*). 1804.   O.P.

Pearce, R. History of the Inns of Court and Chancery. 8vo. *Bentley* (*London*). 1848. pub. 15*s*.   O.P.

Spilsbury, W. H. Lincoln's Inn. 12mo. *Reeves and Turner.* 1850. pub. 6*s*.   O.P
     Its ancient and modern buildings with an account of the library.

Douthwaite, W. R. Gray's Inn; its history and associations. 8vo. *Reeves and Turner.*   7*s. 6d.*

—IV. NATIONAL GALLERY:

Cook, E. T. Popular handbook to the National Gallery. c. 8vo. *Macmillan.*   14*s*.
     Contains a history of the gallery, plan and guide to the rooms, introduction to the schools of painting, critical biographies of the painters, notes on the pictures, etc.

Ruskin, J. Catalogue of Turner's drawings and sketches. 8vo. *G. Allen.*   1*s*.

—V. ST. PAUL'S:

Dugdale, W. History of St. Paul's Cathedral. Ed. Sir H. Ellis. fo. (*London*). 1818.   O.P.
     The quarry for information.

Milman, H. Annals of St. Paul's (historical and biographical). 8vo. *Murray.* pub. 18*s*.   O.P

Longman, W. History of the three cathedrals dedicated to St. Paul in London. 8vo. *Longmans.* pub. 21*s*.   O.P.

Simpson, W. S. Chapters in the history of old St. Pauls. d. 8vo. *Stock.*   7*s. 6d.*

     ,,   Gleanings from Old St. Pauls. d. 8vo. *Stock.*   7*s. 6d.*

—VI. TOWER:

Ros, Lord de. Memorials of the Tower of London. 8vo. *Murray.* pub. 10*s. 6d.*   O.P.
     Historical and descriptive.

Dixon, W. Hepworth. Her Majesty's Tower. 8vo. 4 vols., 15*s*. each. *Hurst.*   60*s*.
     Historical associations.

—VII. WESTMINSTER ABBEY:

Chester, Col. The Abbey registers. 4to. *Harleian Society.*
     Most valuable for reference. Sold only to members, 21*s*. each.

Scott, Gilbert. Gleanings from Westminster Abbey. d. 8vo. *Parker.* pub. 15*s*.   O.P.
     Specially architectural.

Stanley, A. P. Memorials of Westminster Abbey. 8vo. *Murray.* illus.   15*s*.
     Very full of historical information.

Bradley, G. G. The Deanery guide. c. 4to. *Pall Mall Gazette.* illus.   1*s*.
     Contains materials collected from all works on the Abbey.

—VIII. BRITISH MUSEUM:

Nichols, T. Handbook to the British Museum. 8vo. *Cassell.*   21*s*.

LUTHER, *see* CHURCH HISTORY IV.

M.

MACHINERY:

See also ENGINEERING.

Rankine, W. J. M. Machinery and millwork. Ed. W. J. Millar. c. 8vo. *Griffin.* illus.   12*s.* 6*d.*

Reuleaux, F. Kinematics of machinery (mathematical). Tr. A. B. W. Kennedy. i. 8vo. *Macmillan.* illus.   21*s.*

Kennedy, A. Mechanics of machinery. p. 8vo. *Macmillan.* illus.   12*s.* 6*d.*

Unwin, W. C. Machine design, part i. c. 8vo. *Longmans.* illus.   6*s.*

Smith, R. H. Cutting tools. 18mo. *Cassell.*   3*s.* 6*d.*

MADAGASCAR:

Sibree, J. Madagascar. 8vo. *Trübner.*   12*s.*
> Physical geography, geology, exploration, natural history, botany, etc. The best succinct account of the island.

Oliver, S. P. Madagascar. m. 8vo. 2 vols. *Macmillan.*   52*s.* 6*d.*
> Historical and descriptive account of the island, and its former dependencies. A detailed compilation from various sources.

Grandidier, A. Histoire physique, naturelle et politique de Madagascar. 4to. 28 vols. (*Paris*).   £60
> An elaborate and expensive work, with numerous maps and plates, and dealing with the geography, meteorology, ethnography, political and natural history, etc. Still in progress.

MADNESS, *see* MENTAL PHYSIOLOGY I.

MAGIC LANTERN, *see* GAMES III.

MAGNETISM, *see* ELECTRICITY.

MAGNETISM, ANIMAL, *see* PSYCHICAL RESEARCH.

MAHOMETANISM:

See also ARABIA, LITERATURE.

Hughes, T. P. Dictionary of Islam. r. 8vo. *Allen.*   42*s.*
> Encyclopædia of information.

Muir, W. Life of Mahomet. d. 8vo. 4 vols. *Smith, Elder.*   32*s.*
> Also in 1 vol., 14*s.*

Sprenger, A. Das Leben und die Lehre des Mohammed. 8vo. 3 vols. (*Berlin*).   24*s.*

Muir, W. Annals of the early Caliphate. d. 8vo. *Smith, Elder.*   16*s.*

Weil, G. Geschichte der Chalifen. 8vo. 5 vols. (*Mannheim*).   63*s.*

Müller, A. Der Islam. (*Berlin*).   54*s.*

Freeman, E. A. History and conquests of the Saracens. 12mo. *Parker.* pub. 2*s.*   O.P.

Burton, R. A pilgrimage to Mecca and Medina. 8vo. 3 vols. *Longmans.* pub. 21s.   O.P.

Ibn Khallikan. Biographical dictionary. Tr. De Slane. *Oriental Trans. Fund.*   O.P.

MAHOMETAN LAW, *see* INDIA, LAW.

MAJORCA, *see* MEDITERRANEAN.

MALAY ARCHIPELAGO, *see* INDIAN ARCHIPELAGO I.

MALAY PENINSULA :

Colonies et protectorats de l'Indo-Chine. 18mo. *Quantin.*   3s. 6d.
    Tonkin, Cambodge, Cochin Chine, Annam. Vol. iii. of *Les colonies françaises.*

Bowring, J. The kingdom and people of Siam. 8vo. 2 vols. *Parker.* illus. pub. 32s.   O.P.

Anderson, J. English intercourse with Siam in the 17th century. p. 8vo. *Paul.*   15s.

McNair, F. Perak and the Malays. 8vo. *Tinsley.* illus.   21s.

Bird, Isabella L. The golden Chersonese. p. 8vo. *Murray.* illus.   14s.

MALDIVE ISLANDS, *see* INDIAN ARCHIPELAGO III.

MALTA, *see* MEDITERRANEAN.

  ,,   KNIGHTS OF, *see* CHURCH HISTORY III.

MAN, ISLE OF :

—I. GEOGRAPHY, ETC. :

Jenkinson. Practical guide to the Isle of Man. f. 8vo. *Stanford.*   5s.
    A smaller guide by the same author, price 2s. 6d., f. 8vo.

Moore, A. W. Surnames and place names of the Isle of Man. d. 8vo. *Stock.*   10s. 6d.

  ,,   Climate of the Isle of Man. r. 8vo. *Brown (Douglas).*   1s.

Train, J. History of the Isle of Man. *Quiggin (Douglas).* 1845.   O.P.
    Deals with ancient laws, customs, superstitions, etc.

Cumming, J. G. History of Isle of Man (geological). *Van Voorst.* 1848.   O.P.

Statutes of Isle of Man, vol. i.

Keble, J. Life of Bishop Wilson. d. 8vo. 2 vols. *Parker.*   21s.

Harrison, W. Bibliotheca Monensis. *Manx Society (Douglas).*
    Bibliography.
    The Manx Society has issued 31 vols., chiefly reprints of older books relating to the history and antiquities of the Isle of Man. Statistical accounts are published by the Insular Government Office.

—II. LANGUAGE :

Kelly, J. Manx grammar. *Manx Soc.*   10s. 6d.

Cregeen, A. Manx dictionary. *Douglas.* 1835.   O.P.

Kelly and others. Manx-English and English-Manx dictionary. *Manx Soc.*

Manx versions of the Bible. *Brit. and For. Bib. Soc.* 1819. O.P.

Manx version of the book of Common Prayer. *S. P. C. K.* 1s. 6d.

Phillips. Manx version of the book of Common Prayer. Ed. A. W. Moore. *Clar. Press.* in prep.

With introduction on Manx phonetics by John Rhys; the oldest text in the Manx Language.

MANCHURIA, *see* RUSSIA IN ASIA III.

MANURES, *see* AGRICULTURE III.

MAPS, *see* ATLASES.

MARINE ENGINES, *see* STEAM ENGINE.

MARINE INSURANCE, *see* ASSURANCE.

MARITIME LAW, *see* ENGLAND, LAW VIII.

MASONRY, *see* BUILDING.

MATERIALISM, HISTORY OF, *see* PHILOSOPHY II.

MATHEMATICS:

—I. PURE:

See also ALGEBRA, ARITHMETIC, GEOMETRY, *and* TRIGONOMETRY.

Whitworth, W. H. Choice and chance. p. 8vo. *Bell.* 6s.

Todhunter, I. History of the theory of probability. 8vo. *Macmillan.* 14s.

Bertrand, I. Calcul de probabilité. 8vo. *(Paris).* 10s.

Smith, C. Conic sections (elem. analytical). c. 8vo. *Macmillan.* 7s. 6d.

Salmon, G. Conic sections (analytical). 8vo. *Longmans.* 12s.

,, Higher plane curves (analytical). 8vo. *Longmans.* 12s.

Smith, C. Solid geometry (elem. analytical). c. 8vo. *Macmillan.* 9s. 6d.

Frost, P. Solid geometry (analytical). 8vo. *Macmillan.* 16s.

Salmon, G. Geometry of three dimensions (analytical). 8vo. *Simpkin.* 12s

Burnside and Panton. Theory of equations. 8vo. *Longmans.* 12s. 6d.

Todhunter, I. Treatise on the differential calculus. c. 8vo. *Macmillan.* 10s. 6d.

Williamson, B. Elements of differential calculus. c. 8vo. *Longmans.* 10s. 6d.

Todhunter, I. Treatise on the integral calculus and its applications. c. 8vo. *Macmillan.* 10s. 6d.

Williamson, B. Integral calculus. p. 8vo. *Longmans.* 10s. 6d.

Contains Prof. Crofton's valuable essay on Local Probability.

Greenhill, A. G. Differential and integral calculus. c. 8vo. *Macmillan.* 7s. 6d.

Contains those parts of the subject which are of importance to students of physics and engineering.

Carll, L. B. Treatise on calculus of variations. 8vo. *Macmillan.* 21s.

Forsyth, A. Treatise on differential equations. d. 8vo. 14s.

Riemann, B. Partielle Differentialgleichungen. 8vo. 8s.

Contains an extremely good account of the differential equations which are of most importance in physics, with their applications.

Lie, Sophus. Transformationsgruppen. 8vo. 2 vols. *Teubner.*   34*s.*

Vol. i., 18*s.*; ii., 16*s.* Contains the theory of the transformation of differential equations.

Boole, G. Calculus of finite differences. c. 8vo. *Macmillan.*   10*s.* 6*d.*

Ferrers, N. Elementary treatise on spherical harmonics. c. 8vo. *Macmillan.*   7*s.* 6*d.*

Todhunter, I. Elementary treatise on Laplace's, Lamé's, and Bessel's functions. c. 8vo. *Macmillan.*   10*s.* 6*d.*

Heine, E. Kügelfunctionen. 8vo. 2 vols. *Reimer.*   14*s.*

The most complete treatise on the subject.

Salmon, G. Modern higher algebra. 8vo. *Hodges.*   10*s.* 6*d.*

Serret. Cours d'algèbre supérieure. 8vo. 2 vols. *Gautier-Villars.*   20*s.*

Jordan, C. Traité des substitutions. 4to. *Gautier-Villars.*   O.P.

Legendre. Théories des nombres. 4to. 2 vols.   O.P.

Dirichlet, P. G. L. Vorlesungen über Zahlen-Theorie. 8vo.   13*s.* 6*d.*

Tchebicheff, P. Theorie der Congruenzen. 8vo. (*Berlin*).   7*s.*

Kelland and Tait. Introduction to quaternions. c. 8vo. *Macmillan.*   7*s.* 6*d.*

Tait, P. Treatise on quaternions. d. 8vo. *Cambridge Press.*   18*s.*

Grassmann. Ausdehnungslehre. 8vo. *Wigand.*   6*s.*

Brist and Bouquet. Théorie des fonctions elliptiques. 4to. *Gautier-Villars.*   24*s.*

Contains an account of the French theory.

Durege. Elemente der Theorie der Functionen. 8vo. *Teubner.*   O.P.

Contains an account of the German theory.

Thomae, I. Abriss einer Theorie der Functionen. 8vo.   5*s.* 6*d.*

Contains much matter not included in the two former books.

Durege. Theorie der elliptischen Functionen. 8vo. *Teubner.*   9*s.*

Cayley, A. Elementary treatise on elliptic functions. *Bell.* New ed. in prep.

Halphen, G. H. Fonctions elliptiques. 8vo. 2 vols. (*Paris*).   35*s.*

Vol. i., 15*s.*; vol. ii., 20*s.* Contains an account of Weierstrass' methods, and applications to mixed mathematics. Only part is yet published.

Carr, G. S. Synopsis of elementary results in pure mathematics. r. 8vo. *Hodgson.*   4*s.*

A large volume of more than 900 pp.; suitable for reference or revision of bookwork; contains an index to papers on pure mathematics in many British and foreign journals, etc.

—II. APPLIED :

See also ASTRONOMY, ELECTRICITY, PHYSICS.

Greaves, J. Statics for beginners. gl. 8vo. *Macmillan.*   3*s.* 6*d.*

Minchin, G. Statics. 8vo. *Longmans.* pub. 10*s.* 6*d.*   O.P.

Loney, S. L. Elementary dynamics. c. 8vo. *Cambridge Press.*   7*s.* 6*d.*

Williamson and Tarleton. Dynamics. c. 8vo. *Longmans.*   10*s.* 6*d.*

Routh, E. Dynamics of a system of rigid bodies. 8vo. 2 vols., 14*s.* each. *Macmillan.*   28*s.*

Newton, Sir I. Principia. Ed. Thomson and Blackburn. 4to. *Macmillan.*   31*s.* 6*d.*

Besant, W. H. Hydromechanics. f. 8vo. *Bell.* illus.

Part i., "Hydrostatics," 5*s.*

Lamb, H. Motion of fluids. d. 8vo. *Cambridge Press.*   12*s.*

Basset, A. B. Hydrodynamics. d. 8vo. 2 vols. *Bell.*   23s.
Vol. i., 10s. 6d.; vol. ii., 12s. 6d.

Cotterill, J. H. Applied mechanics. m. 8vo. *Macmillan.*   18s

MAURITIUS, *see* INDIAN OCEAN II.

MECHANICS, *see* PHYSICS *and* MATHEMATICS II.

MEDICINE:

> NOTE.—Text-books, as well as special treatises on medicine and surgery, have been purposely omitted, as being useless and even mischievous, until the student has first become acquainted with the groundwork on which they are based, viz.:—anatomy, physiology, chemistry, etc. Some popular works will be found under the heads—ALCOHOLISM, AMBULANCE, ANTISEPTICS, DOMESTIC ECONOMY, HEALTH RESORTS, HOSPITALS, HYGIENE, MENTAL PHYSIOLOGY, NURSING, and VACCINATION.

—I. HISTORY AND BIOGRAPHY:

The healing art ; a sketch of medicine from the earliest times. 8vo. 2 vols. *Ward and Downey.*   25s.

South, J. F. Memorials of the craft of surgery in England. Ed. D'Arcy Power. 8vo. *Cassell.* illus.   21s.

Russell, J. R. History and heroes of the art of medicine. 8vo. *Murray.* pub. 14s.   O.P

Harvey, W. Works. *Sydenham Soc.* 1846-7.   O.P.

Willis, R. Harvey, and his discovery. 12mo. (*Philadelphia*).   4s.

Gross, S. D. John Hunter and his pupils.   6s.

Baron, J. Life and correspondence of Jenner. 2 vols. 1838.   O.P.

Pasteur, his life and labours. By his son-in-law. Tr. Lady Claud Hamilton. c. 8vo. *Longmans.*   7s. 6d.

—II. MEDICAL JURISPRUDENCE:

Guy and Ferrier. Principles of forensic medicine. c. 8vo. *Renshaw.*   12s. 6d.

Taylor, A. Manual of medical jurisprudence. Ed. T. Stevenson. c. 8vo. *Churchill.* illus.   14s.

  ,, On poisons, in relation to medical jurisprudence and medicine. c. 8vo. *Churchill.* illus.   16s.

MEDICINE, VETERINARY, *see* VETERINARY SCIENCE.

MEDITERRANEAN:

Murray's Handbook to the Mediterranean. Ed. R. L. Playfair. p. 8vo. *Murray.*   21s.

Bidwell, C. T. The Balearic Islands. p. 8vo. *Low.* illus.   10s. 6d.

Wood, C. W. Letters from Majorca. 8vo. *Bentley.* illus.   15s.

Tennant, R. Sardinia and its resources. r. 8vo. *Stanford.*   12s. 6d.

Forester, T. Rambles in Corsica and Sardinia. 8vo. *Bohn.* pub. 10s. 6d.   O.P.
With notices of their history, antiquities and condition.

Seddall, H. Malta, past and present. 8vo. *Chapman.*   12s.

Ansted, D. T. Ionian Islands in 1863. 8vo. *Allen.*   16s.

Tozer, H. F. Islands of the Ægean. c. 8vo. *Clar. Press.*   8s. 6d.

Bent, J. T. The Cyclades. c. 8vo. *Longmans.*   12s. 6d.

Spratt, T. A. B. Travels and researches in Crete. 8vo. 2 vols. *Van Voorst.*   40s.

Lang, R. H. Cyprus, history and present resources. *Macmillan.*   O.P.

Mallock, W. H. In an enchanted island. 8vo. *Bentley.*   12s.
A winter's retreat in Cyprus.

MELANESIA, *see* PACIFIC III.

MEMORY, DISEASES OF, *see* MENTAL PHYSIOLOGY I.

MENTAL PHYSIOLOGY AND PSYCHOLOGY:

—I. MENTAL PHYSIOLOGY AND PATHOLOGY:

Carpenter, W. B. Principles of mental physiology. 8vo. *Paul.*   12s.

Wundt, W. Grundzüge der physiologischen Psychologie. 8vo. 2 vols. (*Leipzig*).   18s.
Has been translated into French.

Holland, H. Chapters in mental physiology. 8vo. *Longmans.*   O.P.

Lewes, G. H. Physical basis of mind. 8vo. *Trübner.*   16s.

Ferrier, D. Functions of the brain. d. 8vo. *Smith, Elder.* illus.   18s.

Bastian, H. C. The brain as an organ of mind ("Internat. Scient." ser.). c. 8vo. *Paul.*   5s.

Bain, A. Mind and body ("Internat. Scient." ser.). c. 8vo. *Paul.*   5s.

Ladd, G. T. Elements of physiological psychology. p. 8vo. *Longmans.*   12s.

Maudsley, H. Physiology of mind. c. 8vo. *Macmillan.*   10s. 6d.

  ,, Pathology of mind. 8vo. *Macmillan.*   18s.

Romanes, G. J. Mental evolution in man. d. 8vo. *Paul.*   14s.

Galton, F. Inquiry into human faculty. 8vo. *Macmillan.*   16s.

Ribot, T. Diseases of memory ("Internat. Scient." ser.). c. 8vo. *Paul.*   5s.

  ,, Les maladies de la volonté. p. 8vo. (*Paris*).   2s. 6d.

Down, J. L. Mental affections of childhood and youth. 8vo. *Churchill.*   6s.

Tuke, D. H. Insanity in ancient and modern life. c. 8vo. *Macmillan.* pub. 6s.   O.P.

Mercier, C. Sanity and insanity. c. 8vo. *Scott.*   3s. 6d.

Maudsley, H. Responsibility in mental disease ("Internat. Scient." ser.). c. 8vo. *Paul.*   5s.

Winslow, Forbes. Obscure diseases of the brain and mind. p. 8vo. *Churchill.*   10s. 6d.

Savage, G. H. Insanity and allied neuroses. c. 8vo. *Cassell.*   8s. 6d.

Darwin, C. Expression of the emotions. c. 8vo. *Murray.* illus.   12s.

Lubbock, J. Senses, Instincts, and intelligence of animals ("Internat. Scient." ser.). c. 8vo. *Paul.*   5s.

Romanes, G. J. Animal intelligence ("Internat. Scient." ser.). c. 8vo. *Paul.*   5s.

  ,, Mental evolution in animals. d. 8vo. *Paul.*   12s.

—II. PSYCHOLOGY:

Many of the greater representative works in general philosophy, e.g., those of Locke, Hume, Hartley, and many of the works entered under the heading PHILOSOPHY AND METAPHYSICS are mainly psychological in character. *Mind* and the *American Journal of Psychology* are storehouses of material.

(A) ELEMENTARY.

Sully, J. Outlines of psychology. 8vo. *Longmans.* 12*s*. 6*d*.

,, Handbook of psychology for teachers. p. 8vo. *Longmans.* 6*s*. 6*d*.

Murray, J. Clark. Handbook of psychology. c. 8vo. *Gardner (Paisley).* 7*s*. 6*d*.

Dewey, J. Psychology. 18mo. *Harper.* 6*s*.

Bain, A. Mental and moral science. c. 8vo. *Longmans.* 10*s*. 6*d*.

Lotze, H. Outlines of psychology. Tr. G. T. Ladd. 8vo. *Ginn, Heath.* 4*s*.

Hamilton, W. Lectures on metaphysics. 8vo. 2 vols. *Blackwood.* 21*s*.

(B) ADVANCED.

Mill, Jas. Analysis of the phenomena of the human mind. Ed. J. S. Mill, Grote, and Findlater. 8vo. 2 vols. *Longmans.* 28*s*.

Bain, A. The senses and the intellect. 8vo. *Longmans.* 15*s*.

,, Emotions and the will. 8vo. *Longmans.* 15*s*.

Spencer, H. Principles of psychology. 8vo. 2 vols. *Williams.* 36*s*.

Lewes, G. H. Study of psychology (in "Problems of life and mind"). 8vo. *Trübner.* 7*s*. 6*d*.

Taine, H. On intelligence. Tr. J. D. Haye. 8vo. *L. Reeve.* 18*s*.

Sully, J. Sensation and intuition. 8vo. *Paul.* 10*s*. 6*d*.

,, Illusions ("Internat. Scient." ser.). c. 8vo. *Paul.* 5*s*.

Brodie, B. Psychological inquiries. f. 8vo. 2 ser., 5*s*. each. *Parker.* pub. 10*s*. O.P.

Reid, T. Works. Ed. Sir W. Hamilton. 2 vols. *Longmans.* 30*s*.

METALLURGY:

Percy, J. Metallurgy. 8vo. 4 vols. *Murray.* illus.

The standard work; of great historical value. "Fuel, wood, peat, coal, charcoal, coke, fireclays," 30*s*.; "Lead and part of silver," 30*s*.; "Silver and gold," part i., 30*s*.; "Iron and steel," 30*s*.; "Copper, zinc, and brass," O.P.

Phillips and Bauerman. Elements of metallurgy. sm. 8vo. *Griffin.* illus. 36*s*.

A concise but comprehensive course of metallurgy.

Greenwood, W. H. Manual of metallurgy. p. 8vo. 2 vols. *Collins.* 6*s*. 6*d*.

Roberts-Austen, W. C. Introduction to metallurgy. c. 8vo. *Griffin.* illus. 7*s*. 6*d*.

Bauerman, H. Metallurgy of iron. (elem.). 8vo. *Lockwood.* 4*s*. 6*d*.

For further works on metallurgy of iron and steel, *see* IRON.

Eissler, M. Metallurgy of gold. p. 8vo. *Lockwood.*	9s.
,, Metallurgy of silver. p. 8vo. *Lockwood.* illus.	10s. 6d.
Contains information about the American silver mines.	
Gore, G. Electro-metallurgy. c. 8vo. *Longmans.* illus.	6s.
Mitchell, J. Manual of practical assaying. 8vo. *Longmans.* illus.	31s. 6d.
Beringer, J. J. and C. Text-book of assaying. c. 8vo. *Griffin.* illus.	10s. 6d.
PERIODICAL: *Transactions of the American Institute of Mining Engineers.*	

METAPHYSICS, *see* PHILOSOPHY.

METEORITES, *see* MINERALOGY.

METEOROLOGY:

Bebber, W. J. V. Lehrbuch der Meteorologie. 8vo. *Enke.*	10s.
Scott, R. H. Elementary meteorology (" Internat. Scient." ser.). c. 8vo. *Paul.* illus.	5s

METHODISM, HISTORY OF, *see* CHURCH HISTORY V. (D).

MEXICO:

Conkling, A. R. Guide to Mexico. 12mo. *Appleton.*	10s. 6d.
Including chapter on Guatemala, and Spanish-English vocabulary.	
Cubas, A. G. Cuadro geográphico y estadistico de Mexico.	
Dictionario geográphico y estadistico de la República Mexicana. 5 vols. (*Mexico*).	
Conkling, H. Mexico and the Mexicans. 16mo. (*New York*).	7s. 6d.
Ober, F. A. Travels in Mexico. r. 8vo. *Trübner.* illus.	18s.
Brocklehurst, J. U. Mexico to-day, with account of the pre-historic remains. 8vo. *Murray.*	21s.
Griffin, S. B. Mexico of to-day. 12mo. (*New York*).	7s. 6d.
Charnay, D. Ancient cities of the New World. Tr. r. 8vo. *Chapman.*	31s. 6d.
Travels and explorations in Mexico and Central America, 1857-82.	
Prescott, W. H. History of the conquest of Mexico. p. 8vo. *Routledge.*	10s. 6d.
Bancroft, H. H. A popular history of the Mexican people. 8vo. *Trübner*	15s.
Gooch, F. C. Face to face with the Mexicans. r. 8vo. *Low.*	16s.

MEXICAN WAR (1847-8), *see* UNITED STATES, HISTORY IV.

MICROBES, *see* ANTISEPTICS.

MICROSCOPE:

—I. GENERAL:

Carpenter, W. B. The microscope and its revelations. Ed. Rev. Dr. Dallinger. p. 8vo. *Churchill.*	16s.
Beale, L. How to work with the microscope. d. 8vo. *Harrison.* illus.	21s.
Hogg, J. The microscope; its history, construction, and application p. 8vo. *Routledge.*	7s. 6d.

Davis, G. E. Practical microscopy. 8vo. *Rogue.*   7*s.* 6*d.*

Gosse, P. H. Evenings at the microscope. c. 8vo. *S. P. C. K.*   4*s.*

Colman, W. S. Section cutting and staining. c. 8vo. *H. K. Lewis.*   3*s.*

—II. MEDICAL :

Ranvier, L. Traité technique d'histologie. 8vo. illus.   31*s.* 6*d.*

Lee, A. B. The anatomist's vade mecum. c. 8vo. *Churchill.*   12*s.* 6*d.*
> Most valuable.
> PERIODICAL : *Journal of the Royal Microscopical Society* contains many important reports on the instrument, and its progressive improvement.

MICROSCOPY OF ROCKS, *see* GEOLOGY III.

MIDDLE ENGLISH, *see* ANGLO SAXON.

MILITARY ART, *see* ARMY II.

MILK, *see* DAIRY.

MIND, *see* MENTAL PHYSIOLOGY.

MINERALOGY :

Dana, J. D. System of mineralogy (descriptive). 8vo. *Trübner.*   42*s.*

Phillips, W. Mineralogy. p. 8vo. *Brooke and Miller.* pub. 18*s.*   O.P.
> The two books named above are works for reference.

Miers, H. A. Text-book of mineralogy. *Macmillan.* In press.

Bauerman, A. Systematic mineralogy. c. 8vo. *Longmans.* illus.   6*s.*

  ,, Descriptive mineralogy. c. 8vo. *Longmans.* illus.   6*s.*

Rutley, F. Mineralogy. (elem.). 8vo. *Murray.*   2*s.*

Hatch, F. H. Introduction to the study of petrology: the igneous rocks. 8vo. *Sonnenschein.*   3*s.* 6*d.*

Phillips, J. Treatise on ore deposits. m. 8vo. *Macmillan.* illus.   25*s.*

Brush, J. G. Manual of determinative mineralogy. 8vo. *Wiley (U.S.).*   15*s.*

Des Cloiseaux, A. Manuel de minéralogie. 8vo. *Dunod.*   O.P.
> Vols. i., ii. (I). For reference.

Lapparent, A de. Cours de minéralogie. 8vo. (*Paris*).   12*s.* 6*d.*

Naumann, C. F. Elemente der Mineralogie. Ed. F. Zirkel. 8vo. (*Leipzig*).   14*s.*

Tschermak, G. Lehrbuch der Mineralogie. 8vo. (*Vienna*).   18*s.*

Rammelsberg, C. F. Handbuch der Mineral-Chemie. 8vo. 3 vols. (*Leipzig*).   26*s.*
> Vol. i., 3*s.*; vol. ii., 16*s.*; supplement, 7*s.* For reference.

Groth, P. Tabellarische Uebersicht der einfachen Mineralien. 4to. (*Brunswick*).   7*s.*
> For classification.

Buchner, O. Die Meteoriten in Sammlungen. 8vo. (*Leipzig*).   4*s.* 6*d.*

Flight, W. A chapter in the history of meteorites. 8vo. *Dulau.*   12*s.* 6*d.*

Meunier, S. Météorites. r. 8vo. *Dunod.*   20*s.*

MINING :

Collins, J. H. Principles of mining. f. 8vo. 2 vols. *Collins.*   2*s.*

Callon, J. Lectures on mining. Tr. Foster and Galloway. r. 8vo. 3 vols.
Dulau.   80*s.*
<small>Vol. i., 26*s.*; vol. ii., 36*s.*; vol. iii., 18*s.* Atlas to each vol.</small>

Brough, B. H. Mine surveying. c. 8vo. *Griffin.* illus.   7*s. 6d.*

Hunt, R. British mining. r. 8vo. *Lockwood.*   63*s.*
<small>For history of mining.</small>

Percy, C. M. Mechanical engineering of collieries. 8vo. 2 vols. "*Colliery Guardian*" *Office.* illus.   40*s.*
<small>Vol. i., 15*s.*; vol. ii., 25*s.*</small>

Galloway, R. L. History of coal mining in Great Britain. p. 8vo. *Macmillan.* pub. 7*s. 6d.*   O.P.

Smyth, W. W. Coal and coal mining. 12mo. *Lockwood.*   4*s.*

Lock, C. G. W. Practical gold mining. r. 8vo. *Spon.* illus.   42*s.*

Davies, D. C. Slate and slate quarrying. 8vo. *Lockwood.*   3*s.*

Bowie, A. J. Hydraulic mining in California. r. 8vo. *Spon.*   21*s.*

Sorley, W. R. Mining royalties. d. 8vo. *Frowde.*   1*s. 6d.*

Jevons, W. S. The coal question. 8vo. *Macmillan.* pub. 10*s. 6d.*   O.P.

Merivale, J. H. Notes and formulæ for mining-students. sm. c. 8vo.
Lockwood.   2*s. 6d*

Becker, G. F. Geology of the Comstock lode. (*Washington*).   12*s*
<small>Vol. iii. of monographs of U.S. Geological Survey.</small>

Lord, E. Comstock mining and miners. (*Washington*).   12*s*
<small>Vol. iv. of monographs of U.S. Geological Survey.</small>

Precious metals. (*Washington*).
<small>Report of the tenth census of the U.S. Vol. xiii.</small>

<small>PERIODICALS: *Proceedings* and *Transactions* of the Federated Institute of Mining Engineers. Part i. issued January, 1890. *Proceedings* of the South Wales Institution of Engineers. (Eyre). *Transactions* of the Mining Association of Cornwall. (Redruth).</small>

<small>Reports of H.M. Inspectors of mines and mineral statistics of the United Kingdom are issued by the Home Office. For bibliography see *School of Mines Quarterly*, of Columbia College, New York. Vol. x.; No. 2. January, 1889.</small>

MISSIONS, FOREIGN:

Smith, G. Short history of Christian missions. 8vo. *Clark.*   2*s. 6d.*

Warneck, G. Outline of the history of Protestant missions. Tr. T. Smith.
c. 8vo. *Gemmell.*   3*s. 6d.*

Stowell and Storrow. Missionary work of the Church. c. 8vo. *Snow.*   2*s. 6d.*

Tucker, H. W. The English Church in other lands. f. 8vo. *Longmans.*   2*s. 6d.*

Sherring and Storrow. Protestant missions in India, 1706-1882. c. 8vo.
R. T. S.   6*s.*

Broomhall, B. Evangelisation of the world. r. 8vo. *Morgan and Scott.*
illus.   3*s. 6d.*

Report of the Centenary Conference on Protestant missions, 1888. c. 8vo.
2 vols. *Nisbet.*   6*s.*
<small>Contains a bibliography.</small>

Church Missionary atlas. *C. M. S.* (*Salisbury-square*).
<small>Part i., Africa and Mohammedan lands of the East, 4*s.*; part ii., India, 5*s.*; part iii., Ceylon, China, Japan, and North-West America (in press). Contains copious letterpress.</small>

MOHAMMEDANISM, *see* MAHOMETANISM.

MONASTERIES AND MONASTIC ORDERS, *see* CHURCH HISTORY III.

MONEY, *see* POLITICAL ECONOMY IV.

MONGOLIA, *see* ASIA II.

MONUMENTS, *see* ARCHITECTURE III.

MORAL PHILOSOPHY, *see* ETHICS, MENTAL PHYSIOLOGY II., *and* PHILO-SOPHY.

MOROCCO:

Hooker and Ball. Tour in Morocco and the Great Atlas. *Macmillan.*   21*s.*
  Important from a scientific point of view.

Thomson, J. Travels in the Atlas and S. Morocco; a narrative of exploration. c. 8vo. *Philip.* illus.   9*s.*

Martinière, H. M. P. de la. Morocco: journeys in the kingdom of Fez. c. 8vo. *Whittaker.*   14*s.*
  Contains a bibliography of Morocco from 1844 to 1887, and much general information.

Foucauld, C. de. Reconnaissance au Maroc, 1883–4. 4to. illus.   40*s.*
  Important for the student.

Leared, A. Morocco and the Moors. d. 8vo. *Low.* illus.   16*s.*

Stutfield, H. E. M. El Maghreb: 1,200 miles' ride through Morocco. p. 8vo. *Low.*   8*s.* 6*d.*

Hay, Drummond. Morocco and the Moors: Western Barbary, etc. c. 8vo. *Murray.*   2*s.*

Amicis, E. de. Morocco. 8vo. *Cassell.*   7*s.* 6*d.*
  A series of picturesque sketches.

Playfair, R. L. Bibliography of Morocco. *Royal Geog. Soc.*
  In progress.

MUNICIPAL GOVERNMENT, *see* LOCAL GOVERNMENT.

MUNICIPAL ENGINEERING, *see* HYGIENE.

MUSIC:

—I. HISTORY:

Hawkins, J. History of music. 8vo. 3 vols. *Novello.*   37*s.*
  Vol. i., ii., 21*s.*; vol. iii., 16*s.*

Naumann, E. History of music. Ed. Sir F. Ouseley. 8vo. 2 vols. *Cassell.* illus.   31*s.* 6*d.*

Rockstro, W. S. History of music. 8vo. *Low.*   14*s.*

Hunt, H. G. Bonavia. History of music. (elem.). f. 8vo. *Bell.*   3*s.* 6*d.*

Hullah, J. Transition period (1600–1750). 8vo. *Longmans.*   10*s.* 6*d.*

,, History of modern music. 8vo. *Longmans.*   8*s.* 6*d.*

Chappell, W. Popular music of the olden time. 8vo. 2 vols. *Cramer.*   48*s.*

Musical notation of the Middle Ages. fo. *Masters.*   25*s.*

—II. THEORY AND COMPOSITION:

Cummings, W. H. The rudiments of music. d. 8vo. *Novello.*   1*s*

Banister, H. C. Text-book of music. f. 8vo. *Bell.*	5*s.*
Stainer, J. Primer of harmony. d. 8vo. *Novello.*	2*s.*
Goss, J. Harmony. 4to. *Cramer.*	4*s.*
Macfarren, G. Rudiments of harmony. r. 8vo. *Cramer.*	5*s.*
The last three books make a complete course.	
Richter, E. F. Manual of harmony. Tr. J. P. Morgan. d. 8vo. *W. Reeves.*	7*s.* 6*d.*
Macfarren, G. Six lectures on harmony. 8vo. *Longmans.*	12*s.*
Stainer, J. Theory of harmony. d. 8vo. *Novello.*	7*s.* 6*d.*
Bridge, J. F. Primer of counterpoint. d. 8vo. *Novello.*	2*s.*
,, Double counterpoint and canon. d. 8vo. *Novello.*	2*s.*
Prout, E. Counterpoint. *Augener.*	5*s.*
Higgs, J. Primer of fugue. d. 8vo. *Novello.*	2*s.*
Ouseley, F. A. G. Counterpoint, canon, and fugue. 4to. *Clar. Press.*	16*s.*
Richter, E. F. Canon and fugue. Tr. F. Taylor. 4to. *Cramer.*	5*s.*
Banister, H. C. Lectures on musical analysis. c. 8vo. *Bell.*	7*s.* 6*d.*
Ouseley, F. A. G. Form. sm. 4to. *Clar. Press.*	10*s.*
Stainer, J. Primer of composition. d. 8vo. *Novello.*	2*s.*
Czerny. School of practical composition. Tr. fo. 3 vols., 10*s.* 6*d.* each. *Cocks.*	31*s.* 6*d.*
Prout, E. Primer of instrumentation. d. 8vo. *Novello.*	2*s.*
Berlioz. Instrumentation. Tr. 8vo. *Novello.*	12*s.*
Stone, W. H. Scientific basis of music. d. 8vo. *Novello.*	1*s.*
Taylor, Sedley. Sound and music. ex. c. 8vo. *Macmillan.*	8*s.* 6*d.*

—III. INSTRUMENTAL:

Hiles, J. Catechism of the organ. 4to. *Brewer.*	1*s.*
Hopkins and Rimbault. The organ, its history and construction. 8vo. *Cocks.*	31*s.* 6*d.*
These two books are on organ building.	
Stainer, J. Organ primer. 4to. *Novello.*	2*s.*
Archer, F. Organ tutor. *Novello.*	7*s.* 6*d.*
Best, W. T. Art of organ playing. ob. fo. 2 vols. *Novello.*	10*s.* 6*d.*
Vol. i., 3*s.*; vol. ii., 7*s.* 6*d.*	
Bach. Compositions for the organ. Ed. Griepenkerl and Roitzsch. *Peters.*	
The most accurate and complete edition for advanced students.	
,, Organ works. Ed. J. F. Bridge and J. Higgs. ob. fo. 9 vols. *Novello.*	26*s.* 6*d.*
Vol. i., 2*s.* 6*d.*; vol. ii. to ix., 3*s.* each. In progress. Fingering and pedalling marked with directions for registering. For advanced students.	
Mendelssohn. Organ sonatas. Ed. W. T. Best. ob. fo. *Novello.*	5*s.*
Best, W. T. Arrangements from the scores of the great masters ob. fo. 5 vols. *Novello.*	36*s.*
Also in 100 numbers, 2*s.* each.	
,, "Cecilia." ob. fo. 40 vols., 1*s.* each. *Augener.*	40*s.*
Pauer, E. Pianoforte primer. 4to. *Novello.*	2*s.*
Taylor, Franklin. Pianoforte primer. 18mo. *Macmillan.*	1*s.*
Plaidy, L. Technical studies. 8vo. *Breitkopf and Härtel.*	1*s.*

Bertini. Studies. *Schott.*

Cramer. Sixty studies. Ed. Bülow. 4to.   7s. 6d.

Clementi. Gradus ad Parnassum. fo. *Augener.*   5s.

Mozart's Sonatas. Ed. Agnes Zimmermann. 8vo., 3s. ; fo., 18s. *Novello.*

Beethoven's Sonatas. Ed. A. Zimmermann. 8vo., 5s.; fo., 21s. *Novello.*

    ,,   Sonatas. *Peters.*

Bach's 48 preludes and fugues. Ed. Pauer. 8vo. *Augener.*   4s.

Tours, B. Violin primer. 4to. *Novello.*   2s.

Spohr, L. Violin school. fo. *Cocks.*   21s.

De Swert. Violoncello primer. 4to. *Novello.*   2s.

—IV. VOCAL :

Brown and Behnke. Voice, song, and speech. 8vo. *Low.*   5s.

Mackenzie, M. Hygiene of the vocal organs. c. 8vo. *Macmillan.* illus.   6s.

Garcia, M. Complete school of singing. *Hutchins and Romer.*   15s.

Randegger, A. Singing primer. 4to. *Novello.*   1s.

Concone. Solfeggi. Ed. A. Randegger. 8vo. 4 vols., 1s. 6d. each. *Novello.*   6s.

Wilhem. Manual of singing. Tr. J. Hullah. 8vo. *Longmans.*   5s.

Higgs, J. Two-part solfeggi. 8vo. *Novello.*   1s.

Hiles, J. Catechism of class-singing. 4to. *Brewer.*   1s.

Curwen, J. S. Tonic sol-fa primer. *Novello.*   1s.

Greenwood, J. Lancashire sol-fa primer. d. 8vo. *Novello.*   1s.

—V. CHURCH MUSIC :

Jebb, J. The choral service of the church. 8vo. *Parker.* 1843. pub. 16s.   O.P.

Bridge, J. F. Choral service primer (organ accompaniment). d. 8vo. *Novello.*   2s.

Troutbeck, J. Church choir training. d. 8vo. *Novello.*   1s.

Helmore, T. Primer of plain song. d. 8vo. *Novello.*   2s.

—VI. BIOGRAPHIES, REFERENCE, ETC. :

"**Great** Musicians" series. Ed. F. Hueffer. c. 8vo. 3s. each. *Low.*
    A series of biographies. The best are *Schumann, Mendelssohn,* and *Weber.*

Spitta, P. Life of Bach. Tr. F. Maitland. d. 8vo. 3 vols. *Novello.*   42s.

Rockstro, W. S. Life of Handel. *Macmillan.*   10s. 6d.

Schindler, A. Life and correspondence of Beethoven. Tr. Moscheles. c. 8vo. 2 vols. *Colburn.* 1841. pub. 21s.   O.P.

Rudall. Beethoven ("Great Composers" ser.). c. 8vo. *Low.*   3s.

Jahn, O. Life of Mozart. Tr. P. D. Townsend. d. 8vo. 3 vols. *Novello.*   31s. 6d.

Niecks, F. Chopin as a man and musician. d. 8vo. 2 vols. *Novello.*   25s.

Hiller, E. Letters and recollections of Mendelssohn. Tr. c. 8vo. *Macmillan.* pub. 7s. 6d.   O.P.

Grove, G. Dictionary of music and musicians. 8vo. 4 vols., 21s. each. *Macmillan.*   84s.

Stainer and Barrett. Dictionary of musical terms. 8vo. *Novello.*   **7s. 6d.**
PERIODICALS: *Musical Times.* 3d. monthly. (Novello). *Musical Standard.* Weekly. (Reeves); 9s. per vol.

MYTHOLOGY, CLASSICAL, *see* GREECE, ARCHÆOLOGY.

   ,,   GENERAL, *see* FOLKLORE.

N.

NATAL, *see* CAPE.

NATIONAL GALLERY, *see* LONDON IV.

NATURAL HISTORY, *see* SPORT *and* ZOOLOGY.

It has been found impossible to draw up a list of works under this head, as the lines of demarcation are very vague. Under ZOOLOGY will be found (in addition to scientific treatises) elementary books on animals and their distribution, as well as a short selection of the travels of naturalists. Under SPORT are books dealing with natural history from the sportsman's point of view. The expeditions of naturalists are sometimes valuable as contributions to geographical knowledge: such books are entered under the heads of the countries to which they refer

NAUTICAL TERMS, *see* NAVY II. *and* VI..

NAVY AND SHIPPING:

—I. NAVIGATION:

Lecky, S. T. Wrinkles in practical navigation. 8vo. *Philip.*   **15s.**

Harbord, J. B. Glossary of navigation. 8vo. *Griffin (Portsmouth).*   **7s. 6d.**

Curling, J, J. Coastal navigation. 8vo. *Griffin.*   **2s. 6d.**

Evans, F. J. Elementary manual for deviation of the compass. c. 8vo. *Potter.*   **6s. 6d.**

   ,,   Admiralty manual on the deviation of the compass. c. 8vo. *Potter.*   **4s. 6d.**

Raper. Practice of navigation. 8vo. *Potter.*   **16s.**

Murray, Digby. A-B-C of Sumner's method. 4to. *Potter.*   **5s.**

—II. SEAMANSHIP AND TACTICS:

Nares, G. S. Seamanship. 8vo *Griffin.*   **21s.**

Colomb, P. H. Dangers of the modern rule of the road at sea. 8vo. *Griffin.*   **1s.**

Hoff, W. Modern naval tactics. d. 8vo. *Griffin.* illus.   **10s. 6d.**

Lewal, L. Principes des évolutions navales 8vo. (*Paris*).   **17s.**

Sleeman, C. Torpedoes and torpedo warfare. r. 8vo. *Griffin.*   **25s.**

Noel, G. H. Gun, ram, and torpedo. p. 8vo. *Griffin.*   **8s. 6d.**

Pickard and Fremantle. Nautical terms and phrases; French and English. (elem.). c. 8vo. *Griffin.*   **3s. 6d.**

Smyth, W. H. The sailor's word book. r. 8vo. *Philip.* pub. 7s. 6d.   **O.P.**

—III. NAVAL ARCHITECTURE:

See also YACHTING II.

White, W. H. Manual of naval architecture. 8vo. *Murray.*   24s.

Welch, J. J. Text-book of naval architecture. (elem.). d. 8vo. *Griffin.*   4s.

Sennett, R. Marine steam engine. 8vo. *Longmans.* illus.   21s.
>   For other books on the steam engine, *see* STEAM ENGINE.

—IV. LAW:

Wendt, E. E. Papers on maritime legislation. r. 8vo. *Longmans.*   31s. 6d.

Marsden, N. G. A treatise on the law of collisions at sea. d. 8vo. *Stevens.*   21s.

Arnould, J. Law of marine insurance. Ed. D. Maclachlan. r. 8vo. 2 vols. *Stevens.*   60s.

Carver, J. G. Law of carriage by sea. r. 8vo. *Stevens.*   32s.
>   For further information on insurance, *see* ASSURANCE.

Thring, Lord. Criminal law of the navy. Ed. C. E. Gifford. 12mo. *Stevens.*   12s. 6d.

—V. HISTORY AND BIOGRAPHY:

>   Burchett's *Complete history*, 1720; Entick's *New naval history*, 1757, and Beatson's *Naval and military memoirs of Great Britain*, 1804, are works of reference for naval history.

Yonge, C. D. History of the British navy. 8vo. *Bentley.*   10s. 6d.

Laughton, J. K. Studies in naval history. p. 8vo. *Longmans.*   10s. 6d.

Nicolas, N. H. History of the royal navy (to 1422). 8vo. 2 vols. *Bentley.* 1847. pub. 28s.   O.P.
>   Of great antiquarian interest.

James, W. Naval history of Great Britain. c. 8vo. 6 vols. *Bentley.*   42s.
>   The standard record of naval events, 1793 to 1815.

Roosevelt, T. The naval war of 1812. 8vo. *Putnam.*   12s. 6d.
>   Quite the best history of the American war.

The navy in the civil war. 12mo. 3 vols. *Scribner.*   15s.
>   Vol. i., *The blockade and the cruisers*, by J. R. Soley, 5s.; vol. ii., *The Atlantic coast*, by D. Ammen, 5s.; vol. iii., *The gulf, and inland waters*, by A. T. Mahan, 5s. Best account of the naval part of the civil war.

Norman, C. B. The Corsairs of France. 8vo. *Low.*   18s.

Chevalier, E. Histoire de la marine française pendant la guerre de l'indépendance américaine. 8vo. *Hachette.*   6s. 6d.

Lindsay, W. S. History of merchant shipping. 8vo. 4 vols. *Low.*   50s.

Charnock, J. Biographia navalis. (*London*). 1794.   O.P.
>   The most complete biographical record of the period.

Campbell, J. Naval history of Great Britain (Lives of the admirals). *Stockdale.* 1813.   O.P.

Barrow, J. Naval worthies of Queen Elizabeth. *Murray.* 1845.   O.P.
>   Valuable side-lights on naval origins.

Markham, C. R. Life of Admiral Fairfax. 8vo. *Macmillan.*   12s. 6d.

Dixon, W. Hepworth. Life of Blake. 8vo. *Bickers.*   7s. 6d.
>   More literary than naval.

Penn, G. Memorials of Sir W. Penn. *Duncan.* 1833.   O.P.
>   Valuable as tracing the rise of our naval power.

Markham, J. A naval career during the old war (period 1666–1725).
8vo. *Low.*　　　　　　　　　　　　　　　　　　　　　　　　　14*s.*

Barrow, J. Life of Lord Anson. 8vo. *Murray.* 1839. pub. 14*s.*　　o.p.

Hunt, R. M. Life of Sir Hugh Palliser. 8vo. *Chapman.* 1844.　　16*s.*
　　　Valuable for the great controversy as to Keppell.

Barrow, J. Life of Lord Howe. 8vo. *Murray.* 1838 pub. 12*s.*　　o.p.

Burrows, M. Life of Admiral Lord Hawke. d. 8vo. *Allen.*　　21*s.*
　　　Almost the only modern naval biography of great merit.

Chatterton, Lady. Memorials of Lord Gambier. 8vo. 2 vols. *Hurst.*　28*s.*

Allardyce, A. Memoir of Lord Keith. 8vo. *Blackwood.* illus.　　21*s.*
　　　Valuable to the student of naval strategy.

Tucker, J. S. Memoirs of Earl St. Vincent. 8vo. 2 vols. *Bentley.* 1844.　30*s.*
　　　The best life; parts most interesting and amusing.

Pettigrew, J. J. Memoirs of Lord Nelson. 8vo. 2 vols. *Boone.* 1849.
　　pub. 36*s.*　　　　　　　　　　　　　　　　　　　　　　　o.p.
　　　Remains the most complete life of Nelson. Southey's life cannot be recommended except for
　　　its literary style.

Laughton, J. K. Letters and despatches of Horatio, Viscount Nelson.
8vo. *Longmans.*　　　　　　　　　　　　　　　　　　　　　16*s.*

Dundonald, Earl of. Autobiography of a seaman. c. 8vo. *Bentley.*　6*s.*

—VI. MISCELLANEOUS:

Lewes, V. B. Service chemistry. 8vo. *Whittingham.*　　　　15*s.*
　　　Specially written for sailors.

Brassey, T. The British navy. 8vo. 4 vols. *Longmans.* pub. 21*s.*　o.p.

　　,,　　Naval annual. r. 8vo. *Griffin (Portsmouth).*
　　10*s.* 6*d.* yearly.

Leslie, R. C. Old sea wings, ways, and words. d. 8vo. *Chapman.*　14*s.*

Bedford, F. G. Sailor's pocket-book. 18mo. *Griffin.* illus.　　7*s.* 6*d.*
　　　PERIODICALS: *Nautical magazine* for the merchant service (Potter); *Illustrated
　　　naval and military magazine* for the navy (Allen); *Journal of the Royal U. Ser.
　　　Institution* (Mitchell).

NEEDLEWORK AND DRESSMAKING:

See also COSTUME, HISTORICAL.

　　　Books on dress-making, as a whole, are not to be found, except some special ones on cutting,
　　　issued to their own pupils by inventors of private systems.

Baker, Harriet. Manual of high-school needlework, and cutting out. 12mo.
Griffith.　　　　　　　　　　　　　　　　　　　　　　　　8*s.*
　　　Technical.

Alford, Lady M. Needlework as an art. r. 8vo. *Low.*　　　　42*s.*

Delimont, T. Encyclopædia of needlework. 8vo. *Comptoir Alsacien*
(267, Regent-street).　　　　　　　　　　　　　　　　　　3*s.*
　　　Technical; complete account of all kinds of needlework.

Dolby, A. Church embroidery. 4to. *Chapman.* pub. 12*s.*　　o.p.

　　,,　　Church vestments. 4to. *Chapman.* pub. 21*s.*　　　o.p.
　　　Technical; the only standard books on the subject.

Higgin, L. Handbook of embroidery. 8vo. *Low.*　　　　　5*s.*

　　,,　　Art as applied to dress. sq. 16mo. *Virtue.*　　　　2*s.* 6*d.*

Blanc, C. L'art dans la parure et dans le vêtement. 8vo. (*Paris*). illus.　10*s.*

Palliser, Mrs.　History of lace.　8vo.　*Lon.*　illus.　　21*s.*

The "Queen" lace book.　8vo.　*H. Cox.*　　5*s.*
　　Reprinted from the *Queen*; technical and general.

NETHERLANDS:

For literature, see DUTCH.

—I. GEOGRAPHY:

Murray's Handbook for Holland and Belgium.　p. 8vo.　*Murray.*　　6*s.*

Baedeker's Belgium and Holland.　12mo.　*Dulau.*　　6*s.*

Mahaffy and Rogers.　Sketches from a tour thro' Holland and Germany.
　　ex. c. 8vo.　*Macmillan.*　illus.　　10*s.* 6*d.*
　　Useful as a guide.

Amicis, E. de.　Holland.　Tr. Tilton.　p. 8vo.　*Allen.*　　10*s.* 6*d.*

Havard, H.　Picturesque Holland.　Tr. A. Wood.　d. 8vo.　*Bentley.*　illus.　　16*s.*

　　,,　　Dead cities of the Zuyder Zee.　8vo.　*Bentley.*　illus.　　6*s.*

Blink, N.　Nederland en zyne Bewoners.　8vo.　3 vols.　(*Amsterdam*).　　8*s.* 6*d.*
　　Handbook of geography and ethnology of the Netherlands.

—II. HISTORY:

Kampden, N. G.　Geschichte der Niederlande.　2 vols.　(*Gotha*).　1831.　　15*s.* 6*d.*

Young, A,　Short history of the Netherlands.　d. 8vo.　*Unwin.*　　7*s.* 6*d.*

Ashley, W. J.　James and Philip van Artevelde.　c. 8vo.　*Macmillan.*　　6*s.*

Vanderkindere, L.　Le siècle des Artevelde.　8vo.　(*Brussels*).　　7*s.* 6*d.*
　　Good account of the political and economic conditions of the Netherlands when they were
　　most closely connected with England.

Barante.　Histoire des ducs de Bourgogne.　12mo.　8vo.　(*Brussels*).
　　pub. 23*s.*　　O.P.

Motley, J. L.　Rise of the Dutch republic (to 1584).　d. 8vo.　3 vols.　*Routledge.*　　10*s.* 6*d.*
　　Also 1 vol., 3*s.* 6*d.*

　　,,　　History of the United Netherlands (1584–1609).　c. 8vo.　4 vols.,
　　6*s.* each.　*Murray.*　　24*s.*

　　,,　　Life and death of John of Oldenbarnevelt (1609–23).　2 vols.
　　Murray.　　12*s.*

Pontalis, A. L.　Life of John de Witt (1650–72).　8vo.　2 vols.　*Long-*
　　mans.　pub. 36*s.*　　O.P.
　　Translated from the French.

Wynne, J. A.　Geschiedenis van het Vaderland.　8vo.　(*Gröningen*).　　7*s.*

NEWSPAPERS:

Grant, J.　Newspaper press; its origin, progress, and present position.
2 vols.　*Tinsley.*　　　　　　　　　　　　　　　　O.P.
<small>Interesting, but not always accurate.</small>

Hunt, F. K.　The fourth estate.　2 vols.　*Bogue.*　1850.　　　O.P.
<small>Contributions towards a history of newspapers.　Accurate in its facts.</small>

North, S. N. D.　History and present condition of the newspaper and
periodical press of the United States.　(In " Reports of the tenth
census of the United States, vol. viii., 1884).　*Statistical Bureau*
(*Washington*).
<small>Contains a catalogue of the publications of the census year, 1880.　The best authority on
American newspapers.</small>

Newspaper press directory.　r. 8vo.　*Mitchell.*　　　　　2s.

NEW ZEALAND, *see* AUSTRALASIA IX.

NICARAGUA, *see* AMERICA, CENTRAL.

NIGER, *see* AFRICA III.

NILE, *see* EGYPT I.

NINEVEH, *see* ASSYRIA.

NONCONFORMITY, *see* CHURCH HISTORY V. (D).

NONJURORS, *see* CHURCH HISTORY V. (A).

NORFOLK BROADS, *see* YACHTING III.

NORWAY, GEOGRAPHY, ETC.:

Murray's Handbook for Norway.　p. 8vo.　*Murray.*　　　　9s.

Baedeker's Handbook for Norway and Sweden.　12mo.　*Dulau.*　　9s.

Nielsen, Y.　Handbook.　Tr. from the Norwegian.　12mo.　(*Christiania*).　　10s. 6d.

Du Chaillu, P. B.　Land of the midnight sun.　8vo.　2 vols.　*Murray.*
illus.　　　　　　　　　　　　　　　　　　　　30s.
<small>Journeys through Sweden, Norway, Lapland, and Finland.</small>

Tromholt, S.　Under the rays of the Aurora Borealis.　Ed. C. Siewers.
8vo.　2 vols.　*Low.*　　　　　　　　　　　　　30s.

Laing, S.　Chronicles of the kings of Norway.　8vo.　3 vols.　*Longmans.*
1844.　　　　　　　　　　　　　　　　　　O.P.
<small>A translation of the Heimskringla, with an historical introduction.</small>

NORWAY: LANGUAGE AND LITERATURE:

—I. GRAMMARS AND DICTIONARIES:

<small>The student of Norwegian or Danish (they are essentially the same language), will do
well to begin with Holberg's plays (*see* DENMARK), and then proceed with Asbjörnsen's fairy
tales, Björnson's, Lie's, and Kielland's novels, and Ibsen's prose dramas.　Ibsen's dramatic
poems are more difficult.</small>

Smith and Hornemann.　Norwegian grammar, with a glossary for tourists.
(*Christiania*).　　　　　　　　　　　　　　　2s.

Scharlach.　Concise Norwegian grammar.　12mo.　(*Bergen*).　　2s. 6d.

Geelmuyden and Brynildson. English-Norwegian dictionary. c. 8vo. (*Christiania*).   9*s*.

Rosing, S. Engelsk-Dansk Ordbog. 12mo. (*Copenhagen*).   7*s*. 6*d*.

Larsen, A. Dansk-Norsk-Engelsk Ordbog. 12mo. (*Copenhagen*).   9*s*.

—II. HISTORY AND CRITICISM:

Dietrichsen, L. Omrids af den norske Poesies Historie. 12mo. 2 vols. (*Copenhagen*).   8*s*. 6*d*.

Jæger and Rolfsen. Norske Digtere, en Anthologie. (*Bergen*).

Jæger, H. Norske Forfattere, Literatur billeder. (*Christiania*).

Gosse, E. W. Northern studies ("Camelot" ser.). c. 8vo. *Scott*.   1*s*.
<small>Some account of Norwegian literature before 1814 will also be found in Hansen's *Illustreret dansk Literatur historie*. (*See* DENMARK).</small>

—III. CLASSICS, ETC.:

Welhaven, J. S. Samlede Skrifter. 12mo. 8 vols. (*Copenhagen*).   27*s*. 6*d*.
<small>Lyrical poet and critic.</small>

Wergeland. H. Udvalgte Skrifter. (*Copenhagen*).
<small>The creator of modern Norwegian literature ; poet, dramatist, essayist, etc.</small>

Asbjörnsen and Moe. Norske Folke og Huldre Eventyr. 8vo. (*Copenhagen*).   6*s*.
<small>The Grimm of Norway.</small>

—IV. MODERN NOVELS, DRAMAS, ETC.:

Björnson, B. Fortællinger. 12mo. 2 vols. (*Copenhagen*).   6*s*.
<small>The national poet ; novelist, dramatist, etc.</small>

  ,,   Sigurd Slembe. 12mo. (*Copenhagen*).   5*s*. 6*d*.
<small>His best historical drama.</small>

  ,,   Digte (collection of poems). 12mo. (*Copenhagen*).   4*s*. 6*d*.

  ,,   Paa Guds Veje. 12mo. (*Copenhagen*).   6*s*.
<small>His most important novel of modern life.</small>

Ibsen, H. Peer Gynt. 12mo. (*Copenhagen*).   4*s*. 6*d*.

  ,,   Brand. 12mo. (*Copenhagen*).   4*s*. 6*d*.

  ,,   Et Dukkehjem. 12mo. (*Copenhagen*).   3*s*. 6*d*.

  ,,   Gengangere. 12mo. (*Copenhagen*).   3*s*. 6*d*.

  ,,   Hedda Gabler. 12mo. (*Copenhagen*).   4*s*. 6*d*.
<small>Ibsen is the greatest Norwegian dramatist of the century. *Peer Gynt* and *Brand* are dramatic poems; the next three are prose dramas, of the plays of series generally called his "Social dramas."</small>

  ,,   Hærmændene paa Helgeland. 12mo. (*Copenhagen*).   2*s*. 6*d*.
<small>His greatest historical drama.</small>

Kielland, A. Garman og Worse. 12mo. (*Copenhagen*).   7*s*.

  ,,   Skipper Worse. 12mo. (*Copenhagen*).   6*s*.

  ,,   Sne. 12mo. (*Copenhagen*).   4*s*. 6*d*.
<small>Kielland is a popular, brilliant novelist.</small>

Lie, J. Lodsen og hans Hustru. 12mo. (*Copenhagen*).   5*s*. 6*d*.

  ,,   Kommandörens Döttre. 8vo. (*Copenhagen*).   7*s*.
<small>The Dickens of Norway.</small>

—V. TRANSLATIONS:

Björnson, B. Synnöve Solbakken. Tr. Miss J. Sutter. c. 8vo. *Macmillan*.   6*s*.
<small>His most popular tale of Norwegian peasant life.</small>

Björnson, B. Tales ("Arne," "A happy boy," etc.). Tr. R. Anderson. c. 8vo. 7 vols., 5s. each. *Houghton, Mifflin.*   35s.

,, In God's way. Tr. Miss Carmichael. c. 8vo. *Heinemann.*   3s. 6d.

,, A gauntlet. Tr. H. L. Brækstad. *French.*
A play on modern life.

,, Sigurd Slembe. Tr. W. Morton Payne. c. 8vo. *Houghton, Mifflin.*   7s.
Historical play.

Ibsen, H. Prose dramas. Ed. W. Archer. c. 8vo. 5 vols., 3s. 6d. each. *Scott.*   17s. 6d.

,, Pillars of society, and other dramas ("Camelot" ser.). Tr. W. Archer and Mrs. Aveling. c. 8vo. *Scott.*   1s.

Kielland, A. Skipper Worse. Tr. Earl Ducie. c. 8vo. *Low.*   10s. 6d.

,, Garman and Worse. Tr. Kettlewell. *Paul.*   6s.

Lie, J. The pilot and his wife. Tr. Tottenham. p. 8vo. *Blackwood.* pub. 10s. 6d.   O.P.

,, The Commodore's daughters. Tr. Brækstad and Miss Hughes. *Heinemann.*   3s. 6d.

Asbjörnsen, P. C. Round the Yule-log (folk and fairy tales). Tr. Brækstad. *Low.* illus.   5s.

—VI. BIBLIOGRAPHY, ETC.:

Kraft, J. E. Norsk Forfatter Lexicon (to 1863). 8vo. (*Christiania*).   O.P.

Halvorsen, J. B. Norsk Forfatter Lexicon. r. 8vo. (*Christiania*).
In progress. Nearly half the work has been issued.

Norsk Bogfortegnelse.
From 1814 to date.

NOVELS, ENGLISH:

—I. HISTORY, ETC.:

Dunlop, J. History of fiction. 2 vols., 5s. each. *Bell (Bohn).*   10s.

Masson, D. British novelists and their styles. c. 8vo. *Macmillan.* pub. 7s. 6d.   O.P.

Forsyth, W. Novels and novelists of the 18th century. c. 8vo. *Murray.* pub. 10s. 6d.   O.P.

—II. PRE-VICTORIAN:

Amory, T. Life of John Buncle. p. 8vo. 3 vols. 1825.   O.P.

Austen, Jane. Emma. c. 8vo. *Bentley.*   6s.

,, Mansfield Park. c. 8vo. *Bentley.*   6s.

,, Northanger Abbey, and Persuasion. c. 8vo. *Bentley.*   6s.

,, Pride and prejudice. c. 8vo. *Bentley.*   6s.

,, Sense and sensibility. c. 8vo. *Bentley.*   6s.

,, Lady Susan, and The Watsons. c. 8vo. *Bentley.*   6s.
Also the first five at 2s. each. *Routledge.*

Banim, J. Tales of the O'Hara family. c. 8vo. 3 vols. *Colburn.* 1826.   O.P.

Beckford, W. Vathek. 12mo. *Low.*   2s. 6d.

Behn, Aphra. Oroonoco. c. 8vo. *Thomson.*   1s.

Brooke, H. The fool of quality. c. 8vo. *Macmillan.* pub. 6s. · O.P.

Burney, Frances (Mme. D'Arblay). Evelina. c. 8vo. *Bell (Bohn).* · 3s. 6d.

,, Cecilia. c. 8vo. 2 vols., 3s. 6d. each. *Bell (Bohn).* · 7s.
Also "Evelina." *Cassell.* 2s.

Defoe, D. Adventures of Captain Singleton. c. 8vo. *Bell (Bohn).* · 3s. 6d.

,, Life and adventures of Colonel Jack. c. 8vo. *Bell (Bohn).* · 3s. 6d.

,, Memoirs of a cavalier. c. 8vo. *Bell (Bohn).* · 3s. 6d.

,, Moll Flanders. c. 8vo. *Bell (Bohn).* · 3s. 6d.

Edgeworth, Maria. Absentee. 8vo. *Routledge.* · 2s.

,, Belinda. 12mo. 1803. · O.P.

,, Castle Rackrent. 12mo. 1801. · O.P.

,, Ennui. f. 8vo. *Routledge.* · 1s. 6d.

,, Harrington. f. 8vo. *Routledge.* · 2s.

,, Helen. c. 8vo. *Routledge.* · 2s.

,, Manœuvring. f. 8vo. *Routledge.* · 2s.

,, Patronage. f. 8vo. 2 vols. *Routledge.* · 4s.

,, Vivian. f. 8vo. *Routledge.* · 1s. 6d.

Ferrier, Miss. Destiny. c. 8vo. 2 vols. *Bentley.* · 10s.

,, Inheritance. c. 8vo. 2 vols. *Bentley.* · 10s.

,, Marriage. c. 8vo. 2 vols. *Bentley.* · 10s.
Also 2s. each. *Routledge.*

Fielding, H. Jonathan Wild. 8vo. *Routledge.* · 5s.

,, Joseph Andrews. 8vo. *Routledge.* · 5s.

,, Tom Jones. 8vo. 2 vols., 5s. each. *Routledge.* · 10s.

,, Amelia. 8vo. *Routledge.* · 5s.
Also 3s. 6d., *Bell (Bohn)*; and 2s. each. *Routledge.*

Fielding, Sarah. David Simple. 12mo. 2 vols. 1744. · O.P.

Galt, J. Annals of the parish. f. 8vo. *Blackwood.* · 2s.

Godwin, W. Caleb Williams. c. 8vo. *Bentley.* pub. 3s. 6d. · O.P.

,, St. Leon. c. 8vo. *Bentley.* pub. 3s. 6d. · O.P.

Goldsmith, O. Vicar of Wakefield. r. 8vo. *Nimmo.* col. illus. · 12s. 6d.

,, Vicar of Wakefield. c. 8vo. *Macmillan.* illus. by Hugh Thompson. · 6s.
Also, *Cassells,* 5s. *Bell (Bohn)* (Pocket edition), 3s. 6d. *Routledge,* 1s.

Griffin, G. The Collegians. c. 8vo. *Warne.* · 2s.

Hogg. Confessions of a suicide. f. 8vo. *Nimmo.* · 2s. 6d.

Hook, T. Gilbert Gurney. c. 8vo. *Routledge.* pub. 2s. · O.P.

Hope, T. Anastasius. 12mo. 2 vols., 7s. *Bentley.* · O.P.

Inchbald, Mrs. Simple story. c. 8vo. *Routledge.* · 3s. 6d.

Irving, Washington. Bracebridge Hall. c. 8vo. *Macmillan.* illus. · 6s.

,, Rip Van Winkle. s. 4to. *Blackie.* illus. · 10s. 6d.

,, Tales of the Alhambra. c. 8vo. *Bell (Bohn).* · 3s. 6d.
Also 3s. 6d. *Bell (Bohn)* (Pocket edition); "Rip Van Winkle." 1s. *Routledge.*

Johnstone, C. C. 12mo. 4 vols. 1768. · O.P.

Lee, Sophia and Harriet. Canterbury tales. 12mo. 2 vols. *Bentley.* · O.P.

Lewis, M. G.   The monk.   8vo.   1795.   O.P.

Lockhart, J. G.   Adam Blair.   c. 8vo.   *Blackwood.*   2*s.* 6*d.*

Mackenzie, H.   The man of feeling.   12mo.   *Cassell.*   6*d.*

Marryat, F.   Jacob Faithful.   c. 8vo.   *Routledge.*   3*s.* 6*d.*

  ,,   Japhet in search of a father.   c. 8vo.   *Routledge.*   3*s.* 6*d.*

  ,,   Midshipman Easy.   c. 8vo.   *Routledge.*   3*s.* 6*d.*

  ,,   Peter Simple.   c. 8vo.   *Routledge.*   3*s.* 6*d.*

        Also 2*s.* and 1*s.* each. *Routledge.*

Maturin, R. C.   Melmoth the Wanderer.   4 vols.   1820.   O.P.

Moore, Dr.   Zeluco.   c. 8vo.   1789.   O.P.

Moore, T.   The Epicurean.   c. 8vo.   *Chatto.*   2*s.*

Paltock, R.   Peter Wilkins.   f. 8vo.   2 vols.   *Reeves.*   10*s.* 6*d.*

Peacock, T. L.   Works.   c. 8vo.   3 vols.   *Bentley.*   31*s.* 6*d.*

        This edition includes "Headlong Hall," "Melincourt," "Nightmare Abbey," "Maid

        Marion," " Misfortunes of Elphin," "Crotchet Castle," " Gryll Range."

Radcliffe, Mrs.   Mysteries of Udolpho.   c. 8vo.   *Routledge.*   3*s.* 6*d.*

  ,,   Romance of the forest.   c. 8vo.   *Routledge.*   3*s.* 6*d.*

        Also 2*s.* *Routledge.*

Reeve, Clara.   Old English Baron.   18mo.   *Cassell.*   6*d.*

Richardson, S.   Clarissa Harlowe.   c. 8vo.   *Routledge.*   2*s.*

  ,,   Pamela.   c. 8vo.   *Routledge.*   2*s.*

  ,,   Sir Charles Grandison.   c. 8vo.   *Routledge.*   2*s.*

Scott, W.   Waverley novels.   8vo.   25 vols., 8*s.* 6*d.* each.   *Black.*

   illus.   £10 12*s.* 6*d.*

  ,,   The same.   f. 8vo.   48 vols., 2*s.* 6*d.* each.   *Black.*   illus.   120*s.*

  ,,   The same.   c. 8vo.   25 vols., 3*s.* 6*d.* each.   *Black.*   illus.   84*s.*

        Also 2*s.*, 1*s.* 6*d.*, and 1*s.* per vol. (Pocket edition). *Black*; and 1*s.* per vol. *Bradbury.*

Smith, Charlotte.   Old Manor House.   12mo.   1793.   O.P.

Smith, Horace.   Brambletye House.   c. 8vo.   *Ward.*   pub. 2*s.*   O.P.

Smollett, T.   Humphrey Clinker.   8vo.   *Routledge.*   5*s.*

  ,,   Peregrine Pickle.   8vo.   2 vols., 5*s.* each.   *Routledge.*   10*s.*

  ,,   Roderick Random.   8vo.   *Routledge.*   5*s.*

        Also c. 8vo. 2*s.* each. *Routledge.*

Sterne, L.   Sentimental journey.   18mo.   *Routledge.*   1*s.*

  ,,   Tristram Shandy.   c. 8vo.   *Routledge.*   1*s.*

Walpole, H.   The Castle of Otranto.   18mo.   *Cassell.*   6*d.*

Wilson, J. (Chr. North).   Lights and shadows of Scottish life.   c. 8vo.

   Blackwood.   4*s.*

  ,,   Trials of Margaret Lyndsay.   c. 8vo.   *Cassell.*   2*s.*

—III. VICTORIAN:

       The price of novels varies from 1*s.* to 31*s.* 6*d.*, according to the edition, and different
editions of popular works are constantly being issued. Therefore no attempt has been made
to specify the cost of books in this list. In almost every case, reference to the catalogues of
the larger librarians, such as Messrs. Mudie, or W. H. Smith (London), or Messrs. Douglas
and Foulis (Edinburgh), will give all the information that can be desired.

Abdy-Williams, E. M.—The World Below.

Ainsworth, Harrison.—Old St. Paul's.   Tower of London.

Aldrich, T. B.—Marjorie Daw.

Alexander, Mrs.—The Freres.

Allen, Grant.—In All Shades. The Devil's Die.

Anonymous.—The Dalys of Sodden Fen. Democracy. Atelier du Lys. Mademoiselle Mori. An Australian Girl.

Anstey, F.—Vice Versâ. The Giant's Robe. A Fallen Idol.

Banks, Mrs. G. L.—God's Providence House.

Baring-Gould, S.—Mehalah. Court Royal.

Beaconsfield, Lord.—Coningsby. Contarini Fleming. Henrietta Temple. Lothair. Sybil. Endymion.

Bede, Cuthbert.—Adventures of Mr. Verdant Green.

Besant, Walter.—All Sorts and Conditions of Men. Children of Gibeon. Herr Paulus. Dorothy Forster. Armorel of Lyonesse.

Besant and Rice.—Chaplain of the Fleet. Golden Butterfly. Monks of Thelema. Ready-money Mortiboy.

Betham-Edwards, M.—Felicia.

Black, William.—A Princess of Thule. Strange Adventures of a Phaeton. A Daughter of Heth. New Prince Fortunatus.

Blackmore, R. D.—Lorna Doone. The Maid of Sker. Cradock Nowell. Cristowell. Kit or Kitty.

Borrow, G.—Lavengro, the Scholar, the Gipsy, the Priest. The Romany Rye (sequel to above).

Braddon, Miss.—Ishmael. Vixen. Mohawks.

Bret Harte.—The Luck of Roaring Camp. Flip. In the Carquinez Woods. An Heiress of Red Dog. A Ward of the Golden Gate.

Brontë, Anne.—The Tenant of Wildfell Hall.

Brontë, Charlotte.—Jane Eyre. Shirley. Villette. The Professor.

Brontë, Emily.—Wuthering Heights.

Broughton, Rhoda.—Nancy. Dr. Cupid.

Buchanan, Robert.—God and the Man.

Burnett, Mrs. Hodgson.—That Lass o' Lowry's. Through One Administration. Louisiana.

Caine, T. Hall.—The Deemster. The Shadow of a Crime. The Bondman.

Clarke, Marcus.—His Natural Life.

Collins, Wilkie.—Armadale. The Moonstone. The Woman in White. The Frozen Deep.

Craddock, Charles Egbert.—The Prophet of the Great Smoky Mountain. Despot of Broomsedge Cove.

Crawford, F. Marion.—Mr. Isaacs. Zoroaster. Sarracinesca. A Cigarette Maker's Romance.

Cunnyngham, Sir H.—Chronicles of Dustypore. The Cœruleans. Wheat and Tares. The Heriots.

Cushing, Paul.—The Bull i' th' Thorn.

Deland, Margaret.—John Ward, Preacher. Sidney.

Dickens, C.—Barnaby Rudge. Bleak House. Christmas Carol. David Copperfield. Dombey and Son. Edwin Drood. Great Expectations. Little Dorrit. Martin Chuzzlewit. Nicholas Nickleby. Old Curiosity Shop. Oliver Twist. Our Mutual Friend. Pickwick. Tale of Two Cities.

Edwardes, Mrs. A.—Archie Lovell.

Edwards, Amelia B.—Barbara's History. Miss Carew.

Eliot, George.—Adam Bede. Daniel Deronda. Felix Holt. Middlemarch. Mill on the Floss. Romola. Scenes of Clerical Life. Silas Marner.

Fothergill, Jessie.—The First Violin. Probation. Kith and Kin. A March in the Ranks.

Froude, J. A.—Two Chiefs of Dunboy.

Gaskell, Mrs.—Wives and Daughters. North and South. Sylvia's Lovers. Cranford. Mary Barton. Ruth. Lizzie Leigh.

Gerard, D. and E.—Waters of Hercules. Reata. Lady Baby.

Gibbon, Charles.—The Golden Shaft. Robin Gray.

Gift, Theo.—Lil Lorimer. Dishonoured.

Gissing, George.—Demos.

Grant, J.—The Romance of War. Adventures of an Aide-de-Camp.

Gray, Maxwell.—The Silence of Dean Maitland.

Haggard, Rider.—King Solomon's Mines. She. Jess.

Hardy, Thomas.—Far from the Madding Crowd. The Return of the Native. Under the Greenwood Tree. The Trumpet Major.

Hawthorne, Julian.—Dust. Garth.

Hawthorne, Nathaniel.—Scarlet Letter. Transformation. House of the Seven Gables. Blithedale Romance. Mosses from an Old Manse.

Holmes, O. W.—Elsie Venner.

Hopkins, Tighe.—Nugents of Cariconna.

Howells, W. D.—A Foregone Conclusion. A Modern Instance. The Lady of the Aroostook. Silas Lapham.

Ingelow, Jean.—Off the Skelligs. Fated to be Free. Sarah de Beringer.

James, Henry.—The Bostonians. Roderick Hudson. Daisy Miller. Princess Casamassima. The Tragic Muse.

Jefferies, Richard.—After London. Amaryllis at the Fair.

Keary, Annie.—Oldbury. Castle Daly.

Kingsley, Charles.—Hypatia. Westward Ho! Two Years Ago.

Kingsley, Henry.—Geoffrey Hamlyn. Ravenshoe.

Kipling, Rudyard.—Soldiers Three. The Light that Failed.

Lawless, Emily.—Major Lawrence, F.L.S. Hurrish.

Lee, Katharine.—An Imperfect Gentleman.

Le Fanu, J. S.—Uncle Silas. In a Glass Darkly.

Lever, Charles.—Charles O'Malley. Jack Hinton. Tom Burke of "Ours."

Levy, Amy.—Romance of a Shop.

Lover, S.—Handy Andy. Rory O'More.

Lyall, Edna.—In the Golden Days.

Lynn Linton, E.—The Atonement of Leam Dundas.

Lytton, Lord.—Last Days of Pompeii. The Caxtons. My Novel. Night and Morning. A Strange Story.

Maartens, Maarten.—The Sin of Joost Avelingh.

Macdonald, G.—David Elginbrod.

Macquoid, Mrs.—Patty.

Malet, Lucas.—Colonel Enderby's Wife. A Counsel of Perfection.

Mallock, W. H.—The New Republic.

Martineau, Harriet.—The Hour and the Man.

McCarthy, J.—Dear Lady Disdain. Miss Misanthrope.

Meredith, George.—The Ordeal of Richard Feverel. The Egoist. The Shaving of Shagpat. Diana of the Crossways. Evan Harrington.

Mitford, Miss.—Our Village. Belford and Regis. Tales of Our Village.

Morier, J.—Hajji Baba of Ispahan. Hajji Baba in England. Zohrab the Hostage.

Muloch, Miss (Mrs. Craik).—John Halifax, Gentleman. The Head of the Family.

Murray, D. Christie.—Hearts. John Vale's Guardian.

Norris, W. E.—Major and Minor. Thirlby Hall. The Rogue. Marcia.

Oliphant, Laurence.—Masollam. Altiora Peto. Piccadilly.

Oliphant, Mrs.—Chronicles of Carlingford (5 vols.).
       Intended to be read in sequence; but each volume a complete story.
   Carità. A Beleaguered City. Kirsteen.

Parr, Louisa.—Dorothy Fox.

Payn, James.—By Proxy. Lost Sir Massingberd. The Burnt Million.

Peard, F. M.—A Country Cousin.

Phillips, F. C.—As in a Looking-glass.

Praed, Mrs. Campbell.—The Head Station.

Price, E. C.—The Little One.

"Q."—Dead Man's Rock. Troy Town. The Splendid Spur.

Reade, Charles.—The Cloister and the Hearth. Hard cash. Never Too Late to Mend.

Riddell, Mrs. J. H.—George Geith.

Robinson, F. Mabel.—Disenchantment.

Robinson, F. W.—Lazarus in London.

Russell, W. Clarke.—The Wreck of the "Grosvenor." An Ocean Tragedy.

Rutherford, Mark.—The Revolution in Tanner's Lane.

Schreiner, Olive.—The Story of an African Farm.

Sergeant, Adeline.—Little Miss Colwyn.

Sinclair, Catherine.—Modern Society. Modern Accomplishments.

Shorthouse, J. H.—John Inglesant.

Sime, William.—Cradle and Spade.

Smart, Hawley.—Breezie Langton.

Smedley, F. E.—Frank Fairleigh. Harry Coverdale's Courtship. Lewis Arundel.

Stevenson, R. L.—Treasure Island. New Arabian Nights. The Dynamiters. Kidnapped. The Master of Ballantrae.

Stockton, F. R.—Rudder Grange. The Lady or the Tiger?

Stowe, Harriet B.—Uncle Tom's Cabin. Dred.

Sturgis, Julian.—John Maidment.

Surtees, R.—Mr. Sponge's Sporting Tour. Handley Cross. Plain or Ringlets?

Thackeray, Miss.—The Story of Elizabeth. Miss Angel. The Village on the Cliff.

Thackeray, W. M.—Vanity Fair. Pendennis. Barry Lyndon. The Newcomes. Esmond. The Virginians. Adventures of Philip. The Irish Sketch Book. The Great Hoggarty Diamond. Major Gahagan. The Yellowplush Papers. The Fitzboodle Papers. The Book of Snobs. Lovel the Widower. Denis Duval. Christmas Books.

Trollope, A.—Chronicles of Barset. (6 vols.).
    <small>Intended to be read in given sequence; but each volume a complete story.</small>
    The Prime Minister.

Tytler, Sarah.—Citoyenne Jacqueline.

Veley, Margaret.—For Perceval. A Garden of Memories.

Walford, L. B.—The Baby's Grandmother. Mr. Smith, a Part of his Life.

Ward, Mrs. Humphry.—Miss Bretherton. Robert Elsmere.

Warner, C. D.—A Little Journey in the World.

Warren, Samuel.—Diary of a Late Physician. Ten Thousand a Year.

Whyte-Melville, G. J.—The Gladiators. Kate Coventry. Holmby House.

Wood, Mrs. Henry.—East Lynne. The Channings. Within the Maze.

Woolson, C. F.—Anne. Jupiter Lights.

Yonge, C. M.—Heart's Ease. The Heir of Redcliffe.

NUBIA, *see* EGYPT.

NUMISMATICS:

Head, B. V. Guide to the coins of the ancients. *Quaritch.*	5*s.*
,, Historia numorum. r. 8vo. *Clar. Press.* <small>A manual of Greek numismatics.</small>	42*s.*
Gardner, P. Types of Greek coins. imp. 4to. *Cambridge Press.*	31*s.* 6*d.*
Leake. Numismata Hellenica. 4to.	O.P.
Mionnet, T. E. Description des médailles antiques grecques et romaines. 8vo. (*Paris*). 1837.	21*s.*
Mommsen, T. Histoire de la monnaie romaine. Tr. Blacas and De Witte. 4 vols. (*Paris*).	120*s.*
Babelon, E. Monnaies de la République romaine. 8vo. 2 vols., 20*s.* each. (*Paris*).	40*s.*
Cohen, H. Monnaies frappées sous l'Empire romain. 8vo. 7 vols. (*Paris*).	140*s.*
Evans, J. Coins of the ancient Britons. 8vo. *A. R. Smith.* pub. 21*s.* <small>Intended for students. The introduction, however, would interest every intelligent person. Admirable essays dealing with special subjects. Supplement; 8vo.; *Quaritch.* 12*s.*</small>	O.P.
Ruding, R. Annals of the coinage. 4to. 3 vols. *Bohn.* pub. 84*s.*	O.P.

Henfrey, H. W. Guide to English coins. Ed. C. F. Keary. 8vo. *Bell (Bohn).*   6s.
Suitable as a collector's guide.

Kenyon, R. L. Gold coins of England. 8vo. *Quaritch.*   24s.

Hawkins, E. Silver coins of England. r. 8vo. *Quaritch.* illus. pub. 36s.   O.P.

Atkins, J. Coins and tokens of the British Empire. 8vo. *Quaritch.*   24s.

Hawkins, E. Medallic illustrations of British history. 8vo. 2 vols.
Brit. Museum.   84s.

Patrick, R. W. C. Records of the coinage of Scotland. 4to. (*Edinburgh*).   126s.

,, Medals of Scotland. 4to. (*Edinburgh*).   63s.

Crosby, S. S. Early coins of America. 8vo. (*Boston*).   60s.

Madden, F. W. Coins of the Jews. r. 4to. *Trübner.*   40s.

NURSERY RHYMES, *see* CHILDREN'S BOOKS *and* FOLKLORE.

NURSING:

Nightingale, Florence. Notes on nursing for the labouring classes. f. 8vo.
Harrison.   6d.

,, Notes on nursing. d. 8vo. *Harrison.*   2s.

Lückes, Eva. Lectures on general nursing. 8vo. *Paul.*   2s. 6d.

Humphry, L. Manual of nursing, medical and surgical. p. 8vo. *Griffin.*
illus.   5s. 6d.

Wood, Catherine. Handbook for the nursing of sick children. 12mo. *Cassell.*   2s. 6d.

O.

OCEANOGRAPHY, *see* GEOGRAPHY IV.

OILS AND VARNISHES, *see* INDUSTRIES XIII.

OPTICS, *see* PHYSICS VI.

ORCHIDS, *see* BOTANY *and* GARDENING.

ORES, *see* MINERALOGY *and* GEOLOGY VI.

ORNAMENT, *see* ART VIII.

ORNITHOLOGY, *see* ZOOLOGY VI.

OSTEOLOGY, *see* ZOOLOGY VII.

OTTOMAN EMPIRE, *see* TURKEY.

OXEN, *see* LIVE-STOCK.

OXFORD UNIVERSITY, *see* UNIVERSITIES.

P.

PACIFIC OCEAN:

—I. GENERAL:

Reclus, E. Universal geography. Vol. xiv. (Australasia). i. 8vo. *Virtue.* **21s.**

Wallace, A. R. Australasia. *Stanford.* **20s.**

—II. NORTH PACIFIC:

Findlay, A. G. Directory for the navigation of the North Pacific Ocean. r. 8vo. *Laurie.* **28s.**
With descriptions of its coasts, islands, etc., from Panama to Behring strait and Japan its winds, currents, and passages.

Hopkins, Manley. Hawaii, past, present, and future. 8vo. *Longmans.* pub. 10s. 6d. **O.P.**

Gordon-Cumming, Constance F. Fire-fountains: The kingdom of Hawaii. 8vo. 2 vols. *Blackwood.* illus. **25s.**

Honolulu almanac and directory (annual). (*Honolulu*).

Hager, C. Die Marshall-Inseln und die Gilbert-Inseln. 8vo. (*Leipzig*). **2s. 8d.**

—III. SOUTH PACIFIC:

See also AUSTRALASIA.

Findlay, A. G. Directory for the navigation of the South Pacific Ocean. r. 8vo. *Laurie.* **28s.**
With descriptions of its coasts, islands, etc., from the strait of Magalhaens to Panama, and those of New Zealand, Australia, etc.; its winds, currents, and passages.

Burney, J. Chronological history of voyages and discoveries in the South Sea. 4to. 5 vols. *Payne.* 1803–17. illus. pub. 183s. **O.P.**

Wilkes, C. U.S. exploring expedition to Polynesia and the Antarctic Regions (1838–42). 4to. 28 vols. *U.S. Govt.* illus.

Moss, F. J. Through atolls and islands in the great South Sea. c. 8vo. *Low.* illus. **8s. 6d.**

Romilly, H. H. The Western Pacific and New Guinea. c. 8vo. *Murray.* **7s. 6d.**

Cooper, H. Coral lands. 8vo. 2 vols. *Bentley.* **28s.**
Fiji, Samoa, Tonga, Solomon and Society islands.

Guppy, H. B. The Solomon Islands and their natives. r. 8vo. *Sonnenschein.* **10s. 6d.**

Woodford, C. M. A naturalist among the head hunters. c. 8vo. *Philip.* **8s. 6d.**
Account of three visits to the Solomon Islands in 1884, 1887, 1888.

Gordon-Cumming, C. F. A lady's cruise in a French man-of-war. 8vo. 2 vols. *Blackwood.* illus. **12s. 6d.**
The Samoan, Friendly, and Society islands.

Johnston, A. Camping among cannibals. 8vo. *Macmillan.* **4s. 6d.**
Tonga-tabu, Samoa, Fiji, etc.

Turner, G. Samoa, a hundred years ago. p. 8vo. *Macmillan.* **9s.**
With notes on the cults and customs of twenty-three other islands in the Pacific.

Penny, A. Ten years in Melanesia. p. 8vo. *Wells, Gardner.* **5s.**

Ellis, W. Polynesian researches. 8vo. 2 vols. *Bohn.* 1829. pub. 28*s.*   O.P.

Turner, G. Nineteen years in Polynesia; missionary life and travels. 8vo. *Snow.* illus.   12*s.*

Brenchley, J. Cruise of the "Curaçoa" among the South Sea islands. r. 8vo. *Longmans.* illus. pub. 42*s.*   O.P.

Powell, Wilfred. Wanderings in a wild country (New Britain). c. 8vo. *Low.*   5*s.*

Markham, A. H. Cruise of the "Rosario" among the New Hebrides, etc. 8vo. *Low.*   16*s.*

Imhaus. Les nouvelles Hebrides. *Dulau.*

Colonies de l'océan pacifique. 18mo. *Quantin.*   3*s.* 6*d.*
Vol. iv. of "Les colonies françaises." Wallis, Futuna, Kerguelen, New Caledonia, New Hebrides, Tahiti, Leeward Isles.

Ricci, J. H. de. Fiji. p. 8vo. *Stanford.*   9*s.*

Horne, J. A year in Fiji. d. 8vo. *Eyre.*   5*s.*
Inquiry into the botanical, agricultural, and economical resources of the colony.

Gordon-Cumming, C. F. At home in Fiji. c. 8vo. 2 vols. *Blackwood.* illus.   7*s.* 6*d.*

Murray, T. B. Pitcairn: the island, the people, and the pastor. p. 8vo. *S. P. C. K.*   3*s.*

PAINTS, PAINTING, AND PAINTERS, *see* ART.

PALÆONTOLOGY, *see* GEOLOGY IV.

PALESTINE AND SYRIA:

Murray's Guide to the Holy Land. p. 8vo. *Murray.*   20*s.*

Baedeker's Guide to Palestine and Syria. 12mo. *Dulau.*   20*s.*

Map of Western Palestine. In 26 sheets; mile to inch. *Stanford.*   63*s.* to 210*s.*
A reduced reproduction, 12*s.* to 42*s.*

Conder, C. R. Palestine ("World's Great Explorers" ser.). c. 8vo. *Philip.* illus.   4*s.* 6*d.*
Popular summary of exploration, ancient and modern.

Palestine Exploration Fund; 21 years' work in the Holy Land. 8vo. *Bentley.* illus.   3*s.* 6*d.*
A popular summary of the work of the Palestine Exploration Fund.

Stanley, A. P. Sinai and Palestine. 8vo. *Murray.* illus.   12*s.*

Tristram, H. B. Pathways of Palestine. 2 ser., 31*s.* 6*d.* each. *Low.* illus.   63*s.*

Merrill, S. Travels in Moab, Gilead, and Bashan (1875–7). 8vo. *Bentley.*   16*s.*

Robinson and Smith. Biblical researches in Palestine. 8vo. 3 vols. *Murray.*   36*s.*

Hull, E. Survey of Western Palestine. 4to. *Bentley.*   21*s.*

Survey of Western Palestine. Ed. Palmer and Besant. 7 vols. *Trübner.* illus.   £21
Survey of Palestine Exploration Fund; reference book for students.

Wilson and Warren. The recovery of Jerusalem. 8vo. *Bentley.*   21*s.*

Conder, C. R. Heth and Moab; explorations in Syria in 1881 and 1882. 8vo. *Bentley.*   14*s.*
Published for the Palestine Exploration Fund.

Perrot and Chipiez. L'art dans l'antiquité. (Vols. iv., v., 24s. each). (*Paris*).
The only systematic account of pre-Hellenic antiquities in this class. The Greek and Roman monuments are discussed in architectural works (*see* ARCHITECTURE).

PALI:

Müller, E. Pali grammar. c. 8vo. *Trübner*.   7s. 6d.

Childers, R. C. Pali dictionary. 4to. *Trübner*.   63s.

Fausböll, V. The Jataka. 8vo. 5 vols., 28s. each. *Paul*.   140s.
Stories and folklore in Pali.

Davids, T. W. Rhys. Buddhist birth stories (translation of the Jataka). 8vo. *Trübner*.   18s.
In progress.

Oldenberg, H. Vinaya texts. 8vo. 5 vols., 21s. each. *Williams*.   105s.
Rules of the order.

Rhys Davids and Oldenberg. Vinaya texts; translation of vols. i. and ii. of the last. d. 8vo. 3 vols., 10s. 6d. each. *Clar. Press*.   31s. 6d.

Pali text society publications. 30 vols. *Pali Text Soc.* (22, Albemarle-street, W.). 21s. per annum.
The sacred books.

Wijesinha, L. C. The Mahawansa; Text and tr. into both Singalese and English. 8vo. *Govt. Press (Colombo)*.   43s.
History of Buddhism in India and Ceylon; part i., V. Century, A.D.; part ii., XII. Century, A.D.

PAPER, *see* INDUSTRIES XIV.

PARASITES, *see* ZOOLOGY VI. *and* LIVE-STOCK.

PARISH, *see* LOCAL GOVERNMENT.

PARLIAMENT:

See also ENGLAND, HISTORY I. *and* IV.

May, T. E. Treatise on the law, privileges, proceedings, and usages of parliament. 8vo. *Butterworth*.   48s.

Jennings, G. H. Anecdotal history of the British parliament. d. 8vo. "*Law Times*" *Office* (10, Wellington-street).   15s.

Townsend, W. C. History of the House of Commons (1688–1832). 8vo. 2 vols. *Colburn*. pub. 12s.   O.P.

Palgrave, R. F. D. The House of Commons: illustrations of its history and practice. c. 8vo. *Macmillan*.   2s. 6d.

PARSEES, *see* PERSIA III.

PARTNERSHIP, *see* ENGLAND, LAW VIII.

PATAGONIA, *see* AMERICA, SOUTH.

PATENTS, *see* ENGLAND, LAW VI.

PATIENCE, *see* CARDS.

PATTERN, *see* ART VIII.

PAUPERISM, *see* POLITICAL ECONOMY IX.

PEDAGOGY, *see* EDUCATION.

PENINSULAR WAR, *see* ARMY III.

PERIODICAL LITERATURE:

Poole, W. F. Index to periodical literature. 8vo. (*Boston*).   73*s.* 6*d.*

Poole and Fletcher. First supplement (to Poole's "Index"). r. 8vo. (*London*).   36*s.*

Index of Magazine Articles (annual). "*Review of Reviews*" *Office.*   2*s.*
JOURNAL: *Review of Reviews* (monthly 6*d.*), deals with the periodical literature of the month.

PERSIA:

—I. GEOGRAPHY:

Malcolm, J. Sketches of Persia. p. 8vo. *Murray.*   3*s.* 6*d.*

Wills, C. J. Land of the lion and sun. 8vo. *Macmillan.* pub. 14*s.*   O.P.

,, Persia as it is. c. 8vo. *Low.*   8*s.* 6*d.*

Bassett, J. Persia, the land of the Imâms. 8vo. *Blackie.* Map.   7*s.* 6*d.*

Stack, E. Six months in Persia. c. 8vo. 2 vols. *Low.* Maps.   24*s.*

Benjamin, S. G. W. Persia and the Persians. 8vo. *Murray.* illus.   24*s.*

Goldsmid, F. Eastern Persia, 1870-2. 8vo. 2 vols. *Macmillan.* illus. pub. 42*s.*   O.P.

—II. ARCHÆOLOGY:

Perrot and Chipiez. Histoire de l'art dans l'antiquité; vol. v., Perse. (*Paris*).   24*s.*

Flandin and Coste. Voyage en Perse. 8vo. 2 vols.   12*s.* 6*d.*

Dieulafoy, M. L'Acropolis de Susa; part i. 4to. (*Paris*).   20*s.*

,, L'art antique de la Perse. fo. 5 vols. (*Paris*).   149*s.*

—III. HISTORY, ETC.:

Malcolm, J. History of Persia, to 1800. 8vo. *Murray.*   O.P.

Watson, R. G. History of Persia, 1800-58. d. 8vo. *Smith, Elder.* pub. 15*s.*   O.P.

Benjamin, S. G. W. Persia. *Unwin.*   5*s.*

Vaux, W. S. History of Persia to the Arab conquest. f. 8vo. *S. P. C. K.*   21*s.*
Ancient history from the monuments.

Thompson, W. F. Practical philosophy of the Muhammadan people (Oriental Translation Fund). 8vo. *Allen.*   15*s.*
A translation of the Akhlaq i Jalali.

Haug, M. Essays on the Parsees. 8vo. *Trübner.*   16*s.*

Hughes, T. P. Dictionary of Islam. r. 8vo. *Allen.*   42*s.*

—IV. LANGUAGE AND LITERATURE:

Students should begin with Forbes' *Grammar and reading lessons*, and go on with the *Gulistan*, edited by J. T. Platts.

Forbes, D. Persian grammar, reading lessons, and vocabulary. r 8vo. *Allen.* .... 12*s*. 6*d*.

Clarke, H. W. The Persian manual. 18mo. *Allen.* .... 7*s*. 6*d*.

Johnson, F. Persian dictionary. r. 8vo. *Allen.* pub. 80*s*. .... O.P.

Baretto. Persian dictionary. 8vo. 2 vols. *Allen.* .... 12*s*.

Palmer, E. H. Persian dictionary. sq. 16mo. *Longmans.* ...... 10*s*. 6*d*.

Zendavesta. Parts i. and ii. Tr. J. Darmesteter. d. 8vo. 3 parts. *Clar. Press.* .... 33*s*. 6*d*.
<small>Parts i., ii., 10*s*. 6*d*. each; part iii., 12*s*. 6*d*.</small>

Pahlavi texts. (Vols. v., xviii., and xxiv. of "Sacred books of the East"). Tr. E. W. West. d. 8vo. 3 vols. *Clar. Press.* .... 35*s*. 6*d*.
<small>Vol. v., 12*s*. 6*d*.; vol. xviii., 12*s*. 6*d*.; vol. xxiv., 10*s*. 6*d*.</small>

Firdausi. Shahnama; Persian text, with French translation by J. Mohl. fo. 6 vols. (*Paris*). £25
<small>The translation only, *Livre des rois*. 8vo. 7 vols. 52*s*. 6*d*.</small>

  ,,   Heroic tales; re-told by Helen Zimmern. p. 8vo. *Unwin.* .. 5*s*.
<small>Selections from the Shahnama of Firdausi for children.</small>

Khayyam, Omar. Quatrains; Persian text and translation by E. H. Whinfield. p. 8vo. *Trübner.* .... 10*s*. 6*d*.

  ,,   The Rubaiyat; rendered into English verse by E. Fitzgerald. p. 12mo. *Quaritch.* .... 15*s*.

Lankuran. The Vazír; a Persian play, text, with vocabulary and translation by Haggard and Lestrange. p. 8vo. *Trübner.* .... 10*s*. 6*d*.
<small>A good work for colloquial Persian.</small>

Jalálu 'd Din Muhammad i Rumi. Masnavi i Ma'navi. Tr. E. H. Whinfield. p. 8vo. *Trübner.* .... 7*s*. 6*d*.

  ,,   Song of the reed; the first few stories from the Masnavi. Tr. into verse by Prof. Palmer. 8vo. *Trübner.* .... 5*s*.

Sa'di. Bustan of Sa'di. Ed. and tr. H. W. Clarke. 8vo. *Allen.* .. 30*s*.

  ,,   Gulistan, or Rose garden of Sa'di. Ed. and tr. J. T. Platts. 8vo. *Trübner.* .... 10*s*. 6*d*.

  ,,   With Sa'di in the garden (Chap. 3 of Sa'di's Bustan). Tr. into verse by Sir Ed. Arnold. p. 8vo. *Trübner.* .... 7*s*. 6*d*.

Jami. Yusuf wa Zulaikha. Tr. R. T. Griffiths. p. 8vo. *Trübner.* .. 8*s*. 6*d*.

Persian poetry for English readers (Hafiz, etc.). Ed. S. Robinson. (*Glasgow*).
<small>This includes the "Century of Ghazels" from Hafiz's *Diwan*. Privately printed.</small>

Anvari i Soheili (Fables of Pilpay). Tr. A. N. Wollaston. r. 8vo. *Allen.* .. 42*s*.

Arbuthnot. Persian portraits. 8vo. *Quaritch.* .... 5*s*.

Rieu, C. Catalogue of Persian MSS. in British Museum. 4to. 3 vols. *Sold at British Museum.* .... 25*s*.

PERSPECTIVE, *see* ART VII.

PERU:

Markham, C. R. Cuzco and Lima. 8vo. *Chapman.* pub. 14*s*. .... O.P.

Hutchinson, T. J. Two years in Peru; with explorations of antiquities. 8vo. 2 vols. *Low.* illus. .... 28*s*.

Squier, E. G.   Peru : travel and exploration in the land of the Incas.   8vo.
    Macmillan. illus.   pub. 21s.   O.P.

Markham, C. R.   Peru.   12mo.   *Low.*   3s. 6d.

Paz Soldan, M. F.   Diccionario geográphico estadistico del Peru.
    Imprenta del Estado.

Prescott, W. H.   History of the conquest of Peru.   8vo.   *Routledge.*   5s.

PETROGRAPHY, *see* GEOLOGY III.

PETROLEUM ENGINES, *see* STEAM ENGINE.

PHEASANT REARING, *see* SHOOTING.

PHILIPPINE ISLANDS, *see* INDIAN OCEAN VIII.

PHILOLOGY :

See also the different languages.

Bopp, F.   Vergleichende Grammatik des Sanskrit, Zend, Griechischen,
    Lateinischen, Lithauischen, Gothischen und Deutschen.   8vo.   3 vols.
    (*Berlin*).   42s.
      Best translation is in French by Michel Bréal. *Grammaire comparée des langues indo-
      européennes.* 8vo. 5 vols. (*Paris*). 40s.

  ,,   The same. Tr. Eastwick.   8vo.   3 vols.   O.P.

Wright, W.   Lectures on the comparative grammar of the Semitic
    languages.   d. 8vo.   *Cambridge Press.*   14s.

Müller, F. Max.   Lectures on the science of language.   c. 8vo.   2 vols.
    Longmans.   16s.

Sayce, A. H.   Introduction to the science of language.   p. 8vo.   2 vols.   *Paul.*   21s.

Paul, H.   Principles of the history of language.   Tr. Strong.   8vo.
    Sonnenschein.   10s. 6d.

Müller, F.   Grundriss der Sprachwissenschaft.   8vo.   4 vols.   (*Vienna*).   52s.
      A general philological classification of peoples by languages.

Brugmann, G.   Grundriss der vergleichenden Grammatik der Indo-
    Germanischen Sprachen.   8vo.   (*Strassburg*).
      Vol. i., 10s. ; vol ii. (part 1), 12s.

  ,,   The same. Tr. J. Wright.   8vo.   2 vols.   *Nutt.*   34s.

Fick, A.   Wörterbuch der Indo-Germanischen Sprache.   8vo.   4 vols.
    (*Göttingen*).   45s.
      Vol. i., 14s. ; vol. ii., 14s. ; vol. iii., 7s. ; vol. iv., 10s.   New edition in preparation.

Henry, V.   Comparative grammar of Greek and Latin.   Tr.   *Sonnenschein.*   7s. 6d.

Curtius, G.   Principles of Greek etymology.   Tr. Wilkins and England.
    8vo.   2 vols.   *Murray.*   28s.
      PERIODICAL: *Zeitschrift für vergleichende Sprachforschung* ; ed. Kuhn and Schmidt ;
      pub. bi-monthly ; 16s. per annum.

PHILOSOPHY AND METAPHYSICS :

—I. GENERAL TREATISES :

Lotze, H.   Mikrokosmos.   8vo.   2 vols.   *Clark.*   36s.

  ,,   Metaphysic. Tr. B. Bosanquet.   8vo.   *Clar. Press.*   12s. 6d.

  ,,   Outlines of metaphysic. Tr. G. T. Ladd.   8vo.   *Ginn, Heath.*   12s

Ferrier, J. F. Institutes of metaphysics. c. 8vo. *Blackwood.* 10s. 6d.

,, Philosophical remains. c. 8vo. 2 vols. *Blackwood.* 24s.
Great power of clear illustration.

Grote, J. Exploratio philosophica. 8vo. *Bell and Daldy.* 9s.

Hodgson, S. H. Time and space. 8vo. *Longmans.* 16s.

,, Philosophy of reflection. 8vo. 2 vols. *Longmans.* 21s.

Fiske, J. Outlines of cosmic philosophy. 8vo. 2 vols. *Macmillan.* 25s.

Mill. J. S. Examination of Sir W. Hamilton's philosophy. 8vo. *Longmans.* 16s.

Herbert, T. M. Modern realism examined. 8vo. *Macmillan.* 14s.

Essays in philosophical criticism. Ed. Seth and Haldane. 8vo. *Longmans.*
pub. 9s. o.p.

Balfour, A. J. Defence of philosophical doubt. 8vo. *Macmillan.* 12s.

Bowne, B. P. Metaphysic; a study in first principles. 8vo. *Harper.* 12s. 6d.

Spencer, H. First principles. 8vo. *Williams.* 16s.

Green, T. H. Works. Ed. R. L. Nettleship. 8vo. 3 vols. *Longmans.* 21s.
Very condensed. The memoir in vol. iii. contains a general sketch of his philosophy by the editor.

—II. GENERAL HISTORIES:

Schwegler, A. Handbook of the history of philosophy. Tr. J. H. Stirling.
c. 8vo. *Douglas.* 7s.
Best short and cheap history.

Lewes, G. H. History of philosophy. 18mo. 2 vols. *Longmans.* 16s.

Ferrier, J. F. Lectures on the history of Greek philosophy. p. 8vo. 2 vols.
Blackwood. 24s.
Early part, to death of Socrates, the best.

Erdmann, J. E. History of philosophy. Tr. 8vo. 3 vols. *Sonnenschein.* 42s.
Vols. i., ii., 15s. each; vol. iii., 12s.

Zeller, E. Outlines of history of ancient philosophy. Tr. p. 8vo.
Longmans. 9s.

,, Pre-Socratic philosophy. Tr. S. F. Alleyne. 8vo. 2 vols. *Longmans.* 30s.

,, Socrates and the Socratic schools. Tr. O. J. Reichel. p. 8vo.
Longmans. 8s. 6d.

,, Plato. Tr. Alleyne and Goodwin. p. 8vo. *Longmans.* 18s.

,, Stoics, Epicureans, and Sceptics. Tr. O. J. Reichel. p. 8vo. *Longmans.* 14s.

,, Eclecticism. Tr. S. F. Alleyne. p. 8vo. *Longmans.* 10s. 6d.

Bowen, F. E. Modern philosophy. 8vo. *Low.* 14s.

Lange, F. A. History of materialism. Tr. E. C. Thomas. 8vo. 3 vols.
Trübner. 31s. 6d.

Masson, D. Recent British philosophy. c. 8vo. *Macmillan.* 6s.

—III. SPECIAL AUTHORS:

Plato. Dialogues. Tr. B. Jowett. 8vo. 5 vols. *Clar. Press.* 70s.

Grote, G. Plato, and other companions of Socrates. 8vo. 3 vols. *Murray.* 45s.
Index, 2s. 6d.

,, Aristotle. Ed. Bain and Robertson. 8vo. *Murray.* 12s.

Descartes. " Method " and " Meditations." Tr. J. Veitch. p. 8vo.
   Blackwood.   6s. 6d.

Fischer, K. Descartes and his school. Tr. r. 8vo. *Unwin.*   16s.

Spinoza. Works. Tr. R. H. M. Elwes. p. 8vo. 2 vols., 5s. each. *Bell.*   10s.

  ,,   Ethics. Tr. W. H. White. 8vo. 5 parts. *Trübner.*   10s. 6d.

Martineau, J. Spinoza. 12mo. *Macmillan.*   6s.

Pollock, F. Spinoza. 8vo. *Paul.*   16s.

Bacon, F. Works. Ed. Ellis, Spedding, and Heath. 8vo. 7 vols. *Longmans.*   73s. 6d.

Fraser, A. C. Locke. 8vo. *Blackwood.*   3s. 6d.

Locke, J. Works. d. 8vo. 4 vols. *Ward and Lock.*   20s.
     Also *Bell (Bohn)*, 2 vols., 3s. 6d. each.

Berkeley, Bishop. Works. Ed. A. C. Fraser. 8vo. 3 vols. *Clar. Press.*   42s.
     Fraser, A. C. Selections from Berkeley's Works. p. 8vo. *Clar. Press.* 7s. 6d.

Fraser, A. C. Berkeley. p. 8vo. *Blackwood.*   3s. 6d.

Hume, D. Works. Ed. Green and Grose. 8vo. 4 vols. *Longmans.*   56s.

Kant, I. Critique of pure reason. Tr. Max Müller. 8vo. 2 vols. *Macmillan.*   32s.
     Also *Bell (Bohn)*, 5s.

  ,,   Prolegomena and Metaphysics of natural science. Tr. Bax. 8vo. *Bell.*   5s.

Caird, E. Critical philosophy of Kant. 8vo. 2 vols. *Macmillan.* pub. 18s.   o.p.

Watson, J. Selections from Kant. c. 8vo. *Maclehose.*   7s. 6d.

  ,,   Kant and his English critics. 8vo. *Maclehose.*   12s. 6d.

Wallace, W. Kant. c. 8vo. *Blackwood.*   3s. 6d.

Morris, G. S. Kant's Kritik of pure reason. 16mo. *Griggs (Chicago).*   6s.

Fichte, J. G. Popular writings. Tr. W. Smith. 8vo. *Trübner.*   15s.

  ,,   Science of knowledge. Tr. A. E. Kroeger. r. 8vo. *Trübner.*   6s.

Adamson, R. Fichte. f. 8vo. *Blackwood.*   3s. 6d.

Schelling, F. W. J. von. Transcendental idealism. Tr. J. Watson. 16mo.
   Griggs.   6s.

Hegel, G. W. F. Logic. Tr. W. Wallace. 8vo. *Clar. Press.*   14s.

Stirling, J. H. Secret of Hegel. 8vo. 2 vols. *Longmans.*   28s.

Caird, E. Hegel. p. 8vo. *Blackwood.*   3s. 6d.

Schopenhauer, A. The world as will and idea. Tr. Haldane and Kemp.
   8vo. 3 vols. *Trübner.*   32s.

  ,,   Fourfold root and will in nature. p. 8vo. *Bell (Bohn).*   5s.

Hartmann, E. von. Philosophy of the unconscious. Tr. W. C. Coupland.
   c. 8vo. 3 vols. *Trübner.*   31s. 6d.

Collins, F. H. Epitome of Synthetic Philosophy. *Williams.*   15s.
     An account of Spencer's whole works, published with his sanction.

PHŒNICIA :

Perrot and Chipiez. Ancient art in Phœnicia (vol. iii. of " L'art dans
   l'antiquité "). Tr. W. Armstrong. i. 8vo. 2 vols. *Chapman.*   42s.

Renan, E. Mission de Phénicie. 4to. *(Paris).*   o.p.

Ledrain, E. Notice des monuments phéniciens du Louvre. (Louvre
   catalogue). 18mo. *(Paris).*

Mövers, F. C. Die Phönizier. 8vo. *(Berlin).*   70s.

Kenrick, J. Phœnicia. 8vo. *Fellowes.* illus.   16*s.*

Rawlinson, G. History of Phœnicia. 8vo. *Longmans.*   24*s.*

Pietschmann, R. Geschichte der Phönizier (in Oncken's " Allgemeine Geschichte "). 8vo. (*Berlin*).   12*s.*

Meltzer, O. Geschichte der Karthager; vol. i. 8vo. (*Berlin*).   10*s.*

Smith, R. Bosworth. Carthage and the Carthaginians. c. 8vo. *Longmans.*   10*s.* 6*d.*

PHONOGRAPHY, *see* SHORTHAND.

PHOTOGRAPHY :

> COURSE OF READING : Elementary chemistry and light ; Elements of photography, and the treatise on photography ; Chemical effect of the spectrum ; Pictorial photography and naturalistic photography.

Meldola, R. Chemistry of photography. 8vo. *Macmillan.*   6*s.*

Abney, W. de W. Treatise on photography. c. 8vo. *Longmans.*   3*s.* 6*d.*

  ,, Instruction in photography. 8vo. *Piper and Carter.*   3*s.* 6*d.*

Jones, Chapman. Science and practice of photography. c. 8vo. *Iliffe.*   3*s.* 6*d.*

Emerson, P. H. Naturalistic photography. c. 8vo. *Low.*   5*s.*

Burton, W. K. Modern photography. 8vo. *Piper and Carter.*   1*s.*

Robinson, H. P. Pictorial photography. 8vo. *Piper and Carter.*   2*s.* 6*d.*

Abney and Robinson. Silver printing. p. 8vo. *Piper and Carter.*   2*s.* 6*d.*

Eder, J. M. Chemical effect of the spectrum. Tr. W. de W. Abney. p. 8vo. *Harrison.*   2*s.*

Harrison, W. J. History of photography. 8vo. *Trübner.*   7*s.* 6*d.*

Index to standard photographs (annual). *Review of Reviews Office.*   2*s.*

PHYSIOGRAPHY, *see* GEOGRAPHY III.

PHYSICS :

See also ELECTRICITY *and* MATHEMATICS (APPLIED).

—I. GENERAL TREATISES :

Stewart, Balfour. Primer of physics. 18mo. *Macmillan.* illus.   1*s.*

  ,, Lessons in elementary physics. f. 8vo. *Macmillan.* illus.   4*s.* 6*d.*

Daniell, A. Text-book of the principles of physics. m. 8vo. *Macmillan.* illus.   21*s.*

Anthony and Brackett. Text-book of physics. 8vo. *Wiley (N. York).*   21*s.*

Tait, P. G. Recent advances in physical science. c. 8vo. *Macmillan.*   9*s.*

Thomson and Tait. Treatise on natural philosophy (mathematical). d. 8vo. 2 vols. *Cambridge Press.*   34*s.*
> Vol. i., 16*s.*; vol. ii., 18*s.* Vol. ii. deals with elasticity.

—II. PRACTICAL PHYSICS :

Worthington, A. M. Physical laboratory practice ; 1st course. c. 8vo. *Rivingtons.*   4*s.* 6*d.*

Glazebrook and Shaw. Practical physics. c. 8vo. *Longmans.*   6*s.*

Stewart and Gee.   Lessons in elementary. practical physics.   2 vols.
  Macmillan.   illus.   13*s*. 6*d*.
    Vol. i., 6*s*.; vol. ii., 7*s*. 6*d*.

—III. MECHANICS:

Ball, R. S.   Experimental mechanics.   c. 8vo.   *Macmillan.*   illus.   6*s*

Maxwell, J. Clerk.   Matter and motion (mathematical).   f. 8vo.   *S. P. C. K.*   1*s*

Stewart, Balfour.   Conservation of energy (" Inter. Scient." ser.).   c. 8vo.
  Paul.   5*s*.

—IV. PROPERTIES OF MATTER:

Tait, P. G.   Properties of matter.   c. 8vo.   *Black.*   7*s*. 6*d*.

Thomson, J. J.   Application of dynamics to physics and chemistry
  (mathematical).   c. 8vo.   *Macmillan.*   7*s*. 6*d*.

—V. HEAT:

Stewart, Balfour.   An elementary treatise on heat.   ex. f. 8vo.   *Clar. Press.*
  illus.   7*s*. 6*d*.

Garnett, W.   Elementary treatise on heat.   p. 8vo.   *Bell.*   4*s*. 6*d*.

Maxwell, J. Clerk.   Theory of heat.   c. 8vo.   *Longmans.*   3*s*. 6*d*.

Baynes, R.   Thermodynamics (mathematical).   p. 8vo.   *Clar. Press.*   7*s*. 6*d*.

Clausius, R.   Mechanical theory of heat (mathematical).   Tr. W. R.
  Browne.   c. 8vo.   *Macmillan.*   10*s*. 6*d*.

—VI. LIGHT:

Stokes, G. G.   On light.   (elem.).   c. 8vo.   *Macmillan.*   7*s*. 6*d*.

Wright, L.   Light.   c. 8vo.   *Macmillan.*   illus.   7*s*. 6*d*.
    Deals specially with lecture-room experiments.

Heath, R.   Geometrical optics (mathematical).   d. 8vo.   *Cambridge Press.* 12*s*. 6*d*.

Glazebrook, R. T.   Physical optics (mathematical).   f. 8vo.   *Longmans.*
  illus.   6*s*.

Preston, J.   Theory of light.   8vo.   *Macmillan.*   12*s*. 6*d*.

Roscoe and Schuster.   Spectrum analysis.   m. 8vo.   *Macmillan.*   illus.   21*s*.

Schellen, H.   Spectrum analysis.   8vo.   *Longmans.*   illus.   31*s*. 6*d*.

Lockyer, J. N.   Studies in spectrum analysis (" Inter. Scient." ser.).
  c. 8vo.   *Paul.*   illus.   6*s*. 6*d*.
    A popular work.

Watts.   Index of spectra.   *Heywood.*   13*s*. 6*d*.

—VII. SOUND:

Tyndall, J.   Sound.   c. 8vo.   *Longmans.*   illus.   10*s*. 6*d*.

Taylor, Sedley.   Sound and music.   ex. c. 8vo.   *Macmillan.*   8*s*. 6*d*.

Helmholtz, H.   Sensations of tone.   Tr. A. J. Ellis.   r. 8vo.   *Longmans.* 28*s*.

Rayleigh, Lord.   Theory of sound (mathematical).   2 vols., 12*s*. 6*d*. each.
  Macmillan.   25*s*.

—VIII. REFERENCE:

Lupton, S.   Numerical tables and constants in elementary science.
  ex. f. 8vo.   *Macmillan.*   2*s*. 6*d*.

Everett, J. D. Units and physical constants. gl. 8vo. *Macmillan.*	5*s.*
Clarke, F. W. Table of specific gravities. 8vo. *Macmillan.*	12*s. 6d.*
Landolt and Bernstein. Physikalisch-chemische Tabellen. 4to. (*Berlin*).	12*s.*
Poggendorff, J. Geschichte der Physik. 8vo. *Barth.*	17*s.*

PHYSIOLOGY :

See also MENTAL PHYSIOLOGY.

—I. BOOKS FOR BEGINNERS :

Foster, M. Primer of physiology. 18mo. *Macmillan.* illus.	1*s.*
Huxley, T. Lessons in elementary physiology. f. 8vo. *Macmillan.* illus.	4*s. 6d.*
Milne-Edwards, A. Anatomie et physiologie animales. 16mo. *Masson* (*Paris*).	2*s. 6d.*
Yeo, G. F. Manual of physiology. c. 8vo. *Churchill.* illus.	14*s.*
Bernstein. Five senses of man ("Inter. Scient." ser.). c. 8vo. *Paul.* illus.	5*s.*
Conte, J. le. Sight; the principles of monocular and binocular vision. ("Inter. Scient." ser.). c. 8vo. *Paul.* illus.	5*s.*

—II. GENERAL TREATISES :

Quain's anatomy. Ed. Schäfer and Thane. 8vo. 2 vols., 18*s.* each. *Longmans.* illus.	36*s.*
Foster, M. Text-book of physiology. 8vo. 3 vols., 10*s. 6d.* each. *Macmillan.* illus. The best introduction to the subject.	31*s. 6d.*
McKendrick, J. G. Text-book of physiology. d. 8vo. 2 vols. *Maclehose.* illus. Vol. i., general, 16*s.*; vol. ii., special, 24*s.* Copiously illustrated; contains valuable details as to methods of observation and research.	40*s.*
Hermann, L. Lehrbuch der Physiologie. 8vo. (*Berlin*). Contains chapters of a special excellence on the physiology of muscle and nerve, on vision, and on hearing.	14*s.*
„ The elements of human physiology. Tr. by A. Gamgee. d. 8vo. *Smith, Elder.* Translation of the above.	16*s.*
Handbuch der Physiologie. Ed. Hermann. 6 vols. (*Leipzig*). Vol. i. (two parts, 19*s.*) contains *Physiology of muscle*, by Hermann; *Protoplasm*, Engelmann; *Speech*, Grützner; *Motion*, Fick. Vol. ii. (two parts, 16*s. 6d.*), *Nervous system*, by Hermann, Meyer, Eckhard, Exner. Vol. iii. (two parts, 27*s.*), *The senses*, by Fick, Kühne, Hering, Vintschgau, Funke. Vol. iv. (two parts, 21*s.*), *Circulation and respiration*, by Rollett, Aubert, Zuntz, Rosenthal. Vol. v. (two parts, 28*s. 6d.*), *Secretion, digestion, and assimilation*, by Heidenhain, Drechsel, Maly, Wittich, Mayer. Vol. vi. (two parts, 22*s.*), *Nutrition, generation*, by Voet and Hensen.	137*s.*
Landois, L. Text-book of human physiology. Tr. W. Stirling, with additions. m. 8vo. *Griffin.* illus. A useful book of reference.	34*s.*
Smith, R. M. Physiology of the domestic animals. 8vo. (*Philadelphia*).	28*s.*
Memoirs of the physiology of nerve, muscle, and the electrical organ. Ed. J. Burdon Sanderson. m. 8vo. *Clar. Press.* Contains translations of recent researches by Du Bois Reymond, Hermann, Hering, and others.	21*s.*

—III. PHYSIOLOGICAL CHEMISTRY :

Gamgee, A. Physiological chemistry of the human body. m. 8vo.
    Macmillan. Vol. i., 18s.
       First vol. only has appeared : second vol. now in preparation.

Bunge, G. Physiological and pathological chemistry. Tr. L. Woodbridge.
    d. 8vo. *Paul.*   16s.

Hoppe-Seyler. Physiologische Chemie. 8vo. 4 vols. (*Berlin*).   25s.

   ,,   Physiologische Analyse. 8vo. (*Berlin*).   14s.
        The standard works.

Schützenberger. Fermentation ("Inter. Scient." ser.). c. 8vo. *Paul.*
    illus.   5s.

Halliburton. Text-book of chemical physiology and pathology. *Longmans.*   28s.

—IV. PHYSIOLOGICAL PHYSICS :

Draper, J. O. Text-book of medical physics. r. 8vo. *Churchill.* illus.
    pub. 18s.   O.P.

Gariel and Desplats. Eléments de physique médicale. 8vo. (*Paris*). illus.   10s.

Fick, A. Die medicinische Physik. 8vo. *Vieweg.*   8s.
        The best book on the subject.

   ,,   Mechanische Arbeit und Wärme-entwickelung bei der Muskel-
    thätigkeit. 8vo. *Brockhaus.*   5s.

Helmholtz, H. Handbuch der physiologischen Optik. 8vo. 5 parts,
    3s. each. (*Leipzig*).   15s.
        The best book on the subject.

   ,,   The sensations of tone. Tr. A. J. Ellis. r. 8vo. *Longmans.*   28s.
        The best book on the subject.

PICTURES, *see* ART.

PIG, *see* LIVE-STOCK.

PIGEON, *see* LIVE-STOCK.

PIQUET, *see* CARDS.

PISCICULTURE, *see* FISHING.

PITCAIRN'S ISLAND, *see* PACIFIC III.

PLAIN SONG, *see* MUSIC V.

PLATE, RIVER, *see* ARGENTINE REPUBLIC.

PLATE, GOLD AND SILVER, *see* ARTISTIC PROCESSES IV.

POETRY : VICTORIAN :

—I. SERIOUS :

Arnold, M. Works. c. 8vo. 3 vols., 7s. 6d. each. *Macmillan.*   22s. 6d.
       Also in one volume, c. 8vo., 7s. 6d. ; and selections ("Golden Treasury" ser.), 4s. 6d.

Browning, E. B. Works. c. 8vo. 6 vols., 5s. each. *Smith, Elder.*   30s.
       Also selections, 2 vols., 7s. ; and selections (pocket ed.), 1s.

Browning, R. Works. c. 8vo. 17 vols., 5s. each. *Smith, Elder.* 85s.
    Also selections, 2 vols., 7s.; and selections (pocket ed.), 1s.
        Orr, Mrs. Handbook to Robert Browning's works. f. 8vo. *Bell.* 6s.

Clough, A. H. Works. c. 8vo. *Macmillan.* 7s. 6d.

Longfellow, H. W. Works. c. 8vo. 11 vols. *Routledge.* 42s.
    Also pocket edition. 11 vols., 1s. each. (*Hiawatha* in one volume).

Macaulay, T. B. Lays of ancient Rome. p. 8vo. *Longmans.* 10s. 6d.
    Also at 3s. 6d., and cheaper editions.

Morris, W. The earthly Paradise. c. 8vo. 4 vols. *Reeves.* 40s.
    Also 5 vols., 25s.; and in one volume (double columns; small type), 7s. 6d.
  ,,　　"Guinevere," 8s.; "Jason," 8s.; "Niblungs," 6s.; "Odyssey." Tr. 6s. 6d.

Rossetti, D. G. Works. d. 8vo. 2 vols. *Ellis.* 18s.
    Also in one volume. c. 8vo. 6s.

Swinburne, A. C. Works. c. 8vo. 17 vols. *Chatto.*　·　£6 16s
    "Poems and ballads," first series, 9s.; second, 9s.; third, 7s. "Songs before sunrise,"
    10s. 6d.; "Songs of two nations," 6s.; "Songs of the springtime," 6s.; "Studies in
    song," 7s.; "Century of roundels," 8s.; "Mid-summer holiday," 7s.; "Atalanta," 6s.;
    "Chastelard," 7s.; "Bothwell," 12s. 6d.; "Erechtheus," 6s.; "Mary Stuart," 8s.;
    "Tristram," 9s.; "Marino Faliero," 6s.; "Locrine," 6s.
  ,,　　Selections. f. 8vo. 6s.

Tennyson, A. Works. c. 8vo. 8 vols., 5s. each. *Macmillan.* 40s.
    In one vol., 7s. 6d.; Lyrical poems ("Golden Treasury" ser.), 4s. 6d.

Whitman, Walt. Leaves of grass. p. 8vo. 9s
    Also selections (pocket ed.). c. 8vo. 1s.

Stedman, E. C. Victorian poets. p. 8vo. *Chatto.* 9s.

—II. HUMOUR, DIALECT, VERS DE SOCIÉTÉ, ETC.:

Austin, A. Works. c. 8vo. 5 vols., 5s. each. *Macmillan.* 25s.

Barham, R. H. D. Ingoldsby legends. c. 4to. *Bentley.* illus. 21s.
    Also d. 8vo., 10s. 6d.; c. 8vo., 2s. 6d.; and other editions.

Bret Harte. Works. c. 8vo. *Chatto.* 6s.
    Also selections (pocket ed.). *Routledge.* 1s.

Calverley, C. S. Verses and fly-leaves. d. 8vo. *Bell.* 7s. 6d.
    Also "Fly leaves," 3s. 6d.

Courthope, W. J. Paradise of birds. r. 8vo. *Hatchard.* 7s. 6d.

Dobson, A. Old world idylls. f. 8vo. *Paul.* 6s.

  ,,　At the sign of the Lyre. *Paul.* 6s.

Hood, T. Works. c. 8vo. 2 vols., 5s. each. *Ward.* 10s.
    Vol. i., Serious; vol. ii., Humorous.

Lang, A. Ballades in blue china, 5s.; Rhymes à la mode, 5s.; f. 8vo.
    Paul. 10s.

  ,,　Grass of Parnassus. f. 8vo. *Longmans.* 6s.

Leland, C. G. Hans Breitmann's ballads. f. 8vo. *Paul.* 3s. 6d.

Locker, F. London lyrics. f. 8vo. *Paul.* 6s.

Lowell, J. R. Biglow papers. f. 8vo. *Macmillan.* 4s. 6d.

Lyra Elegantiarum. Ed. F. Locker Lampson. c. 8vo. *Ward.* 2s.

Martin and Aytoun. Bon Gaultier ballads. f. 8vo. *Blackwood.* 5s.

Praed, W. M. Works. c. 8vo. 2 vols., 5s. each. *Ward.* 10s.
    Also selections. *Scott.* 1s.

Smith, Brothers. Rejected addresses. f. 8vo. *Chatto.* 5s.
    Also pocket ed. *Routledge.* 1s.

Traill, H. D. Recaptured rhymes. c. 8vo. *Paul.*　　　　5s.

,,　　Saturday songs. 4to. *Allen.*　　　　3s. 6d.

POISONS, *see* CHEMISTRY IV.

POLABISH, *see* SLAVONIC.

POLAND: LANGUAGE:

For beginning Polish the grammar of Vymazal is recommended; there are selections from Polish literature appended. The student might then read some of the minor poems of Mickiewicz. For a scientific study of Polish, the fine grammar of Malecki is invaluable; it is written in Polish.

Malecki, A. Grammatyka Historyczno-Porównawcza Jezyka Polskiego (*Lemberg*).
Historico-comparative grammar.

Vymazal, F. Grammatik der polnischen Sprache. (*Brünn.*)　　3s. 6d.

Chopzko, A. Complete dictionary of English and Polish. 8vo. (*Berlin*).　20s.

Schmidt, J. A. E. Nouveau dictionnaire portatif Français-Polonais et Polonais-Français. 18mo. (*Leipzig*).　　　　3s. 6d.

Mickiewicz. Konrad Wallenrod. Tr. M. A. Biggs. 18mo. *Trübner.*　2s. 6d.

,,　　Master Thaddeus. Tr. M. A. Biggs. f. 8vo. *Trübner.*　　15s.

POLAR REGIONS, *see* ARCTIC REGIONS.

POLITICAL ECONOMY:

It is difficult to recommend any one course of study which would be convenient to all readers. Generally the student of economics may be advised first to acquaint himself with the broad outlines of the theory of the subject; and then to obtain some substantial knowledge of economic history. After having thus made a general survey of the subject, he will probably have discovered in what direction his special tastes attract him to further study. Whatever may be the particular field ultimately selected, whether that of industrial, commercial, monetary, financial, or other questions, it should be studied with thorough knowledge of the history and statistics of the subject, and with a comprehensive view of all considerations, economic or non-economic, which have any practical bearing upon it. The best information on questions of the day will generally be found, not in set treatises, but in papers communicated to societies and reviews, and in the reports of Commissions (sometimes abstracts of these are available), and in the various official publications.

—I. THEORY:

Walker, F. A. First lessons in political economy. c. 8vo. *Macmillan.*　5s.

Marshall, A. Economics of industry. ex. f. 8vo. *Macmillan.*　　2s. 6d.

Sidgwick, H. Principles of political economy. 8vo. *Macmillan.*　16s.

Marshall, A. Principles of economics. 8vo. *Macmillan.*　　12s. 6d.

Wicksteed, P. H. Alphabet of economic science. gl. 8vo. *Macmillan.*　2s. 6d.
Introduces reader to mathematical conception of subject, and should precede the study of Jevons.

Symes, J. E. Short text-book of political economy. c. 8vo. *Rivington.*　2s. 6d.

Jevons, W. S. Theory of political economy. 8vo. *Macmillan.*　10s. 6d.

Andrews, E. B. Institutes of economics. 8vo. (*Boston*).　　7s.
Specially designed for teachers in schools.

Keynes, J. N. Scope and method of political economy. c. 8vo. *Macmillan.*　7s.

—II. HISTORY OF THEORY:

Smith, Adam. Wealth of nations. Ed. J. S. Nicholson. 8vo. *Nelson*.　　4s.
　　Valuable introduction and notes.

　　,,　　The same. Ed. McCulloch. 8vo. *Black*.　　9s.
　　Valuable historical notes.

Cairnes, J. E. Essays in political economy. 8vo. *Macmillan*. pub. 14s.　　O.P.

Bonar, J. Malthus and his work. 8vo. *Macmillan*.　　12s. 6d.

Ricardo, D. Works. Ed. McCulloch. 8vo. *Murray*.　　16s.

　　,,　　Works. Ed. Gonner. c. 8vo. *Bell* (*Bohn*).　　5s.

Mill, J. S. Principles of political economy. c. 8vo. *Longmans*.　　5s.

Leslie, Cliffe. Essays in political economy and moral philosophy. 8vo. *Longmans*.　　10s. 6d.

Toynbee, A. The industrial revolution. 8vo. *Rivingtons*.　　10s. 6d.

—III. ECONOMIC HISTORY:

Cossa, L. Guide to the study of political economy. 8vo. *Macmillan*. pub. 4s. 6d.　　O.P.

Ingram, J. R. History of political economy. p. 8vo. *Black*.　　6s.

Ashley, W. J. English economic history. c. 8vo. *Rivingtons*.　　5s.

Cunningham, W. English industry and commerce. d. 8vo. *Cambridge Press*.　　16s.
　　Larger edition in course of publication.

Levi, L. History of British commerce (1763–1878). 8vo. *Murray*.　　18s.

Giffen, R. Growth of capital. d. 8vo. *Bell*.　　7s. 6d.

—IV. CURRENCY, BANKING, AND TRADE:

Jevons, W. S. Money and the mechanism of exchange (" Internat. Scient." ser.). c. 8vo. *Paul*.　　5s.

　　,,　　Investigations in currency and finance (1568–1882). Ed. H. S. Foxwell. 8vo. *Macmillan*.　　21s.
　　Contains a bibliography extending from 1568 to 1882.

Walker, F. A. Money, trade, and industry. c. 8vo. *Macmillan*.　　7s. 6d.

Nicholson, J. S. Money and monetary problems. c. 8vo. *Blackwood*.　　10s. 6d.

Walker, F. A. Money. 8vo. *Macmillan*.　　16s.

Liverpool, Lord. Coins of the realm. *Effingham Wilson*.　　5s.
　　The report on which the English gold standard was established.

Horton, S. Dana. The silver pound. r. 8vo. *Macmillan*.　　14s.

Bagehot, W. Lombard-street: a description of the money-market. c. 8vo. *Paul*.　　7s. 6d.

Overstone, Lord. Tracts by. r. 8vo. *Longmans*. 1857–9.　　O.P
　　A collection of important and interesting pamphlets and tracts. Only intended for those who make a special study of the subject.

Gilbart. On banking. Ed. A. Michie. p. 8vo. 2 vols., 5s. each. *Bell* (*Bohn*).　　10s.

Rogers, J. E. T. First nine years of the Bank of England. d. 8vo. *Clar. Press*.　　8s. 6d.

Barbour, D. Theory of bi-metallism. 8vo. *Cassell*.　　6s.

Crump, A. Theory of Stock Exchange speculation. r. 8vo. *Longmans*.　　10s. 6d.

Giffen, R. Stock Exchange securities. d. 8vo. *Bell.*   18*s.* 6*d.*

  ,,   Essays in finance. d. 8vo. 2 vols. *Bell.*   24*s.* 6*d.*
     Vol. i., 10*s.* 6*d.*; vol ii., 14*s.*

Foxwell, H. S. Employment and prices (in "Claims of labour"). 12mo. *Edinb. Co-op. Printing Society.*   6*d.*

Goschen, G. J. Theory of foreign exchanges. d. 8vo. *Effingham Wilson.*   6*s.*

Bastable. Theory of international trade. c. 8vo. *Simpkin.*   3*s.* 6*d.*

Tate, W. Modern cambist. 8vo. *Effingham Wilson.*   12*s.*

Fenn. On the funds. Ed. R. L. Nash. d. 8vo. *Effingham Wilson.*   25*s.*
     The last two books are practical treatises.
     JOURNAL: *Journal of the Institute of Bankers*; monthly; (Effingham Wilson).

—V. FREE TRADE AND PROTECTION:

Fawcett, H. Free trade and protection. c. 8vo. *Macmillan.*   3*s.* 6*d.*

List, F. National system of political economy. Tr. Lloyd. 8vo. *Longmans.*   10*s.* 6*d.*

Taussig, F. W. The tariff history of the United States. c. 8vo. *Putnam.*   5*s.*

Sumner, W. G. History of American protection. 12mo. *Putnam.*   4*s.*

Farrer, T. Free trade *versus* fair trade. p. 8vo. *Cassell.*   2*s.* 6*d.*

Rawson, R. Tariffs and trade of the British Empire. 8vo. *Imp. Fed. League.*   2*s.* 6*d.*

Macneill, J. G. S. English interference with Irish industries. p. 8vo. *Cassell.*   1*s.*

—VI. INDUSTRY AND WAGES:

Walker, F. A. The wages question. 8vo. *Macmillan.*   14*s.*

Howell, G. Conflict of capital and labour. c. 8vo. *Macmillan.*   7*s.* 6*d.*

Brentano, L. History of guilds and trades unions. 8vo. *Trübner.*   3*s.* 6*d.*

Plener, E. von. English factory legislation. 12mo. *Chapman.*   3*s.*

"Alfred." History of the factory movement. 8vo. 2 vols. *Simpkin.* pub. 21*s.*   O.P.

Levi, L. Wages and earnings of the working classes. 8vo. *Murray.*   3*s.* 6*d.*

Giffen, R. Progress of the working classes. d. 8vo. *Bell.*   3*d.*
     Also in *Essays on Finance*, vol. ii.

Price, L. L. Industrial peace. m. 8vo. *Macmillan.*   6*s.*
     Preface by Professor Marshall.

Gilman, N. P. Profit sharing. c. 8vo. *Macmillan.*   7*s.* 6*d.*

Adams, H. B. History of co-operation in the U.S. of America. 8vo. *Macmillan.*   15*s.*

Acland and Jones. Working men co-operators. 12mo. *Cassell.*   1*s.*

Holyoake, G. J. History of co-operation. p. 8vo. 2 vols. *Trübner.*   14*s.*
     See also Reports of the Labour Correspondent of the Board of Trade, and other Board of Trade Publications (*Eyre*); Reports of various Labour Bureaux, U.S.A., especially Massachusetts, Washington, and Pennsylvania; Reports of the principal English Trades Unions, *e.g.*, Engineers, Carpenters, Iron-founders, etc.

—VII. LAND AND MINES:

Pollock, F. The land laws ("English Citizen" ser.). p. 8vo. *Macmillan.*   3*s.* 6*d.*

Probyn, J. W. Systems of land tenure (Cobden Club). 8vo. *Cassell.*   3s. 6d.

Walker, F. A. Land and its rent. f. 8vo. *Macmillan.*   3s. 6d.

Nicholson, J. S. Tenant's gain, not landlord's loss. c. 8vo. *Douglas.*   5s.

Town Holdings: digest of evidence (1886–88). d. 8vo. *Cassell.*   1s.

Sargant, C. H. Urban rating. 8vo. *Longmans.*   6s.

Onslow, Lord. Landlords and allotments. c. 8vo. *Longmans.*   2s. 6d.

Sorley, W. R. Mining royalties. 8vo. *Clar. Press.*   1s. 6d.

Jevons, W. S. The Coal question. 8vo. *Macmillan.* pub. 10s. 6d.   O.P.

—VIII. TAXATION AND FINANCE:

McCulloch, J. R. Taxation and funding. 8vo. *Longmans.* pub. 14s.   O.P.

Baxter, R. The taxation of the United Kingdom. 8vo. · *Macmillan.* pub. 4s. 6d.   O.P.

Wright and Hobhouse. Local government and taxation. 8vo. *King.*   5s.

Goschen, G. J. Reports and speeches on local taxation. 8vo. *Macmillan.*   5s.

Dowell, S. History of taxes and taxation. 8vo. 4 vols. *Longmans.*   42s.

Northcote, S. Financial policy. 8vo. *Saunders.* pub. 14s.   O.P.

Financial statements of Chancellors of the Exchequer (especially W. E. Gladstone). 8vo. *Murray.* pub. 12s.   O.P.

Adams, H. C. Public debts. 8vo. *Longmans.*   12s. 6d.

—IX. SOCIALISM AND FUNCTIONS OF THE STATE:

Jevons, W. S. The state in relation to labour (" English Citizen " ser.). c. 8vo. *Macmillan.*   3s. 6d.

Farrer, T. The state in relation to trade ("English Citizen" ser.). c. 8vo. *Macmillan.*   3s. 6d.

Jevons, W. S. Methods of social reform. 8vo. *Macmillan.*   10s. 6d.

Hadley, A. T. Railroad transportation. 12mo. *Putnam.*   7s. 6d.

Spencer, H. The man *versus* the state. 8vo. *Williams.*   2s. 6d.

A plea for liberty, with introduction by Herbert Spencer. 8vo. *Williams.*   10s.

Rae, J. Contemporary socialism. p. 8vo. *Isbister.*   7s. 6d.

Graham, W. Socialism, old and new ("Internat. Scient." ser.). c. 8vo. *Paul.*   5s.
       Principles and history of socialism.

Ely, R. T. French and German socialism. 12mo. *Trübner.*   3s. 6d.

Noyes, J. H. History of American socialism. p. 8vo. *Trübner.*   15s.

Marx, K. Capital. Tr. Mrs. Aveling. 8vo. 2 vols. *Sonnenschein.*   30s.

Lavollée, R. Les classes ouvrières en Europe. 8vo. 2 vols. (*Paris*).   16s.

Ruskin, J. "Unto this last." 12mo. *G. Allen.*   3s.

  ,,   Munera pulveris. 8vo. *G. Allen.*   13s.

  ,,   Time and tide. 8vo. *G. Allen.*   13s.

Carlyle, T. Chartism, and other writings. 8vo. *Chapman.*   6s.

Kingsley, C. Yeast. c. 8vo. *Macmillan.*   3s. 6d.

  ,,   Alton Locke. c. 8vo. *Macmillan.*   3s. 6d.

" Industrial remuneration conference" report. 8vo. *Cassell.*   2s. 6d.

Booth, C. Labour and life of the people. 8vo. *Williams.*   10s. 6d.

Malthus, T. R. Essay on population. 8vo. *Reeves and Turner.*   8s.

Aschrott, S. P. English poor law system. d. 8vo. *Knight.*   10s. 6d.

Le Play. Les ouvriers européens. 8vo. 6 vols., 5s. 6d. each. (*Tours*).   33s.

Sargant, W. L. Life of Robert Owen. p. 8vo. *Smith, Elder.* pub. 10s. 6d.   O.P.

Jones, L. Life of Robert Owen. 8vo. *Sonnenschein.*   6s.

Seeley, R. B. Memoirs of M. T. Sadler. 8vo. 1842.   O.P.

Hodder, E. Lord Shaftesbury. c. 8vo. *Cassell.*   7s. 6d.

—X. REFERENCE:

Macpherson, D. Annals of commerce. 4to. 4 vols. 1805.   O.P.

Eden, F. M. State of the poor. 4to. 3 vols. 1797.   O.P.

Tooke and Newmarch. History of prices. 8vo. 6 vols. *Longmans.* 1838-57. pub. 52s. 6d.   O.P.

Ruding, R. Annals of the coinage. 4to. 3 vols. *Bohn.* 1840. pub. 84s.   O.P.

Rogers, J. E. T. History of agriculture and prices. d. 8vo. 6 vols. *Clar. Press.*   142s.
  Vol. i., ii., 42s.; vol. iii., iv., 50s.; vol. v., vi., 50s.

Roscher. Political economy. Tr. Lalor. 2 vols. (*Chicago*).   35s.
  Valuable for its foot-notes.

McCulloch, J. R. Literature of political economy. 8vo. *Longmans.* 1845. pub. 14s.   O.P.

Dictionnaire de l'économie politique. Ed. Coquelin. r. 8vo. 2 vols. (*Paris*).   40s.
  New edition in preparation under special headings.

Palgrave, I. Dictionary of political economy.

McCulloch, J. R. Commercial dictionary. 8vo. *Longmans.*   63s.

Bithell, R. Counting house dictionary. p. 8vo. *Routledge.*   5s.

BIBLIOGRAPHY: Royal Statistical Society's Library Catalogue, 2 vols. Classified lists of current bibliography will be found in each number of the *Quarterly Journal of Economics.* Bibliography of works on Socialism and Economics; *Fabian Society*; 1d.

JOURNALS: *Quarterly Journal of Economics.* 8vo. 2s. 6d. each. (Macmillan); *Journal of the Royal Statistical Society* (Stanford); *Political Science Quarterly.* (Frowde). d. 8vo. 13s. yearly.

BLUE BOOKS: Very numerous and most important. Read especially those published by the Statistical Department of the Board of Trade, among which are the Reports of the Labour Correspondent of the Board of Trade Journal. The Reports of Commissions are often most instructive.

POLITICAL PHILOSOPHY:

COURSE OF READING: Begin with Spencer's *Study of sociology*, Tylor's *Anthropology*, Raleigh's *Elementary politics*, and Thorold Rogers' *British citizen.* Political philosophy must be studied in connection with constitutional history (*see* especially ENGLAND, HISTORY III.), and POLITICAL ECONOMY (*q. v.*). Special studies of particular constitutions, *e g.,* Bagehot's *English constitution*, and Bryce's *American commonwealth*, may profitably be read before works on government in general. Books which treat of ideal states should be read in connection with the history of the time that gave them birth.

—I. SOCIOLOGY:

Spencer, H. Study of sociology ("Internat. Scient." ser.). c. 8vo. *Paul.*   5s.

,,   Principles of sociology. 8vo. 2 vols. *Williams.*
  Vol. i. (3 parts), 21s.; vol. ii. (part i.), "Ceremonial institutions," 7s.; part ii., "Political institutions," 12s.; part iii., "Ecclesiastical institutions," 5s.

Tylor, E. B.　Anthropology. c. 8vo.　*Macmillan.* illus.　　7s. 6d.

,,　Primitive culture. 8vo. 2 vols.　*Murray.*　　24s.

Maine, H.　Ancient law. 8vo.　*Murray.*　　9s.

,,　Early history of institutions. 8vo.　*Murray.*　　9s.

Bagehot, W.　Physics and politics ("Internat. Scient." ser.). c. 8vo.
Paul.　　5s.

—II. GENERAL POLITICS:

Raleigh, T.　Elementary politics. f. 8vo.　*Frowde.*　　1s. 6d.

Bluntschli, J. K.　Theory of the state. Tr. 8vo.　*Clar. Press.*　　12s. 6d.
For reference.

Aristotle.　Politics. Tr. Jowett. m. 8vo. 2 vols.　*Clar. Press.*　　21s.
The most famous book on political philosophy.

,,　Politics. Tr. Welldon.　*Macmillan.*　　10s. 6d.

Lang, A.　Essays on Aristotle's "Politics."　*Longmans.*　　O.P.

Burke, E.　Select works. Ed. Payne. ex. f. 8vo. 3 vols.　*Clar. Press.*　　14s. 6d.

Freeman, E. A.　Comparative politics (Royal Institution lectures).
8vo.　*Macmillan.*　　14s.

Pollock, F.　History of the science of politics.　*Macmillan.*　　2s. 6d.

Lewis, G. C.　Use and abuse of political terms. Ed. Wilson. c. 8vo.
Thornton (Oxford).　　6s.

Mill, J. S.　Representative government. c. 8vo.　*Longmans.*　　2s.

—III. FUNCTIONS OF GOVERNMENT:

Locke, J.　Civil government. Ed. Morley. c. 8vo.　*Routledge.*　　1s.
Also in Cassell's "National Library," 6d.

Milton, J.　Areopagitica. ex. f. 8vo.　*Clar. Press.*　　3s.
Also in "Arber's Reprints," 1s.

Mill, J. S.　Liberty. c. 8vo.　*Longmans.*　　1s. 4d.

Spencer, H.　The man *versus* the state.　*Williams.*　　2s. 6d.
The two latter books contain a defence of individualism.

Ritchie, D. G.　Principles of state interference. 8vo.　*Sonnenschein.*　　2s. 6d.
Chiefly a criticism of *The man versus the state.*

Stephen, J. F.　Liberty, equality, and fraternity. d. 8vo.　*Smith, Elder.*　　14s.
Criticism of Mill.

—IV. POLITICAL INSTITUTIONS:

Dicey, A. V.　Law of the constitution. 8vo.　*Macmillan.*　　12s. 6d.

Hearn, W. E.　The government of England. 8vo.　*Longmans.*　　16s.

Bagehot, W.　The English constitution. c. 8vo.　*Paul.*　　7s. 6d.

Rogers, J. E. T.　The British citizen (in "People's Library").　*S. P. C. K.*　　1s.

"English Citizen" series by various authors. c. 8vo. 3s. 6d. each.　*Macmillan.*

Central government (*Traill*); Electorate and legislature (*Spencer Walpole*); Poor law
(*Fowle*); Budget, debt, taxes, rates (*Wilson*); The state and labour (*Jevons*); The state and
trade (*Farrer*); The state and church (*Elliott*); Foreign relations (*Spencer Walpole*);
Local government (*Chalmers*); The state and education (*Craik*); Land laws (*Pollock*);
Colonies and dependencies; India (*Cotton*), and Colonies (*Payne*); Justice and police
(*Maitland*); Punishment and prevention of crime (*Du Cane*).

Dilke, C.　Problems of Greater Britain. c. 8vo. 2 vols.　*Macmillan.*　　12s. 6d.

Bryce, J. American commonwealth. ex. c. 8vo. 2 vols. *Macmillan.*   25s.

Adams and Cunningham. The Swiss confederation. 8vo. *Macmillan.*   14s.

Sergeant, L. Government handbook. l. c. 8vo. *Unwin.*   10s. 6d.

For reference on all the existing constitutions of the world.

—V. IDEAL STATES:

Plato. Republic. Tr. Jowett. 8vo. *Clar. Press.*   12s. 6d.

More, T. Utopia. Ed. Lumby. ex. f. 8vo. *Cambridge Press.*   3s. 6d.

Also in Arber's Reprints, 1s.; and, along with Bacon's *New Atlantis*, and Campanella's *City of the Sun*, under the title of "Ideal Commonwealths," in "Morley's Universal Library." *Routledge.* 1s.

Harrington, J. Oceana ("Morley's Universal Library"). c. 8vo. *Routledge.*   1s. 6d.

POLYNESIA, *see* PACIFIC.

POOR LAW, *see* POLITICAL ECONOMY IX.

POPULATION, *see* POLITICAL ECONOMY IX.

PORCELAIN, *see* POTTERY.

PORTUGAL: GEOGRAPHY AND HISTORY:

See also SPAIN, *for books relating to both countries.*

Murray's Guide to Portugal. p. 8vo. *Murray.*   12s.

Aldama-Ayala, G. de. Compendio geográphico estadistico de Portugal e sus posesiones ultramarinas. (*Madrid*).

Barbosa, V. Monumentos de Portugal. (*Lisbon*).   15s.

Crawfurd, O. Old and new Portugal. 8vo. *Paul.* illus.   6s.

MacMurdo, E. History of Portugal. 8vo. 2 vols. *Low.*   21s.

Balbi, A. Essai statistique sur les royaumes de Portugal et d'Algarve. 8vo. 2 vols. 1822.   O.P.

PORTUGAL: LANGUAGE AND LITERATURE:

The student would do well, after fairly mastering the Grammar, to read Latino Coelho's *Galeria dos varões illustres de Portugal*, the style of which is simple and easy; then he might take Thomas Ribeiro's lovely poem *Dom Jayme*; T. Braga's *Introdução á historia da litteratura portugueza*, and next *O Monasticon* of Herculano. He would then be able to read with ease, and at his own choice, the works of Diniz, Garrett, Castilho, and Thomas Ribeiro. The student must decide for himself at what point he will study Camoens or Sa de Miranda, for while the language and construction of these poets are often archaic, their works, like all great classics, are simple and clear in idea; but he should first make himself acquainted with Portuguese as it is spoken and written at the present day.

—I. GRAMMARS AND DICTIONARIES:

Wall, C. H. Practical grammar of Portuguese. 8vo. *Nutt.*   7s.

On Otto's conversational system. Key 3s. 6d.

Vieyra, A. Grammar of the Portuguese language. 12mo. *Dulau.*   7s.

Braga, T. Grammatica portugueza elementar fundada sobre o methodo historico-comparativo. (*Porto*).   4s. 6d.

Barboza. Grammatica philosophica da lingua portugueza. 8vo. (*Lisbon*).   6s.

Elwes, A. Dictionary of the Portuguese language. 12mo. *Lockwood.*   6s.

Fonseca, J. de. Diccionario franccz-portuguez. 18mo. 2 vols. (*Paris*).   10*s.*

Moraes, Silva A. de. Diccionario da lingua portugueza. Ed. A. J. da Rocha. (*Lisbon*).
New edition now publishing.

—II. HISTORY AND CRITICISM:

Braga, T. Manual da historia e da litteratura portugueza. 12mo. (*Porto*).   4*s.* 6*d.*
By far the best.

Loiseau. Histoire de la littérature portuguaise. 12mo. (*Paris*).   3*s.* 6*d.*

Silva, Pereira da. La littérature portuguaise, son passé et son état actuel. 12mo. (*Paris*). pub. 3*s.* 6*d.*   O.P.

—III. TEXTS:

(A) OLD CLASSICS.

Sa de Miranda. Obras. 4to. (*Lisbon*). 1804.   17*s.* 6*d.*
The second greatest poet: Camoens being the first.

Camoens. Os Lusiadas. 12mo. (*Strasburg*).   3*s.* 6*d.*
A good but cheap edition, with German notes.

,,   Os Lusiadas (critical edition). Ed. J. Gomes Monteiro, etc. i. 4to. (*Leipzig*).   100*s.*
One of the very best library editions; good steel engravings.

,,   The Lusiads. Tr. J. J. Aubertin. p. 8vo. 2 vols. *Paul.*   12*s.*
Best existing translation: text *en face.*

Gil Vicente. Obras. 18mo. 3 vols. (*Lisbon*).   10*s.* 6*d.*
One of the most vigorous and characteristic of the elder classics.

Vieira, Padre Antonio de. Sermoes selectos. Ed. Rolland. 6 vols. *Rollandiana.*   O.P.
These sermons are perfect models of elegance and style.

(B) MODERN.

Castilho, Antonio T. de. A primavera (poesia). 8vo. *De Bulhoes.* 1837.   6*s.*

Ribeiro, T. Dom Jayme (poesia). Ed. Moré. 12mo. (*Porto*).   6*s.*

Almeida-Garrett. Camões. 12mo. (*Lisbon*).   4*s.*

Herculano, A. Historia de Portugal. 8vo. 4 vols. (*Lisbon*).   42*s.*
The Macaulay of Portugal: work incomplete.

Da origem e estabelecimento da Inquisição em Portugal. 12mo. 3 vols. (*Lisbon*).   12*s.* 6*d.*

Deus, João de. Folhas soltas. 12mo. (*Porto*).   4*s.* 6*d.*
A pretty and popular modern poet.

Palmeirim, L. A. Galeria de figuras portuguezas. 12mo. (*Porto*).   4*s.* 6*d.*
Popular modern poet.

—IV. NOVELS:

Herculano, A. O Monasticon. 12mo. 2 vols. (*Leipzig*).   7*s.*
Portugal's best historical novel, but somewhat turgid, and of anti-clerical bias.

Branco, C. C. O Anathema. (*Porto*).
Branco's novels form more than 40 vols. A cheap edition is now being published price in paper, 10*d.* each vol.

Queiroz, Eça de. O primo Basilio. (*Porto*).
Equivalent to the modern French realistic novel.

The Dragon's teeth. Tr. of "O primo Basilio." 12mo. *Ticknor.*   7*s.* 6*d.*

"**Diniz**, Julio," (Gomez Coelho). As pupillas do Senhor Reitor. 12mo.
    Brockhaus.   3s. 6d.
    <small>One of the most beautiful stories of peasant life existing anywhere.</small>

   ,,   Uma familia Ingleza. 12mo. (*Porto*).   7s. 6d.
    <small>Considered to be the author's masterpiece. All Diniz's works are suitable for girls.</small>

—V. BIOGRAPHY AND BIBLIOGRAPHY:

Chagas, Manuel Pinheiro. Portuguezes illustres. 12mo. (*Lisbon*).   2s. 6d.
    <small>Approved by the Board of Public Instruction for the use of students in the higher schools</small>

Coelho, Latino. Galeria dos varões illustres de Portugal. Ed. Corazzi.
    8vo. (*Lisbon*).
    <small>Camoes, 7s.; Vasco da Gama, 2 vols., 14s.</small>

Pimentel, A. de Serpa. Alex. Herculano e seu tempo. 12mo. (*Lisbon*).   4s. 6d.

Silva, J. F. da. Diccionario bibliographico portuguez. 8vo. 14 vols.
    Imprensa National.
    <small>A splendid work. Since the death of the author, Brito Aranha, of the Academy of Science, has continued the publication of this dictionary, which has now reached vol. xiv.</small>

PORT ROYAL, *see* CHURCH HISTORY V. (F).

POSITIVISM:

    <small>The two principal works of Comte may be studied: *Philosophy* (Miss Martineau's abridgment); and the *General view of Positivism* (first part of *Positive polity*, vol. i.); then the criticisms of Mill, Lewes (in *History of philosophy*, vol. ii.), and Spencer (in *Essays*, vol. iii.).</small>

Comte, Auguste. Positive polity. Tr. Beesley and others. 8vo. 4 vols.
    Longmans. pub. 80s.   O.P.
    <small>Vol. i., 21s.; vol. ii., 14s.; vol. iii., 21s.; vol. iv., 24s.</small>

   ,,   Positive philosophy. Tr. and abridged by Miss Martineau. 8vo.
    2 vols. *Trübner.*   25s.
    <small>Six vols. condensed into two.</small>

   ,,   Catechism of positive philosophy. Tr. Congreve. 12mo. *Trübner.*   6s. 6d.

Mill, J. S. Auguste Comte and positivism. 8vo. *Trübner.*   6s.

Caird, E. Social philosophy and religion of Comte. c. 8vo. *Maclehose.*   5s.

Huxley, T. H. Scientific aspects of positivism (in "Lay sermons").
    p. 8vo. *Macmillan.*   7s. 6d.

POTTERY:

Birch, S. History of ancient pottery. 8vo. *Murray.* illus. pub. 42s.   O.P.

Jacquemart, A. History of ceramic art. Tr. r. 8vo. *Low.*   28s.

Chaffers, W. Marks and monograms on pottery and porcelain. r. 8vo.
    Bickers.   42s.

Marryatt, J. History of pottery and porcelain. 8vo. *Murray.* pub. 42s.   O.P.

Franks, A. W. Japanese pottery. c. 8vo. *Chapman.* illus.   2s. 6d.

Audesley and Bowes. Keramic art of Japan. fo. *Howell (Liverpool).*   42s.

Church, A. H. English porcelain; XVIII. century (S. Kensington handbook). p. 8vo. *Chapman.* illus.   3s.

   ,,   English earthenware; XVII. and XVIII. centuries (S. Kensington handbook). p. 8vo. *Chapman.* illus.   3s.

POULTRY, *see* LIVE-STOCK.

POWER-LOOM, CONSTRUCTION OF, *see* TEXTILE FABRICS.

PRECIOUS STONES:

Church, A. H. Precious stones. 8vo. *Chapman.*   2*s.* 6*d.*

King, C. W. The natural history of precious stones. p. 8vo. *Bell.* illus.   6*s.*
Much information as to the knowledge of the ancients.

,,   The natural history of gems. p. 8vo. *Bell.* illus.   6*s.*
Continuation of previous work.

Kunz, G. F. Gems and precious stones of North America. 8vo. *Scientific Pub. Co. (New York).*   52*s.* 6*d.*

Streeter, E. W. Precious stones and gems. d. 8vo. *Bell.* illus.   15*s.*
History and distinguishing characteristics.

PREHISTORIC TIMES, *see* ANTHROPOLOGY II.

PRESBYTERIANS, *see* CHURCH HISTORY V. (B).

PRICES, HISTORY OF, *see* POLITICAL ECONOMY X.

PRIMITIVE MAN, *see* ANTHROPOLOGY *and* FOLKLORE.

PRINTING:

—I. PRACTICE:

Southward, J. Practical printing. d. 8vo. *J. M. Powell.* illus.   7*s.* 6*d.*
Also in two vols., 4*s.* each. The very best book on the subject.

Wilson and Grey. Modern printing machinery. *Cassell.*   21*s.*

Mackellar, T. The American printer. c. 8vo. *(Philadelphia).*   10*s.* 6*d.*
An exposition of letterpress printing as practised in America.

Richmond, W. D. Grammar of lithography. c. 8vo. *E. Menken* (Gray's Inn-road).   5*s.*
One of the few technical books up to its professions.

—II. HISTORY:

Powell, A. C. J. Short history of the art of printing in England. *J. M. Powell.* illus.   O.P.
An exceedingly interesting and well-written sketch.

Skeen, W. Early typography. 8vo. *Quaritch.* pub. 10*s.*   O.P.
Essay on the origin of letterpress printing in the XV. century.

Reed, T. B. History of old English letter foundries. c. 4to. *Stock.*   31*s.* 6*d.*
The only exhaustive work on the subject.

De Vinne, T. L. The invention of printing. *Trübner.*   22*s.* 6*d.*
A work of great interest and value, and shewing considerable research.

Blades, W. Numismatica typographica. *Blades.*   12*s.* 6*d.*
Contains much out of the way information on printing and printers.

,,   Biography and typography of William Caxton, England's first printer. 8vo. *Trübner.*   5*s.*
The text-book on Caxton and his works.

Dibdin, T. F. The bibliographical Decameron. i. 8vo. 3 vols. *(London).* 1807.   O.P.
A highly interesting conversational discourse about early typography, bibliography, engraving, and kindred subjects.

Dickson and Edmund. Annals of Scottish printing. d. 4to. *Macmillan* (*Cambridge*).   42*s.*
> An excellent and dependable history of printing in Scotland from 1507 to beginning of XVII. century.

Ames and Herbert. Typographical antiquities. 4to. 3 vols. (*London*). 1785-90.   O.P.
> A valuable compilation and dependable work of reference for books in the English language; extensively used by later writers.

Johnson, J. Typographia; or the printer's instructor. 24mo. 2 vols. *Longmans.* 1824.   O.P.
> Vol. i., Historical; vol. ii., Practical. An epitome; not required by those who possess Ames and Herbert's *Typographical antiquities.*

Lemoine, H. Typographical antiquities. (*London*). 1797.   O.P.
> A mine of quaint and curious facts.

Willems, A. Les Elzevir, histoire et annales typographiques. 8vo. (*Brussels*). illus.   25*s.*

Didot, A. F. Alde Manuce et l'hellénisme à Venise. 8vo. *Didot.* illus.   7*s.* 6*d.*

—III. REFERENCE:

Ringwalt, J. L. American encyclopædia of printing. i. 8vo. *Lippincott.*   50*s.*
> A good book on the practice of printing.

Timperley, C. H. Dictionary of printers and printing. 8vo. (*Bohn*). 1839. pub. 15*s.*   O.P.
> A useful work of great interest.

Bigmore and Wyman. Bibliography of printing. 4to. 2 vols. *Quaritch.* pub. 105*s.*   O.P.
> The standard work of its kind.

PRINTING, COTTON, *see* TEXTILE FABRICS.

PRISONS:

Her Majesty's prisons. c. 8vo. *Low.*   6*s.*

Wines, F. H. State of prisons. 8vo. *Putnam.*   1*s.* 6*d.*

Eighteen months' imprisonment, by D. S. p. 8vo. *Routledge.*   O.P.

Stoughton, J. John Howard and his friends. c. 8vo. *Hodder.*   7*s.* 6*d.*

Pitman, Mrs. E. R. Elizabeth Fry ("Eminent Women" ser.). c. 8vo. *W. H. Allen.*   3*s.* 6*d.*

Pellico, Silvio. Marchesa Giulia Falletti. Tr. p. 8vo. *Bentley.*   O.P.
> Reformer of Turin prisons.

PROFIT-SHARING, *see* POLITICAL ECONOMY VI.

PROPERTY, REAL AND PERSONAL, *see* ENGLAND, LAW IV.

PROTESTANTISM, *see* CHURCH HISTORY.

PROVENÇAL LITERATURE:

—I. OLD:

Bartsch, K. Chrestomathie provençale. 8vo. (*Elberfeld*).   9*s.* 6*d.*
> Selections; with grammar and glossary (complete in itself). The best book to begin with.

  ,,   Grundriss zur Geschichte der provenzialischen Literatur. 8vo.   5*s.*
> Handbook, with bibliography, and index to all the poems, with the MSS. of each.

Parnasse occitanien.
　Selections, with the old lives of the poets in Provençal.

Glossaire occitanien.　8vo.　(*Toulouse*).　1819.　　　　O.P.

Raynouard.　Lexique de la langue romane.　8vo.　6 vols.　1838.　　O.P.

　　,,　　Choix de poésies des Troubadours.　8vo.　6 vols.　1816.　　O.P.

Diez, F.　Die Poesie der Troubadours.　Ed. C. Bartsch.　8vo.　(*Leipzig*).　6s. 6d.
　An essay on Provençal poetry.

　　,,　　Leben und Werke der Troubadours.　Ed. C. Bartsch.　8vo.　(*Leipzig*).　10s.
　Essays on the different Provençal poets.　These are the two standard works for the history
　of the literature.

Hueffer, F.　The Troubadours.　8vo.　*Chatto.*　pub. 12s. 6d.　　O.P.
　Superficial ; but has more in it than mere bookmaking.

Peire Vidal.　Lieder.　Ed. C. Bartsch.　8vo.　　　　6s.

Bertran de Born.　Sein Leben und Werke.　Ed. Stimming.　8vo.　*Niemeyer.*　10s.
　Separate editions of other poets are published by Niemeyer.

—II. MODERN :

Mistral, F.　Mirèio ; poème provençal avec traduction française en regard.
　12mo.　(*Avignon*).　　　　3s. 6d.

　　,,　　Calendan ; poème provençal avec traduction française en regard.
　(*Avignon*).　　　　6s.

　　,,　　Les isels d'or (Les îsles d'or) ; avec traduction.　(*Avignon*).　3s. 6d.

Aubanel, T.　La Miongrano entre ouberto (La grenade entr' ouverte).
　12mo.　*Maisonneuve.*　　　　O.P.

Roumanille, J.　Lis oubreto en vers.　(*Avignon*).　　　3s. 6d.

　　,,　　Li conte prouvençau.　(*Avignon*).　　　　3s. 6d.

　　JOURNAL : *Revue des Langues Romanes,*
　　　Includes all the dialects of the Langue d'Oc, old and new.　Published since 1870.

PROVERBS, *see* QUOTATIONS.

PSYCHICAL RESEARCH :

Gurney and others.　Phantasms of the living.　d. 8vo.　2 vols.　*Trübner.*　21s.
　Treats of thought transference and apparitions of the living and dying ; together with
　discussions of hallucinations, dreams, etc.

Moll, A.　Hypnotism ("Contemporary Science" ser.).　c. 8vo.　*Scott.*　3s. 6d.

Binet and Féré.　Animal magnetism ("Internat. Scient." ser.).　Tr.
　c. 8vo.　*Paul.*　　　　5s.

Heidenhain, R.　Animal magnetism.　Tr. J. C. Wooldridge.　sm. c. 8vo.
　Paul.　　　　2s. 6d.
　Preface by G. J. Romanes.

Janet, P.　L'automatisme psychologique.　8vo.　(*Paris*).　　6s. 6d.

Bernheim, H.　Suggestive therapeutics.　Tr. C. A. Herter.　8vo.　*Putnam.*　14s.

Tuke, D. H.　Sleep-walking and hypnotism.　d. 8vo.　*Churchill.*　5s.

Seybert Commission.　Preliminary report on modern spiritualism.　8vo.
　Lippincott.　　　　5s.

Wallace, A. R.　On miracles and modern spiritualism.　c. 8vo.　*Paul.*　5s.

Crookes, W.　Researches in the phenomena of spiritualism.　d. 8vo.
　J. Burns.　illus.　　　　5s.
　A record of experiments with various mediums, chiefly D. D. Home.

Zöllner, J. C. F. Transcendental physics. Tr. C. C. Massey. f. 8vo.
    E. W. Allen. illus.   3*s.* 6*d.*
        A record of experiments with the medium Slade, and discussion.

Moses, W. Stainton. Spirit teachings. 8vo. *London Spiritualist Alliance*
    (Duke-street, Adelphi). illus.   3*s.* 6*d.*
        A record of personal experiences in automatic writing, etc.

Home, Mme. D. D. Home ; his life and mission. 8vo. *Trübner.*   12*s.* 6*d.*

Dessoir, Max. Bibliographie des modernen Hypnotismus. 8vo. (*Berlin*).   2*s.*
        Gives the recent books and publications on hypnotism in all languages.
        PERIODICALS : *Proceedings of the Society for Psychical Research* (Trübner) ; usually 2 or 3
        parts a year.

PSYCHOLOGY, *see* MENTAL PHYSIOLOGY II.

PUBLIC HEALTH, *see* HYGIENE.

PUBLIC MEETINGS :

Palgrave, R. F. D. The chairman's handbook. c. 8vo. *Low.*   2*s.*
    Conduct of public meetings.

Q.

QUAKERS, *see* CHURCH HISTORY V. (D).

QUEENSLAND, *see* AUSTRALASIA V.

QUOTATIONS AND PROVERBS :

Grocott, J. C. Familiar quotations. l. c. 8vo. *Routledge.*   6*s.*
Allibone, S. A. Prose quotations. r. 8vo. (*Philadelphia*).   25*s.*
    ,, Poetical quotations. r. 8vo. (*Philadelphia*).   25*s.*
Bohn, H. G. Handbook of proverbs. p. 8vo. *Bell* (*Bohn*).   5*s.*

R.

RACING, *see* HORSE IV.

RACKETS, *see* TENNIS.

RAILWAYS :

Findlay, G. Working and management of an English railway. c. 8vo.
    Whittaker.   7*s.* 6*d.*

Barry, J. W.   Railway appliances ("Text-books of Science").   c. 8vo.
  Longmans. illus.   3s. 6d.

,,   and Bramwell.   Railways and locomotives (engineering).   8vo.
  Longmans. illus.   pub. 21s.   O.P.

Couche, C.   Permanent way and rolling-stock.   Tr. J. Schoolbred.   4to.
  3 vols.   *Dulau.* illus.   £10
  Vol. i., Permanent way, 40s.; vol. ii., Carrying stock, traction, 100s.; vol. iii., Production
  and application of steam, 60s.

Grover, J.   Railway bridges, stations, and culverts, with appendix.   fo.
  Spon.   31s. 6d.

Fidler, T. C.   Bridge construction.   8vo.   *Griffin.* illus.   30s.

Baker, B.   Long span railway bridges.   c. 8vo.   *Spon.*   5s.

Simms, F. W.   Tunnelling.   i. 8vo.   *Lockwood.* illus.   30s.

Balfour-Brown and Theobald.   Law of railway companies.   r. 8vo.
  Stevens.   35s.

Hadley, A. T.   Railroad transportation.   12mo.   *Putnam.*   7s. 6d.

Acworth, W. M.   Railways of England.   8vo.   *Murray.* illus.   14s.

,,   Railways of Scotland.   c. 8vo.   *Murray.*   5s.

,,   Railways of America.   Ed. Cooley.   l. 8vo.   *Murray.* illus.   31s. 6d.

Bradshaw.   Railway manual, shareholder's guide, and official directory.
  Adams (59, Fleet-street).   12s.

RATES AND RATING, *see* LOCAL GOVERNMENT.

REAL PROPERTY, *see* ENGLAND, LAW IV.

REFERENCE BOOKS:

As a rule, books of reference are given under the different heads in the GUIDE. A few
useful books of general reference are added here.

ALMANACS AND ANNUALS.
Whittaker's almanac.   *Whittaker.*   1s.
  With supplement, 2s. 6d.

Hazell's annual.   *Hazell.*   3s. 6d.

British almanac and companion (annual).   12mo.   *Stationers' Company.*   2s. 6d.

BIBLIOGRAPHY.
Best books, The.   p. 4to.   *Sonnenschein.*   30s.
  A classified bibliography of current English and American literature.

English catalogue (annual).   *Low.*   5s.

See also BIBLIOPHILIA.

BIOGRAPHY.
Dictionary of biographical reference.   Ed. L. B. Phillips.   r. 8vo.   *Low.*   31s. 6d.
  Contains 100,000 names, with references to fuller biographies.

Vapereau, G.   Dictionnaire universel des contemporains.   r. 8vo.
  Hachette.   26s.
  Refers to all countries.

Men and women of the time.   Ed. G. W. Moon.   d. 8vo.   *Routledge.*   15s.

DATES AND EVENTS.
Haydn's dictionary of dates.   Ed. Vincent.   r. 8vo.   *Ward, Lock.*   18s.

Irving, J. Annals of our time (1837–1887). 8vo. 2 vols., 18*s*. each. *Macmillan.*   36*s*.

Vol. i., June 20th, 1837, to Feb. 28, 1871 ; vol. ii., Feb. 1871, to June 24, 1887.

Times index (quarterly). sm. 4to. *Palmer.*   10*s*. 6*d*.

Annual register. 8vo. *Rivingtons.*   18*s*.

A summary of domestic and foreign events, legislation, important trials, etc.

DIRECTORIES.

Official Army list (quarterly). 8vo. *Eyre.*   15*s*.

Civil Service directory (annual). d. 8vo. *Allen.*   6*s*.

Colonial Office list (annual). 8vo. *Harrison.*   7*s*. 6*d*.

Crockford's Clerical directory (annual). 8vo. (121, *Fleet-street, E.C.*).   4*s*. 6*d*.

India list, civil and military (half-yearly). 8vo. *Allen.*   10*s*. 6*d*.

Law list (annual). 12mo. *Stevens.*   9*s*.

Medical directory. 8vo. *Churchill.*   14*s*.

Navy list (quarterly). 8vo. *Eyre.*   3*s*.

ENCYCLOPÆDIAS.

Encyclopædia Britannica. 4to. 24 vols., 30*s*. each ; with index, 20*s*. *Black.*   £37

Chambers' encyclopædia. r. 8vo. 10 vols., 10*s*. each. *Chambers.*   100*s*.

In progress ; vols. i. to iv. issued.

MISCELLANEOUS.

Allibone, S. A. Critical dictionary of English literature, and British and American authors. r. 8vo. 3 vols. *Trübner.*   103*s*. 6*d*.

Vol. i., 31*s*. 6*d*. ; ii., 36*s*. ; iii., 36*s*.

Halkett and Laing. Dictionary of anonymous and pseudonymous literature of Great Britain. 8vo. 3 vols., 42*s*. each. *Simpkin.*   126*s*.

Brewer, E. C. Dictionary of phrase and fable. c. 8vo. *Cassell.*   3*s*. 6*d*.

   ,,   Reader's handbook of allusions, references, plots, and stories. c. 8vo. *Chatto.*   12*s*. 6*d*.

Roget, P. M. Thesaurus of English words and phrases. c. 8vo. *Longmans.*   10*s*. 6*d*.

Farmer, J. S. Slang and its analogues. f. 8vo. 5 vols. *Nutt.*   160*s*.

Two vols. issued.

Hotten, J. C. Slang dictionary. p. 8vo. *Hotten.* pub. 6*s*. 6*d*.   O.P.

Almanach de Gotha. 16mo. *Pertz (Gotha).*   7*s*.

Dod's Peerage (annual). 8vo. *Whittaker.*   10*s*. 6*d*.

Haydn's Book of dignities. Ed. Ockerby. d. 8vo. *Allen.*   28*s*.

Year-book of scientific and learned societies of Great Britain and Ireland. 8vo. *Griffin.*   7*s*. 6*d*.

Stock Exchange year-book. 8vo. *Skinner.*   15*s*.

REFORMATION, THE, *see* CHURCH HISTORY IV. *and* V.

RELIGION, COMPARATIVE:

For works on the different religions, in addition to those given below, see BIBLE, BUDDHISM, MAHOMETANISM, POSITIVISM, SANSKRIT, THEOLOGY.

Caird, J. Introduction to the philosophy of religion. c. 8vo. *Maclehose.*   6*s*.

Lotze, H. Outlines of philosophy of religion. Tr. Ladd. *Ginn (Boston).*   3s. 6d.

Pfleiderer, O. Philosophy of religion on the basis of its history. Tr. Stewart and Menzies. 8vo. 4 vols., 10s. 6d. each. *Williams.*   42s.
> Pending the translation of Prof. C. de la Saussaye's *Religionsgeschichte*, vol. iii. of Pfleiderer's work may be taken as an outline of the history of religious thought, naturally dominated by the philosophy of which it forms a part.

Martineau, J. Study of religion. c. 8vo. 2 vols. *Clar. Press.*   15s.

Tiele, C. P. Outlines of the history of religion. Tr. J. Estlin Carpenter. 8vo. *Trübner.*   7s. 6d.
> Comprehensive, with good bibliography to date (1877), but slight and sketchy.

Renan, E. Studies in religious history. c. 8vo. *Bentley.*   6s.

Müller, F. Max. Introduction to the science of religion. c. 8vo. *Longmans.*   7s. 6d.

  ,,   Origin and growth of religion (Hibbert lectures). 8vo. *Williams.*   10s. 6d.

  ,,   Natural religion (Gifford lectures). c. 8vo. *Longmans.*   10s. 6d.
> Prof. Max Müller is well known as the accomplished exponent of a particular theory of the origin and early development of religious ideas.

Tylor, E. B. Primitive culture. 8vo. 2 vols. *Murray.*   24s.
> Development of mythology, philosophy, religion, art, and custom.

Lang, A. Custom and myth. c. 8vo. *Longmans.*   7s. 6d.

  ,,   Myth, ritual, and religion. c. 8vo. 2 vols. *Longmans.* pub 21s.   O.P.
> Mr. Lang and Mr. Tylor are exponents of the anthropological view.

Spencer, Herbert. Ecclesiastical institutions. 8vo. *Williams.*   5s.
> Part of Mr. H. Spencer's great system of constructive philosophy, containing a restatement of the view put forward in *First principles* as to the growth of the religious idea.

Kuenen, A. National religions and universal religions (Hibbert lectures). Tr. P. H. Wicksteed. 8vo. *Williams.*   10s. 6d.
> Judaism, Christianity, Mohammedanism, and Buddhism.

Religious systems of the world, by various authors. p. 8vo. *Sonnenschein.*   7s. 6d.
> Short essays on the distinctive tenets and aims of different denominations or parties.

Réville, A. Prolegomena to the history of religion. 8vo. *Williams.*   10s. 6d.
> Slight and sketchy.

  ,,   Origin of religion (Hibbert lectures). Tr. P. H. Wicksteed. 8vo. *Williams.*   10s. 6d.
> Mexico and Peru.

Renouf, P. Le Page. The religion of ancient Egypt (Hibbert lectures). 8vo. *Williams.*   10s. 6d.

Sayce, A. H. The Babylonian religion (Hibbert lectures). 8vo. *Williams.*   10s. 6d.

Johnson, S. Oriental religions. 8vo. 3 vols. *Houghton (N.Y.).*   75s.
> Vol. i., India; vol. ii., China; vol. iii., Persia; 25s. each.

Williams, Monier. Religious thought and life in India. *Murray.*   10s. 6d.
> Brahmanism and Hinduism.

Smith, W. Robertson. Lectures on the religion of the Semites. 8vo. *Black.*   15s.

Davids, T. W. Rhys. History of Indian Buddhism (Hibbert lectures). 8vo. *Williams.*   10s. 6d.

Dods, Marcus. Mohammed, Buddha, and Christ. c. 8vo. *Hodder.*   3s. 6d.
> Covers similar ground to Dr. Kuenen's *Hibbert Lectures* in a more popular form.

Smith, R. Bosworth. Mohammed and Mohammedanism. c. 8vo. *Smith, Elder.*   8s. 6d.
> Generous and sympathetic.

Wordsworth, J. The one religion. 8vo. *Rivingtons.*   10s. 6d.

Hardwick, C. Christ and other masters. 8vo. *Macmillan.*   10*s.* 6*d.*
> The two last books are written from the point of view of Christian apologetics.

REPORTING, *see* SHORTHAND.

REPTILES, *see* ZOOLOGY.

REVOLVERS, *see* ARMY V.

RIDING, *see* HORSE II.

RIFLE, MILITARY, *see* ARMY V.

  ,,   SPORTSMAN'S, *see* SHOOTING.

RIVIERA, *see* HEALTH RESORTS.

ROADS, *see* LOCAL GOVERNMENT.

ROME: HISTORY (ANCIENT):

See CHURCH HISTORY *and* EUROPE II. *for later history of Rome.*

Mommsen, T. History of Rome. Tr. P. W. Dickson. c. 8vo. 4 vols. *Bentley.*   46*s.* 6*d.*
> Also abridged edition in one vol. c. 8vo. 7*s.* 6*d.*

Smith, W. Student's Rome. p. 8vo. *Murray.* illus.   7*s.* 6*d.*

Merivale, C. History of the Romans under the Empire. c. 8vo. 8 vols., 3*s.* 6*d.* each. *Longmans.*   28*s.*

Capes, W. W. Early Roman Empire ("Epochs of ancient history"). f. 8vo. *Longmans.*   2*s.* 6*d.*

  ,,   Roman Empire of the second century ("Epochs of ancient history"). f. 8vo. *Longmans.*   2*s.* 6*d.*

Gibbon, E. Decline and fall of the Roman empire. 8vo. 8 vols., 7*s.* 6*d.* each. *Murray.*   60*s.*

Smith, R. Bosworth. Carthage and Carthaginians. c. 8vo. *Longmans.*   10*s.* 6*d.*

Hodgkin, T. Italy and her invaders (375 to 553). d. 8vo. 4 vols. *Clar. Press.* illus.   68*s.*
> Vol. i., ii., 32*s.*; vol. iii., iv., 36*s.*

Bury, J. B. Later Roman empire (390-800). 8vo. 2 vols. *Macmillan.*   32*s.*

ROMAN LAW:

> A knowledge of French and German, in addition to Latin, is necessary for any serious study of Roman law. Italian literature on the subject is also rapidly increasing, both in quantity and in importance.

Justinian. Institutes. Ed. J. B. Moyle. d. 8vo. 2 vols. *Clar. Press.*   22*s.*
> Vol. i., 16*s.*; vol. ii., 6*s.*

Gaius. Institutes. Ed. Muirhead. 8vo. *Clark.*   O.P.

  ,,   The same. Ed. E. Poste. d. 8vo. *Clar. Press.*   18*s.*
> These two editions are not equivalent, being on substantially different plans.

Roby, H. J. Introduction to Justinian's Digest. d. 8vo. *Cambridge Press.*   9*s.*

Justinian's Digest, Select titles of. Ed. Holland and Shadwell. 8vo. *Clar. Press.*   14*s.*
> Also sold in parts. Vol. i., 2*s.* 6*d.*; vol. ii., 1*s.*; vol. iii., 2*s.* 6*d.*; vol. iv. (1), 2*s.* 6*d.*; vol. iv. (2), 4*s.* 6*d.*

Muirhead, J.   Historical introduction to the private law of Rome.   d. 8vo.   *Black.*   21*s.*

Hadley, J.   Introduction to Roman law.   p. 8vo.   *Low.*   7*s.* 6*d.*

Hunter, W. A.   Roman law in the order of a code.   8vo.   *Maxwell.*   32*s.*

    ,,   Introduction to Roman law.   p, 8vo.   *Maxwell.*   7*s.* 6*d.*

Dirksen, H.   Manuale juris civilis.   4to.   1837.   O.P.

Grueber, E.   The Roman law of damage to property.   d. 8vo.   *Clar. Press.*   10*s.* 6*d.*
     A commentary on the Digest *Ad legem Aquiliam.*

ROMANY, *see* GYPSIES.

RORAIMA, *see* GUIANA.

ROUMANIA:

See also TURKEY.

Samuelson, J.   Roumania, past and present.   d. 8vo.   *Philip.*   illus.   6*s.*

Walker, Mrs.   Untrodden paths in Roumania.   d. 8vo.   *Chapman.*   illus.   10*s.* 6*d.*

ROUND GAMES, *see* CARDS.

ROWING:

Brickwood, E. D.   Boat-racing ; or the arts of rowing and training.   c. 8vo.   *H. Cox.*   5*s.*
     PERIODICAL: *Rowing Almanac.*   Ed. E. D. Brickwood.   *H. Cox.*

RUNNING, *see* ATHLETICS.

RUSSIA IN EUROPE:

Murray's Handbook.   p. 8vo.   *Murray.*   18*s.*
     Russia, Poland, and Finland, including the Crimea, Caucasus, Siberia, and Central Asia.

Baedeker's Russland (in German).   *Dulau.*   10*s.*

Wallace, D. Mackenzie.   Russia.   2 vols.   *Cassell.*   5*s.*

Beaulieu, Leroy.   L'empire des Tsars et des Russes.   8vo.   3 vols., 6*s.* 6*d.* each.   (*Paris*).   19*s.* 6*d.*

Roskoschny, H.   Russland ; Land und Leute.   4to.   4 vols.   (*Leipzig*).   77*s.*
     Vols. i. and ii. (44*s.*) deal with Russia in Europe.

RUSSIA IN ASIA:

See also ASIA II.

—I. GENERAL:

Reclus, E.   Universal geography, vol. vi.   i. 8vo.   *Virtue.*   21*s.*

—II. CAUCASUS:

Freshfield, D. W.   Travels in the Central Caucasus and Bashan.   8vo.   *Longmans.*   pub. 18*s.*   O.P.

Cunynghame, A. T. Travels in the Eastern Caucasus. p. 8vo. 2 vols. *Murray*.   18*s*.

    Also in Daghestan, and on the frontiers of Persia and Turkey.

Thielmann, Max von. Journey in the Caucasus, Persia, etc. p. 8vo. 2 vols. *Murray*.   18*s*.

Telfer, J. B. Crimea and Transcaucasia. 8vo. 2 vols. *H. S. King*.   O.P.

Bryce, J. Transcaucasia and Ararat. c. 8vo. *Macmillan*.   9*s*.

Abercromby, J. Trip through the Eastern Caucasus. 8vo. *Stanford*.   14*s*.

    With a chapter on the languages of the country.

Wardrop, O. Kingdom of Georgia. 8vo. *Low*. illus.   14*s*.

    Contains a useful bibliography.

Brosset. Éléments de la langue géorgienne. (*Paris*).   12*s*.

Choutinov. Dictionnaire Géorgien-Russe-Français. (*Petersburg*).   72*s*. 6*d*.

—III. SIBERIA AND THE EAST:

Coxe, W. Russian discoveries between Asia and America. 1803.   O.P.

Ravenstein, E. G. Russians on the Amur; its discovery, conquest, and colonisation. 8vo. *Trübner*. illus.   15*s*.

Eden, C. H. Frozen Asia. c. 8vo. *S. P. C. K.*   5*s*.

Nordenskjöld, A. E. von. Voyage of the "Vega." m. 8vo. 2 vols. *Macmillan*. illus.   45*s*.

    Popular edition, c. 8vo., 6*s*. Contains a very full account of the exploration and geography of Siberia.

Long, G. W. De. Voyage of the "Jeannette" 1879-1881. 8vo. 2 vols. *Paul*. illus.   36*s*.

    The ship and ice journals of G. W. De Long (U.S. Polar expedition).

Gilder, W. H. Icepack and tundra. 8vo. *Low*.   18*s*.

    Search for the " Jeannette," and a sledge journey through Siberia.

Melville, G. W. In the Lena delta. Ed. M. Philips. c. 8vo. *Longmans*. illus. pub. 14*s*.   O.P.

    Search for Commander De Long and his companions, with account of the Greeley relief expedition, and a proposed method of reaching the North Pole.

Niemojowski, L. Siberian pictures, from the Polish. 8vo. 2 vols. *Hurst*. illus.   21*s*.

Seebohm, H. Siberia in Asia; natural history, etc., of the valley of the Yenesei. 8vo. *Murray*. illus. pub. 14*s*.   O.P.

James, H. E. M. Journey in Manchuria. 8vo. *Longmans*.   21*s*.

RUSSIA : HISTORY

Ralston, W. R. S. Early Russian history. c. 8vo. *Low*. pub. 5*s*.   O.P.

Rambaud, A. History of Russia. Tr. 8vo. 3 vols. *Low*. illus.   21*s*.

    The best general history in any language except Russian.

Schuyler, E. Peter the Great. 8vo. 2 vols. *Low*.   32*s*.

Tooke, W. Russian Empire under Catherine II. 8vo. 3 vols. *Longmans*. 1799.   O.P.

Bruckner, A. Katharina die Zweite. 8vo. (*Berlin*).   30*s*.

Bernhardi, T. von. Geschichte Russlands (1814–31). 8vo. 3 vols. (*Leipzig*).   30*s*. 6*d*.

    Vol. i., 4*s*. 6*d*.; vol. ii. (1), *s*.; (2), 10*s*.; vol. iii., 10*s*.

Kinglake, A. W.   History of the invasion of the Crimea.   c. 8vo.   9 vols.,
     6*s.* each.   *Blackwood.*   54*s.*

Morfill, W. R.   Russia.   c. 8vo.   *Unwin.*   illus.   5*s.*
     With an account of the sources of Russian history.

Leroy-Beaulieu, A.   L'empire des Tsars.   8vo.   3 vols., 6*s.* 6*d.* each.
     Hachette.   19*s.* 6*d.*

Tikhomirov, L.   Russia: social and political.   Tr. E. Aveling.   d, 8vo.
     2 vols.   *Sonnenschein.*   21*s.*
     Includes an account of Russian village institutions.

RUSSIA : LANGUAGE AND LITERATURE :

     Moser's grammar, or that of W. R. Morfill (which contains a short chrestomathy) should
first be studied. Some of the minor poems of Pushkin might then be read, and then the
novelists; among the translations of these, the French versions are usually to be preferred.
Books marked ∮ are recommended for young people.

—I. GRAMMARS AND DICTIONARIES :

Morfill, W. R.   Grammar of Russian language.   c. 8vo.   *Clar. Press.*   6*s.*

Moser, H.   Grammatik der russischen Sprache.   8vo.   (*Hanover*).   4*s.*

Alexandrow, A.   Complete Russian dictionary.   8vo.   2 vols.   (*St.*
     Petersburg).   32*s.*

New pocket dictionary (English-Russian).   18mo.   *Tauchnitz.*   4*s.* 6*d.*

Nosovich, J.   Slovar Bielorusskago Narechia (dictionary of the White
     Russian dialect).   4to.   (*St. Petersburg*).   10*s.*

—II. HISTORY AND CRITICISM :

Polevoi, P.   Istoria Russkoi literaturi v'ocherkakh i biographiakh.   (History
     of Russian literature in sketches and biographies).   8vo.   2 vols.   (*St.*
     Petersburg).   14*s.*
     Very interesting, like Chambers'.

Rambaud, A.   La Russie épique.   8vo.   *Maisonneuve.*   8*s.* 6*d.*

§**Turner,** C. E.   Modern novelists of Russia.   c. 8vo.   *Trübner.*   3*s.* 6*d.*

Vogüé, E. M. de.   Le roman russe.   12mo.   *Plon.*   3*s.*

§**Ralston,** W. R. S.   Krilof and his fables.   *Cassell.*   3*s.* 6*d.*

Turner, C. E.   Count Tolstoï as novelist and thinker.   c. 8vo.   *Trübner.*   3*s.* 6*d.*

—III. TEXTS AND TRANSLATIONS :

Pushkin, A. S.   Sochineniya (works).   Ed. P. Yephremov.   8vo.   7 vols.
     (*St. Petersburg*).   18*s.*
     The best edition of Russia's most celebrated poet.

     ,,   Poèmes dramatiques.   Tr. Tourguéniev and Viardot.   12mo.
     Hachette.   O.P.

     ,,   Russian romance.   Tr. Mrs. J. B. Telfer.   c. 8vo.   *Paul.*   3*s.* 6*d.*

Lermontov, M. J.   Sochineniya.   Ed. Yephremov.   8vo.   2 vols.   (*St.*
     Petersburg).   12*s.* 6*d.*
     Russia's second greatest poet.

Krilov, J. A.   Basni (fables).   12mo.   (*St. Petersburg*).   2*s.*

Ustrialov, N.   Russkaya Istoriya (Russian history).   8vo.   (*St. Peters-*
     burg).   15*s.*

Zvetkov, A.   Novieshie Russkije pisatelyi.   8vo.   (*St. Petersburg*).   9*s.*

Dostoievski, T. Unizhennie i oskorblennie (The humble and persecuted). 8vo.   9s.

  ,,   Presbuplenie i nakazanie (Crime and punishment). 8vo.   10s. 6d.

  ,,   Les pauvres gens. Tr. Derély. 12mo. *Plon.*   3s.

  ,,   Le crime et le châtiment. Tr. Derély. 12mo. 2 vols. *Plon.*   6s.

  ,,   Souvenir de la maison des morts. Tr. Neyroud. 12mo. *Plon.*   3s.

Tolstoï, Voina i mir (War and peace). 12mo. 3 vols.   15s.

  ,,   Anna Karenina (in Russian). 12mo. 3 vols.   15s.

  ,,   Works. Tr. c. 8vo. 2s. 6d. each. *Scott.*

  ,,   Anna Karénine (in French). 12mo. 2 vols. *Hachette.*   5s.

  ,,   La guerre et la paix. 12mo. 3 vols. *Hachette.*   7s. 6d.

  ,,   Ma religion. 8vo. (*Paris*).   5s.

Tourguéniev. Zapiski okhotnika (Memoirs of a sportsman). 12mo. 2 vols.   6s.

  ,,   Dvorianskoe gniezdo (A nest of noblemen).   O.P.
      May be had in Tourguéniev's collected works, 10 vols., 40s.

§ ,,   Mémoires d'un seigneur russe. Tr. E. Charrière. 12mo. 2 vols. *Hachette.*   2s. 6d.

  ,,   La fumée. 12mo. *Hetzel.*   2s. 6d.

  ,,   Un Bulgare. 12mo. *Hetzel.*   2s. 6d.

  ,,   Terres vierges. 12mo. *Hetzel.*   2s. 6d.

§ ,,   Une nichée de gentilshommes. 12mo. *Hetzel.*   2s. 6d.

  ,,   Pères et enfants. 12mo. *Charpentier.*   3s.
      These five works were translated into French by Tourguéniev himself.

§ ,,   Liza. Tr. W. R. Ralston. 12mo. 2 vols. *Chapman.*   O.P.

§**Nekrasov,** N. A. Red nosed frost. Tr. 16mo. *Ticknor.* illus.   15s.

Gogol, N. Dead souls. Tr. Isabel Hapgood. 12mo. 2 vols. (*New York*).   12s. 6d.

  ,,   Les âmes mortes. Tr. *Hachette.*   2s. 6d.

§**Ralston,** W. R. S. Songs of the Russian people. 8vo. *Ellis and Green.*   12s.

§ ,,   Russian folk-tales. 8vo. *Smith, Elder.* pub. 16s.   O.P.

—IV. MALO-RUSSIAN:

      There is no good German Malo-Russian grammar, and therefore only that by Osadtsa in Malo-Russian can be named. Zelechowski's dictionary is very good.

Osadtsa, M. Grammar. 8vo. (*Lemberg*).   10s.

Zelechowski, E. Ruthenisch-Deutsches Wörterbuch. 8vo. 2 vols. (*Lemberg*).   30s.

S.

SAILING, *see* YACHTING.

ST. DOMINGO, *see* WEST INDIES.

ST. HELENA, *see* ATLANTIC.

SALMON, *see* FISHING.

SAMOA, *see* PACIFIC.

SANITATION, *see* HYGIENE.

SANSKRIT AND BRAHMANICAL LITERATURE:

—I. GRAMMARS AND DICTIONARIES:

Müller, F. Max. Sanskrit grammar. (elem.). Ed. Macdonell. c. 8vo.
   Longmans.   6s.

Whitney, W. D. Sanskrit grammar. 8vo. *Trübner.*   12s.

Edgren, A. Sanskrit grammar. c. 8vo. *Trübner.*   10s. 6d.

Vaidya, L. R. The standard Sanskrit-English dictionary. 8vo. *Trübner.*   10s. 6d.

Apte, V. S. Sanskrit-English dictionary. 8vo. *Luzac.*   18s.

   ,, Student's guide to composition. 8vo. *Luzac.*   5s.

Böhtlingk and Roth. Sanskrit Wörterbuch. 8vo. 7 vols. *Petersburg Acad.*   180s.

—II. HISTORY:

Weber, A. History of Indian literature. 8vo. *Trübner.*   10s. 6d.

Schroeder, L. von. Indiens Literatur und Cultur. 8vo. (*Leipzig*).   18s.

Colebrooke, H. T. Essays on the religion and philosophy of the Hindus.
   8vo. 2 vols. *Trübner.*   28s.

Williams, Monier. Hinduism. 12mo. *S. P. C. K.*   2s. 6d.

Müller, F. Max. India; what can it teach us? 8vo. *Longmans.*   12s. 6d.

   ,, History of ancient Sanskrit literature. *Williams.*   O.P.

—III. TEXTS:

Original Sanskrit texts. Ed. J. Muir. d. 8vo. 5 vols. *Trübner.*   100s.
   Vol. i., 21s.; vol. ii., 21s.; vol. iii., 16s.; vol. iv., 21s.; vol. v., 21s.

Rig-Veda-Samhitâ (Sacred hymns of the Brahmans). Ed. Max Müller.
   4to. 6 vols. *Trübner.*   £15
   Smaller edition; text only. 8vo. 2 vols. *Trübner.* 32s. Also new edition. *Froude.* 105s.

Rig-Veda. Tr. into German and annotated by A. Ludwig. 8vo. 6 vols.
   (*Prague*).   76s.

   ,, Tr. H. Wilson. 8vo. 6 vols. *Trübner.*   119s.
   Vols. i., ii., iii., v., vi., 21s. each; vol. iv., 11s.

Kaegi, A. The Rig-Veda. Tr. R. Arrowsmith. 8vo. *Ginn (Boston).*   7s. 6d.

Ludwig, A. Anschauungen des Veda. 8vo. (*Prague*).   2s. 6d.

"**Sacred** books of the East." Ed. Max Müller. 8vo. 48 vols. *Clar. Press.*
   First series, 24 vols.; second series, 24 vols. (in progress). From 10s. 6d. to 21s. per volume.

Code of Manu ("Sacred books of the East," xxv.). Tr. G. Bühler. d. 8vo.
   Clar. Press.   21s.

Code of Manu. Ed. Jolly. p. 8vo. *Trübner.*   10s. 6d.

Bhagavadgîtâ; text. Ed. Thompson. *W. H. Allen.*   5*s.*

,, ("Sacred books of the East," viii.). Tr. K. T. Telang. d. 8vo. *Clar. Press.*   10*s.* 6*d.*

Sakuntalâ; a play. Ed. R. Pischel. 8vo. *Trübner.*   21*s.*

,, Tr. W. Jones ("Works," ix.). (*London*). 1807.   O.P.

Hitopadesa (fables). Ed. F. Max Müller. 8vo. 4 vols. *Longmans.*   26*s.*
Vol. i., 3*s.* 6*d.*; vol. ii., iii., iv., 7*s.* 6*d.* each.

Mahâbhârata (epic). Sanskrit text. Tr. Pratap Chundra Roy. 8vo. (*Calcutta*).

Râmâyana; text (epic). Ed. and tr. into Italian by G. Gorresio. 8vo. 10 vols. (*Paris*). pub. £12 12*s.*   O.P.

Pânini's Grammar; with German trans. by Böhtlingk. 8vo. (*Leipzig*).   60*s.*

Sanskrit texts; in "Bibliotheca Indica."
The "Bibliotheca Indica" is a collection of oriental works published by the *Asiatic Society of Bengal* (*Trübner*).

Sanskrit series. (*Bombay*).

Haas, E. Catalogue of Sanskrit and Pali books in British Museum. 4to. *Trübner.*   21*s.*
PERIODICAL: *Journal of the Royal Asiatic Society* (Trübner). Another useful journal is the *Indian Antiquary* (Trübner).

SARACENS, *see* MAHOMETANISM.

SARDINIA, *see* MEDITERRANEAN.

SAWMILLS, *see* INDUSTRIES XVI.

SCANDINAVIA, *see* DENMARK, NORWAY *and* SWEDEN.

,,   ANCIENT RACES OF, *see* ANTHROPOLOGY II. *and* III.

SCHOOLS, PUBLIC AND HIGH, *see* UNIVERSITIES.

SCOTLAND:

See ENGLAND *for books dealing with England also.*

—I. GEOGRAPHY:

Baddeley, R. J. B. Scotland ("Thorough guide" series). 12mo. 4 vols. *Dulau.* Maps.   16*s.*
Part i., The Highlands as far north as Inverness, 7*s.*; part ii., Northern Highlands, the mainland north of Inverness, 3*s.* 6*d.*; part iii., The Lowlands, including Edinburgh and Glasgow, 4*s.*: Orkney and Shetland, 1*s.* 6*d.*

Black's Guide to Scotland. f. 8vo. *Black.* illus.   8*s.* 6*d.*
On the whole the fullest guide in one volume.

Murray's Handbook for Scotland. p. 8vo. *Murray.*   9*s.*
Specially valuable for its antiquarian, historical, and literary references.

Geikie, A. The scenery of Scotland viewed in connection with its physical geology. p. 8vo. *Macmillan.*   12*s.* 6*d.*

Grant, J. Old and new Edinburgh. 4to. 3 vols., 9*s.* each. *Cassell.*   27*s.*

—II. HISTORY:

See also CHURCH HISTORY V. (B).

Burton, J. H. History of Scotland to 1748. c. 8vo. 8 vols. *Blackwood*.   63*s*.
Vols. i. to vii., 7*s*. 6*d*. each ; viii., and index, 10*s*. 6*d*.

Chambers, R. Biographical dictionary of eminent Scotsmen. 3 vols.
Blackie.   O.P.

Skene, W. F. Celtic Scotland to 1200. d. 8vo. 3 vols., 15*s*. each. *Douglas*.   45*s*.

Robertson, E. W. Scotland under her early kings (to 1285). d. 8vo.
2 vols. *Douglas*.   36*s*.

Hailes, Lord. Annals of Scotland. 1776.   O.P.

Innes, C. Sketches of early Scottish history. d. 8vo. *Douglas*. pub. 16*s*.   O.P.

  ,, Scotland in the middle ages. d. 8vo. *Douglas*. pub. 10*s*. 6*d*.   O.P.

Skelton, J. Maitland of Lethington. 8vo. 2 vols. *Blackwood*.   28*s*.
A good sketch of Scotland under Queen Mary.

Hosack. Mary, Queen of Scots, and her accusers. 8vo. *Blackwood*.
pub. 21*s*.   O.P.
The best book in defence of Mary.

Goedeke, K. Maria Stuart. (*Heidelberg*).
The most impartial estimate of Mary.

Domestic annals of Scotland (1561 to 1745). Ed. R. Chambers. d. 8vo.
3 vols. *Chambers*.   40*s*.
Vols. i., ii., 21*s*.: vol. iii., 16*s*.

Chambers, R. History of the rebellion, 1745-6. *Chambers*.   5*s*.

Ramsay, J. Scotland and Scotsmen in the 18th century. 8vo. 2 vols.
Blackwood.   31*s*. 6*d*.

—III. LANGUAGE (GAELIC):

Stewart, A. Gaelic grammar. 12mo. *Maclachlan*.   3*s*. 6*d*.

McAlpine, N. Gaelic-English and English-Gaelic dictionary. 8vo.
Maclachlan.   9*s*.
Gaelic pronunciation is given.

McKinnon. Gaelic reader. 12mo. *Maclachlan*.   3*s*. 6*d*.
Part i., 3*s*. 6*d*.

Macintyre, Duncan B. Songs and poems. 18mo. *Maclachlan*.   2*s*.
NOTE: Gaelic texts will be found in Campbell's *Tales of the west Highlands* (Gardner),
and MacInnes' *Folk and hero tales* (Nutt).

—IV. LAW :

No attempt is made to give an account of Scottish law-books on special subjects.

Bell, G. J. Principles of the law of Scotland. Ed. W. Guthrie. 8vo.
2 vols. (*Edinburgh*).   45*s*.

Erskine, J. Principles of the law of Scotland. 8vo. (*Edinburgh*).   21*s*.

Bell's Dictionary and digest of the law of Scotland. Ed. G. Watson.
r. 8vo. *Stevens and Haynes*.   38*s*.
Not by the same author as Bell's *Principles*.

Mackay, Æ. J. Practice of the Court of Session. r. 8vo. *Stevens and Haynes*.   72*s*.

SCULPTURE, *see* GREECE, ARCHÆOLOGY.

SEAMANSHIP, *see* NAVY II.

SEAWEEDS, *see* BOTANY IV.

SENEGAL, *see* AFRICA III.

SERMONS

Alford, H. Sermons. 16mo. *Hodder.*   2s. 6d.

Andrewes, L. Selections. *S. P. C. K.*   O.P.

Arnold, T. Sermons (collected). 8vo. 6 vols., 5s. each. *Reeves and Turner.*   30s.

  ,,   Christian life at school. 8vo. *Longmans.*   7s. 6d.

Barrow, Isaac. Sermons (vol. ix. of " National Library "). *Cassell.*   6d.

Barry, A. Sermons preached at Westminster Abbey. c. 8vo. *Cassell.*   5s.

Beecher, H. W. Plymouth Church sermons. 8vo. 10 vols., 3s. 6d. each. *Dickenson.*   35s.

Beveridge, W. Twenty-six sermons. *S. P. C. K.* (*London*). 1850.   8s.

Binney, T. Sermons preached in the King's Weigh House Chapel (two series). ex. f. 8vo. *Macmillan.*
Congregational.   O.P.

Bradley, C. Sermons selected by G. J. Davies. c. 8vo. *Wells, Gardner.*   3s. 6d.

Brooks, Phillips. Twenty sermons. c. 8vo. *Macmillan.*   6s.

  ,,   The candle of the Lord. c. 8vo. *Macmillan.*   6s.

  ,,   Sermons preached in English churches. c. 8vo. *Macmillan.*
Broad.   6s.

Bull, Bishop. Sermons (vol. i. of " Works "). 8vo. (*Oxford*). 1827.   O.P.

Butler, Bishop. Sermons. 8vo. *Clar. Press.*   5s. 6d.

Butler, H. M. Sermons preached in Harrow School. c. 8vo. *Macmillan.*   7s. 6d.

Butler, A. Sermons (two series). 8vo. *Macmillan.*   15s.

Caird, J. Sermons. 12mo. *Blackwood.*   5s.

Carpenter, W. Boyd. Permanent elements of religion (Bampton lectures). c. 8vo. *Macmillan.*   6s.

Chalmers, T. Select sermons. 12mo. (*Edinburgh*).   1s. 6d.

Channing, W. E. The perfect life. p. 8vo. *Williams.*
Unitarian.   3s.

Church, R. W. Human life and its conditions. Oxford Univ. sermons (1876-8). c. 8vo. *Macmillan.*   6s.

  ,,   The gifts of civilization. c. 8vo. *Macmillan.*   7s. 6d.

  ,,   The discipline of the Christian character. c. 8vo. *Macmillan.*   4s. 6d.

  ,,   Advent sermons. c. 8vo. *Macmillan.*   4s. 6d.

Cox, S. Genesis of evil. 8vo. *Paul.*   6s.

  ,,   Salvator mundi. p. 8vo. *Paul.*   5s.

Dale, R. W. Evangelical revival, and other sermons. c. 8vo. *Hodder.*   6s.

Davies, Llewellyn. The Gospel and modern life. ex. f. 8vo. *Macmillan.*   6s.

  ,,   Warnings against superstition. ex. f. 8vo. *Macmillan.*   2s. 6d.

  ,,   The manifestation of the Son of God. f. 8vo. *Macmillan.*   6s. 6d.

Eyton, R. The true life, and other sermons. p. 8vo. *Paul.*   7s. 6d.

Farrar, F. W. Ephphatha. c. 8vo. *Macmillan.*   6s.

  ,,   Eternal hope. p. 8vo. *Macmillan.*   6s.

Hare, A. W. Alton sermons. p. 8vo. *Isbister.*   10s. 6d.

Hare, J. C. The victory of faith, and other sermons. c. 8vo. *Macmillan.*   6s. 6d.

  ,,   Mission of the Comforter. p. 8vo. *Macmillan.*   7s. 6d.

Holland, H. Scott. Logic and life. c. 8vo. *Rivingtons.*   7s. 6d.

Irving, Ed. Sermons. 3 vols. (*London*). 1828.   O.P.

Keble, J. College sermons. 8vo. *Parker.*   12s.

Kingsley, C. Sermons on national subjects. c. 8vo. *Macmillan.*   3s. 6d.

,,   Village and town, and country sermons. c. 8vo. *Macmillan.*   3s. 6d.

,,   Westminster sermons. c. 8vo. *Macmillan.*   3s. 6d.

Latimer, Bishop. Sermons (in "Arber's reprints").   1s.

Liddon, H. P. Oxford University sermons. c. 8vo. 2 ser., 5s. each. *Rivingtons.*   10s.

,,   Easter in St. Paul's. c. 8vo. 2 vols. *Rivingtons.*   10s.

,,   The Magnificat sermons in St. Paul's. c. 8vo. *Rivingtons.*   2s. 6d.

,,   Some elements of religion. c. 8vo. *Rivingtons.*   2s. 6d.

Maclaren, A. Sermons preached at Manchester. f. 8vo. 3 vols., 4s. 6d. each. *Macmillan.*   13s. 6d.

,,   Week-day evening addresses. f. 8vo. *Macmillan.*   2s. 6d.

Macleod, Norman (Jr.). Simple truths to working people. 12mo. *Daldy.*   2s. 6d.

Magee, Bishop. The Gospel and the age. c. 8vo. *Isbister.*   7s. 6d.

Manning, H. E. Sermons preached before the University of Oxford. 8vo. *Rivingtons.* 1844. pub. 6s.   O.P.

,,   Sermons. 8vo. 4 vols., 10s. 6d. each. *Pickering.* 1850. pub. 42s.   O.P.

Martineau, J. Hours of thought on sacred things. 8vo. 2 vols., 7s. 6d. each. *Longmans.*
Unitarian.   15s.

Maurice, J. F. D. Sermons. 8vo. 6 vols. *Smith, Elder.* pub. 21s.
Broad.   O.P.

,,   Prophets and kings of the Old Testament. c. 8vo. *Macmillan.*   6s.

,,   Social morality. c. 8vo. *Macmillan.*   6s.

Melvill, H. Sermons. 12mo. 2 vols., 5s. each. *Rivingtons.*   10s.

Mozley, J. B. Parochial sermons. c. 8vo. *Rivingtons.*   7s. 6d.

,,   Oxford University sermons. c. 8vo. *Rivingtons.*   7s. 6d.

Newman, J. H. Parochial and plain sermons. c. 8vo. 8 vols., 3s. 6d. each. *Rivingtons.*   28s.

Pusey, E. B. Parochial and cathedral sermons. 8vo. *Smith and Innes.*   6s.

Robertson, F. W. Sermons. c. 8vo. 4 vols., 3s. 6d. each. *Paul.*   14s.

Salmon, G. The reign of law. p. 8vo. *Macmillan.*   5s.

South, Canon. Sermons. 8vo. 4 vols. *Tegg.* 1843. pub. 24s.   O.P.

Spurgeon, C. H. The present truth : a collection of sermons. 8vo. *Passmore and Alabaster.*   7s.

Stanley, A. P. Sermons and essays on the Apostolic age. p. 8vo. *Parker.*   7s. 6d.

,,   Westminster sermons (special occasions). 8vo. *Murray.*   15s.

Stowell, Hugh. Salford sermons. p. 8vo. *Tegg.*   2s. 6d.

Taylor, Jeremy. Sermons (vols. v., vi., of "Works"). 8vo. 1839.   O.P.

Temple, F. Rugby sermons (three series). c. 8vo. *Macmillan.*   16s. 6d.
First series, 4s. 6d. ; second and third series, each 6s.

Thorold, A. W. The claim of Christ on the young (Oxford University sermons). p. 8vo. *Isbister.*   2s. 6d.

Trench, R. C. Shipwrecks of faith. 8vo. *Macmillan.* pub. 2*s.* 6*d.*	O.P.
,, Westminster Abbey sermons. p. 8vo. *Paul.*	6*s.*
Vaughan, C. J. Temple sermons. c. 8vo. *Macmillan.*	10*s.* 6*d.*
,, Oxford and Cambridge University sermons (1861–87). p. 8vo. *Macmillan.*	10*s.* 6*d.*
,, Church of the first days. f. 8vo. 3 series, 4*s.* 6*d.* each. *Macmillan.*	13*s.* 6*d.*
Westcott, B. F. Revelation of the risen Lord. c. 8vo. *Macmillan.*	6*s.*
,, Revelation of the Father. c. 8vo. *Macmillan.*	6*s.*
,, Christianity and social life. c. 8vo. *Macmillan.*	6*s.*
,, Christus Consummator. c. 8vo. *Macmillan.*	6*s.*
,, The historic faith. c. 8vo. *Macmillan.*	6*s.*
Wilberforce, S. Oxford University sermons; three series (1837–70). 8vo. *Parker.*	7*s.* 6*d.*
Wilson, J. M. Sermons preached in Clifton College. c. 8vo. *Macmillan.*	6*s.*
Wright, D. Waiting for the light. p. 8vo. *King.* pub. 6*s.*	O.P.

COLLECTIONS.

British eloquence of the XIX. century. *Griffin.* 1856–8. pub. 21*s.*	O.P.
Contains two series of "Sacred Oratory," one vol. of sermons of the Church of England, and one of sermons of the Presbyterian churches.	
Brogden, J. Illustrations of the liturgy and ritual of the churches of England and Ireland. p. 8vo. 3 vols. *Murray.* 1842. pub. 27*s.*	O.P.
Sermons by eminent divines of the XVII. century.	
Fish, H. C. History and repository of pulpit eloquence. 8vo. 2 vols. (*New York*). pub. 30*s.*	O.P.
British, American, French, German, Greek, and Latin pulpits.	
Knox, G. Family lectures. 1791–5.	O.P.
XVIII. century sermons.	
Practical sermons; selected by A. Watson. 1845–6.	O.P.
Christian institutes; selected by C. Wordsworth. 1837.	O.P.

SERVIA :

See also TURKEY.

—I. GEOGRAPHY :

Denton, W. Servia and the Servians. 8vo. *Bell and Daldy.* pub. 9*s.* 6*d.*	O.P.
Balme, L. J. A. La principauté de Serbie. 8vo. (*Paris*).	O.P.

—II. LANGUAGE :

The beginner might use the short grammar by Morfill, but the works of Danichich in Serbian must afterwards be consulted

Morfill, W. R. Simplified grammar of the Serbian language. c. 8vo. *Trübner.*	4*s.* 6*d.*
Popovich, G. Wörterbuch der serbischen und deutschen Sprachen. 8vo. 2 vols. (*Belgrade*).	18*s.*
Danichich, G. Istoriya oblika Srpskogaili Khrvatskoga Yezika (History of forms of the Serbian or Croatian language). 8vo. (*Belgrade*).	7*s.* 6*d.*
,, Osnove Srpskoga ili Khrvatskoga Yezika (The foundations of the Serbian or Croatian language). 8vo. (*Belgrade*).	9*s.*
Dozon, A. L'épopée serbe. 12mo. (*Paris*).	6*s.* 6*d.*

SEWERAGE, *see* HYGIENE.

SHAKESPEARE :

—I. GRAMMARS AND DICTIONARIES :

Cowden-Clarke, Mrs. Concordance to Shakespeare. 8vo. *Bickers.*   25*s.*

Furness, Mrs. H. H. Concordance to Shakespeare's poems. r. 8vo. *Lippincott.*   18*s.*

Schmidt, A. Shakespeare lexicon. r. 8vo. 2 vols. *Williams.*   31*s.* 6*d.*
Different meanings of words distinguished.

Fleay, F. G. Shakespeare manual. ex. f. 8vo. *Macmillan.*   4*s.* 6*d.*
Useful, but conclusions to be accepted with caution.

Abbott, E. A. Shakespearian grammar. ex. f. 8vo. *Macmillan.*   6*s.*

—II. EDITIONS :

Cambridge edition. Ed. Clarke and Wright. 8vo. 9 vols., 10*s.* 6*d.* each.
Macmillan.   94*s.* 6*d.*
The best authority in the matter of text. The " Globe " edition has the same text.

Globe edition. Ed. Clarke and Wright. 8vo. *Macmillan.*   3*s.* 6*d.*

Leopold Shakspere. 4to. *Cassell.*   3*s.* 6*d.*

Henry Irving Shakspere. Ed. F. A. Marshall. sm. 4to. 8 vols.,
10*s.* 6*d.* each. *Blackie.* illus.   84*s.*
Useful variorum.

New variorum edition. Ed. H. H. Furness. r. 8vo. *Lippincott.*
Very important ; in progress. Seven plays now issued ; 18*s.* each.

First folio. Ed. J. O. Halliwell-Phillips, etc. 8vo. *Chatto.*   7*s.* 6*d.*
Reduced photographic fac-simile, difficult to read.

Reprint of first folio. 4to. *Booth.* pub. 52*s.* 6*d.*   O.P.

Fac-similes of quarto editions. Ed. Furnivall and others. *W. Griggs.*
In progress. 28 vols. published.

Shakespeare's Sonnets. Ed. T. Tyler. 8vo. *Nutt.*   12*s.*
Interesting historical investigation and discussion.

—III. CRITICISM :

Walker, W. S. Critical examination of the text of Shakespeare.
12mo. 3 vols. *J. R. Smith.* pub. 18*s.*   O.P.

Stokes, H. P. Chronological order of Shakespeare's plays. *Macmillan.*   O.P.

Shakespeare's library. Ed. Collier and Hazlitt. 12mo. 6 vols. *Reeves
and Turner.*   20*s.*
Important collection of sources of Shakespeare's plots, etc.

Skeat, W. W. Shakespeare's Plutarch. p. 8vo. *Macmillan.*   6 .

Gervinus, G. G. Shakespeare commentaries. Tr. Miss Burnett. d. 8vo.
Smith, Elder.   14*s.*

Courtenay, T. P. Commentaries on the historical plays of Shakespeare.
p. 8vo. *Colburn.* 1840. pub. 18*s.*   O.P.

Lloyd, W. W. Critical essays on the plays of Shakespeare. f. 8vo. *Bell.*   2*s.* 6*d.*

Hazlitt, W. Characters of Shakespeare's plays. p. 8vo. *Bell (Bohn).*   3*s.* 6*d.*

Jameson, Mrs. Shakespeare's heroines. p. 8vo. *Bell (Bohn).*   3*s.* 6*d.*

Coleridge, S. T. Lectures and notes on Shakespeare. Ed. T. Ashe.
p. 8vo. *Bell (Bohn).*   3*s.* 6*d.*
The portions reported by Collier to be taken with suspicion.

Swinburne, A. C. A study of Shakespeare. c. 8vo. *Chatto.* pub. 8*s*.   O.P.

Chasles, P. Études sur Shakespeare, etc. 12mo. (*Paris*).   O.P.

Dowden, E. Shakspere: his mind and art. p. 8vo. *Paul.*   12*s*.

—IV. LIFE AND TIMES:

Hudson, H. N. Life, art, and character of Shakespeare. c. 8vo. 2 vols., 12*s*. each. *Ginn* (*Boston*).   24*s*.

Halliwell-Phillips, J. O. Outlines of the life of Shakespeare. r. 8vo. 2 vols. *Longmans*.   21*s*.

Fleay, F. G. Chronicle history of the life of Shakespeare. 8vo. *Nimmo*.   15*s*.

Elze, Karl. William Shakespeare; a literary biography. Tr. Miss Dora Schmitz. 8vo. *Bell* (*Bohn*).   5*s*.

Drake, N. Shakespeare and his times. 4to. 2 vols. 1817.   O.P.

Symonds, J. A. Shakespeare's predecessors in the English drama. d. 8vo. *Smith, Elder*.   16*s*.

Simpson, R. The school of Shakespeare. c. 8vo. *Chatto*. pub. 18*s*.   O.P.

Griffiths, L. M. Evenings with Shakespeare. f. 4to. *Arrowsmith* (*Bristol*).   15*s*.
Industrious and useful collection of odds and ends of information.

SHAN STATES, *see* BURMAH.

SHEEP, *see* LIVE-STOCK.

SHIPPING AND SHIP-BUILDING, *see* NAVY *and* YACHTING.

SHOEMAKING, *see* INDUSTRIES III.

SHOOTING:

See also DOG *and* SPORT.

For a knowledge of the construction of shot-guns and rifles, history of development and improvement, read Stonehenge's *Modern sportsman's gun and rifle*; for information on game-shooting, *Shooting* ("Badminton Library"); on wild-fowling, *The wild fowler*, *The fowler in Ireland*, and *Hints on shore shooting*. Hawker's book is somewhat out of date, but contains much that is still useful.

Hawker, P. Instructions to young sportsmen in all that relates to guns and shooting. 8vo. *Longmans*. illus. pub. 18*s*.   O.P.

Payne-Gallwey, R. Letters to young shooters. c. 8vo. *Longmans*.   7*s*. 6*d*.

"Stonehenge." The modern sportsman's gun and rifle. 8vo. 2 vols., 15*s*. each. *H. Cox*.   30*s*.

Greener, W. W. The gun and its development. 4to. *Cassell*.   10*s*. 6*d*.

Dougall. The rifle and how to use it. p. 8vo. *Low*.   10*s*. 6*d*.

Walsingham and Gallwey. Shooting ("Badminton Library"). c. 8vo. 2 vols. *Longmans*. illus.   21*s*.
Vol. i., *Field and covert*, 10*s*. 6*d*.: vol. ii., *Moor and marsh*, 10*s*. 6*d*.

Trumbull, G. Names and portraits of birds which interest gunners. 8vo. *Harper*. illus.   12*s*. 6*d*.
Descriptions and good illustrations.

Folkard, H. C. The wild-fowler. 8vo. *Longmans*. illus. pub. 15*s*.   O.P.

Leffingwell. Wild-fowl shooting. 8vo. (*Chicago*). illus.   10*s*. 6*d*.
Chiefly shooting to decoys. English edition by *Low*.

Payne-Gallwey, R. The fowler in Ireland. 8vo. *Van Voorst.*   21*s.*
Good illustrations; includes decoys.

Long, J. W. American wild-fowl shooting. c. 8vo. *Trübner.* illus.   10*s.*

Harting, J. E. Hints on shore shooting. p. 8vo. *Van Voorst.*   3*s.* 6*d.*
With a chapter on skinning and preserving birds.

Manley, J. J. Notes on game and game-shooting. p. 8vo. *Gill.* illus.   7*s.* 6*d.*

Carnegie, W. Practical game-preserving. d. 8vo. *Gill.* illus.   21*s.*

Oke's Game-laws. Ed. Willis-Bund. p. 8vo. *Butterworth.*   16*s.*
A manual of the law, necessary to shooters; has not been very lately edited, but there is no later text-book.

"Deadfall." Experiences of a game-preserver. d. 8vo. *H. Cox.* illus.   21*s.*

Price, R. J. Pheasant-rearing and grouse-driving. l. p. 8vo. *H. Cox.*   3*s.* 6*d.*

SHORTHAND:

Pitman's system is recommended. The three text-books should be studied in the order indicated in the list.

Pitman, I. History of shorthand. *I. Pitman.*   O.P.
In phonographic characters. Reprinted in common type in the *Phonetic Journal,* 1881.

Levy, M. History of shorthand. 8vo. *Levy* (Mitre-court, Fleet-st.).   5*s.*

Pitman, I. Phonographic teacher. f. 8vo. *I. Pitman.*   6*d.*

   ,,   Manual of phonography (advanced). f. 8vo. *I. Pitman.*   1*s.* 6*d.*

   ,,   Reporter's companion. f. 8vo. *I. Pitman.*   2*s.*
The most abbreviated style.

Levy, M. Taylor's system of shorthand writing. 8vo. *Levy.*   1*s.* 6*d.*
An exposition of Harding's modification of Taylor's system.

Gurney, W. B. Gurney's system of shorthand. p. 8vo. *Butterworth.*   3*s.*
The system employed by the official shorthand writer of the Houses of Parliament, and most of his staff.

Everett, J. D. Shorthand for general use. f. 8vo. *Marcus Ward.*   2*s.* 6*d.*

Reed, T. A. Reporter's guide. *F. Pitman.*   1*s.* 6*d.*
Concerning the duties of the professional reporter.

Westby-Gibson, J. Bibliography of shorthand. l. 8vo. *I. Pitman.*   5*s.*

Rockwell, J. E. The teaching, practice, and literature of shorthand. *Circular of Bureau of Education, U.S., Gov. Printing Office (Washington).*
Contains the alphabets of most shorthand systems.

Panstenographicon. Ed. Krieg and Zeibig. 8vo. (*Dresden*).   24*s.*
Principal systems in all modern languages, each described by a writer of the system; also accounts of Greek and Roman tachygraphy.
PERIODICAL: *Phonetic Journal* (weekly). *I. Pitman.* 1*d.* Printed partly in shorthand, and partly in common type.

SKATING:

Vanderwell and Witham. System of figure-skating. 8vo. *H. Cox.*   7s. 6d.

Adams, D. Skating ("All England" ser.). sm. 8vo. *Bell.*   2s.
Contains a chapter on speed-skating; also a chapter by Miss Cheetham for ladies.

Monier-Williams, M. and S. Combined figure-skating. c. 8vo. *H. Cox.*   5s.

Goodman, N. and A. Fen-skating. c. 8vo. *Low.*   5s.
Contains some history of skating in the Fens, and records of races.

SLANDER, *see* ENGLAND, LAW IX.

SLATE QUARRYING, *see* MINING.

SLAVONIC LANGUAGES AND LITERATURE:

With LITHUANIAN *and* LETTISH. *See also* BOHEMIA, BULGARIA, POLAND, RUSSIA, SERVIA.

The most scientific way of studying the Slavonic languages is to begin with old Slavonic (Leskien's *Handbuch*); and then to go to Russian. Schleicher's *Polabish grammar* (a language now extinct) is invaluable for the scientific study of Slavonic.

Miklosich, F. von. Vergleichende Grammatik der slavischen Sprachen. 8vo. 4 vols. (*Vienna*).   83s.
Vol. i., 20s.; vol. ii., 15s.; vol. iii., 18s.; vol. iv., 30s. A splendid contribution to philology.

,, Lexicon Palæoslovenico-Græco-Latinum. r. 8vo. (*Vienna*).   27s.

,, Dictionnaire abrégé de six langues Slaves (Russe, Vieux-Slave, Bulgare, Serbe, Schèque, et Polonais) ainsi que Français et Allemand. (*Vienna*). pub. £3 3s.   O.P.
Very useful for the comparison of the Slavonic languages.

,, Etymologisches Wörterbuch der slavischen Sprachen. 8vo. (*Vienna*).   20s.
An invaluable book.

Leskien, A. Handbuch der Altbulgarischen (Altkirchenslavischen) Sprache. 8vo. (*Weimar*).   6s.
The most practical grammar of old Slavonic; with chrestomathy.

Pypin and Spasovich. Istoria Slavianskikh Literatur. 8vo. (*St. Petersburg*).
The great work in Russian.

Talvi (Mrs. Robinson). Historical view of the languages and literature of Slavic nations. p. 8vo. *Putnam.*   5s.
Very readable and accurate, but a trifle out of date.

Morfill, W. R. Slavonic literature. f. 8vo. *S. P. C. K.*   2s. 6d.

Schleicher, A. Laut und Formenlehre der polabischen Sprache. r. 8vo. (*St. Petersburg*).   5s.

Cigale, M. Deutsch-Slovenisches Wörterbuch. r. 8vo. 2 vols. (*Laibach*).   21s.

Völkel, M. J. A. Lithauisches Elementarbuch. 8vo. (*Heidelberg*).   3s.

Kurschat, F. Grammatik der lithauischen Sprache. 8vo. (*Halle*).   12s.

,, Wörterbuch der lithauischen Sprache. 8vo. (*Halle*).   22s. 6d.

Schleicher, A. Handbuch der lithauischen Sprache. 8vo. 2 vols. (*Prague*).   14s.

Bielenstein, A. Die lettische Sprache. 8vo. 2 vols. (*Berlin*).   20s.

Ulmann and Brasche. Lettisches Wörterbuch. r. 8vo. 2 vols. (*Riga*).   14s.

SLEIGHT OF HAND, *see* CONJURING.

SLOYD, *see* WORKSHOP.

SOAP, *see* INDUSTRIES XVII.

SOCIALISM, *see* POLITICAL ECONOMY IX.

SOCIOLOGY, *see* POLITICAL PHILOSOPHY I.

SOCIETY ISLANDS, *see* PACIFIC.

SOILS, *see* AGRICULTURE III.

SOLOMON ISLANDS, *see* PACIFIC.

SOMALILAND, *see* AFRICA V.

SOUDAN, *see* AFRICA II. *and* ALGIERS.

SOUTH SEA ISLANDS, *see* PACIFIC.

SPAIN : GEOGRAPHY, ETC. :

Murray's Handbook to Spain. p. 8vo. *Murray.*   20s.

Lavigne, G. de. L'Espagne et le Portugal ("Guide Joanne"). 16mo. *Hachette.*   15s.

Arteche, J. Gomez de. Geografia de España. 4to. (*Madrid*).   10s.

Webster, Wentworth. Spain (in "Foreign countries and British colonies" ser.). c. 8vo. *Low.*   3s. 6d.

Rose, H. J. Untrodden Spain and her black country. 8vo. 2 vols. *Tinsley.*   30s.

Campion, J. S. On foot in Spain. 8vo. *Chapman.* illus.   16s.
    A walk from the Bay of Biscay to the Mediterranean.

Ross and Cooper. Highlands of Cantabria. 8vo. *Low.* illus.   21s.

Ford, R. Gatherings from Spain. p. 8vo. *Murray.*   3s. 6d.

Elliott, Mrs. Diary of an idle woman in Spain. c. 8vo. *White.* pub. 6s.   O.P.

Gilbard. Popular history of Gibraltar, with map and guide. 8vo. (*Gibraltar*).

Riano, J. F. The industrial arts in Spain. c. 8vo. *Chapman.* illus.   4s.

España : sus monumentos, artes, é historia. *Cortezo* (*Barcelona*). illus.
    A description of Spain in provinces; sold separately. Illustrated chiefly from photographs.

SPAIN : HISTORY :

Including PORTUGAL.

La Fuente. Historia general de España. 30 vols. (*Madrid*).

Dunham, S. A. History of Spain and Portugal. f. 8vo. 5 vols. *Longmans.* pub. 17s. 6d.   O.P.

Dahn, F. Die Könige der Germanen. 12mo. 6 vols. (*Würzburg*).   45s.
    Vol. v., vi., deal with the Visigoths in Spain.

Colmeiro, Manuel. Cortes de los antiguos Reinos de Leon y Castilla. (*Madrid*).

Condé, J. A. History of the dominion of the Arabs in Spain. Tr. Mrs. Forster. p. 8vo. 3 vols., 3s. 6d. each. *Bell* (*Bohn*).   10s. 6d.

Poole, S. Lane. The Moors in Spain. c. 8vo. *Unwin.* illus.   5s.

Irving, Washington. The conquest of Granada. *Bell (Bohn).*   3s. 6d.

Chronicle of James I., king of Aragon, 1216–76. Tr. J. Forster. r. 8vo. 2 vols. *Chapman.*   28s.

Life and voyages of Columbus. 8vo. 3 vols. *Cassell.*   7s. 6d.

Prescott, W. H. History of Ferdinand and Isabella. 2 vols. 8vo. *Routledge.*   10s.

Robertson, W. Reign of Charles V. Ed. Prescott. 2 vols. 8vo. *Routledge.*   10s.

Prescott, W. H. Reign of Philip II. 8vo. 2 vols. *Routledge.*   10s.

Ranke, L. von. The Spanish monarchy. Tr. *Whittaker.*   O.P.
A sketch of the constitution, government, and economic failure of Spain under Philip II.

Maxwell, W. Stirling. Don John of Austria. r. 8vo. 2 vols. *Longmans.* pub. 42s.   O.P.

Weiss, C. L'Espagne depuis Philippe II. jusqu'aux Bourbons. 8vo. 2 vols. *Hachette.*   10s.

Coxe, W. History of the kings of Spain and House of Bourbon. 5 vols. (*London*). 1815.   O.P.

D'Aulnoy, Comtesse. La cour et la ville de Madrid vers la fin du 17me. siècle. 2 vols. (*Paris*).
Vol. i., o.p.; vol. ii., 6s. An account of life in the Spanish Court, 1679-80.

Parnell, A. War of succession in Spain, 1702–11. d. 8vo. *Bell.*   14s.

Napier, W. F. P. History of the war in the Peninsula, 1807–14. c. 8vo. 3 vols., 3s. 6d. each. *Routledge.*   10s. 6d.

Cárdenas, F. de. Ensayo sobre la historia de la propiedad territorial en España. (*Madrid*).

Cronicas (in "Biblioteca de autores españoles"). r. 8vo. 3 vols., 12s. 6d. each. (*Madrid*).   37s. 6d.

Historia de sucesos particulares (in "Bibl. aut. esp.," xxi., xxviii). r. 8vo. 12s. 6d. each.   25s.

Navarrette, M. F. de. Coleccion de documentos inéditos para la historia de España. (*Madrid*).
In progress. 93 vols. issued. 8vo. 12s. 6d. each.

Memorias de la Real Academia de la Historia (1796-1888). fo. 11 vols. (*Madrid*).   100s.

Florez, F. H. and others. Espana Sagrada (1754-1879). 4to. 51 vols. (*Madrid*).   £25.
NOTE: Many MSS. of Arabic authors have been edited or translated by F. F. Gonzalez (*España Arabe*), and by Codera (*Biblioteca Arabico-Hispano*).

SPAIN: LANGUAGE AND LITERATURE:

—I. GRAMMARS AND DICTIONARIES:

Del Mar, E. Complete grammar of the Spanish language (key 3s. 6d.) 12mo. *Nutt.*   6s.

Clarke, Butler. Spanish grammar ("Parallel grammar" series). *Sonnenschein.*
In press.

Förster, P. Spanische Sprachlehre. 8vo. (*Leipzig*).   10s.

Velasquez. Dictionary of the Spanish and English languages. r. 8vo. *Trübner*.   24*s.*
Smaller edition. c. 8vo. 7*s.* 6*d.*

Diccionario de la Academia. 4to. *Nutt.*   36*s.*

—II. HISTORY AND CRITICISM:

Ticknor, G. History of Spanish literature. 8vo. 3 vols. *Houghton (U.S.)*   40*s.*

Los Rios, J. Amador de. Historia critica de la literatura española. 4to. 7 vols. (*Madrid*).   O.P.
May be obtained at about 150*s.*

Dozy, R. P. Recherches sur l'histoire et la littérature d'Espagne pendant le moyen âge. 8vo. (*Leyden*).   10*s.*

Hubbard, G. Histoire de la littérature contemporaine en Espagne. 12mo. *Charpentier.*   3*s.*

Tannenberg, B. de. La poésie castillane contemporaine. 12mo. (*Paris*).   3*s.*

Diercks, G. Das moderne Geistesleben Spaniens. 8vo. (*Leipzig*).   5*s.*
The last three books are for literature later than that dealt with by Ticknor.

—III. COLLECTIONS:

Biblioteca de autores Españoles. r. 8vo. 71 vols., 12*s.* 6*d.* each. (*Madrid*).
For students. A new edition, with better print, is in contemplation.

Colleccion de autores Castellanos. 3*s.* 6*d.* each. (*Madrid*).
More modern works.

Biblioteca clasica Española. 1*s.* 6*d.* each. (*Barcelona*).

Coleccion de autores Españoles. 41 vols., 3*s.* 6*d.* each. *Brockhaus.*
Excellent for girls.

Biblioteca Universal. 124 vols., 8*d.* each. (*Madrid*).
Like Cassell's "National Library."

—IV. TEXTS:

(A) POETRY AND DRAMA.

Poema del Cid (" Bibl. Aut. Esp." vol. lvii.). r. 8vo. (*Madrid*).   12*s.* 6*d.*

  ,,   Original text, with French translation, by Damas Hinard. 4to. (*Paris*). pub. 16*s.*   O.P.

Romancero del Cid. Ed. Michaelis. 12mo. *Brockhaus.*   3*s.* 6*d.*

Romanceros (in " Bibl. Aut. Esp." vols. x. and xvi.). Ed. Duran. r. 8vo. (*Madrid*).   25*s.*

  ,,   Ed. Depping. 12mo. *Brockhaus.*   12*s.*

Cantos populares. Ed. F. R. Marin. 12mo. 5 vols. (*Seville*).   30*s.*

Cantares populares (vol. xcvii. of "Bibl. Univ."). Ed. R. Caballero. (*Madrid*).   8*d.*

Poesias populares. Ed. T. Segarra. *Brockhaus.*   7*s.*

Ercilla. La Araucana (vol. xvii. of " Bibl. Aut. Esp."). r. 8vo. (*Madrid*).   12*s.* 6*d.*

Antologia Española. Ed. C. Michaelis. 12mo. *Brockhaus.*   3*s.* 6*d.*

Tesoro del Parnaso Español. Ed. Quintana. 8vo. (*Paris*).   10*s.*

  ,,   de la poesia castellana (vols. xvii., xviii., xx., xxii., and xxx. of the " Bibl. Univ."). 8*d.* each. (*Madrid*).   3*s.* 4*d.*
There is a larger collection in the "Bibl. Aut. Esp."

Espronceda, J. de. Obras poeticas. Ed. Hartzenbusch. 8vo. (*Paris*).   5*s.*

Nuñez de Arce. Gritos del combate, etc. 8vo. (*Madrid*).   4*s.*

Campoamor, R. de. Obras escogidas. 12mo. 3 vols. *Brockhaus.*   10*s.* 6*d.*

La Celestina. Obras (in "Bibl. Univ."). 2 vols., 8*d.* each. (*Madrid*).   1*s.* 4*d.*

Lope de Vega. Comedias escogidas (vols. xxiv., xxxiv., xli., lii., of "Bibl. Aut. Esp."). r. 8vo. 12*s.* 6*d.* each. (*Madrid*).   50*s.*

Calderon de la Barca. Teatro completo (vols. vii., ix., xii., xiv., of "Bibl. Aut. Esp.). r. 8vo. 12*s.* 6*d.* each. (*Madrid*).   50*s.*

,,   Teatro escogido. 12mo. 3 vols. *Brockhaus.*   10*s.* 6*d.*

,,   Select plays. Ed. Norman Maccoll. c. 8vo. *Macmillan.*   14*s.*

,,   Six dramas. Tr. Edward Fitzgerald. 12mo.   O.P.

Trench, R. C. Life and genius of Calderon. ex. f. 8vo. *Paul.*   5*s.* 6*d.*

Lewes, G. H. Spanish drama (Lope de Vega and Calderon). 12mo. *Chapman.* 1846.   O.P.

Ramon de la Cruz. Sainetes. 2 vols. (*Barcelona*).   6*s.*

,,   Sainetes escogidas. (*Madrid*).   O.P.
    Light comedies.

Autores dramaticos contemporaneos. Ed. Novo y Colson. fo. 2 vols. (*Madrid*).   100*s.*
    The modern drama of Spain is worth study. These volumes are a selection of the best play of each author, with introductions by the best Spanish critics.

(B) PROSE: INCLUDING NOVELS.

Mendoza, H. de. Lazarillo de Tormes (1st part in vol. iii. of "Bibl. Aut. Esp."). r. 8vo. (*Madrid*).   12*s.* 6*d.*

Hyta, G. P. de. Guerras civiles de Granada (in the last quoted volume).

Cervantes. Don Quijote de la Mancha (in vol. i. of "Bibl. Aut. Esp."). r. 8vo. (*Madrid*).   12*s.* 6*d.*

,,   The same. 12mo. 2 vols. *Brockhaus.*   3*s.* 6*d.*

,,   The same. Tr. Watts. sq. 8vo. 5 vols. *Quaritch.*   84*s.*

,,   The same. Tr. Ormsby. d. 8vo. 4 vols., 12*s.* 6*d.* each. *Smith, Elder.*   50*s.*

,,   Novelas ejemplares. 12mo. *Brockhaus.*   3*s.* 6*d.*

,,   Numantia. Tr. J. Gibson. c. 8vo. *Paul.*   5*s.*

,,   Viaje del Parnaso, text with tr. by Gibson. c. 8vo. *Paul.*   12*s.*

Caballero, Fernan. La Gaviota. 12mo. *Brockhaus.*   3*s.* 6*d.*

,,   Clemencia. 12mo. *Brockhaus.*   3*s.* 6*d.*

Becquer, G. Obras. 12mo. 3 vols. (*Madrid*).   10*s.* 6*d.*
    These works by Caballero and Becquer form suitable readings for girls.

Valera, J. Pepita Jimenez. 18mo. (*Madrid*).   5*s.*

,,   Doña Luz. 18mo. (*Madrid*).   5*s.*

Galdos, P. Episodios nacionales. 12mo. 20 vols., 2*s.* 6*d.* each. (*Madrid*).   50*s.*
    The *Episodios nacionales* are a series like the Erckmann-Chatrian French novels; *Doña Perfecta*, *Gloria* (2 vols.), and *Marianela* may be specially mentioned.

Luis de Leon. Obras (vol. xxxvii. of "Bibl. Aut. Esp."). r. 8vo. (*Madrid*).   12*s.* 6*d.*

Luis de Granada. Obras (vols. vi., viii., xi., of "Bibl. Aut. Esp."). r. 8vo. 12*s.* 6*d.* each. (*Madrid*).   37*s.* 6*d.*
    Luis de Leon and Luis de Granada were mystics whose works should be read for beauty of style.

Pereda, J. de. Sotileza. 8vo. (*Madrid*).   4*s*

Pereda, J. de. Escenas montañeses. 8vo. (*Madrid*).   4*s.*

  ,,   De tal palo tal astilla. 8vo.   4*s.*

  ,,   El buey suelto. 8vo.   4*s.*

Pereda's works are written in rather difficult Spanish dialect.

Selgas, José. Nona. 8vo. (*Madrid*).   4*s.*

Suitable for girls.

Bazan, E. P. La tribuna. (*Barcelona*).   3*s.*

  ,,   Los pazos de Ulloa. 2 vols. (*Barcelona*).   6*s.*

  ,,   Madre naturaleza. 2 vols. (*Barcelona*).   6*s.*

  ,,   La dama joven. (*Barcelona*).   3*s.*

Alarcon, P. A. de. Un viage en las Alpujarras. (*Madrid*).   5*s.*

Trueba, A. de. Cuentos populares, 3*s.* 6*d.*; Cuentos campesinos, 3*s.* 6*d.*

12mo. *Brockhaus.*

Rather puerile; good for beginners.

—V. SPANISH AMERICA:

Poesias de la America Meridional. Ed. A. J. de Wittstein. 12mo.

Brockhaus.   3*s.* 6*d.*

Poesias mejicanas (vol. xlv. of "Bibl. Univ."). (*Madrid*).   8*d.*

Isaacs, J. Maria. (*Barcelona*).

A South American "Paul and Virginia"; difficult Spanish.

—VI. MISCELLANEOUS:

Quevedo Villegas. Obras (vols. xxiii., xlviii., lxix., of "Bibl. Aut. Esp.").

r. 8vo. 12*s.* 6*d.* each. (*Madrid*).   37*s.* 6*d.*

The Dean Swift of Spain.

Isla, Padre. Obras escogidas (vol. xv. of "Bibl. Aut. Esp."). r. 8vo.

(*Madrid*).   12*s.* 6*d.*

Canovas del Castillo. Obras. (*Madrid*).

Eight vols. already published, 37*s.* They may be had separately; vol. i., *El solitario.*

SPECIES, ORIGIN OF, *see* ZOOLOGY.

SPECTRUM ANALYSIS, *see* PHYSICS VI.

SPIRITUALISM, *see* PSYCHICAL RESEARCH.

SPORT AND TRAVEL:

See also SHOOTING.

St. John, C. Natural history and sport in Moray. r. 8vo. *Douglas.* illus.   50*s.*

  ,,   Tour in Sutherlandshire. c. 8vo. 2 vols. *Murray.* pub. 21*s.*   O.P.

  ,,   Wild sports and natural history of the Highlands. c. 8vo. *Murray.*

illus.   15*s.*

Colquhoun, J. The moor and the loch. 8vo. 2 vols. *Blackwood.* illus.   21*s.*

Knox, A. E. Game-birds and wild-fowl. p. 8vo. *Van Voorst.*   O.P.

  ,,   Ornithological rambles in Sussex. p. 8vo. *Van Voorst.* illus.   O.P.

  ,,   Autumns on the Spey. p. 8vo. *Van Voorst.* illus.   6*s.*

Boner, C. Forest creatures. c. 8vo. *Longmans.* pub. 10*s.* 6*d.*   O.P.

Jefferies, R. Wild life in a southern country. c. 8vo. *Smith, Elder.* 　6s.

　,,　　Red deer. p. 8vo. *Longmans.* pub. 4s. 6d. 　o.p.

　,,　　The gamekeeper at home. c. 8vo. *Smith, Elder.* 　5s.
　　　Also illus. by Whymper, 10s. 6d.

　,,　　The amateur poacher. c. 8vo. *Smith, Elder.* 　5s.

Scrope, W. The art of deer-stalking. r. 8vo. *Murray.* illus. 　o.p.

Grimble, A. Deer-stalking. 8vo. *Chapman.* 　5s.

Collyns, C. P. Chase of the wild red deer. 8vo. *Longmans.* pub. 16s. 　o.p.

Fortescue, J. Stag-hunting on Exmoor. l. c. 8vo. *Chapman.* illus. 　16s.

Smith, T. Diary of a huntsman (fox). *Whittaker.* 1838. illus. 　o.p.

Beard, J. Diary of fifteen years' hunting (hare). Printed for the author. 　o.p.

Macrae, A. Handbook of deer-stalking. f. 8vo. *Blackwood.* illus. 　3s. 6d.
　　　Introduction by Horatio Ross.

Harting, J. E. Essays on sport and natural history. 8vo. *Horace Cox.*
　illus. 　16s.
　　　Shooting, fishing, hawking, etc.

Stuart, C. and J. Lays of the deer forest. 8vo. 2 vols. *Blackwood.* 　o.p.

Rudolf, Prince. Sport and ornithology. Tr. d. 8vo. *Van Voorst.* 　18s.

Boner, C. Chamois-hunting in Bavaria. c. 8vo. *Chapman.* illus. 　o.p.

Wheelwright, H. Spring and summer in Lapland. *Groombridge.* pub.
　10s. 6d. 　o.p.

Davies, E. Wolf-hunting in Brittany. c. 8vo. *Chapman.* 　o.p.

Wheelwright, H. Ten years in Sweden. c. 8vo. *Groombridge.* pub. 16s. 　o.p.

Sanderson, G. P. Thirteen years among the wild beasts of India. i. 8vo.
　Allen. illus. 　25s.

Markham, F. Shooting in the Himalayas. 8vo. *Bentley.* 　o.p.

Baldwin, J. H. Large and small game of Bengal. *Paul.* illus. 　o.p.

Kinloch. Large game shooting. 4to. 2 ser., 21s. each. *Harrison.* Photos. 　42s.

Baden-Powell, R. S. Pigsticking in India. d. 8vo. *Harrison.* illus. 　18s.

Baker, S. W. Rifle and hound in Ceylon. c. 8vo. *Longmans.* 　3s. 6d.

Pollok, J. Sport in Burmah. 8vo. 2 vols. *Chapman.* 　24s.

Baldwin, W. C. African hunting. 8vo. *Bentley.* illus. 　15s.

Baker, S. W. Wild beasts and their ways. 8vo. *Macmillan.* 　12s. 6d.

Selous, F. C. Hunter's wanderings in South Africa. d. 8vo. *Bentley.*
　illus. 　18s.

Bennett, G. Gatherings of a naturalist in Australia. d. 8vo. *Van Voorst.*
　illus. 　21s.

D'Albertis, L. M. Travels in New Guinea. 8vo. 2 vols. *Low.* illus. 　42s.

Dodge, R. J. Hunting grounds of the great west. 8vo. *Chatto.* pub. 21s. 　o.p.

Big game of North America. Ed. G. O. Shields. 8vo. *Low.* 　21s.

Vivian, A. P. Wanderings in the western land. 8vo. *Low.* 　10s. 6d.

King, Ross. The sportsman and naturalist in Canada. r. 8vo. *Hurst.*
　illus. 　20s.

Bromley-Devonport, W. Sport. 4to. *Chapman.* illus. 　16s.

STABLE, *see* HORSE I.

STAGE :

For the Classic Stage, see GREECE, HISTORY III.

Lewes, G. H. Actors and the art of acting. c. 8vo. *Smith, Elder.*   7s. 6d.

Hazlitt, W. View of the English stage. 1818.   O.P.

Fleay, F. G. Chronicle history of the English stage, 1559–1642. 8vo.
Reeves and Turner.   8s.

Hunt, Leigh. Critical essays on the performers of the London theatres. 1807.   O.P.

Lamb, C. Art of the stage, as set out in Charles Lamb's dramatic essays.
Ed. P. Fitzgerald. c. 8vo. *Remington.*   7s. 6d.

Marston, Westland. Our recent actors. p. 8vo. 2 vols. *Low.*   21s.

Morley, H. Journal of a London playgoer. 12mo. *Routledge.* pub. 5s.   O.P.

Cook, Dutton. Nights at the play. c. 8vo. *Chatto.* pub. 6s.   O.P.

Representative actors. Ed. Clark Russell. c. 8vo. *Warne.*   2s. 6d.

Dramatic list. Ed. C. E. Pascoe. c. 8vo. *Allen.*   3s. 6d.
     Memoirs of living actors and actresses.

Actors and actresses of Great Britain and the United States. Ed. Hutton
and Matthews.
     Memoirs of players from the time of Garrick to the present day; with selections from
     criticisms, etc.

Collier, J. P. English dramatic poetry and annals of the stage to the
Restoration. f. 4to. 3 vols. *Bell.*   70s.

Ward, A. W. English dramatic literature to the death of Queen Anne.
8vo. 2 vols. *Macmillan.*   32s.

Archer, W. English dramatists of to-day. p. 8vo. *Low.*   8s. 6d.

Genest, J. Some account of the English stage from 1660 to 1830. 8vo.
10 vols. 1832.   O.P.
     The standard work on the subject.

Doran, Dr. "Their Majesties' servants." d. 8vo. 3 vols. *Nimmo.*   54s.
     Annals of the stage from Betterton to Edmund Kean.

Downes, J. Roscius Anglicanus. 8vo. *Jarvis.* Privately printed.
     Review of the stage from 1660 to 1706.

Dibdin, J. C. Annals of the Edinburgh stage. 4to. *Cameron (Edinburgh).*   21s.

Baker and others. Biographia dramatica. 1812.   O.P.

Lowe, R. W. English theatrical literature, biographical account. d. 8vo.
Nimmo.   18s.

  ,, Thomas Betterton. c. 8vo. *Paul.*   2s. 6d.

Apology for the life of Colley Cibber. Ed. R. W. Lowe. *Nimmo.*   42s.

Fitzgerald, P. Life of Garrick. 8vo. 2 vols. *Tinsley.*   36s.

Boaden, Jas. Life of Mrs. Siddons.   O.P.

  ,, Life of John P. Kemble. 8vo. 2 vols. *(London).* 1825.   O.P.
     Though o.p., very easily obtainable.

Hawkins, F. W. Life of Edmund Kean. 8vo. 2 vols. *Tinsley.*   30s.

Cole, J. W. Life and theatrical times of Charles Kean. p. 8vo. 2 vols.
Bentley.   21s.

Macready's reminiscences and diary. Ed. F. Pollock. c. 8vo. *Macmillan.*
pub. 7s. 6d.   O.P.

Phelps and Forbes-Robertson. Life of Samuel Phelps. 8vo. *Low*.   12*s*.

Hawkins, F. W. Annals of the French stage. d. 8vo. 2 vols. *Chapman*.   28*s*.

,, French stage of the eighteenth century. d. 8vo. 2 vols. *Chapman*.   30*s*.

Gautier, T. Histoire de l'art dramatique depuis 25 ans. 6 vols. (*Paris*).   15*s*.
1858.

Janin, Jules. Histoire de l'art dramatique. 6 vols. (*Paris*).   18*s*.

Vitu, A. Les mille et une nuits du théâtre. (*Paris*).
Eight vols. issued, 3*s*. each. In progress.

STAINED GLASS WINDOWS, *see* ARTISTIC PROCESSES XI.

STEAM AND OTHER HEAT ENGINES:

Anderson, W. On the conversion of heat into work. 8vo. *Whittaker*.
illus.   6*s*.
Practical handbook on heat engines.

Cotterill, J. W. Steam-engine considered as a heat-engine. 8vo. *Spon*.   12*s*. 6*d*.
See also HEAT for works on this branch of the subject.

Perry, J. Steam. 18mo. *Macmillan*.   4*s*. 6*d*.

Weisbach, J. Mechanics of engineering and construction of machines.
Tr. 8vo. *Wiley* (*N.Y.*).   50*s*.
Vol. ii., Heat, steam, and steam-engines.

Rankine, W. J. M. Manual of the steam-engine. Ed. W. J. Millar. c. 8vo.
Griffin. illus.   12*s*. 6*d*.

Clark, D. K. The steam-engine. 4 vols., 12*s*. 6*d*. each. *Blackie*. illus.   50*s*.
A very large number of plates illustrating modern practice.

Northcott. The steam-engine. d. 8vo. *Cassell*.   3*s*. 6*d*.

Rigg, R. Practical treatise on the steam-engine. d. 4to. *Spon*. illus.   25*s*.

Zeuner, G. Value gear. Tr. J. F. Klein. 8vo. *Spon*. illus.   12*s*. 6*d*.

Winton and Millar. Modern steam practice and engineering. 8vo.
4 vols. *Gebbie* (*N.Y.*).   60*s*.
Examples of some of the latest types of engines, etc.

Wilson, R. Steam boilers. 8vo. *Lockwood*.   6*s*.

Traill, T. W. Boilers. 8vo. *Griffin*.   12*s*.
Rules, tables, and formulas of construction.

Seaton, A. E. Manual of marine engineering. d. 8vo. *Griffin*. illus.   18*s*.

Sennett, R. Marine steam-engine. 8vo. *Longmans*. illus.   21*s*.

Jamieson, A. Steam and the steam-engine. c. 8vo. *Griffin*.   7*s*. 6*d*.

Robinson, W. Gas and petroleum engines. 8vo. *Spon*.   14*s*.

STEEL, *see* IRON.

STOCK EXCHANGE, *see* POLITICAL ECONOMY IV.

SUGAR, *see* ECONOMIC PRODUCTS IX.

SULPHURIC ACID, *see* INDUSTRIES II.

SUMATRA, *see* INDIAN OCEAN IV.

SUPERSTITIONS, *see* FOLKLORE II.

SURGERY, *see* AMBULANCE.

  ,,   VETERINARY, *see* VETERINARY SCIENCE.

SURVEYING:

See also ENGINEERING.

Johnson, J. B.   Theory and practice of surveying.   8vo.   *Wiley* (*N.Y.*).   18*s.*

Haskoll, W.   Engineering field-work.   8vo.   *Lockwood.*   27*s.*

Simms, F.   Levelling.   8vo.   *Lockwood.*   8*s.* 6*d.*

Stanley, W. F.   Surveying and levelling instruments.   c. 8vo.   *Spon.*   7*s.* 6*d.*

SWEDEN: GEOGRAPHY AND HISTORY:

See also NORWAY *for books on the Scandinavian Peninsula.*

Murray's Handbook for Sweden.   p. 8vo.   *Murray.*   6*s.*

Geijer and others.   Geschichte Schwedens.   8vo.   6 vols.   (*Gotha*).   42*s.* 6*d.*

Watson, P. B.   Swedish revolution under Gustavus Vasa.   8vo.   *Low.*   o.p.

Stevens, J. L.   History of Gustavus Adolphus.   8vo.   *Bentley.*   15*s.*

Bain, F. W.   Christina, Queen of Sweden (1628–89).   c. 8vo.   *Allen.*   7*s.* 6*d.*

Voltaire.   Histoire de Charles XII.   12mo.   (*Paris*).   2*s.* 6*d.*

SWEDEN: LANGUAGE AND LITERATURE:

—I. GRAMMARS AND DICTIONARIES:

May, A.   Practical grammar of the Swedish language.   12mo.   (*Stockholm*).   6*s.*

Otté, E. C.   Simplified grammar of the Swedish language.   *Trübner.*   2*s.* 6*d.*

Wenström and Lundgren.   Engelsk-Svensk Ordbog.   8vo.   (*Stockholm*).   20*s.*

Björkman, C. J.   Svensk-Engelsk Ordbog.   8vo.   20*s.*

Swedish-English and English-Swedish pocket dictionary.   16mo.   *Tauchnitz.*   5*s.* 6*d.*

—II. HISTORY AND CRITICISM:

Cläeson, G.   Svenska Språkets och Literaturens historia.   8vo.   (*Stockholm*).   3*s.*

Malmström, B. E.   Grunddragen af svenska Vitterhetens historia.   8vo.   5 vols.   (*Örebro*).   37*s.* 6*d.*
    Vol. i., 8*s.* 6*d.*; vol. ii., 7*s.* 6*d.*; vol. iii., 7*s.* 6*d.*; vol. iv., 7*s.*; vol. v., 7*s.*

Ljunggren, G.   Svenska vitterhetens häfder.   8vo.   2 vols.   (*Lund*).   11*s.* 6*d.*
    Vol. i., 9*s.*; vol. ii. (1), 2*s.* 6*d.*

—III. CLASSICS:

Tegner, E.   Frithjofs Saga.   4to.   (*Stockholm*).   illus.   18*s.*
    Epic. Also 12mo., 2*s.*

   ,,   Axel.   12mo.   (*Stockholm*).   6*d.*

   ,,   Samlade Skrifter.   Ed. E. Tegner.   8vo.   7 vols.   (*Stockholm*).   63*s.*
    Tegner's prose works contain some of the finest criticism in the language. His verse is masterly.

Runeberg, J. L.   Fänrik Stals Sägner.   12mo.   (*Stockholm*).   3*s.*

Snoilsky, C.   Dikter.   8vo.   (*Stockholm*).   6*s.*
    Lyric poet. Exquisite style.

Stagnelius, E. J. Samlade Skrifter. 8vo. 2 vols. *(Stockholm).*   9*s.*
Great romantic poet.

Kellgren, J. H. Samlade Skrifter. 8vo. *(Upsala).*   4*s.* 6*d.*
Leader of the classical school.

Wallin, J. O. Dödens engel. 4to. *(Stockholm).*   5*s.* 6*d.*
A celebrated poem.

—IV. NOVELS, ETC. :

Flygare-Carlén, Emilie. Samlade Arbeten. 12mo. 18 vols. *(Stockholm).*   90*s.*

Bremer, Fredrika. Samlade Skrifter. *(Örebro).*

Topelius, Z. Ljungblommer. 12mo. *(Stockholm).*   4*s.* 6*d.*

Strindberg, A. Röda rummet. 12mo. *(Stockholm).*   5*s.* 6*d.*

    ,,   Giftas. 12mo. *(Stockholm).*   5*s.* 6*d.*

Edgren, Anna C. Ur lifvet. 4 series. 12mo. *(Stockholm).*   16*s.*
Living Swedish Novelist.

    ,,   Sanna Kvinnor (a play). 12mo. *(Stockholm).*   2*s.*

Lenngren, Anna M. Samlade Dikter. 4to. *(Stockholm).* illus.   30*s.*
Popular and satirical.

Blanche, August. Samlade Arbeten (novels and tales). 8vo. *(Stockholm).*   57*s.*
A popular and genial novelist.

—V. TRANSLATIONS :

Tegner, E. Frithjofs Saga. Tr. Blackley. d. 4to. *Marcus Ward.* illus.   25*s.*
Edition de luxe.

Bremer, Fredrika. Novels. Tr. Mary Howitt. p. 8vo. 4 vols., 3*s.* 6*d.* each.
Bell (Bohn).   14*s.*

Flygare-Carlén, Emilie. Woman's life. *Bentley.*   O.P.

Topelius, Z. The surgeon's stories ; 5 cycles. 12mo. 6 vols., 3*s.* 6*d.* each.
McClurg (Chicago).   21*s.*

Edgren, Anna C. True women (a play). Tr. Brækstad. *French.*   1*s.*

Geijer, E. G. History of the Swedes. Tr. Turner. *(London).* 1845.   O.P.

—VI. BIOGRAPHY AND BIBLIOGRAPHY :

Biografiskt Lexicon öfver Svenska namnkunnige män. *(Stockholm).*
1835-84.

Linnström. Svenskt Boklexicon. r. 8vo. 2 vols. *(Stockholm).*   £15 15*s.*

SWIMMING :

Cobbett, M. Swimming. ("All England" ser.). sm. 8vo. *Bell.*   1*s.*

Wilson, W. Swimming instructor. p. 8vo. *Cox.*   2*s.* 6*d.*

SWITZERLAND :

—I. GUIDE-BOOKS :

Murray. Handbook for Switzerland, etc. p. 8vo. 2 parts. *Murray.*   10*s.*

Baedeker. Switzerland. 12mo. *Dulau.*   8*s.*

Ball, J. The Alpine guide. p. 8vo. 3 parts. *Longmans.*   21*s.* 6*d.*
Part i., *Western Alps,* 2*s.* 6*d.* ; part ii., *Central Alps,* 8*s.* 6*d.* ; part iii., *Eastern Alps,* 10*s.* 6*d.*
The best of all Swiss guides.

Tschudi, J. V. Der Tourist in der Schweiz und dem angrenzenden Süd-
Deutschland, Ober-Italien und Savoyen. 8vo. *(Zurich).*   11*s.*
The best handbook for Alpine climbers.

Coolidge, W. A. B. Swiss travel and Swiss guide-books. p. 8vo. *Long-mans.*   10s. 6d.
> The *Alpine Journal* should be consulted.

--II. GENERAL DESCRIPTION:

Civiale, A. Les Alpes au point de vue de la géographie physique et de la géologie. 8vo. *Rothschild.* illus.   55s.

Gsell-Fels. Die Schweiz. fo. 2 vols. (*Munich*). illus.   O.P.

Papon, J. Zeichnungen aus der Natur und Volkleben eines unbekannten Alpenlandes. 12mo. (*St. Gall*).   O.P.
> The Engadine.

Osenbruggen, E. Wanderstudien aus der Schweiz. 8vo. 6 vols. (*Schaffhausen*).   32s. 6d.

Christ, H. Pflanzenleben der Schweiz. 8vo. 4 vols. (*Zurich*).   14s. 6d.

Cunningham and Abney. Pioneers of the Alps. 8vo. *Low.*   42s.

Tyndall, J. Glaciers of the Alps. 8vo. *Murray.* pub. 14s.   O.P.
> Narrative of ascents, and discussion of origin of glaciers.

Forbes, J. Works.
> Norway and its glaciers. *Simpkin.* pub. 21s.   O.P.
> Theory of glaciers. *Simpkin.* pub. 10s. 6d.   O.P.
> Tour of Mont Blanc. *Simpkin.* pub. 3s. 6d.   O.P.
> Travels in the Alps of Savoy. *Longmans.* pub. 28s.   O.P.
> The modern theory of the movements of glaciers is due to the investigations and writings of James Forbes. His works deal for the most part with Swiss travel and observations on its glaciers.

Heer, O. Urwelt der Schweiz. 8vo. (*Zurich*).   16s.

Wirth, Max. Allgemeine Beschreibung und Statistik der Schweiz. 8vo. 7 vols. (*Zurich*).   43s. 6d.

Furrer, A. Volkswirthschafts-Lexicon der Schweiz bis jetzt. 8vo. 20 parts. (*Berne*).   32s.
> Appearing in parts; drawn from efficient sources.
> JOURNAL: *Anzeiger für schweizerische Alterthumskunde* (Zurich). Annual. 23 vols. issued.

--III. HISTORY:

Dändliker, K. Geschichte der Schweiz. 8vo. 3 vols. (*Zurich*).   35s. 6d.

Daguet, A. Histoire de la Confédération Suisse. l. 8vo. 2 vols. (*Geneva*).   12s. 6d.

Adams and Cunningham. The Swiss confederacy. 8vo. *Macmillan.*   14s.
> An account of Swiss self-government.

SWORD, *see* ARMS *and* FENCING.

SYMBOLISM IN ART, *see* ART V.

SYRIA, *see* PALESTINE.

T.

TACTICS, *see* ARMY II. *and* NAVY II.

TALMUD, *see* HEBREW.

TAMIL, *see* INDIA, LANGUAGES II.

TANNING, *see* INDUSTRIES XII.

TAPESTRY, *see* ARTISTIC PROCESSES X.

TASMANIA, *see* AUSTRALASIA VIII.

TAXATION, *see* POLITICAL ECONOMY VIII.

TEA, *see* ECONOMIC PRODUCTS X.

TEACHING, *see* EDUCATION.

TEETOTALISM, *see* ALCOHOLISM.

TELEGRAPHY, *see* ELECTRICITY II.

TELEPHONE, *see* ELECTRICITY II.

TELUGU, *see* INDIA, LANGUAGES III.

TEMPERANCE, *see* ALCOHOLISM.

TEMPLARS, KNIGHTS, *see* CHURCH HISTORY III.

TENERIFFE, *see* ATLANTIC.

TENNIS, RACKETS, AND FIVES:

Marshall, J. Annals of tennis. 8vo. *Cox.*   1*s.*

,,   Tennis, rackets, and fives. ("All England" ser.).   sm. 8vo.
Bell. illus.   1*s.*

Heathcote and others. Tennis, lawn-tennis, rackets, and fives. ("Badminton Library"). c. 8vo. *Longmans.*   10*s.* 6*d.*
Admirable as regards "Fives and rackets."

TENNIS, LAWN, *see* LAWN-TENNIS.

TEXTILE FABRICS:

Brooks, C. F. Handbook for the use of cotton manufacturers. c. 8vo.
Spon.   6*s.*

Nasmith, J. Modern cotton spinning machinery. 4to. *Spon.* illus.   15*s.*

Marsden, R. Cotton spinning. sm. p. 8vo. *Bell.*   6*s.* 6*d.*

Sansone, A. Printing of cotton fabrics. d. 8vo. *Heywood.* illus.   15*s.*

Beaumont, R. Woollen and worsted manufacture. sm. p. 8vo. *Bell.*   7*s.* 6*d.*

McLaren, W. S. B. Spinning woollen and worsted. c. 8vo. *Cassell.* illus.   4*s.* 6*d.*

Sharp, P. Flax, tow, and jute spinning. c. 8vo. (*Manchester*).   5*s.*

Quilter, J. H. Trimming and finishing of hosiery fabrics. c. 8vo. *Greening*
(*Bradford*).   2*s.* 6*d.*

Rowlett. Technology of framework knitting. d. 8vo. 2 vols. *Technical
School* (*Leicester*).   30*s*

Brown, A. Construction of the power loom and the art of weaving. f. 8vo. *Simpkin*   3s. 6d.

Ashenhurst, T. R. Weaving and designing of textile fabrics. 8vo. *Simpkin.* 12s. 6d.

  ,, Designs in textile fabrics. c. 8vo. *Cassell.* illus.   4s. 6d

Hummel, J. J. Dyeing of textile fabrics. 12mo. *Cassell.* -   5s.

Crookes, W. Dyeing and tissue printing. sm. p. 8vo. *Bell.*   5s.

THAMES, *see* LONDON I.

THEATRE, *see* STAGE.

  ,, ATTIC, *see* GREECE, HISTORY III.

THEOLOGY:

See also BIBLE.

—I. GENERAL:

Herzog. Encyclopædia of theology. Ed. P. Schaff. i. 8vo. 3 vols., 24s. each. *T. and T. Clark.*   72s.
> Abridged translation of Herzog's *Real Encyclopädie*; rather roughly done, but very comprehensive and useful.

Schaff and Jackson. Encyclopædia of living divines. i. 8vo. *T. and T. Clark.*   8s.
> Useful supplement to the *Encyclopædia.*

Benham, W. Dictionary of religion. 8vo. *Cassell.*   21s.

Arnold, T. Catholic dictionary. d. 8vo. *Paul.*   21s.
> Roman Catholic; a scholarly work.

Outlines of theological study. d. 8vo. *Parker.*   1s. 6d.
> Compiled by a committee. Intended specially for candidates for Anglican orders.

Westcott, B. F. Student's guide to theological examinations at Cambridge. *Deighton, Bell.*
> Specially intended for Cambridge students, and marked by the characteristic exactness and thoroughness of the Cambridge school. New edition in preparation.

Drummond, J. The study of theology. c. 8vo. *Macmillan.*   5s.
> A wide survey of the field from the point of view of a cultivated and very moderate Unitarian; rather deficient in bibliography.

Briggs, C. A. Biblical study. p. 8vo. *T. and T. Clark.*   7s. 6d.
> More limited in its scope, but entering more into detail than any of the above; especially complete in bibliography.

— II. DOGMATIC:

Schaff, P. The creeds of Christendom. r. 8vo. *Hodder.*   63s.
> A history of creeds and confessions of faith, ancient and modern.

Winer, G. B. Confessions of Christendom. Tr. W. B. Pope. r. 8vo. *T. and T. Clark.*   10s. 6d.
> A most convenient synopsis of distinctive doctrines.

Lumby, J. R. History of the creeds. c. 8vo. *Bell.*   7s. 6d.
> Ancient creeds only.

Pearson, J. Exposition of the Apostles' creed. c. 8vo. *Clar. Press.*   10s. 6d.
> Also *Cambridge Press.* 8vo. 5s. This subject has never since been handled with the same exact scholarship and massive learning; but, there are, of course, some positions which are hardly tenable

Westcott, B. F. The historic faith. c. 8vo. *Macmillan.*   6s.
> Lectures on the Apostles' creed. Sermon lectures, but with notes which are full of suggestiveness for the student.

Forbes, A. P. Short explanation of the Nicene Creed. p. 8vo. *Parker.*   6s.
> A clear and readable *resumé* of patristic teaching.

Maclear, G. F. Introduction to the creeds. (elem.). 12mo. *Macmillan.*   2s. 6d.

Browne, E. A. Exposition of the xxxix articles. 8vo. *Longmans.*   16s.
> Not a classic, but the fullest book of the kind available.

Mason, A. J. Faith of the Gospel. 8vo. *Rivingtons.*   7s. 6d.
> High Anglican theories presented in a bright scholarly style, from a point of view partly modern ; but lays equal stress on things important and unimportant, and puts forward matters of private opinion as accepted doctrines.

Shedd, W. G. T. A history of Christian doctrines. 8vo. *Clark.*   21s.
> Presbyterian and Calvinistic, but more elaborate and complete as a system of theology than any work we possess in England.

Hodge, A. A. Outlines of theology. 8vo. *Nelson.*   10s.
> More compendious ; from a similar point of view.

Pope, W. B. Compendium of Christian theology. 8vo. 3 vols. *Wesleyan Conference Office.*   31s. 6d.
> Wesleyan ; covers the whole ground on an ample scale, but rather wanting in the requisite precision of treatment.

Moule, H. C. G. Outlines of Christian doctrine. (elem.). 12mo. *Hodder.*   2s. 6d.
> A remarkably concise summary by an excellent scholar ; from an Evangelical point of view.

Martensen, H. L. Christian dogmatics. Tr. W. Urwick. 8vo. *Clark.*   10s. 6d.
> The original was by a Danish Lutheran bishop ; much used by all parties.

Dorner, J. A. System of Christian doctrine. Tr. 8vo. 4 vols. *Clark.*   42s.
> Probably the most profound work on the subject ; but contains German elements not easily assimilated by Englishmen.

Essays and Reviews. 8vo. *Longmans.*   O.P.
> A manifesto by the Broad Church party, now nearly thirty years old.

Lux mundi. 8vo. *Murray.*   14s.
> A similar manifesto from the younger High Church school at Oxford ; important as an attempt to harmonize the views of that school with critical advance.

Dale, R. W. The old Evangelicalism and the new. c. 8vo. *Hodder.*   6s.
> Presents two stages in the history of Evangelicalism, with all the clearness and force characteristic of the writer, the eminent Congregationalist.

Mackintosh, R. Essays towards a new theology. d. 8vo. *Maclehose.*   12s. 6d.
> An interesting attempt to modify Scottish theology in the direction of Albrecht Ritschl and McLeod Campbell.

Müller, J. Doctrine of sin. Tr. 8vo. 2 vols. *Clark.*   21s.
> The chief authority on the subject.

Dorner, J. A. Doctrine of the person of Christ. 8vo. 4 vols., 10s. 6d. each. *Clark.*   42s.
> Another standard work, but with peculiarly German characteristics.

Liddon, H. P. Divinity of our Lord (Bampton Lectures.) c. 8vo. *Rivingtons.*   5s.

Wilberforce, R. I. Doctrine of the Incarnation. 8vo. *Murray.* 1848.   O.P.
> An early product of the Tractarian movement.

Dale, R. W. The atonement. c. 8vo. *Hodder.*   6s.
> Congregational lectures which have met with wide acceptance and approval.

Oxenham, H. N. Catholic doctrine of the atonement. c. 8vo. *Allen.*   10s. 6d.
> From a Roman Catholic standpoint.

Mozley, J. B. Augustinian doctrine of predestination. c. 8vo. *Murray.*   9s.

Alger, W. R. Critical history of the doctrine of a future state. 8vo. *(Philadelphia).*   18s.
> To this work Dr. Ezra Abbot contributed a specially valuable bibliography.

Luckock, H. M. After death. c. 8vo. *Rivingtons.*   6*s.*
An examination of primitive teaching.

Jukes, A. The second death and restitution of all things. c. 8vo. *Longmans.*   3*s.* 6*d.*
Maintains the limited duration of future punishment.

Pusey, E. B. What is of faith as to everlasting punishment ? c. 8vo. *Smith and Innes.*   2*s.* 6*d.*
A full examination of the tradition of the early church.

—III. APOLOGETICS:

Butler, Bishop. Analogy of religion ; and sermons. c. 8vo. *R. T. S.*   2*s.*
Assumes the truth of some premises which would now be questioned, but must still head any list of English apologetics, if only as a specimen of grave and self-restrained thinking.

Pascal. Pensées. Tr. C. Kegan Paul. c. 8vo. *Paul.*   6*s.*
Also *Bell* (Bohn), 3*s.* 6*d.* Another classic, with a like austere elevation of thought, and greater distinction of style, but less systematic. [For French text, *see* FRANCE, LITERATURE III.]

Fisher, G. P. Grounds of theistic and Christian belief. c. 8vo. *Hodder.*   12*s.* 6*d.*
Probably the best comprehensive treatise on Christian apologetics, extremely clear, temperate and judicious.

Flint, R. Theism. c. 8vo. *Blackwood.*   7*s.* 6*d.*

     ,,   Anti-theistic theories. c. 8vo. *Blackwood.*   10*s.* 6*d.*

Moore, A. L. Science and the faith. p. 8vo. *Paul.*   6*s.*

Temple, F. Relations between religion and science (Bampton Lectures). c. 8vo. *Macmillan.*   6*s.*
Less searching and philosophical than the above, but well representing the average of intelligent opinion.

Hatch, E. Influence of Greek ideas and usages upon the Christian Church (Hibbert Lectures). Ed. A. M. Fairbairn. 8vo. *Williams.*   10*s.* 6*d.*

Bruce, A. B. Chief end of revelation. c. 8vo. *Hodder.*   6*s.*
Deals with modern problems in a modern spirit.

Fisher, G. P. Nature and method of revelation. 12mo. *Scribner.*   7*s.* 6*d.*
A satisfactory little book, especially suited to the present situation.

Liddon, H. P. Some elements of religion. c. 8vo. *Rivingtons.*   2*s.* 6*d.*
On God, the soul, sin, prayer, etc.

Carpenter, W. Boyd. Permanent elements of religion. c. 8vo. *Macmillan.*   6*s.*

Christlieb. Modern doubt and Christian belief. Tr. 8vo. *Clark.*   10*s.* 6*d.*

Luthardt. Apologetic lectures. Tr. c. 8vo. 3 vols. *Clark.*   6*s.*

Jellett, J. H. Efficacy of prayer (Donnellan Lectures). c. 8vo. *Macmillan.*   5*s.*

Lightfoot, J. B. Essays on "Supernatural religion." 8vo. *Macmillan.*   10*s.* 6*d*
Deals with the growth of the Canon, on which see also Salmon's *Introduction* and Westcott on the *Canon,* in BIBLE IV. (A).

Salmon, G. Infallibility of the church. 8vo. *Murray.*   12*s.*
A forcible polemic against Rome.

Gore, C. Roman Catholic claims. c. 8vo. *Rivingtons.*   3*s.* 6*d.*

—IV. DEVOTIONAL WORKS:

St. Augustine. Confessions (Latin text). 18mo. *Nutt.*   2*s.*
Translated, vol. i. of *Ancient and modern library of theological literature.* Griffith. 1*s.*

Thomas à Kempis. Imitation of Christ. 12mo. *Paul.*   2*s.* 6*d.*

     ,,   Imitation, with preface by Canon Liddon. c. 8vo. *Stock.*   6*s.*

Taylor, Jeremy. Holy living and dying. p. 8vo. *Bell* (*Bohn*).   3*s.* 6*d.*

Law, W. Serious call. 8vo. *Griffith.*   1*s.*

Wilson, T. Sacra privata. f. 8vo. *Parker.*   4*s.*

Goulbourn, E. M. Thoughts on personal religion. sm. 8vo. *Rivingtons.*   6*s.* 6*d.*

—V. LITURGICAL:

Bingham, J. Antiquities of the Christian church. 8vo. 10 vols. *Clar. Press.*   63*s.*
A standard treatise, not yet superseded.

Dictionary of Christian antiquities. Ed. Smith and Cheetham. m. 8vo. 2 vols. *Murray.*   73*s.* 6*d.*
Complete for the first eight centuries, which it covers.

Duchesne, L. Origines du culte chrétien. 8vo. *(Paris).*   7*s.*
By far the most scientific survey of the subject.

Palmer, W. Origines liturgicae. 8vo. 2 vols. *(Oxford).* 1839.   o.p.
An older book, dating from the early days of the Tractarian movement.

Swainson, C. A. Greek liturgies. c. 4to. *Cambridge Press.*   15*s.*
Earliest Greek texts, critically edited.

Neale and Forbes. Ancient liturgies. 16mo. *Masters.*   6*s.*
Most accessible edition of earliest Latin texts; unfinished. Translation, 1*s.*

Hammond, C. E. Liturgies; eastern and western. c. 8vo. *Clar. Press.*   10*s.* 6*d.*
Appendix 1*s.* 6*d.*
Greek, Latin, Coptic, Armenian, and Syriac texts : (the last three in Latin translations) ; for the most part not early, but with useful glossary of liturgical terms ; new edition in preparation.

Maskell, W. Ancient liturgy of the Church of England. 8vo. *Clar. Press.*   15*s.*
A collection of service books in use in England before the Reformation.

,, Monumenta ritualia. 8vo. 3 vols. *Clar. Press.*   50*s.*

Blunt, J. H. Annotated Book of Common Prayer. 4to. *Rivingtons.*   21*s.*
A complete commentary on the Prayer Book, now carefully revised.

Procter, F. History of the Book of Common Prayer. c. 8vo. *Macmillan.*   10*s.* 6*d.*
A much used handbook.

Barry, A. The teacher's Prayer Book. 24mo. *Eyre.*   3*s.* 6*d.*
A useful little manual. Also at higher prices, and 16mo.

—VI. HYMNOLOGY :

The student of hymns will, no doubt, also refer to the collected works of the great hymnwriters, Watts, the Wesleys, Cowper, and Newton (the Olney hymns), Keble, Newman, Faber, Bonar, etc.

Duffield, S. W. Latin hymn writers and their hymns. Ed. R. E. Thompson. *Funk and Wagnalls.*   12*s.* 6*d.*
Full and interesting.

Trench, R. C. Sacred Latin poetry. 12mo. *Macmillan.*   o.p.
A selection of Latin hymns, on rather narrow lines, but with scholarly introductions and notes.

Treasury of sacred song. Ed. F. T. Palgrave. c. 8vo. *Clar. Press.*   4*s.* 6*d.*
By far the best anthology of English sacred poetry in the widest sense.

The book of praise. Ed. Earl Selborne. 18mo. *Macmillan.*   4*s.* 6*d.*
A selection numerically larger, by a distinguished scholar, but with less sure judgment both in admission and exclusion.

Moorson, R. M. Historical companion to "Hymns ancient and modern." 24mo. *Parker.*   5*s.*
A concise account of all the writers of the hymns in one of the most popular Church collections; with full texts of the originals of translated hymns.

Dictionary of hymnology. Ed. J. Julian. m. 8vo. *Murray.*
In the press. On a large scale, corresponding to the dictionaries of Christian biography and antiquities.

THERMODYNAMICS, *see* PHYSICS V.

THIBET, *see* ASIA II.

THROAT, MANAGEMENT OF, *see* MUSIC IV.

TIMBER, *see* FORESTRY *and* BOTANY.

TOBACCO, *see* ECONOMIC PRODUCTS XI.

TOOLS, *see* WORKSHOP.

TORPEDOES, *see* ARMY I. *and* NAVY II.

TOTEMISM, *see* ANTHROPOLOGY III.

TRADE, *see* POLITICAL ECONOMY IV. *and* V.

TRADE MARKS, *see* ENGLAND, LAW VI.

TRADES UNIONS, *see* POLITICAL ECONOMY VI.

TRAINING, *see* ATHLETICS.

TRANSCAUCASIA, *see* RUSSIA IN ASIA II.

TRANSVAAL, *see* CAPE.

TRANSYLVANIA, *see* AUSTRIA.

TRAVEL :

Galton, F. Art of travel. p. 8vo. *Murray.* illus.   7*s.* 6*d.*

Lord and Baines. Shifts and expedients of camp life. *H. Cox.* illus.   25*s.*

Hints to travellers; scientific and general. Ed. for the Royal Geograph. Soc. *Stanford.*

In preparation. The most comprehensive and succinct *vade-mecum.*

Manual of scientific enquiry. Ed. R. S. Ball. *Eyre.*   2*s.* 6*d.*

Prepared for the use of officers in H.M. Navy and travellers in general. Originally edited by Sir John F. W. Herschel.

TRAVELS AND VOYAGES, *see* GEOGRAPHY II., SPORT, ZOOLOGY III., *and under the various countries.*

TREES, *see* FORESTRY *and* BOTANY.

TRIGONOMETRY :

Todhunter, I. Trigonometry for beginners. 18mo. *Macmillan.*   2*s.* 6*d.*

 ,,   Trigonometry. c. 8vo. *Macmillan.*   5*s.*

Lock, J. B. Higher trigonometry. 8vo. *Macmillan.*   7*s.* 6*d.*

The last two books may be considered as equivalent.

Todhunter, I. Treatise on spherical trigonometry. c. 8vo. *Macmillan.*   4*s.* 6*d.*

TRIPOLI, *see* ALGIERS.

TROUBADOURS, *see* PROVENÇAL I.

TROUT, *see* FISHING.

TRUSTEES, *see* ENGLAND, LAW V.

TUNIS, *see* ALGIERS.

TURKEY AND BALKAN PENINSULA :

See also BULGARIA, ROUMANIA, *and* SERVIA.

—1. GEOGRAPHY :

Murray. Handbook to Greece. p. 8vo. *Murray.*   24s.
Contains Albania, Thessaly, and Macedonia.

Guide Joanne. De Paris à Constantinople. Ed. Rousset. *Hachette.*   12s. 6d.

,, États du Danube et des Balkans. Ed. Rousset. *Hachette.*
Part i., 12s. 6d. Part ii., in preparation.

Meyers. Der Orient. 12mo. (*Leipzig*).   20s.
Syria, Palestine, Greece, and Turkey.

Boué, A. La Turquie d'Europe. 4 vols. (*Paris*). 1840.   O.P.

Lejean, G. Ethnographie de la Turquie d'Europe. (*Gotha*).   O.P.

Menzies, Sutherland. Turkey: old and new. d. 8vo. *Allen.* illus.   21s.

Laveleye, E. de. Balkan peninsula. Tr. Mrs. Thorpe. d. 8vo. *Unwin.*   16s.

Tozer, H. F. Highlands of Turkey. c. 8vo. 2 vols. *Murray.*   24s.

Brown, H. A. A winter in Albania. c. 8vo. *Griffith.*   10s. 6d.

Asbóth, J. de. Official tour through Bosnia and Herzegovina. 2 vols. *Sonnenschein.* illus.   30s.

Murray's Handbook to Turkey in Asia (with Constantinople). p. 8vo. *Murray.*   15s.

Leonhardi, P. Konstantinopel und Umgebung (in " Europäische Wanderbilder "). 12mo. (*Zurich*).   2s.

Chesney, F. R. Euphrates and Tigris expedition, 1835–37. 3 vols. (*London*). 1850. illus.   O.P.

Tozer, H. F. Turkish Armenia and Eastern Asia Minor. 8vo.   O.P.

—II. HISTORY :

Hammer-Purgstall. Geschichte des osmanischen Reiches (to 1774). 8vo. 10 vols. (*Pesth*). 1827–36.   O.P.
There is also a French translation. 3 vols. (*Paris*).

Zinkeisen, J. W. Geschichte des osmanischen Reiches in Europa. 8vo. 7 vols. (*Gotha*).   83s. 6d.

Creasy, E. History of the Ottoman Turks. c. 8vo. *Bentley.*   6s.
Chiefly an abstract of Hammer.

Poole, S. Lane. Turkey. c. 8vo. *Unwin.* illus.   5s.
An historical sketch.

Freeman, E. A. The Ottoman power in Europe. c. 8vo. *Macmillan.* pub. 7s. 6d.   O.P.
A political essay.

Ranke, L. von. The Ottoman Empire. Tr. 8vo. *Whittaker.* 1843.   O.P.
A study of the causes of its decay in the 16th and 17th centuries.

Holland, T. E. The European concert in the Eastern question. 8vo. *Clar. Press.*   12s. 6d.
Selection of official documents with historical sketch.

—III. TURKISH LANGUAGE:

Müller, A. Türkische Grammatik. 12mo. (*Berlin*).   8*s.*

Redhouse, J. W. English-Turkish lexicon. *Quaritch.*   40*s.*

TUNNELLING, *see* RAILWAYS.

TURBINES, *see* HYDRAULICS.

TYPOGRAPHY, *see* PRINTING.

U.

UNITED STATES: GEOGRAPHY:

—I. GENERAL:

Englishman's guide-book to the United States and Canada. 12mo. *Stanford.* illus.   7*s. 6d.*
With an appendix on shooting and fishing resorts.

Appleton. General guide to the United States and Canada. c. 8vo. *Stanford.* illus.   10*s. 6d.*
Part i., New England, Middle States and Canada; part ii., Western and Southern States.

Spofford. The American almanac (annual). c. 8vo. *Low.*   7*s. 6d.*

Appleton. Guide to summer resorts in the United States. c. 8vo. *Appleton.*   4*s.*

,, Guide to winter resorts in the United States. c. 8vo. *Appleton.*   4*s.*

Atlas of the United States; with text. r. 8vo. *Low.*   10*s. 6d.*
Contains county maps of each state.

Bradshaw. A.B.C. dictionary. f. 8vo. *Trübner.*   2*s. 6d.*
United States, Canada, and Mexico; shewing the most important towns and points of interest.

Stanford's Compendium; North America. Ed. Hayden and Selwyn. l. p. 8vo. *Stanford.* illus.   21*s.*
Contains physical geography, geology, etc., of the United States.

Whitney, J. D. The United States. 8vo. *Little, Brown.*   15*s.*
Physical geography and material resources.

Patton, J. H. Natural resources of the United States. 8vo. *Appleton.*   12*s. 6d.*

King, E. The Southern states of North America. r. 8vo. *Blackie.* illus.   O.P.

Roosevelt, T. Ranche life and the hunting trail. 4to. *Unwin.* illus.   21*s.*
Best book on the subject.

Hewes and Gannett. Scribner's statistical atlas of the United States. fo. *Scribner.*
Maps and diagrams to show present condition, and political, social, and industrial development. Sold only by subscription.

Donaldson, T. The public domain: its history, with statistics, etc. 8vo. (*Washington*). Maps.
Treats fully of the acquirement of territory, the boundaries of the United States at various periods, and the methods of sale and the disposition of public lands.

Colange, E. de. The national gazetteer; a geographical dictionary of the United States. 8vo. *Hamilton, Adams.*   30*s.*
PERIODICALS, ETC.: Publications of the United States' Geological Survey, and of the Smithsonian Institute. (*Washington*). Contain numerous special memoirs of great value to the student of North American geography. The *National Geographical Magazine* (Washington); *Bulletin* of the Geographical Society of Quebec.

—II. LOCAL:

Davidson, J. W.   Florida of to-day.   c. 8vo.   *Stanford.*   illus.   5s.

Barbour, G.   Florida for tourists, invalids, and settlers.   12mo.   *Appleton.*
     illus.   7s. 6d.
        Geography, climate, horticulture, farming, etc.

Porter and others.   The West : from the census of 1880.   8vo.   *Low.*   15s.
        States and territories of the West from 1800 to 1880.

Nordhoff, C.   Northern California, Oregon, and Sandwich Islands.   r. 8vo.
     Low.   12s. 6d.

California of the South.   12mo.   *Appleton.*   illus.   10s. 6d.
        Health resorts.

Elliott, H. W.   Alaska and the seal islands.   8vo.   *Low.*   illus.   16s.

New York illustrated.   8vo.   *Appleton.*   illus.   4s

Dictionary of New York and vicinity.   12mo.   *Appleton.*   Maps.   2s

Bancroft, H. H.   San Francisco.   (*San Francisco*).   2s. 6d

Zacharie, J. S.   New Orleans guide.   *Rand* (*Chicago*).   illus.   1s. 6d.

UNITED STATES: HISTORY :

—I. GENERAL:

Documents illustrative of American history.   Ed. Preston.   8vo.   *Putnam.*   12s.

Bancroft, G.   History of the United States to 1783.   8vo.   10 vols.   (*Boston*).
        Best detailed history ; a scholarly work.

  ,,   History of the United States to 1783.   8vo.   6 vols.   *Low.*   73s. 6d.
        Latest revision, including the "Formation of the Constitution," but without the notes of
        the original ten-volume edition.

Hildreth, R.   History of the United States to 1821.   8vo.   6 vols.   *Harper.*   63s.
        Dry, but trustworthy ; on the Federal side.

Narrative and critical history of America.   Ed. J. Winsor.   8vo.   8 vols., 30s.
     each.   *Low.*   124s.
        Vol. i., Aboriginal America : vol. ii., Spanish explorations and settlements in America
        from 15th to 17th century ; vol. iii., English explorations and settlements in North America,
        1497-1689 ; vol. iv., French explorations and settlements in North America, and those of the
        Portuguese, Dutch, and Swedes, 1500-1700 ; vol. v., The English and French in North
        America ; vol. vi., The United States of North America, part i. ; vol. vii., United States of
        North America, part ii. ; vol. viii., Later history of British, Spanish, and Portuguese
        America. The Appendix gives the manuscript sources of the history of the United States,
        with particular reference to the American Revolution. Written by specialists ; especially
        good on the critical authorities.

Bancroft, H. H.   History of the Pacific States.   r. 8vo.   37 vols., 24s. each.
     (*San Francisco*).

Schouler, J.   History of the United States of America under the Con-
     stitution (1783–1847).   8vo.   4 vols., 10s. each.   (*Washington*).   40s.
        Covers later developments.

McMaster, J. B.   History of the people of the United States (1784–1861).
     c. 8vo.   5 vols., 10s. 6d. each.   *Warne.*   52s. 6d.
        Only two volumes published.

Bryant and Gay.   Popular history of the United States to 1878.   r. 8vo.
     4 vols., 15s. each.   *Scribner.*   60s.
        Full in the early period, but scantier as it comes down to the close of the Civil War. Bryant
        had little to do with the work, and died before a large part of it was written.

Ridpath, J. C.   Popular history of the United States to 1881.   8vo.   (*New*
     York).   illus.   12s.
        The best short history.

Lossing, B. J.   Harper's popular encyclopædia of United States history. 8vo. 2 vols. *Harper.*   48*s.*
     Arranged topically.

De Tocqueville, A.   Démocratie en Amérique. 8vo. 3 vols., 6*s.* each. (*Paris*).   18*s.*

,,   Democracy in America. Tr. c. 8vo. 2 vols. *Longmans.*   16*s.*
     The French original is much to be preferred to the English translation.   .

—II. LOCAL :

American Commonwealths. Ed. H. E. Scudder. 16mo. *Houghton, Mifflin.*
     A series of volumes giving the later history of leading and typical states; 6*s.* each. In progress.

Palfrey, J. G.   History of New England. 8vo. 5 vols. *Low.*   30*s.*

Namsen.   Popular history of California. *Bancroft Co.*

Gayarré, C.   History of Louisiana. 8vo. 3 vols., 20*s.* each. (*New Orleans*).   60*s.* ·

—III. COLONIAL PERIOD :

Fiske, J.   The beginnings of New England to 1689. c. 8vo. *Macmillan.*   7*s.* 6*d.*

Doyle, J. A.   The English in America. 8vo. 3 vols. *Longmans.*   54*s.*
     Vol. i., Virginia, Maryland, and Carolina, 18*s.*; vols. ii., iii., Puritan Colonies, 36*s.*

Parkman, F.   France and England in North America. c. 8vo. 10 vols., 7*s.* 6*d.* each. *Macmillan.*   73*s.* 6*d.*
     "Pioneers of France in the New World" (1572-1635); "The Jesuits in North America" (1634-1670) ; "La Salle and the discovery of the Great West ;" "The Oregon trail;" "Count Frontenac and New France" (1620-1701); "The old régime in Canada" (1653-1763); "Montcalm and Wolfe" (1745-1763), 2 vols. ; "The conspiracy of Pontiac" (1755-69), 2 vols. A series of excellently written books dealing with the contests of the English and French for the possession of North America.

Lodge, H. C.   Short history of the English Colonies in America. 8vo. *Harper.*   15*s.*
     A good summary of the condition of the English Colonies in 1765.

Frothingham, R.   Rise of the republic of the United States. 8vo. *Little, Brown (Boston).*   18*s*

—IV. REVOLUTIONARY PERIOD :

Lossing, B. J.   Pictorial field-book of the revolution. 2 vols. *Harper.*   56*s.*
     Itinerary, with descriptions of battles.

Ludlow, J. M.   War of American independence (1775–83). f. 8vo. *Longmans.*   2*s.* 6*d.* ·
     Brief ; the English view.

Winsor, Justin.   Reader's handbook of the American revolution (1761–83). 16mo. *Houghton, Mifflin.*   5*s.*
     A very full bibliography of the subject.

Fiske, J.   Critical period of American history (1783–9). ex. c. 8vo. *Macmillan.*   10*s.* 6*d.*

—V. 1801–48 :

Adams, H.   History of the United States during the administrations of Jefferson and Madison (1801–17). 16mo. 9 vols. *Scribner.*

De Witt, C.   Thomas Jefferson, étude historique sur la démocratie américaine. 8vo.   6*s.*

Lossing, B. J.   Pictorial field-book of the war of 1812. r. 8vo. *Harper.* illus.   35*s.*

Roosevelt, T.   Naval war of 1812. 8vo. *Putnam.*   12*s.* 6*d.*
     Best history of the United States navy during the war with Great Britain.

Ripley, R. S.   The War with Mexico (1847-8). 8vo. 2 vols. *Harper.* 1849.   O.P.

—VI. THE CIVIL WAR, 1861-5:

War of the Rebellion. Ed. R. N. Scott. 8vo. (*Washington*).
<small>From official records on both sides; not yet complete.</small>

Greeley, H.   The American conflict. r. 8vo. 2 vols. (*Hartford, U.S.*).   40s.
<small>Political history of the war.</small>

Paris, Comte de. History of the Civil War in America. 8vo. 4 vols.,
18s. each. (*Philadelphia*).   72s.
<small>Military history. The best yet published.</small>

Draper, J. History of the American Civil War. 8vo. 3 vols. *Longmans.*
pub. 42s.   O.P.

Nicolay and Hay. Life of Abraham Lincoln. r. 8vo. 10 vols. *Unwin.*   120s.

Stephens, A. H. Constitutional view of the late war between the States.
8vo. (*Philadelphia*).   22s.
<small>The Confederate view.</small>

Johnson, Rossiter. Short history of the war of secession, 1861–5. 8vo.
(*Boston*).   12s. 6d.

Davis, J. Rise and fall of the Confederate government. 8vo. 2 vols.
(*New York*).   40s.

Memoirs of General Grant. 8vo. 2 vols. *Low.*   28s.

Battles and leaders of the Civil War. r. 8vo. 4 vols. *Unwin.*   105s.

—VII. SLAVERY:

Wilson, H. Rise and fall of the slave power in America. 3 vols., 15s. each.
Houghton, Mifflin.   45s.

Garrison, W. P., and F. J. William Lloyd Garrison (1805–79). 2 vols.
Unwin.   30s.
<small>His life told by his children. Complete history of abolition movement in the United States.</small>

—VIII. CONSTITUTION, GOVERNMENT, AND POLITICS:

Bancroft, G. Formation of the Constitution of the United States 8vo.
2 vols. *Appleton.*   25s.
<small>Also 1 vol. 8vo. 12s. 6d.</small>

Curtis, G. T. Constitutional history of the United States (1776–1865).
2 vols., 24s. each. *Harper.*   48s.
<small>Useful account of the Convention proceedings.</small>

Bryce, J. American Commonwealth. ex. c. 8vo. 2 vols. *Macmillan.*   25s.
<small>The best book for the general reader.</small>

Holst, H. von. Constitutional and political history of the United States
(1750–1859). Tr. Lalor and Mason. 8vo. 6 vols. (*Chicago*).
<small>Very full and most valuable to the student, but strongly biassed against Republican
institutions. English translation not yet complete.</small>

Cooper, T. V. American politics (non-partisan) to 1882. 8vo. (*Philadelphia*).   20s.

Johnston, A. United States: history and constitution. c. 8vo. *Blackie.*   4s. 6d.

Federal and State Constitutions. Ed. under authority of Congress, B. Poore.
r. 8vo. 2 vols. (*Washington*).   35s.
<small>Very concise and practically useful manual.</small>

Johnston, A. History of American politics. 16mo. (*New York*).   4s.
<small>Best sketch of American political history; extremely clear and concise.</small>

Cyclopædia of political science and economy; history of the United States.
Ed. J. J. Lalor. 8vo. 3 vols., 30s. each. (*Chicago*).   90s.

"**American** statesmen," series. Ed. J. T. Morse. 16mo. *Houghton, Mifflin.*
J. Q. Adams ; Thomas Jefferson ; John Adams ; Benjamin Franklin ; 6s. each.

—IX. MISCELLANEOUS :

Nordhoff, C. Communistic societies of the United States. 8vo. *Harper.* illus.   20s.

Bolles, A. S. Financial history of the United States from 1774–1885. 8vo. 3 vols. *Appleton.*   48s. 6d.
Vol. i., 12s. 6d. ; vol. ii., 18s. ; vol. iii., 18s.

Sumner, W. G. History of American currency. 12mo. (*New York*).   15s.

Bolles, A. S. Industrial history of the United States. 8vo. (*Norwich, U.S.*).   15s.

Taussig, F. W. Tariff history of the United States. p. 8vo. *Putnam.*   5s.

History of co-operation in the United States ("Johns Hopkins university studies"). Ed. H. B. Adams. 8vo. (*Baltimore*).   18s.
Written by specialists.

Ely, R. T. Labour movement in America. 8vo. *Heinemann.*   5s.

Sprague, W. Annals of the American pulpit. 8vo. 9 vols. (*New York*).   180s.
Biographical notices of American clergymen.

Dorchester, D. Christianity in the United States. 8vo. (*New York*).   24s.
General history of all religious denominations in the United States.

Boone, R. G. Education in the United States ; its history from the earliest settlements. c. 8vo. *Appleton.*   6s.

Porter, Noah. American colleges and the American public. 12mo. *Scribner.*   7s. 6d.
Devoted to the leading colleges only.
    PERIODICALS : *Annual reports* of the Commissioner of Education. (*Washington*). *Circulars of information.* (Bureau of Education ; *Washington*). Short monographs on education generally ; special papers on the United States.

UNITED STATES : LAW :

Story, J. Constitution of the United States. Ed. T. M. Cooley. 8vo. 2 vols. *Low.*   63s.

Hare, J. Clark. American constitutional law. 8vo. 2 vols. *Low.*   63s.

Cooley, F. M. Constitutional limitations. 8vo. (*Boston*).   31s. 6d.

Stimson, F. J. American statute law. 4to. (*Boston*).   42s.
Digested view of State Constitutions.

Kent, J. Commentaries on American law (with notes by O. W. Holmes, Jun.). 8vo. 4 vols. *Low.*   100s.
See vol. i., lectures 20-22, on " Sources of Municipal law."

UNIVERSITIES AND PUBLIC SCHOOLS :

—I. UNIVERSITIES :

Huber, V. A. English universities. Tr. F. W. Newman. 3 vols. *Pickering.* 1843.   O.P.

Laurie, S. S. Lectures on the rise and early constitution of universities. c. 8vo. *Paul.*   6s.

Denifle, H. Die Universitäten des Mittelalters bis 1400. 8vo. (*Berlin*). Vol. i., 21s.

Wordsworth, C. Social life at English universities in the 18th
century. 8vo. *Bell.*　　15*s.*

　　,, Scholae academicae (Studies at the English universities in the
18th century). d. 8vo. *Cambridge Press.*　　10*s. 6d.*

Maxwell-Lyte, H. C. History of the University of Oxford. 8vo.
Macmillan. illus.　　16*s.*

Brodrick, G. C. History of the University of Oxford. f. 8vo. *Longmans.*　　2*s. 6d.*

Lang, A. Oxford. c. 8vo. *Seeley.*　　6*s.*
Historical and descriptive.

Stedman, A. M. Oxford, its life and schools. 8vo. *Methuen.*　　5*s.*
Contributions by resident members of the university. Full information about the schools,
university and college life, etc.

Mullinger, J. Bass. History of the University of Cambridge. d. 8vo.
2 vols. *Pitt Press.*　　30*s.*
Vol. i., 12*s.*; vol. ii., 18*s.*

Bristed, C. A. Five years in an English university. *Low.*　　O.P.
An account of the social life at Cambridge, 1842-7, by an American.

Seeley. Student's guide to the University of Cambridge. f. 8vo. *Bell.*　　6*s. 6d.*

Grant, A. Story of the University of Edinburgh during the first 300 years.
8vo. 2 vols. *Longmans.* pub. 36*s.*　　O.P.

Stubbs, J. W. History of the University of Dublin (1541–1800). d. 8vo.
Hodges, Figgis.　　12*s. 6d.*

Arnold, M. Higher schools and universities in Germany. c. 8vo. *Macmillan.*　　6*s.*

—II. PUBLIC AND HIGH SCHOOLS:

Mullinger, J. Bass. Schools of Charles the Great in the IX. century.
8vo. *Longmans.* pub. 7*s. 6d.*　　O.P.

Furnivall, F. J. Education in early England (Early English Text Society).
Trübner.
Preface to "Early English meals and manners." (d. 8vo. 15*s.*).

Staunton, H. The great schools of England. p. 8vo. *Strahan.*　　O.P.

Our public schools. c. 8vo. *Paul.*　　6*s.*
Eton, Harrow, Winchester, Rugby, Westminster, Marlborough, Charterhouse. Articles
historical and critical; reprinted from *New Quarterly Review.*

The Public Schools, by the author of "Etoniana." 8vo. *Blackwood.*　　O.P.
Winchester, Westminster, Shrewsbury, Harrow, Rugby.

Cotterill, C. C. Suggested reforms in public schools. f. 8vo. *Blackwood.*　　3*s. 6d.*

Maxwell-Lyte, H. C. History of Eton college. 8vo. *Macmillan.* illus.　　21*s.*

Tudor's Charitable trusts. Ed. Bristowe and Cook. r. 2vo. *Reeves
and Turner.*　　38*s.*
Law of endowed schools.
PERIODICAL : *The Public Schools Year Book* (annual). *Sonnenschein.*

V.

VACCINATION :

Warlomont, E. Manual of animal vaccination. Tr. A. Harries. c. 8vo. *Churchill.* illus.   *4s. 6d.*

Crookshank, E. C. History and pathology of vaccination. r. 8vo. 2 vols. *H. K. Lewis.* illus.   *36s.*

Case against vaccination.

Report of the Royal Commission on vaccination. *Eyre.*

VAN DIEMAN'S LAND, *see* AUSTRALASIA VIII.

VARNISHES, *see* INDUSTRIES XIII.

VEDAS, *see* SANSKRIT.

VEGETABLE GROWING, *see* AGRICULTURE I. *and* GARDENING.

VEGETARIANISM, *see* COOKERY II.

VENEZUELA, *see* AMERICA, SOUTH.

VENTILATION, *see* HYGIENE.

VESTMENTS, *see* COSTUME (HISTORICAL) *and* NEEDLEWORK.

VETERINARY SCIENCE:

Robertson, W. Veterinary medicine. *Baillière.*   *25s.*

Williams, W. Veterinary medicine. 8vo. *Churchill.* illus.   *30s.*

  ,,   Veterinary surgery. 8vo. *Churchill.* illus.   *30s.*

Fleming, G. Veterinary sanitary science and police. 8vo. 2 vols. *Chapman.* illus.   *36s.*

  ,,   Veterinary obstetrics. 8vo. *Baillière.* illus.   *30s.*

Steel, J. H. Diseases of the ox. 8vo. *Longmans.* illus.   *15s.*

  ,,   Diseases of the sheep. 8vo. *Longmans.* illus.   *12s.*

Findlay, D. Veterinary medicines. d. 8vo. *Douglas.*   *15s.*

Lord and Rush. Veterinary vade-mecum. c. 8vo. *Homœopathic Publishing Co.*   *15s*

REPORTS *of the Veterinary Department* (Board of Agriculture). *Eyre.*

VICTORIA, *see* AUSTRALASIA IV.

  ,,   NYANZA, *see* AFRICA IV.

VILLAGE COMMUNITIES, *see* ANTHROPOLOGY III.

VINE CULTURE, *see* GARDENING.

VITAL STATISTICS, *see* HYGIENE.

VOICE, *see* MUSIC IV.

VOLCANOES, *see* GEOLOGY II.

VOLUNTEERS, *see* ARMY I.

VOYAGES AND TRAVELS, *see* GEOGRAPHY II., SPORT, ZOOLOGY III., *and under the various countries.*

W.

WAGES, *see* POLITICAL ECONOMY VI.

WALES:

—I. GEOGRAPHY:

Murray's Handbook to North Wales. p. 8vo. *Murray.*   7*s.*

  ,,   Handbook to South Wales. p. 8vo. *Murray.*   7*s.*

Baddeley and Ward. North and South Wales ("Thorough Guide" ser.). *Dulau.*
North Wales, 5*s.* (also in two parts); South Wales and Wye 3*s.* d.

—II. HISTORY:

See also ENGLAND, HISTORY.

Williams, Jane. A history of Wales. 8vo. *Longman.* pub.   •   O.P.

Walter, F. Das alte Wales. 8vo. (*Bonn*).   8*s.*

—III. LANGUAGE AND LITERATURE:

COURSE OF READING: Grammar and exercises, Gweledigaethau y Bardd Cwsg; Ll. y tri Aderyn; Llyvyr Job; the Mabinogion; and D. ab Gwilym.

Rowland, T. Welsh grammar and exercises. 12mo. *Hughes (Wrexham).*   4*s.* 6*d.*

Richards, W. English-Welsh and Welsh-English dictionary. r. 32mo. *Hughes (Wrexham).*   2*s.* 6*d.*
English-Welsh, 1*s.* 6*d.*; Welsh-English, 1*s.*

Evans, Silvan. English-Welsh dictionary. d. 8vo. 2 vols. *Gee (Denbigh).*   40*s.*

Pughe, W. O. Welsh-English dictionary. d. 8vo. 2 vols. *Gee (Denbigh).*   30*s.*
Pryse's edition is the only one in print.

Evans, Silvan. Welsh-English dictionary. r. 8vo. *Spurrell (Carmarthen).*
A, 10*s.* 6*d.*; B, 5*s.* In progress.

Rhys, J. Lectures on Welsh philology. c. 8vo. *Trübner.*   15*s.*
The author has given up his theory of the origin of the Ogam writing, and of the classification of the Celts.

Wynn, Ellis. Gweledigaethau y Bardd Cwsg. Ed. Silvan Evans. c. 8vo. *Spurrell (Carmarthen).*   1*s.* 6*d.*

Lloyd, M. Llyvyr y tri Aderyn. c. 8vo. *Foulkes (Liverpool).*   1*s.*

Llyvyr Job. Tr. Morgan. Ed. J. G. Evans. ex. f. 8vo. *Frowde.*   1*s.* 6*d.*

Text of the Mabinogion, and other Welsh tales from the Red Book of Hergest ("Red Book" ser.). Ed. J. Rhys and J. G. Evans. *Evans (Oxford).*

Text of the Bruts from the Red Book ("Red Book" ser.). Ed. Rhys and Evans. *Evans.*

D. ab Gwilym. Barddoniaeth. d. 8vo. *Foulkes (Liverpool).*   10s 6d.

WAR, *see* ARMY.

WATCHES, MANUFACTURE, *see* INDUSTRIES VI.

WEAPONS, *see* ARMS.

WEAVING, *see* TEXTILE FABRICS.

WESLEYANS, *see* CHURCH HISTORY V. (D).

WEST AUSTRALIA, *see* AUSTRALASIA VII.

WEST INDIES:

—I. GENERAL:

Eves, C. W. West Indies (Royal Colonial Institute Publication). c. 8vo. *Low.*   7s. 6d.

Trollope, A. West Indies and the Spanish Main. 8vo. *Chapman.*   5s.

Kingsley, C. At last; a Christmas in the West Indies. c. 8vo. *Macmillan.*   3s. 6d.

Eden, C. H. West Indies. c. 8vo. *Low.*   3s. 6d.

Silver's West Indian pocket-book. 2 vols. *Silver.*
i., The Leeward and Windward Islands, 2s. 6d.; ii., Jamaica, Hayti, Cuba, The Bahamas, etc., 2s. 6d.

Edwardes. History of the British Colonies in the West Indies. 3 vols. *(London).*   O.P.

Froude, J. A. The English in the West Indies. *Longmans.*   2s. 6d.

—II. LOCAL:

Bulkeley, O. T. Lesser Antilles: a guide for settlers. c. 8vo. *Low.* illus.   2s. 6d.

Ober, F. A. Camps in the Carribees (Lesser Antilles). d. 8vo. *Douglas.* illus.   12s.

Moxley, J. H. S. A West Indian sanatorium and Barbados guide. c. 8vo. *Low.*   3s. 6d.

Hazard, S. Cuba; with pen and pencil. r. 8vo. *Low.* pub. 15s.   O.P.

    ,, San Domingo: past and present; with a glance at Hayti. 8vo. *Low.* pub. 18s.   O.P.

Fortunat, Dante. Nouvelle géographie de l'île d'Haïti. *(Port-au-Prince).*

St. John, S. Hayti; or the Black Republic. c. 8vo. *Smith, Elder.*   8s. 6d.

Léal, F. A. La république dominicaine. *(Paris).*

Sinclair and Fyfe. Handbook of Jamaica. 8vo. *Stanford.*   8s.

Iles, J. A. Burke. Nevis; descriptive account of the island. (*Norwich*).

Collens, J. H. Guide to Trinidad. d. 8vo. *Stock.* illus.   6*s.*

Verteuil, L. A. A. de. Trinidad. 8vo. *Cassell.* pub. 21*s.*   O.P.

WESTMINSTER ABBEY, *see* LONDON VII.

WHEEL-MAKING, *see* INDUSTRIES VII.

WHIST, *see* CARDS.

WINE :

Loftus, W. R. The wine and spirit merchant. *W. R. Loftus.*   5*s.*

Shaw, T. G. Wine, the vine and the cellar. 8vo. *Longmans.*   O.P.

Tovey, C. Wine and wine countries. 12mo. *Hamilton, Adams.* pub. 10*s.*   O.P.

Redding, C. History and description of modern wines. p. 8vo. *Bell* (*Bohn*).   5*s.*

Thudichum and Dupré. Origin, nature, and use of wine. m. 8vo. *Macmillan.*   25*s.*
> Treats also of the viticulture of the various wines-producing districts, and of chemical analysis.

Cocks and Féret. Bordeaux and its wines. c. 8vo. *Nutt.*   10*s.*

Carte générale vinicole. *Féret (Bordeaux).*   6*s.*

Mead, R. B. An elementary treatise on American grape culture and wine-making. 8vo. *Harper.* illus.   O.P.

Reports on wine duties. *Eyre.*
> Committee of House of Commons, 1852, 2 vols., 7*s.* 8*d.* ; 1878-9, 2 vols., 5*s.* 4*d.*

Tennant, J. E. Wine; its use and taxation. *J. Madden.*   O.P.
> An analysis of the evidence before the Parliamentary Committee of 1852.

Gardner, J. Brewing, distilling, and wine manufacture. c. 8vo. *Churchill.*   6*s.* 6*d.*
> British wines.

WOOD-CARVING, *see* ARTISTIC PROCESSES VII.

WOOD-ENGRAVING, *see* ARTISTIC PROCESSES II. *and* ART VI.

WOOLLEN MANUFACTURE, *see* TEXTILE FABRICS.

WORKSHOP :

Tredgold, T. Principles of carpentry. Ed. E. Tarn. 4to. *Lockwood.* illus.   25*s.*

Every man his own mechanic. d. 8vo. *Ward, Lock.* illus.   7*s.* 6*d.*
> Very useful to amateurs.

Sutcliffe, I. D. Handcraft. 4to. *Griffith.*   2*s.* 6*d.*
> On sloyd; gives working drawings and instructions.

Shelley, C. Workshop appliances ("Text-book of Science"). c. 8vo. *Longmans.* illus.   4*s.* 6*d.*

WORSTED MANUFACTURE, *see* TEXTILE FABRICS.

WRESTLING, *see* BOXING.

Y.

YACHTING:

—I. SEAMANSHIP:

Kemp, D.   Yacht and boat sailing.   sup. r. 8vo.   *H. Cox.*   25s.
Complete representation of yachting in all its branches.

Knight, E. F.   Sailing ("All England" ser.).   sm. 8vo.   *Bell.*   illus.   2s.
Scarcely practical enough to be of use except to the general reader.

Davies, G. C.   Practical boat sailing.   l. p. 8vo.   *Gill.*   illus.   5s.

Norie.   Navigation.   r. 8vo.   *Norie and Wilson.*   illus.   16s.

Greenwood, J.   Sailor's seabook.   12mo.   *Lockwood.*   12s.

—II. ARCHITECTURE:

Kemp, D.   Yacht architecture.   *H. Cox.*   42s.

Seaton, A. E.   Marine engineering.   8vo.   *Griffin.*   illus.   18s.
A practical work. Should be studied by the owners of steam yachts.

Kemp and Neison.   Practical boat building.   p. 8vo.   *Gill.*   illus.   2s. 6d.
Suitable to those who do not aspire to design or build anything larger than a 20ft. boat.

Grosvenor, J. du V.   Model yacht building.   l. p. 8vo.   *Gill.*   illus.   5s.

Book of knots.   *Stanford.*   illus.   2s. 6d.

Mackrow, C.   Naval architect's pocket-book.   *Lockwood.*   12s. 6d.
Useful for formulæ and tables.

—III. CRUISES:

Moens, W.   Through France and Belgium (canals and rivers).   8vo.   O.P.

Bagot, A. G.   Yachting in the Mediterranean.   c. 8vo.   *W. H. Allen.*   1s.

Francis, F.   Cruise in the "Lancashire Witch."   c. 8vo.   2 vols.   *Low.*   24s.

Brassey, Lady.   Voyages in the "Sunbeam."   c. 8vo.   *Longmans.*   illus.   7s. 6d.
Also 1s. and 2s., illus.

MacMullen, R. T.   Down Channel.   *G. Wilson* (20, Glasshouse-street).   O.P.

Parry, G.   Cruise of the "Ptarmigan."   d. 8vo.   *W. H. Allen.*   10s. 6d.

Knight, E. F.   Cruise of the "Falcon" to the Pacific.   8vo.   *Low.*   7s. 6d.

Davies, G. C.   Norfolk broads and rivers.   c. 8vo.   *Blackwood.*   illus.   6s.

JOURNALS: *Field*, weekly (*H. Cox*); *Forest and Stream*, weekly (*Broadway, New York*); *Le Yacht*, weekly (*Paris*), 16s. a year.
BIBLIOGRAPHY: Wilson's list of nautical works (*G. Wilson*, 20, *Glasshouse-street, W.*), 1d.

Z.

ZOOLOGY.

Books marked § are suitable for young people.

—I. PRINCIPLES:

Darwin, C.   Origin of species.   c. 8vo.   *Murray.*   illus.   6s.

,,   Variation of animals and plants under domestication.   c. 8vo.
2 vols.   *Murray.*   15s.
Contains the detailed evidence on which the *Origin of species* is based.

,,   The descent of man.   c. 8vo.   *Murray.*   illus.   7s. 6d.
The greater part of the book is devoted to the doctrine of sexual selection.

,,   Expression of the emotions in man and animals.   c. 8vo.   *Murray.*
illus.   12s.

Wallace, A. R.   Darwinism.   c. 8vo.   *Macmillan.*   9s.

§   ,,   Essays on natural selection.   8vo.   *Macmillan.*
New ed. *in press.*

§   ,,   Tropical nature ; and other essays.   c. 8vo.   *Macmillan.*   6s.

Spencer, H.   Principles of biology.   8vo.   2 vols.   *Williams.*   34s.

Haeckel, E.   History of creation.   Tr.; revised Lankester.   p. 8vo.   2 vols.
Paul.   32s.
A popular and somewhat exaggerated account of the evolution theory.

,,   Generelle Morphologie der Organismen.   8vo.   2 vols.   (*Berlin*).   20s.
Important discussion of the principles determining animal form and function.

§**Semper,** K.   Natural conditions of existence as they affect animal life
("Internat. Scient." ser.).   c. 8vo.   *Paul.*   5s.

Müller, F. Max.   Facts and arguments for Darwin.   c. 8vo.   *Murray.*
illus.   6s.

Weissmann, A.   Essays on heredity.   Ed. E. B. Poulton.   d. 8vo.   *Clar.
Press.*   16s.
A translation of a series of essays which have attracted great attention.

Galton, F.   Natural inheritance.   8vo.   *Macmillan.*   9s.

Geddes and Thompson.   Evolution of sex ("Contemp. Science" ser.)
c. 8vo.   *Scott.*   illus.   3s. 6d.
Contains excellent summaries of recent work on the reproduction of the lower animals.

—II. HISTORY AND BIOGRAPHIES:

Carus, V.   Histoire de la Zoologie.   8vo.   *Baillière.*   8s. 6d
Can be had either in French or German. There is no corresponding book in English.

§**Darwin,** F.   Life and letters of Chas. Darwin.   8vo.   3 vols.   *Murray.*   36s.

§**Agassiz,** E. C.   Life of Louis Agassiz.   2 vols.   *Macmillan.*   18s

Wilson and Geikie.   Memoir of Edward Forbes.   8vo.   *Macmillan.*   o.p.

§**Smiles,** S.   Life of a Scotch naturalist (Thos. Edward).   8vo.   *Murray.*   10s.

—III. TRAVELS AND EXPLORATIONS:

§**Darwin,** C.   Naturalist's voyage round the world.   m. 8vo.   *Murray.*   illus.   21s.
Also cheap edition. c. 8vo. 3s. 6d.

§**Wallace,** A. R.   Malay Archipelago.   c. 8vo.   *Macmillan.*   illus.   6s.

§   ,,   Travels on the Amazon.   8vo.   *Macmillan.*   pub. 12s.   o.p.
New edition in "Minerva Library." *Warne.* 2s.

§**Bates,** H. W.   The naturalist on the Amazon.   m. 8vo.   *Murray.*   illus.   7s. 6d.

§**Belt,** T.   The naturalist in Nicaragua.   p. 8vo.   *Murray.*   pub. 12s.   o.p

§**Forbes**, H. O. A naturalist's wanderings in the Eastern Archipelago. 8vo.   21s.
     Low. illus.

§**Haeckel**, E. A visit to Ceylon. Tr. p. 8vo. *Paul.*   7s. 6d.

§**Thomson**, C. Wyville. Depths of the sea. 8vo. *Macmillan.*   31s. 6d.
     A popular account of the earlier dredging expeditions.

§   ,,   The Atlantic. 8vo. 2 vols. *Macmillan.*   45s.
     A popular account of the results obtained during part of the cruise of the "Challenger."

"**Challenger**" reports; narrative of the cruise. Ed. Thomson and Murray.   166s. 6d.
     r. 8vo. 2 vols. *Longmans.*
        Vol. i., 136s. 6d.; vol. ii., 30s.

Moseley, H. N. Notes by a naturalist in the "Challenger." 8vo. *Mac-*
     millan. illus. pub. 21s.   O.P.

Agassiz, A. The three cruises of the "Blake." 8vo. 2 vols. *Low.* illus.   42s.

Coppinger, R. W. Cruise of the "Alert," in Patagonian and Polynesian
     waters. 8vo. *Sonnenschein.*   6s.

Guillemard, F. H. Cruise of the "Marchesa" to Kamschatka and New
     Guinea. 8vo. *Murray.*   21s.

Guppy, H. B. The geology and physical characteristics of the Solomon
     Islands. r. 8vo. *Sonnenschein.*   10s. 6d.

—IV. GEOGRAPHICAL DISTRIBUTION :

Wallace, A. R. Geographical distribution of animals. m. 8vo. 2 vols.
     Macmillan.   42s.
     The most important work on the subject.

§   ,,   Island life. d. 8vo. *Macmillan.*   18s.

Murray, A. Geographical distribution of mammals. 4to. *Day.*   25s.

Trouessart, E. L. La géographie zoologique (in the " Bibliothèque
     scientifique contemporaine "). 12mo. (*Paris*).   3s.

—V. GENERAL TREATISES :

Klassen und Ordnungen des Thier reichs. Ed. Bronn. *Winter (Leipzig).*
     Vol. i., Protozoa; vol. ii., Rotifera; vol. iv., Vermes; vol. v., Arthropoda; vol. vi. (1),
     Pisces; (2), Amphibia; (3), Reptilia; (4), Aves; (5), Mammalia. In progress. On a large
     scale; well-illustrated; and more complete than any English work.

Cuvier, G. Le règne animal. l. 8vo. 20 vols. *Masson (Paris).* 1849.   £80
     The best series of coloured illustrations of animals of all groups.

Brehm, A. E. Thierleben. r. 8vo. 10 vols. (*Leipzig*).   140s.
     The most complete illustrated work on general natural history. Can be had in German or
     French.

"**Challenger**" reports; Zoology. 4to. 32 vols. *Longmans.*
     Prices vary from 30s. to 63s. Many of these reports are of extreme value.

Ray Society's publications. Two series, 8vo. and fo. *Ray Society.*
     Monographs on special groups; admirably illustrated.

Dohrn, A. Fauna und flora des Golfes von Neapel. (*Leipzig*).
     A series of important monographs, with excellent plates, many coloured; in course of publica-
     tion. The 17 vols. already issued may be had for about £40.

Catalogues of the natural history specimens in the British Museum.
     Invaluable for determining species. Sold at the Natural History Museum, also by *Longmans,*
     Trübner, etc.

Memoirs of the Museum of comparative zoology at Harvard College. Ed.
     A. Agassiz. 4to. 15 vols.; various prices. (*U.S.*).
     Also in separate parts, 4s. 6d. to 75s. Some are O.P.

§ **Cassell's** natural history. Ed. Duncan. ex. c. 4to. 6 vols., 9s. each.
    Cassell.   54s.
        Similar to Brehm's *Thierleben*, but on a smaller scale.

" **Riverside** " natural history. Ed. Kingsley. 4to. 6 vols. *Paul.*   126s.

Claus and Sedgwick. Text-book of zoology. 2 vols. *Sonnenschein.*   37s.
        Vol. i., 21s.; vol. ii., 16s. The best student's manual of zoology.

Morgan, L. Animal biology. c. 8vo. *Rivingtons.* illus.   8s. 6d.

Rolleston, G. Forms of animal life. Ed. Jackson. r. 8vo. *Clar. Press.*   36s.

Huxley, T. H. Anatomy of vertebrated animals. p. 8vo. *Churchill.*
    illus.   12s.

    ,,   Anatomy of invertebrate animals. p. 8vo. *Churchill.* illus.   16s.

Gosse, P. H. Marine zoology. f. 8vo. 2 parts, 7s. 6d. each. *Gurney.*   15s.

Balfour, F. M. Comparative embryology. 8vo. 2 vols. *Macmillan.*   39s.
        Vol. i., 18s.; vol. ii., 21s. A book of extreme value to students.

Bell, F. J. Comparative anatomy and physiology. 12mo. *Cassell.* illus.   7s. 6d.

Chauveau and Fleming. Comparative anatomy of domesticated animals.
    8vo. *Churchill.* illus.   31s. 6d.

§**Lubbock,** J. The senses of animals ("Internat. Scient." ser.). e. 8vo.
    Paul.   5s.

§**White,** Gilbert. Natural history of Selborne. Ed. E. Jesse. p. 8vo.
    Bell (Bohn). illus.   5s.
        Also, Ed. Van Voorst and Harting. 8vo. *Bickers.* illus. by Bewick.

§**Wood,** J. G. Common objects of the country. c. 8vo. *Routledge.* illus.   3s. 6d.

§   ,,   Common objects of the seashore. c. 8vo. *Routledge.* illus.   3s. 6d.

Simmonds, P. L. Animal products. l. c. 8vo. *Chapman.*   7s. 6d.

Waterton, C. Essays on natural history. p. 8vo. 3 vols. *Longmans.*   15s.

§**Buckley,** Arabella B. Life and her children. *Stanford.*   6s.

§   ,,   Winners in life's race. *Stanford.*   6s.

—VI. SPECIAL GROUPS OF ANIMALS :

Ray Society's publications. 8vo. and fo. 39 vols., from 2s. to 90s.
    Some are O.P.

Kent, W. S. Manual of infusoria. sup. r. 8vo. 3 vols. *W. H. Allen.*
    illus.   84s.

Hincks, T. British hydroid zoophytes. 8vo. 2 vols. *Gurney.* illus.   42s.

§**Gosse,** P. H. British sea anemones and corals. 8vo. *Gurney.* illus.   21s.

Pennington, A. S. British zoophytes. c. 8vo. *L. Reeve.* illus.   10s. 6d.

Dana, J. D. Coral and coral islands. c. 8vo. *Low.* illus. pub. 8s. 6d.   O.P.

Forbes, E. British starfishes. 8vo. *Gurney.* illus.   15s.

Hincks, T. British marine polyzoa. d. 8vo. 2 vols. *Gurney.* illus.   63s.

Hudson and Gosse. Rotifera. 4to. 2 vols., and supp. *Longmans.* illus.   84s.

Leuckart, R. Parasites of man. Tr. W. E. Hoyle. l. 8vo. *(Edinburgh).*
    illus.   31s. 6d.

Woodward, S. P. Manual of the mollusca. c. 8vo. *Lockwood.* illus.   7s. 6d.

Jeffreys, J. Gwyn. British conchology. r. 8vo. 5 vols. *Gurney.*
        Vols. i. to iv., 12s. each ; vol. v., plates, 57s. coloured ; 32s. plain.

Forbes and Hanley. History of British mollusca. 8vo. 4 vols. *Gurney.*
   illus.   70s.
       With coloured plates, £13.

Reeve and Sowerby. Conchologia Iconica. 4to. 20 vols. *L. Reeve.*
   col. plates.   £178

Harting, J. E. Rambles in search of shells. p. 8vo. *Gurney.* col. illus. 7s. 6d.

Bate and Westwood. Sessile-eyed crustacea. 8vo. 2 vols. *Gurney.* illus. 60s.

Bell, T. British stalk-eyed crustacea. 8vo. *Gurney.* illus. 25s.

Leach. Malacostraca podophthalmata.

§**Huxley,** T. H. The crayfish ("Internat. Scient." ser.). c. 8vo. *Paul.*
   illus.   5s.

§**Staveley,** E. F. British spiders. c. 8vo. *L. Reeve.* illus. 10s. 6d.

Stephens, J. F. Illustrations of British entomology. r. 8vo. 12 vols.
   1828–46.   O.P.

Kirby and Spence. Introduction to entomology. 8vo. O.P.

Hagen, H. A. Bibliotheca entomologica. 8vo. 2 vols. *Engelmann.* 32s.

§**Donovan,** E. Natural history of British insects. 1793–1813. O.P.

§**Schuckard,** W. E. Natural history of British bees. c. 8vo. *L. Reeve.*
   illus.   10s. 6d.

§**Lubbock,** J. Ants, bees, and wasps ("Internat. Scient." ser.). c. 8vo. *Paul.* 5s.

§**Humphrey** and Westwood. British butterflies and their transformation.
   4to. *Chambers.* illus. pub. 31s. 6d.   O.P.

§   ,,   British moths and their transformation. *Chambers.* illus. pub. 84s. O.P.

Scudder, S. H. Butterflies of the Eastern United States and Canada. 4to.
   3 vols. *Houghton, Mifflin.* illus.   £18 18s.

§**Newman,** E. Illustrated natural history of British butterflies and moths.
   sup. r. 8vo. 2 vols. *W. H. Allen.* illus.   25s.
     Separately. Vol. i., "Butterflies," 7s. 6d.; vol. ii., "Moths," 20s.

§**Coleman,** W. S. British butterflies. c. 8vo. *Routledge.* illus. 3s. 6d.

§**Miall** and Denny. The cockroach. d. 8vo. *L. Reeve.* illus. 7s. 6d.

Fowler, W. W. British coleoptera. 4 vols. *L. Reeve.* illus. 64s.
     Superior edition, £10 17s.

§**Curtis,** J. Farm insects. sup. r. 8vo. *Gurney.* illus. 21s.

Ormerod, Miss E. A. Manual of injurious insects. c. 8vo. *Simpkin.* 5s.

Jenyns, L. Manual of British vertebrate animals. *Pitt Press.* O.P.

Günther, A. C. Introduction to the study of fishes. d. 8vo. *Black.* illus. 24s.

Day, F. Fishes of Great Britain and Ireland. i. 8vo. 2 vols. *Williams.* 115s.

Couch, J. History of the fishes of the British Islands. 8vo. 4 vols. illus.
   pub. 84s.   O.P.

Yarrell, W. British fishes. 8vo. 2 vols. *Gurney.* illus. 63s.
     First supplement, 7s. 6d.; second, 5s.
     REPORTS: Reports of the U.S. Commission on fish and fisheries; Reports of the Fishing
     Commission, and of the Fishery Board.

Hopley, Catherine. Snakes; curiosities and wonders of serpent life. 8vo.
   Griffith. illus.   16s.

Bell, T. British reptiles. *Gurney.* illus. 12s.

Cooke, M. C.　British reptiles.　p. 8vo.　*Hardwicke*.　　　　6s.
　　For Indian reptiles, *see* INDIA.

Yarrell, W.　History of British birds.　8vo.　4 vols.　*Gurney*.　illus.　　80s.

§**Saunders**, H.　An illustrated manual of British birds.　d. 8vo.　*Gurney*.
　　illus　　　　　　　　　　　　　　　　　　　　　　　　　　21s.

Bewick, T.　History of British birds.　8vo.　2 vols.　　　　o.p.

Macgillivray, W.　British birds.　8vo.　5 vols.　　　　o.p.

Harting, J. E.　Handbook of British birds.　8vo.　*Van Voorst*.　　7s. 6d.

Seebohm, H.　British birds.　8vo.　4 vols.　*Dulau*.　　　120s.
　　Coloured illustrations of eggs.

§**Morris**, F. O.　Nests and eggs of British birds.　r. 8vo.　3 vols.　*Bell*.
　　illus.　pub. 63s.　　　　　　　　　　　　　　　　　　o.p.

Hewitson, W. C.　Illustrations of British birds' eggs.　8vo.　2 vols.
　　Van Voorst.　　　　　　　　　　　　　　　　　　　84s.

Gray, R.　Birds of West of Scotland.　8vo.　*Murray (Glasgow)*.　　o.p.

Thompson, W.　Natural history of birds of Ireland.　8vo.　4 vols.
　　L. Reeve.　pub. 44s.　　　　　　　　　　　　　　　　o.p.

Vogt, C.　Les mammifères.　Tr. from the German.　4to.　(*Paris*).　　50s.
　　Excellent illustrations.

Bell, T.　British quadrupeds.　8vo.　*Gurney*.　illus.　　26s.

Fleming, J.　British animals.　8vo.　　　　o.p.

Owen, R.　British fossil mammals and birds.　8vo.　*Van Voorst*.　　18s.

Harting, J. E.　British animals, extinct within historic times.　8vo.　*Trübner*.　　8s.

—VII. LABORATORY TEXT-BOOKS:

§**Huxley** and Martin.　Practical biology.　c. 8vo.　*Macmillan*.　　10s. 6d.

Marshall and Hurst.　Practical zoology.　c. 8vo.　*Smith, Elder*.　illus.　　10s. 6d.

Marshall, A. M.　The frog.　c. 8vo.　*Smith, Elder*.　　4s.

Flower, W. H.　Osteology of the mammalia.　c. 8vo.　*Macmillan*.　　10s. 6d.

§**Howes**, G. B.　Atlas of biology.　4to.　*Macmillan*.　　14s.

Parker, T. J.　Zootomy.　c. 8vo.　*Macmillan*.　illus.　　8s. 6d.

Foster and Balfour.　Elements of embryology.　c. 8vo.　*Macmillan*.　　10s. 6d.

Whitman, C. O.　Methods of research in microscopical anatomy.　8vo.
　　(*Boston*).　illus.　　　　　　　　　　　　　　　　　15s.

Lee, A. B.　The microtomist's vade-mecum.　8vo.　*Churchill*.　　12s. 6d.

—VIII. COLLECTORS' MANUALS:

§**Greene**, J.　Insect hunter's companion.　*Sonnenschein*.　illus.　　1s.

§**Kingsley**, J. S.　The naturalist's assistant.　12mo.　(*Boston*).　illus.　　7s. 6d.

Maynard, C. J.　The naturalist's guide.　12mo.　(*Boston*).　illus.　　10s. 6d.

Hughes, W. R.　The marine aquarium.　d. 8vo.　*Gurney*.　illus.　　2s. 6d.

Admiralty manual of scientific enquiry.　8vo.　*Eyre*.　　2s. 6d.

—IX. REFERENCE:

Zoological Record.　(Zoological Soc.).　8vo.　*Gurney*.　　30s.
　　Annual.　Abstracts of papers.

Journal of the Royal Microscopical Society (annual). 8vo. *Williams.*   30*s.*
    Useful abstracts of foreign papers.

Carus and Engelmann.   Bibliotheca zoologica (1700–1860). 8vo. 2 vols.
    Engelmann.   33*s.*

Taschenberg.   Bibliotheca zoologica II. (1861–80). 8vo.   7 parts, 7*s.* each.
    Engelmann.   49*s.*
    In course of publication.

Royal Society's catalogue of scientific papers. 4to. 8 vols., 20*s.* each.
    Royal Society.   160*s.*

Thompson, W. D'Arcy.   Bibliography of protozoa, coelenterata, and worms.
    (1861–83). d. 8vo. *Pitt Press.*   12*s.* 6*d.*

Zoologischer Jahresbericht. Ed. P. Mayer. (*Berlin*).
    Gives abstracts of all zoological papers published in the year.

Scudder, S. H.   Nomenclator zoologicus. 8vo. (*Washington*). pub. 30*s.*   O.P.

Marschall, A.   Nomenclator zoologicus. 8vo.   8*s.*

     PERIODICALS: To the working zoologist periodicals are of greater importance than books.
Philosophical transactions of the Royal Society; *Proceedings* of the Royal Society;
Transactions and Journal of the Linnæan Society; *Transactions and proceedings* of
the Zoological Society; *Quarterly Journal of Microscopical Science*; *Annals and
Magazine of Natural History*; *Nature*, half-yearly vols., 15*s.* each (Macmillan); *Zeitschrift
für wissenschaftliche Zoologie* (Engelmann); *Archiv für microskopische Anatomie* (Max
Cohen); *Morphologisches Jahrbuch* (Engelmann); *Annales des sciences naturelles*
(Masson); *Archives de zoologie expérimentale*; *Archives de Biologie* (Masson).

ZULULAND, *see* CAPE.

INDEX OF AUTHORS.

N.B.—A book appearing on more than one page is only indexed once, except where different editions are named. Authors named only in notes are not indexed.

INDEX OF BIOGRAPHIES AND AUTOBIOGRAPHIES.

ADVERTISEMENTS OF BOOKSELLERS.

ENGLAND AND WALES.

BANGOR.
Jarvis & Foster, Lorne House.

BARNSTAPLE.
Robert Harper, 27, High-street.

BIRMINGHAM.
Edward Baker, 15 & 17, John Bright-street. (10,000 *books of all kinds in stock; catalogues free.*)
Cornish Brothers, 37, New-street.
Midland Educational Company, Ltd. (*New and second-hand books; export.*)

BOURNEMOUTH.
T. J. Powell, Bookseller and Stationer, 71, Commercial-road.

BRADFORD.
W. Cockcroft, Post Office, Girlington, and Belle Vue Post Office, 75, Manningham-lane.

BRIGHTON.
D. B. Friend & Co., 77, Western-road, and 56, Church-road, Hove.
Edward North, 30, Church-road, Hove.
William J. Smith, 41, 42, 43, North-street. (*Largest stock in the county.*)
H. & C. Treacher, 1 & 170, North-street, and 44, East-street.

BRISTOL.
Scholastic Trading Co., Ltd., 34, Bridge - street. (*School and General Booksellers.*)
Thomas Thatcher, 44, College Green.

CAMBRIDGE.
Thomas Dixon, 91, Market-street. (*Depôt of R.T.S and S.P.C.K.*)
Redin & Co., 16, Trinity-street.
William Tomlin, 24, Trinity-street. (*Second-hand Classics and Mathematics.*)

CANTERBURY.
H. J. Goulden, 39 & 40, High-street. Established 1840.

CARDIFF.
Edwin Dobbin, 1, St. Mary's-street. (*Theological and General.*)

COLCHESTER.
T. Forster, 101, High - street. (*Numismatic and Topographical.*)

CROYDON.
Roffey & Clark, Booksellers and Printers, 38, High-street.

DERBY.
Frank Murray, Moray House; also Shakespeare's Head, Leicester; and Regent House, Nottingham. (*Standard Books second-hand.*)

EXETER.
Henry S. Eland, Bookseller, Exeter and Exmouth Library.

FARNHAM.
F. Sturt, Borough.

FAVERSHAM.
William Voile, The Library, 91, Preston-street.

GAINSBOROUGH.
Jasper Hannam.

GUERNSEY.
T. C. Royle, Arcade Library.

GUILDFORD.
Frank Lasham, Publisher and Bookseller, 61, High-street.

HALIFAX.
J. Teal, 7, Crossley-street. (*Miscellaneous and second-hand books; catalogue free.*)

HARPENDEN.
L. Whitehouse.

HARTLEPOOL, WEST.
John Wilson, 19, Church-street.

HEREFORD.
J. Watson Morrison, 1, High Town. (*General.*)

HUDDERSFIELD.
E. W. Coates, 3, Station-street.

HULL.
A. Brown & Sons, 26, 27, and 29, Savile-street. (*Publishers of School Books and Local Literature.*)

KNARESBOROUGH.
Alfred W. Lowe, High-street.

LEAMINGTON.
Midland Educational Co., Ltd., 164, Parade.

LEEDS.
J. W. Bean & Son, 149, Briggate. (*Technical Literature, School and College Books.*)

LEICESTER.

Midland Educational Co., Ltd., 7, Market-street.

LIVERPOOL.

North Western Educational Trading Co., Ltd., Minerva Buildings, Renshaw-street. (*Complete Outfitters to Schools, etc.*)

William Potter, 30, Exchange-street East. (*Second-hand books, and remainders ; catalogue issued at short intervals.*)

Henry Young & Sons, 12, South Castle-street. (*Standard Books, Library editions, Finely illustrated books, Missals and Rare Works in all departments of literature.*)

LONDON.

Richard Amer, Lincoln's-Inn-Gate, Carey-street, W.C. (*Law Books.*)

Henry Burnside, Blackheath, S.E.

W. B. Clive, & Co., 13, Booksellers'-row, Strand, W.C. (*Books for London University Examinations.*)

Congregational Union of England and Wales, Memorial Hall, Farringdon-street. (*Congregational Hymnals, and Theological Lectures.*)

Crosby, Lockwood & Son, 7, Stationers' Hall Court, E.C. (*Publishers of Scientific, Technical, and Educational Books, and Export Booksellers.*)

A. & F. Denny, 304, Strand, W.C. (*Scientific and Medical.*)

Francis Edwards, 83, High-street, Marylebone, W. (*Voyages and Travels.*)

Gilbert & Field, 67, Moorgate-street, E.C.

William Glaisher, 265, High Holborn, W.C. (*New books and remainders.*)

Hachette & Co., 18, King William-street, Charing Cross, W.C. (*French Books.*)

Charles Higham, 27A, Farringdon-street, E.C. (*Second-hand Theological Books of all kinds, ancient and modern.*)

Jones & Evans, 77, Queen-street, Cheapside, E.C. (*All important New and Standard Books ; also Art Books, and L. P. and special editions.*)

LONDON—*contd.*

H. K. Lewis, 136, Gower-street, 136, Gower-street, W.C. (*Medical and Scientific.*)

Moffatt & Paige, 28, Wawick-lane, E.C. *Educational Publishers and Booksellers.*)

David Nutt, 270, Strand, W.C. (*Foreign, Classical, and Theological.*)

H. E. Pearce, 6 and 8, Cleaver-street, Kennington Cross, S.E.

George Philip & Sons, 32, Fleet-street, E.C. (*Geographical, and Technical Books, Maps, Atlases, and Globes.*)

George H. Robinson, The New Book Court, Crystal Palace, Norwood. (*Newest books on day of publication.*)

Walter Scott & Sons, 512, Brixton-road, S.W.

Truslove & Shirley, 143, Oxford-street, W.

William Wesley & Son, 28, Essex-street, Strand, W.C. (*Natural History and Science.*)

John G. Wheeler, 88, Mildmay Park, N. (*Bibles and Evangelical Literature.*)

Wildy & Sons, Lincoln's Inn Archway, Carey-street, W.C. (*Law Books, new and second-hand.*)

A. Wilson (late J. Gilbert & Co.), 18, Gracechurch - street, E.C. (*Standard current Literature ; Books for Workmen's Institutes and Libraries.*)

MANCHESTER.

J. E. Cornish, 16, St. Ann's-square, (*New and old Bookseller.*)

Abel Heywood & Son, 56 and 58, Oldham - street. (*Technical and General.*)

MIDDLESBROUGH.

Smith & Woolston, 22, Wilson-street.

NEWCASTLE-ON-TYNE.

William Beavis, Nelson-street.

NORWICH.

Agas H. Goose, Rampant Horse-street. (*Theological and Archæological.*)

Jarrold & Sons; branches at Cromer and Yarmouth. London House, 3, Paternoster-buildings, E.C. (*Topographical and Antiquarian Works relating to the Eastern Counties.*)

NOTTINGHAM.

R. Allen & Son, Limited, Caxton House, 34, Long-row. (*Farm Account Books, and Almanacks.*)

James Bell, Carlton-street.

OXFORD.

Joseph Thornton & Son, 11, Broadstreet. (*Scholastic and University Books; also Theology.*)

PLYMPTON.

Mrs. Ellen Parish, Bookseller and Stationer, Fore-street, Ridgeway.

READING.

Miss Langley, 37 and 39, Londonstreet. (*A Collection of Ruskin's Works; rare and valuable editions; Circulating Library.*)

William Smith, 109 and 111, Londonstreet. (*Miscellaneous books, new and second-hand.*)

ST.-LEONARD'S-ON-SEA.

Whittaker & Williams, Royal Victoria Library.

STOCKPORT.

Henry Dooley, 22, Lower Hillgate. (*Old and new bookseller.*)

TAUNTON.

Barnicott & Son, Fore-street. (*Publishers of " The Country Gentleman's Reference Catalogue."*)

Alexander Hammett, 53, North-street.

THIRSK.

Zaccheus Wright, Market-place.

TORQUAY.

Arthur Westley, 10, Strand. (*Publisher of Torquay Guides, Plans, and Maps.*)

ULVERSTON.

Mrs. S. J. Whitham, 47, Marketstreet. (*Bookseller and Circulating Library.*)

WARWICK.

Henry T. Cooke & Son, 9, Highstreet.

WELLINGBOROUGH.

Dennes Bros., Booksellers and Printers. (*Depôt for the S.P.C.K.*)

WIGAN.

James Starr, 43 and 45, Wallgate, and North Western Station Approach. (*New and second-hand books.*)

WISBECH.

Leach & Son.

WOODBRIDGE.

John Loder, Stationers' Hall.

WORCESTER.

Deighton & Co., 53, High-street. (*Domesday Books, Worcestershire and Local Histories.*)

SCOTLAND.

ABERDEEN.

D. Wyllie & Son, Booksellers and Stationers, 247, Union-street, and Bridge-street. (*Local, Antiquarian; First Editions; Circulating Library.*)

ARBROATH.

Mrs. Sutherland, 219½, High-street (*Literature of every class.*)

EDINBURGH.

George Adam Young & Co., 102, South Bridge. (*Second-hand Foreign Literature, especially Hebrew and Greek.*)

Andrew Elliott, 17, Princes-street. (*General Bookseller and Publisher.*)

R. W. Hunter, Theological Book Depôt, 19, George IV. Bridge. (*Theological and General Litera-*

EDINBURGH—*contd.*

ture, new and second-hand; catalogues post free.)

Macniven & Wallace, 138, Princesstreet. (*New and second-hand books; library.*)

James Thin, Bookseller, 55, South Bridge. (*All departments, new and second-hand.*)

GLASGOW.

Robert L. Holmes, Wholesale Bookseller, 3 and 5, Dunlop-street.

James Maclehose & Sons, 61, St. Vincent-street. (*Booksellers to the University.*)

John Smith & Son, 129, West Georgestreet. (*Law, Scientific, and Maps.*)

Alexander Stenhouse, College Gate, Hillhead. (*University, Medical, and General; new and second-hand.*)

IRELAND.

BELFAST.
  William Mullan & Son, 4, Donegall-place. (*Educational and General.*)

COLERAINE AND PORTRUSH, Co. Derry.
  Miss Woods.

DUBLIN.
  Hodges, Figgis & Co., 104, Grafton-street. (*Booksellers and Publishers*

DUBLIN—*contd.*
  to the University of Dublin: Sole Agents in Ireland for the sale of Government publications.)
  William McGee, 18, Nassau-street. (*College, School, Law, and Medical.*)

PRINTED BY HARRISON AND SONS, ST. MARTIN'S LANE, LONDON.

9 789354 216978